The Corrupter of Boys

THE MIDDLE AGES SERIES

Ruth Mazo Karras, Series Editor
Edward Peters, Founding Editor

A complete list of books in the series
is available from the publisher.

The

CORRUPTER
OF BOYS

Sodomy, Scandal, and
the Medieval Clergy

DYAN ELLIOTT

PENN

UNIVERSITY OF PENNSYLVANIA PRESS

PHILADELPHIA

Published by
University of Pennsylvania Press
Philadelphia, Pennsylvania 19104-4112
www.upenn.edu/pennpress

Printed in the United States of America on acid-free paper

10 9 8 7 6 5 4 3 2 1

A Cataloging-in-Publication record is avaiable from the Library of Congress

ISBN 978-0-8122-5252-1

CONTENTS

The Corrupter of Boys

Introduction

While each church district had its idiosyncrasies, the pattern was pretty much the same. The main thing was not to help children, but to avoid "scandal." That is not our word, but theirs; it appears over and over again in the documents we recovered. . . . Special agents testified before us that they had identified a series of practices that regularly appeared, in various configurations, in the diocesan files they had analyzed. It's like a playbook for concealing the truth.

—Pennsylvania grand jury report, August 2018

I suspect most historians have moments when the past becomes overly present —so much so that it seems more than mere coincidence; it seems uncanny. In May 2002, the news broke that Catholic priests in Boston were guilty of multiple incidents of child abuse. As if this was not horrific enough, it turned out that the ecclesiastical authorities were aware of this abuse but did nothing to punish the offenders. Instead they kept silent about these offenses, coercing the victims and their families into doing likewise, and simply moved the offending clerics to different parishes.[1] I remembered that a similar solution had been anticipated by the thirteenth-century scholastic Henry of Ghent, who raised the question of what a superior should do in the event that he learns through confession that one of his subordinates is a threat to his parishioners. The answer: keep silent and, when the opportunity arises, move him. I began to wonder if this degree of ecclesiastical subterfuge in concealing clerical vice had been in place long before the multiple scandals that rocked the Boston church and the world. This was the uncanny moment that led to the writing of this book.[2]

As I was completing my research, more and more instances of abuse came to light, and the members of the public were aghast. Catholics and non-Catholics alike kept asking what could have gone so horribly wrong, or, as a recent editorial in the *New York Times* put it: "How have so many pedophiles been allowed into the priesthood? How could bishops have so consistently looked the other way?"[3] The editor was responding to the recent report of the grand jury convened to investigate the clerical abuse of minors in six dioceses in Pennsylvania. The ecclesiastical archives revealed that church authorities had concealed the fact that three hundred priests were responsible for abusing around one thousand children. The jurors were convinced that there were many more such cases of abuse that would never come to light. The editorial in the *Times* presumed that the multiple tragedies detailed in this report were simply failings of the contemporary church, which, of course, they were. But by this point, my research had convinced me that the questions raised in the editorial were not apposite. The irresponsible manner in which the church hierarchy handled these cases of child abuse was not the exception, but the rule. The report from Pennsylvania had only helped to confirm my dark premise: what we are witnessing in the contemporary church is no aberration but a continuation of a practice that spanned centuries.

This might seem like an unlikely position to maintain given the decentralization of premodern religious structures. There was no monolithic "church," as there is now. Rather there were many disparate interest groups manifesting rivalry and contestation throughout the church hierarchy. Parish priests did their best to keep themselves and their parishes under the radar of their suffragan bishop, even as suffragans strove to guard their diocese from interference by the archbishop. Monastic orders struggled to resist episcopal oversight. The growing power of the papacy instigated a new set of rivalries throughout the high and later Middle Ages. The mendicant orders, responsible to the pope alone, were bitterly resented by the secular clergy for their incursions into the parochial system and especially feared and hated for their roles as inquisitors of heresy. For their own part, members of the different mendicant orders roundly despised one another. Meanwhile, the rising national monarchs resisted papal power, and their bishops rallied around them.

And yet, the clergy was united in certain salient ways that would ultimately foster an enduring culture of ecclesiastical subterfuge. In the fourth century, clerics began to distinguish themselves from members of the laity by virtue of augmented claims to holiness. Because clerical celibacy was key to this distinction, religious authorities of all stripes—patristic authors, popes, theologians, canonists, monastic founders, and commentators—became progressively sensitive to sexual scandals that involved the clergy and developed sophisticated tactics for concealing or dispelling embarrassing lapses. The fear of scandal dictated certain lines of action and inaction, the consequences of which are painfully apparent today. This book discusses how the scandal-averse policies, which existed at every conceivable level of the ecclesiastical hierarchy, in conjunction with the requirement of clerical celibacy, resulted in the widespread sexual abuse of boys and male adolescents.

This is a difficult topic that religious authorities were loath to acknowledge, then as now. In the Middle Ages, when clerical activists like Odo of Cluny (d. 942), Peter Damian (d. 1072), and Ivo of Chartres (d. 1115) attempted to alert the authorities to this problem, they were ignored or, as in Damian's case, even chastised for their indiscretion. This conspiracy of silence is still in effect. Not only do contemporary religious authorities resist prosecuting members of the clergy, but attempts to sanitize these crimes are embedded in the extant records. For instance, in the findings of Pennsylvania's grand jury, the crime of rape is consistently characterized by church authorities as "inappropriate contact" or "boundary issues."[4] It is noteworthy that the modern church's pattern of concealment and prohibition even pertains to clerical sins committed centuries before. In 1995, Filippo Tamburini, a priest and former archivist at the Vatican, edited a collection of premodern cases from the papal penitentiary (a tribunal for grievous sins reserved for the papacy) under the sensational title *Santi e peccatori* (Saints and sinners). Tamburini was chastised and threatened with a number of censures by Archbishop Giovanni Battista Re, "minister of the interior" of the Holy See.[5] The inclusion of incidents of clerical sodomy was deemed particularly objectionable. This manner of response is of long standing and, as discussed in Chapter 5, finds eloquent expression in a euphemism that arises in the high Middle Ages: "the sin not fit to be named."

The widespread suppression of clerical scandal at every level of the ecclesiastical hierarchy was not based solely on self-interest; there was an altruistic side to this taboo. The term "scandal" is derived from a Greek word meaning "to cause another to stumble." If an individual's actions somehow occasioned sin in another, even if whatever they said or did was not sinful in and of itself, the perpetrator was nevertheless guilty of scandal.[6] This perspective was not simply grounded in ecclesiastical expediency but had strong scriptural support. Christ had famously set a child in the midst of the apostles and said, "unless you be converted and become as little children [*sicut parvuli*], you shall not enter into the kingdom of heaven. . . . But he that shall scandalize one of these little ones [*unum de pusillis istis*] that believe in me, it were better for him that a millstone should be hanged about his neck, and that he should be drowned in the depth of the sea" (Matt. 18:2–3, 6).[7] Over time, canonists and theologians would determine that the more influential the person, whether by virtue of rank or reputation, the greater his ability to scandalize, and the greater the culpability he would accrue for occasioning scandal. As the clergy's moral authority grew over time, it was progressively invested with a heightened capacity to scandalize. This meant that the suppression of clerical sins was not simply pragmatic, but praiseworthy. As early as the seventh century, a cleric who hid his sin and hypocritically posed as a holy man was widely believed to be less sinful and, to most religious authorities, such behavior was considered infinitely preferable to the cleric who sinned openly.

These same authorities were much more inclined to conceal the clergy's sexual relations with other males over their involvement with females and for good reason. From a theoretical standpoint, same-sex relations in any form were considered much more sinful, and hence more scandalous, and this would justify a salubrious concealment for the public good. In practical terms, however, relations between two males, especially between two members of the clergy, were easier to conceal and, from this perspective, less scandalous than would be a priest's relationship with a woman. From an institutional standpoint, the clergy's relations with other males posed much less of a threat than comparable relations with females, since wives or concubines and their offspring not only represented an economic drain on ecclesiastical property but also tended to divide the clergy's loyalties. During the eleventh-century papal reform and its aftermath, it was the married clergy who were persecuted, while clerical same-sex relations were tacitly tolerated and, in some circles, celebrated. We shall see that it was very rare for a cleric to be charged with same-sex relations before an ecclesiastical tribunal during the period under consideration. In fact, most of our knowledge of same-sex relations in premodern Europe is drawn from secular criminal tribunals. For although members of the clergy were exempt from secular jurisdiction, clerics were nevertheless periodically apprehended for sodomy by secular authorities.

The evidence of these tribunals overwhelmingly indicates that same-sex relations in the premodern world paralleled the model of classical pederasty in which the active party (i.e., the penetrator) was older and more powerful.[8] These sources, in conjunction with scattered literary representations and rare instances of prosecution by ecclesiastical tribunals, suggest that the model of pederasty pertained to both clerical and secular society. The church's ongoing toleration of clerical pederasty may seem at odds with Christianity's reputation as defender of children, evident in its condemnation of classical same-sex relations through the introduction of concepts like *paidopthoria* (violation of children) or *corruptor puerorum* (corrupter of boys). I would contend, however, that the prime motivation behind such sanctions was never the welfare of children. What was really being condemned was same-sex relations. Pederasty just happened to be the form that such relations assumed, and these condemnations would have been issued regardless of whether they benefited children. This might seem like a shocking contention—especially for premodern historians of childhood, who are still resisting Philippe Ariès's argument that the premodern world had no conception of childhood.[9] Some of this scholarly resistance is legitimate; there is little doubt that medieval society was aware of childhood as a unique stage of development. But I also think this resistance has overemphasized the positive attitudes toward children over the negative. For the perception of childhood was deeply riven—especially when it came to church authorities.

This bifurcation can be projected backward onto Christ's comments on scandal and children, in which he used different terms to symbolize two discrete but related conceptions of childhood. The child whom Christ upheld as a model citizen for the kingdom of heaven is described as the sinless *parvulus*; the one who is in danger of being scandalized is the corruptible *pusillus*. Different authorities often chose to emphasize one of these aspects of childhood over the other. For John Chrysostom (d. 407), childhood was a time of sexual innocence, which he associated with the angelic life. The child's easy access to salvation was because "the soul of the little child is pure from all the passions. He does not bear a grudge against those who have hurt him, but approaches them as friends as if nothing had happened."[10] This accorded with the fond remembrances of Gregory of Tours (d. 594), who grew up in the household of his maternal great-uncle, Bishop Nicetius of Lyon (d. 573). Not only does Gregory present the child himself as presexual, but he refuses to entertain the possibility that a child could be the object of sexual desire.

> I remember in my youth, when I was beginning to learn how to read, and was in my eighth year, that [the bishop] ordered my unworthy self to come to his bed, where he took me in his arms with the sweetness of paternal affection; holding his fingers on the edges of his garment he covered himself with it so well that my body was never touched by his blessed limbs. Consider, I beg you, and note well the precaution of this man of God, who abstained thus from touching a child's body, in which he could not have had the least glimmer of concupiscence nor the least incitement to impurity. And when there might be a real suspicion of impurity, how much more did he avoid temptation![11]

Gregory's representation is deeply invested in a vision of childhood innocence, not to mention the purported respect that such innocence should inspire in adults. Yet in the tug-of-war between the innocent *parvulus* and the corruptible *pusillus*, it is the latter that often wins out in ecclesiastical discourse—especially in the West. For the flip side of childhood innocence is the child's undisciplined mind, which rendered him especially susceptible to sin.[12] This grim view is epitomized by Augustine (d. 430), who maintained that no one was without sin: "not even the infant which has lived but a day upon the earth." Far from being immune to the passions, Augustine points to the inchoate rage and jealousy that infants experience, arguing that "in the weakness of the infant's limbs, and not its will, lies its innocency."[13]

This apprehension of childhood finds expression in different discourses throughout Latin Christendom. In the *Life of St. Anthony* by Athanasius (d. 373), for example, the boy's first sign of sanctity was his deliberate avoidance of other children.[14] Evidence for the duration of this view is ubiquitous. In a twelfth-century otherworldly vision, allegedly visited on the ten-year-old Alberic of Settefrati (b. ca. 1100), the angelic guide gives an Augustinian-inflected explanation of the babies being tortured in hell: "There are many who think that infants and little children have no sin, nor do they imagine that when they die they will suffer any punishment, but this is not the case *because even an infant of one day is not without sin* and such children cannot be entirely without sin, often saddening the mother or hitting her in the face."[15] The waywardness of children could even provoke divine retribution. In the early 1360s, when the second visitation of the bubonic plague was believed to target children especially, an anonymous treatise on the Ten Commandments construed this susceptibility as punishment for the disrespectful treatment of parents.[16] It is possible that this widespread clerical view of a child's innate propensity to evil blunted the clergy's sense of tragedy over his premature sexual initiation.

Although predatory clerics had easier access to boys, clearly underaged females did not escape unscathed. The sources make it difficult to discern the sexual abuse of girls, however. As we shall see, the ecclesiastical authorities showed considerable ambivalence to boys but at least paid attention to their perversity: penitentials penalized them for their sexual (same-sex and masturbatory) "games"; adolescents were stigmatized by church councils, Carolingian capitularies, canon law, and later pastoral theologians for their lewdness; and monastic communities showed intermittent awareness of the sexual victimization of younger boys by their seniors. Girls do not occasion parallel concern. I have found no indication that girl-children were considered at risk of molestation in female communities, although there is occasional uneasiness over same-sex relations. The monastic rule for nuns by Donatus of Besançon (d. after 658), for example, contains the following indictment: "It is forbidden that any take the hand of another for affection whether they stand or walk around or sit together. She who does so, will be improved with twelve blows. And any who is called 'little girl' [*juvencula*] or who call one another 'little girl,' forty blows if they so transgress." The appellation "little girl" is clearly a term of endearment versus a reference to age.[17]

In the above example, the question of age deflects analysis, and this is true of many ecclesiastical sources. The penitentials epitomize this problem, despite the fact that sins are hierarchically determined in terms of gender and rank. The term *puella* (girl) is entirely deracinated from age and used to designate any unmarried woman. The *Penitential of Finnian*, for example, warns that any cleric at one time married who returns to his wife and begets more children is every bit as sinful as someone who had been a cleric from his teenage years and fornicated with a "foreign girl" (*cum puella aliena*). *Finnian* also maintains that a layman who defiles a nun (*puella Dei*) is punished more harshly if he begets a child with her than if he does not.[18] According to the *Chapters of Theodore*, a *puella* already betrothed to someone cannot be married to another.[19] The *Penitential of Theodore* regards the sin of fornication by a widow or *puella* of equal severity and deserving of the same penance, which is uniformly less than what would be meted out to a woman who has a husband.[20] *Theodore* also accords a *puella* of fourteen years with power over her own body, while at the same time maintaining that she is under her parents' control and cannot independently become a nun until she is sixteen or seventeen.[21] In the *Penitential of Bede*, a youth (*adulescens*) who has sex with a *puella* is punished less harshly if he is under the age of twenty.[22] The *Penitential of Hubert* adopts a sliding scale of penance for a cleric touching the breast or the filth (*turpitudinem*) of a *puella* or *mulier*, which waxes in proportion to the perpetrator's rank in the ecclesiastical hierarchy.[23]

Even in questions of incest, an area in which girl-children would seem especially prone to victimization, age is rarely a factor.[24] One of the few instances of incestuous abuse of a child in penitentials, arising in the *Penitential of Bede*, assigns penance to a mother who simulates intercourse with an infant son. There are, however, no parallel age markers for the abuse of prepubescent girls by relatives.[25] If we widen our purview to include spiritual incest (sex between a godparent and godchild), there is a memorable exemplum from the *Dialogues* of Gregory the Great (d. 604) in which a godfather died soon after seducing his goddaughter (described as a "certain young daughter," *juvencula quaedam filia*), and flames are seen issuing from his tomb.[26] Gregory tells the story to prove the existence of hellfire, however, while later canonists will mobilize it against the evils of spiritual incest. It is not used to decry the abuse of an underage female, however, which seems to fall well below the legalistic consideration of Christian disciplinarians.[27] As a result, the sexual objects/victims discussed in the course of this analysis are almost exclusively boys and adolescents.

This book is divided into two parts. Part I consists of five chapters demonstrating how the tacit toleration of clerical sodomy evolved from late antiquity until the late thirteenth century. Chapter 1 addresses the problem of clerical sin in the early church. Through an examination of conciliar legislation, patristic letters, and penitential culture, it argues that the ban against a cleric doing public penance, although originally intended to hold a cleric to a higher moral standard, ultimately ushers in a culture of secret sin and concealment. The second chapter addresses boys as sexual objects in late antiquity and the early Middle Ages: first in classical pederasty and then in clerical culture. As we shall see, many church authorities are clearly cognizant of the sexual temptation afforded by boys and youths. But the very temptation that boys afford aligns them with women with similar results: the boys themselves are often blamed for their inadvertent seductiveness. The first two chapters are written with a view to establishing precedent, which means that I occasionally depart from a strict chronological movement in favor of a topical approach. The chapters do not engage changes in secular or ecclesiastical society at any length.

Chapter 3 examines the eleventh-century papal reform—particularly the dynamics between the papal reformers, consistently accused of sodomy and the unreformed married clergy. It is in this context that Peter Damian's polemic on clerical purity for the clergy is considered: how his initial attack on the culture of clerical sodomy, significantly centered on the abuse of sacraments rather than individuals, is eventually abandoned for the more politic attack on clerical wives. Chapter 4 sets the ecclesiastical authorities' tacit toleration of clerical same-sex relations alongside clerical chroniclers' efforts to direct suspicions of sodomy away from the clergy. It begins with the clergy's flagrantly homoerotic poetic culture at the end of the eleventh and beginning of the twelfth century and some very rare instances of resistance. It then turns to contemporaneous ecclesiastical chroniclers who project accusations of sodomy onto secular rulers hostile to church reform in the Anglo-Norman milieu. Chapter 5 addresses the reluctant acknowledgment in various clerical sources that same-sex relations had, indeed, become a problem among the clergy. Beginning with the rise of oblique visionary critiques, it then turns to the twelfth-century milieu of Peter the Chanter and his cohort, engaging their heightened concern about clerical sodomy and their deliberate measures to ensure its eradication. The Chanter's efforts to curb clerical sexual vice were defeated by new theological developments, however, some of which were generated by his own initiative. An examination of some of the pastoral theologians in the Chanter's circle, as well as some prominent thirteenth-century scholastics, demonstrates how the growing emphasis on the seal of confession, compounded by a new sensitivity to scandal, made it increasingly difficult to bring a corrupt cleric to justice.

Part II begins with a brief prologue addressing the eventual admission of the prevalence of clerical same-sex relations by religious authorities over the course of the thirteenth century and, despite the best efforts at obfuscation by many of these same authorities, among the laity. Even though there was a burgeoning of church tribunals, however, evidence for the prosecution of clerical same-sex offenses is sparse, bespeaking ecclesiastical reluctance. The exculpatory mind-set that sustains this reluctance is illuminated by a foray into alternative tribunals, such as the papal penitentiary. This forum provides a disturbing window into clerical familiarity with pederasty, suggesting a tolerance for this offense among members of the clergy that contrasts sharply with the often vigorous resistance of their sexual targets as well as the extreme antipathy to such relations among the laity. The prologue is followed by a final four chapters examining a series of exemplary cases from the high and later Middle Ages in which same-sex relations between an older male (generally the aggressor) and a younger male were subjected to some kind of judgment in an external tribunal. These occur in milieus in which boys and adolescents would have been especially at risk: the monastery (Chapter 6), the choir (Chapter 7), the schools (Chapter 8), and the episcopal court (Chapter 9). In each of these venues I have attempted to emphasize aspects of the culture that could be turned to the advantage of a sexual predator, such as hierarchical considerations, living arrangements, and especially the prevalence of corporal punishment.

The different chapters of Part II are united by the unusual circumstances under which reluctant church officials were pressured into prosecuting clerical offenders. As we shall see, such cases are few and far between. The reader should thus be forewarned that the nature of the evidence requires some geographical and chronological leaps. Hence the final chapters address cases from France, Germany, England, and Italy. The fragmentary nature of the records from episcopal registers and courts prior to the fourteenth century also means that a number of the cases discussed are quite late. Indeed, the last chapter addresses an extended disciplinary case from early sixteenth-century Italy. Admittedly, so capacious a net is hardly ideal, but the subject itself is elusive, which has determined this challenging scope. And yet, while these chapters seek to examine concrete cases, innuendo and euphemism are intrinsic to most medieval discussions of sodomy. As a result, my interpretation of some of the materials in these chapters must necessarily remain speculative.

Most scholars will agree that the study of sexual practices in the premodern world has become something of a semiotic minefield. John Boswell learned this the hard way in the course of the reception of his seminal work *Christianity, Social Tolerance, and Homosexuality: Gay People in Western Europe*. Although an instant best seller, the book was almost immediately criticized for the employment of the anachronistic term "gay" in its subtitle, which was widely perceived as projecting a dangerous culture of sameness across the ages. The designation "gay" was also thought to imply that the subjects of Boswell's narrative had a fixed sexual orientation.[28] In our post-Foucauldian world of social construction, this latter premise has been largely rejected, even as there is a widespread recognition that the very categories "homosexual" and "heterosexual" are modern constructs.[29] These are crucial distinctions. Today many, if not most, people believe that a married man who engages in same-sex practices is "in the closet," repressing his true sexual preferences, yet such an assumption is quintessentially modern.[30] The evidence suggests that premodern individuals did not identify themselves by sexual orientation but were more inclined to focus on the act, especially who did what to whom: who was the active subject (the penetrator) and who was the passive object (the one being penetrated)?[31] For the present study in particular, it is especially important to reject any presupposition of sexual orientation. The males I will be discussing are, for the most part, professional celibates, many of whom live in communities of men with little or no access to women. We can only suppose that much of their sexual initiative is contingent on their environment.[32] In this sense, clerical predators are similar to the inmates of modern prisons in which many men who consider themselves heterosexual nevertheless engage in homosexual practices. For the Middle Ages, however, in recognition of the fact that terms like "homosexual" and "heterosexual" are anachronistic, I have tried to avoid them in favor of more neutral expressions like "same-sex activity" and "male-female relations"—although, admittedly, no such descriptors existed at the time.

The term "sodomy," though widely used throughout the premodern period, is also rife with ambiguity. Although by the later Middle Ages, this will become the preferred way to describe male same-sex relations, especially in a legal context, the term was nevertheless applied to any number of prohibited sexual acts—same-sex and male-female alike—throughout the Middle Ages. When I use the term "sodomy" or the adjective "sodomitical," it will refer to same-sex relations between males, unless otherwise specified. By the same token, there are a number of favored euphemisms like "the sin against nature" and "the sin not fit to be named" that were routinely employed when alluding to same-sex relations. Although such innuendoes effectively project an aura of prohibition, they remain inadequate conduits for stable meaning and do not express precisely what activity is being censured.[33] But despite such ambiguities, this is the only historical vocabulary of record at my disposal. I have attempted to choose the terms that best reflect the usage of my various sources, clarifying what actually is being condemned whenever possible.

I recognize that this study goes against the grain of contemporary historical narrative or literary analyses of sexual relations between men in the Middle Ages, which have often been celebratory or defiantly eulogistic. John Boswell pointed to the undeniable clerical homoerotic subculture of the high Middle Ages as evidence that same-sex relations were once tolerated in a number of ecclesiastical venues. The existence of this widespread toleration is impossible to contest. Yet where Boswell saw the "Triumph of Ganymede," I tend to see the "Triumph of

Jupiter"—that Ganymede was not a youth whose abduction by a god allowed him to realize his sexual potential in his role as celestial cupbearer, but a boy who was dominated by an older and more powerful entity and forced into sexual servitude.[34]

Boswell also posits a secular correlative for this clerical efflorescence of same-sex culture in his matter-of-fact assertion of a love affair between the English king Richard Coeur de Lion and the French king Philip Augustus. Some scholars, like William Burgwinkle, likewise accept this relationship unquestioningly and even attribute a conspiratorial denial among historians for refusing to give Richard a place in history as one of the first medieval kings who overtly had a sexual relationship with another male.[35] But I remain skeptical. The description of their passionate attachment is, after all, based on a single source. But more to the point, the possibility of a sexual relationship between Richard and Philip seems just as implausible as the putative relations between Philip I, the king of France, and the youthful bishop of Orléans, which I discuss (and, I hope, debunk) in Chapter 4. While there is considerable evidence in Mediterranean regions that same-sex practices between males continued to be relatively common after the fall of Rome, in the secular north, charges of sodomy were politically lethal. Ecclesiastical authors chose to impugn select monarchs with such charges precisely because of the laity's aversion to such relations. Furthermore, the evidence for Richard and Philip's love affair is thin. There is only one brief account of their allegedly impassioned relations, describing how the two men ate at the same table by day and occupied the same bed by night. The larger context for this revelation, however, was the bewilderment of Henry II, Richard's father, at the attachment between the two younger men. I am inclined to agree with Stephen Jaeger's view that Henry was astonished at (and concerned by) his son's affection for the French monarch, given the rivalry between England and France.[36] But even if this report of the monarchs' behavior did constitute a wry insinuation of same-sex relations, it was based entirely on clerical innuendo and could be construed as a less explicit version of the sodomitical allegations that we will see were lobbed against Richard's much less popular forebear William Rufus by monastic chroniclers in an attempt to disparage him. It is also worth noting that the supposedly amorous relationship between the two princes was remarked upon in 1187, when Richard and Philip were both grown men—Richard being around age thirty and Philip twenty-two. Practically all the evidence for same-sex relations between males in the Middle Ages, north and south, adheres to the model of classical pederasty, which involves a mature man and a beardless youth.[37] The idea of two adult males consensually having sex would have been considered a highly unusual, and possibly revolting, prospect. If the public believed that Richard Coeur de Lion was implicated in such a relationship, he may well have met with the same terrible fate as Edward II, whose trials a number of scholars attribute to his same-sex proclivities.[38]

The model of pederasty that shapes same-sex relations in the Middle Ages does not constitute the kind of usable past that historians of sexuality, including myself, were hoping for. This is not to deny that there may have been many instances of caring and committed relations between mature men and their youthful lovers in the premodern world.[39] Mathew Kuefler has further contested the presumption that pederast relations were necessarily abusive, pointing to cultures that foster and even institutionalize relations between adults and pubescent or even prepubescent boys, anticipating potential social benefits.[40] Of course, some of the relations I discuss may have been consensual, even if during a period when boys could marry at fourteen and girls at twelve, the criteria of consent are distinct from our own. But social historians who have written in the wake of Boswell—scholars such as Guido Ruggiero, Michael Rocke, and Christian Berco, to name but a few—have examined alternative sources to those enlisted by Boswell, particularly court proceedings. What has emerged is a very different picture of same-sex relations in the premodern world—one that is steeped in violence.[41] Nor was Boswell unaware of this somber potentiality. When exploring Dante's decision to put some sodomites in purgatory and others in hell, Boswell reasons that the ones consigned to hell were guilty of rape.[42]

The association of clerical same-sex activity with violence, or at best coercion, is present throughout the Middle Ages. In the early Middle Ages, monastic and penitential sources make frequent references to the sexual abuse of boys. In the thirteenth century, the Dominican canonist Paul of Hungary referred to the sin of sodomy as "the sin of homicide just as is said of Cain in Genesis: *the voice of thy brother's blood crieth to me from the earth* [Gen. 4:10]. It is the sin of oppressors—that is, of those who oppress others.[43] We shall see that the fourteenth-century constitutions of Cluny project a parallel violence on same-sex relations, stigmatizing "whoever imposes the sin against nature through malice on his brother."[44] Finally, there is the lurid case of Donato Piermaria Bocco, vicar-general to the bishop of Pistoia and subject of Chapter 9, who by his own admission raped the younger clerics of his household with impunity, sometimes inflicting unspeakable damage. Thus, while I empathize with Mark Jordan's desire to place the clerical sodomite in the same quasi-martyred position as the witch or the heretic, I would argue that this realignment would in many, if not most, instances be inappropriate.[45]

The persistence of a climate of clerical sexual abuse over centuries was fostered by canon law, which tended to minimize clerical same-sex relations while maximizing the dangers of clerical scandal. Gratian's twelfth-century *Decretum* and key supplemental texts (the so-called new law) continued to be authoritative until 1917. At this point the Code of Canon Law was introduced as a compendium of past law. In both the original code and its 1983 revision, the concern over scandal continues to intrude on the subject of clerical discipline. I believe that the same clerical prerogatives and privileges that were formulated in late antiquity and the medieval era are still at the center of what it is to be a member of the clergy today, as well as the impetus to protect these privileges. Such a contention will doubtless cause some readers to approach this book with a certain apprehension. As connoisseurs of change, historians are understandably suspicious of any claims of continuity that span more than a millennium. The profession has also overwhelmingly turned against books that attempt to analyze multiple centuries—concerned that such an undertaking flattens out historical difference en route to the creation of some specious master narrative. Contemporary trends favor studies that focus on a single century or less and depend primarily upon one set of sources. Such historical tastes are certainly a contributing factor in the rise of microhistory. But the problem that I want to analyze requires a wider terrain. Interestingly, the scope of John Boswell's seminal book and his formidable range of sources provided inspiration in this respect. Despite our fundamental differences in approach and conclusions, I have found the very existence of such a book enabling. It is embedded in the conviction that there are certain patterns of continuity and change that can only be discerned through a wide-angle lens.

I also recognize that my acknowledgment of the very contemporary events that led to the writing of this book renders me susceptible to charges of undue bias and "presentism," which could, in turn, prejudice the reader against the book. From this perspective, it would certainly have been wiser to remain silent: to present the evidence and allow readers to draw their own conclusions about possible connections between past and present. This was the modus operandi recommended by the press's two anonymous readers. But while undoubtedly a less contentious approach, the idea of obscuring the reasons behind why I wrote this book struck me as rather spineless. I also think that challenging the efficacy of a historical work because it was prompted by current events is parallel to questioning whether the past can shed light on the present. It is precisely the reluctance of historians to point to the resonance between past and present that is fast rendering our discipline irrelevant. So this book unabashedly posits a tragic continuity between the clerical sexual abuse that was tacitly tolerated in the medieval church, protected by theologians and canonists alike, and the abuse we are now witnessing in the contemporary Catholic Church.

There are some who might point out that the Catholic clergy's history of sexual abuse is by no means singular, drawing attention to other recent instances in which people in a position of trust have likewise preyed upon the weak and vulnerable. The scandal regarding Penn State coach Jerry Sandusky is just one of the more prominent in a long series of revelations about the endemic abuse of minors in the world of sports.[46] In many of these secular contexts, people in positions of authority were prepared to look the other way and tolerate the behavior of these culprits. Even though this might seem like the same basic situation that we find in the contemporary Catholic Church, there are two significant differences. First, clerical abusers had the advantage over their secular counterparts by virtue of an ancient and hallowed system that was created to protect them in order to protect the reputation of the clergy at large. Second, no secular abuser has the personal cover of the sexually predatory priest, who, over time, became imbued with an aura of holiness that helped to obscure any personal deficiencies. He alone could administer the sacraments deemed so essential to the salvation of the faithful. He alone had access to the secret lives of not just potential victims, but their entire families, by virtue of the sacrament of penance. And he alone stood in the place of Christ—an entity who was not just credited with founding a religion but was believed to be God incarnate.

PART I

CHAPTER I

The Scandal of Clerical Sin

For many sinners are corrected, as was Peter, many tolerated,
as was Judas, and many are not known until the Lord should
come and illuminate the hidden things of the shadows and
manifest the thoughts of the heart.
—Augustine, Sermon 351 (as cited in the *Collectio Dacheriana*)

There are many ways to write the history of the evolution of Christianity in
Latin Christendom. One possible method would be to trace the growing distinction between the clergy and laity or, to put it another way, by chronicling the
rising prestige of the clergy and the ever-expanding scope of clerical privilege.
Nowhere is this privilege more apparent than in religious authorities' preoccupation with clerical sin and their efforts at containment.

Sin was considered to be an offense against God that required expiation
through penance. Yet how this expiation was effected at any given time in the
period under question is a matter of scholarly contention.[1] The traditional narrative maintains that the only penance available to sinners in the early Christian
era was public. But, according to conventional wisdom, sometime in the sixth
or seventh century the shame and humiliation of public penance was believed
to have taken its toll, giving way to private confession, where penance would be
assigned by a confessor in private. Recent scholarship now recognizes that there
were many different types of penance that coexisted in late antiquity and the
Middle Ages and that public penance never entirely disappeared.[2] Even so, why
these misconceptions first came into being is understandable. The earliest
sources discuss a public ritual for penance, while the contours of private penance
only begin to take shape some centuries later. And, for our purposes, it is certainly significant that the rise of this private penance is inseparable from questions surrounding clerical sin. Not only does the clerical sinner have a central

role in the evolution of private penance, but it is through him that the different ramifications of public versus private penance are negotiated.

The sources suggest that public penance was reserved for someone guilty of a truly grievous sin, such as adultery, homicide, or apostasy. The sinner was first formally excommunicated, which suspended him or her from participating in communion and from contact with the faithful. Thereafter, dressed in sackcloth, the penitent would stand at the door of the church until he or she was formally reconciled by the bishop through the laying on of hands.[3] Initially, this opportunity for reconciliation was perceived as a major concession on behalf of God. In the words of Tertullian (d. 220): "although the gate of forgiveness has been shut and fastened up with the bar of baptism, [God] has permitted *it* still to stand somewhat open. In the vestibule He has stationed the second repentance for opening to such as knock . . . but never more because the last time it had been in vain."[4] In other words, Tertullian perceived penance as a solemn undertaking that, like baptism, could not be repeated.[5]

Yet public penance was not for everyone. As Mayke de Jong has suggested, public penance constituted a spectacle in which the performers were invariably people of rank—whether by virtue of birth or office. In other words, it was centered around individuals who had reputations to lose.[6] A cleric was certainly believed to be possessed of this kind of visibility in early Christian communities. But this very visibility ensured that his relationship to penance was a vexed one. The complexity surrounding clerical penance is already apparent at the Spanish Council of Elvira in the fourth century. Elvira is believed to be the first convocation of bishops which ever articulated a series of canons, and clerical sin is already a prominent concern. Canon 18 maintains that "bishops, priests, and deacons, if—once placed in the ministry—they are discovered [*detecti fuerint*] to be sexual offenders [*sint moechati*], shall not receive communion, not even at the end."[7] Essentially, what is being mandated is deposition for the errant cleric with no hope of being admitted to penance and, hence, no hope for reconciliation. Sexual misdemeanors further bar a cleric from advancing in orders: young men guilty of sexual indiscretion are not to be ordained as subdeacons "inasmuch as they might afterwards be promoted by deception to a higher order." Furthermore, anyone guilty of a grave sin that only came to light after ordination was to be removed from office.[8] Yet the canons are not entirely intractable when it comes to the quotient of sin committed before entrance to the clergy. Canon 76 determined that a deacon who was discovered to have committed a mortal sin prior to his ordination and confessed voluntarily was assigned three years penance, but fifteen years penance if he were denounced.[9] The deacon whose sin was revealed through denunciation, moreover, was only readmitted to communion alongside members of the laity, which, in this period, represented a form of clerical degradation.[10]

Admittedly, Elvira presents a problem in any discussion of historical precedent because so many details involving the council remain mysterious. For
instance, although the council was believed to have occurred in the first decade
of the fourth century, it eludes precise dating. Furthermore, Maurice Meigne
has recently argued that only the first twenty-one canons pertain to the original
proceedings of the council, and that the rest represent a compilation of later
conciliar action taken in the Iberian Peninsula.[11] Nor is there much evidence
that Elvira was widely known before it was incorporated into canonical collections in the ninth century. Even so, canon 18, one of the canons that Meigne
judges authentic, advances the stern view that a bishop cannot be admitted to
penance, while the other canons extend parallel sanctions to the lower clergy.

In canon 18, the following rationale is provided for excommunicating bishops who were public sex offenders: "because of the scandal and the heinousness
of the crime." Yet a crime that predates the individual's entrance into the clergy
was clearly not considered as damaging—either to the reputation of the clergy
or to the "little ones" who might be scandalized by his behavior. This relative
tolerance for a sin that was committed prior to ordination was sustained at the
Council of Neocaesarea (315), which argued that ordination itself effaces earlier
sins. The individual in question could retain his office, but not preside at Mass.[12]
Over the course of the century, however, there is a new initiative to put the
cleric beyond reproach that reaches into his past. There was no toleration for
errors committed before ordination at the Council of Nicaea (325), which specified deposition for anyone already ordained who confessed to a mortal sin prior
to ordination. Even if the unfortunate cleric had managed to procure penance
and absolution through the laying on of hands, this illicit act would not amelio-
rate the situation: "for the catholic church vindicates only what is above
reproach."[13] By the same token, anyone who had lapsed during the persecution
and had subsequently been ordained by error was likewise deposed.[14]

Mum's the Word

Despite the epoch-making status of Nicaea as the first ecumenical council, its
canons did not circulate in the West until sometime after 545.[15] Yet any link
between the clergy and public penance, even if undertaken prior to ordination,
was eradicated in the fourth century during the course of the Donatist crisis.
From a Donatist perspective, priests who had succumbed during the time of the
persecutions, whether through handing over holy books to the secular authorities or full-scale apostasy, were no longer priests. Their sacraments were invalid,
and they should be made to do public penance.[16] Optatus, bishop of Milevis

(d. 397), the most important orthodox exponent against the Donatists, described what he perceived as their mistreatment of the priesthood in vivid terms: "You have found boys; you have wounded them with penance so that none could be ordained. . . . You have found deacons, presbyters, bishops; you have made them laics; acknowledge that you have ruined their souls."[17] The clerics in question "lived on after this as human beings, but as priests who held God's honours they were killed by you." This was an extreme position. Not only did Optatus perceive canonical penance as a discipline incompatible with the clerical state, but he attempted to place the clergy above human tribunals altogether, arguing: "You shall not touch, [God] says, my anointed ones. . . . God has reserved his own property for his own judgment."[18] Optatus's anti-Donatist writings were destined to leave a deep impression on Augustine, who would argue that ordination, like baptism, was indelible. For this very reason "the hand [of reconciliation] should not be imposed on them in public—lest an injury be done the Sacrament, not the man."[19] So although Augustine never said that a priest was beyond human judgment, and hence ineligible for penance, his deference to the sacrament of ordination elicited the same results.

The problem of clerical sin was picked up by the bishops of Rome, who were gradually asserting their authority over the other bishops in the western half of the Roman Empire and its aftermath. In 384, the same year that Optatus was revising his treatise, Siricius became pope. Under Siricius, the prohibition against a cleric doing penance would become still more categorical. In the course of his letter to Bishop Himerius of Tarragona, he writes: "Just as it is not conceded to a cleric to do penance, so also after penance and reconciliation it is not permitted for any layman to obtain the honor of the clergy." Though acknowledging that these former sinners were now "purified of all the contagion of sin," nevertheless, as "former vessels of sin," it was inappropriate for them to be bearers of the sacrament.[20] Siricius's two-part interdict is both old and new. The prohibition against a former penitent being admitted to the clergy was implicit in conciliar bans against anyone formerly guilty of a mortal sin entering the clergy. But the pope's injunction against clerical penance is more equivocal. While denying atonement for a cleric's past transgressions, a possibility still available at Elvira, Siricius does not say explicitly that the guilty cleric should be deposed. It is possible that Siricius was attempting to hold the priesthood to a higher standard and that his prohibition against clerical penance should be taken to imply that a cleric who is guilty of so grave a misdemeanor as to require public penance would automatically be deposed. But the prohibition against clerical penance could also suggest a similar view to that of his contemporaries Optatus and Augustine, with their concern for the dignity of the priesthood. Perhaps Siricius wished to spare the clergy the kind of constrained and career-ending penance associated with Donatist circles.

Siricius's injunction against clerical penance received additional ballast from Pope Leo I (d. 461) in his response to a series of questions posed by Bishop Rusticus of Narbonne concerning disciplinary matters—many of which were penitential. When Rusticus asked whether a priest or deacon who acknowledged his crime could seek public penance through the laying on of hands, Leo responded: "It is contrary to the custom of the Church that they who have been dedicated to the dignity of the presbyterate or the rank of the diaconate, should receive the remedy of penitence by the laying on of hands for any crime; which doubtless descends from the Apostles' tradition, according to what is written, 'If a priest shall have sinned, who shall pray for him?' And hence such men when they have lapsed in order to obtain God's mercy must seek private retirement, where their atonement may be profitable as well as adequate."[21] Thus Leo reiterates Siricius's ban on a cleric doing public penance, tracing it (erroneously) to apostolic times and attempting to ground it in scripture. He also points to a potential solution for the dilemma presented by the sinful cleric that, arguably, requires neither deposition nor public penance, but a less shameful expiation in private.[22]

Again, it is possible that the scenario Leo sketches presupposes deposition and that the reference to a "private retirement" betokens a monastery, where the disgraced cleric may undertake penance in private.[23] Yet Leo's response could also be applied to the situation of a priest whose transgression was concealed, and his reference to a private retreat carried with it a recommendation for performing penance in secret.[24] The rationale would be to spare the priest, not to mention the priesthood, the humiliation, and to avoid scandalizing the community. Similar motives seem to have informed Leo's censorious letter to several bishops, whom he had recently learned were insisting that prospective penitents confess their sins in public—something that Leo perceived as unprecedented. According to Leo's assessment, although their penance was public, penitents should be permitted to confess their sins privately. To do otherwise was to invite much more than shame and humiliation; it could even potentially put the penitents' lives at risk.[25] This response is in keeping with Leo's reputation for empathy for the sinner, urging other bishops to exercise a parallel clemency.[26]

Yet even if Leo intended that the errant priest be deposed, his comments were open to other interpretations. Optatus, for example, was a proponent for discretion. He was not denying that the priests who lapsed during the persecutions had sinned. He was, however, objecting that Donatists made these sins public by insisting on penance, automatically reducing them to lay status. But what if a sin was secret? Did Leo believe it could be atoned for in secret, preserving the dignity of the individual priest and the clergy at large? I would posit a tentative "yes" on the basis of the authority he cites. In order to strengthen the prohibition against a priest doing public penance, Leo had further enlisted this ostensibly biblical text: "If a priest sins, who shall pray for him?" This was an interesting choice. We know from Augustine's anti-Donatist texts that the Donatists used this text to argue that a priest's purity was integral to the efficacy of the sacrament. A priest who was guilty of a mortal sin was irretrievably fallen; hence, "if the people shall sin, the priest shall pray for them: but if the priest shall sin, who will pray for him?"[27] Leo's appropriation of this text makes a different point—one that was not focused on the sin per se, but on its publicity. Either way, the citation is apocryphal. The biblical passage that comes closest is a verse from 1 Kings 2:25: "If one man shall sin against another, God may appeased on his behalf: but if a man shall sin against the Lord, who shall pray for him?"[28] The fact that the passage in question constituted severely bowdlerized scripture did not seem to bother anyone.[29] The Donatist substitution of "priest" for "man" was a rather opportunistic way to invalidate the consecration of a sinful priest. But the fact that orthodoxy kept the Donatist change, while subtly subverting its meaning, is more opportunistic still.

Let us suppose that Leo was proposing private penance for the priesthood. This advice would doubtless have seemed unremarkable to his correspondent, the bishop of Narbonne, because Gallican councils had already been admitting priests to penance for some two decades.[30] The impetus toward clerical penance, moreover, corresponded with the growing distinction between the clergy's hidden transgressions and their manifest sins. As early as 442, the Second Council of Vaison urged bishops to admonish their sinful subordinates privately, bringing them to compunction in secret.[31] But secrecy is the key word here. In sixth-century Gaul, a cleric whose sin was manifest could be deposed and sent on a quasi-penitential retreat.[32] The Council of Marseilles (533), for example, will pronounce against Bishop Contumeliosus of Riez for his alleged sexual transgressions, deposing and sending him to a monastery for penance. But it is important to note that the bishop's deeds were widely known (*fuerant devulgata*) and that Contumeliosus had publicly confessed, throwing himself on the ground with sorrowful lamentation, and gratefully accepting deposition with the opportunity to do penance.[33] A century later the emphasis on the publicity of the sin (and the implicit scandal) versus the sin itself will become even more marked. The bishops assembled at the Council of Châlons (between 639 and 654) wrote a letter to Theudorius, bishop of Arles, reproving him for his written acknowledgment of certain unspecified enormities and for publicly agreeing to do penance. The agreement, allegedly written in his own hand, was witnessed by a number of his subordinates. It is suggestive that the assembly did not rebuke Theudorius for his misdeeds, nor for his nonattendance at the council (which could, in itself, be grounds for deposition), but reprimanded him for his public profession of sin and acceptance of penance. He was thus suspended from office until a council could convene to hear his case.[34]

Gaul further witnessed a blurring of the lines between different kinds of penance, shifting the boundaries between private and public. When commending the tenacity of public penitents, Caesarius of Arles (d. 542) observes that "one who does public penance could have performed it privately," but he goes on to reflect upon the wisdom of the sinner's choice, thereby securing the prayers of the faithful.[35] It was also becoming an increasingly common practice for individuals to be admitted to the penitential state on their deathbeds.[36] But what about the person who, eyes trained on heaven, confessed all his sins yet did not happen to die? The Council of Gerona (517) addressed this possibility, determining that any person who had received the viaticum on his deathbed as a penitent, and later recovered, could enter the priesthood, provided he confessed no "manifest" wickedness. But those who "accepted penance so that they confessed publicly a mortal sin that they perpetrated are never able to enter the clergy or receive ecclesiastical honors because they marked themselves by their own confession."[37] This might seem overscrupulous. How public was a deathbed confession, after all? The answer, clearly, is: public enough to become a disqualifying factor.

Living with Sin

The necessity of private penance for the clergy represented much more than the simple recognition of the inevitability of clerical sin: it was an admission that however wicked a given cleric might be, religious authorities still preferred that his turpitude remain secret. This may have been the realpolitik of Latin Christendom, but it was still a difficult position to justify. This job fell to Augustine. Over the course of his career, Augustine had argued effectively that government, persecution, war, and even prostitution were but necessary evils in this fallen world. In the course of his controversy with the Donatists, Augustine would succeed in adding the clergy's secret sins to this sorry list. Augustine made it abundantly clear not only that orthodoxy had the capacity to accommodate a high degree of clerical sin but also that such an accommodation was without ill effects. Hence, when denouncing the teachings of Petilian, the Donatist bishop of Cirta, Augustine is at pains to divorce the purity of the Eucharistic sacrament from the impurity of the priest, arguing that "if a bad man offer sacrifice to God, and a good man receive it at his hands, the sacrifice is to each man of such character as he himself has shown himself to be, since we find it also written that 'unto the pure all things are pure' [Titus 1:15]."[38]

Although Augustine may seem to be setting a disappointingly low bar for clerical morality, for the future of the faith, his position is the only viable one. If the sacrament of baptism could be undone by the officiant's secret sin, the entire community of the faithful would be destabilized.[39] Yet in the process of making this argument, Augustine necessarily paints his church in exceedingly somber hues. Hence, the priesthood, united by a common anointment with chrism, takes its name from Christ, but holy orders "can exist among the worst of men, wasting their life on the works of the flesh, and never destined to possess the kingdom of heaven."[40]

Augustine's florid characterizations of sinful clerics clearly made an impression on his Donatist interlocutor Petilian, who assumed that these allusions to clerical turpitude were references to specific instances. Such naïveté was clearly frustrating to Augustine: "as though . . . such cases were not constantly occurring everywhere on either side!" Instead, he insisted that many clerics engaged in considerable subterfuge, "wish[ing] to be thought good, though really bad, and to be reputed chaste, though really guilty of adultery . . . and so the Holy Spirit, according to Scripture, was fleeing from them [Wisd. 1:5]."[41] Likewise, when Petilian cites the expulsion and readmission of a cleric guilty of the "sin of the men of Sodom" as a typical instance of orthodox laxity, Augustine defends his church by arguing that deposed clerics constitute "a multitude dispersed throughout the earth."[42] One of Augustine's more ingenious moves was to turn the Donatist fixation with sacerdotal purity into an indictment for only glorying in men's virtues, rather than God's. Indeed, orthodoxy's inestimable values are reflected in the fact that "the wicked [are] bodily intermingled with the good." Augustine's church, confident in God's grace, is a place where "among us, whatever wicked men are either wholly undetected, or, being known to certain persons, are yet tolerated for the sake of the bond of unity and peace, in consideration of other good men to whom their wickedness is unknown, and before whom they could not be convicted, in order that the wheat may not be rooted up together with the tares."[43] Augustine's "good men" have much in common with Christ's "little ones." In fact, they may be even more fragile, potentially corrupted not only by example but by the mere knowledge of an inchoate evil in their midst. From this perspective, there was clearly a merciful logic to suppressing any and all information concerning the sins of oneself or others—especially for members of the clergy. To do otherwise would needlessly put others at risk.

Augustine's heightened degree of tolerance for clerical sin is not restricted to his contentions with the Donatists. It is also apparent in his reflections on what will eventually be referred to as fraternal correction—the charitable responsibility of every Christian to rebuke wrongdoers so that they might amend.

Fraternal correction is based on Christ's advice: "If thy brother shall offend against thee, go, rebuke him between thee and him alone. . . . And if he will not hear thee, take with thee one or two more: that in the mouth of two or three witnesses every word may stand" (Matt. 18:15–16). Even so, this rather forgiving approach pertains to the sins of all the faithful. There was, however, an apostolic tradition that was specifically addressed to the problem of sinful clerics that was not as lenient. Two or three witnesses were required to convict a priest, with maximum publicity following his conviction: "Them that sin reprove before all that the rest also may have fear" (1 Tim. 5:19–20).

Augustine would ultimately allay some of the tensions between the merciful principles behind fraternal correction and the Pauline injunction for denunciation and public shaming. He argues that the model of public denunciation (which he significantly deracinates from the priesthood and applies to every sinner) was limited to public crimes. In contrast, the private rebuke of fraternal correction pertained to secret sin, with the rationalization that "where the evil happens, there should it die." Otherwise, Augustine contends, the person who seeks to expose the offense for disciplinary purposes is acting not like a corrector but as a betrayer. In pursuit of his point, Augustine adduces the example of the newly married Joseph, who, upon discovering Mary's pregnancy, chose not to expose her shame to others.[44] This will become a key text to discussions of fraternal correction in the high Middle Ages.

Fraternal correction became the very cornerstone of clerical discipline, presented as the model for how bishops were to correct their clergy.[45] It was equally important in the monastic world. Yet, given the challenges of communal life, fraternal correction was padded by additional measures aimed at sparing the sinner public rebuke. Both the Rule of St. Augustine (423) and the Rule of St. Benedict (ca. 520), for example, add the interim step of bringing the offense to the superior in the hopes that the offender could be corrected privately, unbeknownst to the rest of the community.[46] Later commentators on Benedict's rule will elaborate this process, developing a penitential program that will be referred to as the *disciplinaria regularis*.[47] The same degree of compassion and discretion is recommended for individual monks grappling with their own sins. According to the Benedictine Rule, "should the matter be a secret sin of the soul, let him tell such a thing to the abbot alone, or to a spiritual father; for they know how to cure both their own wounds and the wounds of others without disclosing or publishing them."[48] The monastic rule of Isidore of Seville (d. 637) provides a rationale for this secrecy, arguing that only sins committed openly need to be corrected openly lest their evil deeds influence others to do likewise.[49] This is in keeping with Isidore's conviction that a person who sins openly is doubly guilty insofar as he not only perpetrates the sin but also teaches it to others.[50]

Compassionate discretion could manifest itself in strange ways. This is certainly true when it comes to some of the spiritual counsel of the earliest monks, commonly referred to as the desert fathers. These freelance ascetics lived in the Syrian and Egyptian deserts in the third and fourth centuries. In the context of their loosely structured communities, fraternal correction was supplanted by an alternative teaching that focused on suspending judgment. The teaching of Abba Poemen, who was nicknamed "The Shepherd," is a case in point. "A brother questioned Abba Poemen, saying, 'If I see my brother committing a sin, is it right to conceal it?' The old man said to him, 'At the very moment when we hide our brother's fault, God hides our own and at the moment when we reveal our brother's fault, God reveals ours too.'" Poemen also warns against the mandate to "give witness of that which your eyes have seen" (Prov. 25:8), arguing, "even if you have touched it with your hands, do not give witness." This is supported by a cautionary tale about a monk who believed that he saw one of the other brothers fornicating with a woman. The outraged monk shouted at and kicked the perceived offenders, only to realize that he was upbraiding a sheaf of corn. The fathers were also encouraged to practice such compassionate forbearance on themselves. Apparently whenever Abba Paphnutius revealed his sinful thoughts to his spiritual elders, he always received the same counsel: "Wherever you go, do not judge yourself and you will be at peace."[51] These gnomic utterances would continue to circulate throughout the Middle Ages.

Private Confession

Many reasons were advanced for the prohibition against the public penance of the clergy. Early councils perceived it as a dangerous mechanism for reversing depositions; Siricius and Leo I (probably) perceived penance as beneath the clergy's dignity; Augustine argued that penance dishonored not the man but the sacrament. But perhaps the most radical view was expressed by Bishop Optatus: that God's anointed could only be judged by God alone. This view would again be articulated by Isidore of Seville—someone who was destined to become a more mainstream authority. But by this time, the issue of the clergy's public penance was largely put to rest. Isidore's contention moved beyond the arena of clerical sin to accommodate clerical crime: secular people had no right to accuse priests, who were subject to a higher justice.[52]

By the Carolingian period, private confession and penance had become an integral part of clerical life. The penitential process was increasingly structured around penitentials—a genre of pastoral literature originating in Ireland that spread to the Continent.[53] These works were basically manuals created for the use of the priest hearing confession, assigning penalties for individual sins. There was no agreed upon standard, however, as to which sin merited what penance; indeed, some of the more scrupulous penitential works confused the matter further by citing several different opinions concerning the appropriate penance for a given sin. By the ninth century, penitentials were under attack by at least some Carolingian authorities—not only for their many inconsistencies but also for their uncertain authorship and purported leniency for grievous sins.[54]

Despite the wide acceptance of private penance, there were lingering fears over its efficacy. In particular, there was concern that private penance was insufficient in atoning for the more serious sins. And as for the truly egregious sinners: did they, in fact, need to confess their sins at all, or would confession to God alone suffice? Over the course of the ninth century, a new reformist literature emerged that attempted to grapple with these fears.[55] These new works were determined to sidestep the pitfalls of penitentials by basing their pronouncements on unimpeachable authority. They also paid greater attention to the penitential process, both the manner in which confession was undertaken and the nature of the penance to be imposed. For instance, Theodulf (d. 821), a member of Charlemagne's inner circle and later bishop of Orléans, gave detailed instructions to his clergy about how to question a penitent about the eight principal vices, including strategies for extracting confession from the recalcitrant. An individual too ashamed to confess should be reminded that confession was not necessary for God—who already knows everything that we do, say, and think—but was essential to the sinner's salvation, lest the devil accuse us on Judgment Day of a neglected sin. If the penitent claimed not to remember his sins, he should be interrogated, gently and with finesse, lest he be introduced to some hitherto unknown vice.[56]

Despite efforts at a degree of homogeneity, there were still areas of substantial disagreement among authorities. Theodulf himself was equivocal about the scope of private confession, advising his priests: "Capital and mortal sins ought to be wept for publicly according to the institution of the canons of the fathers. Yet we do not deny that mortal sins can be paid for by secret satisfaction."[57] Opinions also diverged over the necessity of confessing to a priest or whether confession to God alone would suffice—a problem alluded to at the reformist Council of Châlons (813).[58] Again, Theodulf of Orléans is of two minds. He acknowledges that a priest can provide the sinner with helpful counsel. Yet he also makes a case for confession to God alone, arguing that the more we remember our sins in this manner, the more God is inclined to forget them.[59]

Hrabanus Maurus (d. 856), abbot of Fulda and later archbishop of Mainz, was unabashedly concerned with the implication of such issues for the clergy and approached these matters directly under the rubric of "Concerning those who after receiving holy orders commit capital crimes." While Theodulf seemed prepared to remain equivocal, Hrabanus pressed for answers, and his clerical focus prompted him to be much more decisive. Clearly aware of the advantages of keeping the sins of the clergy private, he upholds the efficacy of private expiation for the cleric who committed a capital crime either before or after ordination. "Those whose aforesaid evil crimes are committed secretly in the presence of the eyes of God but hidden from others should confess and accuse themselves of having grievously sinned in the presence of a priest, who will lead them in penance—if they are truly penitent, and fight to purge themselves through fasts, alms, and sacred prayers with tears. Even to these people the hope of pardon from the mercy of God ought to be promised, with their rank preserved."[60]

Hrabanus's deference to clerical rank does not end here. In the treatise *On the Institution of the Clergy*, Hrabanus repeats a salient point from Isidore of Seville that it was customary, presumably in Visigothic Spain, for priests and deacons to make their confession to God alone, without loss of office.[61] In Hrabanus's consideration of the matter of a priest guilty of a capital crime, he took it upon himself to extend the Visigothic option to the Frankish clergy. The capstone to Hrabanus's argument countenancing the clerical sinner "whose sins are secret, nor can they be manifestly declared by anybody" is a citation of Gregory the Great's letter to a certain Secundinus—a recluse who, allegedly confused by the conflicting canons of various councils, had appealed to the pope as to whether a priest guilty of a mortal sin could somehow regain his rank. The compassionate pontiff is encouraging. "After due satisfaction we believe that a return to an office is possible for you, as the prophet says: 'Will he who fall not succeed in rising again?' and 'Will he who has turned away not turn back?' [Jer. 8:4]. He also says to the sinner: 'On whatever day you shall turn back and weep for your sins, then shall you be saved' [Isa. 30:15]." In fact, the letter as a whole is a veritable wellspring of reassurance upon reassurance: that Christ came to justify, not destroy sinners; that the lost lamb was more precious than all the other ninety-nine; and that Peter, prince of the apostles, was guilty of something far worse than a sin of the flesh: he denied Christ yet continued as an apostle.[62]

This advice complements Isidore of Seville's judgment noted above: that the secret sinner was less culpable than the individual who sinned openly—a view that Hrabanus cites with approval elsewhere.[63] It also corresponds to the underlying face-saving strategies intrinsic to the concept of fraternal correction—particularly with its monastic adumbrations. Yet, as plausible as such expressions of comfort might be, they were not written by Gregory the Great. In fact, the legendary pontiff was not particularly tolerant of clerical sin, expressing outrage at the rumor that errant priests, deposed for sins of the flesh, had been readmitted to their offices, penance or no penance.[64] Pope Gregory did, however, write a letter to someone named Secundinus that consisted primarily of praise for the hermit's upright life, along with efforts to allay any perplexity he might suffer over current theological disputes. The version of Gregory's letter that Hrabanus relied upon, however, contains a pseudonymous interpolation, written at some point in the eighth century, which recasts the honorable anchorite as a fallen priest, anxious to regain his rank in holy orders.[65]

The forgery was a canny endeavor that offered something for clerics of all stripes. Consider the situation of the priest who was the secret sinner. While not prepared to face the consequences of making his offense public, he was nevertheless fearful that the hypocrisy of concealment would increase his degree of culpability in God's eyes. But here was a letter written by a saintly pope that offered not just solace for the contrite priest but scriptural justification for the subterfuge of concealing his sin. From the standpoint of religious authorities, Pseudo-Gregory's sentiments were equally gratifying. Their aversion to scandal was developing apace with an increasingly self-protective stance. Hence, when it came to the clergy, a secret sin, no matter how heinous, was infinitely preferable to public scandal. In short, any authority that promoted the efficacy of clerical self-correction was a godsend. It is little wonder that the Pseudo-Gregorian interpolation appealed to all the subsequent canonists of note.

As the view that mortal sins could be atoned for privately gained traction in clerical circles, new texts suddenly appeared in its support. A forged decretal attributed to Pope Callixtus (d. ca. 223) argued that whoever doubted that such covert reconciliations were possible was challenging the church's celebrated right of binding and loosing (Matt. 18:18). "Callixtus," for his own part, believed "without hesitation, that both the priest of the Lord and other believers may return to their honors after a proper satisfaction for their error, as the Lord Himself testifies by His prophet: 'Shall he who falls not also rise again?'[Jer. 8:4]."[66] Centuries later when Anselm, archbishop of Canterbury (d. 1109), was asked whether an unchaste priest can resume his office, he appealed to both these texts.[67]

But there was also hope for a priest whose sin was known only to a handful of clerics and, hence, contained. A fabricated decretal, misattributed to the Council of Gangra (340), provides very painstaking directions on how such an individual may be reconciled.

> A priest, if he committed fornication, although according to the canons
> of the apostles he ought to be deposed, nevertheless, according to the
> authority of blessed Pope Silvester, if he did not remain for a long time in
> this vice, and if he brought forth his confession voluntarily, may rise again
> in ten years if he does penance in this fashion. For three months in a
> private spot removed from others, he lives only on bread consumed in the

evening; however, on Sundays and auspicious feast days, he may be restored by a little wine and fish and legumes, without meat, fat, eggs, and cheese. Wearing sackcloth, he should lie on the ground day and night imploring the mercy of the omnipotent Lord. At the end of three continual months he may leave, nevertheless he cannot appear in public lest the faithful flock suffer scandal through him. Nor ought the priest to do penance publicly, like a layperson. Afterward, with his strength somewhat restored, he should complete a year and a half on bread and water, except Sundays and auspicious feasts, on which days he is able to have wine, fat, eggs, and cheese, according to the canonical measure. After a year and a half, lest he grow bitter, he may partake of the body and blood of the Lord. And let him be present for the [kiss of] peace singing in the choir in the last place. He should not approach the altar and, according to blessed Clement, he should only undertake minor offices. From this point until the completion of the seventh year, he should always fast on bread and water for three legitimate days a week, except during Easter. With the cycle of the seventh year complete, if his brethren, among whom he did penance, praise him for his worthy penance, according to the authority of blessed Pope Callixtus, the bishop can recall him to his old office. Clearly it ought to be done singing a psalm on a Monday, or giving a denarius to the poor as an act of redemption. With seven years completed, moreover, he should continue to fast on Fridays on bread and water, with no intervening respite until the end of the tenth year.[68]

This canon first surfaced in Gratian's *Decretum* (ca. 1140). Although its ultimate origin has yet to be determined, my guess would be that it originated in the Carolingian period, which was an especially propitious time for forgeries.

The Carolingian Dichotomy

> It is contained in the ancient law, that whoever has not given obedience to the priests should either be stoned outside the camp by the people, or with his neck beneath the sword should expiate his presumption by his blood [Deut. 17].
> —The False Decretals[69]

Although private expiation for clerical sin was gaining momentum, there were clear limits on its scope: the sin must be hidden as opposed to manifest. Indeed, the distinction between hidden and manifest sin was an underlying principle in

Augustine's motto: "Where the evil happens, there should it die." The natural corollary to this view was expressed in his parallel statement that "if the sin is in the open, correct it publicly, so that he will amend, and others should be afraid."[70] It was during the Carolingian reforms, however, that the hard and fast rule that private sins be corrected privately and public sins be corrected publicly first emerged. This principle, frequently referred to by scholars as the "Carolingian dichotomy," was first stated in a penitential written circa 800.[71] In 813, it was reiterated by a series of councils organized at Charlemagne's behest.[72] The reformed penitential literature also accommodated this newly articulated norm. Theodulf makes this distinction with respect to a priest who committed adultery.[73] In a similar vein, Hrabanus Maurus writes: "It seems to me that a distinction ought to be made that those who were detected or caught publicly in perjury, theft, fornication, or other crimes of this sort should, according to the things instituted by the sacred canons, be deposed from their rank because it is a scandal to the people of God to have such people placed over them who it is agreed are vice-ridden beyond the limit."[74] Indeed, Hrabanus demonstrated a consistent awareness of the scandal that would ensue if a publicly sinful priest were not chastised. The year before writing his manual, a great council, presided over by Louis the German, was held in Hrabanus's own bishopric of Mainz. The council set a precedential procedure for the thorny problem of a priest who is infamous, but where sufficient legal proof of his malfeasance is lacking.[75]

In short, reform brought with it a heightened sense that public sins promoted scandal and a growing apprehension of the lay response to such affronts.[76] The laity could only be appeased if the sinner made public amends.[77] Yet bringing the errant cleric to justice was a vexed issue. For while the laity was subjected to the laws of secular and ecclesiastical tribunals, the clergy was theoretically answerable only to the latter.[78] Clerical exemption from secular courts was an ancient prerogative. St. Paul had insisted that Christians not litigate against one another in the secular courts of pagans (1 Cor. 6:1), the result being that bishops became the de facto judges for altercations among the faithful. With the Christianization of the empire, Paul's prohibition against secular litigation lost its salience. Even so, the Christianized emperors still recognized the clergy's exemption from secular courts, and their edicts were duly noted in the fifth-century Theodosian Code—the font of Roman law in the West until the twelfth century.[79] Church councils would, in turn, censure any cleric who attempted to appeal an ecclesiastical sentence in secular courts.[80] There were also venerable legal traditions that discouraged and hampered cases against the clergy. The pastoral letters already stipulated that accusations against men in holy orders should not be easily entertained and that any charge against a priest required a minimum of two or three witnesses (1 Tim. 5:19). The relative privilege of the cleric charged with a crime increased over time.

The *Collectio Dacheriana* (ca. 800), a compendium of canons drawn from councils and papal decrees at the very heart of the reforming initiative, testifies to the difficulty of enforcing the public correction of the manifest sins of the clergy. The prologue openly embraces the principle: "If a sin is not only a great evil for oneself, but also a scandal to others, and it seems to the [presiding] priest to the advantage of the church, [the sinner] should not refuse to do penance in the presence of many, or even all the people. . . . For what is more infelicitous or perverse than not to blush from a wound that cannot be hidden, and to blush more at the bandage?"[81] And yet the second book of *Dacheriana*, which is focused on matters of procedure against a cleric, dedicates itself to delimiting, discrediting, and at times even threatening potential accusers. It opens by denouncing any clerics who conspire against priests and bishops through swearing false oaths[82] and malicious accusers of all stripes[83] and by insisting on background checks for both the accusers and the accused.[84] Excommunicates, serfs, former serfs, and those deemed infamous are all excluded from making accusations or testifying against a cleric, as are actors, heretics, flagrant sinners, heathens, Jews, or anyone who might be excluded from bringing a case in civil courts.[85] It was further stipulated that anyone who failed to prove a charge was not permitted to accuse or give evidence in any other case.[86] An accuser, who must be a minimum of fourteen years of age, was not permitted to produce any witnesses from his own household.[87] Any case in which a layperson accuses the clergy, especially bishops, should be scrutinized carefully; if the party's character is in any way questionable, the accusation should be ignored.[88] The word of a fractious cleric who seems to litigate too often should be taken with a grain of salt. Furthermore, no cleric should be compelled to testify against his will.[89]

The privilege of the bishop was especially marked. Because lowborn people, frequently "not of good life," were inclined to attack their betters—bishops in particular—their accusations were often summarily dismissed.[90] With a view to "silenc[ing] the right of accusing within our ranks," the bishop could disregard any charge that one cleric brought against another if he deemed it too trivial, and he was even permitted to punish the brother bringing the accusation.[91] A humble cleric who falsely accused his confrere was excommunicated until he was on his deathbed,[92] while a bishop who falsely accused another was deposed.[93] The bishop's authority was theoretically inviolate: if he were to condemn a cleric of any degree, no congregation or individual, no matter what rank, was permitted to defend him.[94] The pontiff's princely prerogative was likewise reflected in the number of judges required to hear a case against him. In the event that the offense arose between synods, his case had to be heard by twelve other bishops.

A priest in a parallel predicament only merited six bishops, while a deacon, a scant three.[95]

If the *Dacheriana* testifies to the difficulty in proceeding against the clergy, let alone members of the higher clergy, the situation was about to become exponentially worse with the introduction of a corpus of forgeries known as the Pseudo-Isidorian or False Decretals. Written in the Frankish Empire in the mid-ninth century, this clever set of forgeries was a conglomeration of fake decretals by legendary popes mixed in with real synods supplemented by invented canons and reasonable-sounding capitularies allegedly issuing from the revered Charlemagne.[96] Although the forgeries contributed to a reformist agenda, their particular purpose seems to have been the defense of the rights of suffragan bishops against their metropolitans, in particular, and the rights of the clergy from lay incursions, in general. In this latter context, Paul Fournier argues that the authors were combating what they perceived as the widespread abuse of accusations engineered to chase bishops from their sees and despoil the church.[97] Hence Pseudo-Isidore's intervention provided additional inoculation to the clergy's already heightened degree of immunity, and this was especially true for the episcopacy. In this context, the apostolic admonition that the launching of any accusation thus "should be made a matter of great difficulty" is not just cited with approval but emerges as a foundational principle.[98] An errant bishop should first be corrected privately by his subordinate clergy, probably members of his household that he would have ordained. He only comes to trial if he proves incorrigible.[99] According to the reckoning of Pope Zephyrinus, it required seventy-two witnesses to convict a bishop, testifying before up to twelve judges of the bishop's choice. The actual sentence, however, was ultimately resolved in Rome.[100] No one of an inferior clerical office could accuse a bishop, and certainly no layperson could.[101] The accuser who did not carry his point risked the loss of his property.[102] Priests, as well as their supporters, who conspired against bishops, were to be degraded and pronounced infamous.[103] The prescribed deference to episcopal authority is well expressed with a warning from scripture: "Whoso casts a stone on high, it will fall upon his own head [Eccles. 27:17–30]."[104]

Although undoubtedly enhancing clerical privilege, the False Decretals also put superiors attempting to prosecute delinquent clerics in a terrible bind. The double-edged nature of the False Decretals is revealed by the plight of Archbishop Hincmar of Reims, who in an attempt to streamline procedure, was writing a treatise on criminous priests sometime in the 870s. Occasionally, the forgeries worked in Hincmar's favor. The treatise opens credibly with a capitulary in the voice of Charlemagne. Although in reality a part of the forged capitularies assembled by the otherwise unknown Benedict the Levite, it nevertheless presents the problem of priests believed guilty of a crime as a matter of some urgency—especially "when there is no proof, and they will always deny it."[105]

But the False Decretals also thwarted Hincmar. The frustrated bishop complains about the alleged decretals of Pope Sylvester mandating that "no layperson should dare to bring a charge against a cleric, and no priest against a bishop, no deacon against a priest, no subdeacon against a deacon" and so on. The fictive decrees further specify that the highest leader (*praesul*) cannot be judged by anyone whosoever as "the disciple is not above the master" (Matt. 10:24)—a principle that, in fact, seems to inform Pseudo-Isidore's reckoning throughout the False Decretals. In the spirit of the decrees of Pseudo-Zephyrinus cited above, "Sylvester" mandates an impossibly high tally of witnesses which increase in number according to the rank of the cleric accused. Finally, "Sylvester" further curtails possibilities of procedure by refusing to allow laymen and clerics to testify against one another.[106] Hincmar did his best to challenge such exacting requirements, arguing that these decretals were not authorized by orthodoxy and pointing out perceived inconsistencies. (He seems especially exercised by the requirement that a lay accuser be married, urging the superiority of chastity over marriage.)[107]

Since canon law eschewed the death penalty, deposition was the ultimate punishment reserved for public sin. From a practical standpoint, however, deposition was a tenuous proposition, especially when it came to bishops. Gregory the Great recounted the depredations of Paul, bishop of Doclea, who had admitted to "sinful bodily crime" "among other evil acts." Paul was duly deposed but returned to invade the bishop's palace and remove church property.[108] As noted earlier, Contumeliosus of Riez was deposed by the Council of Marseilles, over which Caesarius of Arles presided. Yet Contumeliosus foiled his judges by staging a forcible return to his see, buttressed by an appeal to the pope.[109] An appeal to Rome could squelch even the most propitious prosecution. According to Christine Kleinjung, the break between Hincmar of Reims and his nephew, namesake, and suffragan bishop, Hincmar of Laon, only occurred when the latter appealed to Rome. The younger Hincmar was eventually deposed at the Council of Douzy (871) and soon after blinded—a drastic move that would block either a trip to Rome or a possible resumption of office.[110]

Even the lower clergy could confound their superiors through an appeal to Rome. Hincmar presided over a case in which a priest had attempted to kill, but only succeeded in mutilating, his accuser—the brother-in-law of a woman the priest had debauched. The offending priest denied the affair with the woman altogether, and Hincmar was prepared to accept his word, reasoning "what he denied, I left to God." In fact, there was no manifest proof of the affair, and Hincmar was content that the delinquent priest openly confessed to attempted murder—an act that was witnessed by many. But the priest countered with an appeal to Rome. Although we do not know the outcome of this appeal, it is possible that Hincmar's sentence was overturned.[111] The False Decretals had reinforced the efficacy of such appeals, contributing to what was doubtless a growing conviction among ecclesiastical authorities that it was impossible to keep a bad man down.

The Clergy: Discreet and Discrete

There is much that is not known about the rise of private penance. One aspect, however, is clear: its development was intrinsically bound up with the sins of the clergy and the need to create a forum where the fallen cleric could atone for his sins in secret. Private penance permitted a sinful priest to pose as a holy man. Any compunction that he may have felt over this kind of hypocrisy, moreover, was allayed by authoritative reassurances that it was more charitable to conceal one's sins than risk corrupting others. Canon law was complicit with this toleration of clerical offenses. While an offense that became public theoretically required action on behalf of church authorities, any disciplinary action was inhibited by the basic contours of clerical privilege as expressed through a compendium of patristic writings, papal decrees, conciliar acts, and perspicacious forgeries.

This sizable bulwark of privilege was in place by the mid-eighth century. Authors like Regino of Prüm (d. 915) and Burchard of Worms (d. 1025) would become important conduits for their inclusion in the works of eleventh- and twelfth-century reformers.[112] Hence, the decrees of Siricius and Leo I, banning public penance for the clergy, and parallel interventions discussed above, found a place in Gratian's *Decretum*.[113] These texts acquire new and different meanings over time. The authors of the False Decretals, for instance, had emphasized the clergy's right of appeal to Rome as a ploy to evade the jurisdiction of their metropolitan bishops during a time when the popes were weak; when the papacy was on the rise, such appeals would help consolidate its power.[114] Likewise, when Hrabanus deployed Pseudo-Gregory's reassurances that a fallen priest could regain his office, it was contextualized around the plight of a secret sinner. Deracinated from its context in later canonical collections, these reassurances could be read as a freestanding promise of resumption of office for even the most depraved clerics.[115]

Scholars have observed that the strict division between clergy and laity can function as a set of blinders, obscuring historical patterns: that from the perspective of popular religion and heresy, for instance, it makes much more sense to approach religious culture in terms of the local community, consisting of both clergy and laity, standing together to confound the outsider.[116] But in the arena of clerical misdemeanors and their consequences, the clergy stands together— not just as a discrete group but as one for which discretion was of paramount importance. As we shall see, both types of clerical discretion would only increase with time.

CHAPTER 2

The Trouble with Boys

Men who sexually abuse boys (*strupatores puerorum*) shall not
be given communion even at the end.

—Council of Elvira

This chapter argues that the culture of pederasty that was customary in the
classical world was covertly sustained among the medieval clergy. Considering
that early Christian religious authorities were intolerant of same-sex relations,
this might seem like a bizarre contention. The shameful and unnatural relations
between two males or two females are presented as divine punishment for the
sin of idolatry in Paul's letters (Rom. 1:23–27).[1] Paul will also include practitioners of same-sex relations among the different types of sinners barred from
salvation (1 Cor. 6:9–10)—an attitude echoed in the pastoral epistles (1 Tim.
1:8–10). The Council of Elvira and other authoritative sources would sustain
these prohibitions in their condemnations of Roman pederasty.

Yet it is the age dissymmetry implicit in pederasty that has often misled
scholars into believing that the Christian sanctions against same-sex relations
were instituted as measures to protect children.[2] There is little to support this
view. With few exceptions, the church fathers seemed indifferent to the plight
of children, tending to emphasize their innate corruptibility over their innocence. A parallel insensitivity was also apparent in the monastic milieu. Because
medieval monasteries received children as oblates, monastic authorities necessarily paid greater attention to children than did most patristic writers. As one
might expect in an all-male community of professional celibates, children were
vulnerable to sexual predation. Monastic officials were well aware of this and
did what they could to insulate the children from the sexual overtures of older
monks. If a rape did occur, however, it was generally the victimized child who
was singled out for blame as opposed to the older predator. By the same token,

when Carolingian reformers addressed the problem of same-sex relations in religious communities, their outrage was generated by the heinousness of the act, while the exploitation of children was ignored. The chapter concludes with an important exception to this pattern from the Iberian Peninsula.

The Late Antique Culture of Pederasty

> In Capri's woods and groves [Tiberius] contrived a number of
> spots for sex where boys and girls got up as Pans and nymphs
> solicited outside grottoes and sheltered recesses. . . . He
> acquired a reputation for still grosser depravities that one can
> hardly bear to tell or be told, let alone believe. For example,
> he trained little boys (whom he called his little fishes) to come
> and go between his thighs when he went swimming and tease
> him with their licks and nibbles; and babies, fairly strong but
> not yet weaned he would put to his penis as though to the
> breast, being by both nature and age rather fond of this form
> of satisfaction.
>
> —Suetonius, *Lives of the Caesars*

Suetonius's depiction of the sexual habits of Tiberius (d. 37 CE) was clearly intended to shock and repel.[3] But even if the writer invented these perversities, they point to a dismal truth: that for certain children there was no possibility of a presexual childhood in the classical world. This is also implicit in same-sex relations, where the model of pederasty determined the partnering of a mature male, who played the active role, and a beardless youth, who was passive.

In late antique same-sex relations, the roles assigned to the elder male as the active party and the younger male as passive did not brook reversal. To be penetrated was not only considered effeminate and degrading but eventually became illegal after a certain age. Any grown man who played the passive role was not only disgraced but incurred a fine.[4] Yet while this model not only accommodated but foregrounded children as licit sexual objects, it was framed within carefully circumscribed limits. There were rules that governed which children could be solicited sexually and which were off limits, and these rules were structured on the basis of class and age. The Romans divided childhood into two stages: *infantia*, which ranged from birth to seven years, and *pueritia*, which extended from seven to fourteen.[5] Freeborn males were protected from sexual advances until the age of fifteen, at which point the young man received his toga of manhood. The violation of freeborn girls or boys under the age of fifteen was punished harshly.[6] Yet there seemed to be few scruples over sexually engaging with children even in the first period of childhood, provided that the object of desire was licit. Indeed, much greater stigma seemed to be attached to adultery than to pederasty.[7]

But the letter of the law was often at variance with social realities. Marriage practices are a case in point. Girls could legally marry at the age of twelve—two years younger than the legal age for men. In practice, however, marriages were arranged for much younger girls, and some of these unions were consummated: there are several inscriptions concerning girls who married as early as six or seven, and one papyrus refers to a child bride who became a mother at nine.[8] It was also possible to pay lip service to the law, while at the same time embracing proscribed behaviors. The pagan rhetorician Libanius (d. 393) gives vivid accounts of young boys, unwisely taken to feasts by their fathers, who were mauled and seduced by mature men.[9] And yet there were rumors that Libanius himself engaged in pederastic relations.[10]

Slaves were accorded no protection from sexual predation. Indeed, a free-born boy wore a white amulet (*bulla*) to indicate that he was sexually unavailable, distinguishing him from the slave boy who potentially was.[11] The Romans also abandoned unwanted children; those that survived probably ended up in brothels.[12] And there was no particular stigma attached to the relations between mature men and very young slave children. Martial (d. ca. 102) wrote several erotic poems for his slave Erotion, a girl of five. In a similar vein, Ausonius (d. ca. 395) rhapsodizes over his girl slave Bissula.[13] Although these relationships were in all probability sexual in nature, this does not necessarily mean that they included penetrative sex: Christian Laes has argued that this would have been considered inappropriate for children under ten years of age because it could harm the child.[14] Yet, if there is any truth to Suetonius's depiction of the aging Tiberius, some very young children could be abused in ways as ingenious as they were perverse. If we assume that the emperor's victims were slave children or the offspring of poor parents who were forced to sell their children, no law would have been broken.

The accessibility of children as sexual objects was a sufficiently venerable, and presumably acceptable, tradition in the classical world that the *Didache*, a second-century text purporting to represent apostolic tradition, had to coin the term *paidophthoria* ("the violation of children") in order to condemn the practice.[15] As the epigraph at the opening of this chapter suggests, the Council of Elvira treats this practice as an irreconcilable sin, denying communion to men who engage in sex with boys, even on their deathbeds. This injunction is one of the later canons that Meigne has argued were additions to the actual deliberations of the council.[16] If Meigne is correct, it would mean that pederasty was not initially singled out as a pressing concern. This would not be surprising. As we shall see in Chapter 3, the overwhelming concern of Elvira was the regulation of sexual relations between males and females: Canon 71 is the only one that mentions children explicitly. Although pederasty receives the harshest penalty meted out by the council, moreover, this degree of opprobrium is hardly singular. The same punishment is visited upon Christians who lapse into idolatry (cc. 1, 2, 6); women who unilaterally leave their husbands (c. 8); parents who marry their daughters to pagans (c. 17); clerics who occasion sexual scandal (c. 18); adulteresses who abort their fetuses (c. 63);[17] adulterous wives who refuse to abandon their lovers (c. 64); clerics or laymen who fail to repudiate their adulterous wives (c. 70); men who marry their stepdaughters (c. 66); and members of the laity who assail clerics with false accusations (c. 75).

Yet it is on the basis of such interventions that scholars of Christianity have perceived the church as the champion of children.[18] It is difficult to construe either the *Didache*'s interdict against *paidophthoria* or Elvira's parallel move against *stupratores puerorum* as measures taken on behalf of children per se, however, since it is impossible to separate same-sex relations between males from sexual relations between adult males and boys in this period. Christian initiative is further undermined by the fact that the censures against violating boys appear at a time when pagan moralists were likewise distancing themselves from same-sex relations.[19] The Latin translation of the fourth-century *Apostolic Constitutions* ordains: "You shall not corrupt boys [*non corrumpes pueros*] for this wickedness is contrary to nature, and arose from Sodom"—emphasizing the contravention of the laws of nature over the boys' welfare.[20] By the same token, authors from the time of Tertullian had used Socrates's attraction to boys, an attraction the philosopher admitted to but claimed to have repressed, as a critique of the chastity associated with the pagan philosophical tradition. Tertullian's pro-Christian apologia was that "the Christian confines himself to the female sex," but it does not take up the question of age.[21] Nor, for that matter, did Christian moralists object to sexual relations with extremely young girls.[22] Significantly, when Augustine was pressured to marry by his mother he chose a girl of ten—someone he found sufficiently pleasing that he was prepared to wait for two years until she was of legal age.[23]

Not every Christian was blind to the question of the age dissymmetry implicit in pederasty, however. The church father John Chrysostom (d. 407) had studied with Libanius and afterward exhibited marked hostility to both same-sex relations between males and his former teacher. Stephen Morris explores a possible connection between the two antipathies, asking whether John himself had at one time been subjected to Libanius's sexual advances. The historian Sozomen (d. ca. 447), however, implies that John's hostility was grounded

in religious differences.[24] In any event, John seemed very much aware of how the sexual profligacy of the empire impinged upon the young. In a treatise addressed to the paterfamilias decrying the lax education of young boys, John launches an impassioned attack on same-sex relations in Antioch—a phenomenon that he describes as "a new and lawless lust" that threatens to supplant sexual relations with women. Despite the censure of both natural and Roman law, John argues that such relations were sufficiently rife that Antioch outstripped Sodom in its depravity. Courts, parents, and pedagogues seemed complicit in their toleration of such depravity. Mature men preyed upon the young, circumventing their parents and tutors with bribes or by force.[25] Nor were such predators confined to the pagan community: even those with the benefit of divine instruction and scripture "have intercourse more fearlessly with young boys than with prostitutes! . . . But the parents of the children who are being violated bear it in silence."[26] John's radical solution to this problem was monasticism.[27] Even if the children came to dwell in the monasteries for their education alone and did not remain to become monks, at least they would have had a decade—or better still, two—to develop morals strong enough to withstand the onslaught of debauchery from the outer world.[28]

Chrysostom is exceptional in several respects. Although censorious attitudes toward pederasty were on the rise in the empire, it was unusual to describe such relations as a new phenomenon, and one can only suppose that Chrysostom's purposes were somehow rhetorical.[29] Furthermore, very few were naive enough to advance the monastery as a safe haven for preserving the sexual purity of the young. Even so, Chrysostom is distinct for his sensitivity to the vulnerability of youth, which otherwise seems to be lacking among Christian theologians and lawgivers alike. As already suggested, Christian moralists were, and would continue to be, much more intent on regulating heterosexual relations. It is telling, for example, that while commenting on Socrates's predilection for boys, John Cassian (d. 435) expresses much greater horror at Diogenes's casual remark to an adulterer about to be put to death for its tacit promotion of prostitution: "You should not purchase with your death what is freely sold."[30]

At first glance, the secular legislation of the Christian emperors seems to have taken a much harsher position against the sexual abuse of children than we have seen hitherto. According to the chronicler John Malalas, the emperor Justinian (d. 565) made an example of two bishops accused of the corruption of boys. Both were tried and found guilty. One was tortured extensively and then exiled; the other had his genitals amputated and paraded around on a litter. The emperor further decreed that all "those detected of pederasty should have their genitals amputated," resulting in many arrests and mutilations. The subsequent treatment of same-sex relations in the Justinian Code demonstrates parallel severity.[31] Yet chronicle and code alike exhibit the same tendency to collapse the corruption of boys with the censure of same-sex relations. This bias is also reflected in the severe edict of 390, incorporated into the Theodosian Code, which threatened anyone playing the passive role with the death penalty. The law is directed at adult men: the violation of boys was passed over in silence.[32]

The legalistic failure of the Christian emperors to consider the boy child in his own right was tacitly abetted by patristic prejudice against children—an attitude complemented by a pronounced bias against childbearing and reproduction, generally. Initially, the expectations of the second coming of Christ and the end of the world led authorities like St. Paul to challenge the need for further offspring (1 Cor. 7:29). In the fourth century, the procreative impetus of the faithful was further dampened by panegyrics on virginity in which authors like Ambrose (d. 397) and Jerome (d. 420) portrayed a grim and unlovely image of reproduction.[33]

In particular, the impact of Augustine on Western thought must again be considered. Admittedly, his praise of virginity was temperate when compared with colleagues like Ambrose and Jerome. And yet his decidedly negative view of childhood was compounded by an increasingly pessimistic understanding of the sex act, a view that reached its final form over the course of his struggle with the Pelagians. While the Pelagians urged that human nature was good and that a child born of Christian parents would be saved, Augustine not only argued that male-female intercourse could not be performed without sin, but formulated the doctrine of original sin, which was transmitted sexually at conception and consigned the unbaptized child to the flames of hell. But such extreme views were already apparent in his bleak statement regarding the birth of his own child, Adeodatus: "of me was there naught in that boy but the sin [in his making]."[34] Significantly, Augustine framed Jupiter's abduction of the beautiful Ganymede in terms of the illegality of the god's lust, not evoking any special empathy for the victim.[35]

The Age of the Desert Fathers

While there is little doubt that Christianity promoted a more restrained sexual ethos, this did not necessarily work to the benefit of the child. Indeed, the child's sexual vulnerability was additionally challenged with the development of monasticism. The desert fathers arose at a time when both the Eastern and Western church still permitted a married clergy. They were thus distinguished by their unique commitment to chastity, which was frequently enacted through an avoidance of women that bordered on fanatical. This did not just mean shunning physical proximity to women: authorities like Cassian believed that the devil used memories of women to gain access to the mind of the monk, a process that might begin innocuously enough with reminiscences about one's mother but then escalate. All memories of women must therefore be cast out.[36] The physical avoidance and mental suppression of women left a void, however, and this void was filled by boys. It is in this context that we see a further transformation in the semantic valence of the child. For if the *parvulus* was a positive symbol, and the *pusillus* was ambivalent, the *puer* (boy) in monastic culture was, like the woman, a source of temptation and, hence, active corruption. It is significant that, while St. Anthony triumphed over a demon in female form, the spirit of fornication appeared before him as a black child ("puer horridus atque niger"). The demon was, presumably, described as *horridus* for his success in inspiring lust in holy men—an achievement he trumpeted with glee.[37]

There was a fluidity between boys and women in desert culture that did not require explicit articulation. Nor was there a heightened opprobrium for succumbing sexually to one over the other. The very rigor of the desert fathers' sexual discipline had a blunting effect: with no legitimate sexual outlets, degrees of sinfulness became muted. As a result, when it came to fornication, women, boys, and even donkeys were, for all practical purposes, on an equal footing.[38] This lack of differentiation between the temptations afforded by women and boys alike is exemplified in the terms in which the legendary Paphnutius (d. after 399) turned away a youthful monk from the community: "I do not allow the face of a woman to dwell in Scetis [an eremitical valley in Egypt], because of the conflict with the enemy."[39] The assumption that boys are an unequivocal danger to all ascetics is amply represented through many terse epigraphs scattered throughout the *Vitae patrum*. "He who gorges himself and talks with a boy has already in his thought committed fornication with him."[40] "When you see a cell built close to the marsh, know that the devastation of Scetis is near; when you see trees, know that it is at the doors; and when you see young children, take up your sheep-skins and go away."[41] "Be aware of your faults, do not judge others but put yourself below everyone; do not be friendly with a boy nor with an heretical friend."[42] "A man who lives with a boy, and is incited by him to no matter what passions of the old man, and yet keeps him with him, that man is like someone who has a field which is eaten up with maggots."[43]

The ubiquity of such sentiments had the effect of normalizing the "corruption of boys" in ascetical discourse. These alleged remarks suggest that the very reflex that favored ascetical isolation also fostered something akin to a group narcissism, as callous as it was self-protective. The intention is to stigmatize monks who risk compromising their chastity, with no sympathy for the boys who inadvertently threaten it. The result is a culture in which the welfare of the monk and the good of the child are pitted against one another. Take the example of the wife of a monk, abandoned and indigent, who showed up at her husband's cell with their two children. Unable to provide for both, she insisted that the monk take the boy. Father and son proceeded to live together in one cell, a situation that fostered suspicions of incestuous fornication wherever they went. The son finally put an end to these rumors by bathing in a lake "full of nitre [potassium nitrate]," which left him horribly deformed. Yet the boy's sacrifice was approved by a saintly elder who, now that the boy had the appearance of a leper, likened him to an angel. The tacit implication is that the boy, sensual matter out of place, was somehow at fault all along.[44]

The same could be said of John the Persian's account of a certain boy demoniac who came to the fathers to be healed. An old monk "saw a brother sinning with the boy, but he did not accuse him; he said 'If God who has made them sees them and does not burn them, who am I to blame them?' "[45] Intended to demonstrate the ideal of ascetic forbearance toward the sins of others, this story also exemplifies the imperviousness to being scandalized, which, in this context, is represented as an essential component of sanctity.[46] But it also reveals a notable indifference to the claims of children. The monk's use of the plural implies that both parties were equally at fault.

The Monastic Milieu

Eventually, the heroic age of the desert fathers gave way to communal living under a rule.[47] We have seen that John Chrysostom idealized the monastery as providing a bulwark to safeguard the young boy's chastity, but V.A. Kolve's assessment is probably more realistic: "cenobitic (communal) monasticism—the Middle Ages' highest ideal of the religious life—almost against its will created the most fertile field imaginable in which same-sex desire might grow, while proscribing and punishing its physical expression."[48] In contrast to the child-rejecting stance of the desert fathers, cenobitic monasteries welcomed children, who could be dedicated as child oblates while still in their infancy. In the East, the child who grew up in a religious community seems to have had an opportunity to choose whether to remain in the monastery when he or she came of age.[49] But in the Rule of St. Benedict, promoted by the Carolingian reformers and destined to become the template for Western monasticism, the procedure for oblation was much more formal, as was the level of commitment: "If any man of good station offer his son to God in the monastery and the boy himself is still very young, let his parents draw up the petition which we mentioned above [vowing to accept the monastic life]. And then at the Offertory let them wrap the petition and the boy's hand in the altar cloth and so offer him. As regards property, let them promise in the same document under oath that they will never of themselves, or through an intermediary, or in any way whatever, give him anything or provide him with the opportunity of possessing anything."[50] In other words, the child is severed from all former ties to the secular world.[51] The oblate belonged to the community and was the responsibility of the community as a whole. The rule ordained that "boys [under fifteen] are to be kept under discipline at all times and by everyone."[52] When this injunction is repeated elsewhere, it is further stipulated that such discipline should be accomplished "moderately and with prudence" and that monks who "treat[ed] the boys with immoderate severity" would themselves be disciplined.[53]

Benedict was of the opinion that "human nature itself is drawn to pity . . . toward old men and children" and that concessions should be made for "their weakness."[54] Indeed, there is good reason to commend Benedict's moderation and discretion when it comes to children.[55] One of the rule's seventy-two "tools of good works" was "to love the young."[56] Yet there is little doubt that Benedict and his commentators tend to emphasize the weak, potentially corruptible, and corrupting *pusillus* over the innocent *parvulus*, the paradigm for the elect. In the monastic tradition, children were not born good but were made good. Because children were too young to understand the gravity of penalties like excommunication (essentially ostracism from the community), "let such offenders be punished with severe fasts or chastised with sharp stripes, in order that they may be cured."[57] Benedict's heirs elaborated upon this logic. In his commentary on the rule, Abbot Smaragdus of St.-Mihiel (d. ca. 840) drew upon the wisdom of Solomon, which propounded that "Folly is bound up in the heart of a child, and the rod of correction shall drive it away" (Prov. 22:15). The seventh-century rule of Isidore of Seville, like its Benedictine counterpart, sought the "discipline of the lash" to curb a young boy's excesses.[58]

Since oblates were expected to adhere to the monks' rigid schedule, their very modus vivendi appears rather stark—even punitive.[59] Concessions to age were remarkably few: they were permitted to eat meat, but there was little leeway in other areas. The commentary of Hildemar of Corbie (d. 844) recommended that oblates be taken to a field to play for an hour once a week or once a month—as the master saw fit.[60] Hildemar's extensive glosses on the rule suggest that the care of the young became an area of increasing concern, which was especially articulated over the sleeping arrangements. Benedict had preferred that the monks all sleep in one room with a lantern kept lit throughout the night. If there were too many people for one room, a senior monk was to be assigned to supervise groups of ten or twenty. Benedict also advised that the beds of younger monks be interspersed with the elder. While Hildemar believes that Benedict expressed his concerns about same-sex relations obliquely in "dignified language," Hildemar himself forgoes subtle subtexts and innuendo, stating plainly that the prescribed sleeping arrangements were safeguards against sodomy. "Because that crime is the most abominable. For that reason, Benedict anticipated that crime lest, God forbid, it might ever occur." Even so, Hildemar clearly felt that Benedict's provisions were not equal to the problem. Hildemar multiplies the single guardian for ten boys into three or four senior monks.[61] A boy is not permitted to go anywhere on his own without one of these guardians.[62] The guardian is there when the child urinates; the guardian is also present to assist in washing off the semen from a boy's nocturnal emission. As to the gainsayers who object that at no point does Benedict require this level of vigilance, Hildemar responds that they have a flawed understanding of the rule.

The child oblate's vulnerability to sexual predation looms large in monastic commentaries. Although Benedict's rule contains no discussion of sexual infractions, there is a section regarding the punishment of certain "graver sins"—sins that the saint once again discreetly refrained from naming. We have already seen that, while admiring Benedict's discretion, Hildemar did not seek to emulate it. In his discussion of the graver sins, Hildemar specifies: "If a brother, from his fifteenth year onward, should seize a small boy [*parvulum*] and commit fornication with that child [*illo infantulo*], the child should be beaten with rods and chastised for this."[63] In contrast, the assailant, if a first-time offender, is given a light penance—especially if drunk at the time. Despite its presence among the "graver faults," this kind of assault is only treated as such in the event of a repeat offense ("two or three times"), in which case that individual is barred from the priesthood. If the repeat offender is already ordained, however, he must refrain from saying Mass for two years.[64]

Hildemar's surprising clemency toward the sexual aggressor reflects medieval perceptions of the life cycle. The fact that the assault on the child is envisioned as being perpetrated by a fifteen-year-old rather than a mature monk corresponds to the widespread acknowledgment of the male's predilection toward sin and lust during *adulescentia*—the period immediately following *pueritia*.[65] Basil the Great (d. 379) hence cautions would-be ascetics as follows: "If you are youthful in body or mind, fly from intimate association with comrades your own age and run away from them as from fire. . . . At meals take a seat far away from your young brother; in lying down to rest, let not your garments be neighbor to his; rather, have an elderly brother lying between you. When a young brother converses with you or is opposite you in choir, make your response with your head bowed lest, perchance, by gazing fixedly into his face, the seed of desire be implanted in you."[66] Like Basil, Hildemar regards the lust of an adolescent monk as natural and to be expected—hence, always already exculpated.[67]

The matter of eligibility to the priesthood also determined a degree of leniency toward the sexual sins of adolescents. When Benedict wrote his rule, the regular and the secular clergy tended to be discrete categories: monks were rarely ordained priests. With the progressive merging of the categories of priest and monk, there was an increased emphasis on sacerdotal purity for the purposes of performing the Mass. The relatively light penance that a youthful corrupter of boys might initially receive is, in fact, out of deference to his potential as a priest, the natural corollary for which would be secrecy about any sexual lapses.[68] As Hildemar knows only too well, anyone who has committed one of the more scandalous "graver sins" would be excommunicated and incur public penance, in which case that person was automatically barred from the priesthood. He thus offers this shrewd counsel: "Anyone, therefore, with responsibility for excommunication must consider the individual and the fault, because although for all graver faults the rule appears to provide that anyone guilty thereof should perform penance through exclusion from the church, the refectory, and fraternal company, yet a discerning and prudent abbot will distinguish on an individual basis whose advancement to holy orders is blocked by public penance and whose not."[69] Nor were such scruples unique to Hildemar; they were shared by other commentators under the rubric of *De gravoribus culpis.*[70] Hildemar's parallel deference to members of the community who were already ordained is underlined by the citation of a forged decretal attributed to Pope Sylvester, requiring forty-four witnesses before a priest could be condemned for an offense.[71]

The greater penalty for the victimized child is puzzling: I can only offer some possible rationales, none of which is mutually exclusive. One possibility involves Old Testament law, which required that both males involved in sexual relations be punished by death (Lev. 20:13). But Bernadette Brooten has argued that the ancient Jews were more inclined to regard the younger passive party as deserving of death and to let the elder active party go free. The reasoning is that the active party at least "remained culturally masculine."[72] Perhaps a similar mentality prevailed in all male communities. Another option would be the dissonance between a child who had been sullied by abuse and the purity that he was meant to represent. By the Carolingian period, the child oblate had become associated with Samuel, who was offered to the temple as an infant and was understood as both a living sacrifice and a model for the priest or bishop growing up in the church.[73] Perhaps stripped of his innocence, the oblate was no longer considered a worthy offering to God, nor, corrupted at so early an age, was he a prime candidate for the priesthood. Whether or not the boy was in some way complicit with his assailant was seemingly incidental. The pollution of the child himself might be compounded by the question of his assailant's possible ordination: not only has the child lost his value as an offering, but his seductive presence may have compromised an otherwise promising candidate for the priesthood. A final hypothesis involves the possible persistence of antique theories regarding the etiology of same-sex desire. Aristotle's *Nichomachean Ethics* divided males who desired males into two groups: those who were made this way by nature and those who became that way by habit. The latter group consists of those abused in childhood.[74] The punishment that the abused child received might be precautionary, reflecting the fear that this early violation might condition him to seek out parallel encounters. This final option is supported by Hildemar's comment that if the child lives an "honest life," by which he means specifically "never falls into this sin" again, he may still accede to the "honor of the priesthood."

As Lynda Coon has suggested, this harsh treatment of child oblates demonstrates that the forces of gender and sex are impossible to dispel—even from an all-male community. As we saw with the desert fathers, boys under the age of fifteen were, like women, both tempting and weak/subordinate, and this had a "destabilizing and solidifying" effect on the community. According to Coon, the punishment of the violated oblate stigmatizes his female-like weakness and carnality.[75] The prevalence of same-sex rape in a community of males parallels similar instances that occur in the contemporary prison system, in which a hierarchical gender system is likewise maintained by violence against the weak.[76] In this context, it is noteworthy that Hildemar likened the monastery to a prison—though this is probably not what he had in mind.[77]

The growing concern about sodomy finds interesting expression in visionary forays into the afterlife. This is certainly not the first time that the visionary genre had been used as a scourge against sexual offenders.[78] But by the Carolingian era, such visionary interventions were few and far between, especially ones that focused so pointedly on the sexual vices of the clergy.[79] In 824 Heito, a monk and former abbot at the monastery of Reichenau, recorded the revelations of the elderly monk Wetti, who had once presided over the monastic school. While Wetti was languishing on his deathbed, his soul was conducted through a series of (largely punitive) otherworldly wonders by an angelic guide. The first site along Wetti's visionary journey was a lofty mountain range, surrounded by a river of fire that contained the tormented souls of clerics, many of whom Wetti recognized. They were strapped together with their concubines, while waves of flame were lapping against their genitals.[80] Yet despite this dramatic staging of clerical concubinage, the angel insisted that, out of the many vices afflicting humanity, the sin *contra naturam* offended God the most. Indeed, there was considerable danger of the "sodomitical wickedness chang[ing] the dwelling place of God into a shrine for demons." This analogy had the advantage of operating both on an individual level (i.e., the body as temple for the Holy Spirit), but also collectively whereby the shrine was associated with the monastery.[81] When the angel returned to the subject of sodomy later in the vision, Wetti observed that the angel "noted the rest of the vices to be shunned only once. But this pestiferous sickness against nature, suggested to the soul by the scheming of the devil, he repeated must be avoided five times and more." Immediately thereafter, Wetti raised the question of why in his own time so many people were dying from the pestilence, and the angel responded that the pestilence was widespread because of the immensity of the people's sins. Both the sequence and wording could imply that the pestilence—characterized as the "pestiferous sickness against nature"—was on a continuum with the discussion of sodomy. But whether Wetti was referring to an actual epidemic, the epidemic of sodomy, or a combination of the two, the pestilence was represented as a divine sign auguring the end of the world.[82] That same year, Walafrid Strabo (d. 849), one of Wetti's former students, would produce a much longer versification of the vision that contrasted the momentary sweetness of the "frenzy of pleasure" in sodomy with the eternal pain of hellfire.[83]

The normalization of same-sex desire in monasteries is apparent in a series of scenarios penned by Ælfric Bata (fl. 1000) involving an older monk and a young boy. They are prosaic scenes: a visit to the lavatory, a compliment about the boy's hair, drinking wine, and comments on the wine horn.[84] But these banalities are all highly, and seemingly deliberately, eroticized. This sexualization and ultimate victimization of the young is exemplified in the life of St. Euphrosyne (d. ca. 475), whose vita, originally written in Greek, was translated into Latin in the eighth century, inspiring a number of vernacular translations. Like most saints' lives, this vita is best interpreted as a reflection of communal values rather than mined for empirical facts. Euphrosyne, allegedly an Alexandrian virgin of twelve years of age, was being pressured to marry against her will. In order to preserve her virginity for God, she disguised herself as a male and entered a community of monks—the rationale being that she was less likely to be discovered and reclaimed by her father in a male community. She took the name Smaradagus, posing as a one-time palace eunuch in order to account for her delicacy. The abbot considered Euphrosyne/Smaradagus too young to be left alone and entrusted her/him to a senior monk, who took the young monk to his cell. Fortunately, the senior was "a holy and impassible man"—a salient description considering what was to follow. When the beautiful Euphrosyne/ Smaradagus entered the church with the other monks "the devil incited many with bad thoughts . . . so that everyone was annoyed with the abbot for letting him in." The abbot acknowledged to the young monk that her/his beauty would "be the ruin of the weak brothers" and that he must commit her/him to solitary confinement.[85] And so, the blameless Euphrosyne/Smaradagus endured monasticism's ultimate punishment: life imprisonment, the same punishment that would have been meted out to the runaway oblate.[86]

Penitentials and the Games Boys Play

The tendency to blame the victim of a same-sex assault, so characteristic of monastic writers, echoes the perspective presented in penitentials with their ham-fisted sense of reparation.[87] For, despite the ostensible intention of tailoring appropriate tariffs to particular sins, penitentials are marked by an overwhelming tendency to conflate categories of sin. Such conflations mirror the monastic milieu, which gave birth to this genre: as with the desert fathers, the blanket condemnation of all forms of sexual activity has the effect of muting degrees of sinfulness. Hence, one sixth-century penitential states, "Those who commit fornication with a woman who has become vowed to Christ or to a husband, or with a beast, or with a male, for the remainder [of their lives] are dead to the world and shall live unto God." This presumably means that the sinner must do perpetual penance. Yet not much later, the same penitential assigns only three years of penance to anyone who fornicated with a beast, or a sister, or another man's wife, or was planing to poison someone.[88]

Penitentials are, however, consistent in at least one respect: the image of the innocent *parvulus* is obscured by the acute perception of the malleable, and hence more dangerous, *pusillus*. In addition to the expectation that boys would misbehave, there is also the presumption that this misbehavior would be manifested sexually. In fact, the *Penitential of Cummean* even has a special section dedicated to the sexual misdemeanors of the young, euphemistically entitled "On the Games of Boys" (*De ludis puerorum*)—a category that accommodates males well into *adulescentia* up to the age of twenty.[89] Some of these games, like masturbation or sexually engaging with peers, are deemed voluntary. But the inclusion of the sexual abuse of minors among these games not only trivializes these assaults but could even suggest that the author is tacitly identifying with the older predator, who is "playing" with his passive prey. Hence, "a small boy misused by an older one, if he is ten years of age, shall fast for a week; if he consented, for twenty days."[90] The differentiation between consensual sex and rape does not eclipse the fact that once again the child is being blamed. Perhaps the canon carries with it the Augustinian view that rape is invariably pleasurable and that the child at some point consented to an act that was initiated by violence.[91] There is no mention of the assailant's penance. Nor is this an isolated instance. Other penitentials treating same-sex rape continue in this vein well into the eleventh century.[92]

The Heinousness of the Act Versus the Question of Age

Carolingian reforms gave rise to a flurry of legislation on clerical chastity, which included condemnations of same-sex relations. Born of a common agenda, these indictments sought to magnify the consequences of such depravity by pointing to disastrous biblical precedents. The baleful reputation of the city of Sodom looms large in this context, where "the enemy of humankind" is credited with introducing the sodomitical vice (Gen. 19).[93] The Council of Paris (829) raises the stakes by incorporating the extra-biblical tradition that it was not just Sodom and Gomorrah that were the objects of God's wrath, but that all five cities of the plain were destroyed for sins against nature. Increasing the pool of disaster exponentially, the council even claims that this same perversity was responsible for the flood. This reading eschews the biblical explanation that the flood was provoked by the miscegenation of the angelic sons of God and the daughters of men (Gen. 6:6), instead positing that the antediluvian offense was caused by same-sex relations. This opportunistic masculinization of the daughters of men complements the feminization of the child oblate in a monastic milieu. With even less justification, the council attributes parallel wrongdoing to the 400,000 members of the Israeli army who suffered defeat at the hands of Benjamin and his men (Judg. 20:17–21).[94]

The capitularies of the so-called Benedict the Levite, another set of Carolingian forgeries, lent their authority to this censorious enterprise. One capitulary warns that same-sex relations and bestiality, acts described as *contra naturam*, bring plague and famine in their wake—just as surely as they brought down God's wrath on the five cities of the plain.[95] Another attempts to align divine vengeance with a more recent genealogy: namely, that God sent the scourge of the Saracens to chastise the regions of Spain, Provence, and Burgundy for sexual aberrations, and that France and Italy should amend their deviant ways while there was still time.[96]

The Carolingian legislators also turned to the ancient Council of Ancyra as a template for the condemnation of same-sex relations. The pertinent chapters meted out punishment for sexual offenders on the basis of age—lessening the penalty for youths under twenty and increasing it for men over fifty.[97] These considerations were also incorporated into a number of the Carolingian interdicts.[98] The *Admonitio generalis* (789), outlining the necessary collaboration of church and state, is the first capitulary to address the problem of same-sex relations, suggesting that Charlemagne himself was apprised of the prevalence of this vice. The context was to alert priests to the problem in potential penitents. "It was found at the Council of Ancyra (314) that those who sin against nature with quadrupeds or men warranted a strict and harsh penance. On this account bishops and priests, to whom the judgment of penance is enjoined, should try in every way to prohibit or uproot this evil from practice."[99]

Clearly there was a growing consensus among secular and religious authorities that same-sex relations between males was a pressing concern. But where were these offenders that Charlemagne sought to stigmatize? Hildemar was of the opinion that same-sex activity was not indigenous to the cloister but was imported by monks who had grown up in the secular world and entered the monastery as adults. If an oblate was properly raised, he would never fall into this kind of sin.[100] But as understandable as Hildemar's stance might be, by the time that he was writing it was probably a minority position. Already in 802, Charlemagne had turned the vector of blame against the regular clergy:

> For the most pernicious report has reached our ears that many abominable and unclean fornications are already found in the monastery. It is sad and disturbing that it is able to be said without great exaggeration that from the arena where the greatest hope of salvation to all Christians is believed to arise—that is, from the life and chastity of the monks—there is the detrimental rumor that some of the monks are said to be sodomites. Whence we ask and enjoin that they should strive to keep themselves from this evil with every caution. And it should be known to all that, since this evil is by no means tolerated anywhere in our entire kingdom, it should meet with even less toleration among those who desire to promote chastity.[101]

Charlemagne concludes by threatening unheard of (but unspecified) measures of vengeance against not only the perpetrators but also those who tacitly consent to such acts. There are other indications of similar concerns about the situation in monasteries. The Synod of Aachen (816) states explicitly that monks are not to be beaten nude before the gaze of the brothers, whatever their offense.[102] The false capitularies of Benedict the Levite, moreover, describe a veritable invasion of sexual aberrations and vexations to the servants of God of both sexes that include fornication, incest, *sodomiticasque luxurias.*[103]

Although the Council of Ancyra did heighten the punishment for same-sex relations on the basis of the offender's age, it made no effort to differentiate

between pederasty and sexual relationships between grown men or between consensual and nonconsensual sex. Neither did the Carolingians. It seems likely
that the question of age did not present itself because the age dissymmetry of
same-sex relations was rendered normative by classical models, and this was
sustained by the patterns of abuse in monasteries. The sexual objectification of
the boy would be further abetted by the perception of the child as a creature of
sin and enticement, foregrounded by the monastic and penitential tendency to
punish the victim of rape. This prejudice is also apparent in Carolingian legislation. The Council of Aachen (816) had stern views about the unruliness of boys
who were brought up and educated among a college of canons, admonishing
"the rectors of the churches . . . to watch carefully the boys and adolescents who
are entrusted to the congregation to be educated and nourished, so that they are
bound by the yokes of ecclesiastical discipline and their lascivious age [*lascivia
aetas*] prone to sinning finds no place where they can rush into the villainy of
sin."[104]

And yet, there was a strain in monasticism that still emphasized the child's
innocence, implicit in his apparent lack of guile. St. Columbanus (d. 615) allegedly extolled the child, saying: "He does not persevere in anger, he is not spiteful, he does not delight in the beauty of women, he says what he thinks."[105] It
may seem difficult to reconcile the idealization of childhood as a time of asexual
purity with the alternative view of childhood as a time of sexually precocious
perversity, but it is not difficult to imagine how so divided a view of the child
might obstruct a sympathetic assessment of his vulnerability and victimization.
An exclusive focus on the vision of childhood purity might occlude an honest
recognition of the evil that could befall a child oblate. By the same token, the
concentration on a child's proclivity to evil might foreground his implication in
sinful acts of the flesh, even those that were involuntary, as deserving of punishment. Whatever the psychological impact of this bifurcated view of the child,
there is little doubt that the alleged heinousness of same-sex relations of any
variety undermined possible exoneration for a resisting child.

The sudden Carolingian concern over same-sex relations is not surprising.
The circle surrounding Alcuin (d. 804), the monk from York who was the head
of Charlemagne's palace school, was distinguished by close affective bonds
between its members. Indeed, Alcuin's poetry and letters to his students are
sufficiently charged with emotion and laden with erotic metaphors that a number of scholars have speculated that Alcuin may have at one time been sexually
active with other males.[106] Homosocial eroticism also animates certain writings
of Hrabanus Maurus, who was, as we have seen, a key figure in the Carolingian
reform.[107] Yet the expression of desire, consciously or unconsciously, is not necessarily incompatible with a commitment to its suppression. Alcuin made a

sharp distinction between fornication with women versus men. When comparing the destruction of Sodom with God flooding the earth, he argues that Sodom warranted destruction by fire "because the natural lust with women is condemned by a lighter element [of water], as it were: but the sin of lust against nature with males is vindicated by the conflagration of the harsher element. In the former instance, the land purified by water will grow green again, but in the latter, consumed by flames, it dries out eternally sterile."[108] Not only did Alcuin play a role in shaping the *Admonitio generalis* of 789, but he also wrote a censorious letter upbraiding a former student for persisting in the "filthy practices of boys."[109]

Iberian Exceptionalism

The monastic mentality reflected in penitentials as well as commentaries on the Benedictine Rule demonstrate a notable lack of empathy for the young boy who is forcibly violated and a disturbing laissez-faire toward older offenders, especially adolescents. We noted earlier that Benedict refrained from discussing sexual transgressions altogether, and it was his successors who filled in this lacuna. Other monastic founders were more forthcoming than Benedict. The fourth-century rule of the Eastern ascetic Pachomius attempts to forestall inappropriate relations before they happen, rebuking anyone who has been caught laughing, playing, or developing friendships among boys of a tender age (*amicitias aetatis infirmae*).[110] Pachomius's indictment was incorporated into two little known Western rules: the *Regula orientalis* (late fifth century, perhaps from Italy) and the sixth-century Frankish Rule of Tarn.[111]

But the most notable efforts to protect boys from sexual predation come from the monastic rules of the Iberian Peninsula. These rules not only exhibit an awareness of same-sex predation, but they are prepared to mete out punishment on the basis of suspicion alone. Nor did they assume that adolescents, with their raging passions, were the sole abusers. As was seen with the Eastern Rule of Pachomius, Iberian rules also demonstrated a special sensitivity to what is now referred to as the predator's "grooming" of his victim. The Rule of Isidore of Seville, for example, condemns anyone joking with small boys (*cum parvulis jocaverit*), considering such behavior among the graver sins deserving of excommunication. The length of the punishment is left to the abbot, however, with the recommendation "that those who are known to have sinned more grievously should be punished with harsher severity."[112]

Yet the most explicit and censorious condemnation of the solicitation of children occurs in the rule of Fructuosus (d. 665), the Visigothic bishop of

Braga and metropolitan archbishop of Galicia. His rule for the monastery of Compludo articulates an uncompromising position on brethren who prey on boys—one that is unparalleled in the entire monastic tradition.[113]

> Any monk who seduces children or youths, or is apprehended in a kiss, or gazing longingly, or any other filthy scenario, once clearly proven through the most trustworthy accusers and witnesses, should be publicly beaten, his tonsure removed, and made to stand in the open, shaved bald, enduring contemptuous opprobrium, with his face smeared with the spit of all, while sustaining the insults of all. He should be imprisoned, bound in iron chains and tormented in anguish for six months; for three more years through each and every week he should be sustained on only the smallest amount of barley bread, not to be consumed until the evening. Then, in the custody of a spiritual man, he should do manual labor on the farm, segregated. He should engage in continuous prayer; subjected to vigils, tears and, with humility, ask for pardon with penitential laments. He will walk in the monastery always in the care and solicitude of two spiritual brothers, with no extensive private conversation or counsel with the young.[114]

Fructuosus does not go as far as the Council of Elvira, which ordained that seducers of boys die excommunicated. Even so, his judgment had no room for the kind of equivocation demonstrated in the case of first-time offenders that is present in Hildemar's commentary. In addition, Fructuosus is seemingly indifferent to Augustine's insistence that a private offense be corrected privately, using the shame-inducing spectacle as a clear deterrent.

Fructuosus's zeal for the monastic life was preeminent, resulting in the foundation of nine monasteries in all. We know nothing about these foundations, however, apart from the two rules that he drafted. Compludo's rule was especially unique in its rigor, scrutinizing much more than the actions of the monks and attempting to enter into their thoughts.[115] "None shall conceal his thoughts, his visions, his dreams, and his own negligence from an elder, nor the occasions when he is moved by shame or the desire to harm."[116] This solicitude naturally carries over into monastic sleeping arrangements. Fructuosus stipulates that "a space of one cubit shall separate each bed, lest incentives of lust be aroused by the closeness of bodies."[117] The abbot or prior shall change bed assignments twice a week. No one is permitted to speak in the dark, while "no younger monk shall approach the bed of another."[118] The prior (second in command to the abbot) was required to stand in the center of the dormitory until the monks were asleep, at which point he would pass silently by each bed

in turn to see who was sleeping and who was engaged in idle chatter, so that
"by observing the actions of each more closely, he may learn how to treat the
character and merits of each."[119] By the same token, the prior was expected to
rise before the other monks for the customary reciting of psalms at midnight so
that he "may diligently visit the couch of each before they get up . . . that he
may see for himself how each one is sleeping."[120]

Fructuosus's vigilance against same-sex predation did not emerge from a
vacuum. We have seen that the Rule of Isidore of Seville excommunicated any
monk who joked with children. We find a parallel intransigence in other Iberian
venues. The Council of Toledo (693) evokes God's wrath against the doomed
city of Sodom, ordaining that lay offenders should suffer the consequences of
secular law, while bishops, priests, and deacons who practice this filthy act
against nature should be degraded and perpetually exiled. Both clerics and lay
perpetrators were barred from communion until their deathbeds.[121] Toledo's
severity could gesture toward a legacy of opprobrium that can be traced back to
Elvira. By the same token, secular law unilaterally punished males who sleep
with other males (*masculorum concubitores*) with castration and perpetual imprisonment.[122] Although Boswell has presented this degree of secular intolerance as
singular, the evidence of monastic rules and conciliar action suggest that these
attitudes were more broadly based.[123]

In less than a century, Visigothic Spain would be overwhelmed by Islamic
forces. Even so, Fructuosus's very explicit indictment of the sexual predation of
children would be granted a significant afterlife through its appropriation by
other sources. It enjoyed particular celebrity in the Frankish kingdom, where it
was repeated in full by Smaragdus's commentary on the Benedictine Rule.[124]
Consisting chiefly of assorted quotations from various authorities, this commentary was not as practical or systematic as the parallel works of Hildemar or Paul
the Deacon. Even so, Smaragdus also includes the passage from Isidore's rule
that places the onus of responsibility on the aggressor and presents the child as
more deserving of protection than punishment.[125] Soon after, the passage from
Fructuosus was included in the concordance of religious rules compiled by Benedict of Aniane (d. 821). This was a significant inclusion. Prior to the ascendancy
of Benedictine monasticism, most Western monasteries did not follow a single
rule, but drew upon a number of rules. Despite Benedict of Aniane's role in the
spread of Benedictine monasticism, his concordance continued this tradition,
presenting the different rules as complementary to one another.[126]

Fructuosus's prohibition eventually crossed over to the secular clergy. It
appeared in the influential manual of Regino of Prüm, written at a bishop's
behest, where it picked up the added luster of a misattribution to St. Basil the
Great.[127] From Regino the now Pseudo-Basilian passage entered the canonical

collections of Burchard, bishop of Worms (d. 1025), writing around the millennium, and, a century later, Ivo, bishop of Chartres (d. 1115).[128] In both collections, the passage was buttressed by the few other canons that treated the abuse of minors, such as Elvira.[129] Yet neither the Pseudo-Basilian/Fructuosus canon nor any of the other related texts made it into Gratian's all-important collection *Decretum*. This is in spite of the fact that Burchard and Ivo were his two major fonts.

How do we explain the sudden disappearance of one of the most forceful condemnations of same-sex relations in monasteries and undoubtedly the most important canon pertaining to the protection of minors? As Chapter 3 will argue, this was a politic decision on behalf of church authorities. Rather than looking inward to the threat of same-sex relations among the clergy, they directed their attention outward to the threat of the clergy's sexual relations with women.

CHAPTER 3

The Problem with Women

Let us also pray for our concubines.
For they are our judges and rule us with an iron rod,
And whose treachery consumes our wealth.
                    —A satirical fifteenth-century *oratio*

Whenever church authorities attempted to clamp down on the clergy's sexual relations with women, it was the clerical wives and concubines who bore the brunt of the attack. We shall see that this general truism is borne out over time. The Western impetus toward clerical celibacy ensured that the sexual activity of nubile women was carefully scrutinized and generally cast in an oppositional light from early days. This is already apparent at the fourth-century Spanish Council of Elvira—a precocious indication of religious authorities' efforts to distinguish themselves from pagan mores through a sharp turn toward sexual asceticism.[1] Over a third of its canons directly concern sexual matters—thirty out of eighty-one to be exact. There are twenty-two canons concerning the sexual infractions between laymen and women, thirteen of which explicitly focus on female sexual offenders;[2] one addresses the lapse of consecrated virgins, and three address the proper allocation of nubile women.[3] Women are also indirectly invoked for their powers of corruption: a man who marries his late wife's sister is excommunicated for fifteen years; if he marries his stepdaughter, he is denied communion, even on his deathbed.[4] Additionally, five canons are dedicated to ensuring the purity of the clergy by restricting different types of contact with women.[5] Of course, women were stigmatized for a range of nonsexual offenses as well, from whipping their maidservants to death to sending or receiving personal letters.[6] To Samuel Laeuchli's mind, the skewed ratio of prohibitive canons directed at women (one-fourth by his count) was a function of the clergy's repressed sexuality, resulting in a "constant desire to punish the women with whom they came into contact."[7]

As intimated earlier, there is much about the Council of Elvira that is uncertain. But whatever Elvira's precise status, it nevertheless suggests that the struggle for clerical celibacy was moving to the forefront of clerical discipline, and this would be reflected in an increasing tendency to regard women as a threat.[8] For instance, the Council of Nicaea did not mandate clerical celibacy.[9] Even so, there are two canons bearing on sexual discipline that should be construed as the kind of fallout resulting from the increased emphasis on clerical chastity. Canon 1 was directed against men who castrated themselves, presumably in an effort to make themselves "eunuchs for God"; canon 3 condemned clerics who kept suspect women in their households, permitting only a mother, sister, aunt, or persons beyond suspicion.[10] Canon 3 addressed the problem of the *virgines subintroductae*: consecrated virgins who lived in chastity with members of the clergy for domestic reasons. The crisis of the *virgines subintroductae* constituted the first public sex scandal to be bruited about in Christian circles.[11] Even though this form of ascetic cohabitation was initially noted and condemned in the mid-third century by Cyprian, bishop of Carthage, the practice proved intractable and was the object of many scornful treatises both before and well after Nicaea, all of which were laced with misogynist polemic.[12] Local councils would subsequently reiterate the categories of women permissible in clerical households.[13]

Toward the end of the fourth century, when the impetus for clerical chastity was championed by Rome, Pope Siricius would again play a pivotal role. In his response to Himerius of Tarragona, already discussed in the context of penance, Siricius maintains that married clergy are obliged to be sexually abstinent from the time of their ordinations and that those who continue to beget children with their wives are in error—a position that he reiterates on other occasions as well.[14] This view was sustained by a number of patristic writers, particularly St. Ambrose (d. 397).[15]

The accelerated quest for celibacy addressed clerical noncompliance with a series of ingenious punitive measures that frequently targeted the clergy's female companions and offspring. Spain was once again at the vanguard of sexual purity. A number of Spanish councils declared that priests or deacons who continued to "to live obscenely" with their wives should be imprisoned and made to do penance, usually until the end of their lives. The women, moreover, should be sold by the bishops as slaves and the proceeds distributed among the poor.[16] At least one council applied the principle of the sins of the fathers being visited on their sons, insisting that "children born in such pollution would never receive their inheritance, but also would remain in perpetual servitude of that church of which priest or minister they were born in ignominy."[17] The Council of Gerona (517) attempted to circumvent such problems altogether by insisting that all interactions between clerics and their estranged wives be witnessed by a third party.[18]

Although the Gallican councils of the sixth and seventh centuries were zealous in their legislative efforts for clerical celibacy, they were not as severe as their Spanish counterparts. For instance, they stopped short of reducing clerical families to servitude.[19] Yet they frequently built upon Spanish conciliar legislation in interesting ways. The Gallican Council of Tours (567) developed an adumbration of Gerona's introduction of a third party as witness to clerical couples, insisting that a lector or one of the canons should take turns bedding down with priests, deacons, and subdeacons who were suspected of secretly harboring their wives. Those who refused to cooperate with this initiative should be whipped. The priest overseeing the lectors who refused to punish them should be deprived of communion for thirty days. Any priest or deacon discovered with his wife should be deposed, excommunicated for a year, and reduced to lay communion.[20]

Clearly the clerical wife was perceived as a particularly noxious thorn in the side of the clergy. Catapulted from the conjugal bed and roundly reviled, she retained all of the liabilities of marriage with few of the advantages. We saw that Elvira punished the cleric who did not instantly expel his wife for adultery, even after conjugal relations had ceased. While the lay husband who tolerated his wife's adultery could eventually be admitted to penance, his clerical counterpart would be deprived of communion even on his deathbed "lest the instruction of enormities seem to proceed from those who ought to be an example of a good life."[21] The Council of Toledo (380) attempted a different approach, insisting that clerical husbands guard their errant wives—constraining them at home, where they would be compelled to undertake salubrious fasts or work on behalf of the poor. The delinquent wife's penitential status rendered her something of a spiritual untouchable, however, and her clerical husband was forbidden to dine with her.[22]

Yet, as irksome as the clerical wife's status most certainly was for everyone concerned, it was impossible to discard, even as a widow. The Council of Braga (572) insisted that any clerical widow who remarried should be excommunicated, shunned by clergy and laity alike, and only allowed to receive communion on her deathbed.[23] A woman's sexual past could also impinge upon clerical purity through a bizarre understanding of sexual ancestry: a previous marriage to a widow or a divorcée was deemed an impediment to orders, and any cleric who had temporarily concealed this taint must be summarily expelled.[24] Indeed, priests were even barred from attending a marriage feast for a second wedding, and those who disobeyed were forced to do penance.[25]

Much of the above legislation presupposes that clerical couples would continue to cohabit and live in chastity after the husband's ordination.[26] Indeed, authorities as far-ranging as the *Apostolic Canons*, Leo I, and Gregory the Great insisted that priests continue to cohabit with their wives, lest they be left destitute.[27] But clearly chaste cohabitation between clerical spouses was difficult to monitor. Over time, sacerdotal wives came to be presented as insidious instruments of diabolical seduction. Gregory of Tours, for example, describes how, subsequent to the difficult transition to chastity, the wife of Urbicus, bishop of Clermont-Ferrand, "was filled with the Devil's own malice . . . for he inflamed her with desire for her husband and turned her into a second Eve." The hapless husband succumbed. As clerics struggled with their chaste vocation, their continued attachment to wives was construed through the lens of ignominy and defeat. The historian Flodoard (d. 966) recounts how Genebaud (d. ca. 555), bishop of Laon, would visit his estranged wife on the pretext of religious instruction. When the instruction eventuated in a series of unwanted children, the father demonstrated his remorse by assigning them penitential names like Latro (thief) for his son or Vulpecula (little fox) for his daughter. But select clerics were presented as transcending such travails by virtue of their exceptional sanctity. In a vita by Venantius Fortunatus (d. 609), Hilary, bishop of Poitiers (d. 363), dispels familial tensions by successfully praying for the death of both his wife and daughter.[28]

The Capacious Clerical Closet

The struggle for clerical celibacy is a dark story, marked by unintended effects and tragic consequences. By insisting on absolute chastity, Western religious authorities were, in essence, constructing a capacious closet that accommodated all manner of sexual behaviors: male-female, male-male, human-beast, solitary acts, and the places in between. The sexually active cleric was forced to be furtive, not unlike the female adulteress with whom he was believed to share a set of common crimes. The Council of Elvira was but one articulation of the widespread association between adultery and infanticide or abortion, perceiving these as desperate measures undertaken by a woman who had conceived in her husband's absence.[29] The Council of Lérida (546) includes clerics who had relations with women as abettors of infanticide and abortion, punishing them with copious penance and permanent deposition.[30] Zubin Mistry describes this canon as "an earlier manifestation of a more enduring concern."[31]

And yet, despite this early awareness of its often lethal consequences, religious authorities continued their drive for celibacy, inadvertently fostering abortion and infanticide. The *Penitential of Finnian*, arguably the oldest surviving penitential, stigmatizes "one of the clerical order [who] falls to the depths of ruin and begets a son and kills him."[32] Yet the fornicating cleric is permitted to maintain his office—provided it only occurred once and his crime is "concealed from men but known before God." Furthermore, while acknowledging that infanticide greatly increases a cleric's culpability, Finnian nevertheless assigns the same penance to a clerical fornicator who murders his offspring as is given the cleric who fathers a child but spares his life.[33] Nor is Finnian singular in rewarding a clerical culture of furtiveness. The *Penitential of Columbanus* assigns seven years of exile to any cleric who "has fallen to the depth of ruin and begotten a child," but only three to a clerical fornicator who has not begotten a child and whose offense "has not become known among the people."[34]

Although produced during a time of Carolingian reform when penitentials were under attack, the ninth-century *Penitential of Pseudo-Theodore* remains very much an "old style" penitential that subscribes to a similar pattern of subterfuge.[35] Clerics who fornicate can make amends through penance, in contrast to a priest who publicly "takes an extraneous wife with the people's awareness," who is deposed.[36] The cleric who engenders a child is punished more severely than one who does not.[37] Pseudo-Theodore also remarks upon the development of a greater degree of clemency for such offenses. Formerly the cleric who attempted to conceal his fornication by murdering his offspring was removed from office in order to do penance, but "now it is more humanely determined that he should do penance for ten years, and never be entirely without penance."[38] The threat that sexual activity with women presented to clerical discipline skews the scale of justice in more overt ways: the cleric who marries after ordination is afforded the same ten years of penance as the cleric who commits infanticide. Meanwhile, penalties for relations that are, technically, considered more aberrant are either lightened or suppressed altogether. Hence, the bishop who fornicates with a quadruped only merits seven years penance—though this penalty is increased to ten years if the practice is habitual.[39] It is certainly suggestive that Pseudo-Theodore omits same-sex relations altogether.

In short, religious authorities constructed a culture in which secrecy was rewarded, while open relations with women were inevitably ruinous. A return to Bishop Contumeliosus's trial at the Council of Marseilles demonstrates this point. Accused of "many filthy and dishonest things,"[40] Contumeliosus confessed and was condemned by the council. At no point was the nature of the "filthy and dishonest things" to which he confessed made explicit, however. When Caesarius of Arles appealed to Rome about the appropriate penalty for Contumeliosus, the pope recommended deposition and removal to a monastery, appending a set of canons to justify his decision. In the context of these canons, it becomes clear that the bishop's primary offense was returning to his wife.[41]

It is hardly surprising that a number of clerics would turn away from the subterfuge and crime implicit in relations with women, seeking sexual release with other males. This was in spite of the universal recognition that same-sex relations were more sinful than simple fornication with women, or even adultery. As was the case with Alcuin, many penitentials differentiated between "natural" (i.e., male-female) and "irrational" fornication (i.e., anything else).[42] According to some reckonings, a cleric's "natural" fornication could be atoned for by years of private penance, while "unnatural" fornication could not even be atoned for privately. Such offenses warranted deposition, compounded by years of penance.[43] But frequently the different degrees of sinfulness got lost. The Council of Ancyra (314) had aligned same-sex relations between males and sex with quadrupeds. The Latin tradition would throw incest into the mix.[44] The late fourth-century *Apostolic Constitutions* anathematized adultery, pederasty, and fornication as a unit.[45] Many penitentials would classify bestiality and same-sex relations under the rubric of "irrational" fornication. A parallel assimilation occurs in the rite for making a bishop. The apostolic representative directs the archdeacon to inquire of the candidate if he had committed any of the four "capital" crimes stipulated by the canons: "*arsenoquita*, that is, [having sex] with a male; with a consecrated handmaiden of God . . . ; with a four-footed animal; or if he had the wife of another man."[46]

But out of the panoply of possibilities for sexual lapses among the clergy, it was relations involving women that were actively pursued. The consequences of persisting in a clerical marriage, as had Bishop Contumeliosus, seemed more momentous than the fleeting instances of sodomy that we know about. And their mention is, indeed, fleeting. In the late fourth century when the drive for clerical celibacy was beginning in earnest, the Donatist bishop Petilian criticized orthodox bishops for deposing a clerical sodomite only to readmit him soon after. Gregory the Great called for an investigation into the idolatry and sodomy (in that order) of the priest Sisinnius of Reggio.[47] Was Sisinnius really a sodomitical idolater or was he being slandered with the ancient association of sexual sins and idolatry articulated by Paul in Romans 1:23–27?[48] It is impossible to say. If the matter was pursued, we never hear about it.

Even so, there were those who rejected this model of studied ignorance—especially in the monasteries where the abuse of children seems to have been an unpleasant but pervasive phenomenon. This point is painfully made by Odo of Cluny (d. 942) in a work entitled *Occupatio*. Divided into seven books that correspond to the progress of creation, the poem begins with the formation of the angelic host, and ends in the present day where all manner of vice flourishes and the end of the world is imminent.[49] Although the association between monasticism and the *vita angelica* was ancient, Odo of Cluny was particularly invested in this association.[50] Lapses from the chaste ideal, and sodomitical lapses in particular, were especially heinous.

> Alas, for shame! In cloisters, once founded with a zeal for stability, where brothers serve in one another's presence as guardians for each other, it is disgraceful to receive a propitiatory offering [i.e., an oblate] in front of the other brothers, while here in the lord's school insanity rages. A boy is offered up like Samuel to be nurtured and become strong in the sacred disciplines, by one who has earlier been steeped [in this tradition], retaining its flavor as if sealed in a jar, and [the child] learns the good in the same way a stick is bent through use. But then someone corrupts the gift of Christ and drowns him—someone who had received him in order to nourish him in the Lord; someone whom Satan inflamed, through whom he casually profanes the boy. Just as a soul is better than the body, so is [the child's corrupter] worse than Herod. For [the corrupter] destroys a soul that will continue to live; but [Herod] destroys only flesh that will die.[51]

The mention of Herod refers to his slaughter of the Holy Innocents (Matt. 2:16–18), an allusion that periodically occurs in indictments of clerical sodomy.[52] But Odo, recognizing that he had entered upon uncharted and somewhat dangerous territory, concluded his diatribe with the apologetic reflection: "Saying such things upsets chaste ears." He comforted himself with the fact that "Paul often said things that he acknowledged to be evil."[53]

Peter Damian and the *Book of Gomorrah*

Odo began his career as a canon of St.-Martin of Tours and only entered the Cluniac order as an adult. His poignant indictment of same-sex relations is focused on the monastery, pointing to the age dissymmetry and climate of abuse that had been targeted in the Rule of Fructuosus and accepted with resignation in Benedictine commentaries.[54] But although the greatest awareness of same-sex offenses was shown by monastic authors, there is no reason to think that such relations were restricted to the cloister. Rather of Verona (d. 974) reverses the career trajectory of Odo, beginning as a Benedictine oblate in Hainaut, and eventually becoming bishop of Verona. He complained that the local clergy cohabited with women in order to dispel suspicion of the worse sin of sodomy. Hence, he reflects: "How damned is the whole order of clerics if there is none among them who is not either an adulterer or an *arsenoquita* [a male who sleeps with males]?"[55]

Peter Damian (d. 1072) was responsible for the most sustained and methodical critique of same-sex practices within the clergy, which he referred to as sodomy, in a work that would later be referred to as the *Book of Gomorrah*. Like Rather and Odo, Peter had a foot in both clerical worlds.[56] He had spent a number of years as a secular cleric and scholar, only to be converted to monasticism as an adult.[57] Yet while Rather and Odo criticized the clergy for same-sex abuses in the context of larger works, the *Book of Gomorrah* was exclusively devoted to the problem. Its focus was singular and unrelenting; its descriptions were sometimes embarrassingly graphic; its language was extraordinarily heated and flamboyant. But while the *Book of Gomorrah* may, on the surface, seem like an uncontrolled rant, it is, in fact, a difficult, subtle, and original work. The very singularity of the subject matter, the contrasts between the incendiary rhetoric and subtle argumentation, and assumptions about Damian's own background have given rise to a series of misconceptions that have obscured why Damian wrote the book and what was really at stake for him. For instance, scholars have tended to assume that the *Book of Gomorrah* was an indictment of monastic mores.[58] This is a natural supposition—especially if one considers that the demographic evidence indicates that the number of child oblates had reached its high point in eleventh-century monasticism.[59] Yet while his experience in the monastery may have been instrumental in heightening Damian's sense of crisis, he did not single out the monastery as a particular center of vice. In fact, Damian tends to idealize, not excoriate, the monastic life.[60] His focus is instead on same-sex relations as rife among members of the ordained clergy— particularly priests and bishops. Yet, in a period when an unprecedented number of monks were becoming ordained as priests, this would additionally obscure the work's focus.

Another misconception about the *Book of Gomorrah* is that it was intended as a targeted attack upon older clerics who prey upon the young, much in the same tradition as Odo of Cluny.[61] But this certainly was not Damian's primary concern and, arguably, not much of a concern at all. Instead, the *Book of Gomorrah*'s indictment of the higher clergy was a function of Damian's sacramental orientation and his incumbent efforts to ensure the integrity of the sacraments. This was not a unique preoccupation, especially with respect to the Eucharist. The increasing number of monks becoming priests was, in fact, one of the most striking testimonials to the heightening of Eucharistic devotion, as was the concern with ritual purity. Odo of Cluny's *Collationes*, a work with which Damian was familiar, also required a very high standard of ritual purity for ministers of the altar.[62]

Damian was, indeed, preoccupied throughout his career with the question of sacramental purity, but this concern was not restricted to the Eucharist. In 1046, several years before the appearance of the *Book of Gomorrah*, Damian had written a treatise denouncing efforts to reduce the prohibited degrees in marriage from seven to four. From his perspective, the canon lawyers in favor of this amendment were "introducing the filth of incest under the title marriage . . . [and] attempting to defile the stainless chastity of the church."[63] The treatise was written in the querulous and aggressive tone of an apologist for tradition. In it we see the first contours of the template that Damian would refine in his later polemical works also bearing on sexual purity. It was an extensive treatment. But to those who would accuse him of verbosity, Damian insisted that "it is imperative to write these things so that the cancer which daily grows larger as it creeps along may not spread its contagion through the vitals of the Church." Hence, he urged clerics to "withstand this deadly disease like men lest its deadly leprosy spread."[64]

At the time it was written, the treatise on incest had been Damian's longest work to date and certainly his most passionate. The *Book of Gomorrah* was its natural successor. Written with even greater vehemence and at considerably greater length, the *Book of Gomorrah* redeployed both the mechanisms of incest and the language of disease and corruption to vilify same-sex relations. Damian's central argument is based on the principal of sacramental filiation—a concept indebted to the impediments to marriage created by a blood relationship, as well as to the spiritual affinity arising between godparents and the children they sponsor in baptism. The *Book of Gomorrah* posits that parallel impediments are created by the sacraments of ordination and penance. This would render same-sex relations between two clerics, one the administrator and the other the recipient of the sacrament, a much worse travesty than parallel transgressions between members of the laity. Hence, Damian's scorn for the bishop who would, "by his lust, consign a son whom he has spiritually begotten for God to slavery under the law of satanic tyranny" turns upon the fact that the prelate has entered into sexual relations with someone whom he had ordained.[65] Such abuse is parallel to the man who assaults his own daughter or a spiritual daughter, only much worse. For the bishop who "commits sacrilege on a son and incurs the crime of incest" is also "violating the law of nature on a male." The same pertains to the confessor corrupting his penitent, who is his spiritual son.[66]

Damian's argument was original and precedential. Incest taboos were developed to regulate marriage. Hitherto, religious authorities had exclusively applied them to relations between male and female parties, probably seeking offspring, who, more often than not, were members of the laity.[67] In service to the sacraments, however, Damian appropriated and extended these prohibitions to accommodate clerical same-sex relations. This was already daring. Yet, he was prepared to go even further than this. In addition to the sacrilege visited upon the sacraments of ordination and penance, Damian was intent on showing how this depraved brand of incest united two priests by blood, threatening the very efficacy of the Mass. This unusual claim first emerges in the course of a convoluted meditation on the polluting effects of blood, concluding with Isaiah's pronouncement "Your hands are covered with blood" (Isa. 1:15). The prophet's words epitomize God's rejection of tainted offerings.[68] The analogous refusal of the sodomitical priest's offerings is demonstrated by a medical excursus: "In fact, if we also carefully study the nature of this [sodomitical] vice and recall statements of physical scientists, we find that the discharge of semen has its origin from blood. For, as by agitation of the winds sea-water is converted into foam, so also blood is turned into liquid semen by handling the genitals."[69] Contemporary canon law maintained that extramarital intercourse created a blood relationship between the couple that would constitute an impediment against either party marrying a relative of the other party within the prohibited degrees.[70] The explicit identification of semen and blood invites the reader to make the logical, but tacit, association: that anal intercourse between a bishop and cleric that he has ordained or between a confessor and his penitent is not just transgressing against the grid of spiritual affinity that Damian is seeking to impose; through the act of intercourse, they actually become related by blood.

Damian's sacramental focus changes the way in which the passive party, a potential victim of same-sex abuse, is presented. Although Odo of Cluny was likewise convinced that a cleric's unchaste practices undermine the sacrament of the altar, his condemnation of same-sex practices does not engage sacramental issues, but is entirely focused upon the abuse of the young. In contrast, the impediments created by ordination and their impact on the sacraments are at the heart of Damian's censure, which means that sexual predators and victims alike are identified on the basis of hierarchy and priority in the religious life, not age. This is, perhaps, not surprising since, as Kathleen Cushing has demonstrated, in the reformers' lexicon, age was a question of spiritual growth versus years.[71] Even so, the horror of spiritual fathers joining themselves to spiritual sons tends to obscure the potential abuse of the oblate, who had been foremost in Odo's treatment.

But though Damian himself seems relatively indifferent to questions of age, some of the sources he enlists are not. In particular, he cites in full the harsh punishment mandated by Pseudo-Basil (i.e., Fructuosus of Braga) for any monk deemed a potential threat to the young.[72] The deployment of this passage needs to be put in context, however. It is preceded by a lengthy attack on penitentials for their random and, overall, lenient treatment of same-sex relations.[73] Fructuosus's uncompromising indictment of same-sex relations is the most dramatic and authoritative source available for countering penitential laxity. Damian's criterion for selection is underlined by the reflection that follows the Pseudo-Basil/ Fructuosus text: "Here the sodomite should seriously consider whether he is worthy to serve in any ecclesiastical office, since this sacred authority judges him to be deserving of such ignominious and degrading treatment." If a kiss merits such a severe penalty, how much more ignoble is actual intercourse between males. "Therefore, since Basil commands that he who is guilty of this sin must undergo severe public penance, and Siricius forbids a penitent to enter the clerical state, it evidently follows that whoever is wantonly polluted with the disgraceful filth of uncleanness with a male is not worthy to perform ecclesiastical offices."[74] In short, the Pseudo-Basil/Fructuosus text was evoked as ammunition for the degradation of adult clerics. It was not enlisted in pursuit of a child's well-being. Indeed, questions regarding age or the consensual versus nonconsensual nature of the sex act are not considered.

There is no doubt that Damian's treatise is *sui generis*. There had been plenty of treatises denouncing suspect practices between males and females—the crisis of the *virgines subintroductae* being a case in point. But there was no precedent for a full-scale treatise denouncing same-sex relations, let alone among the clergy. Damian is aware of the singularity of his work but presents it as a necessary measure for averting scandal: "the befouling cancer of sodomy is, in fact, spreading so through the clergy. . . . It would be better for them to perish alone as laymen than, after having changed their attire but not their disposition, to drag others with them to destruction, as Truth itself testifies when it says, 'But if anyone is a cause of stumbling to one of these little ones, it is better for him to be drowned in the depths of the sea with a great millstone around his neck.'"[75]

Damian is also aware, however, that his perception of what constituted scandalous behavior among the clergy, and what should be done about it, may be out of step with the opinion of contemporary religious authorities. As his conclusion makes clear, he is deliberately breaking with the ecclesiastical authorities' preferred mode of minimizing scandal, instead deferring to his own conscience. "If, indeed, this small book should come into the hands of any one whose conscience rebels and who perhaps is displeased by what is contained above, and he accuses me of being an informer and a delator of my brother's crime, let him be aware that I seek with all my being the favor of the Judge of conscience."[76] Peter likens his denunciation and excoriating tones to the church fathers in their fight against heresy.

The treatise was explicitly intended for Leo IX, who was elected on February 12, 1049. Peter's treatise is believed to have been written in the latter half of the same year. The timing is suggestive. In October, Leo held a synod in Reims. At his request, a certain Peter, described by the only chronicler to discuss the synod as a deacon of Rome, acquainted the assembly with the issues at hand, which were recorded in the following order: simony, lay investiture, the misuse of church buildings, incestuous marriages, men abandoning their legitimate wives and forming invalid second marriages, monks and priests fallen from their holy propositions, clerics bearing arms, the pillaging and unjust imprisonment of the poor, the sodomitical vice, and the heresies that have risen up in various areas.[77] The very prominence of issues like incestuous marriages, invalid second marriages, and sodomy suggests that the deacon in question was, almost certainly, Peter Damian.[78] The primary position that Damian was assigned at the council further points to his probable influence in setting the agenda.[79] The synod concluded with a series of injunctions—the last of which condemned those practicing sodomy.[80]

Whether or not the *Book of Gomorrah* was written before or after the synod, it is nevertheless clear that Damian perceived the pope as a natural ally. The entire treatise was fraught with a sense of urgency, arguing that only the intervention of the Holy See could "curb this unbridled evil."[81] Yet the pope's response was tepid. Damian had urged that all same-sex activity was deserving of deposition, including masturbation.[82] This final offense accommodated both mutual masturbation and solitary initiatives—presumably because a cleric bringing himself to orgasm was still engaging in a same-sex activity that resulted in a sinful shedding of semen/blood and was capable of compromising the Mass. In response, Leo IX, "acting more humanely and relying on divine mercy," countered that clerics guilty of acts like mutual masturbation or femoral intercourse should be restored to their offices with due penance. He did, however, agree that anal intercourse should incur deposition.[83] Nor was Damian disappointed in the opposition he had anticipated. In yet another letter to Leo IX, the beleaguered monk defends himself against his many detractors objecting to the *Book of Gomorrah*—probably his scandalized confreres.[84]

Leo IX did not act, nor did Damian's treatise circulate. Pope Leo's successor, Alexander II, may have been even more sensitive to the treatise's potential for scandal. According to Damian, the pontiff borrowed a certain work, ostensibly to have it copied. "But at night he took it away without my knowledge and stuffed it into his book chests. . . . And when I complain about these things . . . his mouth bursts forth with laughter while his hand boxes my ear."[85] Many scholars have interpreted Damian's letter of complaint to a friend as pertaining to the *Book of Gomorrah*.[86]

The Sexual Reorientation of Peter Damian

Papal responses aside, the *Book of Gomorrah* was badly timed: at least initially, the problem of simony (the selling of church offices) trumped the issue of sexual purity from the perspective of the reformers.[87] In terms of length and sense of urgency, however, the *Book of Gomorrah* suggests that Damian perceived sodomy as probably the worst vice assailing the clergy and certainly the worst sexual vice. From the perspective of degrees of sinfulness, he was, of course, correct. Yet, Damian was suffering under the illusion that deference to his own conscience justified speaking out, thereby transforming the clergy's private vice into public scandal. Other outspoken critics of the clergy were not so naive. In Rather of Verona's indictment of clerical incontinence, for example, he was especially outraged by public indiscretions: "For hidden sins kill only those who commit them, but public sins both kill the committers and injure those witnessing them."[88] Ultimately, Damian would bend to the ecclesiastical imperative that privileged the threat of scandal over the promptings of the individual conscience. He would come to recognize that if his attack on clerical sodomy had the capacity to scandalize so many of his colleagues, it must be hidden from the public at all costs. After the *Book of Gomorrah*, Damian fell silent on the subject of clerical sodomy. His unabated passion for clerical purity was redirected: in his future literary horizon, the sexual vices of the clergy were strictly male-female.

There was a ten-year hiatus between the *Book of Gomorrah* and the beginning of Damian's prolonged war against clerical marriage. During the interim, the reformers had only made a few symbolic feints aimed at clerical families.[89] But with the accession of Nicholas II to the papacy in 1059, Damian believed the time was ripe. Just as he had greeted Leo IX with the *Book of Gomorrah*, Damian addressed a treatise on clerical celibacy to Nicholas during the first year of his pontificate, attacking incontinent bishops for their sexual involvement with women.[90] His fight for sacerdotal and sacramental purity was still driven by flamboyant rhetoric, asking uxorious bishops: "What business have you to handle the body of Christ, when by wallowing in the allurements of the flesh you have become a member of the antichrist?"[91] Yet the treatise also bears witness to Damian's hard-won sense of discretion. Not only was the male-female dynamic less scandalous, but Damian was careful to articulate a number of comforting disciplinary norms: that "a prudent silence is maintained concerning clerical sexuality for fears of insults from laymen." He even seemed to recognize the possible virtue of this silence, echoing the compromise implicit in the Carolingian dichotomy: "if this evil were secret, silence could perhaps be condoned." But this only prepared the way for the contention that, because the fault of incontinent bishops was so public and widespread, the "offenders [must] be properly branded with infamy."[92]

Damian seems to have struck the right chord, and the pope was responsive. In the same year, Nicholas would hold a Lateran Council excoriating clerical marriage, perhaps inspired by Damian's treatise.[93] Soon Damian was emboldened to go beyond clerical authorities to seek secular support in the fight against clerical marriage. This was a risky undertaking, and he knew it. In his letter to Adelaide, Duchess of Turin, Damian protects himself by noting that he had written to the bishop first, lest he be accused of "publiciz[ing] to women what should have been handled in the sacristy."[94] Yet the very publicity of clerical concubinage empowered Damian, bestowing a de facto imprimatur on his work that had been withheld in a parallel indictment of same-sex relations. Damian's sexual reorientation was doubtless abetted by the discovery that it was easier to make a compelling case against sacerdotal relations with females than with males. This might seem counterintuitive given the greater gravity of same-sex relations. The subject of "unnatural" sex also lent itself to more opportunities for outlandish polemic—a factor that Damian, who admits to a penchant for scurrility, would have doubtless appreciated.[95] These rhetorical possibilities were not lost on Damian: his *Book of Gomorrah* seized on opportunities to exploit the potential gender-trouble ensuing from same-sex relations. Hence, the clerical sexual aggressor makes "a mistress of a cleric or a woman from a male."[96] Likewise, he argues that prostituting a monk is no different from violating a nun, since "he who fouls male thighs would, if nature so allowed, achieve with a male with the same act of insane, unbridled lust as he would with a woman."[97]

But Damian's rhetorical sallies were hampered by the constraints of his same-sex construct in a number of ways. To begin with, Damian's case against the monstrosity of same-sex relations ultimately depended upon the model of incest between males and females, and this would render its application to relations between men awkward—even polemically "unnatural." Second, Damian had implied that the exchange of semen somehow created a covert blood relationship between clerics—an obscure argument at best. In contrast, the case for the corruption of the bloodline through incest between men and women, or even through spiritual affinity, was much more compelling because of the possibility that offspring could result from such perverse acts of intercourse. Third, there were considerations in the symbolic register. Despite the mandate for clerical celibacy, the male-female binary would continue to be applied to clerics figuratively. As Megan McLaughlin has argued, Damian deftly exploited the traditional imagery of bishop as bridegroom to emphasize the incestuous (not to mention adulterous) implications of episcopal incontinence.[98] Fourth, the fact that women were already considered polluting in and of themselves was a salient factor. Gregory the Great had argued against the view that a menstruating woman should be barred from church, but the taboo nevertheless reasserted itself in penitential tradition.[99] Although skeptical of penitentials, the reformers had redoubled their efforts to distance women from holy things, even forbidding nuns to handle vessels and fabrics associated with the altar.[100] So the allegation that the sacraments were compromised by the celebrant's touching "the private parts of harlots" may have seemed more compelling than contact with the private parts of other clerics.[101] Fifth, the scandal implicit in exposing hidden sins bears repeating. Damian had learned the hard way that if the clergy's sexual vice was to be excoriated, it was infinitely preferable for it already to be public rather than private, and for it to be a natural rather than unnatural vice.

A sixth reason is the ease with which Damian could sink into the venerable tradition of clerical misogyny.[102] From a historical standpoint, it was customary to stigmatize the clergy's familiarity with women, to blame women for any ensuing illicit relations, and to take action against them. Hence, in later attacks on clerical marriage, Damian abandoned the incest framework altogether, reflexively turning to the familiar patterns of censure that had become canonized over time. This polemic first arose in the struggle against the *virgines subintroductae* and had become a familiar discourse. Damian had already demonstrated a metaphoric predilection for this kind of gendered invective in the *Book of Gomorrah* when he imagined: "This utterly diseased queen of Sodom renders him who obeys the law of her tyranny infamous to men and odious to God. . . . She defiles him in secret and dishonors him in public."[103] "The diseased queen of Sodom" is a wonderfully capricious construction. But it was, after all, much less problematic to associate the female "harpies flying about the sacrifice of the Lord to snatch those who are offered to God and cruelly devour them" with real women, as became possible in his polemic against clerical marriage.[104]

With a time-honored target like clerical wives, Damian could apply his rhetoric to promote concrete measures. To Adelaide, Duchess of Turin, he advised that she leave the disciplining of clerics to the bishops, instead "apply[-ing] the vigor of your worldly power to the women" who were not wives but concubines or prostitutes. Invoking the example of Jael, who hammered a tent peg into the skull of Sisera (Judg 4:21), he enjoined Adelaide to likewise "pierce the head of the devil . . . and destroy the source of all impurity who prevents clerics from participating in the joys of heaven."[105] Seemingly inspired by the Draconian measures of ancient Visigothic councils, Damian makes the dubious claim that Leo IX ordered that clerical wives become slaves of the Lateran Palace. Damian, for his part, hoped that "every bishop may acquire as slaves of his diocese all the women in his territory that he finds living in sacrilegious unions."[106]

The seventh and final reason moves beyond polemic into the personal realm. Damian had a dim view of marriage, clerical or lay, because of its inescapable carnality. This prejudice undoubtedly assisted his polemical reorientation. As repellent as the institution may have been to him, however, it was nevertheless a subject to which he had dedicated considerable thought. This was unusual for this period. In fact, there had been no treatises dedicated to the subject of marriage since patristic times.[107] And yet Damian wrote two: in addition to the treatise on incest discussed above, Damian also wrote a second work on the proper times for marriage. Both works were consistent with his preoccupation with purity, approaching marriage as something potentially polluting that needed to be contained. Consanguineous unions were vehicles for "introducing the filth of incest under the title marriage . . . [and] attempting to defile the stainless chastity of the church." This was especially egregious: "with divine judgment close at hand, when men should be wholly persuaded to renounce the pleasures of the flesh, they are wantonly encouraged to enter incestuous marriages."[108] By the same token, marriages contracted during Lent, even if unconsummated, were invalid.[109] In addition to defiling a holy season, such unions would remain illegitimate after Lent had passed, thereby polluting the entire church. Although ostensibly defending marriage, Damian characteristically takes this opportunity to delimit intercourse. The treatise on Lenten marriages invokes the apocryphal tradition that John the Evangelist was called away from his marriage at Cana by Christ, interpreting Paul's license to marry to the opposite purpose (1 Cor. 7:1–2): "But while first declaring that it is a good thing for a man not to touch a woman, and then decreeing that because of immorality each man should have his own wife, the wise teacher undoubtedly proposes celibate marriage."[110]

Nor is it surprising to learn that Damian's view of marriage was strictly postlapsarian. This contradicts the assertions of Augustine, who, in response to the many detractors of marriage in late antiquity, pronounced marriage the natural bond of human society, projecting the institution back into Eden.[111] In contrast, Damian argued that marriage was introduced when humanity was in decline. According to his reckoning, all humanity descended from Adam, yet as the "race was extended and the bonds of relationship grew weaker, . . . to restore the flickering fire of mutual love, the contract of marriage was thereupon introduced."[112] In the above instance, Damian's unforgiving theology of marriage was delivered in an unusually optimistic mode. More characteristic is Damian's letter to Duchess Adelaide of Turin alluded to earlier. In the course of enlisting her support against unlawful clerical marriages, Damian reminded himself at the end of the letter that the duchess was in doubt about the validity of her own marriage: was it, in fact, lawful to make a second marriage? He allayed her apprehensions with the rather dour assurance that marriage would cease to exist in heaven.[113] Elsewhere, he drew attention to the conundrum of "why the canons decreed that a man who has remarried may never be promoted to the priesthood, but that a priest who has committed fornication may be recalled to his former office after he has done penance"—a prohibition that he ultimately defended on the basis of the "mystical norms of the true priesthood."[114] Not surprisingly, Damian characteristically inverted normative views of fecundity and sterility, aligning married clergy with animals whose testicles have been crushed and hence rendered inappropriate offerings to the Lord (Lev. 22:24).[115]

Yet Damian's change in focus from clerical same-sex relations to clerical concubinage was not just premised on what was politic or argumentatively feasible, or even on his personal misgivings about marriage. His reorientation was facilitated by the discovery of an important theological rationale. Damian had justified his vehemence in the *Book of Gomorrah* by comparing his vitriolic tone with the rhetoric deployed by the church fathers in the prosecution of heresy. If clerical marriage/concubinage was somehow rebranded as a heresy, it would easily outstrip sodomy in its degree of sinfulness and in the potential threat it presented to the faith. Damian's treatise attacking incontinent bishops does just that: such pontiffs are implicated in the heresy of the Nicolaitans. Damian seems to have been the first of the papal reformers to use this term, but he was not the first orthodox authority.[116] The Council of Tours (567) pronounced clerics who consorted with women as Nicolaitans "as it is read: *That heresy of priests that first arose from priests.*"[117]

Although the alleged quotation seems to have been the invention of the conciliar fathers, the Nicolaitans themselves had a home in scripture. In the Apocalypse, there is a heretical group known by this name associated with fornication and eating the meat of idols who are described as despised by God and a stumbling block (*scandalum*; Rev. 2:6, 14ff.). These Nicolaitans, active early in the Christian era, were associated with gnostic and antinomian tendencies. It is believed that the sectarians opportunistically aligned themselves with the deacon, Nicolas—one of the seven deacons ordained by the apostles (Acts 6:5)—because of a tradition associated with his name. According to Clement of Alexandria (d. ca. 215), Nicolas was married to a beautiful woman of whom he was very possessive. When reproached by the apostles, he made the ascetic gesture of not only giving up his wife but offering her to the others in marriage and insisting that one ought to "abuse the flesh." While the so-called gnostic Nicolaitans took this as permission for libertine behavior, Clement goes on to relate that no one took Nicolas up on his offer: his wife remained unsullied, and their children remained virgins, raised in ascetic renunciation.[118]

This story was repeated by Eusebius (d. before 341), who likewise associates Nicolas's willingness to sacrifice his wife with his ascetic ideals.[119] But most Western fathers construed Nicolas's renunciation in antinomian terms. According to Augustine, Nicolas "was condemned for jealousy over his most beautiful spouse. He acquitted himself, it is said, by permitting that she be used by whomever wished. Because of this deed, it turned into the most depraved sect with an undifferentiated use of women." Other religious authorities followed suit.[120] So the ascetic deacon went down as a profligate in the annals of history. In a similar reversal, the Council of Tours resourcefully seized upon this ancient sect, remembered for the way it abused the exclusivity of marriage, to stigmatize clerics who clung to their wives. In threatening tones, the council excoriated the unchaste priest who dared consecrate the body of Christ, perceiving the resurfacing of this heresy as a penalty for society's sins.[121]

Damian first mentions the "heresy of the Nicolaitans" in his treatise to Nicholas II, where he refers to both the deacon "who boldly taught that clerics of every rank should be married" and the heretical sect of the Apocalypse.[122] His personal experiences with the married clergy would only sharpen his sense of the heretical outrage they presented, even as the biblical legacy of the Nicolaitans became aligned with contemporary politics. In December of 1059, shortly after Damian completed this treatise, Nicholas II sent him on a reform mission to Milan, where clerical marriage and simony were rife. A letter describing the mission to Archdeacon Hildebrand, the future Gregory VII, gives a careful reckoning of wherein lies their heresy: "These [clerics] first become fornicators as they enter this kind of sordid union, but then are rightly called Nicolaitans when they defend this deadly disease with arguments they think bear authority. A vice, indeed, turns into heresy when it is defended by arguments dependent on false doctrine."[123] Damian's dismay over this alleged heresy was heightened by his visit to Turin in 1064, when he discovered that the bishop, though himself chaste, tolerated a married clergy. Soon after, Damian issued a sharp letter of reproach in which he again alleged that the priests who attempt to defend their marriages "by slyly asserting that their position is based on established truth" were heretics. This time, however, Damian aligned married priests with the German anti-reform movement and their antipope Honorius II—formerly Cadalus, bishop of Parma. If the heretical clerics were to win the day, then the Nicolaitans should be renamed Cadalaitans in honor of the venal antipope who "will loosen the bonds of lust according to their plan."[124]

Married Heretics, Orthodox Sodomites,
and Reverse Accusation

> There was in that time almost through all of the kingdom of
> Germany a grave scandal and widespread complaint
> concerning the incontinence of the clergy. Nor did it lie
> hidden; but *it was a harlot's forehead* for them and they *wouldst
> not blush* [Jer. 3:3]. This matter reached the ears and vision of
> the Roman pontiff who condemned and prohibited this
> enormity with decrees and letters. And the bishop [Altmann]
> approved and rejoiced.
>   —Anonymous life of Altmann, bishop of Passau (d. 1091)

> Whoever deprives the clergy of women, in whatever way,
> Makes deacons and priests into sodomites.
> —Anonymous poem from a thirteenth-century manuscript[125]

    The term "Nicolaitan" caught on. Subsequent writers would cite Damian's
definition with approval, and married clerics were thenceforth branded as heretics.[126] The laity was incited to violence against the married priesthood and
urged to boycott their Masses.[127] In a series of anti-reform treatises, the "heretical" clergy would counter reform rhetoric with charges of sodomy in the reformers' camp—ironically assuming the mantle that Peter Damian, that ur-
proponent of clerical purity, had let drop.[128] Some also attempted to repel the
charge of heresy with a strategy that Carolyn Dinshaw has referred to as "reverse
accusation."[129] Both of these tactics are present in the first and most famous of
the defenses of clerical marriage—the *Rescript*. This treatise was addressed to the
pope, but it is not clear which one. It was either written around 1060 in response
to Nicholas II's strictures against clerical marriage or around 1075 in response to
Gregory VII's reissuing of Nicholas II's earlier ruling. Augustin Fliche believes
that the *Rescript* was written in reaction to Peter Damian's writings against
clerical marriage, particularly the treatise addressed to Nicholas II.[130] The author
identifies himself as a bishop named Ulrich. Since the dates for potentially eligible bishops named Ulrich do not align with the circumstances associated with
the treatise, however, the author is generally referred to as Pseudo-Ulrich.[131]
    The anonymous author's defense is grounded in scriptural and patristic
sources. The manner in which he wields these authorities in the course of his
argument has been amply analyzed by scholars.[132] What has received less attention is the way Pseudo-Ulrich introduces the question of heresy as a subtle, but

important, leitmotif—a historically recurring heresy that is associated with clerical celibacy and haunts the clergy's past, present, and future. The question of
heresy is first raised to rebut what is represented as one of the reformers' leading
contentions: that clerical celibacy was first imposed by Gregory the Great—a
claim that Peter Damian did, in fact, make.[133] Pseudo-Ulrich's response to this
assertion is derisive: "I laugh at their temerity but grieve at their ignorance. For
they are ignorant that the dangerous ordinance of this heresy [*huius heresis*],
mandated by the holy Gregory, was afterwards atoned for by him with the
deserved fruit of penance." The author proceeds to recount how, after making
the decree, the pope found the heads of more than six thousand infants floating
in his fishpond. Recognizing that his edict against clerical marriage was responsible for this carnage, Gregory "straightway condemned the decree, praising the
apostolic counsel that it is better to marry than burn, adding for his own part:
it is better to marry than furnish the occasion for death."[134]

Anne Llewellyn Barstow perceives the apocryphal tale of Gregory's fishpond
as a distinct flaw in Pseudo-Ulrich's otherwise scrupulous choice of authorities.[135] She has a point. One might counter, however, that although the story
may be apocryphal, it nevertheless functioned as an exemplum, pointing to a
historical reality: the link between clerical celibacy and infanticide, which, as we
have seen, was repeatedly emphasized in penitential tradition. It also capitalizes
on the resonance between past and present by focusing on the ill-considered
efforts of church authorities to impose celibacy on the clergy. This resonance
would be amplified if Pseudo-Ulrich was, in fact, writing around 1075—during
the pontificate of Gregory VII. Not only had the latter-day Gregory commemo-
rated his forebear by assuming his name, but, according to I. S. Robinson's
estimate, over half of the patristic and canonical references in Gregory VII's
correspondence were from the registers of Gregory the Great.[136] But even as
Gregory VII was attempting to honor Gregory the Great and emulate his merits,
Pseudo-Ulrich demonstrates that he was also at risk of repeating the saint's worst
mistake. The tale of the fishpond follows a series of biblical texts authorizing
clerical marriage, demonstrating that, by going against established scripture,
even a holy pontiff could make an error in judgment.[137] From this authoritative
platform, Pseudo-Ulrich warns the pope that his role is to admonish rather than
compel "lest through a private precept . . . you will be found at odds with both
the Old and New Testament." In short, because the present-day pope insists on
preferring a "private precept" to scripture, he is revisiting Gregory the Great's
"heresy," which will give rise to the same tragic consequences.[138] So if Pseudo-
Ulrich was, in fact, writing during Gregory VII's pontificate, his strategic con-
vergence of the saintly pontiff and his latter-day namesake would have rendered
the heresy that forbids clerics to marry doubly "Gregorian."

Up until now, Pseudo-Ulrich's evocation of heresy has been subtle: the saintly pontiff repented his heretical doctrine, even as the present pope, victim of the same heresy, should likewise repent. The potentially volatile charge of heresy is then diffused by several passages from Augustine in favor of clemency. The first one is particularly evocative: it is from Augustine's letter to the proconsul of Africa, urging that the heretical Donatists be corrected, not killed.[139] It is unclear whether Pseudo-Ulrich was aligning the married priesthood with the heretical Donatists or with the papal reformers. An argument could be made for either: on the one hand, the married priests, like the Donatists, were in the more vulnerable position with respect to both secular and religious authorities; on the other hand, the reformers' uncompromising position on clerical chastity was not unlike the unbending rigidity of the Donatists. Contextually, it is also possible to interpret Pseudo-Ulrich's evocation of Augustine as an appeal for a kind of détente that would secure clemency and toleration for both opposing camps. Pseudo-Ulrich is not without hope that such a solution is possible: he is aware that the pope has shown discretion in other areas of life, and, hence, "we do not despair that you will quickly correct this perversity of intention."[140] To do otherwise would be to court disaster.

Pseudo-Ulrich further argues that the reformers were in danger of instigating the same crisis that had been narrowly averted in biblical times. Neither Christ nor Paul had mandated chastity. In fact, the apostle understood that many who were incapable of such a discipline nevertheless pretended to embrace chastity, wishing to please men over God. The results were tragic: some fell into incest, pursuing their fathers' wives, while others "did not shrink from the embraces of beasts and men." To ensure that this sickness did not turn into an epidemic, Paul determined that every man should have his own wife (1 Cor. 7:2).[141] Now once again there are hypocrites who dare disparage the chaste marriages of the clergy—all the while reveling in adultery, incest, and "the most wicked embraces of males, for shame!" For they claim that "it is more honest to be implicated with many secretly than openly—namely, in the knowledge of men—to be bound with one." These so-called reformers are likened to Pharisees, who do all things on account of men, not God (Matt. 23:5).[142] They are the very infidels that Paul had warned were the harbingers of the end of time: heretics who embrace the doctrine of devils and forbid marriage (1 Tim. 1–4). With their pharisaical madness, the entire clergy would "be turned into fornicators, adulterers, and the most wicked ministers of other depravities along with them who skillfully contrived to bring this heresy into the church—like the blind leading the blind."[143]

Pseudo-Ulrich invented the Gregorian heresy to counter Damian's invention of the Nicolaitan heresy, deliberately fighting fire with fire. In fact, the anonymous author, arguably, had access to a superior flame. What, after all, is the obscure heresy of the Nicolaitans: the patristic slander regarding a deacon from the Acts of the Apostles cobbled together with meat-eaters from the book of Revelation? How could it possibly compare to the very clear warning that the end of time would be heralded by hypocritical heretics who forbade marriage? From Pseudo-Ulrich's perspective, the "heresy" that both popes were in danger of promulgating was invested with apocalyptic power capable of bringing about the end of the world.

No one followed up on Pseudo-Ulrich's ingenious invention of the Gregorian heresy.[144] Yet anti-reform rhetoric was united by a common tendency to associate the reform movement with chronic hypocrisy and sexual profligacy, particularly the sin of sodomy. Sometimes sodomitical relations are alluded to obliquely. Hence the canons of Cambrai, protesting against the renewed persecution of married clergy under Gregory VII, write: "It is said that these men [reformers] abominate marriage because they irreverently and impiously practice what is both abominable and nefarious."[145]A certain priest named Andrew, speaking on behalf of the entrenched married clergy of Milan, reportedly argued that, by forbidding wives, the reformers were authorizing fornication, adultery, and "that detestable vice, because of which some of you pretend to live so chastely, dismissing wives with false religion."[146] The poet Serlo of Bayeux (fl. 1095), a self-avowed son of a priest who was dismissed from his paternal benefice, is among the most strident critics of the reform movement, claiming: "Now men of filthy, adulterous, sodomitical lives / Who perform furtive acts, bark [latrant] about shameful things in us." While framing new laws to the detriment of clerical children, the reformers themselves are becoming progressively more depraved:

> The most harmful things recede ever further from [the reach] of law!
> Should [the law] not pursue their sodomitical lives with grievous
>   punishment?
> But such acts go uncensored, whereby the clergy is destroying itself and
>   its laws.[147]

Those who resisted reform presented themselves as the defenders of marriage, an honorable institution contracted in the open, against the attacks of pharisaical sodomites, who sought covert gratification among themselves. But reformers did what they could to delegitimize this offensive, arguing that clerical marriages were not marriages and that clerical wives were, in fact, whores. They also experimented with reverse accusation. According to Landulf the Senior (d. 1110), the deacon Ariald (d. 1066), a popular preacher and reformer, accused the

Milanese clergy of committing "under the pretext of false religion innumerable adulteries and many and diverse sodomitical fornications."[148]

In view of the Milanese clergy's life or death struggle to keep their wives, the accusation of sodomy may seem rather strained. But there was a more compelling case to be made in the secular sphere. Reformist chroniclers began to train their reverse accusations at the very apex of anti-reform secular power—the German emperor Henry IV (d. 1106)—constituting the first in a series of sodomitical slurs to be turned against secular rulers.[149] Sometimes clerical chroniclers approached the subject warily. Lampert of Hersfeld (d. between 1082 and 1085) simply says that Henry "gave himself precipitously to all manner of shameful acts, with the harness of modesty and temperance broken."[150] Wido of Ferrara ventures more, noting that the emperor "greatly rejoiced in the company of boys [*puerorum*]—especially beautiful ones," but refrains from pronouncing on whether Henry had actually committed "that sin" as others claim.[151] Manegold of Lautenbach (writing ca. 1085) is less circumspect about the emperor's vices, claiming that, out of Henry's many perversions, "the turpitude that surpasses all of these is abandoning the natural use of women and using men. I could name many names if the matter was not known equally to all. Why should I shy away from speaking when he practically did it in public? And it's better to say it than do it."[152] Several chapters later, Manegold circles back to that "most wicked kind of sin—the filth of which pollutes everyone who hears . . . the singular uncleanness of sodomitical impurities," describing it as a contravention of divine and natural law. Even a dog only has sex with a female of its own kind, and if it were discovered to behave otherwise, it would instantly be put to death.[153]

Sodomy was certainly not the only sexual offense that the emperor was credited with. In keeping with the time-honored principle of casting every possible aspersion at an adversary in the hopes that something sticks, Henry's critics also accused him of a wide variety of abuses with women. This was, of course, useful, as it allowed those in the reform camp to present themselves as the defenders of marriage. Manegold accuses the emperor of seducing and defiling many women, as his many illegitimate children attest. The fact that he debauched both of his sisters, one a nun and the other a virtuous matron, "is no rumor since there were witnesses."[154] Bruno, a cleric from Magdeburg and chronicler of Henry's war with the Saxons, rendered a spirited account of Henry's failed attempt to inveigle one of his courtiers into seducing his queen—a noble and beautiful woman whom the emperor despised—hoping to catch her in adultery. (He was more successful with his sister, the nun, whom he constrained physically while he watched another defile her.)[155]

Such charges served a practical function during Henry's lifetime. So heightened a degree of sexual profligacy would render the emperor infamous and, hence, unfit to rule.[156] Gregory VII was certainly prepared to capitalize on Henry's ill-fame, referring to the monarch's "unheard-of wickedness and manifold iniquities."[157] Henry's sexual misconduct was apparently used as a pretext for the Saxon rebellions,[158] while Manegold unabashedly presents Henry's behavior as grounds for deposition. Rumor of Henry's sexual depravity resonated long after his death. An anonymous chronicler of Disibodenberg (ca. 1147) conflates the emperor's heretical simony with sexual trafficking. Hence, he sold Constance, Bamberg, and Mainz for money; Regensburg, Augsburg, and Strassburg for military help; the abbey of Fulda for adultery; and the episcopacy of Namur, "what is wicked to say and hear, he sold for sodomitical uncleanness."[159]

It was certainly not unusual to impugn a monarch for matters sexual. Gregory of Tours was a scrupulous chronicler of Merovingian debauchery. The Carolingian emperor Lothair II (d. 869) was famously reprimanded for his scandalous attempts to divorce his wife Theutberga—a case that Manegold himself draws upon to demonstrate papal power over monarchs.[160] Peter Damian relates how the incestuous marriage of Robert the Pious (d. 1031), king of France, resulted in a son with the head and neck of a goose, and how the marriage of Emperor Otto I (d. 973) to his godmother drew down the vigorous condemnations of his own son, the saintly bishop of Mainz.[161] But the imputation of sodomy was something new. Over the course of the high and later Middle Ages, it was destined to be one of the most effective ways of undermining a monarch.

Reverse accusation may have been effective for its preemptive force, but it was hardly subtle. More interesting was the reformers' semiotic retooling and redeployment of the term "sodomy," which, as is evident by Damian's usage, was used less and less to signify a miscellany of sexual prohibitions and was becoming progressively associated with same-sex relations between males. For instance, in the course of defending the lay boycott of Nicolaitan Masses, the anonymous *Epistle on the Sacraments of the Heretics* equates the offerings of married priests as "cursed bread" and wine from "the vine of the Sodomites."[162] In a similar vein, the theologian Gerhoh of Reichersberg (d. 1169) aligns the unreformed church with the time that Lot perforce lived among the people of Sodom, who were none other than the Nicolaitans. Eventually, the members of the true church, who were enslaved by the king, turned on the king and his armies and slew them with the sword of the Holy Spirit, finally "wresting the church from the hands of the Sodomite clerics, namely the Nicolaitans."[163] In short, at a time when the term "sodomy" was beginning to resolve itself as same-sex activity, some of the more inventive reformers were resisting, attempting to associate the term with the practices of the married clergy.

Reforming Referendums

Gerhoh's clever realignment of the Nicolaitans with the biblical Sodomites provides an intriguing window into orthodox denial. If the reforming papacy had turned a deaf ear to Damian's disturbing wake-up call regarding the existence of widespread sodomy among the clergy, the writers of reform-minded canonical collections were equally hard of hearing. The *Collection in Seventy-Four Titles* (ca. 1050) was one of the earliest reform manuals. And yet the section "On the Cleanness of Priests and the Continence of the Clergy" contains only canons prohibiting clerical marriage and Nicaean-inflected reiterations of the women acceptable in a priest's household. There are no canons mentioning clerical sodomy.[164]

The focus on clerical relations with women in the *Collection in Five Books*, written sometime between 1063 and 1085 by a member of the reformist party, is especially striking. The second book addresses the lives of secular and regular clergy alike, addressing questions of sin, criminal procedure, penance, and punishment. A full 72 of its 203 canons are either injunctions about avoiding sexual temptation or efforts to address situations in which a cleric had already succumbed.[165] The only sexual sins treated involve women, however. This is in spite of the fact that the author drew heavily on a wide array of sources that highlight sodomy, such as penitentials. He also uses Smaragdus—the Carolingian commentator who had cited several canons bearing on the abuse of children, including the Pseudo-Basil/Fructuosus canon. Yet when referring to "the more grievous sins"—a term that in monastic culture was often a euphemism for same-sex relations or bestiality—the only sins specified are with women.[166] Even the *Vision of Wetti* makes an appearance. It will be remembered that Wetti's angelic guide repeatedly identified sodomy as the most dangerous threat to humanity and claimed that its ubiquity presaged the end of the world. Yet the passage that proved irresistible to our anonymous canonist is, predictably, the one depicting fornicating priests, bound to stakes in the river of fire, facing their female partners in sin.[167] Possible exceptions to this male-female trend are not only few and far between but also extremely muted.[168] The cumulative message was that the eleventh-century clergy had no problem with same-sex relations— only with women. Apart from Leo IX's initial interdict against sodomy at Reims in 1049, where Damian's presence probably influenced the agenda, there was no legislation enacted against sodomy at any subsequent reform councils.[169]

The willingness to overlook the issue of clerical sodomy meant that the situation of the child oblate and his vulnerability to sodomitical predators, so poignantly evoked by Odo of Cluny, was never addressed in the reformers' abundant canonical collections. This was not due to any lack of authoritative sources. The huge compendium of Burchard of Worms, *Decretum* (before 1023), included a section on irrational intercourse in which both the Pseudo-Basil/Fructuosus passage and parallel warnings from the rule of Isidore of Seville appear.[170] The ninth-century False Decretals contained a canon, probably based on Elvira, that denied communion to the corrupter of boys.[171] The eleventh-century reformers were especially indebted to the False Decretals, which both numerically and ideologically constituted Anselm of Lucca's most important source.[172] And yet neither Anselm, nor any other canonist in the reforming circle, made reference to it. Damian was alone in his attempt to introduce the Pseudo-Basil/Fructuosus text, with its unforgiving treatment of monks perceived as child abusers. Even so, Damian's use of the passage was opportunistic, introduced to protect sacraments rather than children, and the *Book of Gomorrah* was soon suppressed.[173] Children were generally below the purview of the reformers. Any attention they did receive either focused on the original sin that marred their entry into the world or their heightened capacity for venality.[174] The major exception was the issue of clerical children, who were pronounced bastards, disinherited, and barred from the priesthood.

*   *   *

When Odo of Cluny raised the issue of clerical sodomy, it was about protecting children. Over a century later when Peter Damian addressed the same matter, it was about ritual purity. Despite their disparate rationales, these two men were the exceptions. For most religious authorities, concern about same-sex relations among the clergy was negligible, especially when compared with their vociferous expressions of the dangers women presented to clerical chastity. This chapter has explored this discrepancy. The early church councils consistently foregrounded the threat of wives and concubines over the evidence of same-sex relations within their own ranks. But this pattern is epitomized during the eleventh-century papal reform by Peter Damian's failed attempt to draw attention to same-sex relations among the clergy. Damian will subsequently redirect his reforming zeal against the more palatable vice of clerical marriage, which he ingeniously classifies as a heresy. But the reformers' disinclination to prosecute clerical same-sex relations was not lost on their critics: anti-reform polemicists will accuse the reforming party of hypocritically targeting the married clergy, all the while fostering same-sex relations among their own ranks. The reformers will attempt to deflect such charges through a variety of tactics, such as accusing the reform-resistant German emperor of sodomy or fiddling with the semiotics of the word so it could be applied to clerical marriage. Reforming councils and

canonical collections alike are silent over the issue of clerical sodomy, a silence
that speaks volumes.

The reformers may have wanted chastity, but they were prepared to settle
for celibacy. Married priests and their families were the obvious losers. But there
were also the many children entrusted to the clergy for care, particularly child
oblates, who paid a price.

CHAPTER 4

Sodomy on the Cusp of the Eleventh
and Twelfth Centuries

By the beginning of the twelfth century, clerical marriage had become a licit scandal, by which I mean that it was one sexual offense that moralists did not fear talking about. This point is driven home by Honorius Augustodunensis (d. ca. 1154) in two treatises excoriating the married clergy. Under the salient title *Apostates* he writes: "The Lord singled out these [married clergy] deserters when he called down a terrible curse on them: *Woe to the world because of scandals. For it must needs be that scandals come: but nevertheless woe to that man by whom the scandal cometh* [Matt. 18:7]. For they are the scandal of the entire church and an obstacle of all those turning to God. They are like homicides—hence God's curse. . . . And that *Woe* will occur in that place [hell]."[1] A second work, also addressing the sin of clerical marriage, is entitled *Offendiculum*—an equally telling title that literally means stumbling block and was often used interchangeably with the word "scandal."[2] The twelfth century also saw confirmation of Damian's perception that the administration of the sacraments transformed the priest into the recipient's spiritual father: for writers like Honorius and Gerhoh of Reichersberg, the married clergy and their wives were not mere fornicators but incestuous fornicators.[3] The essential illegality of such relations was confirmed when, after centuries of prevarication, the Second Lateran Council (1139) declared clerical marriage altogether invalid.[4]

This chapter examines the discrete same-sex cultures that were believed to have arisen in the wake of the papal reform. I begin with the unabashed flourishing of homoerotic poetry and lyric in the cathedral schools of northern France and its facilitation of a brand of pederastic nepotism among the higher clergy. I will then turn to the ambiance of the Anglo-Norman court where clerical chroniclers claim that same-sex relations were rife, examining possible factors that gave rise to such claims.

Bishops Who Hate Love Songs

[Sodom] is a sin many can imitate
Since it needs only beautiful boys of tender years.
                    —Twelfth- or thirteenth-century graffiti

Vile youth occupies episcopal halls, youth slippery in body,
flighty at heart like the wind.
                                        —Bernard of Cluny[5]

The routing of the married clergy was immediately followed by a flourishing of
homoerotic literature in clerical circles—a phenomenon that John Boswell
dubbed "The Triumph of Ganymede."[6] The evocation of Ganymede seems
appropriate, regardless of whether the phenomenon is perceived as a triumph.
The homoerotic poetry of the twelfth century exhibited—indeed, embraced—
the same dissymmetry in age and power represented in the myth and typical of
ancient pederasty.[7] And so Ganymede was elevated from his patristic status as
illicitly abducted minor to eloquent spokesperson for same-sex relations. In a
poetic debate pitting relations between males against relations between males
and females, Ganymede's sparring partner is none other than Helen of Troy—an
even more famous rape victim from antiquity.[8] The work is playful and witty.
Yet, at the risk of sounding churlish, there is an undeniable irony in the choice
of these celebrated rape victims for extolling erotic pleasure. Admittedly, it is
doubtful that most modern readers would perceive the irony, while twelfth-
century audiences, in thrall to the Ovidian tradition, would almost certainly
not.[9] Ovid's *Heroides*, which was one of the staples of the cathedral school curriculum, consisted of a series of painful rebukes from women who had been abandoned by men. Yet a number of these women had originally been abducted,
raped, or won as booty by the very men whose loss they were bemoaning. By
the same token, the penitential tradition situated the sexual abuse of a boy under
the category of *ludus*, or "game," but this term becomes a common euphemism
for same-sex relations generally in the twelfth century.[10] Such paradoxes should
serve as a reminder that the boundaries between eros and abuse were drawn
differently in the past. Yet, they should also make one mindful of who was
responsible for delineating the playing field in the first place.

This homoerotic poetry is all in Latin, bespeaking its clerical provenance.[11]
There is nothing apologetic about the verse. Some poems circulate anony-
mously, as is the case with the debate between Helen and Ganymede. But some
of the most celebrated verse was written by men who had achieved prominent
positions in the ecclesiastical hierarchy. Marbod of Rennes (d. 1123) is a case in

point. First appointed as master at the cathedral school of Angers, in 1097 he was elevated to the bishopric of Rennes in Brittany. Much of Marbod's verse is characterized by a cynical and provocative edge. In one poem, he urges an absent friend that he should hasten his return if he wants to keep his "boy" (*puer*), who is being courted by another:

> And if a boy can be tempted there is good reason to worry that he can
>   be netted.
> . . . .
> Give up the castle if you want to keep your puppy.[12]

In another poem, which describes "a certain boy / Who could easily enough have been a pretty girl," Marbod cautions that:

> A handsome face demands a good mind, and a yielding one,
> Not puffed up but ready for anything.
> The little flower of youth is fleeting and too brief;
> It soon withers, falls, and knows not how to revive.
> This flesh is now so smooth, so milky, so unblemished,
> So good, so handsome, so slippery, so tender.
> Yet the time will come when it will become ugly and rough,
> When this flesh, dear boyish flesh, will become worthless.[13]

The boy's flawless beauty is described at length, only to be contrasted with the uncouth manner in which he resists overtures of love.

Baudri of Bourgueil (d. 1130) is another prolific poet who lingers over the beauty of boys. First abbot of the Benedictine monastery of St.-Pierre in Dol, he was later elevated to the archbishopric of Dol. Baudri's age-specific eroticism is even more marked. In a satirical poem to a youth named Alexander, Baudri taunts that "time and age will harden [his] cheeks" and that a "beard is stealing the boy from himself."[14] This is probably the same Alexander who is the subject of Baudri's lament, describing him as:

> An adolescent, he had not yet lived twenty years
> . . . .
> He was a canon at Tours, a boy of great talent.[15]

But Baudri's most sensual effort is addressed "To a Youth Too Proud," whose voice, "sounding as sweetly as a nightingale's,"

. . . could be a boy's or a girl's;
You will be another Orpheus, unless age injures it—
Age which distinguishes girls from boys,
When the cheek is clothed with the first down of young manhood
. . . .
The touch of your snow-white body sports with my hands.[16]

Both poets seem to have eventually renounced their poetical efforts, perhaps regarding them as incompatible with ecclesiastical advancement.[17] But if such verses at some point became an embarrassment to their authors, they are, arguably, even more embarrassing to modern scholars. In his attempts to locate a past tolerance for same-sex relations in the church that could act as an exemplar for the present, Boswell urges the case for poetic license, maintaining that the designation "boy" need not be taken at face value.[18] Others, such as Jean Leclercq, apologize for the erotic components of such verse by pointing to the fervent emotions expressed in monastic letters and noting that there is only one vocabulary for different types of love.[19] Erotic overtones are also an inevitability in any exegesis on the Song of Songs, a favorite text for monastic commentary.[20] Another approach is to acknowledge the erotic nature of such verse, but to argue for its sublimation to a higher purpose. For instance, Stephen Jaeger perceives Baudri's provocative poem to the surly youth not in terms of seduction but as pedagogical encouragement: "this is one of many texts in which the erotic is invoked as a goad to learning. The teacher/poet, stirred by the student's beauty, moves from the language of courtship to that of moral instruction."[21] Baudri takes the youth to task for his abrasive behavior, but, as Jaeger notes, he also praises him for "refus[ing] to be Jove's Ganymede. / And I pray you not be corrupted in loving."[22] Even so, it would be perverse to insist that all of Baudri's celebrations of youthful beauty were pedagogic. He significantly concludes his lament on the death of the youth Alexander by asking God to forgive him "if his beauty and age brought stains upon him / . . . You who gave him both."[23] In another poem on the same subject, Baudri writes: "the paltry glory of his beautiful flesh begins to stink, / But forgive, God, what he may have ill deserved."[24]

However we choose to construe this celebration of boyish beauty, it was representative of a powerful current amid the clergy that was strenuously resisted by some. We will examine two cases of such opposition. Both are bishops; both are located in northern France—the epicenter of erotic verse. The first case involves Manasses I, the archbishop of Reims (d. after 1081)—an old-style, worldly type of prelate that papal reformers were committed to wiping out. Manasses was no paradigm of virtue. He was a greedy and aggressive simoniac, who was frequently accused of despoiling the churches and monasteries of his see.[25] But it is possible that his notorious dereliction of duty and inexhaustible greed might have been overlooked had he shown due subordination to his superiors. In 1077, Manasses refused to appear at a council in Autun when he was summoned by Hugh, bishop of Die and eventual archbishop of Lyon and Gregory VII's most puissant legate. This lapse precipitated Manasses's eventual deposition.[26]

To Hugh of Die, the archbishop of Reim's failure to appear was clearly a case of contumacy. Manasses had his own version of events, however. In a letter to Gregory VII, Manasses explained how he had been framed by a different Hugh, this one being the bishop of Langres and a relative.[27] According to Manasses, the bishop of Langres was fond of going to various cities where he indulged in a lustful, louche lifestyle, listening to male singers and their songs about boyish lovers. When he returned home, he brought these filthy songs with him, and proceeded to sing them to his friends. Although Manasses was ashamed to share such filth with Gregory's "great majesty," he felt compelled to give a salient sample: "Come beautiful and tender one / With flesh as soft as a girl." Manasses claimed to be especially distraught over the musical tastes of the bishop of Langres because, in addition to being a blood relative, he was also one of Hugh of Die's most trusted counselors. Yet despite Manasses's express disgust for such lyrics, he feared they would be his undoing. Apparently, the dissolute bishop of Langres became apprehensive that the very verses that he had put in circulation would bring infamy on his name. As a result, the wily bishop began to attribute the verses to his relative Manasses—presumably in spiteful retaliation for Manasses's righteous revulsion. Over time, Hugh of Langres became progressively more vindictive, alleging he would rather die than let Manasses remain in his bishopric. Such sentiments were, allegedly, not idle threats: Hugh of Langres began to conspire against Manasses, amassing his enemies. Their plan was to take advantage of the opportunity afforded at the council at Autun to destroy the archbishop of Reims totally. This was why Manasses feared to attend the council.[28]

The great canonist Ivo, bishop of Chartres (d. 1115), probably had very little in common with his peer Archbishop Manasses except a shared aversion to the kind of love songs that seemed to be circulating everywhere. Ivo clearly saw these verses not as expressions of platonic love but as symptoms of an unrestrained carnality that went hand in glove with a rarefied simony that the reformers had failed to stigmatize: a quasi-nepotistic simony in which the currency was not coin, but flesh, and in which the people advanced were not nephews but boyish lovers. In 1098, Ivo wrote a letter to his friend, Hugh of Die—the very legate whose council had been scorned by Manasses—objecting to the recent promotion of a certain John to the bishopric of Orléans on precisely these grounds.[29] He recounts how Archbishop Ralph II of Tours had struck a deal with the French king Philip I, promising to preside at his Christmas coronation provided that the king gave his permission for John to be made bishop of Orléans.[30] John had already been ordained archdeacon by the late bishop of Orléans, also named John, despite considerable local opposition. Ivo writes: "This matter is no secret for the king of the French testified to me publicly that he was the lover [*succubus fuerit*] of the aforesaid John, and so he published this, spreading rumor in neighboring cities with the result that he accepted the nickname of Flora from his fellow canons, after a certain famous concubine."[31] This passage has been interpreted by historians as King Philip's sensational admission that he had enjoyed the sexual favors of the redoubtable John the Younger.[32] This is not only a serious misinterpretation of the text, but also one that makes no sense. As the sorry example of Henry IV suggests, and as contemporaneous aspersions cast on the Anglo-Norman court will confirm, there was no surer way of besmirching a secular ruler than through accusations of same-sex relations. Much of Philip I's reign was famously marred by the bitter struggle that ensued from his attempt to repudiate his first wife and marry a second. Ivo of Chartres was one of the few ecclesiastical authorities bold enough to resist the king's "adultery" from the outset. Not only did Ivo refuse to attend the wedding, which he perceived as invalid, but he even paid the consequences of his implacable intransigence through temporary imprisonment.[33] The past spring, moreover, Hugh of Die had placed an interdict upon France because of Philip's failure to separate from his second wife.[34] Why would Philip voluntarily antagonize Ivo, his sworn enemy, by publicly flaunting a sodomitical affair with a member of the higher clergy, let alone actively assist in spreading the rumor? Such an admission becomes all the more unlikely since the language used implies that the king played the sexually passive role.

The French king's putative admission to such relations is generated by confusion over who was the subject in the phrase *succubus fuerit*—a highly unusual but nevertheless evocative way to describe a sexual act. *Cubare* means to lie down; when joined with *suc-*(or *sub-*), it literally means "the one who lies underneath."[35] Ivo apparently confronted the king with the flagrant relations between young John and the late bishop of Orléans, hoping the king would condemn the promotion of anyone so patently unfit for the episcopal office. The king responded by saying that he was well aware that the younger John had slept with (or under) his first patron, John the Elder. Then Ivo goes on to say that the younger man had spread the salacious nature of this relationship among his fellow canons with naughty glee.

Later in the same letter to Hugh of Die, Ivo makes explicit reference to the fact that Ralph, bishop of Tours, had supplanted the late bishop of Orléans as young John's sexual partner—a charge that Ivo will repeat subsequently in a letter to the pope.[36] But the existence of such a relationship between Ralph and the younger John is already implied by the highly unusual words Ivo first uses to characterize Ralph, the bishop of Tours. Ralph is described as *paedagogus et incubus* of the church of Tours.[37] In classical times, the *paedagogus* was a slave who accompanied children to school. Eventually, the word had shed its servile quality and was used as a synonym for teacher or master, accentuating the implicit hierarchy in age and experience over the student. In this context, it is noteworthy that one of Ivo's chief objections to the appointment of the younger John was his extreme youth.

Ivo also referred to the archbishop of Tours as an *incubus*, a malign spirit who was believed to prey sexually on women.[38] Its dominant position in the sex act is again implicit in the verb from which it was derived: *incubare* (to lie upon).[39] This designation is clearly derogatory, pointing to the manner in which Ralph dominated and corrupted both his episcopal see and the younger John. In supernatural parlance, moreover, the *incubus* finds its feminized counterpart in the *succubus*, which, as we saw, is how Ivo characterizes the younger John. The *incubus/succubus* alignment simultaneously points to the sexual hierarchy implicit in their perverse gendering (*incubus* as dominant male penetrator; *succubus* as submissive entity being penetrated). Both creatures, however, are demons.[40]

Finally, the linguistic coupling of Ralph, the *incubus* of Tours, with the John the Younger, *succubus* to the late bishop of Orléans, conveys the depravity of this three-way relationship as only a canon lawyer could. The two senior clerics were sodomitically sharing one youth and, hence, sexually mingling their blood via semen. This perverse form of consanguinity is compounded by the blood relationship between Ralph of Tours and the late John the Elder of Orléans, who were brothers—a fact well known to Hugh of Die.[41] Ivo linguistically parses the brothers' incest by implying that Ralph of Tours played the role of *incubus* with John the Younger of Orléans, even as the youth had formerly played *succubus* to John the Elder. This, of course, means that John the Elder shares the role of *incubus* with his brother Ralph, even as Ralph shares in the spoils of the *succubus*, John the Younger, who formerly consorted with Ralph's late brother. There are also varying degrees of spiritual incest at work. Sexual infractions against clerical vows of celibacy were progressively deemed incestuous. The sacrament of ordination created additional spiritual bonds between the bishop and the individual being ordained. One brother ordained young John as deacon, the other ordained him as bishop. Hence, both older men were spiritual fathers to the same son. For either of the two brothers to have sex with John would be to violate his spiritual paternity, making his sodomitical relations even more abominable. For both of them to have sex with young John was to further unite the two brothers in some dark and unspeakable spiritual affinity.

When Ivo again evokes the image of the pedagogue later in the same letter, a pederast dynamic is even more apparent, as is the suggestion of sexual abuse. "The youth [*juvenis*], commanded by the king and forced by the archpriest of Tours, is thrust into the aforesaid church, and is thus under the archbishop of Tours, like a boy under a pedagogue. If he [the young John] is standing, he dares not to sit without [the archbishop of Tours] either ordering him or agreeing to let him sit, for [the young John] is said to have submitted himself to the most filthy uses."[42] In this context, the work of the *paedagogus* and *incubus* have become interchangeable: the archbishop of Tours dominates the younger man. But this dynamic is not simply sexual: Ivo states that he is convinced that the younger John's elevation was engineered so that Ralph could control the dioceses of both Tours and Orléans.[43]

Yet despite the seeming pathos of young John's situation, and the representation of him as being forced to endure unspeakable acts, Ivo nevertheless labels John a *succubus*—a diabolical entity complicit with his corrupter with the potential to corrupt others. This is borne out in Ivo's account of his reputation. "Many filthy and nefarious things" were alleged against John, though Ivo acknowledges that suitable witnesses were probably lacking for a conviction. Even so, Ivo remains convinced that "the said adolescent [*adolescens*] . . . is a most ignominious person and shamelessly defamed in all the neighboring churches," which should suffice for removing him from office.[44] Evidence of his perfidy is especially apparent by his participation in the erotic world of clerical lyric. Adolescents throughout the cities and countryside sang about "how [John] often sang to his lovers [*concubini*] and listened as they sang them [the songs] back to him."[45] In the event that Hugh of Die was incredulous about the veracity of these charges, Ivo reverted to the same strategy adopted by the redoubtable Manasses: he included a little ditty in his letter that was written by John about his sexual conquests. The song has not survived.

In his remonstrance against young John and his episcopal patrons, Ivo of Chartres selects his words carefully in order to demonstrate just how this particular strain of diabolical simony works. The term *incubus* is hardly a usual term for referring to a bishop, even as *succubus* is a bizarre way to designate a human lover—same-sex or otherwise. This is the sole appearance of these demonically inflected terms in Ivo's entire correspondence. *Paedagogus* appears only rarely and is invariably used in a pejorative sense.[46] The rigidly hierarchical nature of these terms suggests that Ivo's distaste for all forms of homoerotic expression is at least partially predicated on his sensitivity to the question of age. He is clearly aware that boys like the younger John were typical of the age dissymmetry implicit in clerical pederasty. But once a youth like John has been corrupted, he will pass this corruption along to others. In his letter to Urban II, Ivo again complains about how John the Younger's many concubines popularized his songs, which were, in turn, picked up by "filthy youths" (*foedis adulescentibus*), "who were singing them in the highways and the byways." Ivo concludes his letter to the pope with another ditty, this time a rueful satire written by the canons of Tours. It turns on the ironic fact that the younger John was elected bishop on the Feast of the Holy Innocents—the feast associated with the carnivalesque tradition of electing a boy bishop. "We are electing a boy [*puer*], while observing the feast of the boys. / We do not follow our custom, we only follow our monarch's orders."[47] The irony is heightened by the association of Herod's slaughter of the Holy Innocents with the clergy's sexual abuse of boys.[48]

We do not know at what age John was made archdeacon or how long he remained in the post before he was made bishop. John Boswell has argued that Ivo's concern over the younger John's age was exaggerated; that John was at least twenty-five—the traditional minimum age for becoming a deacon.[49] But it is noteworthy that a more accommodating view was gaining ground that regarded twenty as the minimum age for becoming a deacon, at least if no other more suitable candidate was available, a position that Ivo argued on at least one occasion.[50] This probably means that John was under twenty. Ivo's choice of vocabulary is also suggestive. Although he enlists ambiguous terms like *adolescens* (a state that could technically last anywhere from fifteen until twenty-eight),[51] he also uses *puer* to describe the younger John. Nor would this be the first time that Bishop Ralph of Tours had sought to advance an underage favorite. In 1076, Gregory VII had to override the bishop's choice for bishop of Dol, another suffragan diocese subordinated to Tours, describing Ralph's candidate as a youth (*iuvenis*).[52]

Despite Ivo's apparent agitation over such relations, it is important to remember that he was very much the exception. His urgent concern about clerical pederasty likewise clashed with the reformers' relative nonchalance.[53] The papal legate, Hugh of Die, clearly did not share Ivo's concerns about the see of Orléans. Nor were Hugh or Urban II disturbed by the salacious songs that seem to have been relayed by the bishop of Chartres as incontrovertible evidence of corruption. The same could be said for the implacable Gregory VII, who was clearly unmoved by Manasses's complaint against Hugh of Langres—the latter being a reform sympathizer as well as a dilettante in clerical same-sex erotica. Nor was Gregory's laissez-faire attitude reserved for reformist clergy alone. The

chronicler Wido of Ferrara took the pontiff to task for failing to discipline
Henry IV's legate, Bishop Ulrich of Padua—that "bilge water of all vices"—who
was accustomed to "abuse boys in his mouth."[54] Boswell finds the "apparent
indifference to the homosexual behavior of the institutional church during this
century . . . all the more remarkable because it was precisely this time that the
most strenuous efforts were made to enforce clerical celibacy."[55] But the married
clergy would not have found this indifference remarkable at all. It corroborates
what they had said about the reformers' practice of punishing clerics involved
with women but ignoring same-sex infractions among their own ranks.

This pattern of condemning the clergy's relations with women but ignoring
their same-sex relations even seemed to pertain when the clerics engaging in
same-sex relations were totally corrupt. Both Manasses of Reims and Ralph of
Tours were reprobate simoniacs and deemed repellent by their peers. According
to Guibert of Nogent, Manasses was wont to say: "It would be good to have the
arch-episcopacy of Reims, if one didn't have to say Mass."[56] It was disgust for
Manasses that impelled the saintly Bruno (d. 1101), one of the canons of the
cathedral of Reims, to strike out alone and found the Carthusian order in the
wilds. By the same token, the poet Geoffrey of Vendôme (d. 1132) asserted that
Ralph of Tours was a liar who had "almost the entire world decrying, but no
one vindicating, his many perverse and dishonest works."[57] But the two bishops
met with very different fates. Manasses, who was repelled by clerical same-sex
eroticism, was suspended by Hugh of Die in 1078 and ultimately deposed in
1080.[58] He ended his life as an exile, dying unreconciled with the church.[59] But
Ralph hung onto his bishopric, despite his flagrant affair with and unlawful
promotion of his late brother's *succubus*. Likewise, John the Younger—the sod-
omotical protégé of the two brothers, lived until 1135, presiding over the bishopric of Orléans for almost forty years.[60] This is in spite of the fact that, according
to Ivo of Chartres, young John's see was purchased for him by his parents,
implicating him in the more conventional kind of simony.[61] Ivo had attempted
to redress this situation by appealing to the king, the papal legate, and the pope
himself—all to no avail.

Ivo also took an ineffectual swipe at Baudri of Bourgueil, someone well
known for his homoerotic paeans. In the same letter to Hugh of Die that pro-
tested the younger John's elevation, Ivo described Baudri's aborted efforts at
simony. Baudri allegedly arrived at the king's court at Christmas "open-
mouthed, open-handed," secure that he would be able to purchase the bishopric
of Angers, just as the queen had promised. It turned out, however, that his
enemies had deeper coffers and could afford to pay more than could the abbot.[62]
But such peccadilloes did not ultimately impede Baudri, who was, as we have
seen, eventually accorded the bishopric of Dol in 1107.[63] Ivo had much greater

success in securing the deposition of Stephen of Garland, a prelate whose name was linked with sexual scandal, from the church of Beauvais. As Ivo complained to Paschal II (d. 1118), Stephen was not even in major orders when he assumed his see. In addition, he was "an illiterate, a gambler, a womanizer [*mulierum sectatorem*], and had been declared infamous as a public adulterer."[64] Stephen's sexual excesses, however, were with women.

When it comes to his works of canon law, Ivo is again out of step with his fellow reformers, citing a number of authorities that explicitly address the sexual violation of minors.[65] As mentioned earlier, not only did the long overlooked Pseudo-Basil/Fructuosus passage make an appearance, but this was buttressed by a number of like-minded decrees, such as the indictment of the corrupter of boys at Elvira, as well as outright condemnations of sins against nature.[66]

Monks Who Hated Curls

Here's a help. Sounds crazy. When you pretend it's in the right hand, you have to believe it.
—Magician Slydini on the art of misdirection

Repression is effected not by means of amnesia but by a severance of the causal connections brought about by a withdrawal of affect. These repressed connections appear to persist in some kind of shadowy form . . . and they are thus transferred, by a process of projection, into the external world, where they bear witness to what has been effaced from consciousness.
—Sigmund Freud, "Notes Upon a Case of Obsessional Neurosis"[67]

Ivo and Manasses were not alone in their resistance to clerical same-sex eroticism. A number of clerical authors wrote what might be described as "backlash" poetry, lamenting the celebration of same-sex relations and the culture of sodomy.[68] The sin of sodomy also gave rise to some ominous portents. In 1083, the chronicler for the Benedictine abbey of Ottobeuren reported an unprecedented heat wave in which not only men but even fish perished. This is followed by the comment: "In this time, sodomitical crimes were especially perpetrated."[69] And, as will be seen below, Hugh of Flavigny (d. after 1114) cites a series of grisly portents that culminate in a cleric who is impregnated through sodomy.

And yet, at the turn of the century it was not the clergy but the secular courtiers of the Anglo-Norman world who were, arguably, the most notorious sodomites in Latin Christendom. Much of the blame seemed to reside with King William II (d. 1100), whose cognomen was Rufus—allegedly a blatant sinner who refused to reform his own behavior or that of his courtiers. Of course, it is sometimes difficult to know what exactly Rufus was being accused of because the disapprobation of chroniclers was often conveyed through dark innuendo. The Benedictine chronicler Eadmer (d. ca. 1126), a disciple of Anselm, archbishop of Canterbury (d. 1109), is a case in point. In Eadmer's biography of Anselm, the first meeting between the king and the bishop after the coronation is fraught with carefully choreographed occlusion. The meeting began well, with the king's warm greeting and some cheerful talk. But then Anselm asked to see Rufus in private, and, once the two men were alone, he began to "rebuke the king for those things which were reported about him: nor did he pass over in silence anything which he knew ought to be said to him. For almost everyone in the whole kingdom daily talked about him, in private and in public, saying such things as by no means befitted the dignity of the king."[70]

If Eadmer is rather circumspect about the nature of the king's objectionable behavior in his vita of Anselm, he is more forthcoming in his *History of Recent Events in England*, in which we learn incrementally that the problem has something to do with sodomy.[71] Eadmer prefaces a disagreement between Anselm and the king by observing that it had become customary for courtiers to wear their hair long, like women, and walk with a mincing gait, "glancing about them and winking in an ungodly fashion." Nor was Anselm oblivious to this perceived abnormality. One of his first acts as archbishop was to excoriate such behavior in a sermon delivered at the beginning of Lent, with good effect. Many were inspired to cut their hair and resume a more manly bearing. Those who would not reform were suspended both from receiving the Lenten ashes on their forehead and from the benefits of Anselm's blessing. It was in this context that the archbishop approached the king to request that the practice of church councils be renewed to curtail various crimes. The king responded in anger that he would attend to these matters when he saw fit, before asking, in a mocking tone, what the archbishop intended to speak about at such a council. Anselm immediately replied, "That most shameful sin of sodomy," which was spreading so quickly that "the whole land will . . . become little better than Sodom itself." But Anselm's words "found no home in the heart of the King," who would hear no more on the subject.[72]

The monk William of Malmesbury (d. ca. 1140) gives a slightly more empathetic portrait of William Rufus, describing him as "a man of high principles, which he himself obscured as in the process of time he became unduly harsh; in such a way did vices creep into his heart little by little in place of virtues that he could not tell the difference."[73] The problem originated in the king's misguided liberality, which not only bankrupted the treasury but also disrupted the rule of justice. This, in turn, had a deleterious impact on the court:

> The noose itself was slackened from the bandit's neck if he had promised something to the king's advantage. The knightly code of honour disappeared; courtiers devoured the substance of the country people and engulfed their livelihood, taking the very food out of their mouths. Long flowing hair, luxurious garments, shoes with curved and pointed tips became the fashion. Softness of body rivaling the weaker sex, a mincing gait, effeminate gestures and a liberal display as they went along, such was the ideal fashion of the younger men. Spineless, unmanned, they were reluctant to remain as Nature had intended they should be [*enerues, emolliti, quod nati fuerant inuiti manebant*]; they were a menace to the virtue of others and promiscuous with their own. Troops of effeminates and gangs of wastrels went around with the court; as a wise man said, with good reason "The court of the king of England is not the abode of majesty but a brothel of perverts."[74]

When Anselm attempted to intervene, he found himself unable to rally the bishops of the land. In fact, he so failed in his efforts at reform that he voluntarily left the country.[75] William of Malmesbury again places the blame for the court's decadence on the king's misguided generosity and unwillingness to correct vice. Such laxness redounded on the king's reputation "to his great and indelible discredit; which in my opinion he thoroughly deserved, for a man would never expose himself to such disgrace, who had once bethought him of the great kingdom he was called to rule. So I veil the topic in these few bald and hasty words, because I am ashamed to speak of so great a king, and I am devoting my efforts to refuting or palliating the evil spoken of him."[76]

The Norman monk Orderic Vitalis (d. ca. 1142) spreads the net of iniquity more broadly, heaping scorn on William Rufus's elder brother Robert Curthose, Duke of Normandy (d. 1106). According to Orderic, the sodomitical decadence of Robert's court had already been foretold to Robert's mother, Mathilda, when she consulted a German hermit/visionary.[77] Sadly, this prophecy was fulfilled: during Robert's rule, "sodomy [*uenus sodomestica*] walked abroad unpunished, flaunting its tender allurements and foully corrupting the effeminate [*molles*], dragging them down to Hell." The bishops threatened the offenders with anathema; clerics preached repentance—all to no avail.[78] This rampant feminization of the Norman aristocracy was abetted by Fulk, Duke of Anjou, who, in order to disguise his deformed feet, had introduced pointed-toed shoes—an innovation that hastened the decline of the already effeminate aristocracy.[79]

Orderic first broaches the subject of William Rufus to establish the king's wanton and lascivious character (*proteruus et lasciuus*), and its effect on his subjects, who imitated his corrupt morals.[80] So when the decadent footwear spread from Normandy to the English court, there was no hope of royal intervention. Orderic moves seamlessly from an indictment of "frivolous fashion" to the courtiers' lax sexual morals. "Effeminates [*effeminati*] set the fashion in many parts of the world: foul catamites, doomed to eternal fire, unrestrainedly pursued their revels and shamelessly gave themselves up to the filth of sodomy [*sodomiticis . . . spurciciis*]." Rejecting the counsel of priests, the corrupt courtiers wore their hair like women and donned long, tight tunics.[81] When Orderic returns to the subject of the king, he segues directly from his oppression of the poor to the fact that "he never had a lawful wife, but gave himself up insatiably to obscene fornications and repeated illicit couplings [*frequentibus moechis*]. Stained with his sins, he set a culpable example of shameful debauchery for his subjects."[82]

Such charges of sodomy and effeminacy among the nobility have lent themselves to various interpretations. To Gábor Klaniczay, they represent fallout from the rapid spread of fashion around the turn of the eleventh century and its destabilizing effect on traditional social semiotics.[83] This premise corresponds with the scholarly consensus that the changing parameters of secular and ecclesiastical spheres created a crisis in masculinity around this time.[84] Mathew Kuefler has further suggested that such charges of sodomy reflect the church's efforts to undermine the homosocial culture of the military aristocracy.[85] While all of these theories are eminently credible, they do not address the question of why the Anglo-Norman milieu was especially vulnerable to such charges. Yet there were, indeed, special factors at work that recommended England as a propitious destination for sodomy—at least from a rhetorical standpoint. As we saw in the previous chapter, the first pointed charges of sodomy against a Western monarch arose against Henry IV, the emperor who was rash enough to have strenuously resisted papal reform, and these changes were driven by a clerical polemic of blistering heat. Whatever the sexual predilections of the German monarch, it is undeniable that accusations of sexual depravity in general, but sodomy in particular, were used strategically by his ecclesiastical enemies. The same is true of his contemporary William Rufus, who resisted not just papal reform but the authority of religion on many levels—a resistance that would secure his legacy as a sodomite.

The seeming accord among the earliest historians for the Anglo-Norman court should not eclipse the tight genealogy at work. William of Malmesbury was probably only four years old at the time of William Rufus's death. Although Orderic Vitalis would have been twenty-five at the time of the king's death, he lived in Normandy and rarely left his cloister.[86] Both historians were indebted to Eadmer, loyal propagandist to his beloved archbishop and the first to chronicle both William Rufus's villainous opposition to Anselm's authority and facilitation of sodomy throughout the English court.[87] Eadmer's bias had probably already begun to spread during Anselm's lifetime among their continental confreres. As the former abbot of the Norman monastery of Bec, Anselm was already known abroad. Indeed, if we are to believe Eadmer's account, Anselm had become something of a celebrity early in his career, "mak[ing] himself beloved by all good men, so that a good report of him spread not only throughout Flanders and all neighboring lands. His reputation even crossed the sea and England was filled with it."[88] During his troubled time as archbishop of Canterbury, Anselm twice left England for the Continent in self-imposed exile, always with the faithful Eadmer in tow.[89] Although Anselm's stated objective was to consult the pope, he was also a consummate politician who managed to appear in visible venues such as Cluny and the Council of Bari, where he helped to refute the heresies of the Greeks. Eadmer's account is triumphal: "Where he came he was met by crowds of people, gatherings of clergy and armies of monks, who acclaimed him with joy and enthusiasm."[90] Even if Eadmer is exaggerating, the exiled archbishop was certain to elicit sympathy in religious circles, rendering his peregrinations something of a prerelease press tour for Eadmer's writing. After Anselm's death, the earliest requests for Eadmer's vita came from the continental communities who had known Anselm, while the work's dissemination in England was much slower.[91] Later chronicles will continue to favor William Rufus as their whipping boy because of his treatment of the church. Hence when Herbert of Clairvaux, writing after 1170, refers to "a certain English king by the name of William, a carnal and libidinous man who greatly oppressed the churches in his land," he cites the "noble historian Eadmer" by name.[92] Anselm would be expeditiously canonized largely owing to Eadmer's efforts.[93]

Eadmer clearly despised the king and depicted the tensions between the king and the archbishop as unrelenting, especially when it came to financial matters. According to Eadmer, the king's first open quarrel with Anselm was on the Christmas following his ordination when the pontiff refused to despoil his tenants in order to offer the king a gift of one thousand pounds for his munificence.[94] Rufus was also described as an unapologetic simoniac who, as soon as a given prelate died, would immediately put his office up for sale.[95] Alternatively, he was said to leave offices empty to better conscript the foundation's revenues. When reproached by Anselm, the king responded: "What business is that of yours? Are not the abbeys mine?"[96] Rufus, who had doled out various church properties to his favorites during the see of Canterbury's long vacancy, asked Anselm to make these alienations permanent. Anselm declined.[97] Of course, a monastic chronicler like Eadmer was either unable to see the king's position or refused to. The rising national monarchies were all cash-strapped, with no legal formula for taxation. Naturally monarchs would attempt to turn church appointments into revenue.[98] The king clearly believed it was within his rights to require money from the archbishop—one of his tenants in chief. Nor was this the only way in which Anselm would seem wanting. The king, about to set out on a campaign, was frustrated over the underequipped troops that Anselm supplied. Eadmer, however, adduced this example as proof of the king's insensitivity toward an unworldly man of God.[99]

But what stands out especially in Eadmer's writings is the king's resistance to any papal influence over the English episcopacy, refusing to let Anselm go to Rome for the archiepiscopal pallium. Rufus argued his position with puckish sophistry: "We have not found him [Anselm] to be so lacking in counsel in what needs to be done, that he must needs consult the pope, nor subject to any grave sin, for which he must implore his absolution."[100] Instead, Rufus furtively arranged for the pallium to be brought to England, harboring the hope that he could appoint a different archbishop.[101] Later, when Anselm continued to ask leave to go to Rome and consult the pope about some of the difficulties he was encountering, the king refused.[102] When Anselm finally left without permission, the king attempted to strip him of his rank and possessions.[103] Anselm's loyalties were complex: he wanted to uphold the dignity of the see of Canterbury, even if this meant resisting the expansion of the authority entrusted in papal legates, yet he looked to the pope as a potential father figure to whom he could apply for advice. But however conflicted his attitude toward the papacy might be, it was very clear that Anselm's first loyalties were not to the monarchy.[104] To William Rufus's mind, such an attitude seemed contumacious, and he responded accordingly, confiscating the honors that he believed that he had bestowed upon Anselm.[105]

Because William died in a hunting accident at the relatively early age of forty-four, chroniclers and historians interpreted his death—one that deprived him of last rites—as punishment for his sinful ways. Eadmer, who was at Cluny with Anselm at the time, reports that there were many portents in England anticipating the king's death. But Eadmer was privy to Abbot Hugh's dream, which allegedly occurred before news of Rufus's death had arrived. Hugh dreamed that "the king had been accused before the throne of God, judged, and had the sentence of damnation passed upon him."[106] Whether or not the portents that Eadmer alluded to were real, subsequent chroniclers would have had no trouble fabricating the kind of ominous signs that one would expect to augur the death of a king whose damnation had been witnessed by a holy abbot. Several sources mention a fountain that flowed with blood in the days leading up to the king's death.[107] The chronicler Florence of Worcester (d. 1118) builds upon reports of the portentous fountain, adding devastating floods that swept entire villages away. More menacing still was the rumor that the devil himself had appeared "in a horrible shape" and was seen speaking to the king on a number of occasions in the woods.[108]

But the portents reported by the Benedictine abbot and historian Hugh of Flavigny are without a doubt the most memorable—not only because they continue after the king's death but for their scandalous nature.[109] The year following the king's demise, a priest named Peter, a chaplain of the royal chapel, became pregnant—allegedly inseminated by a series of male partners. Peter carried this burden secretly for a year until he publicly confessed to a sin that was now beyond concealment, begging that his "uterus" be opened (*aperiri sibi uterum*). When no one dared to fulfill this bizarre entreaty, the hapless priest went into labor and died in a frenzy. At his own request, Peter was buried as an excommunicate, outside the cemetery "in the grave of an ass."[110] Prior to his interment, the cadaver was opened, and a monster with the contours of a human was discovered within.[111]

The story about the pregnant priest is but a prelude to the real focus of Hugh's animus: the priest's brother Gerard, whom Hugh claimed had been appointed archbishop of York by William Rufus. According to Hugh, Gerard was a devil worshipper. He sacrificed a pig to his diabolical master, who ordered him to invite as many people as possible to a great feast so he could serve them the pig, presumably in order to enslave their souls. Fortunately, Gerard's chamberlain, concealed nearby, overheard his master's diabolical machinations, buried the cursed pig and substituted another, and denounced him to the new king, Henry I. Hugh maintained that everyone already knew that Gerard was unfit to be archbishop. Indeed, he had done impure things ever since he was a boy (*quae a puero impura extitisset*) without making any amends. The same year, fetid blood once again appeared in the prescient fountain, and the clerics in the king's chapel began excommunicating the sodomites on Sundays and every feast day.[112]

Hugh of Flavigny is the exception here insofar as his account of the English court was probably not indebted to Eadmer.[113] In fact, Hugh claimed to be in England in time to see the chain of horrendous marvels surrounding the death of William Rufus. Yet while Hugh may have been an independent voice, he was hardly an impartial one. In 1096, Hugh was a member of the legatine commission sent to England by Urban II with the dual purpose of reconciling William Rufus with his brother Robert, Duke of Normandy, and reproaching William for his blatant simony and failure to prosecute Nicolaitism. But the mission was derailed. As mentioned earlier, Rufus had sent his own legation to Urban II, the progress of which had been assisted by a present of ten marks of gold—at least according to Hugh. Thus, when Hugh and his fellow legates were about to get down to business, suddenly, out of nowhere, William's messenger returned with a papal legate, Walter, bishop of Albano, bearing the pallium for Anselm. Hugh's legation was dismissed in a preemptory fashion, and he was left shocked and disheartened by what he perceived as the corrupt collusion between England and the papacy.[114] Eadmer tells us that one of the two clerics sent by William Rufus on the surreptitious mission to bring back the pallium from Rome was none other than Gerard—Hugh's necromancer-archbishop.[115]

Gerard was a king's man.[116] Not only did he serve as Rufus's chancellor, but he had held the same position under his father, William the Conqueror. He was also indebted to the monarchy for his preferment in the church: William had made Gerard bishop of Hereford, and Henry I (not Rufus, as Hugh of Flavigny had alleged) would promote him to archbishop of York.[117] Gerard's priorities were in evidence when he led Rufus's sly expedition to get the pallium, and once again when he was later sent to Rome on behalf of Henry I over the question of lay investiture.[118] The archbishop's unequivocal loyalties doubtless fed the dark rumors that circulated about him. William of Malmesbury characterized Gerard as a "master of craft,"[119] a man given to lust and unsavory readings. Every afternoon he would read Julius Firmicus Maternus (a pagan astrologer) in secret, from which he gained a reputation for adhering to the dark arts. Like his former master William Rufus, Gerard died suddenly without the benefit of sacraments with a book of "curious arts" on his pillow. The cathedral canons would not allow him to be buried in the church and "would barely allow a sod to be ignominiously cast on the body outside the door."[120] To Hugh of Flavigny, Gerard epitomized the venality of the English court, which Hugh had witnessed firsthand.[121] Peter, the pregnant chaplain of the royal chapel, and his brother Gerard, the archbishop who dabbled in the dark arts, were but symptoms of a corruption that emanated from a debased monarch. The fact that the entire English clergy was infected was apparent in their adherence to the king over the papacy.

Yet while Hugh of Flavigny may have been a reformer at heart, his representation of sodomy among the clergy flags him as an outlier among clerics sympathetic to reform—not unlike his contemporary Ivo of Chartres. It was, as we have seen, much more typical for the married clergy to accuse the reformers of sodomy. But such accusations did not receive an airing from Eadmer. This is in spite of the fact that Normandy, where Anselm had spent so much of his career, was the vanguard of resistance to clerical celibacy, giving rise to a number of treatises defending clerical marriage.[122] The poet Serlo of Bayeux, the disinherited son of a priest, and one of the most scathing critics of the reformers' sodomitical hypocrisy, is a case in point. Serlo was a contemporary of both Anselm and Eadmer. It is difficult to believe that neither the bishop nor his retainer was unaware of reform casualties, like Serlo and his cohort, or their critique. It is equally unlikely that they would have been oblivious to the clerical celebration of same-sex eroticism emanating from the continental cathedral schools. The same holds true for the other chroniclers, particularly the Norman Orderic Vitalis.[123] Yet they chose to excoriate sodomy among secular courtiers, thus misdirecting attention away from the clergy. In fact, considering the attention paid to the sodomitical laity by contemporary chroniclers, it is curious that the sexual vices of the clergy garner so little interest. For Eadmer, this may have something to do with the fact that Anselm had made remarkably little headway with the entrenched married clergy of England, as was the case with Lanfranc before him.[124] On the one occasion when Eadmer does mention clerical incontinence, it is consorting with women that is at issue.[125]

Thus far I have been focusing on how the Anglo-Norman chroniclers embraced misdirection as a deliberate strategy for drawing attention away from the problem of clerical sodomy. In the case of Anselm and his milieu, however, there may also have been deeper motives at work. It is possible that the emphasis on the same-sex transgressions of secular courtiers resulted from the projection of their own unfulfilled and disavowed sexual desires.[126] As was the case with Alcuin and his students, Anselm and his cohort have occasionally been singled out by historians for skirting that fine line between carnal and spiritual love in their relations with one another.[127] It bears reiterating that professions of love are at the very heart of monastic letters, and there is no way of discerning what libidinal transgressions may be concealed within fervent expressions of emotion. Indeed, on a discursive level, many monastic authors seem to revel in the ambiguity over what kind of love is being offered or solicited. Stephen Jaeger has argued that this purposeful cultivation of ambiguity represents a deliberate rhetorical device for some authors. For others, however, it may be that, under the pretext of tantalizing their reader, they succeed in confounding themselves: that by availing themselves of the ambiguous vocabulary of eros, they are facilitating the dangerous slippage between spiritual and carnal love.

Eadmer provides an unusually detailed account of Anselm's close emotional relations with members of his community, unabashedly commending Anselm's boundless affection for the young males under his tutelage. Such affection is seemingly exemplified in Anselm's relationship with a difficult protégé named Osbern. When Anselm's appointment as prior of Bec met with considerable resistance from Osbern, Anselm went to great lengths to render the youth more cooperative. "He began with a certain holy guile to flatter the boy with kindly blandishments; he bore indulgently his boyish pranks, and—so far as was possible without detriment to the Rule—he allowed him many things to delight his youth and to tame his unbridled spirit." As the boy began to blossom, Anselm "showed a more tender affection to him than to any other; he nursed and cherished him, and by his exhortation and instruction he encouraged him in every way to improve."[128] This was clearly at odds with monasticism's traditional suspicion of any close interaction between monks and younger members of the community. Although the rule followed at Bec is no longer extant, the *Monastic Constitutions* of Lanfranc, Anselm's mentor whom he had succeeded as prior at Bec and later as archbishop of Canterbury, help fill this lacuna. The *Constitutions* were written for the monks of Canterbury Cathedral; Lanfranc claimed to have drawn upon the most reputable rules of his day, and surely Bec was a major source.[129] But far from relaxing the customary vigilance exercised over the young, Lanfranc's *Constitutions* called for an even higher degree of sequestration. Child oblates and novices alike were so deliberately isolated that only specified persons were permitted to make a sign or smile at them.[130]

There are instances in which Eadmer presents Anselm as adhering to these norms, observing salubrious distance in his dealings with the young. For instance, when a young monk was troubled by excruciating pain in the genitalia, Anselm felt compelled to inspect the ailment, but took the precaution of bringing with him one of the brethren, "a very old and pious man," before conducting an examination.[131] When it came to Osbern, however, Anselm, who "loved his son more than you could believe possible," is presented as incapable of maintaining similar boundaries—whether physical or emotional. This is especially apparent in the circumstances surrounding Osbern's death. "As [Anselm] used to relate with tears, just as he was hoping that the youth [*juvenis*] would bring much profit to the church, he was seized with a serious bodily infirmity and confined to bed." Anselm's attendance at the sickbed was tireless: "diligently he looked after his [Osbern's] body, and his soul likewise."[132] As Osbern was on the brink of death, Anselm made him promise to return, if possible, to report on how he fared in the afterlife.[133] When the boy died, the weeping prior withdrew from the other brothers to "where he might more freely pour out prayers for him." Eventually, exhausted by his tears, Anselm fell asleep, at which point Osbern appeared with reassurances of his salvation. But the relationship was far from over. Anselm "did not withhold from his dead friend the offices of that holy love that he had bestowed upon him while he was alive." He said a Mass for Osbern's soul every day and wrote to religious personnel far and wide in order to procure prayers on his friend's behalf. Although Eadmer never seems to question the extent or tenor of Anselm's devotion, he nevertheless manages to convey that Anselm's confreres did not share in his complacency. The other monks were clearly dismayed at the extent of Anselm's mourning and "blamed him for giving way to weakness." That Anselm's feelings for Osbern had been the source of considerable envy, and doubtless resentment, is suggested by the fact that several of the monks "devoted themselves body and mind to Anselm's service, hoping to succeed to Osbern's place in his affections." Anselm thanked them, but was now determined to become "all things to all men, that he might save all" (cf. 1 Cor. 9:12).[134]

Becoming "all things to all men" seems to imply that Anselm would no longer indulge himself by favoring one brother over another. Brian Patrick McGuire, in fact, argues convincingly that no one ever succeeded Osbern in Anselm's affections.[135] Even so, after Osbern's death, Anselm wrote a series of passionate letters to three successive favorites. One letter in particular, addressed to the monk Gilbert, intimates that there had at one time been a physical dimension to their relationship. Hence, Anselm anticipates how "when we see each other again we should once more revive, face to face, lip to lip, embrace to embrace, our forgotten love."[136] McGuire argues that Anselm may have permitted himself to invest this degree of passion in his relationship with Gilbert precisely because Gilbert was independent and relatively undemanding.[137] But his relationships with the monks Gundulf and Maurice, who made greater claims on Anselm, exhibited the kinds of trajectories reminiscent of unhappy love affairs: Anselm would begin with passionate declarations of love; follow up with apologies for not writing, coupled with reassurances of his undying affection; and ultimately devolve into silence.[138]

Although Eadmer often seems to celebrate Anselm's relations with the younger monks, he nevertheless suggests that Anselm was sometimes called upon to justify this devotion. Immediately following the detailed account of the relationship with Osbern, Eadmer relates that Anselm's "chief care was for the adolescents and youths [*adolescentibus atque juvenibus*], and when men asked him why this was, he replied by way of a simile. He compared the time of youth to a piece of wax of the right consistency for the impress of a seal. 'For if the wax . . . is too hard or too soft it will not, when stamped with the seal, receive the perfect image.'" But it is noteworthy that such impressions go both ways. In a flowery letter to Gundulf, Anselm writes: "How could I forget you? How could someone imprinted on my heart like a waxen seal slip out of my memory?"[139] Such emotive language was restricted to males. Unlike his near contemporaries, Peter Damian or Bernard of Clairvaux (d. 1153), Anselm extended no affective flourishes to his female correspondents.[140]

Is possible that Anselm's spiritual love for his special friends had at one point devolved into carnal love? There is evidence that might suggest such a lapse. Early in his monastic career, Anselm wrote a meditation entitled *Lament over Virginity Wickedly Lost* in which he bemoans the erstwhile marriage between his once virginal soul and Christ, forfeited because of some unnamed transgression.[141] There is no way of knowing if the meditation is referring to a physical lapse and, if so, of what nature. Fornication is referred to as "the defiler of my mind; the means of losing my soul," perhaps suggesting that the more fragile construct of mental virginity is at issue.[142] Or his lament could be purely metaphoric. In the *Dicta Anselmi*, utterances recorded by the devoted companion who replaced Eadmer, potential threats to the soul are frequently cast in sexual terms. The insufficiently vigilant soul that falls prey to temptation is deemed a fornicator, even as its entertainment of unclean thoughts is the equivalent to succumbing to words of adultery.[143] But although Anselm's meditation may be laced with metaphor, his grief, perhaps over something as intangible as spiritual purity, is presented as substantial, even as his remorse seems relentless. Bewailing his "inconsolable loss; hence intolerable torment," Anselm reproaches himself in visceral terms for having "willingly rushed into the infernal mire of stench," preparing himself for the fires of hell that he so richly deserves.[144]

Of course, Anselm's misery could be retrospective, associated with an event from his pre-monastic past. After all, Anselm did not embark upon religious life until the relatively late age of twenty-six.[145] It is certainly plausible, even likely, that he had acquired some sexual experience before entering the cloister. After becoming a monk, however, impassioned correspondence aside, such a prospect seems doubtful. Indeed, if Eadmer's testimony is to be trusted, the post-conversion Anselm was revolted by sex. This aversion is powerfully expressed through Anselm's vision of a river "into which flowed all the purgings and filth of the whole earth." The river "sucked into itself" everything in its path. Men and women were caught up in "obscene twisting and turning" (*obscenam revolutionem illorum*)—a movement that, as McGuire notes, is an ugly simulation of sexual passion. Yet, when Anselm learns that the river's denizens not only endure being nourished by its polluted water, but actually delight in it, he responds indignantly: "How can that be? Would anyone rush to take such a filthy drink? If nothing else, a sense of shame would hold him back." Anselm is mercifully led away from the horror of the roiling river and shown a vision of true monastic life "where the walls of the cloister were covered with the most pure and shining silver."[146] The filth of the river may well be a reaction to a sexual past, but there seems to have been no room for such experiences in Anselm's ideology of the cloister.

We should be mindful, however, that the projection of same-sex desire onto secular courtiers does not require sexual activity on behalf of the individuals engaged in projecting. On the contrary, the process is stimulated by the repression of any such activity.[147] Furthermore, the action being projected is necessarily the source of some ambivalence. Some of Anselm's more passionate letters are addressed to youths that he probably did not know well, if at all, written to encourage them in their monastic vocation. From R. W. Southern's perspective, Anselm's florid expressions of love exist on a continuum with prayers addressed to a saint or God: "But in the latter, the reality of the ideal object was guaranteed in advance; in his letters of friendship it was a subtle blend of fact and imagination."[148] Even though these imaginative exercises of devotion and love may be divorced from any possibility of physical realization, that does not preclude a residue of unfulfilled desire, even if it is a desire from which Anselm would naturally recoil. Yet it would be this very residue that was ripe for projection onto the secular court. Assuming Eadmer's representations are to be trusted, Anselm's very prioritization of same-sex relations as the chief concern assailing the kingdom suggests that some degree of projection was at work. It is certainly odd that an archbishop would blurt out accusations of sodomy almost immediately upon meeting his monarch for the first time and then would continue to hammer away at the issue in subsequent meetings. Perhaps Anselm supposed that, without the enabling restraint of a vow of chastity, courtiers might succumb to the temptation that he had himself experienced, indulging freely in sodomitical excesses. Seen from this perspective, the king's resistance does not necessarily imply any complicity with sodomitical courtiers. It could signify that he did not consider sodomy to be a particular problem at court.

Despite Eadmer's efforts to present sodomy as a purely secular affair, Anselm himself may not have been so sanguine. After, the king's death, Anselm was finally permitted to call a church council at which he deposed clerical sodomites and declared lay offenders infamous in that order. Sodomites were, additionally, to be excommunicated every Sunday in all the churches throughout the land.[149] Anselm is unique among his fellow clerics for taking such an initiative against sodomy in this period. Even so, the married clergy received the lion's share of attention at the council, while a subsequent council focused exclusively on the problem of married clergy.[150]

But what about William Rufus, the main target of the monastic chroniclers' aggressions? Apart from their accusations, there is nothing else in the historical record to suggest that William Rufus had sexual relations with other males, any evidence to the contrary being circumstantial. William of Malmesbury reports that Rufus wore his hair long, parted "window style" (*fenestrata*) in the center and, like most of the military aristocracy, was probably something of a dandy.[151] He never married but, as Emma Mason argues, men of royal and noble families often deferred marriage. If a king waits until he is politically puissant, he is in a better position to negotiate a politically advantageous union.[152]

In addition to his resistance to reform, Rufus also seems to have had personality traits that would render him especially susceptible to clerical slander, chief among them being an irreverent sense of humor. This is a topic to which William of Malmesbury, in particular, drew frequent attention.[153] When Anselm would confront the king with some scandalous (but unspecified) report about his behavior, the king would guffaw, claiming he could not control rumors but that "a holy man should not believe such stories."[154] Nor did Rufus do himself any favors if he did, in fact, apply his impious wit to the alleged portents of his death. A certain monk was said to have dreamed that the king entered a church with his usual surly demeanor before grabbing the crucifix with his teeth. He had almost gnawed off both the arms on the figure of Christ, when it suddenly began fighting back, kicking the king so hard that he fell over backwards. Flames issued from the prostrate monarch's mouth. When the dream was reported to the king, however, he roared with laughter: " 'He's a monk,' he said, 'and has these monkish dreams with an eye to the main chance. Give him a hundred shillings.' "[155] The suddenness of Rufus's death was but divine confirmation of his general perfidy.

Finally, Rufus's obstreperous attitude toward Anselm and the papacy was further cast into relief by the reputation of his pious father, William the Conqueror (d. 1087). William of Malmesbury acknowledges this explicitly when he describes Rufus as "a prince unquestionably without peer in our own time had he not been overshadowed by his father's greatness."[156] The Conqueror manifested what David Bates has described as "theatrically demonstrative piety,"[157] and he did his best to cultivate the friendship of popes and monastic reformers alike. This investment paid off: Alexander II (d. 1073) bestowed the papal banner on William, essentially authorizing the invasion of England.[158] Although ruthless when it came to the property of the conquered English nobles, the new king was wise enough to leave church holdings unmolested and was rewarded by ecclesiastical writers for his forbearance. Rufus's reputation was further damaged by his successor, Henry I, who paid lip service to eschewing the policies of his brother, all the time expanding upon them.[159]

The unfortunate emperor Henry IV shared in the affliction of a notably pious progenitor. His father, Henry III (d. 1056), had been so deeply committed to church reform that he appointed Leo IX, the first in the line of reforming popes.[160] If pro-papal chroniclers like Lampert of Hersfeld had attempted to argue that the sexual infamy surrounding Henry IV made him unfit to rule, English chroniclers went further still: William Rufus was living proof that greed and antipathy toward the church was synonymous with sexual license, with a strong suggestion of sodomy. Such a ruler was not simply ungodly but scandalous in the literal sense. His depraved example either corrupted the courtiers directly or abetted the corruption of the entire court. Yet the sudden ubiquity of same-sex relations among Anglo-Norman courtiers is as suspicious as it is convenient.[161] While a clerical culture of same-sex relations was flourishing across the channel, the Anglo-Norman court, with its reform-averse monarch, presented a unique opportunity for the deflection of charges of sodomy from the clergy and provided a target for the projection of their own unfulfilled desire. Like illusionists practiced in the art of misdirection, Anglo-Norman chroniclers ensured that their audience was looking the wrong way: not at same-sex relations within clerical culture, but at depraved rulers and their courtiers—with their flowing hair, tight tunics, and curly shoes.

CHAPTER 5

Confession, Scandal, and the "Sin Not Fit to Be Named"

As sins are weighed, so are they punished.
Greater punishments for greater sins, and lesser for lesser.
Thus copulation performed by members of a single sex,
A crime less serious than none, is punished more severely than
    any other.

—Marbod of Rennes

The eleventh-century papal reform and its aftermath saw an unprecedented flourishing of canon law that was deeply preoccupied with clerical discipline. Yet the compiler of these collections paid little heed to sexual infractions among the clergy that did not involve women. The one exception was, as we saw, Ivo of Chartres, whose efforts to counteract sexual nepotism among the clergy was corroborated by the inclusion of canons relating to the abuse of children in his work. Yet any gesture Ivo may have made in this direction would eventually be swept away by Gratian's *Decretum*, which was destined to supplant previous collections of canon law. Gratian represented a continuation of the reformers' tendency to focus on the clergy's sexual relations with women, while placing few obstacles in the way of the ongoing celebration of relations between males. As Boswell has noted, the *Decretum*'s prohibitions against same-sex relations were sparse.[1] Both Elvira's condemnation of the corruption of boys and the Pseudo-Basil/ Fructuosus canons are absent, despite Gratian's indebtedness to Ivo. A later recension of *Decretum* would include two potentially palliative canons from Roman law, however: one prosecuted anyone who attempted to debauch males or females; the second was against those who corrupted boys, girls, or women. But the fact that these were secular rulings, with the debauchment of boys elided with girls and women, mediated against their effectiveness with regard to clerics who preyed upon boys.[2]

There were other canons that did address sins *contra naturam*, but they were introduced in what can only be described as an obfuscatory manner under the umbrella question of whether a husband can dismiss his wife for fornication. One passage from Augustine's *Confessions* condemns unnatural acts, which are defined as "the kinds of things the people of Sodom do." The second passage, also emanating from Augustine but misattributed to Jerome, is less circumlocutious: "Natural [sexual] usage is licit in the marriage bed, but illicit in adultery. But usage against nature is always illicit and beyond a doubt more shameful and filthy, which is what the Apostle argues, wishing to convey that in both men and women it is more damnable than if they sinned by natural usage in adultery or fornication."[3]

There is nothing extraordinary about including a section on sins against nature in a discussion of marital sex. Such terms are still widely used to describe various nonprocreative sex acts or impermissible postures between men and women, as is the term "sodomy." Yet the one instance in which Gratian does address the question of unnatural acts between members of the same sex, again with regard to the dismissal of one's wife for fornication, is as oblique as it is disturbing. Gratian cites a passage from the treatise *On Abraham* in which Ambrose is attempting to justify why Lot was prepared to offer his daughters up to the lascivious people of Sodom and Gomorrah as a substitute for the travelers he was sheltering in his house—the ones that the men outside wished to "know," that is, to violate sexually. The answer is simple: "Lot offered the chastity of his daughters for, although the impurity [of the gesture] was shameful, nevertheless it was less shameful to have sex according to nature than against nature."[4] True, same-sex relations are unequivocally condemned, but in a manner that draws attention away from the original offense by substituting one crime for another. Since the girls were unmarried and undoubtedly young, moreover, Ambrose's determination again belies the early church's reputation for championing the young against the sexual predation of their elders. Ivo had clearly found Ambrose's verdict jarring, surrounding it with four passages questioning Lot's right to prostitute his daughters in this way.[5] Because Gratian does not include these canons, this equivocation is also absent, and Lot's decision goes unchallenged.[6]

Lot was prepared to prostitute his daughters to avoid a worse evil. From a rhetorical standpoint, Gratian's treatment employs a similar dodge, sanitizing the sexual misdemeanors of the clergy. In contrast to the handful of canons condemning same-sex relations, muffled in a section on marriage, Gratian dedicates four entire *distinctiones* to the issue of clerical marriage and concubinage, with a total of seventy-four canons.[7] In a *distinctio* that is explicitly concerned with disciplining the unchaste clergy, nineteen canons forbid relations with women, while the remaining four use the gender- and age-neutral term "fornication."[8] As was seen with the eleventh-century reformers, the only sexual threats that matter come from outside the clergy, not from within. The real problem is the women—now extraneous in every way. There is nothing in Gratian's work that associates same-sex practices with the clergy.

Envisaging Clerical Sin

If concerns about clerical same-sex relations were ignored by mainstream authorities, they returned through the back door in the burgeoning genre of visions. We have already seen that Wetti, the Carolingian visionary-cum-monk, bore mystical witness to the ubiquity of sodomy among the clergy in the ninth century. Wetti's concern was something of an anomaly for his age: most contemporaneous visionaries seemed content to use their visions to settle old scores, envisaging their adversaries suffering in hell.[9] But from the eleventh century onward, Wetti's preoccupation with sexual sins returns with a graphic luridness that gains momentum over time. The first in a succession of monastic visionaries is an anonymous monk of Auxerre, whose vision was recorded by Ansellus, the *scholasticus* of Fleury, sometime between 1032 and 1052. The visionary is raptured and taken to the infernal regions on Palm Sunday, where he watches as Christ harrows hell, releasing the souls that have been purged of their sins so they could advance to heaven.[10] In compliance with Christ's orders, a demon guides the monk safely through various hellish threats encountered on their return to the monastery. Once they arrive safely, the demon solicits a place in the monk's bed as a reward. As strange as these bedfellows may seem, this arrangement does not seem to be charged with erotic overtones but merely facilitates the strange conversation that ensues. When asked about why people were being released from hell before Judgment Day, the demon alleges that such releases were customary and occur every year during Easter week. According to the demon's reckoning, there were at present quite a number of sinful religious personnel (including sacrilegious bishops, undisciplined abbots, and nuns bearing "baby clerics") who had served time in hell and were eligible for release. But for such captive souls to qualify, they would have needed to acquire some merit while on earth and to have living friends who were willing to make satisfaction on their behalf. There were, however, some sinners for whom there was no hope, and those "sinning against nature" (*contra naturam peccantes*) were among them.[11]

Hugh of Flavigny, the Benedictine abbot and papal legate thwarted by the machinations of William Rufus, was also an early exponent of otherworldly visions with a sexual charge. This is hardly surprising: it was, after all, Hugh who recounted the story of Peter, the pregnant priest who died in horror. But in a vision that Hugh claims to have occurred almost a century earlier, clerical sin is more encrypted. In 1011, a monk from the French monastery of St.-Vaast died after a three-day illness. The monks were just completing the funeral observances when the deceased began to call upon God and the saints in a barely discernible voice.[12] The corpse then proceeds to relate the otherworldly peregrinations of his soul under the escort of Archangel Michael.[13] Yet wherever the soul is led, be it heaven or hell, the soul is in constant anxiety, ever entreating the angel to let him return to his brethren, to which the angel invariably responds that this was the Savior's decision. One of the more memorable stops features a huge conglomeration of wailing souls, submerged up to their waists in boiling waves. Demons in the shape of horses, dogs, and all manner of creeping things torture these souls, whose faces are averted even as their voices are raised in lament, "for these were the faults of a graver nature [*gravioris culpae*]." Clearly this category is an allusion to the rubric *De gravioribus culpis* from the Benedictine rule, a euphemism for mortal sins like same-sex relations, which Benedict himself was too discreet to name, but subsequent commentators were not. The angel is more of Benedict's persuasion, however, listing the graver sins as homicide, fornication, adultery, sacrilege, "and the wretched end of those who delighted in the shameful movement of body and voice [*eorum miserabili interitu, impudendo gaudebant vocis et corporis gestu*]." Such a description suggests that these souls were associated with the kind of musical enterprises already witnessed in homoerotic circles. It could also signify a precocious condemnation of polyphony, a musical form arising in Carolingian times that became especially prominent in the twelfth century. Polyphony featured a harmonic merging of male voices that came to be associated with same-sex relations.[14] That these souls are implicated in the "graver sins" suggests that their offense encompasses something more than mere singing and dancing.[15] Michael does not say if this latter group is clerical or lay, but they are returned to what is referred to as the "malignant" (or, possibly, narrow) hell (*malignus infernus*), which allegedly contains "adulterers, perjurers, false bishops, false priests, [and] false monks."[16]

Most painful to the soul, however, are Michael's veiled prognostications about the spiritual state of the soul's confreres, living and dead. "I tell you that just like a lion roaring, the devil is among your brothers," the angel warns. The evidence adduced is that the devil willed one of the monks to strangle a living boy (*puerum vivum*). The soul knows this to be true because he was still alive when this sorry event occurred. When he asks if the brother will be saved, the angel answers in the negative: the homicidal monk refuses to make a true confession.[17] The subject is not pursued any further, yet the reader cannot help but wonder why the monk would not confess. What could be a worse sin than murdering a boy? A plausible, even likely, answer is that sexually assaulting a boy and then murdering him in order to conceal the assault would be considerably worse. As the evidence of penitentials suggests, this would hardly be the first time that a cleric murdered a child to cover up a sexual lapse. Such an oblique reference to a criminal sex act would be in keeping with the visionary's overall discretion. He often withholds names, while the intensity of the tortures he witnesses is expressed more through the wailing of distressed souls than through the graphic laceration of body parts. This is in contrast to the anonymous vision that Hugh of Flavigny recounts from 1012, the following year, when another sick monk from the same monastery goes on a journey with St. Michael. This later visionary endures a quasi-pornographic vision of the otherworld in which the breasts of whores are devoured by serpents and the like.[18]

The degree to which a vision is sexually explicit and how this is communicated varies widely among visionaries. Sometimes the visionary relates that both men and women guilty of sins of the flesh are lacerated in the offending members, leaving the rest to the reader's imagination.[19] Others are more meticulous. When the Augustinian canon Peter of Cornwall recounts a vision of hell experienced by a certain Aisli in 1170, he is careful to specify which sinners warrant being tortured in the genitalia. Among the usual suspects (adulterers and fornicators), we also find the *molles*—literally, "soft" or "weak." This term, evoking effeminacy, was traditionally used to designate both same-sex relations (particularly the passive role) and masturbation.[20] The *Vision of Tnugdal* (1149), recorded in a Bavarian monastery by an Irish monk named Marcus, features an especially ingenious punishment for incontinent religious personnel. A fire-breathing dragon-like creature, sporting both an iron beak and claws, stands on a lake of ice. The monster first devours souls, only to give birth to them again, perpetuating an eternal life cycle of birthing and cannibalistic eating. The reborn/regurgitated souls, both male and female, are returned to the lake pregnant with viperlike fetuses tearing at their entrails. The parturition is excruciating. Serpentine progeny are born not just through the genitalia of the various souls; they burst forth from all parts of the body—replete with burning heads, iron beaks, fiery tongues, and hooked stingers in their tails. The doomed denizens of the frozen lake are also attacked by their own genitalia, which, in snakelike forms, gnaw at their innards. Naturally, the visionary is anxious to know what acts in life these souls could have perpetrated to warrant such horrors, but the angelic guide refuses to reveal the nature of their sexual transgressions. Even so, the mode of punishment is telling. The fact that not just the female but also the

male souls become pregnant suggests a strange feminization of the male, bringing to mind the fate of the pregnant priest.[21] The infernal vision of the Cistercian monk William (ca. 1153) likewise traffics in innuendo. Hence, monks and
nuns "lay in the unclean and shameful acts of fornication in the manner of brute
animals."[22] It is probable that the traditional elision of bestiality and sodomy is
at play here.[23]

Even as the punitive aspect of the visions becomes more detailed over time,
the visionary's willingness to name certain offenses diminishes. This pattern
culminates in the vision of the monk of Eynsham (1196) in which the sin that
one is led to assume is same-sex sodomy warrants its own special corner of hell:
a place filled with black smoke and fetid smells, where the inhabitants are rent
by fire-breathing snakes and eaten by worms.[24] Demons goad the souls with
fiery prods, preliminary to casting them into the fire. The unfortunate souls
melt like metal only to be reformed, forced to undergo the gruesome procedure
again and again.[25] The souls are further raped repeatedly by misshapen monsters.
The narrator is so horrified that he can barely look at the suffering souls, expressing shock and disbelief that any Christian would ever voluntarily engage in a
vice that would warrant such a punishment.[26] The only individual the visionary's soul recognizes is both male and a cleric—a most learned doctor of law
who had instructed many students.[27] The soul is filled with surprised dismay:
he had seen the lawyer recently and assumed that he was alive and well. But the
wretched shade reveals that he had died recently, suddenly, and tragically—
overthrown by his own vanity: "with the devil deceiving me, I was ashamed to
confess so filthy a sin lest I should be despised among those to whom I appeared
splendid and glorious."[28] The lawyer was thus damned by his refusal to name
his sin. The ghostly lawyer's shame is echoed by the monk's delicacy, who
characterizes the offense as "a sin not fit to be named" (*scelus quod nec nominari
decet*).[29]

A Cistercian miracle collection from the 1170s suggests that a reluctance to
name the sin could cause it to recede altogether. In the cemetery of an unnamed
monastery, the mournful voices of deceased monks could be heard, all of whom
were condemned by virtue of their stubborn retention of private property. The
moral attached to this exemplum is unusual. The anonymous author posits that,
once monks move from unity to a desire for singularity, this appetite cannot be
satisfied by simple excesses in food or clothing. They soon begin to indulge in
"the most unspeakable depravities [*nefandis pravitatibus*] that they scarcely dare
to confess for shame." No sin is specified, but the author is probably referring
to the kind of sexual excesses that the monk of Eynsham refused to name. A
subsequent hand attempted to efface this moralization, suggesting that even this
degree of innuendo was discouraged.[30] Thirty years later, Conrad of Eberbach's

Exordium magnum would incorporate many of the materials from the earlier collection into a more polished and homogeneous whole.[31] At this juncture, any sin too shameful to confess is much too shameful to be associated with the Cistercian order. Instead, the exemplum of the unconfessed sin is assigned to a laywoman.[32]

The murky circumlocutions and euphemisms deployed in the above visions are typical of the noncommittal nature of this subcategory of the visionary genre. Visions of the afterlife are comparatively tame and a relatively safe place from which to launch a critique. After all, whatever the extent of the clerical presence in hell, there is still comfort to be derived from the fact that only individual clerics are being censured, not the entire clergy. The potential for scandal is further blunted by the posthumous nature of the revelation: the clerical perpetrators are most certainly dead, and the majority are anonymous. The fact that the visionary himself is a passive figure in the hands of a supernatural guide further exonerates him from any blame that might otherwise be incurred for the troubling nature of his disclosures. The visionary is also protected by the fact that his journey into the next world is usually recorded (or, perhaps, invented) by someone else—a mere amanuensis who is, allegedly, even less responsible than the passive party upon whom the vision is visited. In an age that places a very high premium on authority, it is also noteworthy that these near-death experiences are, for the most part, undergone by historical nonentities.

The remarkable visions of the Benedictine abbess Hildegard of Bingen (d. 1179) challenge these tacit conventions. In contrast to the ailing anonymous monks and their angelic escorts, Hildegard was a prophet who received her mandate directly from God while still in a lucid and relatively robust state. This is not entirely unique. Orderic Vitalis has already introduced us to another German visionary who used his prophetic powers to predict the decadence of the Norman court. His vision was primarily an *ad hominem* attack on the secular elite in which sodomy served as a symptom of misrule. But Hildegard's condemnation of same-sex relations not only implicates the clergy in the sin of sodomy but, like Peter Damian before her, presents this transgression as a threat to the sacraments. In her first visionary work, *Scivias* (1142–1151), the emphasis on clerical celibacy coexists with the view that the priest's ability to function sexually with women is central to his ministry. Women cannot be priests because they cannot impregnate themselves but require a man to conceive. "Therefore, just as the earth cannot plow itself, a woman must not be a priest and do the work of consecrating the body and blood."[33] In this instance Hildegard's celebrated "gender complementarity," often progressive and gender-bending, is unflinchingly retrograde.[34] Males and females are distinct, and their gender should be instantly discernible: "the man displaying manly strength, and the woman womanly weakness." Hildegard's gender conservatism is expressed both in a censure of cross-dressing and in what is referred to as a contrary manner of fornication (*contrarietate fornicationis*) with men "chang[ing] their virile strength into weakness of contrariety [*in mollitiem contrarietatis*], rejecting proper male and female roles."[35] In the later *Book of Divine Works* (1163–1174), God registers his disdain for humanity's perverse sexual initiatives by flooding the earth—echoing the Carolingian view that the quintessential antediluvian vice was not angelic miscegenation with the daughters of men but same-sex relations between males.[36] Chroniclers cited, and would continue to cite, Hildegard's divinely inspired indictments of sodomy with grim satisfaction.[37]

Hildegard's investment in a priesthood that is celibate yet ideologically coupled with women is on a continuum with her conviction that the world had entered into a "womanish age," wherein men, in general, had become soft and the clergy weak and effeminate.[38] In fact, Hildegard's entire prophetic mandate is derived from the clergy's spiritual and moral failure—a dire situation that provoked God to entrust Hildegard, a member of the weaker sex, with his message.[39] In a famous letter excoriating the laxness of the clergy, Hildegard chides her clerical audience in the following terms: "Blessed and sealed in the celestial persons, you ought be the little habitation redolent of myrrh and incense, in which God also dwells. But you are not so. Rather, you are quick in your pursuit of puerile lust [*ad lasciuiam puerilis etatis*]. . . . You do whatever your flesh demands." Given the dim view of boyish sexual "games," this may well be an allusion to same-sex practices.[40]

The Birth of a Euphemism

Hildegard's frankness was exceptional. The more oblique approach, which accommodates the near-death experiences of her male colleagues, was much more typical. And this type of discretion is above all signaled with the emergence of the euphemism "the sin not fit to be named."[41] Although twelfth-century in provenance, this designation was heir to a rich ideological legacy. There was, for example, the concept of the "unspeakable"—one of several definitions attached to the term *nefandus*. Bede (d. 735) referred to the same-sex relations as something "unspeakable" (*nefandus*)—the same adjective used in the Cistercian miracle collection for unnamed depravities.[42] *Nefandus* is not exclusive to sodomy, however, but was widely applied to anything deemed depraved, sacrilegious, or unlawful. The Council of Chalcedon (451) applied *nefandus* to simony; Alcuin associated it with the worldly filth trampled down by the virginal mind; for

Abbo of Fleury (d. 1004), it pertained to the reviled opinions of heretics or the Saracen race.[43]

Even so, the designation of "Sodom" had a special purchase on the unspeakable because the word itself was believed to be etymologically enveloped in a shroud of silence. Jerome applied descriptors like "beast," "silent," and "blind" to the name "Sodom."[44] Subsequent authors would provide variations on this theme. Some, like Hrabanus Maurus, perceived "blindness," "beast," and "silence" as a unit: the sinner is a silent beast, blindly pursuing his old vices.[45] The Benedictine monk Haymo of Auxerre (d. 853) interpreted the term Sodom as "mute" with apocalyptic overtones: those who do not dare confess Christ in the time of Antichrist.[46] In contrast, Guibert of Nogent compared the mute beast of Sodom with those who hypocritically conceal carnal intentions.[47]

Yet while the association of Sodom and "silent" may be ancient, silent was precisely what the biblical Sodomites were not. According to scripture, the sin of the Sodomites raised a clamor to heaven (Gen. 18:20). The prophet Isaiah construed this clamor as an unacceptable brazenness, prompting him to rebuke sinners who "proclaimed abroad their sin as Sodom" (Isa. 3:9).[48] The twelfth-century biblical *glossa ordinaria* believed Isaiah meant that such sins should be hidden lest they corrupt others like a stench. The gloss also included the Septuagint's reading, which stressed that a righteous sense of shame should forestall the revelation of such a sin.[49] Because the papal reformers eschewed the subject of same-sex relations altogether, they (arguably) took Isaiah's critique very much to heart: Peter Damian's *Book of Gomorrah* was suppressed, even as Ivo of Chartres's initiative to forestall sodomitical nepotism was ignored. We have also seen that, apart from Archbishop Anselm's anomalous ordinances, the subject of sodomy was not raised at any ecclesiastical council between Reims in 1049 and Lateran III in 1179.

This triumph of suppression over expression will be further abetted by the conflicted currents of twelfth-century theology regarding questions of conscience that were especially rife in Parisian intellectual circles. Our starting point is Peter Abelard (d. 1142), who defined sin as an interior contempt for God, meaning that it could only be fully perceived by God. Thus Abelard maintained that a sinner who confessed to God alone could be forgiven for his sins, provided that confession was accompanied by true contrition.[50] Yet Abelard, who had learned the hard way that society necessarily punished outer sins over those that remained concealed, recognized that, for the public good, manifest sin must be punished more harshly.[51] Hence, the malefactor who created a scandal must be publicly chastised in proportion to the degree of scandal, even if he were innocent in the higher tribunal of intentionality.[52] The disjunction between hidden and manifest sin is foregrounded in Abelard's *Sic et non* when he poses the question of whether it is better to sin secretly or in the open, listing a series of authorities for and against either position. In favor of the secret sin, Abelard, like the Carolingians before him, found a champion in Isidore of Seville.[53]

These tensions will be taken up by yet another Parisian master named Peter—Peter the Chanter (d. 1195).[54] In the Chanter's *Summa on the Sacraments and Counseling of the Soul*, "scandal" is defined as when someone brings about the ruin of another through the indignation he or she has generated by either word or deed.[55] Because scandal is a sin so often at odds with the intentions of the offender, however, it is difficult to assess. To demonstrate the complexity of the issue, the Chanter provides a series of casuistic exempla involving the clergy and the impact of their behavior on the laity. Supposing, for example, that someone saw the Chanter himself performing an inessential act, such as walking around at leisure. Someone might see him and say, "Look at the cleric playing," and be scandalized. Did the Chanter sin mortally? The answer is yes because, as the Chanter attests: "If I pursue an unnecessary work and accidentally kill a man, I am guilty of homicide. By the same token, if I pursue an unnecessary task and cause someone to be scandalized, accidentally killing his soul, I am guilty of scandal."[56] Thus in order to avoid scandalizing, "We ought to abstain from all things licit which are able to be omitted—provided we preserve the truth of life, doctrine, and justice." This triad of truths was destined to become the critical touchstone for assessing when scandal cannot be avoided and, hence, was permissible.[57]

The Chanter was the first religious authority to treat scandal as a sin in its own right. This attention to scandal undoubtedly sharpened the distinction between the hidden and the manifest and further emphasized the so-called Carolingian dichotomy, which determined that someone who offended publicly was bound to make public reparations. Again, the Chanter adduces these points through casuistry focused on clerical behavior. Supposing that a priest defied a king for a noble cause, and everyone was aware of it, but then, out of fear, the priest perjured himself, abjuring his good deed. Or what about a repentant bishop who was widely known for simony? How might he repent? In neither instance would God be satisfied unless the scandalized people were placated first. This could only be achieved by resignation from office and public penance.[58] The other side of the coin, however, is the Chanter's view that what the laity did not know would not hurt them. Hence he maintains that a sinning cleric could preach, as long as his sin was concealed.[59]

Despite his apprehension of scandal, however, the Chanter did not seem to share Augustine's sanguine view that the church could accommodate a plethora of sinners—especially when it came to clerics committing sodomy. From the Chanter's perspective, there were only two sins in which the clamor ascends to

God from the earth: murder, an allusion to how the voice of the murdered Abel was heard in heaven (Gen. 4:10), and sodomy.[60] As the fate of the doomed city of Sodom indicates, so grievous is this vice that God withheld his characteristic patience and goodness, destroying the perpetrators with heavenly fire, presaging the hellfire to which they were destined and removing the possibility of penance.[61] The perpetrators of this sin were like the names of Sodom and Gomorrah—that is, mute from the praise of God and bitter over the enormity of their sin. Out of detestation of the sin, God turned the area into the Dead Sea—a place of waste where no fish swims, nor boat sails, and where the very fruits of trees vanish into dust at the slightest touch.[62] Not surprisingly, the Chanter found the church's tacit policy to let sleeping sodomites lie deeply offensive, marveling that sinners who are punished so grievously by God "remain untouched by the church, and that the individual is punished lightly whom God punishes so harshly."[63]

Clerics Confessing Clerics

> Anyone who has the appearance of holiness, and who by word
> or deed destroys others, would be better off hiding his
> misdeeds under an outer show of holiness until his death. This
> is preferable than for someone engaged in holy offices to
> manifest a fault that could be imitated by others. Because it is
> better that he is the only one to fall and suffer punishment.
> —*Glossa ordinaria*, twelfth century[64]

The Chanter's complaint was heard in high places. In 1179, the Third Lateran Council would legislate that any cleric guilty of "unnatural vice" be either expelled from the clergy or confined to a monastery to do penance, and these strictures would be reiterated at Lateran IV (1215).[65] There is little doubt that Peter the Chanter was one of the prime movers behind this anti-sodomitical initiative.[66] Not only does his work make frequent reference to Lateran III, but the Chanter was well known to the presiding pope, Alexander III, who frequently relied upon his legal expertise.[67] In capturing papal attention over the issue of clerical sodomy, Peter the Chanter had succeeded where Peter Damian had failed. Perhaps now that clerical marriage had been outlawed, the church would at last be able to clean house and tackle "the capacious clerical closet." The timing seemed right.

And yet, the rising distinction of the priesthood and a growing sensitivity to scandal conspired to undermine any meaningful initiative. The Chanter was clearly sensitive to this dynamic: it was no accident that his exempla demonstrating the hazards of scandal invariably concerned the impact of the ill-considered behavior of the clergy on the laity. Indeed, the Chanter had helped to advance the nexus of clerical prestige and scandal. Both he and his students were the intellectual force behind the legislation mandating annual auricular confession to a priest at Lateran IV, thus prevailing over Abelard's contritionist view. This new emphasis on the confessor as a direct conduit to God raised the prestige of the priesthood exponentially, simultaneously stoking the potential for sacerdotal scandal.[68]

There is no doubt that the Chanter's followers continued to be preoccupied with the issue of clerical sodomy. Indeed, his student Robert of Courson (d. 1219) considered the vice so pernicious and ubiquitous that he was in favor of Lateran IV abolishing clerical celibacy altogether.[69] But the Chanter's students did not write as canon lawyers determining discipline in the external forum, but as pastoral theologians—experts in the internal forum, the realm of conscience. Their groundbreaking confessors' manuals reflect this orientation. Like penitentials before them, these manuals were written to assist priests in hearing confession. Yet, in line with the mandate of Lateran IV, the new penitential ethos required that the confessor adopt a more comprehensive approach, understanding who the penitent was and the circumstances surrounding his sin, before assigning an appropriate penance. This process required a heightened degree of flexibility, discretion, and empathy.[70]

Confessors' manuals also ushered in the movement away from the kind of austerities inflicted on the sinners of yesteryear, meaning that the most venerable canons condemning the sexual abuse of minors were out of date both in terms of degree of harshness and of degrees of publicity. It is noteworthy that the only members of the Chanter's circle to cite uncompromising indictments of same-sex activity were Robert of Flamborough (d. after 1213) and Thomas of Chobham (d. 1233 × 1236), both Englishmen. Their nationality may not be a coincidence since the evidence from later ecclesiastical courts suggests that sodomy charges were exceptionally rare in England, perhaps betokening a heightened degree of intolerance.[71] Both cited the Pseudo-Basil/Fructuosus canon regarding the *insectator puerum*—the canon that called for an unusually humiliating public penance that would maximize the offender's punishment.[72] In addition, Robert of Flamborough cites Elvira's sanction against the corrupter of boys along with a penitential canon degrading and assigning penance to clerics who fornicated "against nature.[73]

But while Peter Damian had argued against penitentials on the basis of their inconsistency and excessive leniency, the majority of theologians in the Chanter's circle challenged the penances of these ancient works as too strict.

Indeed, several scholars puzzled over the reasons behind the severity of earlier times. Alan of Lille (d. 1202) posited that the fervent faith of the early church explains this rigor, although he muses that human nature must have been stronger back then. For his own time, however, Alan argues that penance ought to be tempered, just as a doctor adjusts his medicines lest they be excessively harsh.[74] Peter of Poitiers of St.-Victor (d. ca. 1215) echoes these sentiments, indicting contemporaries who included the antiquated penitential canons in their manuals. It has been suggested that the penitential of Robert of Flamborough was Peter's particular target.[75] If so, Peter was preaching to the chorus: even Robert of Flamborough, one of the few to cite the Pseudo-Basil/Fructuosus passage, argued that these ancient canons were too stringent and needed to be mitigated with mercy.[76]

This ultimately more sin-friendly perspective is exemplified in an anecdote related by Thomas of Chobham concerning a monk who had committed a sin that he would rather die than confess to his abbot. The abbot would not grant the monk leave to confess to anyone else, however. Hence, when the monk died, the abbot refused him burial in the cemetery. This story is followed by an indictment of the Cistercian order for its rule requiring all incoming monks to make a life confession of every sin ever committed to the abbot. Although the purpose was to ensure that the abbot knew what kind of life each monk had lived and to what sins they were prone to better protect them from relapses, Thomas complains that many good men were sent away from the order because they did not want the abbot to know all their secrets.[77]

The new empathy for the sinner is also reflected in the unflappable attitude of the ideal confessor—a quality sometimes demonstrated through memorable examples. Robert of Flamborough provides a mock dialogue between a confessor and his penitent, a subdeacon, in which the confessor's a dogged thoroughness coexists with a blasé lack of judgment.

> *Priest.* Have you sinned with a man?
> *Penitent.* With many.
> *Priest.* Did you introduce any innocent parties to this?
> *Penitent.* Three scholars and one subdeacon.
> *Priest.* Tell me how many you abused and how often and your rank
>   and their rank.
> *Penitent.* I am a subdeacon and [I did it with] three subdeacons for half
>   a year; and a married man once.[78]

This represents but a fraction of the promiscuous subdeacon's conquests.

While writing for the internal forum, however, the Chanter's students had nevertheless internalized his emphasis on scandal. Thomas of Chobham argues that the Lord is often more offended by the publication of the sin than through the actual sin itself, citing the prophet's opprobrium of those who "proclaimed abroad their sin as Sodom, and they have not hid it" (Isa. 3:9). In contrast, one who sins privately only kills his or her own soul, while through scandal the souls of others are harmed and, perhaps, the entire church.[79] This would suggest that scandal-inducing sins, like sodomy, would be better left to the confessional.

But despite sacramental confession's prophylactic role in scandal-aversion, scandal only required an audience of one, and the confessional relationship met that requirement. The Chanter was the first to make this association. We have already made note of his concern that an unwary cleric could inadvertently scandalize the secular world by aimless perambulation. In a confessional context, however, the Chanter—sensitive to the risks involved for a professional celibate hearing the sins of a sexually active laity—perceived the potential for scandal as running in the opposite direction. For instance, at a time when there were no confessional boxes to conceal the penitent from the confessor, the confessor might be scandalized by a female penitent's beauty.[80] Yet there was even greater danger in what the priest might hear. To that end, the Chanter momentarily assumes the perspective of the lay penitent when he asks: "if any [penitent] has a simple priest who would be easily corrupted if he were to make new discoveries in sin, particularly in the 1,000 different ways of having sex, should he confess the sins as well as their circumstances to him?" The answer is probably not.[81]

Subsequent confessors' manuals would again reverse the vector of corruption by considering the question of how the confessor could scandalize the penitent by asking questions about sexual sins, perhaps even inadvertently inducting him into the sin. The sin of sodomy was considered especially volatile. The extremely popular guide *Peniteas cito peccator* (Sinner you should repent quickly), probably written by William de Montibus (d. 1213), who also studied at Paris during the Chanter's tenure, captures the clerical conundrum in the succinct verse:

The wounds of the flesh should be examined carefully.
Any sin against nature should never be expressed.
Lest a simple person were to agree to an irregularity
About which he knew nothing [and] is thus taught to do.[82]

Even a penitent who already had experience with same-sex relations was not impermeable to corruption. Robert of Flamborough rounds off his mock dialogue between a confessor and a penitent with the following advice: "Afterward he can be asked if he ever sinned against nature to a greater degree by having someone in an extraordinary manner. If he asks 'extraordinary in what way?' I

do not answer him; he might consider doing it. I should never mention something to someone who is able to use it as another opportunity for sin." Another
version of the manual volunteers that this kind of inadvertent coaching "happens frequently."[83]

Soon specialized manuals designed for hearing clerical confessions emerge
that internalize these different trajectories for corruption. Robert Grosseteste (d.
1253), bishop of Lincoln, who was associated with a number of the Chanter's
students, notes unequivocally in his extremely popular manual *Templum Dei*
that the clergy is particularly afflicted with the problem of sodomy.[84] Grosseteste
was also the probable author of *Perambulavit Judas* (Judas walked around), a
treatise instructing monks on how to prepare for confession. It features an imagi-
nary monk who agonizes over confessing "how I dared to offend in myself and
in others with unchaste touch." He seems especially attuned to the danger of
scandalizing his confessor: "Nor did I show reverence in the presence of God by
doing that which I blush to confess, because the weak hearing such things are
capable of being scandalized."[85]

The heightened awareness of scandal also increasingly limits the kinds of
penance that could be assigned. For instance, the *Speculum penitentis* (Mirror of
the penitent) of William de Montibus recognizes "the burning passion of sodomy"
(*incendium sodome*) as one of the sins particularly afflicting monks and the challenges that this vice presents for the confessor.[86] "When we have to assign penance
for the grave [*gravibus*] and hidden sins of religious . . . we are put in a tight spot,
aware of just how difficult it is to know what should be enjoined on them or
how."[87] Because members of religious communities are already burdened by the
weight of the rule, excessive penance is eschewed. And yet, as William observes, it
is precisely because of considerations such as these that many confessors give
exceedingly light penances for some of the most grievous sins, resulting in unfortunate relapses. Although William aspires to providing correctives to this gloomy
prognosis, his prescribed penance for serious sexual offenses, like adultery or sodomy, consists largely of genuflections and prayers. He counsels against assigning a
fast that exceeds communal norms because this would run the risk of exposing the
gravity of the penitent's sins. Any fasting is, therefore, limited and largely gestural.
Hence, the culprit is told that on Fridays, he should abstain from whatever food
accompanies the bread (*companagium*), but should still eat the bread "so that he
eat something in order to avoid scandal."[88]

The anti-sodomy legislation of Lateran III and Lateran IV ensured that the
concern with sodomy spread beyond the schools of northern Europe. But as
the concern spread, it brought with it the many contradictions and confusions
associated with sodomy and its stigmatization. This is exemplified in the manual
of Paul of Hungary—a Dominican canonist writing in the early thirteenth

century who was clearly influenced by the Chanter. In this work, alarm over sodomy predominates: it receives more space than all the other sins combined.[89] Sodomy is presented as a ubiquitous and unmitigated evil "from which evil things arise, and arise daily."[90] In sheer heinousness, it outstrips fornication, adultery, and even incest with one's mother. Like Hildegard before him, Paul construes sodomy as a particular affront to God in its violations of nature's laws.[91] Not only was sodomy the reason that God flooded the earth, but it continues to be the source of famine and pestilence.[92]

While clearly imbibing the sense of urgency that the Chanter brought to the discussion, Paul invests the word itself with such potent power to scandalize that his confessional guidelines devolve into hysterical and self-contradictory nonsense. Sodomy is so horrendous that the word should not be said out loud, lest both the mouth of the speaker and the ears of the listener be polluted. By the same token, a simple discussion of the vice causes any good angel to flee the area, even if the speakers were not practitioners of this vice. Yet, despite these implacable taboos, nobody can be absolved of this sin unless they name it explicitly.[93] Any sodomite who dies impenitent is buried in hell.[94]

Paul of Hungary's treatment of sodomy epitomizes how the nexus of sodomy, scandal, and confession competed against one another, vividly demonstrating how and why the euphemism "the sin not fit to be named" had become permanently imprinted on the vice by the thirteenth century. And, as we shall see, an unnamable sin that is difficult to confess is also well-nigh impossible to prosecute. This is doubtless not what Peter the Chanter intended.

The Demon in the Cloister Versus Knowing as God

> Special agents testified before us that they had identified a series of practices that regularly appeared, in various configurations, in the diocesan files they had analyzed. It's like a playbook for concealing the truth. . . . [The sixth one is] if a predator's conduct becomes known to the community, don't remove him from the priesthood to ensure that no more children will be victimized. Instead, transfer him to a new location where no one will know he is a child abuser.
> —Pennsylvania grand jury report, August 2018[95]

One of the most distinctive features of the new penitential ethos that has yet to be mentioned is the heightened degree of secrecy enjoined on the confessor. In Carolingian times, if a confessor recognized that a penitent was a threat to others on the basis of his confession, it was possible for him to intervene. Hildemar, for example, anticipates a situation in which an abbot is about to ordain one of the monks who is guilty of one of the "graver sins." In such a case, the confessor is permitted tacitly to warn the abbot.[96] The eleventh century, however, will witness the growing emphasis of what will eventually become known as the "seal" of confession. Significantly, there is little discussion of such a thing before then, and it is around this time that penalties for revealing a confession first begin to be formulated.[97] The treatise *On Concealing Confession* by Lanfranc (d. 1089) is especially precedential in this regard. It not only binds the confessor to total secrecy concerning the penitent's sins, but also forbids any revelation that might raise suspicion about the nature of the penitent's sins. Even if the penitent refuses to reform, the confessor is still bound.[98]

The casuistry surrounding the confession of clerics reflects this growing insistence on the inviolate nature of the confessional forum. Peter the Chanter considers the situation of a cleric of good reputation, about to be elected to a position of authority, but whom the priest has learned in the course of confession is deeply depraved or, worse still, even a heretic. Supposing the electors wish to consult the confessor? Should he refuse to give counsel, all the time knowing that the person in question would do a great deal of harm to the souls of his subordinates? Supposing the confessor were to hint that the candidate was not suitable for the position: wouldn't this compromise the secrecy of the confession and damage the penitent's reputation?[99] Or what about a bishop who learns through confession that his chamberlain is a sensualist and a fornicator? On the one hand, it would be difficult to remove him without arousing sinister speculation. On the other hand, by retaining such a scoundrel in office, the bishop not only risks personal infamy but also jeopardizes many souls.[100]

Despite the palpable risks, the Chanter determines that in each of these instances, the confessor is required to hold his peace. He cannot avail himself of the kind of cryptic comments that Christ routinely made, such as "one of you will betray me." Nor can he drop hints through offhand generalizations like "our priests are worse than our deacons." A grimace or expression that in some way betrays the confessor's mind-set is also explicitly ruled out. Basically, no disclosures are licit. Even so, the Chanter remains ambivalent. Amid these heightened sanctions, some degree of permeability still lingers on in his mind. Hence he concludes that the priest must remain silent "except when a faithful soul is endangered." In such an instance, "hinting or revealing is not so much an uncovering of a confession as [attending to] the care of souls."[101]

The Chanter was not alone in his determination. The canonist Huggucio (ca. 1188), one of the most famous commentators on Gratian's *Decretum*, believed that the priest was permitted to denounce an unrepentant criminal in court.[102] Thomas of Chobham maintained that if a penitent revealed that he was about to commit a violent crime, the confessor was allowed to warn one of the penitent's relatives or close friends, who might then deter him.[103] Lateran IV would do away with all equivocation on this score, however, threatening anyone who betrayed the sinner "by word or sign or in any other way" with deposition from office and perpetual penance in a strict monastery.[104] Hence, in later manuals, if a confessor becomes aware that his clerical penitent presents an imminent danger, the most he can do is to enjoin his superior to watch his flock.[105]

When it came to the confession of clerics, the seal of confession would become the stuff of nightmares, constituting a clear roadblock to meaningful action in the face of corruption. Robert of Courson presents a wrenching portrait of the confessor's powerlessness when confronted by a truly evil colleague: "For it happens frequently that someone approaches the penitential forum whose root is corrupt, the infected fruit of a putrid branch, in whom there is a demon that cannot be expelled by either prayer or fasting." This individual has exploited his position to the fullest, robbing the poor and depleting church resources. If such a penitent were to approach the confessor in apparent sincerity, the confessor would be obliged to enjoin fasts, prayer, and alms, knowing full well that this would not expel the demon, whose venom has suffused the very roots of the penitent's being. Robert has nothing but contempt for the prelate who elevated this unworthy in the first place. By choosing to promote this "demon," he has thereby killed the souls of all the ailing people placed in his trust. Yet, as ubiquitous and desperate as the situation clearly is, Robert acknowledges that he has no light to shed on this problem, except that if the penitent is, indeed, repentant, the only fitting penance would be for him to resign his position and return all the money he has stolen.

Robert goes on to consider the frequent situations in which that same demon is present in the cloister—impervious to prayer and fasting. In fact, it often happens that a given monastery is entirely supported by rapine, simony, and similar crimes. Against this background of corruption, Robert imagines the scenario in which an individual monk is conscience-stricken about the way in which the monastery is sustained. What advice does the confessor give? Does he tell the monk to stay at the monastery? To leave at once? Or to seek the advice of his abbot? Supposing the confessor tells him to stay. He is essentially condemning the monk to a sinful life of ill-gotten goods. In advising the penitent to leave, however, the confessor would have to assume responsibility for transferring the monk to a more appropriate cloister or hermitage. But what if no cloister can be found, except yet another one already infected with rapine? Or perhaps there are no other religious options in the area. Another possible solution would be to send the monk to the abbot for counsel. But the abbot, in all probability permanently corrupted by graft and venality, would doubtless threaten the monk with excommunication—a penalty that, as he reminds the monk, only he would be able to lift. Such risks might argue that the monk should stay put. And yet, Robert recognizes that to make someone act against his conscience results in the most grievous sins.[106]

The tortured speculation about the seal and its capacity to protect clerical vice reaches its apex in the sophisticated casuistry of Henry of Ghent (d. 1293), a secular master at the University of Paris and one of the greatest scholars of his generation.[107] Henry dedicated a series of quodlibetal questions to the problem of clerical vice, as revealed in the course of confession, and related problems. One quodlibet is especially poignant. An abbot knows through confession that one of his monks, who has the care of souls, is a corrupter of his parishioners. Is he bound to recall him? The case is by no means clear. On the one hand, Henry cites Lateran IV's prohibition against revealing confessions; on the other hand, he argues that if the abbot remains silent, he is essentially consenting to evil deeds that might otherwise have been prohibited. Ultimately, the seal wins out. For even if the abbot in question were ordered to speak the truth to his superior about something he learned in the course of confession, he can and should remain silent. This silence is justified by an intricate understanding of different ways of knowing in a confessional context. The confessor cannot speak to what he has learned about the clerical penitent's sins in the course of confession because he knows these things not as a man but as God. By the same token, he cannot move the evil pastor on the basis of what he knows as God; any action would have to be based upon what the confessor knows in his everyday persona as abbot—a public minister of God, but still only a man. Henry does, however, introduce a final persona that provides a bridge between the priest's roles as God and man: that of *secretarius*, or confidential clerk, of God. It is in the capacity of *secretarius* that the confessor can form the private intention of moving the monk, and then leave it to his persona as abbot, the public minister, to do the deed. But circumstances have to be just right.

> In the public eye, the [abbot] must have a reason and opportunity for moving him without scandal or suspicion. . . . Even if there was the slightest possibility that someone else, aware of the deed, would be scandalized, he can't be moved—even though it would be for the best. . . . In this case the business should be committed to God, with the firm conviction that [God] would not permit evil acts to be done by the man, unless it was somehow just for those evil things to occur and

God, who is all powerful, knew how to ordain those [evil] things to good.[108]

Henry's resolution splits the confessor into four different persona: the man, who knows nothing of the evil and is powerless to act; the confessor, who knows as God does, but cannot act on this knowledge; the *secretarius* of God, who can form a private resolution to move the monk, should the right circumstances arise; and finally the abbot, who, in consultation with the *secretarius*, can move the monk when the opportunity presents itself.

Of course, Henry does not bother to state the obvious: if the confessor was a simple priest, as opposed to an abbot, he is only possessed of two personae: the man, who knows nothing, and the confessor, who may see like God, but can do nothing.

The Use and Abuse of Fraternal Correction

There are, presumably, less fraught ways, of correcting the errors of your fellow clerics than by confession. The most obvious is through the medium of fraternal correction. As we have seen, this concept was based on the scriptural injunction to admonish one another privately, only revealing the offense to others if the perpetrator refuses to amend (Matt. 18:15–17). But when and how it should be applied would become the source of heated discussion. Peter the Chanter presents the possibility of an errant monk, guilty of only a trifling offense, being scandalized when confronted with his error. If his punishment is too severe, moreover, this would undermine the truth of justice. In such instances, it would be preferable to remain quiet, though the Chanter does acknowledge the possibility that the sinning monk who does not receive a timely reprimand might devolve from bad to worse.[109] The Chanter's student Peter of Poitiers despaired of the effectiveness of even timely interventions. He perceived the secular canons of Paris, who lived a common life under the Augustinian Rule, as irreparably riddled with vice. On the rare occasion that any attempt was made to correct a brother in chapter, the others, equally polluted by the same crime, would loudly protest whatever judgment the superior saw fit to visit on the culprit because, as Peter says with contempt, there was "great concord among the weak [*molles*]."[110] The use of the word *molles* is, of course, evocative of homosexuality.

The fine line between the need for correction and scandalizing the offender was explored by various scholastic theologians, who never tired of introducing ever-greater complexities. Although Thomas Aquinas (d. 1272) believes that fraternal correction is a duty, provided it is undertaken in the spirit of charity, he nevertheless warns against the dangers of public denunciation—especially of a cleric.[111] An anonymous quodlibet of 1278 queries "whether someone is bound to correct his brother or neighbor when he knows or sees him misbehaving. And this question has two or three components: is an inferior seeing a superior misbehaving bound to correct him, or bound to correct everyone, or is no one bound to correct anybody?"[112] The correct answer is that we are all bound to correct others out of charity. But how this principle might pertain to a superior in need of correction is qualified: if the superior is moving toward some kind of error or infidelity, and there is no one of authority on hand to whom he can be denounced, then the subordinate, in the most humble manner possible, must step up.[113]

In Henry of Ghent's hands, the complexities of fraternal correction reach a high-water mark with potentially fearful consequences. Henry considers the hypothetical case of a monk who secretly knows that one of his brethren has committed a mortal sin. Considering the gravity of the sin, would it be permissible for the person who apprehended the offense to bypass a private warning and go straight to the offender's superior? Henry begins by deploying two analogies—one arguing for and one against bypassing private admonition. On the one hand, immediate denunciation is likened to the error of a medical doctor who withholds the best medicine, which is, in this case, a private warning. On the other hand, a bailiff is permitted to arraign a prisoner and bring him to the king for correction without a private admonition. Hence, if an individual were to learn that that someone else is harboring a secret and grievous wound, it would be appropriate to bypass discussion and summon a doctor—an analogy from the Rule of St. Augustine.[114]

Henry upholds the first position. A private warning is central to fraternal correction, aiming at the sinner's reformation before the sin results in "scandalizing infamy [*scandalizantem infamiam*]." The hope is that the sinner, once privately confronted with his sin, will turn away from it—either from confusion or from fear of punishment. If the warning is administered suddenly, the sinner should, ideally, experience a "rapture of the heart," causing him to desist from his sin before it is revealed to others. The biblical gloss likewise warns against the danger of omitting the private admonition mandated by scripture (Matt. 18:15), "lest a person corrected publicly loses a sense of shame, and remains in the sin."[115]

But scripture also dictates that if the sinner does not respond to private admonition, the person aware of the sin should call one or two witnesses so the offender can be corrected in their presence. (The Augustinian Rule is in basic conformity with this, but advises that the monk be brought before the abbot for correction first.) If this fails, only then should the offending monk be brought before the community.[116] Henry is skeptical, however. Since the sin is not public, he doubts whether the offender's sin should be revealed to anyone not already aware of it. Even a limited revelation to two or three others compromises the offender's reputation. At the same time, Henry recognizes that such concealment could compromise the health of the church. In fact, Augustine's rule presents the exposure of sin as an act of mercy to the sinner, while maintaining silence was allowing his wound to fester.[117]

Bent on discretion, however, Henry ultimately embraces the position articulated in Augustine's sermon on fraternal correction: that someone who publicly denounces a crime is behaving like a betrayer rather than a corrector.[118] Even if the offender refuses to make amends privately, the would-be corrector should take his cue from Joseph's discretion over Mary's pregnancy and not proceed further. Joseph did not accuse Mary, waiting until others learned independently about her offense.[119] Likewise, a concerted effort at correction can only be attempted once others are apprised of the situation independently. But the move to a group intervention is not automatic: if the other would-be correctors only know of the individual's sin by rumor, they should not be accorded any further details. If the superior is one the cognoscenti, he should summon the sinful monk for correction. It is only if the culprit denies the offense that others may be summoned for a conviction. Then, if the sinner refuses discipline, he must be cast out.[120]

Henry likewise resists the view that, once the case has gone beyond admonition, the alleged culprit's reputation ought to be disregarded entirely and the people who might benefit from knowledge of his offense be apprised. Again, he upholds the clemency and discretion apparent in Joseph's treatment of Mary.[121] Indeed, Henry goes so far as to argue that the revelation of the convicted sinner's offenses to the public only refers to the two or three witnesses necessary for his conviction, not the congregation at large.[122]

In short, from Henry's perspective, if the sin is only known to one person, whether a superior or a subordinate, it is impossible to move beyond a private admonition. Some might argue that the alleged sinner's superior should be informed, as his admonition would be the most effective. Henry, however, believes that this kind of humiliation would only make a person worse. After the secret warning, the matter should be left with God. There are those who maintain that if a hidden sin is harmful to others, whether a particular individual or society at large, the perpetrator should be denounced to his superior. Henry acknowledges that such an action might be justified, but notes that the denunciation was no longer in the realm of fraternal correction and the virtue of charity and its effects. Rather it pertains to public rather than individual justice.[123]

This line of inaction does not mean that Henry was entirely insensible to potential dangers: "Certain hidden sins . . . incline to the detriment of the neighbor and the public good, [so] some say that if the delinquent is not corrected by [the prelate] privately, the sin ought to be revealed by public denunciation." Once again, he refutes this view. "For although [this solution is] technically licit, it is not the good of the delinquent which is principally sought, but the good of the public; it does not comply with the precept of fraternal correction in which the good of the delinquent is principally sought."[124] To Henry's mind, deference to the sinful cleric trumps public safety.

*   *   *

The prophetess Hildegard of Bingen broke with decades of visionary innuendo, forcefully presenting clerical sodomy as a threat to the sacraments. Denouncing the present-day clergy as effeminate, she besought them to put aside their "pursuit of puerile lust." Soon after, Peter the Chanter would decry sodomy, attempting to disrupt the tacit toleration of religious authorities. As his influence at Lateran III would suggest, he looked to the external forum, the judicial arm of the church, to eradicate sodomy. And yet any such disciplinary initiative the Chanter may have hoped for was undermined by his other points of emphases: the augmented role of the priesthood, scandal, and the seal of confession—issues that ultimately canceled one another out. The fear of scandal would ensure that many of the clergy's most grievous sexual sins be consigned to sacramental confession. This was especially true in the wake of the papal reform, when clerical celibacy had become the most potent symbol of clerical superiority. In Robert of Flamborough's articulation of sacerdotal prowess, the priest was a walking symbol of his chaste vocation: the white alb represented purity of the soul; his belt, chastity. The bishop wore three tunics: the white linen tunic signified purity; the silk tunic—the work of worms, which were believed to be generated spontaneously without coitus—represented chastity and humility; the third was the color of hyacinth, indicating airy serenity.[125] A priest who fell from this holy standard, especially through the ubiquitous but increasingly heinous sin of sodomy, would be encouraged to conceal this lapse. Theologians progressively presented such subterfuge as the most righteous line of action. But this view also coincides with a shrewd pragmatism, exemplified by the quip by Thomas of Chobham in his summary regarding sexual sin and scandal: "if you can't be chaste, be careful."[126]

PART II

Prologue

When sodomy emerged from the clerical closet, it was a strange coming out party. While the sin itself was roundly excoriated, clerical sinners appeared to be extremely thin on the ground, and instances of prosecution would remain rare. This prologue explores the distance between the growing awareness of clerical sodomy by society at large and ecclesiastical authorities' reluctance to take any substantive measures.

The Clerical Closet Opens

There is no doubt that by the thirteenth century, theologians and canon lawyers alike were at last recognizing what Peter Damian had maintained centuries before: that sodomy was rife among the clergy. Following the lead of Peter the Chanter, confessors' manuals were quick to identify the problem, and other authorities demonstrated a parallel sensitivity. The Dominican canon lawyer Paul of Hungary identified sodomy with the devotional disaffection of clerics and monks who refused to mortify their flesh. Even so, Paul gave pride of place to courtiers who, deprived of women, turned to sodomy.[1] When Hostiensis (d. 1271) came to write his *Summa* of canon law, however, there was no prevarication. The subject was introduced under the rubric: "Clerics commonly sin by incontinence which is against nature."[2]

In the hands of theologians, sodomy became more openly castigated than ever before, its ancient status as "unnatural act" being corroborated and supplemented by current intellectual trends. Twelfth-century Neoplatonism had spawned a ubiquitous adulation of nature in the schools. The thirteenth-century scholastic turn to Aristotle did not diminish this reverence, but grounded it in a more "scientific" ethos. Dominican theologians were at the forefront of this movement. Thomas Aquinas would argue that the unnatural vice was the worst kind of lust, "flout[ing] nature by transgressing its basic principles of venereal use."[3] Because the order of nature is divine, this sin was even worse than sexual acts that harm others, like adultery and rape, since it constitutes a direct affront to God.[4] Aquinas's views were subsequently popularized in the confessional world by the influential manual of the Dominican theologian John of Freiburg (d. 1314).[5]

Other more accessible Dominican writers also helped to heighten this discourse of stigmatization. The *Speculum morale*, attributed to Vincent of Beauvais (d. 1264), will echo the view that sodomy is an attack on the natural order and a direct attack on God, the "ordainer of nature."[6] Thomas of Cantimpré (d. 1272) prefaced his discussion of sodomy with Aristotle's remarks on man's shameful singularity: no other species of animal ejects its semen outside the proper vessel (i.e., female), making the sodomite worse than a beast. Thomas also generated authorities who accentuated dire soteriological consequences. Jerome had argued that the sin against nature was so vile that Christ was compelled to postpone his Incarnation. Augustine had allegedly claimed that the sodomitical enemies of nature perished with the Incarnation.[7] Anyone who persisted in this sin past the age of thirty-three—the span of Christ's lifetime—would never be freed from it, unless by divine intervention.[8] Thomas had known a man afflicted with this vice whose very footsteps burned the verdure of the field upon which he trod.[9] Nor can the morning dew settle on the places where such a sin was committed.[10] In fact, an acquaintance reported that Peter the Chanter knew of a place where two clerics had unnatural intercourse, rendering the spot dry and sterile in perpetuity.[11] Like the Chanter before him, Thomas attempted to awaken the doomed city of Sodom from its symbolic slumber by dwelling on the wasted landscape upon which the city once stood.[12] The behavior of the biblical Sodomites is parallel to those who "have gone astray from the womb; they have spoken false things" (Ps. 57:4). Although the people who had rejected the womb were traditionally interpreted as heretics in biblical exegesis, Thomas seems to have intended a double entendre. On the one hand, sodomy was becoming increasingly associated with heresy. On the other hand, men "gone astray from the womb" could be understood to have literally rejected the womb for perverse pleasures. The duplicity of the ancient citizens of Sodom is mirrored by modern-day sodomites who, overwhelmed by shame, rarely confess their unnatural acts. Thus, "it is with good reason that Sodom is interpreted as mute. As long as they are mute, the Holy Spirit cannot enter them."[13]

Dominican William Peraldus (d. ca. 1271) anticipates still more pernicious consequences for sodomy. Just as the lifeless waters of the Dead Sea are expressions of God's punishment, Peraldus argues that sodomy has the capacity to destroy human nature itself.[14] For to be one with God means to be one with nature, hence acknowledging that God's creation of man resists modification. When a male is so perverted by lust that he makes himself into a woman, however, he renders himself unrecognizable as part of God's creation—transgressing against a law that even brute animals observe. So while other kinds of lust have the capacity to reduce individuals to the level of animals, unnatural vice places them below animals. Sodom is mute because these bestial males are rendered mute on the Day of Judgment. "For they are not able to excuse themselves through ignorance since nature teaches a law and those who transgress it become brute animals." This degree of human debasement was the reason that Christ deferred his incarnation.[15]

Despite this seemingly open acknowledgment of sodomy, however, some ecclesiastical authorities still expressed frustration with the church's toothless response. Franciscan canonist and theologian Astesanus d'Asti (d. ca. 1330) points out that since sodomy was a capital offense in the old law, it necessarily becomes a more serious crime in "the time of grace when human nature was assumed by the Son of God." Hence he commends the vigilance exercised by secular authorities, who punish sodomy with "fire and the sword," maintaining that both those who perpetrate sodomy as well as those abetting the vice should suffer these consequences. For this reason Astesanus urges that "the ecclesiastical judge ought to punish it more severely than other forms of wickedness." And yet, due punishment is allegedly hindered by the fact that the "sacred canons passed over [the sin of sodomy] out of detestation of such a great crime and outrage because it ought not to be named."[16]

Considering the number of prominent sanctions against sodomy promulgated over the centuries, one might conclude that Astesanus either was ill-informed or erroneously believed that the handful of canons on sodomy featured in contemporary canon law was somehow exhaustive. Although it seems unlikely that our author was either this ignorant or this naive, he is nevertheless representative of the kind of lenience that he appears to decry: complicity by discretion. This discretion facilitates his anachronistic presentation of the early church, which ignores milestone councils like Elvira or Ancyra. Even so, discretion will remain the zeitgeist of the high Middle Ages. Lateran III had condemned "that incontinence which is the sin against nature on account of which *the wrath of God came down upon the sons of disbelief* [Eph. 5:6]."[17] In contrast, Lateran IV stigmatizes "every vice involving lust, especially that on account of which *the wrath of God came down* from heaven *upon the sons of disobedience*."[18] Although embellishing the scriptural citation, the canon excises the phrase "sin against nature," instead preferring the catchall term "incontinence."

Lay Responses

> Let a friar of some order
> pass the night with you
> either your wife or your daughter
> this (friar) will seek to violate
> or your son he will prefer
> as (he prefers) the fork of a strong (boy)
>   —Anonymous fifteenth-century carol[19]

For most lay audiences, especially in northern Europe, the charge of sodomy was toxic. This is why it was deployed by writers like Eadmer and Orderic Vitalis to disparage rulers who resisted reform. As Mathew Kuefler has discussed, the twelfth century saw the flourishing of vernacular romance in which the possibility of same-sex relations between members of the military aristocracy are alluded to only rarely, but always with suspicion and contempt.[20] Even the sexually explicit fabliaux veer away from sodomy, while one very rare allusion elicits extreme aversion.[21] Sodomy even had the capacity to incite mob violence. Andrew Miller analyzes the attack on Roger of Pont l'Évêque, the archbishop of York, positing that the mob slashed Roger's episcopal capa in order to expose his buttocks—a graphic allusion to the bishop's past pederasty. Miller draws attention to John of Salisbury's letter of 1178, which recalls the alleged circumstances of this charge with gusto.[22]

> The Caiaphas of today . . . had doted excessively on Walter, a boy of handsome face (not to say enjoyed sinful intercourse [*nefario concubitu*] with him); but when his beard grew, and he blabbed with tongue too loose the unnatural and wicked deeds he had suffered, he had his eyes put out, and when he accused him [the bishop] of the crime the same arch-devil corrupted judges in the secular courts and had him hanged. . . . Thus he rewarded the long complaisance of his old love: first he seduced the wretched youth; then, to make him more wretched still, because he repented his consent to such sordid and filthy behavior, he mutilated and blinded him; finally, to bring his wretchedness to its height, because he made such noisy protest as he could of his misfortunes, he had him murdered by hanging on a gibbet. . . . Right down to this day to the Church's frequent shame and contempt the sad tale is told.[23]

John was hardly an impartial witness. As a member of the household of the late Thomas Becket, archbishop of Canterbury, John blamed Roger for inciting Becket's death.[24] Since the crime is not corroborated by any other source, John may well have invented the entire episode. Even so, the story is built on the assumption that the reader was no stranger either to incidents of clerical pederasty or to the lay outrage over clerics who abused youths with impunity. Nor was this instance of mob violence over pederasty unique. In 1286, a man named Conrad Nantwinus, returning from a pilgrimage to Rome, was accused of debauching a boy in Wulfrathausen. Despite the pilgrim's theoretical exemption from secular law, Conrad was seized and roasted on a grill in the manner of St. Lawrence as preliminary to be being burned at the stake. Miracles immediately ensued attesting to his innocence, and he was proclaimed a saint.[25]

Secular legislation against sodomy took a persecutory turn in the high Middle Ages. As early as 1120, Baldwin II issued a series of laws condemning sins of the flesh in the hopes of averting any more natural disasters from befalling the fragile kingdom of Jerusalem.[26] Four of the twenty-five canons were directed against sodomy; two addressed forced penetration, and in one instance the anticipated victim was a child (*infans*). All sodomites were to be burned, except for a culprit who was prepared to denounce himself.[27] In the following century, secular authorities begin actively to pursue men engaged in same-sex relations, and the narrowing of the term "sodomy" begins to reflect this focus. Initially, the references are desultory. A German chronicle mentions that German king Rudolf I had the lord of Haspisperch burned for sodomy in 1277; ten years later, a man named Niger de Pulis was burned for sodomy in Parma.[28] Yet the initiative against sodomy was destined to become more systematic. Throughout Europe, sodomy was treated as a capital offense punishable by being burned alive.[29] Many cities in Italy set up special tribunals. Secular society also became sensitive to the impact of sodomy on the natural world. Hence, in the fourteenth century sodomites became automatic scapegoats for the plague and other disasters.[30]

Despite the church's efforts to the contrary, the laity had come to recognize sodomy as "the clerical vice." Examples of such an awareness abound. The thirteenth-century *Bible moralisée*, written in the vernacular for the French royal family, depicts wicked bishops who engage in shady money deals as being punished through divinely inflicted sodomy. The vice is illustrated by the bishops embracing diminutive male figures, a number of whom are tonsured.[31] The sodomites of Dante's *Inferno* (after 1302) are described as "great men, high / In the Church," while Andrea de Mozzi, archbishop of Florence, is named explicitly.[32] In Boccaccio's *Decameron* (1349 × 1352) the papal curia is reported to be rife with the vice, even as a traveling knight who agrees to share a room with an abbot finds himself being molested by his roommate.[33] In a miracle of the Virgin entitled "Of a prest that lay be a nonne," the illustrator of the Middle English Vernon manuscript coyly swapped the nun for a monk.[34]

Charges of sodomy continued to be used opportunistically, but with a different vector. While eleventh and twelfth century chroniclers had disparaged monarchs by allegations of sodomy, by the end of the thirteenth century, secular leaders would turn the tables on the clergy, wielding accusations of heretically inflected sodomy against highly placed religious. Philip the Fair of France (d. 1314) used this conjunction of depravities against the redoubtable Boniface VIII,[35] and eventually against the entire Templar order.[36] There was nothing new about the association between heresy and sexual depravity. The church fathers had routinely made this association. But by the later Middle Ages, sodomy would become the special marker of heretics.[37] Indeed, in fourteenth-century Navarre, when a man was put to death for sodomy, he was described as committing "heresy of the body."[38]

The widespread association of the clergy and sodomy stoked anticlericalism and dissent throughout Latin Christendom. The English Lollards' critique is especially interesting in this regard. In their Twelve Conclusions (1395), boldly nailed to the walls of Westminster, "the Third Conclusion, sorrowful to hear, is that the law of continence annexed to the priesthood, that in prejudice of women was first ordained, induces sodomy in all of Holy Church. We excuse ourselves [for naming sodomy] by [its appearance in] the Bible against the suspect decree that says we should not name it."[39] Clearly, the taboo against naming sodomy was sufficiently compelling as to convince the Lollards that there was an actual conciliar decree forbidding its utterance. But even if they were technically mistaken, they correctly recognized the connection between refusal to name an offense and ecclesiastical inaction.[40]

Ecclesiastical Tribunals

It was highly unusual for a cleric to be accused of sodomy before any ecclesiastical tribunal. This is in spite of the fact that, by the end of the thirteenth century, the church had developed sophisticated ways of monitoring clerical behavior, even as the forums dedicated to prosecuting clerical misdemeanors had evolved. The burgeoning of canon law in the twelfth century was followed by the development of ecclesiastical courts that operated on many different levels from the mid-thirteenth century onward.[41] As subsequent chapters demonstrate, records of episcopal visitations to the parishes and subject monasteries of a given diocese also become more meticulous. The mother houses of the increasingly centralized religious orders will send visitors to its different priories who would, in turn, refer the most egregious offenses to the general chapter. Universities and colleges also keep records concerning any disciplinary action meted out to its members.

The prosecution of misdemeanors like sodomy would, in theory, have been further facilitated by the thirteenth-century movement from the accusatorial system of criminal law to the inquisitional procedure, allowing the bishop to launch an ex officio case against an unchaste cleric. Traditionally, two or three witnesses were required for the prosecution of a cleric.[42] In the high Middle Ages, however, canon law adopted a less stringent standard of proof for prosecuting manifest clerical offenders, especially those accused of incontinence.[43] Even so, the risks for a member of the laity to bring a charge against a cleric were great. It could result in a countersuit against the laypersons who launched the case. For instance, when the Pisan priest Fabio was denounced to the bishop's court by some of the senior members of his church for certain unspecified crimes, it was noted at the time the charges were first brought that the priest would have a chance to clear himself through canonical purgation, at which point the court should proceed against his accusers.[44] Indeed, Guy Geltner notes that the bishop of Lucca routinely punished parishioners by bringing counter-suits for defamation against anyone who dared to accuse one of his clerics.[45]

Given the difficulty of bringing charges against a cleric, members of the laity frequently took justice into their own hands.[46] From this perspective, Abelard's castration for the seduction of Heloise is not that unusual: ecclesiastical records bear witness to many instances in which outraged members of the laity castrate clerics for their sexual indiscretions.[47] As the spontaneous attacks on the bishop of York or on the hapless pilgrim Conrad Nantwinus would suggest, heinous sexual acts like pedophilia could also excite mob violence against offending clerics. In the thirteenth century, a Premonstratensian conversus from Orte was found guilty of bestiality and buried alive, alongside the bodies of the animals he had defiled.[48]

Yet the rules for charging an incontinent cleric were framed around two decretals addressing clerical concubinage, which is telling: for the vast majority of instances in which clerics were disciplined by ecclesiastical courts continued to be for sexual infractions with women. These punishments were considerable and extended far beyond the courtroom.[49] The children resulting from these illicit relations were heavily stigmatized for the scandal they afforded. Thirteenth-century French councils insisted on the removal of clerical bastards from their fathers' home. Reports of a squalling infant could result in the presumed father's suspension. There were also weighty prohibitions against clerical bastards assisting at, or even approaching, the altar.[50] They were, of course, barred from the priesthood—at least in theory.[51]

The disciplinary proclivities of church officials are highlighted in a remarkable series of registers from the bishop of Lucca's criminal court, recently
brought to light by Guy Geltner. There are forty-four registers in all, ranging
from 1347 to 1400, probably constituting the longest unbroken span of this type
of source—certainly for Italy and probably for the Continent.[52] Yet, as Geltner
points out, these records tend to foreground the clergy's dereliction of duty,
destruction (or depletion) of church property, or acts of violence over sexual
offenses, and none of the cases he examines involves sodomy.[53] My own cursory
examination of these sources points to the unsurprising conclusion that the only
instances in which members of the clergy were arraigned for sexual offenses were
when their behavior caused a scandal. The clerics of Lucca were hardly saints:
in addition to instances of concubinage, there were also a number of flamboyant
cases of rape and abduction.[54] Yet instances involving married women seemed
especially egregious, occasioning greater scandal. One memorable instance
occurred in 1353 when the rector of Sant'Andrea of Montecarlo, ironically named
Justus, invoked demons to compel one of his parishioners—Nuta, wife of a
certain Corsenus Perdo—to come to his house. Once there, the priest violated
her repeatedly. Nuta was gagged and could not call for help. Nor was escape
likely, since she was imprisoned in some sort of cellar surrounded by a ditch. As
one might expect of the devil's protégé, Justus's affront to the marriage bond
was complemented by a marked hostility to reproduction. The priest told Nuta
repeatedly that he would ensure that the fetus (whose existence he somehow
gleaned) would never see the light of day. Justus was further accused of baptizing
a child "in the name of the devil." After admitting to the charges, he was fined,
deposed, and imprisoned in the episcopal jail to do penance for three years.
Upon his release, he was exiled from the diocese of Lucca.[55]

The sacerdotal necromancer allegedly had sex with his resistant, yet presumably enchanted, captive day and night for twenty-two consecutive days without
ever exciting the suspicions (or at least the complaints) of her husband. This degree
of obliviousness must have been magically induced: in a culture where privacy was
at a premium, it would be very difficult to conceal a cleric's cohabitation with a
woman for any length of time—especially if there was an aggrieved husband
involved. In contrast, sodomy could be undertaken much more discreetly. This is
especially true if both parties were members of the clergy and either the relationship was consensual, or the passive party was successfully suborned. Even if relations between two clerics were discovered by clerical authorities, such an offense
would generally be beneath the purview of the courts, where the ubiquitous
Augustinian principle of "where the evil happened, there let it die" found a com-
plement in the canonical principle that "the church cannot judge hidden things."
Hence a cleric might well escape formal chastisement, let alone deposition, unless

his offense were public.[56] The imperative of heightened publicity would especially pertain in districts in which sodomy seemed anomalous. England is a case in point. According to Richard Wunderli's analysis of London church courts, only 1 of over 21,000 defendants was accused of sodomy between 1470 and 1516, and only one defamation suit entailed a sodomitical slur.[57]

Yet the sparsity of cases that did come to trial should perhaps be taken as an inverse indicator of just how odious the offense was considered to be in England. In 1408, a terse entry in the archbishop of Canterbury's court register notes that the rector of Bordofale was accused of sodomy by an eyewitness (*secundum videntem*).[58] Presumably the person in question had made enough noise to ensure that the rector was summoned before the court. Since there was only one witness, however, the rector was probably allowed to clear himself by canonical purgation—the standard procedure when a cleric was accused of a public crime or was otherwise defamed, but where concrete proof was lacking. The accused cleric would proclaim his innocence by oath, also producing a number of oath supporters (often seven, but the number could vary) who would attest to his good reputation.[59]

This is precisely how a case brought before the episcopal court of York was resolved in 1407. Richard Benet, a chaplain of Langtoft, was accused of sodomy with several males: Russeton Schyphyrd, George Saluayn, and Andrea Raper. The charge itself is unusual. But what makes Benet's case singular is that the individuals he allegedly had sex with were characterized as *senibus*: not just grown men, but "old" or, at the very least, "mature" men. The penalty was deposition and loss of benefice, as well as a humiliating public penance: Benet would be required to stand at the front of the parish church of Langtoft from the beginning of the Mass until the elevation of the Host for six consecutive Sundays, dressed in sackcloth and bearing a wax candle that weighed a pound. He would then be required to repeat this penance for six Sundays in the parish church of Kyllam—presumably because Andrea Raper was from Kyllam. Benet appeared to protest his innocence. The requisite evidence seems to have been lacking, but he may also have been helped by the fact that his sexual partners were described as "old men." Such a characterization was so out of keeping with normal expectations for objects of any recognizable expression of libidinousness that it may have struck the judges as a spurious and malicious accusation. A week later, Benet appeared with twelve compurgators, six chaplains and six villagers from Langtoft, and purged himself canonically.[60]

The rarity of sodomy cases in Italian church tribunals is especially noteworthy given the prolix evidence in their secular counterparts, as will be seen below. It is always conceivable that some of the cases brought before ecclesiastical courts did entail sodomy, but the charge was hidden in plain sight. For instance, a certain Guido, a priest and chaplain of Pisa who was also a member of a local monastery, was repeatedly called before the episcopal court for his wandering. In parallel disciplinary cases, we are given some idea of what the errant cleric was up to: that he was out roaming the town, playing dice, haunting taverns, sleeping with prostitutes. But in Guido's case, there are no details. Instead, there is an emphasis on his returning to his room, which is "at the front of the refectory, within the cloister of the church, and to remain in it continually." Although the vicar-general at one point stipulates that Guido should not leave the monastery unaccompanied by another monk, a second iteration of just where exactly his room was located begs the question of whether some of Guido's wanderings were undertaken in the monastery. This is certainly possible: as we shall see in Chapter 6, an amorous Cluniac monk was accused of uncovering and stroking his fellow monks while they slept. Whatever Guido may have been up to, the other monks found his behavior sufficiently noxious that they were prepared to cut him loose. The bishop's vicar, moreover, found Guido's behavior serious enough to threaten him not only with excommunication but with the loss of his prebend if he did not mend his ways.[61]

The sparse evidence for church disciplinary action against clerics accused of sodomy has led some scholars to assume that sodomy was not particularly widespread among the clergy or, at least, its prevalence was much exaggerated.[62] Yet if instances of sodomy were often overlooked in the external forum, there is fragmentary evidence to be found in the papal penitentiary—the one tribunal addressing matters involving the internal forum, which allegedly corresponds to the realm of conscience. First arising in the thirteenth century, the papal penitentiary was the office responsible for absolving certain heinous sins reserved for the pope alone, as well as common irregularities like clerical bastardy.[63] The earliest known formulary for the penitentiary, compiled from materials spanning the years 1234 to 1243, contains one letter from what was apparently a series of letters from an anonymous abbot concerning a difficult situation that arose in his monastery. An old monk had made advances to a youth (iuvenis), who retaliated by castrating him. Although commending the youth's commitment to chastity, the pope's representatives nevertheless saw his response as excessive and required the abbot to set an appropriate penance for this violent act. (Even so, the papal officials noted that the youth's progress in holy orders should not be interrupted.) The officers of the penitentiary demonstrated less sympathy for the youth's would-be seducer, who, in keeping with Lateran III, was to be thrust into a monastic prison. The elderly monk had been despicably persistent in his pursuit of the youth, even to the point of using the sacrament of penance as a mechanism of seduction. The abbot emphasized, however, by way of exoneration, that the would-be seducer was never given the opportunity to practice this "abominable sin." Perhaps the abbot's exculpatory mind-set had something to do with the rather bizarre rubric assigned to the case in the formulary: "Concerning the cleric or regular who was mutilated through no fault of his own."[64] In contrast to the unforgiving attitude of earlier authorities like Fructuosus, the principle of mens rea was clearly not embraced by whoever was responsible for the rubric.

This case, along with other instances of sodomy, was presumably included in the formulary for its exemplary nature. One can only assume that this scenario—at least in its general contours, if not its specifics—was not extraordinary. In fact, a case from Filippo Tamburini's notorious edition possesses a similar profile to the case of the elderly monastic predator preserved in the formulary, but with a very different outcome. In 1461, a Cistercian monk, once again described as a *iuvenis*, was forced by his abbot to commit sodomy. The youth brought the case before their superiors, but was subsequently manipulated by the abbot's friends and relatives into withdrawing his complaint and signing a document attesting that he had made the accusation out of malice. The young monk was subsequently imprisoned, presumably for bearing false witness. As fate would have it, his cellmate was none other than the abbot who, though exonerated for the sin of sodomy, was nevertheless imprisoned for a number of other crimes. The young monk managed to break out of prison and put aside his habit—"not for the sake of apostasizing but for safety." He headed for the Roman Curia to seek absolution for sodomy, perjury, and apostasy so he could be free of the stain of infamy. He also asked to be moved from his original monastery to some other Benedictine monastery "where benevolent receivers were to be found."[65]

As the above exempla suggest, the only cases referred to the papal penitentiary were the ones that gave rise to considerable scandal. In the normal course of events, clerical sodomy would be revealed in the context of sacramental confession and, as a reserved sin, be referred to the local bishop. But such referrals may be more reflective of theory than practice. In the later Middle Ages, theologians such as Jean Gerson (d. 1429) challenged the growing number of reserved sins, arguing that this phenomenon only served to inspire fear in the penitent.[66] It is entirely possible that many confessors felt the same way and absolved their penitents regardless of whether or not a sin was reserved. But let us suppose that a discreet case of sodomy, by which I mean one that was only known through the medium of confession, for some reason found its way to the papal penitentiary. In such an instance, the seal of confession would ensure that sinner and sin alike would leave no parchment trail.[67]

It is not surprising that clerical sodomy leaves so light an imprint upon ecclesiastical tribunals. As Helmut Puff puts it, "theologically normative texts loudly prescribed silence on sodomy. . . . Thus it is not surprising to hear so little about actual same-sex behavior among the clergy in ecclesiastical court-rooms" or, I would add, in any ecclesiastical forum.[68] And so, while the gravity of clerical sodomy would seem to dictate prosecution, the very enormity of the sin, and incumbent potential for scandal, would urge suppression. The threat of scandal invariably trumped the heinousness of the sin. Hence, sodomy was only prosecuted in the event that the scandal could not be contained, in which case failure to prosecute ran the risk of even greater scandal. What follows in the final four chapters are some very atypical cases in which prosecution was judged the lesser of two evils. The cases occur within four settings in which boys or youths were especially vulnerable to sexual predation: the monastery, the choir, the school, and the episcopal curia.

CHAPTER 6

The Monastery

"What, I ask you, is to be done with them [the boys in the monastery]? They are incorrigible ruffians. We never give over beating them night and day and they only get worse." Anselm replied with astonishment: "You never give over beating them? And what are they like when they grow up?" "Stupid brutes," he said. To which Anselm retorted, "You have spent your energies rearing them to good purpose. From men you have reared beasts."

—Eadmer, *The Life of St. Anselm*

The conversation in this chapter's epigraph took place between Anselm of Canterbury and another abbot renowned for his piety.[1] Anselm's resistance to corporal punishment was unusual, but not unique. Here is another telling vignette: Othloh (d. ca. 1070), a monk at St. Emmeram's in Regensburg, was still quite young when he was appointed as a teacher at the monastery's school, where he was made responsible for what he referred to as the "detested discipline of boys." He observed that several of the older boys took it upon themselves to chastise the younger boys and were often very rough. But interfering with such systemic abuse had its own consequences. When Othloh upbraided one of the offenders "who seemed especially violent," the boy was so dismayed and saddened by the public rebuff that the sensitive Othloh, in turn, experienced considerable guilt, which soon spiraled into a spiritual crisis. Othloh feared that he had abused his authority and despaired of ever making adequate reparations to the older boy. Fortunately, God intervened, prompting the youth to seek out Othloh and ask forgiveness for his error. But he also begged that, in the event he inadvertently committed future transgressions, Othloh correct him in private.[2]

These anecdotes underline an obvious point that nevertheless bears repeating: the extreme vulnerability of a child, or even an adolescent, in a monastic context—disciplined at the discretion of whoever was placed in authority and isolated from family and friends. We have seen that the Benedictine Rule held that fasts and vigils were too subtle for children and mandated beatings. The tenor of monastic discipline created a pecking order of the beaters and the beaten, fostering the culture of bullying that Othloh of Regensburg had observed. Yet his efforts to intervene by singling out one of the worst offenders had unanticipated results. In his own words: "Hitherto, I was ignorant of some-one else's particular fragility, and I believed that there was no harm in whatever manner I berated an obtuse adolescent, who was subject to me by law." The suffering experienced by bully and would-be corrector alike could have been averted had Othloh but observed the monastic principle of fraternal correction. And yet, we have seen the way in which fraternal correction both concealed and deferred punishment—often indefinitely—potentially enabling abusers of many different stripes.

Monastic authorities had recognized from early days that the rigors of monastic life would render the young inclined to trust anyone who treated them with simple kindness. The Visigothic rules of Isidore and Fructuosus considered an adult joking with or even looking at children as one of the most serious offenses conceivable. The English *Regularis concordia* (972) warned the monks and abbot alike against embracing or kissing youths or children, urging that their "affection for them be spiritual" and that they "love children reverently with the greatest circumspection." On no account should any monk arrange to be alone with a child on some spiritual pretext. Even the master especially entrusted with the care of the children could not be alone with a boy unless a third party was present.[3] Over time, monastic customaries set progressively higher standards for the probity, chastity, and purity of the guardian.[4] Bernard of Cluny, writing between 1060 and 1090, assigned four masters to the dormitory, each bearing a stick and a lantern, to preside over elaborate arrangements for sleeping and for nighttime visits to the lavatory. The stick ensured that the masters never touched the boys with their hands. If a boy was sleeping uncovered, he was poked with a stick and told through sign language to cover himself up. If a boy failed to wake up promptly, the master could prod him with a stick or yank his hair.[5] Other brethren were kept at arm's length: a stick-bearing guardian even followed a sick child into the infirmary.[6] No one could offer the children water for washing their hands unless the person offering the water was "of good character and mature age."[7] Children were barred from exchanging the customary kiss with visiting monks—an interdiction that Bernard's contemporary Ulrich extended to the kiss of peace during Mass. Even the abbot was not to be trusted. At the end of the daily meeting of chapter, when the children would ask for his blessing,[8] the abbot was "always guarded when he is with children"—keeping his hood drawn over his eyes until the blessing was complete.[9]

In Lanfranc's *Constitutions*, the isolation of the oblate is truly wrenching.

> [When reading] they shall sit apart from one another, in such a way
> that no-one can touch his neighbour either with his hands or his
> clothes. No child shall make a sign to another, nor say a word to him,
> unless the master can see and hear him. . . . Whithersoever the children
> go a master shall be between every two. . . . When the abbot is present
> in choir no one shall strike a child, or cause him to strip for flogging,
> unless the abbot so orders. When the abbot is away the cantor may
> beat them for their faults in performance [in choir] that fall under his
> jurisdiction; in all other small matters the prior shall punish them.
> Wherever they may be, no one save the persons mentioned above shall
> make a sign to them, or smile to them. No one shall enter their school
> or speak to them anywhere unless permission has been granted.[10]

Such scrupulous attention is also meant to restrain childhood perversity. The nature of this attention at Cluny has led Isabelle Cochelin to remark that "the Cluniac discourse on *pueritia* is derogatory."[11] Even so, the activity of children was sufficiently scrutinized that no one could reasonably challenge Bernard of Cluny's boast that "no child of a king could be raised with greater attentiveness [*diligentia*] at the palace than any small boy at Cluny."[12]

The awareness of the potential sexual jeopardy in which monastic children were placed was expressed through a number of different media. A capital on the Benedictine abbey church of La Madeleine at Vézelay (ca. 1125–1130) vividly portrays the abduction of Ganymede by Jupiter in the shape of an eagle. The screaming child is suspended upside down with the devil cheering in the background, while his parents look on in horror. Ilene Forsyth has interpreted this capital as an indictment of monks who preyed upon oblates—an interpretation that is supported by its placement in front of the entrance to the monastic precincts.[13] In a similar vein, V. A. Kolve has argued that a monastic play from Fleury entitled *The Son of Getron* is a psychologically charged warning against same-sex relations. Like the myth of Ganymede, the story turns on the abduction of a boy, Adeodatus, to serve as cupbearer—in this case not to a pagan god, but to a pagan tyrant. Although the tyrant admires the boy's purity, leaving him unmolested, his melancholic longing for Adeodatus is an ominous warning that the master's respectful state of sexual détente had its limits. The boy is eventually snatched away by St. Nicholas (an appropriate advocate insofar as one of the saint's first miracles was rescuing two girls from prostitution) and returned to the mother. The fact that the roles of Adeodatus and the mother were probably assigned to younger monks would have added poignancy to the scene.[14]

A final vignette is offered by Gilles of Corbeil (d. before 1224), a canon at Notre Dame, the foremost physician of the medical faculty at Paris, and a member of Peter the Chanter's circle. He imagines a boy, too young to be separated from his nurse and still childishly lisping his words, who is forced into religion. His uncle, the bishop, is prepared to make him a church canon, and the boy's parents are grateful. The uncle, however, is an incorrigible lecher. He secretly sends for his nephew, enticing him with gifts. He enlists spies to discover what the child particularly likes for purposes of bribery. "A great and insupportable burden descends on the [child's] little shoulders, under the power of which an older breast would fail." First, there is guilt presumably over the illicit presents, which he would be bound to conceal. There is, however, "another hidden reason more compelling by far. It disturbs him more, striking and goading him."[15] When the parents come for the child's investment, they are shocked to see how he kicks and screams when he is led before his uncle.[16]

The Seductive Youth

> Elsewhere we saw the same sort of disturbing disdain for
> victims. In the Diocese of Pittsburgh, church officials
> dismissed an incident of abuse on the ground that the 15-year-
> old had "pursued" the priest and "literally seduced" him into
> a relationship.
> —Pennsylvania grand jury report, August 2018[17]

Instances of empathy for children in the religious life are, arguably, the exception, not the rule. Most allusions to the mythical cupbearer were not so trenchant as the Vézelay capital. We have already seen that Ganymede was a pliable object of desire in the clerical poetry of the period. Likewise, a capital at Clermont-Ferrand portrays Ganymede as a serene and compliant youth.[18] The sexual obligations associated with Ganymede's cup-bearing responsibilities were clear to everyone, apparently devoid of any capacity to scandalize. In fact, Glenn Olsen has drawn attention to capitals in Romanesque churches and cloisters that depict anal intercourse, sometimes explicitly in the context of pederasty.[19]

Gilles of Corbeil couches his story about the underage canon in defiant language: "I will utter aloud what has been repressed by the silence of the speechless tongue, buried and shut in. But the entire outrageous matter refuses to be enclosed by shadows, to be hidden among unacknowledged matters by a joke. It insists that the listener's jocular whispers be expelled, his laughter be interrupted by a loud noise ringing in his ears."[20] Gilles is alluding to the way in which the question of sexual predation upon the young was often deflected through humor. This was something of a monastic truism. For instance, in the miracle collection of the Cluniac abbot Peter the Venerable (d. 1154), a half-dozing monk listens as demons compare notes about their varying degrees of success in the instigation of sin. A vulture-shaped demon, so fat that he can barely stand, complains that he could make no headway with the Cluniac monks due to their extensive prayers and liberal sprinklings of holy water. But his comrades had spent their time more productively. One seemingly routine triumph occurred: "Going through a certain monastery, we brought it about that the master of the school committed fornication with one of the boys." At this point, another demon notices the onlooking monk and rebukes the hitherto unsuccessful vulture-demon: "But what is your business, you idler? Stand up and at least cut off the leg of the monk who . . . extends it beyond the bed in a disorderly fashion."[21] The fornication between a teacher and student at a monastic school seems no more remarkable than the unruly postures of a sleeping monk.

Cloistered sex with a minor takes an especially ribald turn under the direction of Walter Map (d. ca. 1210), a secular cleric at the court of Henry II and an outspoken critic of monastic culture. Map relates how a visiting Cistercian abbot was musing aloud while at table over the failed miracle of the recently deceased Bernard of Clairvaux (d. 1153)—a monk who had not just been a celebrity in the Cistercian order but was one of the most influential men in all of Europe. According to the abbot, a desperate father had besought Bernard's help for his ailing boy, but when Bernard arrived at the man's abode the boy was already dead. The saint dramatically prostrated himself on the boy's body in prayer. When he arose, however, the boy just lay there, still dead. At this point Walter could not resist quipping: "Then he was the most unlucky of monks . . . I have heard before now of a monk throwing himself upon a boy [puer], but always, when the monk got up, the boy promptly got up too."[22] The abbot blushed in mortification, while the others at the king's table chuckled.

Peter the Venerable's anecdote draws upon the well-known buffoonery of demons for its salience. Yet his unspoken presumptions about sexual sin has much in common with the attitudes of the desert fathers: boys, like women, are presented not in their own right, but as sources of temptation. If the boy in question is not actually responsible for the monk's sin, he is nevertheless the material through which the demon brought about the monk's fall. The boy is treated not as a victim in Peter's anecdote but as a stumbling block—a source of scandal. In an anonymous poem, the monastic child is even more pointedly the object of blame:

> The morals of the young are not corrupted in the cloister
> Often the older brothers are molested by them.
> Anyone who defends the young and does not reprove them
> is frequently duped and falls into a trap.[23]

The humor of this biting verse might seem to reside in a deliberate inversion of an accepted truism: everyone knows that it is monks who corrupt boys, and not vice versa. And yet this effort to cast the boys as aggressors is not entirely outré. The anonymous poet's sentiments parallel the sodomitical plague visited upon the bishops in the *Bible moralisée*, discussed above. The errant (but passive) bishops are punished by being actively embraced by boys; later the reformed (and now active) bishops are depicted as literally casting the boys away from them. Both instances are grounded in an alternative truth that seems to have been subscribed to in certain clerical circles.

In Walter Map's tale, the evocation of the boy, whether dead or alive, is again purely instrumental: the Cistercian abbot's exemplum presents the boy as a vehicle (albeit one destined to disappoint) for revealing Bernard's sanctity; the quick-witted inversion renders the boy a vehicle for demonstrating monastic depravity. Map's quip exemplifies the Freudian contention that a joke is always at someone's expense—in this case, it would seem to be the Cistercian abbot and, by analogy, monks everywhere. The distance of almost a millennium offers a different perspective, however: one trusts that the modern reader would regard the tales of both Peter the Venerable and Walter Map as stories told at the expense of the child.

Cistercians and Children

If our hypothetical modern reader happened to be a historian of monasticism, however, he or she might well argue that Map lobbed his charge of pederasty at the wrong order. Like the other "new" orders that arose in the late eleventh century, the Cistercians eschewed child oblation, instead requiring adult recruitment.[24] But the rather murky origins of the Cistercian order veers from this crisp textbook account. Although founded in 1098, the earliest documents, responsible for representing and shaping the order's ethos, emerged incrementally over the course of the twelfth century.[25] The earliest statute addressing the question of age, traditionally dated as 1134 but probably drafted sometime later, stipulated that a novice must have completed his fifteenth year before entering the order.[26] Very soon chronological age proved an insufficient standard. In 1154, however, the general chapter, the order's administrative arm that met annually, would further ordain that "if any novice of fifteen or more has a face or an entire body that casts suspicion on his age," he could be expelled by the abbot of Cîteaux, who presided over the entire order, during one of his visitations.[27]

Since the Cistercians technically followed the Benedictine Rule, the exclusion of children is a distinct break with tradition. And yet there is no statement by the founders or in the early statutes justifying the exclusion of children and prepubescent youths. Based on earlier Benedictine commentaries, it would stand to reason that the founders perceived children as a threat to monastic discipline, which would include the sexual temptation they represented to their seniors. Although this motive is never acknowledged, the aforementioned statute of 1154 comes close. The pointed appeal to appearance versus chronological age is suggestive, bringing to mind the legend of the hapless cross-dressed novice Euphrosyne/Smaragdus, who was kept under lock and key so as not to corrupt her/his elder confreres. Later statutes corroborate this sense of caution. In 1157, the official age of entrance was raised from fifteen to eighteen, granting the abbot the right to expel an underage novice.[28] Four years later it was further specified that a novice must be "of greater stature and a more manly age."[29] Even so, the order ultimately fell away from this degree of scrupulosity, generally permitting the child or youth who had been prematurely admitted to stay, but punishing the one who was responsible for his admission.[30] Hence, a French prior admitted a boy who was under fifteen; another in Galicia admitted a boy of twelve. Such transgressions were initially deemed light faults that could be expunged by fasting.[31]

In the twelfth century, the specter of same-sex incontinence was not raised, except by innuendo.[32] Case in point is the repeated emphasis on monkish manliness. One of the earliest statutes, traditionally ascribed to 1134, insisted that men sing with virile voices and not in a "feminine manner with ringing sounds or, as is commonly called, in falsetto [*falsis vocibus*] as a wanton actor imitates"— probably resisting the controversial practice of polyphony.[33] In 1157, the same year that entrance to the order was raised to eighteen, it was also ordained that "no one should be made abbot with an excessively young or boyish face [*nimis juvenis et puerile facie*]." Brethren were also expected to keep one another at arm's length. In 1182, the custom whereby the abbot received a kiss when he returned from travel was roundly condemned as indecent.[34] When a statute explicitly banning sexual infractions finally made an appearance in 1189, its terms were suggestive: "if anyone is apprehended in manifest contagion of the flesh, he should be absolutely expelled from that house from which he sinned, never to return there, according to the custom preserved by our holy fathers thus far."[35] The canon seems to imply that the sin was committed within the monastic precincts, which might argue for a same-sex component.[36] Although this canon may well be the custom of the founding fathers, as was claimed and would be repeated after 1189, this is nevertheless its first formal appearance.[37]

Actual punishments for what were possibly sexual infractions begin to make an appearance in the thirteenth century, though the exact nature of the offenses is not always clear.[38] What, for example, are we to make of the Thuringian monk who was accused of "certain filthy and unheard of things, not fit to be said or related,"[39] the Slovinian abbot who was deposed (twice) on account of his filthy infamy (*propter turpem infamiam*),[40] or the Hungarian abbot deposed for his "shameless dissolution" (*inhonestum dissolutionem*)—the sole explicit charge against him being that he struck the naked buttocks of certain monks with his bare hand.[41] It is only in 1220, however, when a lay brother was ejected from his monastery for an unspeakable vice (*vitium indicibile*) that we can be relatively certain that the offense being addressed involved same-sex activity. The offending lay brother was sent to another community, where he was to be imprisoned.[42]

The above punishment seems to be a conflation of the 1189 Cistercian statute, ordaining expulsion from the house, and the Lateran ruling that mandated monastic imprisonment for sodomy. Soon it would be regarded as expedient to dispense with the sinner altogether. The 1189 statute insisted that someone apprehended in "manifest contagion of the flesh" be expelled from a particular priory; a ruling of 1221 ordained that anyone convicted of the sodomitical vice (*sodomiticum vitium*) should be expelled from the order, never to be readmitted. Monastic authorities found it difficult to stick to this resolve, however. Three years later an addendum was added, allowing someone convicted of sodomy, but on the verge of death, to be admitted to the infirmary of the poor, but expelled in the event that he recovered.[43] In 1229, the "unspeakable vice" was listed as one of the egregious crimes that merited imprisonment, with no mention of expulsion.[44]

This indecision continued throughout the thirteenth century. In 1242 the general chapter reiterated that those apprehended in the unspeakable vice be incarcerated, adding, "with every opportunity removed [*omni occasione remota*]." The chapter also attempted to put pressure on the noncompliant abbot or prior by barring him from approaching the altar until he brought the sodomite to justice.[45] Furthermore, the general chapter of 1267 lessened the evidentiary requirements for an indictment of sodomy. Although three trustworthy witnesses were still mandatory, each of them could have been the sole person to witness a particular occurrence of the offense. Those found guilty "by filthy and notable signs of the vice" were to be bound in chains and segregated from the others. They were no longer allowed to wear the habit, nor were they permitted to shave. The reference to "filthy and notable signs" suggests that circumstantial evidence was deemed acceptable.[46] But, predictably, the problem did not go away. Six years later "a great and indecent clamor about that worst and most unspeakable vice assailed the ears of the general chapter many times." This crisis initiated a return to the discipline of 1220: it was determined that anyone convicted of sodomy be cast out of the order, with his name recorded by the prior to ensure that his offense never be forgotten.[47]

As the danger of same-sex relations became more explicit, the illicit introduction of minors was presented in increasingly ominous terms. In 1201 the noncompliance of a number of houses on the matter of age was cited as giving rise to "the gravest scandals." As a result, a monastic superior who knowingly accepted underage novices suffered irreversible deposition.[48] The following year, however, the general chapter mitigated this harsh decree. It was now ordained that any prior or subprior responsible for admitting an underage novice should be moved to another house, never to return.[49] Either way, the original edict and the more forgiving version would both have the effect of separating the prior or subprior from whatever underage novice he illicitly admitted, suggesting that the transgression was linked to an objectionable partiality on the part of the monastic official.[50]

Clearly such measures proved insufficient. A ruling of 1231 made it clear that the admission of an underage monk would no longer be tolerated as a fait accompli and that the original rule of expulsion must be enforced. First, however, it must be ascertained that the expulsion of such an individual would serve the "utility and honor of the order." Before leaving, the child must be subjected to a kind of testing that is compared with the "proving of spirits—if they are of God" (1 John 4:1).[51] In other words, an approximation of the process for distinguishing divine from diabolical inspiration must be applied to the boy himself. In a scandal-averse religious climate, such measures made sense: a child who was ejected from the monastery could be a dangerous variable. Cistercians were forbidden to reveal the sins of their confreres to the outside world or to commit them to writing, and those who disobeyed this interdict were deemed infamous.[52] But the child monk who has been expelled from the monastery could no longer be compelled to remain silent. The boy might well reveal the vices of his brethren, thereby aligning himself with the false prophets and their diabolical master. Clearly if the child seemed predisposed to defame the order once expelled, he must be stopped. How this might be achieved is a question that is not addressed. But it is possible that the powers that be would judge that allowing him to remain in the order, perhaps at another house, would be the safest route—in this way serving the "utility and honor of the order."

Even if the Cistercian age requirement had been universally observed, however, the monastic precincts continued to accommodate children. One canon,
which forbids that children be raised in the cloister, nevertheless stipulates that
the children hired in the monastic workshop as weavers or tanners should be at
least twelve.[53] There were also an unspecified number of boys (*pueri*) who trav-
eled with an abbot's entourage, entering into the discussions of the general
chapter by virtue of the disruption they created. In 1241, four such boys, attending their respective abbots at the general chapter, were dismissed for beating up
a conversus.[54] The general chapter of 1251 found their singing and raucous
behavior so annoying that they considered appealing to the secular arm.[55] Nevertheless, there were also monks who clearly doted on these boys. There was a
prohibition against dressing children elaborately (*curiose*) by outfitting them
with stitched sleeves, gauntlets, or little sharp knives.[56] Abbots attending the
general chapter were enjoined not to overpay their boy attendants.[57] And any of
the monastic brethren who attempted to join the boys for a meal were promptly
punished.[58]

Monastic Discipline: The Case of Cluny

In the mid-eleventh century, children between the ages of three and fourteen
would have constituted about a fifth of the entire population in a Cluniac community.[59] Around the same time that the new orders were emerging, however,
Cluny was likewise attempting to introduce strictures regarding age.[60] Abbot
Peter the Venerable issued a set of statutes that are unique for providing the
rationale behind each one. When Peter raised the bar for investing a monk to
the age of twenty, he volunteered the following motive: "The reason behind this
institute was the ill-considered and excessively hasty way of accepting children
who, before they have anything of rational intelligence, are dressed in the garb
of sacred religion, and mixed with others. Everyone is disturbed by their inept
childishness; and as I am quiet about certain things, I sum up many things
briefly; and they [the children] advance practically nothing [by early profession]
in themselves, and impede the religious dedication of others not a little, and
indeed sometimes excessively."[61] Admittedly, this statute mostly addresses the
disruptive presence of children. Despite their elaborate liturgy, Cluny placed a
high premium on silence, even elaborating an intricate sign language for its
maintenance.[62] The presence of both children and adolescents was bound to
subvert that kind of discipline. Yet Peter's resolve to be "quiet about certain
things" also suggests that boys were a source of sexual scandal, and this is corroborated elsewhere. For instance, Peter introduced "two mature and serious brothers" to police the dormitory at night.[63] In another statute, Peter stipulates that

in the event that a prior is moved from one priory to another, he is not allowed to take any personal servants. The reason he gives is that such a move engenders "sinister suspicion of certain things that ought not to be spoken, or rather not just a suspicion, but a proven certainty."[64] A later statute issued by Abbot Hugh V (1205/6), went even further, barring the abbot from having a personal servant.[65]

But most of Peter the Venerable's reform initiative failed, including his efforts to raise the age of monastic profession.[66] Child oblation continued at Cluny until the end of the thirteenth century.[67] The record abounds in references to monks too young for ordination to the priesthood, even though the bar was now lowered to the minimum age of twenty.[68] In addition to ubiquitous references to "youths," there are many references to "boys" (*pueri*), one reference to a boy monk (*puer monacus*; could this suggest that the child in question had taken his life vows?),[69] and even mentions of "little boys" (*pueri parvi*).[70]

As with the Cistercians, the sin not fit to be named was, indeed, not named in early Cluniac customaries or statutes. Such discretion was by no means universal in other Cluniac-authored media, however. Bernard of Cluny (not to be confused with the author of the eleventh-century customary) was the author of the incendiary work *On Contempt for the World* (ca. 1140), which maintained that "the flame and the ardor of Sodom are wickedly common. No one conceals or represses this wickedness. . . . Also, the filth of Sodom is openly seen, countless Ganymedes are swarming . . . Oh shame! castles and towns are full of this filthy plague, indeed sacristies are no less full."[71] Not only was Bernard a monk at Cluny during Peter the Venerable's abbacy, but the poem in question was dedicated to the abbot.

There is no denying that Bernard's poem is a heated and extended rant, with a message as apocalyptic as it was apoplectic. And yet, we have already seen that some two centuries earlier, at a time when Cluny was still in its reforming vigor, Odo, the second abbot of Cluny, had decried the abuse of oblates by their elders.[72] It was not until 1292, however, that the general chapter saw fit to address the question directly in the context of a list of reasons for excommunication. The statute in question indicted "whoever imposes the sin against nature through malice on his brother."[73] Again in 1301, under Abbot Bertrand I, the same sanction was issued as an official statute: "[We excommunicate] all those who would inflict the vice against nature on his brother through malice, and we understand malice by the fact that he does not wish to follow what he [the abuser] inflicted or by the fact that he [the accuser] failed in proving [the abuse]."[74] As with penitentials and Carolingian commentators alike, this statute recognizes that rape was an ongoing problem in monastic culture. But the statute differs from these earlier sources by punishing the perpetrator versus the victim. This could signify a change in sensibility—one that the modern world would regard as progressive. But it should be remembered that the victim envisaged in these earlier sources was a child who, according to Benedictine lights, was best taught by flogging. The underlying assumption seems to be that the child either provoked or enjoyed the assault, or perhaps both. Despite the fact that Cluny was by no means a child-free zone, officials broke with monastic tradition by making efforts to redress the wrongs visited upon a victim of rape. So it may be that Bertrand was imagining an older victim, which could account for the more sympathetic view.

Yet even though rape is singled out in the above statute, the burden of proof rested upon the victim, who ran the risk of incurring penalties for an unsuccessful case, and the presumed slander behind the unsuccessful suit demonstrated a "malice" that is assimilated with rape. In keeping with canon law, legal proof required two or three witnesses in good standing, which made the successful prosecution of sexual offenses extremely difficult. This doubtless would have deterred many would-be accusers. The statute was clearly issued in order to prevent the crime rather than to solicit a denunciation after it was committed. In fact, one manuscript in which this statute appears includes a round condemnation of those who resort to "writings and rolls and schedules and public instruments," thereby handing over documents full of infamy and denigration to their legal advisers and fautors.[75]

The statute's emphasis on rape does not mean that consensual relations were in any way condoned. In fact, Abbot Bertrand specified that "the vice against nature . . . comprehends every libidinous touch of the two males" and, parallel with the discipline of the secular clergy, was considered sufficiently serious to be included among the reserved sins that only the abbot of Cluny could absolve.[76] Indeed, the above statute intonates that the very gravity of a sodomy charge rendered it a lethal weapon for monks to deploy against one another.

Evidence for actual instances of sodomy emerges from the visitations to Cluniac priories that begin to be undertaken in the thirteenth century. Prior to this, the abbot of Cluny had convoked meetings of the general chapter, which was an assembly of all Cluniac priors at the motherhouse, to discuss matters of common concern.[77] In 1231, however, Gregory IX mandated a reorganization of Cluny's general chapter based on the Cistercian model.[78] The refurbished chapter, which met annually, would become the order's chief deliberative body, to which even the abbot was answerable. Every year, the chapter would appoint visitors, two of which were assigned to each of the ten Cluniac provinces. These visitors would make the rounds to each of the priories in a given province, assessing their spiritual and corporeal condition, and report back to the general chapter.[79] The record of these visitations would be handed over to the *diffinatores*, who were essentially judges determining the appropriate recommendations for a community, as well as the penalties for individual offenders.[80]

Despite the constraints that were theoretically imposed by the cloister, the vast majority of sexual offenses reported to the visitors involved women.[81] Nor did such relations, however scandalous, seem particularly unusual. In 1279, for example, a certain Brother Peter was said to keep a woman in town;[82] another monk, also named Peter, was believed to have had a child with a woman in town;[83] and a subprior, who supposedly fathered a child, went ahead and married the mother.[84] In 1291, a prior was said to have married a young girl and then proceeded to build her a house with the order's money.[85] In 1385, another prior was accused of keeping a woman of ill fame in the monastery.[86] In 1326, Brother Robert allegedly not only fathered a child with a prostitute, but was said to amuse himself further by hanging out in taverns, eating meat, and singing songs that denigrated the order.[87] In 1386, one prior was defamed with a woman named Ambrosia: the couple apparently had several children, whom the prior hoped to make monks.[88] In 1374, a number of priors, administrators, and monks throughout the French countryside were charged with engaging in "a dangerous mixing of the sexes," keeping suspect women in their houses, and, hence, "giving rise to scandal and infamy."[89] In 1367, a husband in Namur complained to the visitors about a monkish Lothario's relationship with his wife.[90]

Many sexual infractions concerning women were steeped in violence, fomenting even greater scandal. In 1280, a Lombard prior, with the reputation of being corrupt and nepotistic in the traditional sense of the word, allegedly went around town dressed like a soldier. He gave rise to "great, or rather the greatest scandal," when he attempted to rape a certain *conversa*.[91] In 1310, a French monk, who had raped a woman and wounded her father, remained at large with a band of armed malefactors.[92] Still more heinous was the 1316 case of a French monk who abducted a married woman who was pregnant. He raped her multiple times, on Easter night no less, and she aborted four days later. The local Franciscans fanned the flame of scandal by preaching sermons against him.[93]

This is just a small window into the scandal and mayhem that could arise when monks engaged in sexual relations with women. By comparison, the number of cases in which a monk is charged with sodomy is low, even remarkably so. The low count may, to some extent, be predicated on the traditional aversion to naming sodomy explicitly. The records seem to eschew even circumlocutions like "the sin against nature" or "that sin not fit to be named," probably masking same-sex offenses by the word *incontinentia*—a conveniently vague term also applied to offenses with women.[94] Sometimes the degree of punishment could perhaps indicate a same-sex component. For instance, certain monks who were defamed of incontinence received the routine punishment stipulated in the rule (*regulariter puniatur*).[95] But as a reserved sin, sodomy required a visit to the motherhouse. Hence in 1274, when two French monks from the same house were cited for unspecified incontinence and summoned to Cluny, this could signal the presence of a same-sex component.[96] The absence of any specific charge is also sometimes suggestive. Take, for instance, the cases of "Brother Peter of Montleyry, who scandalized the order in many ways, just as it was said by his prior in chapter, [who] went to Cluny to be punished at the judgment of his order"; or the incorrigible fugitive Brother Theobald, who "generated many scandals . . . for the order," and was supposed to be captured and sent to Cluny.[97]

Flamboyant but vague adjectives may also furnish clues. For instance, a French monk was summoned to the general chapter for his "misdeeds, offenses, and enormities";[98] a fugitive from Germany was defamed for "the most ignominious sin and infinite other crimes";[99] an inquisition against a French prior was inconclusive, "except [in demonstrating] that he was gravely defamed of incontinence."[100] The *diffinatores* also ordained that certain young monks from Gascony be separated and sent to other priories as soon as possible "on account of fault and excesses."[101] These cases are so riddled by circumlocution that the nature of the offenses are occluded—probably purposefully so.

Out of the years that I have examined, which span from 1259 to 1408, I found only four cases in which a monk was openly accused of sodomy, and in three of these the reportage is terse and nebulous. For instance, we are only introduced to the 1313 case of Brother Ralph, a monk from Crespin in the Tarn region of France, when it is already in its final stages before the *diffinatores*. Brother Ralph had already been summoned to Cluny and accused of "that ignominious vice *for which the wrath of God came down upon the sons of disobedience*," echoing the biblical censures of sodomy cited at Lateran III and Lateran IV. An inquest had already been undertaken and a list of articles drawn up concerning his alleged guilt. When asked to respond to the articles, Ralph denied the charges in their entirety, denouncing the witnesses who had testified against him, and then proceeded to purge himself canonically. Ralph seems to have had superior connections compared to his accusers. He managed to procure "better witnesses, in number and in dignity," who attested to his good fame and claimed that "the initial infamy arose from malicious and determined actors hating him and [their] deception." Ralph was declared innocent, and his good name restored.[102]

We have no other details about Ralph's situation. Yet whether or not he was guilty, his case demonstrates how a spurious charge of sodomy could be used to destroy a monk's reputation. This should be borne in mind with respect to the second case, which turns on a set of accusations brought against the Lombard prior of Vertemate by his disgruntled subordinates in 1280. The visitors' report suggested a high degree of dysfunctionality at the monastery. The Divine Office was no longer performed; nor were the customary distribution of alms and other acts of charity maintained. The monks alleged that this was the fault of the present prior, Durant. In the halcyon days before the prior's arrival, they complained, everything was done properly; now nothing was. Neither the abbot nor his brother William bothered to maintain the traditional fasts. Their failure to perform the Divine Office was "because their Divine Office was to eat, drink, and give themselves over to lust."[103]

Prior Durant's sexual tastes were allegedly eclectic. There were two priests who witnessed first Lord Bernard and later Lord Agardus (who are not mentioned again in the report) in the prior's bed "doing together what is not permitted to say." The other charges point to a different kind of dissolution: the prior had not lived in the priory for some time, but dwelt far away in the home of laypeople, where he ate with women. As a result, "he brought scandal and expense to himself and to the whole Order of Cluny he brought scandal and expense." The prior also manifested simoniacal tendencies, admitting two new monks to the priory for money. Both were supposedly unqualified: one was over forty (the implication being that he was in his dotage), and the other was a Humiliati, ignorant of both letters and chant. In addition, the prior squandered the monastery's resources and involved himself in shady business deals. It was either the prior or his brother who had stolen a series of articles from the monastery: books, wine, hay, pigs, "all destined for his female lover [*amica*] who lived in the village of Covernus, where the prior likewise lived." A prior from another house alleged that he saw the prior and his brother with a pretty woman in the prior's room, where they were shut up for a long time.[104] Yet Brother Oldratus also claimed to have seen the prior with a male servant "standing in his chamber just as if he were with some woman." To top things off, the prior and his brother were violent brawlers: they attacked Brother Nicholinus with a sword, even though they were in sacred orders. The victim was left all bloodied, with his clothing lacerated.[105]

How much of this testimony can be taken at face value? Eight years earlier, the visitors had, indeed, declared that the prior of Vertemate was both incontinent and a poor administrator, and recommended that he be moved elsewhere. Two years later, the priory of Vertemate was described as impoverished and in debt, while the prior was allegedly responsible for removing a certain anchoress from her cell.[106] Since the prior was not named, it is impossible to know for certain if this was, in fact, Durant. Chances are, it was. Either way, at the time of the visitation of 1280, the prior clearly had plenty to hide. He attempted to stop the visitation, and, when that failed, he ordered the monks not to cooperate. The visitors nevertheless proceeded, insisting that the prior sit in chapter with the rest of the monks under pain of excommunication. Paying no heed, Durant left.

The prior's culpable behavior was indisputable. And yet there was something suspicious about the united invective of the community. At the outset, the visitors had listed the monks who testified: Peter, Roland Paxentius, Oldratus, John, and Nicholinus—"all monks of the said house." The only monk present who was actually eyewitness to the prior's most spectacular depravities, however, was Brother Nicholinus, the victim of assault. It is significant that neither of the prior's purported lovers (Bernard and Agardus) was present. Nor were the two anonymous priests who had seen them in the prior's bed. The prior of Olzate, who allegedly witnessed the prior and his brother enclosed with a pretty woman, was not present to repeat his testimony. Durant's brother William likewise seems to have been absent as, in all probability, were the newly professed monks who had entered the order through simony—the members of the community most likely to vouch for the prior. There were also some strange discrepancies in the various testimonies. The activities witnessed in the prior's bedroom seem at odds with the charge that he was living far from the monastery and, as we later learn, in the village of Covernus, where his *amica* (the erstwhile anchoress?) lived. It seems likely that the prior's *amica* was his concubine.

The squandering of the monastery's resources and the articles stolen by the prior and his brother take up about two-thirds of the testimony, which suggests that the real source of grievance was financial: the prior mismanaged the priory and stole in order to support his concubine. Even so, Durant seemingly retained his position despite what appears to have been years of mismanagement, embezzlement, and concubinage. Clearly the monks were desperate to get rid of him, hoping that the charge of same-sex relations would succeed where his other vices had failed to get a meaningful reaction from the authorities. But the visitors had their doubts about this univocal testimony, and this was apparent in their closing remarks: "All the monks on this matter, nevertheless, said all those things. But I did not inquire about their reputations [*de statu personarum*], since I would not have been able to know the truth from them, nor did the prior wish to say anything about the aforesaid things."[107] Clearly the visitors' report did not have much of an impact. The following year, the visitors observed that the monastery was in shambles and that the prior no longer resided there.[108] In 1286, the visitors note that the *diffinatores* had recommended the prior's removal, yet he was still there.[109]

The case against the Lombard monk Benedict was much more definitive. In 1299 he confessed to being an incontinent thief and brigand. Benedict further admitted both to leaving the monastery at night for the express purpose of sinning and to restraining a certain woman in the monastery for three days. He also committed the sin of sodomy ("nec non peccatum sodomicum commiserit"). Although the admission of sodomy is clear enough, the context renders it uncertain as to whether the act involved another male or a female. The *diffinatores* determined that Benedict be taken to Cluny under the custody of his prior and imprisoned for life. The gravity of his punishment, echoing what was mandated in Lateran III, could point to same-sex sodomy, since the same acts with a woman were generally regarded as less heinous.[110] Given Benedict's multiple offenses, it is impossible to say.[111] One thing is certain, however: Benedict's sodomy would never have come to light had he not so thoroughly scandalized the surrounding countryside.

But it is only with the fourth instance, the most detailed of them all, that we can say with any degree of assurance that it was same-sex relations that were at issue. The case occurred in 1303 at the Swiss priory of St.-Victor, a community that, like the priory of Vertemate, had suffered a series of external reversals. The monastery had been in debt for years.[112] Some of its possessions had been wrongly relinquished to a local knight, and the sacristan was at a loss for how to remedy the situation. To make matters worse, the son of the knight, who happened to be a monk at a neighboring abbey, kept attacking the prior and his community, seizing men and property on the flimsy pretext that this aggression was in some way justified by virtue of a letter from St.-Victor's former prior. Their troubles were further compounded by their flamboyant subprior, Brother Jordan, who was defamed for practicing "the vice against nature." Apparently, Jordan did nothing to conceal his sexual proclivities. He would repeatedly kiss two brothers in particular, both inside and outside church, "holding their vile parts and [doing] other unchaste things." Nor was this behavior limited to the priory; it was also enacted in the city of Geneva, where he was defamed "among good and serious men" of the said vice.

The community at large complained that Jordan would end his public displays of affection with the boisterous (not to mention ominous) comment that he and his companions should exercise "that vice" on the other monks—one at a time, over and over. He reassured his acolytes that it was a greater sin to know women than men, adding the practical consideration that two males who sinned together could always absolve one another. For an entire winter Jordan kept his confreres awake, forcing them to participate in a sing-along of secular tunes. As a result, the monks were so sleep deprived that they didn't dare to sing *Salve Regina* in a loud voice (*in alta voce*) at Compline, lest their ineptitude create a scandal. Sometimes the other monks were so tired that they did not wake up for Matins and had to celebrate it at dawn. When not keeping them awake with singing, Jordan found other ways to annoy the community: by night, he was wont to uncover his sleeping confreres, stroking their legs and backs.[113]

Before the monks had even finished their testimony, Jordan had fled the monastery, ignoring his prior's insistence that he stay. But Jordan's hasty departure was doubtless motivated by the fact that he recognized one of the visitors. After Jordan's flight, Brother P. de Brussinez revealed that he had already encountered him on an earlier visitation. De Brussinez was therefore asked if he could shed any light on the present situation:

> [He] responded that in his visitation to Germany a good three years ago, he found him [Brother Jordan] in a priory called Thierenbach where he dwelt with the prior, and that Brother Jordan ensnared a certain youth [*juvenis*] with many words and made him sleep with him in his bed totally *nude*, saying to the youth that if he acquiesced to his words and deeds, he would give him a good gown and certain other things. The youth responded by asking what he wished to do to him. The aforesaid Jordan said that he wished to know him carnally in two ways and began *kissing* and embracing him. The youth fled, almost naked, and reported those things to the prior and the household. In fact, the visitor said to the prior that he should send Jordan to the next general chapter, but he did not come to the chapter.

The words "nude" and "kissing" are underlined by the scribe.[114]

The case is exceptional—if only for the fact that not only is Jordan's offense named, but his behavior is described in such detail. Even so, some predictable patterns further illuminate why, in all probability, most cases of monastic sodomy never come to light, as well as why this one did. After the incident in Thierenbach, Jordan ignored the summons to Cluny that he had incurred for the reserved sin of sodomy. Instead, he simply moved. Although Jordan may have made the move on his own initiative, it was a familiar clerical strategy. Henry of Ghent had advised the superior who discovered through sacramental confession that one of his subordinates was a corrupt pastor that the culprit should be moved. It was also a common solution among the Cluniacs. Hugh V had mandated that "if anyone were to be plagued by scandal in one place, he should be transferred to another place and a more reputable person be substituted in his place."[115] This line of action was especially germane in instances of incontinence with women since it separated the monk from the female source of sin. In Jordan's case, his illicit move from Basel to Geneva put about 150 miles between himself and the scene of the crime, and the two priories were also in two different Cluniac provinces.

And this is how Brother Jordan evaded almost certain incarceration at Cluny. In all probability, Brother Jordan did not act alone, but was helped by his former prior. Thierenbach was a two-person priory.[116] This was not unusual: many Cluniac communities contained just a prior and one other monk.[117] The prior of Thierenbach was alone when Jordan first arrived: it would be natural for him to rejoice at the prospect of a companion, even as it would be natural for the two men to come to rely on one another. Because of the scandal Jordan had occasioned, the prior was forced to testify against him. Even so, he may well have shrunk from the prospect of Jordan's imprisonment. Perhaps the prior rationalized that Jordan's case was not much different from other cases of "incontinence" he was familiar with. Or perhaps Jordan's case even seemed less egregious: after all, Jordan did not get very far in his attempted seduction of the youth. Let us suppose that the prior did wish to help Jordan escape: the obvious route would be to move him. Even so, an authorized move would be difficult to effect. Jordan could not just have walked into another priory and claim a place as a Cluniac monk without some kind of recommendation. A Cluniac monk was not even authorized to travel without a letter from his prior.[118] It is possible that the prior wrote a letter introducing Jordan to the prior of St.-Victor's and asking that he be received as a monk in that house. Or maybe Jordan took it upon himself to borrow the prior's seal and forge the requisite letter.[119] Either way, any request for another house to receive Jordan would have been against the rules. The statutes forbade any house to accept a monk from another priory whose "excesses merited expulsion."[120] But even if Jordan's offenses had not been so serious, there was other legislation that would invalidate such a move. A statute of 1200 chastised priors for sending difficult monks to different houses just to get rid of them. In 1277, moreover, such moves were forbidden without the permission of the abbot of Cluny or one of his representatives, and any house to which a monk was illicitly sent should not receive him.[121]

But the situation of Jordan is living proof that the statutes were not always followed. Besides, Jordan had qualities that may well have recommended him to the monastery on the receiving end. First and foremost was his flair for music: it seems very likely that someone who was so intent on keeping his brethren awake with secular ditties was fond of singing and probably also had a good voice. Cluny was famous for its liturgy, which could occupy as much as eight hours of the monk's day.[122] Masses, particularly Masses for the dead, had traditionally been an important source of revenue for Cluny.[123] Furthermore, Jordan's glib remark that sacerdotal lovers had the advantage of being able to absolve one another suggests that he was already ordained to the priesthood, which would increase his value to the community. The visitors commonly recommended that monks who had reached the required age be ordained so that they could begin to bear their expected sacerdotal burden. When there was an insufficient number of priests at a given priory, moreover, the visitors would routinely recommend that monks who had yet to be ordained be exchanged for priests from another priory.[124] The priory of St.-Victor's probably could have used the sacerdotal support. Only six of St.-Victor's twelve monks were priests. If there were only five priests when Jordan arrived, he might have been very welcome. And Jordan clearly had the ability to ingratiate himself. In three years he had risen from being a mere newcomer with a flair for music to the position of subprior.

But familiarity breeds contempt. If Jordan had at one time seemed like a godsend, his flagrant behavior, though perhaps conducive to the amorous musical circles of twelfth-century Orléans or to the polyphonic masterminds of Paris, was out of step with a thirteenth-century Cluniac priory in Geneva. Although Jordan's evening pranks may have been titillating at first, when news of his high jinks spread "among good and serious men," his fate was sealed. In this respect, Jordan's case is representative. We have seen that a charge of sodomy was occasionally used in an effort to get rid of a hated confrere. Jordan's case suggests that the charge of sodomy was only formally made and seriously pursued by monastic authorities when a situation was either known or threatened to become known to secular society. Jordan created a scandal in Germany when he attempted to seduce a secular youth, barely escaping imprisonment. St.-Victor's gave him a chance to start anew. It seems as if Jordan initially focused his libidinal interest on his confreres, suggesting that he was reaping the benefits of a larger, and tantalizingly youthful, monastic community. The fact that five of his confreres were not priests means that they were, almost certainly, under twenty. Indeed, even if Jordan's sexual partners had been ordained to the priesthood, this did not necessarily mean that they had reached the age of twenty: since the thirteenth century, there was an ever-increasing number of dispensations for candidates who were a few years shy of the theoretical benchmark.[125] But Jordan had no discretion and began to solicit males outside of the cloister. This meant that he had become a distinct liability for St.-Victor's and was ripe for denunciation at the next visitation.

Cluniac Discretion and Its Limits

Guy de Valous, a historian of Cluny, is right in noting that although the lay world clearly believed that monks were especially prone to sins against nature, there is very little evidence to sustain such a belief at Cluny. According to Valous, these registers yield ten cases at best.[126] After having examined the same records, I would have to say that this count is high—especially since in the four cases I found, three may have been trumped-up charges. At this juncture, the sparsity of evidence for clerical sodomy should come as no surprise. But Cluny also had special protections to help ensure that what happened at Cluny, stayed at Cluny. First and foremost was the foundational charter of 910, which freed Cluny from the interference of the local bishop. In contrast, unaffiliated religious foundations depended on episcopal tribunals for discipline and would, as we saw with the Pisan community determined to keep one wandering monk in his own bed, occasionally denounce their most ornery members.

But sexual relations between monks of any order abiding in the same monastery would have existed on an entirely different plane than sexual offenses that became public: an insular plane that would leave no record. It is noteworthy that Bertrand I saw fit to make a statute against sodomitical rape at the general chapter in 1301—this is in spite of the fact that the visitations, which had begun in 1259, witnessed but two instances of sodomy. It may be that in many cases of conventual intramural sex, even if one party was initially suborned, sexual relations eventually became consensual or, if not consensual, would evolve into a state of tacit subordination that would probably come to an end when the youth became a man. In the event that the relationship came to the notice of a third party, the witness was, in theory, to be guided by the benign dictates of fraternal correction. A private warning might ensue; if that proved ineffective, the prior should be informed, and so on. In theory, the prior would be required to denounce the offending monk to the visitors, who would, in turn, refer his case to Cluny. But one wonders how many priors would actually do this—especially considering the way an individual monk's behavior was perceived as reflecting on the community as a whole. Even if the offending monk had been denounced in chapter, moreover, such proceedings were considered sacrosanct, and the attendant monks were bound to silence. This kind of discretion was ingrained in monastic tradition generally. But in order to ensure its observance, Cluny's general chapter, fearful of the ensuing scandal, issued a number of statutes against revealing any secret of correction occurring in chapter to an outsider. Superiors were encouraged to apply the harshest discipline for any infractions against this rule of discretion.[127]

The general chapter also leveled heavy penalties against brethren who presumed to defame the order to laypeople.[128] Monks were prohibited from appearing before a secular court to pursue a quarrel or make a denunciation, and such a move was listed under the general chapter's summary of reasons for excommunication.[129] Later abbots became still more proactive in terms of damage control. The behavior of Cluniacs studying in Paris was carefully monitored lest it give rise to infamy and scandal.[130] When the visitor of France conducted an inquest in 1386, he found the college rife with incontinence, violence, and gambling. The visitor sent a letter to the abbot recommending that a number of students be expelled for their offenses, "even if concerning the hidden things, which are many, we remain quiet."[131] In 1393, Abbot Henry I articulated what matters should be brought before the general chapter: "the grave things . . . which cannot be sufficiently or easily corrected by [local authorities], or what things were proved or brought to public notice through rumor."[132] This degree of discretion was reflected in the behavior of the visitors, who would recommend punishment to any monk who spoke about his community's problems to outsiders, especially to laypeople.[133] Peter the Venerable had attempted to ban secular servants from the monastic precincts because of their garrulity and their possible detraction of the order.[134] Such precautions were redoubled over time. In one case, the visitors even required that a woman who was rumored to have denigrated the order be expelled from the village.[135]

Naturally, this mentality was internalized by members of individual priories. It was considered a serious offense to deceive the visitors as to the actual state of dilapidation or the extent of the debt of a given priory, but this did not deter priors from trying.[136] Durant, the crooked prior of Vertemate, ordered his community not to cooperate with the visitors. Another prior found it necessary to chain up a conversus (who by virtue of his lay status was already an outsider of sorts) in a remote tower to prevent him from talking with the visitors.[137] This degree of subterfuge was also applied to the sins of individuals, especially when it came to incontinence. There were a number of instances in which priors denied the rumors that a given monk was unchaste, only to be punished for disobedience when the truth came out.[138] In 1260, the prior of St.-Victor, the community that would later house the redoubtable Jordan, was summoned to Cluny and punished for failing to correct his subordinates, generally, but in concealing the excesses of one monk, in particular.[139] The subsequent denunciation of Jordan suggests that the community had learned its lesson.

Cluniac discretion also seems to have increased over time. It is noteworthy that the dates for the four cases in which the charge of sodomy is (relatively) unequivocal range from 1280 to 1313: a thirty-three-year window. After that, cases of incontinence fall precipitously, while there are no explicit charges of same-sex activity. Priors known for scandalously deflowering virgins or for their prolific progeny are still cited.[140] There are, however, many more "excesses" or "enormities" alluded to but not specified.[141] The self-protective instincts of individual priories could account for aspects of this pattern. But there is also a notable shift in the focus of the *diffinatores*: the later visitors seem much more concerned about the fabric of the individual priories than in the sins of their denizens, suggesting that the trials of the fourteenth century—particularly war-fare and plague—were taking their toll.[142]

The fourteenth century also saw the illicit introduction of private rooms within the dormitory—structures the *diffinatores* roundly eschewed, ordering their destruction.[143] We have no way of knowing what went on in these rooms, but illicit privacy is clearly conducive to illicit sex. This impetus toward privacy is complemented by a parallel move to secrecy among monastic authorities themselves—a phenomenon that is already apparent in the late thirteenth cen-tury. For instance, the last line in a 1293 visitation in France reads: "We heard some secret things concerning a certain monk dwelling there which ought to be revealed to the abbot alone."[144] On another occasion, some monks created a scandal by abusing their prior "shamelessly and disgracefully" (*turpiter et inhon-este*), for which visitors suggested "grave penalties and perpetual imprisonment." What they did, however, remains unspecified, muffled behind enigmatic biblical analogies.[145] Charges of incontinence also began to be pursued by private inqui-sition, the results of which were sent to the abbot of Cluny under seal.[146] In some instances, there is no indication what the offense might have been, yet the concern for the secure delivery of the sealed articles was so pronounced that one can only assume that the contents were, indeed, volatile.[147] In short, the sin that is not fit to be named probably receded into sealed accounts of inquests only fit to be read by a spiritual elite and then destroyed.

Thus far we have been focusing on sodomy as a crime that is denounced as such. But it was also a mortal sin that could only be absolved through sacramen-tal confession to a priest. Subprior Jordan had boisterously claimed that two sodomitical brothers had the advantage of absolving one another for their sin—Peter Damian's worst nightmare. In fact, theologians had by now determined that such an absolution would be invalid.[148] Furthermore, even if a Cluniac monk were to confess the sin of sodomy licitly, his confessor, however sympa-thetic, theoretically could not absolve him of a sin reserved for the abbot. The same would go for a prior presiding over a daily chapter meeting at which the sin of sodomy somehow came to light. There were heavy sanctions against any illicit person who attempted to involve himself in the reserved sin of another, and such sanctions were expanded over time. The only exception would be if the sinner was at the point of the death.[149]

A Cluniac monk, tortured by his hidden sodomitical past, had to denounce himself to the visitors in order to reach the abbot. Clearly only a very scrupulous and supremely penitent individual would contemplate this drastic solution. Yet we do find several individuals who embraced this form of spiritual self-immolation. In 1313, a German prior and one of his monks accused themselves of incontinence together (*ad invicem*). An inquisition was ordered and the results were sent to the abbot of Cluny under seal. The way the sin is described suggests that it was not an instance of same-sex intercourse, but probably mutual masturbation. This is corroborated by the fact that the *diffinatores* ordered an inquisition rather than immediately summoning them to Cluny. Presumably the inquisition would ascertain the degree of their culpability.[150] In 1263, however, an English monk from Lenton accused himself of the "worst vice" (*de vicio pessimo*) and was ultimately imprisoned for life.[151] The *diffinatio* refrains from naming the sin, yet the severity of punishment suggests sodomy. By denouncing themselves to the visitors, these penitent monks were using the visitation as an extension of the confessional. The visit to Cluny could mean years of penance and prison, but it would also mean absolution and peace.

*   *   *

The great age of oblation ended in the eleventh century. Thereafter, monastic authorities were progressively hostile to the presence of underaged monks, and yet they continued to be an issue at both Cistercian and Cluniac foundations. A number of sources suggest that the presence of boys was not just a distraction, but a dangerous sexual distraction for the older brethren. In addition to the insinuations of monastic constitutions, there were also writers like Walter Map who made salty dinnertime conversation about sodomitical monks. Nevertheless, explicit condemnations of sodomy were slow to appear in monastic statutes. In the Cistercian order, the first ordinance condemning sodomy appeared in 1221—more than a century after the order's alleged founding. Although the Cluniac order was founded in 910, the first ordinance against sodomy was issued in 1292. It specifically (and exclusively) addressed the question of sodomitical rape and would be reissued nine years later. Both orders exacted the maximum penalty for sodomy.

The latter-day appearance of such ordinances bespeaks reluctance. One assumes that this legislation was driven by something, yet actual cases involving sodomy are few and far between. This discrepancy might prompt some scholars to conclude that monasteries had no particular problem with sodomy and that any claims to the contrary represent more smoke than fire. But in a monastic culture, where innuendo and subterfuge were embraced as strategies essential to an order's survival, the flip side of the adage seems more appropriate: that where there is smoke, there is also fire.

CHAPTER 7

The Choir

Music and musical instruments ought to be greatly feared. For
they soften and break the hearts of men.
— William Peraldus, *Summa aurea*

Even if Peter the Venerable had succeeded in raising the age of entrance for a
Cluniac monk to twenty, it would hardly have rendered Cluny a child-free zone.
Peter himself waived the age requirement for choirboys, whom he referred to as
"little scholars" (*parvi scholares*).[1] Under Abbot Bertrand I, the number of boys,
which had been limited to six since the twelfth century, was raised to twelve in
the early fourteenth century, with six masters to supervise them. The statute
itself is couched in acerbic apology, making it clear that this innovation is "for
the worship and praise of God, and that the true fervor of religion and devotion
be extolled in the church of Cluny, and not for dissipation, vices and other
inconvenient things to be entirely avoided and totally amputated."[2]

Cluny is not unique in its liturgical dependence on children. References to
boy choirs reach back to Merovingian times.[3] In traditional Benedictine communities, liturgical training became a key component in the education of a
monk. Over the course of the eleventh century, when oblation was at its peak,
child oblates gained a progressively more prominent role in the monastic liturgy.[4] As with other aspects of monastic training, corporal punishment loomed
large. The Benedictine Rule says expressly that children should be whipped for
mistakes in chanting.[5] Hence in Bernard of Cluny's customary, boys who made
mistakes—whether by incorrectly chanting the psalms, falling asleep, or being
distracted—were punished accordingly. With frock and cowl removed, they
would be beaten with sticks that were prepared ahead of time either by the prior
or the special master assigned to oversee liturgical performance. Such punishment was to be administered immediately, as soon as a given office was over,

unless there happened to be laypersons present.[6] With the decline of oblation in the twelfth century, the number of choristers necessarily dropped significantly.[7]

This chapter focuses on the boys' choirs that developed at most major churches and cathedrals in the high and later Middle Ages. That the chorister might be an object of sexual desire for members of the clergy is not surprising in view of his relative accessibility, his youth, and the sensual temptation afforded by his voice. The boy's high vocal range could only contribute to the ongoing eroticization and feminization of young boys apparent in monastic culture. Hence, in the ninth-century monastic church of Corvey, the dangerous allure of the choristers is alluded to in a fresco that represents Ulysses being tempted by the sirens, strategically positioned just above where the boys sang.[8] Sometimes the criteria for selecting choristers may have contributed to their appeal. The statutes of Norwich Cathedral required that the boys be "of elegant stature."[9] The desire for attractive choristers may have been a tacit criterion in many, if not most, choirs. Since children were often called upon to represent angels in liturgy and liturgical drama, it would be appropriate for them to be pleasing to the eye.[10] But choristers were also assigned female parts that accented their vulnerability. Carissa Harris's analysis of the sixteenth-century Ritson manuscript, a collection of songs produced for choristers at Exeter, suggests that the boys were routinely assigned the roles of female victims of rape—a convention that Marjorie Woods has demonstrated also pertains to the instruction of grammar.[11]

The chorister's tractability was secured by the corporal punishment that went part and parcel with musical training.[12] The boys were taught plainchant through the Guidonian scale: a mnemonic system in which different parts of the hand were assigned different syllables, which, in turn, signified different notes. Theoretically, the choirmaster could point to a part of his hand and elicit the desired results from his singers.[13] But this method still required attention and a good memory. At Wells, a student who fails to apply himself is first warned kindly; the second time, sharply; but thereafter, "if necessity arises, [ought] to be flogged—as Solomon says: *Stupidity is rooted in the heart of the boy and the rod of discipline puts it to flight.*"[14] The fourteenth-century Middle English poem "The Chorister's Lament" features two reluctant choristers who acknowledge their complete incompetence with regard to the Guidonian scale, a problem compounded by an inability to sing on key. The master responds by alternately abusing them verbally and boxing their ears.[15] In the "Lamentation of Boys Learning Prick-Song" (i.e., written music), a woeful chorister claims: "Out of our buttokes we may plucke the stumpes thus long!"[16]

And yet, the position of chorister was a coveted one. Although sometimes chosen from elite and well-connected families,[17] in many cases it was customary to recruit children from indigent families, so choristers were frequently referred to as "poor boys."[18] In addition to room and board, they also received a rudimentary education. Sometimes the choir was a stepping-stone to church office: a famous example is Liudprand of Cremona (d. 972), who was said to owe his preferment to the beauty of his voice. And, indeed, many retired choristers received jobs as vicars or chaplains in chantries.[19] Even so, the chorister's life was probably fraught with anxiety about the future. For while subjected to many of the same constraints as the monastic oblate, the chorister nevertheless had none of the oblate's security. When a boy's voice changed, his position disappeared and he would be required to leave the relatively sheltered community in which he had lived for much, if not most, of his life.[20]

Gerson and the Corruptible Chorister

While in monastic discourse the sexual allure of the prepubescent boy was a constant undercurrent, when it came to secular choristers, this problem was rarely addressed directly. There is, however, a preoccupation with the child as vulnerable, easily scandalized, and eminently corruptible—an attitude exemplified in the writings of Jean Gerson that would eventually be reflected in the rule that he wrote for the choristers of Notre Dame. Gerson's biases already announce themselves some seven years earlier in the title of his short treatise—*A Protest Against the Corruption of Youth* (ca. 1402). This work constitutes an impassioned appeal first to secular and ecclesiastical authorities but ultimately to God, who is called upon in his cleansing wrath to ensure that children are protected from early corruption by the negligent or louche behavior of adults. His argument follows the contours of Jeremiah's pronouncement that someone who has been taught evil can no more turn away from this course than can an Ethiopian change the color of his skin or a leopard his spots (Jer. 13:23). Even as a new mirror can be stained by a corrosive influence, soft wax ruined, or a young shoot twisted and deformed, so it is with a boy, who is soft and tender, and easily bent toward vice. Every day his body and soul are afflicted by filthy and disgusting images of outer things. The greater the exposure, the greater the impression these images leave upon his imagination.[21] Very soon, the boy becomes irrevocably altered. Gerson anticipates that, even when the boy has become an old man, these unhealthy images would continue to afflict his soul—however much he may consciously struggle to reject them. Following in Christ's stead, Gerson calls down woe upon anyone who would infect, and hence scandalize, one of these little ones. But a thousand times woe should be visited on any authority figure, whether parent or superior, who corrupts a child through some casual joke or impious comment. For, as Juvenal says, it is the domestic, day-to-day realm that has the most potential for corruption and where quotidian incidents make the greatest impression on the soul. Even Alexander, conqueror of the entire world, could not avoid the vices of Leonidas, his teacher, who infected Alexander as a little boy.[22]

Gerson takes particular umbrage at the "shameful and nude images, which venal things are exposed in shrines on holy days" and result in the "most filthy corruptions among little boys and adolescents."[23] He may be referring to the (arguably) ribald brooches and medallions of graphic body parts that proliferated in this period. A popular motif was the depiction of penises and/or vaginas on pilgrimage—delineated as standing upright, entirely autonomous, with staff and scrip. Such artifacts were apparently sold at churches and shrines alongside genuine devotional objects—possibly with an apotropaic function, though it is equally likely that their aim was to satirize genuine devotional objects.[24] Gerson maintains that adults who expose children and adolescents to such images—be they impious mothers, deceitful maids, or abandoned snickering fathers (with their dirty songs, obscene gestures, and disgraceful habits)—may as well be sacrificing them to the idol Beelphegor (Baal). These shameless adults persist in this behavior even in sacred places or on holy days, in addition to "many other abominable habits—things which are filthy to think about, let alone write about." Such individuals surpass the vice-ridden denizens of Sodom and Gomorrah in degree of corruption.[25]

Some four years later, Gerson took the opportunity to expand on the dangers of the easily perverted child in the treatise *On Drawing Little Children to Christ*.[26] From Gerson's perspective, annual confession during Easter week, mandated by Lateran IV, was insufficient to get to the "bottom of all things" since the priest was bound to be too rushed for proper interrogation. And such in-depth questioning was necessary. "Indeed in childhood, how many children, seduced by diabolical madness, either do or suffer many enormities and abominable things, the kind of things they do not recognize or dare to speak of unless forewarned and interrogated."[27] Young penitents require a special finesse. Gerson claims that three-year-old penitents admitted to him that they had never confessed their sins before because of the insensitive approach of the confessor.[28] In contrast, Gerson insists that the confessor win the child's trust through good humor, judicious praise, and a loving fraternal manner.[29]

The tone of this treatise is defensive: Gerson recognizes that most people do not think confession necessary for toddlers. Such gainsayers tend to perceive childhood as a time of innocence, while Gerson clearly does not. When arguing the case for puerile confession to a lay audience, Gerson adduces an example from Gregory the Great's *Dialogues* in which a carelessly brought up five-year-old is suddenly taken ill and sees devils coming for his soul upon his deathbed. He utters a blasphemous epithet and dies. Gerson also notes, somewhat wryly, that none of the children from Sodom were spared.[30] Hewing close to the unyielding Augustinian position, Gerson maintains that all children are imbued with original sin, even a one-day-old infant.[31] Elsewhere, Gerson notes that confessors need not fret about putting ideas into a child's head since, due to the "corruption of nature," boys of three or four were already inclined to masturbate, initially not recognizing it as a sin. Even when too young to ejaculate, the child can lose the virginity of his soul—perhaps even more completely than in the case of a youth visiting a prostitute. But as the pleasure increases with age, the habit becomes ingrained and can even lead to sodomy. For this reason, children must be constantly warned against touching their genitals by parents and teachers alike.[32] Because of their innate propensity toward perversity, a dangerous lasciviousness could easily be triggered by ordinary stimuli. Gerson thus advises parents not to hold or kiss their naked children, "especially in a private place." (One assumes he means in a private location, but the phrasing is ambiguous.) He also counsels that the child be taught to resist such embraces and, when subjected to them, immediately confess. Even if the incident makes no impression upon the child at the time, he might still be irreparably corrupted, just like the ignorant beast that is burned for the sin of bestiality committed by a human. Subject to inchoate influences such as these, the child could have no peace without confession.[33]

Despite Gerson's invective against irresponsible adults, it is very clear that he regards children as the chief corrupters of other children. Boys who teach one another to masturbate will then engage in mutual masturbation, which Gerson perceives as a type of sodomy.[34] Young boys and girls who are, in legal parlance, "capable of deceit" (generally around the age of seven) should never share a bed with an older relative. Nor should they touch their own naked bodies. In fact, Gerson opines that no other animal is harmed as easily as through the "mutual contagion" that one child spreads to another. Just as a single beast can infect the entire herd, so a depraved adolescent can pollute his entire cohort. The individual responsible for initiating sinful practices must be discovered through careful interrogation. If he cannot be corrected, he must be expelled.[35] Gerson's periodic allusion to the animal kingdom takes a despairing turn when he decries contemporary children as entirely vice-ridden, with filthy habits worse than beasts.[36]

Gerson's treatise *On Drawing Little Children to Christ*, described above, is imbued with the spirit of pessimism. Some five years later, Gerson will pen his rule for choristers (1411), which begins with a more optimistic turn. For instance, *On Drawing Children to Christ* had opened with the reflection that

Christ's solicitude for children demonstrated that "the company of boys and adolescents is not a worthless portion of the church."[37] In contrast, the opening of his rule describes the choristers' contribution as the "most beautiful and shining portion of the church." The boys themselves are compared with Samuel and their office is described as angelic.[38] Even so, the core beliefs that boys are not only easily corrupted but are the chief agents in corrupting one another remain unchanged. In his prohibition against the choristers socializing with extraneous boys, Gerson again makes the argument that one vicious beast infects the entire pack, adding, "especially when someone is perversely inclined and inducted to the most enormous sins, which ought not to be named."[39] Not surprisingly, there is also considerable emphasis placed on confession—"not just once each year, but four or six times, on the solemn feasts"—along with attention to soliciting a priest adept at hearing the confessions of children. The boys are "to guard themselves safely from all shamelessness in the thought of the heart, in the speech in the mouth, and in the filthy touching of an act." Dissolute songs are condemned, as is descant—at least after a boy's voice had broken.[40]

Many of the practical aspects of the rule resemble a monastic regimen. For example, the boys ate in silence. They were carefully sequestered from the outside world. Considering Gerson's preoccupation with boyish impurity, it is perhaps surprising that they slept two to a bed—an expedient that may reflect spatial or budgetary considerations. There is a light in front of the statue of the Virgin to ensure that "they perform only those deeds which can and ought to be seen in the light." Nor are the boys allowed to meet privately through secret assignation.[41] They are also expected to practice a version of fraternal correction, drawing attention to any wrongdoing by another boy.[42] An apprehension of the corrosive influence of adults is reflected in the admonition that clerics and chaplains from outside were not allowed to speak to the boys without one of the masters present.[43]

The choirmaster is presented as guarantor of the choristers' good behavior. He must be "the most incorruptible of men" because, as Horace often repeated, a disciple invariably imitates his master. Juvenal maintains, moreover, that domestic vices have the greatest impact on the young, thus the greatest deference is owed to the boy lest he imitate a sin that he sees. This includes filthy and obscene words, dissolute gestures or touches, and wicked deeds. The master must be free from all other worries so that he can focus entirely on the boys and ensure that no inappropriate relations be formed—as much with individuals in town as among other members of the choir. Uncompliant boys should be compelled by blows or sent to the superiors for discipline. And woe to the boy who misleads others since, as Christ testifies, "a millstone should be hanged about his neck that he should be drowned in the depth of the sea" (Matt. 18:6).[44] The slippage is subtle, but telling: the familiar biblical verse that shows solicitude over the little child being corrupted is now being turned against the unruly child who is being cited as a potential source of corruption.

The English Chorister

> Teacher, do you think it is clever
> To beat us in this way every day
> as if you were the lord of the town?
> We would rather leave school
> and each take a different occupation
> than remain under your control.
> —Anonymous carol from a Lincoln Cathedral manuscript[45]

Gerson's rule is unique in its inclusion of the ideology that informs its various strictures. As we turn our attention to England, we find that comparable provisions for choristers, though more cursory, demonstrate parallel concerns. The statutes of Wells Cathedral, drawn up in 1459, likewise insist that the master of the choristers be learned, a deft judge of a boy's ability, but "above all let the master be chaste in his life that he may give a stainless example of purity to his boys and that he may the more firmly correct them in the event of any impurity." Both the choirmaster and his undermaster must ensure that at no time should the boys be instructed in music "which tends towards or has the air of the lascivious or the impure."[46] The light in the boys' dormitory should burn all night "in order that the master or undermaster may see the manner or posture in which the boys are lying whenever it be necessary. . . . But above all it is most certainly to be overseen with the utmost diligence that decent behavior of every kind is maintained in the boys' room, and that no trace of ejaculation [*micture*] or anything untoward or unfitting is left or done there." Every week, two choristers were selected to report on the wrongdoings of their cohort.[47]

The practice of many, if not most, English churches was to recruit their choristers from indigent families, and the boys were often housed in the almonry.[48] This was initially the case at Lincoln Cathedral, whose statutes provided for twelve boys to be supported by the alms of the cathedral canons.[49] In 1264, however, the situation was further regularized: there were to be twelve boys, selected by the precentor or his delegates, who would be assigned fixed pensions of two marks per annum and live in common in their own house. A master would be appointed from outside the chapter to instruct and supervise them.[50]

Although the same ordinances were theoretically in effect in the fifteenth century, the records give a sense that the boys of Lincoln Cathedral were, for the most part, neglected. In a visitation of 1432, Bishop William Gray upbraided choristers who, rather than perfecting their grammar and singing, wandered around aimlessly, and threatened to divide an errant boy's stipend among the rest of his cohort.[51] The canons, for their part, insisted that someone should be put in place to govern the choristers who, left to their own devices, "almost every day . . . spend their time in drinkings and other unseemliness, wherefrom they slip into diverse ill-doings to the scandal of the church."[52] The selection process for the boys also seems to have devolved into a matter of partisanship with its attendant evils. Hence in 1434, when adjudicating a fight between the cathedral chapter and its dean, Bishop Gray stipulated that the boys must be free "of requests and favors owed to some and the corruptions of others."[53]

When William Alnwick succeeded Gray as bishop of Lincoln two years later, the dean and his chapter were still at each other's throats.[54] In 1437, less than a year after he had assumed office, Alnwick's own visitation of the cathedral was greeted by a barage of accusations and counteraccusations.[55] The boys' choir contributed to the institutional mayhem. According to one witness, the precentor failed to control the choristers, who wandered around at will. The boys themselves were remiss at memorizing their chants, were rude to the superiors, and were a general bother to everyone.[56] Others blamed the precentor for the choir's uneven chanting.[57]

Yet when the choristers themselves are called upon to testify, the picture of brazen heedlessness gives way to a sense of youthful pathos. There was a unanimous outcry against the precentor's efforts to control visits with friends and relatives, a power that they claimed belonged to the seneschal.[58] Some boys begged for fuel in the winter and scarves against the wind.[59] Others complained about not receiving their stipends.[60] Still others noted, woefully, that for breakfast on Fridays and Saturdays, they used to receive a concoction of honey, flour, and milk, along with their bread, but that this treat had been taken away by the seneschal, and now they only received bread.[61] The choristers were frequently beaten up by some of the younger members of the vicars choral, who would allegedly smack their heads for no apparent reason.[62]

The vicars choral was a peculiarly English institution, composed of a group of clerics who were each assigned to represent one of the canons in the event that the incumbent was temporarily traveling, did not want to wake up for night offices, or was a perpetual absentee. At Lincoln Cathedral, the vicars choral consisted of somewhere between thirty-eight and forty members.[63] Here, as elsewhere, they were presented as an unruly lot, repeatedly accused of incontinence,[64] laughing and talking during divine office, and entering and exiting the choir at will.[65] The precentor, who was responsible for keeping them in order, purportedly did not bother to attend services himself, so the vicars were not fined for their comings and goings, as was mandated.[66] The vicar's second-class standing was emphasized by the fact that he was not permitted to appear in public if the incumbent were present.[67] This is in spite of the fact that the appointment as canon at cathedrals and collegiate churches alike was essentially a sinecure at which the incumbent was not required to perform pastoral duties. This meant that the vicars necessarily assumed their responsibilities.[68] It was thus typical for the vicars to take out their frustrations on the choristers, who were universally bullied. At Lincoln, this was not limited to simple smacks of the head: in 1395, the vicar John Austeyn seems to have captured and detained nine of the boys in his house. (Austeyn eventually confessed and promised to reform himself.)[69] This pattern of harassment is similar to what we have seen by the older boys in the monasteries. The younger vicars were probably not much older than the choristers.[70] In fact, at Lincoln and elsewhere, an errant vicar might receive the infantilizing punishment of being made to stand in the boys' choir.[71]

But the disturbances in Lincoln were nothing compared to the crisis in the boys' choir that awaited Bishop Alnwick in Leicester at the Collegiate Church of St. Mary in the Newarke.[72] According to the founding documents of 1355–1356, there were supposed to be six choristers at St. Mary's, selected and overseen by the sacristan, and supported by a fixed stipend. As at Lincoln Cathedral, the boys were expected to live, eat, and sleep in their own house within the church precincts.[73] But by the time of Bishop Alnwick's visitation in 1440, whatever discipline might have existed had clearly broken down, and the choristers seemed dangerously neglected. Alnwick's injunction states: "it stands disclosed to us that the choristers . . . do in these days wander about almost without a leader and spend their time in gaddings-out and other breaches of discipline, making no virtuous profit in any wise." The sacristan was warned under pain of excommunication to attend to them more carefully when they were not in church, supervising their instruction, and redoubling corporal punishment so that "living under the rod, they may have power to go forward from strength to strength."[74]

But dereliction of duty aside, the most compelling evidence of mayhem was the fact that several of the boys had been seduced by an unscrupulous canon. Bishop Alnwick was alerted to this scandal at the very beginning of his visitation by the dean (head of the college of canons) William Walesby.

Master John Dey, canon of the place, is defamed of the vice of sodomy with Thomas Craven, chorister in the same, who has confessed, and

with one of the surname of White, a canon of Repton, and with Henry
Cravene, and with John Burley, chorister, to some of whom he gave
long boots that they should conceal such offences; and he is a haunter
of public taverns, even to drunkenness and vomiting. Let inquiry be
made of William Bentley, late the said master John's cook, now with
sir Henry Rose, canon, and of sir William Derby, the same master
John's vicar, and of John Welforde, who dwells with sir Henry Rose,
canon, and of sir Henry Syleby vicar to the same [Rose].[75]

Variations of these charges were echoed by others.[76]

When John was summoned the same day and informed of the accusations,
he "denie[d] all such guilt, declaring that if these two youths will bear witness
against him, he will make renunciation of all his benefices in the world."[77] John's
defiant protest expressed confidence that the two choristers summoned would
say nothing to incriminate him. Hadn't he, after all, bought them long boots?
The next day, John was again summoned along with the various individuals
that the dean had recommended for questioning. John was dismissed while the
witnesses were interrogated. The recorded testimonies were terse, but to the
point.[78]

> Thomas Craven, a chorister of fifteen years (etc.) says less than half a
> year ago he swore that he lay nude three times in bed with Master John
> Dey at night, who was nude, where and when the said Master John
> Dey put his erect virile member between the legs of the one testifying
> and acted as if he were with a woman until the one testifying felt liquid
> leave the member of that Master John.

> John Burley, a chorister of fifteen years (etc.) says that around the Feast
> of St. Michael the Archangel, more than a year ago but on which night
> he cannot remember, he, the one under oath, lay nude with the same
> Master John, who was nude, in his bed when and where the same
> Master John made the one under oath get up on the stomach of Master
> John and to bite the lower lip of the same John, and then the same
> Master John, with his member erect, rubbed and poked the one
> testifying around the navel and his virile parts; when the one testifying
> was asked if he could feel some liquid leave the member of the said
> John, he said no. The one who was testifying was asked if he had [done
> this] many times or if only once with the said John Dey, he said yes
> [he had done this many times] and that he never felt the member of
> the said John except the first time, and he [John Dey] after often

embraced and kissed the one testifying and made him bite the lips of the said John Dey.

Dey's vicar, the twenty-year-old John Welforde, also testified. Welforde confessed to having sex with John Dey the previous year in early autumn. Dey embraced and kissed Welforde many times "and then touched him with his erect virile member, poking and rubbing the one testifying above the stomach, around the navel. Asked if he felt any liquid leave the member of the said John, he answered no."

The interrogation was focused entirely on what sexual transgressions took place, discerning their gravity against a scale of perversity not unlike the one that Peter Damian had earlier proposed to Leo IX.[79] If this was, in fact, the case, it was doubtless a relief to the bishop that John Dey did not always seem to have ejaculated, nor did penetration occur. It is also noteworthy that, although the ages of the boys with whom Dey had sex were duly given, there was no particular emphasis on their youth or vulnerability, as was sometimes the case in secular tribunals.[80] Apart from the gift of boots, the witnesses were not examined about any degree of pressure Dey might have exerted, or to what degree these relations may have been consensual. The fact that the bishop did not seem to have attempted to prosecute any of John's partners/victims might suggest that they were exonerated by virtue of Dey's role as initiator, but this is by no means certain. It is possible that the bishop deliberately left any disciplinary action in the hands of the dean.

In addition to the testimony of John's sexual partners, there were three other witnesses who could corroborate their statements. William Bentley, the twenty-three-year-old cook who had once worked for Dey, but was now living with Henry Rose, was actually an eyewitness. Bentley had observed Dey on a number of occasions with various youths through a "snekhole" in the door, watching and listening as the naked Dey "lasciviously embraced and kissed the said youth as if he were a woman." Bentley made it clear that such behavior soured his opinion of Dey and, although the rest of his testimony is effaced, probably precipitated his departure from Dey's household. Bentley also complained about Dey to William Derby, Dey's vicar, in elliptical terms. When Derby pressed him for details, Bentley described Dey's habits as "vile and filthy and the very worst and on account of their filthiness he abhorred telling about them," leaving little doubt about the nature of Dey's offenses. Derby also claimed that Henry Craven, a chorister, reported "similar things in a similar way" about Dey. (The fact that Henry was not summoned along with the other choristers could suggest that he was no longer at St. Mary's.)[81] According to Henry Rose's vicar Henry Syleby, both the choristers Thomas Craven and John

Burley reported their encounters with Dey in basically the same terms that they would later use at the inquiry.[82]

Later that afternoon when the bishop revealed the results of the inquest to John Dey, the latter had nothing to say in his own defense and was speedily convicted in the presence of four other canons: Halywelle, Fysshewyck (the dean's lieutenant), Chelle, and Rose.[83] On December 3, 1440, John Dey was brought before the bishop and the case against him rehearsed. Dey was ordered to appear before the bishop or his appointee the following Saturday at the church of Liddington, where he would receive the bishop's final deliberations concerning "the damnable and hateful vice of sodomy, by the name whereof alone the air is defiled." This second meeting would consider Dey's offense in the light of what "the sacred canons and the decrees of the holy fathers prescribe." We never learn what additional penalties Dey may have incurred, but we do know that he was formally deposed from his canonry and prebend.[84] It was a substantial punishment, conforming to what Lateran III stipulated for secular clerics. Although Dey had said he would renounce all his benefices should the implicated youths testify against him, he was not required to forfeit his living outside of Leicester since no wrongdoing had been discerned there.[85]

The charge of sodomy was sufficiently uncommon in England that the scribe recording the inquest reflexively wrote down "the detestable vice of simony," only to cross it out and write "sodomy."[86] The rarity of the case is corroborated centuries later by the reaction of A. Hamilton Thompson, the editor of Alnwick's visitations and many other documents associated with the diocese of Lincoln, who repeatedly underlined its exceptionality. Thompson's edition is a face-to-face Latin-English translation. Yet he is so disturbed by the case that he left some of the proceedings against Dey in Latin and omitted the interrogation of the witnesses altogether. But despite such evidence of dismay, medieval and modern, it would be naive to assume that Dey was the only clerical sodomite who had ever been detected by his confreres. Instead, his denunciation to the bishop seems to have resulted from an unusual configuration of personal and circumstantial considerations. Before Dey was accused of sodomy, he had already created a public scandal by frequenting taverns and drinking excessively. Dey's dissipation also manifested itself in more concrete ways. More than one person noted that Dey did not repair his house and "it well-nigh threatens decay beyond repair; for he devours all his goods, ever giving the rein to gluttony."[87]

Considering Dey's undisciplined habits and drunkenness, it is unlikely that he was a good employer, and this doubtless contributed to his downfall. Both Dey's vicar, whom Dey had debauched, and his former cook had not only testified against their master but decamped to the establishment of Canon

Henry Rose. Another leading witness was Rose's vicar, Syleby. In fact, Rose's entire household knew something to Dey's discredit. Although Rose's establishment may have been a hotbed of anti-Dey sedition, however, it is significant that Rose remained above the fray, leaving it to the two vicars and a layman to lead the charge. Indeed, when it was Henry Rose's turn to report on the wrongdoings of his fellow canons to Alnwick, he only said that the dean "has corrected all that there was to correct."[88] Nor was Rose named as a witness against Dey. Considering the heightened awareness of the various members of his household, it seems unlikely that Rose was ignorant of Dey's sexual activity. It is possible, however, that Rose was ambivalent about making such a charge against a fellow canon. It is, indeed, significant that the only clerical witnesses cited were Derby and Syleby, who were both vicars, perhaps underlining the endemic tensions between the vicars and the canons.

The other canons were hardly models of good behavior, which is doubtless reflected in the fact that St. Mary's was Alnwick's longest and, arguably, most fraught visitation. According to John Bramburghe's testimony, Henry Rose, who had harbored the vanguard against Dey, nevertheless had certain things in common with Dey: "haunt[ing] taverns and [Rose] has recourse to the town of Leicester, to the great scandal of the church."[89] But John Bramburghe, who had complained about the state of Dey's house, also claimed that Rose was defamed with two married women.[90] And this was just the beginning. John Shiryngham was accused of adultery with the wife of a certain Ryggesmaydene.[91] Ralph Welles committed adultery with one woman and fornicated with two others, each of whom bore his children.[92] Robert Matfene was himself defamed with a certain Elizabeth, who dwelt by the south gate of Leicester, and who was pregnant by him, as well as with two other women.[93] The same Robert would, in turn, accuse Richard Kempsale (vicar) of cavorting with the sister of John Broghtone, who conveniently lived by the gate of the college close.[94]

All of these men were allowed to clear themselves through canonical purgation on the basis of their oath alone.[95] This option was not available to Dey because of the overwhelming amount of evidence against him. According to the new, less stringent, criterion of canon saw, multiple witnesses to different events could count as proof. Hence, the testimonies of the choristers and the vicar who confessed to having sex with Dey would have been sufficient for conviction. But the fact that Bentley had witnessed many of these encounters through the "snekehole," in conjunction with the testimony of any one of Dey's sexual conquests, would also have fulfilled the older criterion of two or three witnesses. Furthermore, Bentley shared what he saw with the vicars Syleby and Derby, who were also confidantes to several of the eyewitnesses.[96] In this respect, the practice of the English church deviated from the standard Romano-canonical rules, allowing people who were not eyewitnesses to testify.[97] So their evidence would also have been factored in.

The overwhelming evidence made it impossible for Bishop Alnwick to look away, as he had done before. At his 1438 visitation to Markby Prior, for example, Alnwick was confronted by the case of Brother John Alforde who, like Dey, was hardly an exemplary citizen: he left the cloister without permission; skipped meals; verbally abused his brethren;[98] and haunted taverns, where he drank with laymen.[99] Furthermore, Alforde was said to be "so malicious that, if any one have transgressed against him, he bears this in his heart, ever watching for some time or another when he may be able to take his revenge."[100] (John Alforde, for his part, retaliated by complaining "that silence is kept nowhere according to the rule, and that religious discipline is not observed, and this is because of the subprior's heedlessness.")[101] But the most common charge brought against Alforde was the one first brought by the cellarer: "secular youths do lie in the dormitory among the canons, and some with canons in the same beds, and especially John Alforde."[102] This rather murky charge gives the impression that all the monks were prone to this behavior. But this tendency to generalize could be the cellarer's tactic for circumventing Alforde's vengeful ways. Significantly, when two other brethren corroborated the cellarer's report, they made it perfectly clear that the only real offender was Alforde.[103]

As suspicious as Alforde's behavior might sound, nobody actually witnessed a sex act. So there was not the kind of incontrovertible evidence that William Bentley and his supporters had garnered against John Dey. The only discipline meted out to Alforde was a "warn[ing] under pain of excommunication that henceforward he shall admit no persons to sleep with him in the dorter or out of it, save only in the imminence of pressing and unavoidable necessity."[104] John Alforde may be an embarrassment, and even a scandal in the making, but he was not yet a scandal. A bigger problem, at least the only thing explicitly identified as scandalous, was that "the secular folk, and women especially, have overmuch and suspect recourse to the inner precincts, and even to the cloister buildings, of the priory, to the sore scandal of the house."[105]

Propter puerum

The case of John Dey, and his predatory behavior with choristers, is not unique.[106] In 1475 John Stocker, a chaplain of the cathedral of Basel, was convicted by an episcopal court for committing sodomy with the chorister John Müller, who lodged with him.[107] In Basel, it seemed to be customary for the choristers to live with the canons and act as servants within their households. According to Müller's testimony, Stocker first approached him to ask if he had found a master yet. The boy answered no, and Stocker took him to his house. Müller was initially assigned his own room. About two weeks later, however, Stocker asked him if he was frightened to be alone at night. When Müller acknowledged that he was, Stocker invited him to sleep in his own room in a separate bed. During the next two weeks, Stocker did his best to seduce the boy, telling him over and over that he had never seen a boy so handsome and that, ever since he had first seen him in choir, he could not take his eyes off him. But when Stocker asked the boy if he would have sex with him, Müller refused, arguing that it was a terrible sin for which they both could be burned. Stocker seemed to have laughed this off: not only did he deny that sodomy was a sin, but he maintained that if the authorities were to burn all the sodomites in Basel, there would hardly be fifty men left in the city. Over time, Stocker became more and more insistent and eventually raped the boy. The attack was violent: Müller testified that he bled for three or four days, but when he complained to Stocker of the harm he had sustained, the canon responded that he did not give a damn. When Müller confided in the maid, she urged him to leave.[108] But Müller was somehow convinced that Stocker would not repeat his attack. He was wrong. Two days after Müller had spoken to the maid, Stocker raped him for a second time, again leaving him bleeding for three or four days.[109]

At this point others seem to have become apprised that something was wrong. Some of the canons told Müller that he should leave Stocker's house. Likewise, the schoolmaster from the church of St. Leonard's approached Müller and asked if he liked his master and whether he was friendly with him. When the boy answered in the affirmative, the master told him to "take care that he does not hurt you as he has hurt the other two children." When Müller asked who they were (perhaps he was already thinking of launching a suit and wanted corroboration), the master would not reveal their names. Eventually Müller did decide to go, taking his leave of Stocker and returning his keys. Stocker's reaction was to claim that the boy had done him a great harm that he could never repair. It is not clear what Stocker meant by this. Perhaps he was referring to his unreciprocated feelings for Müller; perhaps Stocker knew that Müller had already told others about the assaults. Either way, Stocker enjoined the boy to say nothing to anyone about his private matters. The day before Müller testified, another canon also warned the boy that he should not say anything about Stocker, but leave things as they were.[110]

Müller must have made some kind of a formal accusation because Stocker was called in to testify. He admitted to "florenzing" (i.e., sodomizing) the boy on fourteen different occasions, but claimed that their relations were consensual, and that Müller was immediately ready and willing. It is hard to know what to make of the discrepancy between Stocker and Müller's testimony regarding the number of sexual encounters. Possibly Stocker inflated the number to make it seem as if Müller had, in fact, been eager—at least in the beginning—and that their relationship was consensual. But Stocker resisted the rumors in circulation regarding his attempts to debauch other boys. Instead he claimed that Müller was his first sexual encounter of this sort, and that he had never even attempted to sodomize any other man or boy. Nor was he aware of this kind of behavior in others.[111] Stocker ended his testimony with the following justification: that he had sex with a boy so he could continue to be considered a pious priest because "women are even less tolerated by his masters and friends."[112] This comment speaks volumes about the extent to which clerical celibacy had simply come to mean "unmarried" rather than "chaste" in certain quarters. To Stocker's mind, he could maintain his reputation among other clerics provided he kept his sexual sights on males.

The bishop's vicar-general condemned Stocker to perpetual imprisonment. Because Stocker had influential friends and family, however, there was a successful appeal to the bishop, and Stocker's sentence was commuted into a fine of 150 guilders, deposition from all benefices, a mandatory trip to the pope's curia for absolution, and perpetual exile from German lands.[113] Stocker was made to sign a very detailed confession that began by identifying him as "John Stocker, priest and sodomite."[114]

Stocker's case became notorious. It was taken up by a local chronicle, in which his one victim became two. In this context, we learn that, like John Dey, Stocker was probably unpopular with his colleagues. He would allegedly eavesdrop and spy on his fellow canons, reporting everything he learned to the higher authorities. Soon he was rewarded for his efforts and appointed head chaplain. In this capacity, Stocker not only received augmented (and lucrative) liturgical responsibilities, but he also was put in charge of distributing daily stipends to the other canons. Growing overly confident, Stocker began to argue with his colleagues, badgering them about their behavior in choir and withholding their funds. After many such altercations, Stocker was discovered by the dean of the chapter's assistant in the sin of sodomy with two students and imprisoned. One of the students confessed to the dean that he had slept with Stocker many times. As in the case of John Dey, the ill will of his fellow canons may have been compounded by the testimony of a servant whom Stocker had fired, presumably because of what she had seen. Indeed, this woman was allegedly able to report some "astonishing things." According to the chronicler, Stocker confessed his crime in the course of his inquest and was subsequently handed over to the lord of Basel, who stripped him of all his goods.[115]

What makes Stocker's case unusual was not that a priest committed sodomy, but that a priest was brought to trial for sodomy before a church tribunal.
As Helmut Puff has shown, clerics were periodically picked up for sodomy by
the secular authorities in Germany. But when they handed the offenders over
to church authorities to be disciplined, as they were obliged to do, no action
was taken.[116] In Stocker's case the archbishop's tribunal finally did something.
Indeed, the negative publicity of the Stocker trial seems to have made something
of an impression on local church authorities. Suddenly, they began keeping
track of clerical infractions involving same-sex relations, and even developed a
special moniker for describing them: *propter puerum,* "on account of a boy."[117]

*   *   *

There are clear parallels between the situation of the boy chorister and the
child oblate. Indeed, before the twelfth century, the two categories frequently
overlapped. As seen with monastic sources, the rules written for choristers
exhibit the same tendency to stress the corruptible and corrupting aspects of
boyhood over innocence: the *pusillus* over the *parvulus,* as it were. This especially
comes into focus when Jean Gerson's rule for choristers at Notre Dame of Paris
is seen through the lens of his writings on children. But one of the major conditions separating the chorister from the oblate was the heightened vulnerability
of the former. Not only did the chorister lose his position once his voice
changed, but the records suggest that a number of boys' choirs were in disarray
and that the boys themselves were frequently neglected. This neglect could
assume many forms: the choristers of Lincoln Cathedral may have been under-
fed, badly clad, and frequently bullied. But neglect could manifest itself in still
more ominous ways. At a collegiate church in Leicester, the canon John Dey
seduced a series of choristers. In Basel, where choristers did not live together but
were expected to find their own lodgings, boys were especially at risk. John
Müller ended up in the home of the cathedral canon John Stocker, who raped
the chorister (if you credit his testimony) on more than one occasion.

These cases would probably never have been brought to justice were it not
for special attending circumstances. Dey was unpopular with the other canons
and had already created a scandal in town. But prosecution was probably contingent on the testimony of the outraged layman, William Bentley—Dey's former
cook who was not prepared to let the matter drop. Although the dean promptly
introduced the matter at the beginning of the episcopal visitation, it is significant
that none of Dey's fellow canons presumed to testify against him. In contrast,
John Stocker was probably brought down by the courage of one of his victims,
the chorister John Müller. As was clear by their many allusions, the proclivities

of Stocker were well known to his colleagues and, if the contemporaneous chronicler is to be believed, Stocker was not even particularly popular with them. But they did nothing to put an end to Stocker's abuse. Indeed, on the day before the trial, Müller was warned by one of the canons to let the matter drop. In short, the canons were prepared self-protectively to close ranks around Müller, even if this meant countenancing a series of sodomitical rapes. There was one thing that they would apparently not have tolerated, however, at least according to Müller's testimony, and that was any involvement with a woman. As long as Stocker limited himself to boys, he remained a pious priest. Nor is this the last time that we shall see such a view expressed.

CHAPTER 8

The Schools

> Now consider a boy of tender years and little knowledge,
> unable to distinguish between good and evil, or even to
> understand you when you talk about such things. Here indeed
> the wax is soft, almost liquid, and incapable of taking an image
> of the seal. Between these extremes is adolescence and youth,
> aptly tempered between the extremes of softness and hardness.
> If you teach him, you can shape him as you wish.
> > —Eadmer, *Life of St. Anselm*

> If he is evil, he is not a teacher; if he is a teacher, he is not evil.
> > —Augustine, *On Free Will*

Medieval pedagogy was riddled with eros. The first rule of the classroom was love of the teacher, who was presented as the embodiment of virtue, inspiring adulation and emulation.[1] The actual curriculum of the schools was rife with illicit passion. Young boys cut their teeth on Ovid's *Heroides* and his *Ars amatoria* when learning grammar.[2] The study of grammar and rhetoric also engaged the darker side of the emotional spectrum by focusing on classical rape narratives, often requiring young boys to identify with the victim—a practice that was already noted with choristers.[3]

The pedagogical ideology that underwrote the selection of what, from a modern perspective, might seem like surprising choices, was partially indebted to mnemonic theory, which held that scenes involving sex and violence were more easily retained in memory.[4] Interestingly, it was the more sexually explicit material that was considered suitable for younger, but not older students.[5] Hence, the commentaries on the classical homoerotic texts that Tina Chronopoulos has examined, which tend to downplay or even efface same-sex relations altogether, were probably intended for an older audience.[6] On the one hand, this policy reflects a shrewd pragmatism, which determined that the most suggestive material be withheld from the age group that was most likely to be distracted by its sexual content. On the other hand, this meant that the more salacious material was introduced to children when they were at their most impressionable. Marjorie Woods has argued for the psychological utility of these texts: that they recommended themselves to students by virtue of "their unreality, their elements of projection and wish-fulfillment."[7] Even so, if a curriculum normalizes sexual aggression, the degree of "unreality" in the models employed is not necessarily stable. To the younger and weaker boys, the ones encouraged to identify with the female victims, these narratives might suggest that resistance to sexual violence was ultimately useless and thus urge resignation.[8] And at least some of the students, subsequently empowered by age and rank, might be emboldened to go beyond "projection and wish fulfillment" to become seducers and rapists.

It was materials such as these, imbued by their own peculiar pedagogy, that laid the groundwork for the twelfth-century's efflorescence of same-sex love poetry discussed above. Of course, in at least some of these works the kind of love expressed remains ambiguous. It bears reiterating that the very nature of Christian letters often makes it impossible to discern with any certainty when *caritas* has crossed over into *eros*—a problem compounded by the centrality of erotic verse to the core curriculum. Baudri of Bourgueil, whose suggestive poetry addressed to boys was discussed earlier, is a case in point. When M. L. Stapleton identifies Baudri as one of the earliest poets "who truly internalized Ovid's erotic conventions," this could imply that he was something of a living textbook, an amorous monk, or both.[9] And then there are Baudri's poetic disclaimers that the emotions portrayed in his verse were fabricated and that he himself was untouched by love. Of course, as Stapleton points out, such disclaimers are also Ovidian, which adds yet another layer to the onion-like configuration of poetic semiotics.[10]

The Cathedral Schools

Let Chartres and Sens be destroyed, where Adonis prostitutes
    himself
According to the law of the whorehouse: there are shameful
    acts of intercourse with males [*stupra maris*] there.
Infected by the same vice, the noble and distinguished city
Of Paris is happy to be married to a soft and delicate master.
But more than all these monstrous towns, you, Orleans,
Are ruined by your reputation for this sin.[11]

—Anonymous twelfth-century poem

Whatever we make of the poetry of Baudri of Bourgueil and his cohort, the belief that the schools were dens of same-sex iniquity was ubiquitous, and this generated alarm about the victimization of students by their masters. When Ivo of Chartres was decrying the sexual relationship between the youthful John, bishop of Orléans, and his mature lover, the bishop of Tours, John is described as "under the archbishop of Tours, just like a boy under a pedagogue."[12] A number of writers put these concerns into verse. Godfrey of Winchester (d. 1107) writes:

That you pursue boys, love them, and are loved by them
Is worthless activity, not for a man; it's bird-hunting for a fool.
Did I say you love them? Yes, if hate can manifest as love,
Or if deluding them with clever traps of love.
You teach sin and put curbs on sinning;
. . . .
To enter into sin, they always pay with a gift,
And to get you to conceal the deed, they pay again with a gift.
The fault is yours that their lives and reputation suffer;
Your fault that they lose their good name and esteem.[13]

Walter of Châtillon (d. 1180) likewise decries the dangers for students:

When they are young, sons of the nobility
Are sent to France to become scholars;
Corrupters of youth recruit them with coaxing or cash.[14]

Poverty would have enhanced the student's vulnerability. In his satirical poem *Architrenius*, John of Hauteville (d. 1199) depicts the life of Parisian students in the most abject terms, describing their overall poverty, threadbare clothes, terrible lodgings, and starvation rations.[15]

The anti-sodomy polemic of Peter the Chanter and his students was a response to the sexual abuse of students. Boys from all over Europe and the British Isles were flocking to Paris, many as young as fourteen. The cathedral schools and the later universities also had close ties with the parochial grammar schools, where the boys would be even younger.[16] It is significant that Thomas of Chobham, one of the Chanter's students, describes the office of schoolmaster as "very dangerous"—especially with respect to teaching boys, though the reasons he gives are circumspect.[17] The abbey of St.-Victor, which housed some prominent members of the Chanter's circle, had been given the authority for hearing the confessions of Parisian students, and this task could well have heightened their awareness of same-sex activity.[18] We have seen that the Chanter and his cohort were so apprehensive about the clergy's sexual vices that some wanted the general council to dispense with clerical celibacy altogether.[19] Robert of Courson, in particular, argued that, while vows of continence might have benefited the church in the past, now they only served to foster sodomy, immorality, and, ultimately, damnation. Robert also recognized how sodomitical relations gave rise to nepotisim, so "while the lord took away their children, the devil conferred an abundance of nephews" who would, in turn, be advanced through simony.[20] While in the high Middle Ages "nephew" becomes a code word used to designate clerical bastards,[21] Robert is referring to the kind of sexual nepotism discussed in Chapter 4, which was, to his mind, even more corrosive. The Chanter was likewise sensitive to how enforced celibacy put the young at risk. When discussing sodomy, his *Verbum adbreviatum* evokes a salient passage from Jeremiah's lamentation over the devastation of Jerusalem: "They abused the youths [*adolescentes*] indecently: and the children [*pueri*] fell under the wood" (Jer. 5:13).[22]

Some members of the Chanter's circle capitalized on the unabashedly erotic nature of the curriculum to incorporate sexual prohibitions into pedagogy. Alan of Lille's *The Plaint of Nature* is a celebrated case in point. Not only was it written by someone who was both educated and taught at the schools, but the work was destined to be incorporated into the curriculum.[23] Grammar and grammatical explanations of different parts of speech had a long history as a medium for wordplay and punning; Alan exploited this tradition of double entendre to decry same-sex relations.[24] The despairing persona of Nature describes humanity's perversity in terms of "the active sex shudder[ing] in disgrace as it sees itself degenerate into the passive sex. . . . He is subject and predicate: one and the same term is given a double application. Man here extends too far the laws of grammar."[25]

As unique as Alan's *Plaint* was, it was nevertheless representative of a larger movement that was afoot. We have seen that in the wake of the papal reform—when the idealization of clerical same-sex love was at its height, and most church authorities mutely stood by—the visionary genre had been used to indict sodomy. Alan's choice of the medium of a poetic dream vision was certainly no accident and could be construed as a self-conscious effort to extend this earlier initiative—albeit a somewhat ironic one. Nor was Alan's use of sexualized wordplay to indict sodomy singular. Abbot and poet Gautier of Coincy (d. 1236) launches an extensive rant against hypocritical clerics who pretend chastity, all the while destroying nature by joining "hic a hic" (i.e., "this [male] to this [male]). He is confident that God will erase such miscreants from his Book of Memory.[26] Parisian physician and cathedral canon Gilles of Corbeil looked to grammar for his arraignment of

> the good many men wishing by an irregular law
> To be made grammarians while they often stick
> To similar articles.[27]

The Goliard poem *Priscian's Rule* likewise appeals to grammar when articulating the association between clerical celibacy and sodomy.[28]

Peter the Chanter perceived Parisian sodomitical tendencies as so pervasive that even the liturgy was being compromised. As the "chanter" (cantor, or precentor) of Notre Dame of Paris, Peter was responsible for supervising liturgical activities.[29] Paris was at the center of the rapid development of polyphony (i.e., two or more lines of independent melody) in the twelfth century, in contrast to the traditional plainchant.[30] The Chanter and his cohort were appalled by polyphony's sensual linking of male voices in harmony, clearly associating such musical innovations with same-sex relations.[31] Nor were their suspicions entirely without grounds. Bruce Holsinger has demonstrated that Master Leoninus (d. ca. 1201), the celebrated musician associated with the development of polyphony, was also a master of same-sex erotic verse.[32] In contrast, Peter of Poitiers reports with grim satisfaction that the Chanter had alleged that God would prefer the sound of dogs barking in church over the singing of the cathedral canons of Paris, presumably alluding to their polyphony.[33] When a *conductus* was written in honor of the Chanter, it was, not surprisingly, monophonic.[34]

Peter the Chanter's concerns spread well beyond theological circles. The medical doctor Gilles of Corbeil, alluded to above, adopted Peter's reform program wholeheartedly, even setting some of the *Verbum adbreviatum* to verse in his satirical poem *Hierapigra ad purgandos prelatos*. Literally "a laxative for purging prelates," the *Hierapigra* excoriated the clergy for their sodomitical ways, comparing them to unreasoning beasts.[35] Like Robert of Courson, Gilles strenuously resisted the papacy's redoubled efforts to enforce clerical celibacy, arguing that many clerics compelled to leave their wives "cultivate the old ways and renew the acts of ancient time, with enormities buried. And they do worse things and depraved error springs forth."[36] The reference to "ancient days" evokes the specter of pederasty.

The anti-sodomy discourse at Paris becomes more explicit over time, especially with respect to the abuse of children. A university sermon from 1230, significantly written for the Feast of the Holy Innocents by an anonymous Franciscan, begins with the many occasions in which scripture extolls the innocence of childhood, urging the audience to emulate the innocents in their purity.[37] Clerical purity and impurity are associated with the instructions God gave to Noah regarding permissible and impermissible food: he is permitted to eat of all living things except meat with blood (Gen. 9:3–4). The eating of bloody meat is then equated with temporality and lust, vices widespread among the contemporary clergy and exemplified in the sin of sodomy, which is presented as cannibalistic. "The vice of the Sodomites [*Sodomorum*] is so mixed with blood that a man is scarcely able to rebound from this sin; such ones are the enemies of all the little children [*parvuli*] born—and not only of God, but of every man." The sin of the Sodomites deferred the Incarnation, even as it perverts the natural order.[38] A child should not be abused but honored, just as the Holy Innocents who follow the lamb (Apoc. 14:4).[39]

"The Intemperate Rod"

> Since thou at school thy teacher's blows hast known,
> Thou'lt better bear thy father's angry tone.
>
> —*Distichs of Cato* [40]

For centuries, pedagogical beatings had been the stuff of nightmares. Augustine lived in fear of being beaten at school, praying to God to spare him the rod, but to no avail. Meanwhile, his usually doting parents laughed at the stripes left behind by the rod, regarding them as an essential component in the process of transforming an unruly child into an obedient student. Later Augustine would rationalize that the human race, represented by Adam, was being beaten by God for its own good. Such salubrious beatings force humankind to look heavenward to the Lord, even as the slave looks up at the whip in the hand of his master.[41] Othloh of St. Emmeram's entrance into religion, although (one hopes) ultimately a source of joy, was precipitated by the vision of a fierce man who beat

him mercilessly. Later as a teacher, he lived in dread of disciplining his students.[42] Peter Damian was partial to flagellation as an ascetic practice, even
writing a treatise in its praise. Yet he clearly drew a distinction between its
voluntary and involuntary administration, characterizing an anonymous critic
as someone who "so arrogantly wields his intemperate rod over pupils that as
yet he has been unable to attract any students."[43]

Teachers were urged to use moderation in their floggings, but such admoni-
tions hardly provided an exacting standard. Guibert of Nogent claimed to have
been beaten daily, literally the whipping boy for his master's frustration over his
own incompetence.[44] Ecclesiastical tribunals testify to even worse abuses. In
Lucca, for example, one priest who was a "teacher of boys" beat a very young
child (designated as *infans*) so severely that he was said to be in danger of death.
The situation was sufficiently serious that the bishop's vicar assiduously investi-
gated these charges, interviewing the weeping mother in person. The priest
confessed to wrongdoing and paid a fine of ten pounds. Yet no efforts were
made to bar him from receiving further students.[45]

It goes without saying that a beating could be used to solicit sex coercively.
As Carissa Harris has noted, in one anonymous carol the boundary between
corporal punishment and sexual violence seems purposefully amorphous.

> My master pepered my ars with well good spede;
> Hit was worse than fynkyll [fennel] sede;
> He wold not leve till it did blede—
> Myche sorow have he for his dede!
> What vayleth it me thowgh I say nay?[46]

The last line, "what vayleth it me thowgh I say nay?"—repeated as a refrain
throughout—is ambiguous. It could refer to corporal punishment; it could refer
to coerced sodomy. Both were painful, but resistance was deemed futile in either
case. The relationship between corporal punishment and sexual abuse is more
clearly drawn in the anonymous seventeenth-century *Children's Petition*, allegedly presented to the Speaker and some members of the House of Commons in
protest to the harsh discipline of the English schools. Comparing themselves to
the angels sheltered by Lot against the men of Sodom, the "Children" claimed
"our sufferings are of that nature as makes our Schools to be not merely Houses
of Correction, but of Prostitution, in this vile way of castigation in use, wherein
our secret parts . . . must be the Anvil exposed to the immodest eyes, and filthy
blows of the smiter."[47]

Despite its questionable legacy, no authority challenged the necessity of
corporal punishment, which was considered essential to the learning experience.[48] This is especially the case with the teaching of grammar—a child's first

induction into the world of learning for which the universal symbol was a cluster of birch sticks in the master's hand.[49] The figure of Grammar appears as such in the famed sculptural program on the west facade of the cathedral of Chartres and would continue to be represented in this manner well beyond the Middle Ages.[50] Regular floggings were considered an essential rite of passage in the scholarly community. Indeed, Oxford and Cambridge even required that the newly minted master publicly beat a "naughty boy" as proof of his pedagogical prowess.[51]

Corporal punishment was an obsessive concern in the English exercise books that were used for Latin training in grammar schools, dating from the fifteenth century. These student compilations consisted of a series of phrases in English, Latin, or both for purposes of practicing translation. One such book dedicated an entire section to the subject of the master and his rod. Some of the passages were written in the voice of an apprehensive boy, who works to please the master "lest he be angry and avenge his anger on us";[52] who rejoices in the master's toothache because it keeps him absent;[53] and, when considering the punishment that he himself has experienced, doubts that there was ever a person who "trespassed so greatly that he deserved to be punished in this fashion."[54] Some passages were written in the voice of a seasoned scholar, reflecting that "some think themselves too old and too big to be beaten with a rod. . . . However, when I first came to this university, there was no difference in the correction between the big and the small."[55] It is, however, the master who has the last word, maintaining that "there is nothing that I desire more than to use soft and easy discipline with scholars, if only I thought it would profit them. But some would never learn if they were sure that they would never be beaten."[56]

The above exercise book is comparatively well organized: parallel works tended to be much more haphazard, both in terms of sequence and content. Nicholas Orme, who has edited a volume containing a number of these exercises, posits that these works were probably based on other compilations or dictation and, as such, are more representative of a school than of an individual.[57] Even so, there is one exercise book in his collection, originating in Oxford circa 1483 but copied in Winchester, that distinguishes itself in format and, I believe, in tone.[58] While the other exercise books tend to favor short phrases, the Oxford work is arranged in much longer paragraphs; the connection between subjects reads like a practicum in free association, imparting something of a stream-of-consciousness effect. This arrangement could, of course, reflect the initiative of the Winchester copyist. But even if this were the case, decisions over what sentences to combine and where to introduce paragraph breaks are still salient ones. The introduction of idiosyncratic personal information also heightens the sense of free association. Hence we find obscure non sequiturs like

"Stop shaking me, for I do not desire to trifle with you. My sister was delivered before the right time and therefore she miscarried."[59] However jarring the juxtaposition of such statements may be, it nevertheless creates the sense of a point of view from which to observe the dynamics of a classroom: the favoritism, the antipathies, the bullying, and the public shaming.

Throughout the book, the dominant perspective is that of a student who prides himself on being one of the master's favorites, setting him apart from his fellow students. One chapter reads: "My master has me in greater repute than any of the children inhabiting the school / his school, thus: I am more acceptable to the master than any other child inhabiting his school."[60] Although this particular book is written primarily in Latin, another passage enlists both languages to make its point: "The master gives me credit, [which means] in English: the master makes much of me."[61] Being one of the master's favorites could have an adverse effect on that student's standing with his peers, however. This variable is reflected in the following sequence: "I will please my master not less well than my father. All my schoolfellows regard me as infamous." Then there is the cryptic effect of a radical shift in persona midsentence: "I have never fixed my gaze upon any boy who more fully desires himself to go in motion with you."[62] Nothing is clear about this utterance, apart from an eerie longing—whether projected, internalized, or something in between—for an unspecified union.

But what especially seems to distinguish the favored student from the others is that he is spared from beatings. "The inner chambers of my heart are made heavier by the sorrows of my comrades, who were soundly beaten today for [their] response, so that he [the master] imposed every shoot of a flexible rod everywhere on their bottoms."[63] "The master often consigns to oblivion the faults of children whom he finds good at learning and continuously labouring about teachings. . . . Granted that my master spares me for unfinished duties, no-one should be surprised among all my comrades, since I am reputed a good learner of the faculty of grammar. . . . One of my school fellows is to be beaten by the master for committing an enormous offense [*enorme delictum*]; when he is beaten in public, the whole school will beware in turn of deviating in that way [*taliter declinare*]. It is good to confess our sins."[64] It is impossible to know what "enormous offense" is implied or how it would be inferred by medieval readers. But the failure to name the sin could signify a sexual excess—perhaps sodomy—that somehow became public. And the use of the verb *declinare* points to a grammatical fault but also resonates with the association between irregular grammar and sex.

But it would seem that a "reputed good learner," who was an acknowledged favorite, also ran the risk of becoming something of a thug. "I whom my schoolfellow feared am I who shall fear the master."[65] Fear of the master might serve to harness aggression. "My schoolfellow . . . blushes so much that he lacks firmness in his [facial] expression. Unless fear of the master constrained me more than fear of [your] person, I would constrain you by the nose so that blood appears all around it."[66] Clearly a propensity for bullying—perhaps spawned by a sense of privilege—could place a student's special status in jeopardy: "I am plainly prohibited from threatening my schoolfellows who are not as strong in the body as me. I was almost beaten for favouring my schoolfellow; since then I am his friend."[67] But a student who is spared the pain of the rod, is not always spared the humiliation of verbal reproach. "The master delivered abusive words to me in the presence of outsiders. My teeth grow wet."[68] In the arena of the classroom, moreover, even the teacher's pet still lived in constant fear of a beating. This nebulous fear animates a dreamlike sequence of suggestive juxtapositions and confused grammar. The exuberant "the master makes much of me," cited above, is followed by the following: "I went abroad an equestrian and came home a pedestrian. He by whom I am once beaten slightly will never be he by whom I shall be beaten, unless I were beaten by him so slightly that anyone might never be beaten by me."[69]

After this chapter, the tone changes dramatically, as does the content, and this continues for the last quarter of the exercise book. Proverbs, tidbits about courtship, and snippets of nonsense eclipse the classroom altogether until the penultimate entry: "The master can better beat than teach."[70]

Teachers and Students

Although the schools were perceived as fostering their own brand of pedagogic pederasty, we have little by way of specifics. In fact, the best-known teacher-student liaison associated with the intellectual ambiance of twelfth-century Paris is between Abelard and Heloise. Of course, there are limits to what this relationship can tell us about student life. The student was female, hence ineligible for the schools, and her rapport with her teacher was *sui generis*, to say the least. Nevertheless, this celebrated relationship is grounded in familiar pedagogic dynamics, the imprint of which would remain throughout their lives. Abelard was already established as a famous teacher at the cathedral school of Notre Dame when he solicited a position as tutor in Fulbert's household for the express purpose of seducing his prospective student, Heloise. Fulbert, "ambitious to further his niece's education in letters," gave Abelard "complete charge" over Heloise, urging him to "punish her severely" if he found her idle. In Abelard's words: "I was amazed by his simplicity—if he had entrusted a tender lamb to a ravening wolf it would not have surprised me more. In handing her over to me to punish as well as to teach, what else was he doing but giving me freedom to realize my desires, and providing an opportunity, even if I did not make use of it, for me to bend her to my will by threats and blows if persuasion failed?" Presumably many a predatory teacher could have availed himself of similar opportunities "to realize [his] desires." Abelard did beat Heloise, though he only made reference to doing so after they had become lovers. Indeed, corporal punishment was so central to medieval pedagogy that Abelard claimed to have struck Heloise "to avert suspicion." Yet the blows that he administered were purportedly "prompted by love and tender feeling rather than anger and irritation and were sweeter than any balm could be."[71]

Sweeter to whom, one might ask? And supposing Abelard had begun beating his student before they became lovers? Such a possibility becomes all the more ominous if one attributes the twelfth-century exchange of letters between two anonymous lovers, ostensibly a male teacher and his female student, to Abelard and Heloise, as do a growing number of scholars. Recently, Barbara Newman has made a compelling argument for the authenticity of the letters, adducing the correspondents' intimate knowledge of contemporaneous French poets from the Loire Valley (particularly Baudri of Bourgueil) and the almost certain Parisian provenance of the letters.[72] At some point in the course of the exchange, the relationship seems to have been sexually consummated, but when and how this occurred remains a matter of some debate. Barbara Newman believes that the student was seduced at a relatively early stage in the correspondence, perhaps implicit in the woman's resigned reference to "having given up everything," and her sudden slavish submission to her lover's authority.[73] Constant Mews, however, posits that a particular exchange, occurring approximately halfway into the correspondence, points to a forced consummation. The teacher acknowledges that he was the guilty party since he "compelled her to sin." The woman responds by attempting to end the relationship, concluding her letter: "Farewell. Your wisdom and knowledge have deceived me, so from now on, let our writing perish."[74] If the letters are authentic, and we accept Mews's somber reading, this would not have been the only time that Abelard resorted to violence as a means to sexual fulfillment. After the couple's preemptory entrance into religion, Abelard did what he could to reconcile Heloise to her religious vocation by disparaging their sexual past. To this end, he made the following admission: "Even when you were unwilling, resisted to the utmost of your power and tried to dissuade me, as yours was the weaker nature I often forced you to consent [to sexual intercourse] with threats and blows."[75]

If we were to waive temporarily the anomalous gender of the student, what we are left with is the story of a mature teacher, exalted for his academic prowess who, with callous premeditation seduced a youth—probably in his midteens at most. Of course, we do not know Heloise's exact age and whether she was still at such a susceptible stage in life. The traditional dating for her birth would place her at somewhere between fifteen and seventeen years of age when she first met Abelard, while Abelard would have been around thirty-six. More recently, M. T. Clanchy has argued that Heloise was about ten years older than previously thought.[76] If this is correct, Heloise may have had the advantage over the average male student in terms of years. Even so, the teacher-student hierarchy would have persisted. If, moreover, we now reintroduce the question of gender, her pedagogic subordination would be compounded by gender discrimination and female physiology alike. Unlike a male student, Heloise could never evolve to become a master and hence equal in stature to Abelard. And there is little question that her eventual pregnancy was a liability, despite Abelard's account of her alleged exaltation at the prospect of a child. For after Abelard impregnated his student, he insisted on marrying her, becoming her master in a different and even more authoritative way. From this new position of dominance, he could pressure his student/wife into taking the veil so that he could get on with his career.[77]

The story of Abelard and Heloise appears toward the end of the next century in Jean de Meun's continuation of *The Romance of the Rose* (1269 × 1275). Heloise is extolled for her exemplary rejection of marriage; the fact she was once Abelard's student is never mentioned.[78] One could interpret this cavalier omission as a sign of disapproval, but I think it unlikely that Jean de Meun would have seen anything remiss in the way their relationship began. As a scholar who had probably studied at Paris, Jean would have been conditioned by the classical narratives that shaped the school curriculum for grammar. Some of these are what Marjorie Woods has described as "heroic rapes," in which the assailants were gods or demigods. There were also seduction narratives, in which the boundaries between persuasion, coercion, and rape are indistinct.[79] And, in fact, Jean de Meun's romance arguably ends with the rape of the Rose and her ensuing pregnancy.[80]

While Abelard and Heloise's saga may tell us something about a student's vulnerability to sexual advances, it does nothing to illuminate the heightened concern with sodomy that mobilized Peter the Chanter and his circle. Yet, despite the alarm expressed in contemporaneous poetry, it is very rare to find traces of such relations in the official record. The occasional chronicle might allude to the vice in general terms. In 1198, we are told that a certain priest named Volcus, who was credited with many miracles, preached penance to the vice-ridden city of Paris, which was especially riddled by sodomy.[81] Franciscan theologian Roger Bacon (d. 1292), who described carnal lust as against the nature of human dignity and deleterious to the pursuit of wisdom, delivered a much more pointed indictment of academic mores.[82] Bacon believed that once men indulged certain vices, they become progressively blinded to lust "just as was proved this year when many theologians in Paris, who teach theology, were banished from the city and the kingdom of France for many years, publicly condemned on account of sodomitical vileness."[83] Bacon wrote these words in 1271 while still teaching at Paris. Yet there is no hint of this disgrace in the official record. Indeed, actual trials for sodomy in a university context were almost unheard of. This is not really surprising, especially in northern Europe where medieval universities were ecclesiastical institutions equipped with their own courts and jails to keep scandal at bay.[84] It is significant that the only sexual scandal recorded in the Parisian *Chartularium* was the rape of a woman committed in Meaux in 1329, and this is probably because the university and the episcopal court of Meaux went head to head over questions of jurisdiction.[85] Yet the authorities were quick to discipline any theologian that somehow veered into heresy and left prolix records to that effect.[86]

Occasionally, one stumbles across the kind of suspicious innuendo that we have witnessed in monastic statutes. For instance, in 1205 the abbot of the canons of St.-Victor issued a charter addressed to the University of Paris concerning a certain unnamed priest who had been accused of "many things" and whose growing infamy required that he abjure Paris. After the bishop who expelled him was deceased, he returned without permission. Very soon that priest "of intolerable infamy and perverse life" attracted the notice of the current bishop, who had him seized and incarcerated—a punishment that might suggest sodomy.[87]

A similar question mark hangs over a letter written to an anonymous master by Robert Grosseteste sometime between 1232 and 1234, when Grosseteste was teaching at Oxford. He begins with the declaration that he can no longer love the recipient "*in* Christ, but *because* of Christ, since, as a rumor is emphatically and stridently proclaiming about you, you are not *in* Christ. For the dangerous and putrid infection of lewdness has cut you off from the body of Christ and made you one with the body of the old enemy."[88] Such language implies that some kind of sexual lapse is at issue, and this is confirmed when Grosseteste later reminds his correspondent of his vow of chastity. In addition, Grosseteste dwells on the fact that the nameless sinner is "neither strong, very beautiful in appearance, [is] wasted by diseases and many different toils, consumed by old age, gray-haired, wrinkled of face, near to the grave." Such deprecations not only imply that the letter's recipient should be past such base desires, but also that the object of his correspondent's desire was probably considerably younger.[89] Despite such allusions, the sin is not named. Still, there is none of the usual misogynist rhetoric associated with clerical celibacy that generally attends sexual lapses involving women. But if sodomy is at issue, one might have expected a degree of frankness from the pastoral theologian who, as we have seen, acknowledges on more than one occasion that this vice was widespread among the clergy. Perhaps when confronted with a concrete situation involving a close acquaintance, however, the bishop's clerical code of discretion was activated.

One of the most explicit indictments of a teacher-student relationship is found amid Thomas of Cantimpré's scare stories about the impact of "the sin against nature" on the natural order. A youthful companion, whom Thomas characterized as "dear, chaste, and good," was not at school long before he was seduced by one of the masters. The student's ensuing sexual indiscretions were hardly a secret since he was warned by Thomas, his family, and other friends about the infamous reputation he was developing, and they all urged repentance. The youth died cursing his seducer, with visions of hellfire before his eyes.[90] Despite the apparent widespread awareness of this relationship, Thomas makes no mention of any disciplinary action taken against the student or, more important, his master.

There are, however, two exemplary cases from ecclesiastical tribunals that shed light on same-sex dynamics in medieval education. The first is familiar to medievalists: the testimony of Arnold of Verniolle, made famous in Emmanuel Le Roy Ladurie's *Montaillou*. Arnold was a subdeacon and apostate from the Franciscan order who was tried for heresy and sodomy before Jacques Fournier, bishop of Pamiers, in 1323. His trial showcases the vulnerability of the average student to sexual predation.[91] Arnold himself had been sexually victimized at an early age. According to his own testimony, he was either ten or twelve years of age when he was sent to board at Master Pons's grammar school in Pamiers. Initially, he shared his bed with a certain Arnold Auriol who must have been somewhat older since Arnold commented that he was already shaving. When the older Arnold thought young Arnold was asleep, "embracing [him], he would put his virile member between his thighs, moving himself as if he were with a woman" until he ejaculated. Arnold testifies that because he was "a boy [*puer*] then, the said act was unpleasant for him; but for shame he did not dare reveal it to anyone." After enduring the elder Arnold's nightly abuse for six weeks, the school moved and Arnold was obliged to share a bed with Master Pons, who left him alone.[92]

As an adolescent, Arnold would, in turn, prey upon students. According to the testimony of a Carmelite cellmate in whom Arnold confided while he was awaiting trial, when Arnold was himself studying at Toulouse he accepted students for private tuition. A woman sent her very little son (*filium parvulum*) "who could already recite seven psalms" for instruction. This description could imply that the boy was even younger than Arnold had been when he was first sent away to Master Pons's school. Arnold "abused the boy, committing the crime of sodomy with him" ("dicto puero abutebatur, comitendo cum eo dictum crimen sodomie").[93] When Arnold was arrested, he was between thirty and thirty-two years of age. Although still preying upon students, he now targeted older boys—youths between the ages of fifteen and nineteen who were enrolled in the faculty of arts at the University of Pamiers.[94]

The students' relative poverty gave Arnold considerable leverage over them, which he exploited in any way he could. One especially ingenious ploy was the offer of free room and board with a certain cathedral canon, a position that came with special requirements. Although this job was dangled as bait before a number of youths whom Arnold found sexually attractive, the most fulsome account of the canon and his peculiar habits occurred in the course of Arnold's seduction of the student William Roux. According to Arnold's testimony, William came to his house in need of help: he was financially dependent on this brother, who, he had just learned, would no longer support his studies. William asked if Arnold knew of any cleric who would take him into service, and who would also listen to him recite his lessons.[95] Arnold told him about a certain Maurand, a canon of St.-Sernin of Toulouse and prior of Lavelanet, who needed someone to carry books for him back and forth between the school and his home. But before going any further, Arnold made William swear that he would not reveal the canon's secrets. When William accordingly swore, Arnold told him that he had heard that the canon sometimes kissed and embraced youths and afterward he would put his penis between their thighs and perpetrate that sin, "and if perchance you should stay with him, it will be necessary for you to put up with [this behavior]." William allegedly answered that he was willing and admitted to having already had a sexual relationship with a certain squire. When Arnold offered to demonstrate what kind of acts the canon would require, William was agreeable, and they went up to Arnold's room to have sex.[96]

William's version of events gives a somewhat expurgated account of the canon and his habits. Apparently, Arnold told William that the canon was prone to drunkenness, which often resulted in physical violence. If William were to live there, he would have to put the canon to bed. He would also have to procure women for the canon. William would, however, be expected to share a bed with the canon during the winter months and do whatever else the canon required—with no other specifications. In the summer, William would be expected to rub his feet around noon. Arnold then invited William to his house to show him books, at which point he offered him a place to stay. Once the two of them were inside and leafing through a certain book, Arnold cried out: "Look what it says in the decretals!" William could not as yet read Latin, so Arnold translated for him: "it says that if a man should lie with another man, and because of the heat of their bodies their semen flows, it is not so grave a sin as if a man carnally knows a woman, because . . . nature requires this and it makes a man healthier."[97] William expressed skepticism that sex with a man was less sinful than with a woman, but Arnold was adamant, insisting on the authority of the decretals. At this point, Arnold allegedly threw William to the ground and forcibly had sex with him. Arnold then insisted on William doing the same to him or else he would not permit William to leave.[98] Since the youth had a number of sexual encounters with Arnold after their initial engagement, the degree of compulsion is, perhaps, exaggerated. In their second meeting, however, when William claims to have been raped at knifepoint, Arnold will later admit to using force on William, but denied that he had raped him: he was just testing the younger man, although he never specifies for what.[99]

Arnold proved himself to be an opportunistic master of manipulation on many levels, brimming with offers and promises that were never fulfilled. The job with the canon was probably a fiction, though the canon was real enough, prompting the bishop to ask Arnold the obvious question: did Arnold know for a fact that Canon Maurand practiced sodomy? It turned out that Arnold's evidence was circumstantial. On one occasion, he ran into one of the canon's servants who had been hired to fetch books. The servant apparently wanted to leave the canon's service because he was expected to rub the canon's feet, and once the canon was warmed up (*calefactus*), or possibly aroused, the servant was supposed to hug and kiss him, and put him to bed. Arnold just assumed the canon practiced sodomy. Although it is entirely possible that Arnold did not know the canon, let alone have any power to fill vacancies in his household, the pretense provided the requisite bait for his trap. The servant's grumbling, moreover, provided him with a core story that Arnold could embellish for the vetting and grooming of desirable youths.[100] Arnold also invented other incentives. He frequently offered to procure women for the students, something that he never followed through with.[101] In fact, even in small interpersonal matters, Arnold tended to disappoint. Arnold had promised William Roux that he would loan him books and give him a knife if he would have sex with him.[102] But when the sex was over, it was Arnold who borrowed William's volume of Ovid. Meanwhile, when William attempted to take the promised knife, Arnold told him that he could not have that particular one, and that Arnold would find him another knife.[103]

Arnold admitted that he had told William Roux that sodomy was a lesser offense than sex with a woman but denied that he had shown William or anyone else a book of decretals making such a statement.[104] Although Arnold only seems to have used this argument on William Roux, Arnold also was said to espouse other complementary doctrines. For instance, he argued that sodomy was no worse a sin than fornication, a view he expressed often.[105] This assimilation of sodomy and fornication, however convenient, was more than a mere ploy: it was one of Arnold's core beliefs that he maintained throughout his interrogation.[106] When asked whether this elision of sins was tactical for purposes of seduction, Arnold denied it, claiming that the various youths with whom he had sex all acted voluntarily.[107] Arnold also attempted to diminish sodomy's sinfulness by aligning it with masturbation in degree of gravity, and further claiming that these two sins were common throughout the religious orders.[108] This was a question Arnold could speak to with some authority. He was, after all, a Franciscan (though, admittedly, not in good standing), who, according to his Carmelite cellmate, claimed that sodomy was so ubiquitous among the Franciscans that a certain unnamed friar felt compelled to leave. Arnold then went on to defame his former Franciscan brethren for their sodomitical ways, thereby fulfilling every religious order's worst nightmare about the capacity for indiscretion by a disgruntled former member. He wound up by claiming that if the bishop were to arrest everyone infected with the vice, he would be required to round up at least three thousand people—an assertion that resonates with John Stocker's views.[109]

Arnold's strategies of seduction were overall quite successful. In less than a year, he had managed to seduce the students William Roux, William Bernard, John Ioc of Gaudiès, and an anonymous apprentice from Toulouse.[110] Like most predators, Arnold looked for weaknesses that he could exploit. William Roux is a case in point. His brother had stopped supporting him and he was struggling to find a job or apprenticeship in order to continue his studies. The anonymous lodger had come from Toulouse to work with a shoemaker but was told upon arrival that there was no room for him in the master's house. In other words, he literally had no place to stay. In William Bernard's case, Arnold won his trust by leading him to believe that he was connected with members of the boy's family. When William said he was from Gaudiès, Arnold responded that he knew a student there, who turned out to be William's second cousin. Was this a coincidence or had Arnold been stalking William, hoping to acquire information that would render him more pliable? It is impossible to know. But in the course of the precoital conversation about the lascivious canon, William jumped at the chance to become his servant, which could suggest that William had a precarious living situation as well.[111]

Both William Roux and William Bernard were exceptionally timid sinners. To the scrupulous William Roux, who believed sodomy was "a grave sin and a heresy," Arnold offered to procure a lenient Franciscan to hear his confession. Even though Roux, who either did not know or did not care that sodomy was

a reserved sin, would remind Arnold plaintively about the confessor, no such
individual was ever produced. At one point when Roux refused to have sex with
Arnold, the offer of the confessor was spitefully withdrawn.[112] William Bernard
was equally apprehensive. After committing sodomy with Arnold, both Bernard
and John Ioc approached Arnold together to ask if sodomy was, in fact, a heresy.[113] Playing upon such scrupulous susceptibilities, Arnold would routinely
swear his sexual conquests to secrecy, an oath that William Bernard took very
much to heart. When the bishop asked if he had confessed the sin of sodomy to
anyone, William Bernard answered that he could not confess because Arnold
had made him swear that he would reveal this sin to no one else and that he
was afraid of committing perjury.[114] Most of Arnold's targets were around eighteen, but William Roux was sixteen; William Bernard was only fifteen.

William Pecs and William Boyer, however, two students called in by the
inquisitors who were clearly being groomed by Arnold, did not succumb to his
efforts at seduction. Arnold approached Pecs outside the church and immediately began to tell him about the canon. When they were later by themselves
near the Carmelite convent, Arnold bragged about how he had celebrated many
Masses and even asked Pecs if he would assist him at Mass. Later, Arnold would
try to convince Pecs to make a confession to him. But, although his trajectory
may have been tentatively plotted, Arnold never actually propositioned Pecs.
This may be because Arnold had only met with Pecs once and did not want to
act precipitously. Or it may be because, at nineteen years of age, Pecs was older
than Arnold's other victims. This may have rendered Pecs less attractive to
Arnold, made Arnold more circumspect, or both.[115]

The testimony of William Boyer, a student of eighteen or thereabouts, is
especially noteworthy because it suggests that Arnold had considerably less
influence over a strong-minded and self-assured youth. But it is also significant
that Boyer appears to have been in a stable living situation, which probably
made it more difficult for Arnold to manipulate him. It is probably for similar
reasons that Arnold feared exposure by a certain youth from Moissac with whom
he had committed sodomy—someone "of good family."[116] Be that as it may,
William Boyer and Arnold seemed to know each other quite well and spent the
better part of at least one day together. According to Boyer, he was attending
Mass with Arnold at which some women that they both knew were also present.
When Arnold later asked Boyer with whom, from the various women they had
seen, Boyer would prefer to have sex, the youth simply answered that this was
inappropriate conversation for a graveyard (i.e., consecrated ground). Then
Arnold asked which sin was greater, masturbation or sodomy. When Boyer
replied that he did not know, Arnold volunteered that both sins were extremely
common among the religious orders. Boyer, though surprised to hear this,

merely responded "Is that so?" and kept walking. When Arnold once again attempted to turn the conversation to sex, seemingly intent on learning whether Boyer preferred women to men, he brought up the prospect of intercourse with the widow Bartholmea, who is described as Boyer's mistress (*domina*). Boyer responded that he really did not care for such things. After lunch they took another walk, during which Arnold asked Boyer: "If you had a woman here, what would you do to her?" Boyer's answer was "Nothing." Arnold seemed to have taken this as a promising sign because he suddenly embraced Boyer, kissing him on both cheeks. But Boyer, who had apparently not been attempting to signal interest in a same-sex encounter, told Arnold to leave him alone. Arnold's last overture was to bring the conversation around to confession. Boyer had confided that his confessor had initially withheld absolution at his last confession, and Arnold, not surprisingly, was curious to know what the sin in question was. Boyer's preemptory answer was that it was forbidden to reveal such things. Finally, when Arnold offered to hear Boyer's confession, the latter responded that he had already confessed that year and, besides, Arnold was not a priest.[117] Boyer may even have attempted to interfere with Arnold's efforts to seduce others. On a later occasion, when Boyer heard that a boy *(puer)* at school had made his confession to Arnold, Boyer challenged Arnold on this issue, once again reminding him that he was not a priest.[118] Arnold was certainly aware of Boyer's position as servant or apprentice in Lady Bartholomea's household, which was probably why he never bothered to introduce the canon of St.-Sernin into the conversation.

Arnold's appearance for sodomy before an ecclesiastical tribunal, and one dedicated to heretical inquisition no less, was a decided an anomaly. For what attracted the attention of inquisitor Jacques Fournier was not so much Arnold's sodomy as his illicit incursions into the sacraments. There was abundant evidence that Arnold was fond of posing as a priest, offering to hear the confessions of his potential quarry.[119] Masquerading as a confessor was bad enough, but the most damning of Arnold's offenses was donning priestly garments and saying Mass.[120] Although Arnold attempted to deny this charge, there were too many witnesses who had heard him make this claim. The appropriation of the priestly role, doubtless helped along by a series of inefficacious libertine doctrines, added up to heresy. The question of sodomy was probably secondary, but it was a crime that fit in well with the increasing assimilation of the two charges. It was a combination that made Arnold's punishment particularly harsh. He was degraded from the clergy, imprisoned in chains, and restricted to a diet of bread and water.[121]

A second case is from the register of Merton College, Oxford, concerning Richard Edmund, a member of the college accused of sodomy.[122] On July 21,

1492, Edmund, Bachelor of Arts and Fellow of the College, was accused of "sins against nature." The following list of charges was presented to Edmund by the warden and an assembly of masters:

1. Inciting and provoking various and different youths to the sin against nature, some once and some you wretchedly abused on various occasions unto the greatest peril of your soul and the immense scandal of our college, and not a little infamy.
2. Visiting suspect spots within the university, one spot in which you are particularly suspected of unchaste behavior in peril of your conscience and the greatest scandal to our house.
3. Indulging in nocturnal prowling within the university to the scandal of the college and you plotted and incited others to do this with you.
4. Often laying outside the college suspiciously unto the great scandal and infamy of the college.

Edmund was asked to indicate in writing of which offenses he was guilty. He was encouraged to take two or three days to deliberate, especially since admitting to the first article would result in automatic expulsion. Although Edmund claimed he did not want a deferment, he nevertheless pondered the articles at some length. Finally, in the presence of the warden and the assorted masters, he wrote "Sic" beside the first and most grievous charge, and "Non" beside the others. The warden immediately sent the other masters out of the room and asked Edmund who first introduced him to this sin. Edmund answered that it was someone now dead, but one that the warden had known well. Then the warden asked Edmund on his conscience how often he indulged in that "worst crime." "With greater frequency of late," was Edmund's response.

The warden had heard enough and called back the witnesses to report to them "secretly" what he had been told. It was not his intention to report this sin to any higher authority for fit punishment, however. In fact, he especially wished to take counsel over what line of action would adequately "preserve the honor of the said bachelor." Edmund was then dismissed from the meeting. In the ensuing couple of days, it came to the attention of the warden that Edmund had "begun to excuse himself over the article concerning the sin against nature, claiming that the warden and the other witnesses had lied. He denied the crime entirely and all the other things that he had conceded earlier." The warden was disturbed by the rumor. On July 27, he gathered together six of the senior masters to assist him, as required by statute, and recalled Edmund, who again denied the charge. Asked why he had written "Sic" beside the article, Edmund claimed it was because he had been told that the warden already had enough witnesses for conviction.

In light of Edmund's denial, the warden took more time to deliberate on how best to proceed. On the last day of the month, Edmund was again called before the warden and in the presence of the other six masters, yet again asked about the first article. Edmund persisted in denying the accusation. This is in spite of the fact that Edmund had allegedly admitted his guilt to Master Richard Rawlins the day after his initial hearing, even revealing the identities of various youths whom he had "incited to the said crime and whom he abused." Hence, despite his denials, Edmund had confessed on two different occasions. The college also had the testimony of one of the boys whom Edmund had "induced to the said sin."

The masters unanimously agreed to expel Edmund in the following terms: "we concede to you the favor of remaining until Christmas, for the honor of the college; but after that we expel you from our college on account of your demerits which were sufficiently proved by the college in our presence. And we declare you are expelled in perpetuity." Afterward, Edmund sought grace on his knees, again confessing to the first article and confirming his guilt in the nefarious crime. He also named four youths whom he had seduced.[123]

The procedure was scrupulous, deliberate and, perhaps most important from the college's perspective, discreet. Edmund's trial was an entirely in-house process, which, in keeping with the merciful principles of fraternal correction, was extremely deferential to the reputations of defendant and institution alike. Edmund was permitted to remain at the college until Christmas, an additional five months, in order to avert suspicion. Indeed, the college was so successful in suppressing the scandal that Edmund appears on the list of newly made masters in the faculty of arts on February 12, 1483—a mere month and a half after he left Merton.[124]

Around the time of Richard Edmund's trial, the college was threatened by a second scandal involving another bachelor, this one named Richard Holt. In 1490, Holt received his first formal warning against frequenting "suspect spots." Such behavior had already occasioned "great infamy" for the college, and he was threatened with expulsion.[125] Over time, more evidence piled up. A few months later, Holt's name appeared in one of the college's "scrutinies"—events not unlike monastic chapter meetings during which the fellows of the college were expected to report on the wrongdoings of the other members. The specifics were never recorded, however.[126] The following year, Holt was accused of certain "enormities" at another scrutiny: "namely the frequent game of tennis, and this in public places, excessive familiarity with his senior students, visiting suspect places . . . excessive frequenting of places of ill-repute and wandering around the village." These offenses were compounded by being tardy or absent from church on feast days and an overall disregard for his studies.[127] In 1492, six days after Richard Edmund's expulsion, Richard Holt received a second warning to leave off his dishonest games and suspect perambulations under pain of expulsion.[128] The statutes stated that a third warning meant automatic expulsion. Holt postponed what he clearly saw as an inevitability by seeking permission to leave college, a permission that was granted—he was even permitted to keep his fellowship.[129] Sometime over the course of the next two and a half years, Holt married and necessarily resigned from the college.[130]

The manner in which the two Richards of Merton behaved was not all that different. Both were seen in suspect places; both brought scandal upon the college. Holt's overfamiliarity with seniors could be a coded way of conveying a suspicion of sodomy. Yet while Edmund received a form of summary justice that resulted in expulsion, Holt had the benefit of multiple warnings. The fact that Holt eventually married could suggest that, if he were guilty of any sexual infractions, at least some of them might have been with women. If that was the case, the college's relative leniency is all the more surprising considering the general tendency of church tribunals to prosecute the clergy's entanglements with females and ignore the ones with males. This double standard probably pertained to Merton as well. It is significant that when the warden asked Edmund who introduced him to sodomy, Edmund responded that the person in question was one the warden knew well. Although in all likelihood Edmund was signaling that he had been seduced by another member of the college, the warden did not pursue this matter any further. But this code of silence only seemed to pertain when such behavior was discreet, and Edmund's was not. It seems quite likely that the official response to the two Richards was parallel to what we already saw with respect to the two Johns scrutinized by Bishop Alnwick of Lincoln: John Dey's offense was too flagrant to ignore; John Alforde's behavior was more equivocal and, hence, still possible to ignore, or even contain. In a university setting, moreover, in which many students as well as members of the faculty alike could be in minor orders, a college with a problem fellow like Holt could get lucky: he could still leave the clerical fraternity and marry.

CHAPTER 9

The Episcopal Curia

The Jew mounted a horse, and rode off with all possible speed
to the court of Rome. . . . [He] cautiously began to observe
the behaviour of the Pope, the cardinals, the other Church
dignitaries, and all the courtiers. . . . [P]ractically all of them
from the highest to the lowest were flagrantly given to the sin
of lust, not only of the natural variety, but also of the
sodomitic, without the slightest display of shame or remorse.
—Boccaccio, *Decameron*

In Northern European sources, there are scant references to sodomy, while in
Italy they abound. Assuming that there is some degree of correspondence
between representation and actual practice, we can only speculate about the
reasons behind these regional differences. It is possible that the relative normalization of same-sex activity lingered in the Italian peninsula since classical times,
but it certainly would have been abetted by the high proportion of bachelors
and the custom of late marriage for men in Italian cities.[1] All of Europe seemed
to recognize an Italian predilection for sodomy. For instance, a Belgian chronicler learned firsthand from a lay brother who had once served in an army that
the sodomitical infamy of the Lombards was revealed by the unbearable stench
of their corpses.[2] The chronicler further claimed that Florentine authorities,
anticipating the natural world's revulsion, ordered that the land upon which
sodomitical acts were known to have occurred be laid waste.[3] Indeed, Florence
was so particularly associated with sodomy that its name was transformed into
a euphemism for sodomitical penetration all over Europe. Hence, in Germany
John Stocker confessed to "florenzing" the choirboy John Müller.[4]

Yet as commonplace as the offense might be in Italian cities, in theory
sodomy was still perceived as a terrible crime that could incur castration or even

the death penalty as punishment, though these harshest sentences tended to be reserved for instances of child abuse.[5] Eventually, various Italian cities would aggressively search out and prosecute those guilty of sodomy. The Florentine authorities created the Office of the Night, a special tribunal for rooting out sodomites, the initiatives of which have been carefully examined by Michael Rocke. Part police force and part tribunal, the office endured from 1432 to 1502. As a lay tribunal that was free from the constraints of due process, the Office of the Night encouraged anonymous accusations, which were usually dropped into baskets attached to Florentine churches as well as the churches of the nearby towns under Florence's control.[6] Its records remain a vivid testimony to just how common sodomy seemed to be in mainstream Italian culture.[7] Members of both the secular and the regular clergy periodically become entangled in the skein of the Office of the Night's surveillance, rendering this tribunal, as well as parallel secular initiatives in other regions of Italy, the most prolix source of evidence for clerical sodomy, certainly in the Italian peninsula and probably for all of western Europe.[8] Even so, the Office of the Night and corresponding tribunals in other cities had no jurisdiction over religious personnel, but the activity of guilty clerics was duly noted. The Florentine priest Venturo, for example, confessed to a string of sodomitical relations. He admitted to being sodomized by a certain Laurentio near the Guelph Bridge and by two clerics attached to the church of San Cresci, noting that his sexual relations with these parties lasted for three months and eight months respectively. Venturo's encounters with the clerics of San Cresci took place in a bed located in the church of San Cresci itself. The choice of locale was especially heinous because semen was considered polluting: any spilling of seed inside church precincts would require reconsecration. Yet, the officers stated explicitly that they had no legal competence over the priest, and the matter was referred to the archbishop.[9]

    In 1433, the Office of the Night also took it upon itself to ensure the decency of the monasteries, an ambitious task to be sure. Monastic discipline was, as we have seen, largely internal and many orders were exempt from even the visitations of the diocesan bishop. But monasteries were hardly immune to the threat of anonymous denunciation, even, or perhaps especially, from members of their community. For instance, in a case that vindicates the Cluniac apprehension of the division of the dormitory into separate rooms, we learn that Brother Andreas, a member of the prestigious Franciscan basilica of Santa Croce, occupied the third room in the lower part of the monastery, and that he had been sodomizing the friar in the adjoining room for at least three months.[10] But sexual liaisons with individuals from outside the community were much more vulnerable to disclosure. Hence we learn that in 1494, several Calmaldolese friars from the same house had sodomized a youth named Benvenuto in a special room that everybody in the community seemed to know about, almost as if it were unofficially reserved for that purpose. It is unclear whether Benvenuto was prostitute: some of the monks paid him; others did not.[11]

Occasionally, the Office of the Night's frustration over clerical disorder eventuated in formal appeals to ecclesiastical authorities. In 1470, Antonino, archbishop of Florence, received a letter from a group of disgruntled Florentine officials bespeaking secular frustration with the church's studied unawareness of clerical incontinence: "Most reverend and just father . . . our magistracy is entrusted with . . . obviating, as much as possible, the horrible vice of sodomy. Wishing to fulfill a part of our duty, we have arrested several young boys who have been sodomized not only by students, but also by numerous priests. This was made known to the representative of your most reverend lord, yet nothing has been done about it. For this reason we are most scandalized."[12] In this context it is noteworthy that the same bishop to whom this letter was addressed had remanded the legislation of his saintly forebear, also named Antonino, archbishop of Florence between 1446 and 1459. The remanded statutes included indictments of not only sodomy but also clerical concubinage.[13]

Although the intemperate behavior of some Florentine clerics remained a challenge for the Office of the Night, it had even less leverage with clerics from outside the diocese. Baldassarre, a cleric from Pisa attached to the church of Santa Liberata, was said to have "committed more buggery than the most beautiful whore of Chiasso." When Baldassarre denied these charges, the officers noted that the entire neighborhood would testify to his turpitude and it would be on the officers' consciences were they to release him. But Baldassarre was eventually released anyway.[14] When charges were deemed credible, the miscreant cleric was supposed to be sent back to his own diocese for punishment. Yet the successful return of an undesirable cleric required the cooperation of the episcopal authorities in his home diocese. Not surprisingly, this cooperation was difficult to coordinate. In July of 1492, the officers wrote the bishop of Pistoia that Lapo di Lodovicho, a youth from Prato of about fifteen or sixteen years of age, confessed "freely and without any violence" (i.e., torture) that he had been sodomized by four different priests from Prato over many months.[15] When a month went by with no word from the bishopric of Pistoia, of which Prato was a component, the officers saw fit to issue a tacit reproof that "having received no notice from our reverend lord, we wonder whether you have not received the said letters."[16] Such disciplinary actions were generally in the hands of the bishop's vicar-general, the bishop's second-in-command. Indeed, the powers of this office had become so far-sweeping, that the appointment of a wicked or an incompetent man could put the entire diocese at risk.

A Bishop and His Vicar

While Peter the Chanter was musing over the various implications of scandal when applied to the clergy, he considered the augmented capacity of the bishop to scandalize. What if a bishop created a scandal among the laity by virtue of his sumptuous trappings—the fine clothes, the horses, and the team of lawyers especially trained in coercing the laity? One might think that at the time that the Chanter was writing—when apostolic poverty was on the rise, including its heretical exponents—he might see the wisdom in tempering such ostentatious displays of wealth. And yet, the Chanter makes the opposite case. The bishop who felt compelled to put aside his opulent personal effects or diminish his entourage was behaving unwisely since these very actions could jeopardize the truth of justice. For if the bishop dressed meanly, behaved abjectly, and had no attendants to do him honor or to punish delinquents, he would no longer command the laity's respect. This could jeopardize the well-being of the diocese and ultimately place the people at risk. In fact, the Chanter will go on to argue that, even if a prelate has a penchant for overly extravagant clothing, this fault is to be preferred over efforts to diminish his rank. Ostentation renders subordinates more obedient, which is all to the good. Indeed, the Chanter determines that the overdressed prelate is actually deserving of merit.[17]

The Chanter was asserting that a bishop was a prince in his own right and had to be perceived as such. In this context, it is significant that from the late eleventh century, the episcopal residence was referred to as a palace.[18] The holdings of Italian bishops, in particular, increased exponentially in the wake of the papal reform.[19] The bishop's good fortune would naturally be reflected in public displays of wealth and the size of his household.[20] In the thirteenth century, a new and still more princely type of bishop began to emerge: someone who was not elected by the cathedral chapter; whose appointment gestured toward powerful connections outside the diocese.[21] Niccolò Pandolfini (d. 1518) fits this profile to perfection. He was born to a patrician family in Florence, became a canon of the cathedral, and studied law in Bologna, where he received his doctorate. He was recommended as bishop of Pistoia by Giuliano della Rovere, the future Julius II (d. 1513), and approved by Lorenzo de' Medici—the Magnificent (d. 1492). Niccolò was ordained bishop of Pistoia in 1474 and would remain in this position until his death, yet his career always reached beyond Pistoia. He was well connected with the papacy, serving in the papal curia and even acting as papal nuncio. Altogether, Niccolò served under eight different popes, enjoying various degrees of preferment. This culminated in 1517 when he received his cardinal's hat from Leo X.[22]

Niccolò Pandolfini also distinguished himself as a patron of the arts and clearly wanted to be remembered as such: it is widely believed that the figure of Gregory the Great in Ghirlandaio's *Sacra conversazione* was a portrait of Niccolò, who had been involved with the painting's commission.[23] As his best and last act of patronage, Niccolò commissioned an elaborate marble tomb for himself. But the project was abandoned, and the tomb left unfinished shortly before his death, probably because he ran out of money. For, in addition to his interest in the arts and generous benefactions to churches and charities, the bishop also struggled to make elaborate gifts to Leo X, being careful to honor his patron pope.[24]

The office of bishop of Pistoia could not have been an easy one. Florence had begun to exercise considerable control over Pistoia already in the thirteenth century, and the city succumbed to Florentine rule in 1401.[25] Florence also cast a long shadow over the bishopric of Pistoia. It is significant that Niccolò's predecessor was Donato de' Medici (d. 1474), the brother of Lorenzo the Magnificent. Pistoia was also famous for a political factionalism steeped in violence. From this vantage point, Stephen J. Milner perceives Niccolò as an unfortunate choice as bishop, describing him as "a career cleric constantly seeking to expand the jurisdiction of his bishopric, its income and fiscal immunities," as "singularly argumentative," and as someone who perceived his position as "merely a stepping stone to a Cardinal's hat."[26] Of course, it is also possible to construe Niccolò's efforts as the mark of an effective steward of Pistoia's episcopal patrimony, pushing back against Medici encroachments and what he perceived as excessive exactions.[27] And this is how he seems to have been remembered in Pistoia. With no fitting tomb to receive him in his see, Niccolò's body was ultimately taken to Florence for burial in the Badia. But the city of Pistoia remembered his long pontificate with reverence, still marking the day of his passing two centuries later by solemn obsequies in the cathedral.[28]

Niccolò was a busy man who was constantly on the move between Rome, Bologna, and Florence. This probably meant that he would rely heavily on his vicar-general for the day-to-day running of the diocese.[29] Since the thirteenth century, the vicar-general had begun to wield full episcopal power when the bishop was absent. Over the course of the fourteenth century, however, the power associated with the office increased and the vicar-general was also empowered to act on behalf of the bishop even when the bishop was in residence.[30] This rendered the vicar-general every bit as puissant as the bishop when it came to diocesan affairs. Like the bishop, he was able to corroborate monastic elections, grant dispensations, provide dimissory letters, arrange for ordinations, call synods, confer various kinds of licenses, and oversee the purgation of episcopal prisoners or their release from jail. He could also take the lead in episcopal visitations to the parishes and religious institutions of the diocese.[31] Sometimes a bishop might also have an assistant that was called the *officialis*, who was assigned the more limited function of presiding over the bishop's court for a period of time. Although vicar-general and *officialis* are two titles that are often confused, in Italy they were frequently deemed one and the same thing.[32] When the two offices coexisted, however, the *officialis* was subject to and could have been dismissed by the vicar-general.[33] The bishop's curia in Pistoia did not seem to have an *officialis*, at least not under Pandolfini. So when the bishop was either absent or indisposed, the vicar-general would automatically preside over his court.

The vicar-general would thus be at the very top of the administrative pecking order of the episcopal household. He would also have his own clerics, who were especially selected to serve him. Of course, a priest need not be of a particularly elevated status in order to acquire a servant. The unfortunate living arrangements between John Müller and John Stocker suggest that the cathedral choirboys in Basel doubled as servants for the canons. Maurand of Toulouse, the allegedly lascivious canon of St.-Sernin, likewise required a servant for fetching his books.[34] Some of these clerical retainers could be quite young—tonsured, but not yet ordained to major orders. It was before the eyes of young clerics such as these that Arnold of Verniolle had dangled the prospect of employment with the nefarious canon. These positions were in many ways akin to apprenticeships, only rather than learning a craft, the young clerics were learning how to conduct themselves for a career in the church. In Italy, it was common to have written contracts between the older cleric and the youth whom he took into his service that stipulated the number of years the apprenticed cleric would serve his older mentor. Giampaolo Cagnin describes the terms of such an agreement. In 1340, for example, Giovanni di Nascimbene of Monselice, who had just turned eighteen, signed a contract with the priest Pietro, rector of the church of San Lorenzo of Treviso, for five years "for staying, dwelling, inhabiting and learning the art and office of the clerical state." The priest would instruct him for a specified period of time, providing him with food and clothing. Giovanni would be expected to live in the priest's house, to serve the priest "day and night," and promise not to rob him or leave before the stipulated time had elapsed. If Giovanni in some way broke the contract, the priest would elicit damages. In this case, the responsible party would be Niccolò di Ventura from Florence, who backed Giovanni to the sum of one hundred lire di piccoli. Cagnin speculates that Giovanni's training would involve knowledge of grammar, rhetoric, scripture, and, possibly, a bit of theology and canon law. Because Giovanni received no salary and, as yet, had no benefice, he was supported by his clerical mentor and was, for all practical purposes, completely at his mercy.[35] Although most of these boys were probably in their mid to late teens, it is noteworthy that a boy was eligible for ordination to the minor clergy as door-keeper or acolyte as early as seven.[36]

The power invested in the bishop's vicar, in conjunction with the vulnerability of the younger members of his household, is key to understanding the 1507 trial of Donato Piermaria Bocco, former vicar-general to the bishop of Pistoia.[37] Donato's trial represents another of those very rare instances of a cleric being tried before an ecclesiastical court on sodomy charges—although these were by no means his only offenses. His high rank makes the case even more singular. We know little about Donato's background, apart from the fact that he was originally from Florence and at some point had received a doctorate in canon law, as would be appropriate for someone in his elevated office.[38] It is not clear what year Donato assumed his post. We do know, however, that it was sometime after October 16, 1484, because before that date the position of vicar-general of Pistoia had been held by Giovanni Damiano de Beccis of San Geminiano, a canon of Volterra, who also held a doctorate in canon law.[39] We know that Donato was vicar-general in 1505 when he attempted (unsuccessfully) to interrogate a popular holy woman named Dorotea da Lanciuole.[40] But we do not know when Donato was actually dismissed. In the extant trial record, Donato was first cited before Iacobo Pucci de Centis, a canon of the cathedral and the newly appointed vicar-general of Bishop Pandolfini, in August 1506, but his trial did not begin until March 1507. Since several of the witnesses relate events that occurred only a year before the trial and specify that Donato was still presiding as vicar, clearly his dismissal was recent. So Donato could have occupied the position of vicar-general anywhere between late 1484 and the summer of 1506.

Donato's dismissal was not only warranted, but long overdue—especially from the perspective of an ambitious bishop who was necessarily protective of his own *fama*. Donato was loose-lipped and spiteful and derived particular pleasure from spreading slanderous stories about his employer, the bishop. Many of the allegations put in circulation by Donato were of a serious nature. For instance, he claimed that the bishop only undertook visitations for profit and that simony was the rule at the episcopal court.[41] If anyone received some kind of position in Rome, the bishop would launch a lawsuit to detain him and insist on getting paid off before the reluctant defendant could depart.[42] But Donato's position as vicar-general also made him privy to highly sensitive information, which, if leaked, could have done the bishop considerable harm, even if the information in question was invented or distorted. Donato did not flinch from regaling his confidants with damaging snippets from court cases, nor did he shy away from naming names. Hence, he spread the rumor that the bishop refused to act in a marriage case because it was supported by a cleric named Lodovico Antonio di Ambrosio who was allied with the Dominicans; that the bishop refused to prosecute a certain priest named Bernardino, even though he was known to forge documents and clip money; and that the bishop broke the law for the sake of Francesco di Prato (who, Donato says derisively, was a mere layperson) and against Thomasio Pippi Lei, who Donato believed should have been chosen as his replacement.[43]

More portentously, Donato claimed that the bishop would never take legal action against a member of the Cancellieri family, only against the Panciatichi. This was a very serious indiscretion because Donato was referring to a case of disputed livestock that was currently before the bishop's court. What made matters still worse were the identities of the disputants and their history. The Panciatichi (Ghibelline) and Cancellieri (Guelf) had dominated the social and political landscape of Pistoia with their infighting since the thirteenth century.[44] Violence had once again broken out between the two factions in 1498 and continued until 1502. The catalyst was a contested appointment that was key to controlling the hospital of San Gregorio—one of the city's most important religious institutions. Pandolfini was directly implicated in the crisis because it had been his job to choose between the two sets of candidates put forward by the feuding families. It was widely believed that Pandolfini did, in fact, favor the Cancellieri—in spite of the fact that Lorenzo de' Medici, the all-powerful ruler of Florence, favored the Panciatichi.[45] So for Donato to maintain that the bishop would invariably side in favor of the Cancellieri provided dangerous confirmation to widespread suspicion.

Donato invented a shifting set of alibis to justify his treachery toward the bishop. According to his friend, Lord Castellano di Castellani, Donato frequently claimed that he wished to leave the bishop's service, but that he feared that the bishop would become violent.[46] On one occasion he alleged that the bishop bore Donato a grudge for a robbery he had endured at the hands of a servant who had just left Donato's service. Sometimes Donato blithely justified his slander by claiming the bishop was cheap, and that the salary for the vicar-general was rotten. In fact, Donato maintained that all the previous vicar-generals had left the bishop because they felt disparaged and underpaid, and that these chagrined predecessors had likewise taken comfort in complaining about their employer. Like his predecessors, Donato also believed that he was being treated with general despite and little honor, and he planned to leave as well.[47]

Once Donato realized that the bishop had caught wind of his wrongdoings and that he would soon be forced to leave Pistoia, he threw all caution to the wind and set out to destroy the bishop's reputation in earnest.[48] (He also started stealing from him.)[49] But the vicar-general's malice was as fulsome as it was unrelenting, eddying out well beyond the bishop to include all of his subordinates. Donato claimed that the bishop's entire curia was venal, unjust, and would do anything for money.[50] He maintained that the whole episcopal household was full of gamers who did nothing but play dice day and night, asserting that the bishop himself could only tolerate gamblers, blasphemers, and other vice-ridden individuals who were rotten to the core, and had little patience for anyone else. Donato even offered up the names of the Pistoian priests whom he deemed most depraved.[51] When visiting Florence with some friends, Donato sharpened his invective, maintaining that the Pistoian clergy were infidels who didn't believe in Christ, but that this was the least of their crimes.[52]

Donato's precarious job security also seems to have resulted in dramatic mood swings. Sometimes he was full of bravado about his future prospects, confident about acquiring another position as vicar-general and anticipating his future revenge on the bishop of Pistoia with relish—or in his terms: "I know a certain a little devil [i.e., Donato] who will castigate another bigger devil [i.e., the bishop]."[53] But at other times Donato would besiege his friends with pathetic laments, begging them to find him a position as vicar-general elsewhere. To this end, Donato forged certain letters that he hoped would help him secure a post either in Viterbo or in Volterra, entrusting the forgeries to Castellano di Castellani.[54]

In the course of Donato's testimony it emerges that the trial of 1507 was not his first: the bishop had already tried his irascible vicar-general and found him guilty. We do not know the specific charges. We only know that the bishop had, indeed, learned of some of Donato's "offenses and crimes" (*delicta et scelera*), and this probably precipitated proceedings to remove him from office.[55] In the wake of his deposition, Donato withdrew to the monastery of Mount Olive in Pistoia—voluntarily, according to his own account—planning to appeal the sentence but attesting to overall good spirits now that he was finally out of the bishop's grasp. Meanwhile, Donato continued to spin his web of lies around the unsuspecting monks. For instance, Donato falsely claimed not only that he had been forced into religion, but also that the greedy prelate seized upon the opportunity to despoil Donato of his clothing, pens, and books.[56] Donato also fantasized about the kind of hostile political climate that would bring about Pandolfini's downfall: that he would lose his bishopric because of his enmity with the Florentine *gonfaloniere della giustizia*; that he was on the wrong side of at least two Florentine cardinals;[57] and that he was not a particular favorite with Pope Julius II.[58] When confronted with the abundant evidence of his impressive slander campaign, Donato freely acknowledged that his many calumnies against the bishop and clergy of Pistoia were groundless, instead representing products of his prodigious malevolence.

Whether invented or not, Donato's accusations so closely mirror his own conduct that they are probably best understood as instances of projection, albeit of a particular kind. In Chapter 3, we discussed cases in which clerics unconsciously repressed prohibited behavior, projecting it onto others. In Donato's case, however, sanctioned behavior was clearly not repressed, but embraced, acted out, and internalized. Ultimately, such reprehensible conduct not only seems to have become a new norm for Donato, but he projected it onto others: it was his standard for how he believed anyone would behave, given the opportunity. The number of wrongdoings to which Donato admits is legion, testifying to the extent of his power. The range of matters for which Donato accepted bribes is especially indicative: two florins to resolve a matrimonial case in the husband's favor (although Donato complained that the man never paid up);[59] two florins for the dissolution or confirmation of any marriage;[60] four lire for cases involving a dispensation from the fourth or fifth degree of consanguinity, something which seemed to be frequently required in the hill country;[61] six florins from the family of a nun who had left the monastery of San Michele to coax the nuns into receiving her back (but they steadfastly refused, and he never got paid);[62] an unspecified amount from another family for sending one of its members back to a monastery in which he was never actually professed and where the monks did not want him;[63] three gold florins for an apostate friar who wanted to stay in Pistoia;[64] three lengths of black satin in order to leave a priest and his concubine unmolested; eighteen lire for the favorable settlement of an inheritance case;[65] twelve grossoni for forcing someone to sell his grain unwillingly;[66] three lire for absolution from homicide; six or eight grossoni for absolution from arson (which prompted a scribal note in the margin as a reminder to ask just how many cases he absolved as well as how much money he got);[67] and many bribes for absolving instances of abortion and infanticide.[68] Donato also solicited money from anyone who sought to appeal a debt as well as from anyone seeking to have a debt annulled.[69]

In the course of the various visitations that he undertook on behalf of the bishop, Donato not only enriched himself by overlooking a wide range of parochial irregularities,[70] he also extorted money for accepting candidates to orders or the transmission of benefices.[71] Donato also proved especially successful at corrupting a succession of *operarii*—officials in charge of the fabric of the various parish churches, who kept some of the money delegated for repairs and equipment for themselves, but turned most of it over to him.[72] On the rare occasion, Donato might make an effort to to disguise his greed. During a visitation of a female religious community, for example, the abbess offered him a florin, but

Donato made a virtuous show of refusing the bribe, instead asking that the money be bestowed upon a member of his entourage. The abbess obliged, and Donato pocketed the florin the moment the abbess was out of sight.[73]

This list of Donato's misdemeanors is representative, but by no means exhaustive. Yet, as unsympathetic as Donato may sound, however, he was not without friends. Once he had embarked on his path of open revolt against the bishop, Donato shared everything the bishop did or contemplated doing with his best friend, Bernardo Taviani.[74] Then there was Paolo, the chanter who hid a chalice behind the altar dedicated to Corpus Christi and then ran off with it.[75] Donato must have been attached to Paolo because he was dismayed by his arrest and became despondent over his subsequent imprisonment.[76] But then Donato, with the help of his friend Bernardo, a gifted forger, sprang Paolo out of prison, reversing the bishop's express orders.[77] A marginal note in the trial record adds that Donato had probably been fully aware of Paolo's theft at the time, choosing to look the other way. Paolo's escape from prison was clearly successful as the note concludes wryly: "I still don't have him in hand."[78]

Donato's most trusted confidant was, arguably, the local nobleman Castellano di Castellani, alluded to above. It was with Castellano that Donato shared the bulk of his anti-episcopal slander, and it was upon Castellano that Donato particularly depended for securing another position. Even so, Donato's loyalty was hardly unshakable. When, for example, he got ahold of some compromising information about Castellano, Donato's abundant malice was ignited. A certain servant who worked in the convent of San Giorgio di Cusina revealed that Castellano was having an affair with the abbess. This salacious piece of gossip was not only confirmed by the testimony of Lorenzo di Lottheringho della Stupha—one of Donato's own clerics—but then seconded by the alleged "nephew" of the said abbess.[79] The nephew also noted that the illicit couple had contrived certain secret signs for signaling when one of them wanted to have sex. Rather than keeping this affair to himself, as would a good friend who also happened to have unconscionable morals, Donato suddenly assumed the role of the most scrupulous officer of the bishop. He told the bishop about Castellano's dalliance with the abbess, with predictable results: the bishop sent Donato with a message for Castellano, insisting that he stop frequenting the monastery immediately on pain of imprisonment. But, as Donato told his judges, Castellano did not stop visiting the abbess, instead arguing that the monastery was in Empoli, and therefore not under the bishop's jurisdiction.[80] Predictably, Donato did not let on that he was, in fact, the one responsible for betraying Castellano to the bishop. Rather, he called the bishop a traitor—showing Castellano letters authorizing Donato to arrest him for his liaison with the abbess.[81] Yet Donato, an Iago figure if there ever was one, did not leave the matter there. When

Castellano was visiting a friend in Pistoia, Donato went to see him and, "with evil intent in mind and spirit," fallaciously told Castellano that the bishop, wearing a cheerful expression, had absolved Castellano. His friend was, of course, very relieved.[82]

Donato's attitude toward Castellano is puzzling, but it may have something to do with his basic contempt for the laity. One of Donato's complaints against Bishop Pandolfini was that he bent the law, or at least showed clemency, for someone "who was a mere layperson."[83] Perhaps the prospect of a layman having sex with the abbess, a woman consecrated to God, was repulsive to Donato. Apparently, Donato told the abbess's nephew repeatedly, almost in tears, that he would be ashamed to have so debauched a relation.[84] Or perhaps his behavior was grounded in a different kind of aversion: in a time and place where sexual orientation was still flexible, Donato remained, as we shall see, unequivocal in his tastes. He was seemingly only interested in sex with males. Perhaps he lacked sympathy, or even felt revulsion, for intercourse between the sexes and found Castellano's attachment repellant. Clearly Donato would stop at nothing to assist someone like Paolo the chanter. In contrast, not only was Donato responsible for reporting Castellano to the bishop, but he repeatedly returned to the subject of the affair between Castellano and the abbess during the course of his inquest. Was this simply spiteful behavior or did Donato somehow believe that by turning into an unofficial informant he might warrant a degree of clemency? Whatever Donato's intention, his testimony clearly made an impression on his listeners. Immediately following his confession, the scribe jots down a reminder for the inquisitors to check up on Castellano's behavior.[85]

Sodomy and Rape

> There are certain things you just don't believe can happen to
> a man, you get me? But I know now that sexual violence
> against men is a huge problem. Everybody has heard the
> women's stories. But nobody has heard the men's.
> —Eunice Owiny, refugee counselor, Kampala, Uganda[86]

Donato's sexual practices were on a continuum with the rest of his criminal profile—only his depravity was marked not only by his characteristic lack of conscience but by an inordinate capacity for brutality. The testimony of Lorenzo Pietro Giovanni of Florence, a chaplain at the hospital of Santa Maria del Ceppo dei Poveri, gives an account that is both graphic and poignant, attesting to

Donato's cruel appetites.[87] Two years earlier, when Lorenzo occupied the position of the bishop's chaplain, the vicar-general came to his room. At the time, Donato employed the cleric Lorenzo di Lotteringho della Stupha, the same servant we met earlier attesting to Lord Castellano's affair with the abbess. Donato requested that the chaplain come and examine Lorenzo, who seemed to be suffering from a torn anus (*ruptus culus*). When Donato led the chaplain to his chamber, the latter lit a candle and examined the young cleric. His anus was, indeed, badly damaged. The chaplain told the boy that he needed to go to the hospital of Santa Maria del Ceppo dei Poveri, where they would wash the wound with wine and orange peels, disinfect it with a copper extract, and bandage him. But the chaplain did not participate in the care of the young Lorenzo, nor did he know who had or what became of the boy.[88]

The unfortunate Lorenzo was in an impossible position because Donato supported (*tenebat*) him. Lorenzo was not alone in this regard. Iacopo Bernardino di Buti (nicknamed "the Spaniard"), a cleric in Pistoia, likewise testified to being abused sexually three or four times by Donato when he was in his employ.[89] Even clerics who were not members of the episcopal household were afraid to resist the vicar-general's overtures. A Pistoian priest named Niccolò testified that about two years earlier, when he had certain essential business to conduct with the vicar-general, he went to his room in the episcopal palace. Donato closed the door, grabbed Niccolò, and sodomized him. It only happened on the one occasion, and Niccolò claimed that he tried to resist. But he ultimately gave in because of Donato's intimidating office.[90] The priest Bernardino, who was affiliated with the church of San Felice of Pistoia, was sodomized by Donato the night of his visitation to the parish two years earlier. Since then, he had been sodomized three times in Donato's chamber.[91]

A handful of witnesses was produced to testify against Donato. But most of the evidence for Donato's sexual excesses was revealed by the man himself. His testimony resembles an even darker version of *Madamina*—the famous catalog of Don Giovanni's sexual conquests from Mozart's opera—only Donato's list itemizes rapes rather than seductions. The worst sufferers were Donato's own clerics, doubtless handpicked to suit his sexual tastes. Donato seconds the testimonies of both Lorenzo di Lotteringho and Iacopo "the Spaniard." He admits to sodomizing Lorenzo "continuously, day and night," acknowledging the damage he had done to his anus and noting that the wound had to be attended to secretly "day and night" for a long time. He also confirmed sodomizing his cleric Iacopo "the Spaniard" many times. Donato even confessed to relations with clerics who had worked for him but who had not been called to testify. Three years earlier, he had sodomized the Florentine Baronio Mormorai multiple times, as well as Nicolino di Piero Boso. In fact, Donato acknowledged that he had sodomized every cleric who ever worked in his chamber. He preyed upon members of the bishop's personal household as well, sodomizing the bishop's barber some three years earlier.

Despite Donato's formal training and disciplinary position, his sexual braggadocio won out over the traditional fear of scandal that was second nature to most clerical authorities. His testimony confirmed what other witnesses had already attested: that Donato made no effort to limit his sexual activity to the episcopal palace but was prepared to force himself on clerics throughout the diocese. Although he did not seem to remember the priest Niccolò, perhaps because it was a single encounter, he did corroborate what Bernardino di Pratense had to say about his sodomatical activities, though with some differences. Donato claimed to have sodomized Bernardino "lots and lots, many times," while Bernardino himself testified that this only occurred on four occasions. The threat that Donato presented to the Pistoian clergy also extended to their families. He admitted to sodomizing the "nephew" of the priest, Lodovicho di Vannozo of Pistoia. Two years earlier, he had sodomized Iacopo, the little son (figluolo) of the priest Nanno Poli, ripping him so badly that he needed medical attention for many days.

Donato spent a good deal of his time in Florence, where he persisted in his sexual excesses. A year and a half before the trial, Donato crept up on Alberto di Giugni of Florence and assaulted him while he slept. He sodomized a certain Bartholomeo di Thomaso Fescobaldi; Rafaele, one of the clerics retained by whoever his host was, an infinite number of times; he also attested to sodomizing another Rafaele—this one being the son of a Florentine furrier. Ten years before the trial, Donato also sodomized the knight Francesco del Pavese, who at that time was a cleric. Donato winds up his testimony by admitting to having sodomized many more males than the ones named, but he could no longer remember their names or ranks.[92]

Donato's sexual predation did have some limits, however. With the exception of Rafaele, the son of the Florentine furrier, and the bishop's barber (who one assumes was a layman), Donato seems to have confined his sexual overtures to other members of the clergy. This could, in part, be a reflection of his clerical snobbism: the age-old tendency to clump laici and illiterati together.[93] But it also reflects Donato's pragmatic recognition of the individuals over whom he exercised the most control—the ones, he assumed, who would not dare speak out against him. The objects of his dreadful desire were usually not far advanced in holy orders. In fact, only two of Donato's victims were identified as priests— Niccolò, the Pistoian priest who had come to the episcopal palace on business, and Bernardino di Pratense of San Felice, whom Donato first encountered in the course of a visitation. Although ordained to the priesthood, they could still

have been quite young: the age requirement for ordination to the priesthood in
Latin Christendom had sunk to around twenty, while Italy tended to advance
clerics at an even earlier age. But supposing that some of his sexual conquests
were not particularly young, supposing they were pushing thirty: Donato was
clearly no gentle lover pitching woo; he sexually subdued weaker males with
force and violence. From an aesthetic standpoint, it might be more pleasurable
for him to have sex with younger males, but from the point of view of rape as
an act of violence and domination, even mature men might have been satisfying
conquests.

The fact that Donato raped with impunity for years, apparently with no
fear of denunciation, is not really as surprising as it might seem. Any youthful
hopeful employed in his chambers was removed from the care and surveillance
of family, yet following in a career trajectory that was predetermined by his
family. The boy's relatives were paying to have him apprenticed to a priest: that
the priest in question should be the vicar-general to the bishop would be a
particular coup. Since Donato was a practiced extortionist, one can only assume
that he exacted top lire for such a position. Familial expectations, the contract
entered into, and the money paid would all conspire to secure the silence of the
young cleric. We saw in the previous chapter that the adolescents exploited by
Arnold of Verniolle were suborned into silence by fear and shame alone. Someone like Lorenzo di Lotteringho della Stupha, contractually bound and horribly
wounded in ways he could never have anticipated, would have been more
ashamed still. Had Lorenzo dared to speak out, it is difficult to imagine that his
family would have stood by in silence while he suffered continual abuse from
his employer. For even in a culture that was inured to the pederastic contours
of same-sex relations, the mistreatment that Lorenzo endured would probably
have been perceived as intolerable.

Donato had other ways of securing silence as well. As vicar-general, Donato
would be responsible for punishing flagrant sexual offenses. We have seen that
in the context of the alleged affair between his friend Castellano and the abbess,
Donato feigned the role of a scrupulous disciplinarian. Sodomy was, of course,
a much worse sin than fornication—even with a nun. Although the church
could not impose the death penalty, in some Italian dioceses public penance was
required for sodomy in order to maximize the offender's humiliation.[94] But
Donato did what he could to subvert his disciplinary responsibilities in this
regard. When a group of youths was apprehended by a secular official for sodomy, for example, Donato offered to claim that the boys were clerics and, hence,
not under secular jurisdiction, provided they would each pay him four silver
florins. On at least one occasion, however, circumstances seemed to have forced
Donato's hand, and he was required to discipline some clerics caught for

sodomy—probably because the case had become a scandal. Donato had them whipped but took no other action. Whatever the attendant circumstances, Donato felt compelled to justify his actions to Castellano, supporting the supposition that the offense was known to the public. He claimed that the bishop did not want him to proceed against the canons in Pistoia because they were all great sodomites. Later in his confession he withdrew these allegations against the canons, saying that these charges were but other examples of his efforts at defamation through spiteful fabrications.[95] This was ever Donato's default justification for his treacherous tongue. Yet if one considers that Donato was being tried by the vicar-general of his former employer, the very bishop he had disparaged, it was certainly prudent to disavow his ongoing vilification of the diocesan clergy. Even so, the fact that Donato was allowed to persevere in his reign of terror for some years suggests that the clergy of Pistoia were no strangers to sodomy and even found a way to tolerate Donato's abuses.

Back to the Future

> Presley is a violent man. . . . He managed to work his will and
> way by fear, intimidation, charm and deception, all the classic
> signs of a hardcore predator. How he managed to escape for
> so many years defies reason and understanding.
> —Bishop Donald Trautman's petition to the Vatican for the
> laicization of Erie priest, William Presley, 2006

The diocesan officials of Erie, Pennsylvania, had known since at least 1987 that Father William Presley had abused many minors, and yet he remained active in the ministry for another sixteen years. Bishop Trautman was the presiding prelate for thirteen of these years. His alleged bewilderment over how Presley could have "managed to escape" for so long was disingenuous, to say the least—especially when one considers that Trautman was the primary abettor of the predator's prolonged "escape" tactics. When Trautman reported Presley's abuse to the secular authorities, as the present-day church is theoretically obliged to do, he contained the scandal to the best of his ability. Before contacting the district attorney, Trautman preemptively curtailed the diocesan inquest regarding the extent of Presley's abuse to ensure that no new cases would be discovered. Thus the bishop was able to claim: "We were unaware of these allegations until they came to light only a few years ago. As a result, no criminal charges were ever brought forward because the statute of limitations had expired."[96]

Did Bishop Pandolfini know about his vicar-general's exploitation of younger clerics before the trial of 1507? It is difficult to imagine that he did not. Of course, what he could have done to remedy the situation was perhaps contingent upon how he learned about the abuse. What if he learned about Donato's depravity in the same way that Peter the Chanter's hypothetical bishop had learned that his chamberlain was a sensualist and a fornicator—through sacramental confession? If that were the case, the bishop would be paralyzed. Without corroborating evidence, it would be impossible to remove Donato from office without scandal, no matter how many souls were imperiled.

But most of Donato's depredations took place in the episcopal palace—a grim two-story structure, built in the eleventh century and still extant. It is imposing, but not colossal. The outer walls are extremely thick, but the floors and inner barriers are wooden.[97] It is difficult to believe that no one knew that these boys were being assaulted—that no one heard anything behind a door or through a floor. Or even if no one heard, it is impossible to believe that no one talked. One wonders, for instance, about Lorenzo Pietro Giovanni, the bishop's chaplain, who was brought in by Donato to give his opinion on the damage he had inflicted on his poor servant, Lorenzo di Lotteringho della Stupha. As a witness to such harrowing maltreatment, it would seemingly make sense for the chaplain to mention this abuse to the bishop—especially if the chaplain acted as the bishop's sometime confessor, or vice versa. Let us give them the benefit of the doubt. Let us imagine that the chaplain had mentioned the problem to the bishop or that the bishop had made the discovery on his own. It is always possible that either the chaplain or the bishop first attempted the expedience of fraternal correction. Supposing one of them had spoken privately with Donato, but the latter failed to heed his warning. Perhaps his would-be corrector then proceeded to gather several brethren to confront collectively the vicar-general with his sins. Yet if such a private intervention ever took place, it clearly was not effective. In theory, that would mean that Donato, as an unrepentant and continual offender, should be publicly denounced and tried. But supposing that the would-be correctors subscribed to Henry of Ghent's view: that if they were to advance the case to the next level and make the offense public they would be acting against charity? Such a persuasion could forestall further action. Yet even if Donato's accusers did not subscribe to this view, it was nevertheless a convenient position to espouse if they were determined to avoid scandal.

But there were also other avenues available for contending with Donato's sexual terrorism. Together the two Lorenzos, victim and witness, met the criteria for canonical proof and could have formally accused Donato. This path was also fraught with danger, however. The bishop was a busy man who was often away from his see, and it was probably difficult to get an audience without going through his vicar-general. And even if the two Lorenzos did manage to meet privately with the bishop in order to bring charges against Donato, would they have been heeded, even if they were believed? Lorenzo, the chaplain, was at least ordained to the priesthood. But the other Lorenzo was young, still in minor orders, and a servant of the accused—just the type of malcontent whose testimony had traditionally been disparaged in canon law and could be easily discounted.

The two Lorenzos were not possessed of sufficient gravitas to bring down a vicar-general, and such an attempt was probably never even contemplated. The younger cleric was indentured to Donato. Pleasing the vicar-general was central to his future career. And unless the younger Lorenzo was prepared to reveal the physical harm he had sustained, he would doubtless be apprehensive about the kind of reception he would meet were he to return to his family or patron before the agreed upon time. For his part, the chaplain seemed all too intent on distancing himself from the younger Lorenzo: he says explicitly that he did not attend him in his illness (although Donato initially appealed to him because of his medical expertise) and never saw him again after that traumatic night two years earlier—in spite of the fact that the two Lorenzos both technically lived under the same roof. By the time of the trial, moreover, the chaplain had left the service of the bishop to take up a new chaplaincy at the hospital of Santa Maria del Ceppo dei Poveri, leaving behind the scene of the crime. We do not know exactly when or why Lorenzo, the chaplain, left. Perhaps his glimpse into the vicar-general's sinister appetites precipitated his exodus. It was, after all, disgust with the decadence of Archbishop Manasses's curia at Reims that prompted the canon Bruno to strike out on his own and found the Carthusians. Yet the chaplain's departure was more likely a different kind of career move: the hospital of Santa Maria del Ceppo was Pistoia's richest religious institution, possessing twice the budget of the episcopacy.[98]

It is doubtful that either of Donato's trials was precipitated by accusations of sodomy. As we saw in the case of the hapless Franciscan apostate Arnold of Verniolle, sodomy was incidental to the more serious charge of heresy, even as it was secondary to the case for official corruption and defamation that was brought against the vicar-general of Pistoia. The succession of events, as well as the line of questioning, suggests that it was probably Donato's libelous tongue that prompted the bishop to explore his dereliction of duty. It seems all too likely that the question of sodomy was never raised at the first trial—although one assumes that Donato's sexual excesses were common knowledge. If the authorities had been intent on punishing Donato for sodomy at this juncture, why was he not imprisoned? Why was he left to his own devices after his dismissal? Clearly the bishop just wanted Donato gone. But to dismiss him, yet allow him to remain at large in Pistoia, was a miscalculation. The stream of slander against the bishop continued after Donato's deposition, and it was this continuance that probably precipitated another trial. The second time around, while Donato's inquisitors were still more focused on the wrongdoings he had committed in an official capacity than on his sexual abuses, the charge of sodomy had become useful. It was the checkmate that could silence Donato once and for all.

Donato was a cooperative witness, confessing to every sin of which he was accused and then some. We do not know what the final verdict was. But one would assume that his judges had learned their lesson from the first trial and realized that Donato was too dangerous to go free. They could have leapt upon the abundant evidence for sodomy as an opportunity to put away this depraved cleric forever by imprisoning him for life. And yet they did not. In 1515, the Dominican Francesco Onesti da Castiglione wrote to the vicar-general of Pistoia for an account of the aborted interrogation of Dorotea da Lanciuole that Donato had attempted in 1505. The vicar-general obliged, providing a detailed account in a letter and identifying himself as none other than Donato Bocco, doctor of canon law.[99] Onesti's request came some eight years after Donato's second trial. In other words, Donato not only managed to elude imprisonment, but even succeeded in regaining his position under Bishop Pandolfini.

Conclusion

Whenever a strict pattern of purity is imposed on our lives . . .
if closely followed [it] leads to hypocrisy.
                              —Mary Douglas, *Purity and Danger*

The word "Sodom" has been traditionally associated with words like "mute" or
"silence." Some historians of sexuality have lingered over the tragedy of this
silence for the men who were unable to express their sexuality openly or even
confess their sins except through euphemisms. This book has attempted to draw
attention to another set of silences: the ecclesiastical authorities' centuries of
silence about the clergy's predation on the young and the ensuing efforts to
silence the victims. These efforts are especially palpable in the monastic world.
The Carolingian commentator's advice to an abbot that an adolescent who sexually assaulted a younger boy should not be assigned public penance if he seemed
a promising candidate for the priesthood; Peter the Venerable's efforts to end
oblation at Cluny, couched in a determination to remain "quiet about certain
things"; a Cistercian abbot's politic decision to waive the rules and not expel an
underage monk who might talk; and the equivocal references to nebulous
offenses in monastic statutes, concealing more than they reveal. In this context,
the silence that was at the very center of monastic discipline suddenly seems
laced with a sinister irony. By contrast, the business of silencing was not always
articulated so clearly as a policy in the church's secular tribunals. The officials
simply refused to prosecute offending clerics, including those who were caught
in the act by secular authorities.

It was in the wake of the eleventh-century papal reform, when the premium
on clerical purity ran high, that the telling euphemism "the sin not fit to be
named" first emerged. Although ostensibly introduced as an epithet of disapprobation, it also gestured toward the historical forces that brought it into being.
On the one hand, there were statutes and canons that were unequivocally repres-
sive, truly seeking to extirpate this perceived evil. On the other hand, the euphemism was inseparable from the church's reflexive instinct to suppress scandal.

The actual prohibition against naming the sin operated like a covert license for church authorities to ignore it altogether. It might be tempting to associate "the sin not fit to be named" with the Clinton administration's tactical policy of "Don't ask, don't tell" regarding gays in the military, but that would be a mistake. The studied reticence of the Clintonian policy may have been damaging to the individuals forced to suppress their true identities, while doing nothing to allay the prejudice against individuals perceived as gay. But the policy it replaced, which had required active pursuit of gays in the military, was far worse. Though recognizing it as an imperfect solution, Clinton nevertheless perceived this tactical silence as preliminary to the full acceptance of gays in the military. In other words, he was anticipating a time when relations between two consenting adults would be accepted. In contrast, the tactical silence surrounding the medieval church's "sin not fit to be named" did not anticipate a better future, but merely maintained a sordid status quo. Nor was this silence generated for the benefit of two consenting adults, but to help conceal the relations between a sexually dominant adult and an often resistant child or adolescent.

It is possible that "the sin not fit to be named" became more ubiquitous with the papal reform's suppression of clerical marriage and its aftermath. In the wake of the reform, the emergence of a clerical subculture that celebrated the love of boys could be construed as triumphal. The clerics who indulged in same-sex relations were not chastised, even as the clerical poetry celebrating same-sex love circulated without constraint. But sexual practices are often situational. It is possible that many clerics turned to boys in order to fill the emotional and physical void left behind by the departure of wives and children. The absence of legislation regarding sodomy in the course of the eleventh-century reform and its aftermath may even signal a tacit consensus among religious authorities that this manner of substitution was permissible, regarding it as less disruptive than clerical marriage, and hence, from a practical standpoint, the lesser of two evils. When clerical sodomy was eventually prohibited at Lateran III, all the equivocation implicit in the euphemism "the sin not fit to be named" stood in the way of any meaningful prosecution. Even so, this evolving dialectic between prohibition and tacit permission did not go unnoticed. The English Lollards explicitly challenged the taboo surrounding the articulation of the term "sodomy," seeing a direct link between verbal suppression and the continuance of covert predation.

The relationship between clerical celibacy and clerical pederasty is undeniable. It was recognized by the persecuted married clergy of the eleventh century and by reformers like Robert of Courson alike. The same awareness is also implicit in the sometimes strained defenses that clerical defendants contrived to justify their sodomitical ways. Arnold of Verniolle alleged that sodomy was a lesser offense than heterosexual fornication with a female for purposes of seduction; John Stocker claimed to have turned to sodomy because it was more acceptable to his clerical colleagues than were relations with a woman; and Donato Piermaria Bocco alleged that the bishop of Pistoia did not even bother to discipline clerical sodomy, which was rampant among his canons.

Meanwhile, the church did what it could to make clerical concubinage into the real scandal. The efforts, which began in the fourth century and were redoubled in the ninth, became especially compelling from the eleventh century onward. Despite the propaganda of various clerical reformers, however, the "scandal" of clerical marriage was always something of a stretch. It is true that as long as celibacy remained the rule, and an important element in claims to clerical ascendancy, clerical marriage or concubinage provided fuel for anticlericalism. But what exactly was the nature of the stumbling block that clerical marriage presented to members of the laity, who were themselves married? In the high and later Middle Ages, the clergy's illicit relations with women were considered so routine that many parishes in England tried to insist that a prospective priest take a concubine rather than corrupt the parishioners' wives and daughters.[1] Alsatian peasants were likewise protective of their wives and urged priests to marry, excoriating the bishop of Basel for leaving behind twenty children by different mothers.[2] In parts of Italy, the laity was also extremely accepting of clerical wives. Daniel Bornstein's study of an episcopal visitation in fourteenth-century Cortona identifies one parish in which all of the priests had female companions except one—the only one who was roundly criticized by his flock. The parishioners were much more concerned with how the parish was run than with clerical concubinage.[3]

But if members of the laity were not really scandalized by clerical marriage, the evidence suggests that this was not the case with clerical pederasty. Their revulsion for this form of sexual expression was doubtless fostered by parental fear for their children—a feeling that some clerics might have empathized with but, unless they were widowers or had in some way assumed responsibility for any children they might have fathered, could never entirely share. The apprehension was especially strong in northern Europe, where the vestments of a sodomitical bishop were mutilated to expose his buttocks and a pilgrim suspected of child molestation was martyred. Such instances of mob violence provided yet another good reason for church authorities not to name—or prosecute—clerical sodomy.

The clergy seems to have been shaped by a different ethos than the laity, however. Since clerics were not permitted to father children, it is hardly surprising that they were discouraged from cultivating positive attitudes toward them. From the time of the desert fathers, clerics were deterred from forming affective bonds with children, who were aligned with women because of the temptations they afforded. The rules of Fructuosus and Isidore severely chastised monks who smiled at, joked with, or demonstrated any signs of affection for children. The monks of Reichenau projected their own desires onto children, associating the choristers with sirens. Commentators on Benedict's rule and writers in the penitential tradition alike punished boys who were raped rather than their more mature assailants. In the later Middle Ages, clerical authorities like Jean Gerson continued to devalue children, emphasizing their innate sinfulness that only worsened as they developed into adolescents. The clerical consensus was that children's perversity was best curbed by corporal punishment. In short, one of the unexpected consequences of compulsory celibacy may have been to encourage the clergy to invest more deeply in the Augustinian tradition, which stressed the pliable *pusillus* over the innocent *parvulus*.

Since clerical authorities' attitudes toward children vacillated between suspicion and obliviousness, this ultimately meant that the sexual abuse of children and adolescents was beneath their purview. We have seen that the early initiative to end pederasty was, in fact, focused on the sinfulness of same-sex relations rather than the exploitation of the young. Church councils seldom addressed the subject of children, except when it came to punitive measures against clerical bastards. Peter Damian's passionate invective against sexual relations between members of the clergy was focused on the sacramental hierarchy of who ordained whom: the question of age was never addressed. Gratian's *Decretum* downplays the issue of sodomy, while children appear only fleetingly and are never the subject of sustained focus.[4] This degree of indifference not only failed to protect the young, but probably abetted their sexual exploitation.

Finally, clerical offenders of all stripes were supported by a disciplinary framework that was developed to suppress scandal and protect the church's reputation. The emergence of private auricular confession is inseparable from the issue of clerical sin—allowing the sinner to do penance in private without forfeiting his position. In the high Middle Ages, the ironclad seal of confession emerged, rendering a superior, who might become aware of the sins of one of his subordinates through confession, powerless. The principle of fraternal correction was likewise elaborated in such a way that only the most egregious and public offenses received public admonition and punishment, while some authorities argued against this degree of exposure altogether. When Peter the Chanter and his circle attempted to stigmatize the ubiquity of clerical sodomy, a problem that was dramatically foregrounded by the flood of young students to the cathedral schools, the result was ecclesiastical legislation without enforcement. In fact, the Chanter inadvertently made matters worse by introducing scandal as a freestanding sin, solidifying the premise that it was less sinful to conceal a sin like sodomy than to acknowledge it publicly. This kind of discreet hypocrisy especially pertained to someone in holy orders.

It may seem rash to argue for any meaningful continuity between the late Middle Ages and modern times, considering the gaping chasm of some four hundred years between when my study ends and the travails of the present-day church begin.[5] One might suppose that central aspects of clerical culture would have changed substantially after the medieval era, and that any systemic abuses were addressed in subsequent reform. Since, for example, the clergy's sexual profligacy (including sodomy) had been an essential plank in the Protestant Reformers' platform, it seems reasonable to expect that church authorities, cognizant of this critique, would have seen the Council of Trent (1545–1563) as an opportunity to end clerical authorities' self-protective reflex that eschewed scandal and fostered covert sexual abuse among the clergy.

It is impossible for me, as a medieval historian already chronologically stretched to my limits, to fill in the missing centuries on my own. Fortunately, there is an array of secondary literature to draw upon. Apparently Trent itself did not address the question of clerical same-sex relations, although, predictably, it had much to say about clerical concubinage.[6] The council did, however, mandate that clerics guilty of heinous (but unspecified) crimes were to be degraded and handed over to the secular arm, ensuring the death penalty.[7] Previously such drastic measures had been reserved for deposed clerics accused of heresy. In the wake of Trent, moreover, the zealous reforming pope Pius V issued the bull *Horrendum illud scelus* in 1568, which applied Trent's extreme punishment to clerics found guilty of the "vice against nature."[8]

There is evidence that such heightened scrutiny was felt, but only in the short term. Richard Sherr analyzes a case in Loreto from 1570 in which a canon was defrocked and decapitated for his sodomitical relations with a choirboy at the determination of the cardinal bishop who was the Protector of Loreto—a punishment that, to my knowledge, was never meted out for clerical sodomy alone in the pre-Tridentine world.[9] Sherr reasons that the cardinal's insistence on so severe a punishment was because the case occurred in the shadow of Trent and because of his awareness of the stern reformist attitudes of Pius V. But Pius died in 1572. Six years later when another choirboy from Loreto made similar accusations against some priests, there was a different pope, and the same cardinal was content to have the offenders defrocked.[10]

In Spain, Tridentine reform was notoriously enforced by the Spanish Inquisition, a tribunal that spanned from the pre-Tridentine fifteenth century to the nineteenth century, providing detailed records regarding sexual mores. Although initially intended to eradicate heresy, the Inquisition soon extended its jurisdiction over sodomy cases—an expansion doubtless facilitated by the progressive slippage between heresy and sodomy.[11] But rather than seeing marked amelioration in the wake of reform, the patterns of clerical same-sex relations seem to be consistent with medieval antecedents. Hence, St. Theresa of Avila (d. 1582) writes that "a friar and a nun have more to fear from the very ones in their convents than from all the demons put together," perhaps suggesting that things had gotten worse since Trent and that monastic morality in religious communities of both sexes was on the decline.[12]According to Stephen Haliczar's assessment of the records from the kingdom of Valencia, clerics represented 18.9 percent of the total number of individuals accused of sodomy. They were still, however, a difficult group to bring to justice, remaining beyond the reach of the secular arm. Many of the accused, moreover, gained exemption from the Inquisition's jurisdiction and were released to more lenient church tribunals.[13] Christian Berco not only found that there was a disproportionate number of clerics denounced for sodomy, but that clerics were widely perceived as presenting a dangerous sexual threat to adolescent boys. Even so, clerics also tended to receive much lighter sentences.[14] Other scholars have suggested that the number of clerical offenders was higher than the records indicate, particularly for members of religious orders, whose offenses remained underreported or unprosecuted.[15] The Inquisition's records suggest that priests continued to generate bizarre rationales as justification for clerical pederasty. A Franciscan friar was publicly whipped and imprisoned for a year for not only denying that sodomy was sinful, but for claiming that "fornicating with boys was something holy and just." A noble from Catania claimed to have been taught by a theologian that "whoever has carnal knowledge of handsome boys does not commit a sin."[16] The priest Juan Brunete scandalized the people of Moya by declaring that "it was not a mortal sin to have sex with men because he could not have it with women."[17] Same-sex relations continued to adhere to the model of coercive pederasty. According to William Monter, who examined approximately one thousand cases, "the nearly invariable pattern of relationships was between older men and adolescents, between dominator and dominated." Around one hundred of these cases involved child abuse.[18] Timothy Mitchell's study of nineteenth- and twentieth-century Spain attests to the continuance of this grim pattern.[19]

It is also possible that church reform had some unfortunate and unintended long-term consequences. The Council of Trent forcefully reaffirmed the traditional insistence on clerical celibacy and the sacrosanct nature of the clergy.[20] This doubling down has led some scholars to speculate on the ways in which Trent may have further enabled the sexual crisis in the contemporary church.[21] It has also been suggested that the council's introduction of the seminary as the vehicle for sacerdotal training, and the prevalence of sodomitical relations therein, was a contributing factor to sexual abuse in the present-day church.[22]

Past Present

The medieval legacy of sexual exploitation of minors casts a long shadow over the modern-day church. Clerical celibacy continues to provide cover for the sexual abuse of minors by the clergy, even as clerical authorities persist in concealing such offenses. Seen through this harsh light, the modern-day church could well be construed as a time capsule for abandoned or discredited ideologies. Perhaps the *longue durée* of clerical pederasty has been facilitated by an ongoing internalization of Christianity's darker view of children and youths. This is not implausible given the church's traditional resistance to change: in certain respects, clerical culture may have remained frozen in time, much like clerical vestments.

Modern church authorities have attempted to explain the contemporary scandal by the phenomenon of "clericalism"—a distorted sense of clerical entitlement resulting in the exploitation of the weak. At a recent meeting at the Vatican focusing on the protection of minors in the church, Colombian cardinal Ruben Salazar Gomez decried clericalism, accusing complicit bishops who attempt to downplay or conceal the acts of a sexually abusive clergy as behaving like salaried workers and not living up to their true vocations.[23] Clerical offenders and their abettors have also been compared with the executives of Enron, likewise awash in corporate narcissism.[24] Despite such modern analogies, however, the conditions informing the clerical sense of entitlement, and the code of silence that sustains it, are embedded in the very fabric of church doctrine from at least the fourth century, increasing over time.[25] Indeed, the degree of secrecy surrounding clerical vice has sharply risen over the course of the twentieth century. Both the 1917 Code of Canon Law and its 1983 revision maintain that a cleric's hidden offense should never be brought to light by public penance; penalties for clerical infractions are lightened, or alleviated, if there is a risk of scandal; and judges are encouraged to excuse first-time offenders.[26] Contemporary canon law forbids superiors from utilizing any knowledge gained through sacramental confession for decisions pertaining to administration or governance. This closes off Henry of Ghent's tactical solution for the abbot who, in the capacity of God's secretary, could look for an opportunity to move his sinful charge.[27] Especially alarming, however, are certain significant omissions that occurred in the 1983 revision of the code, which provide even more secure cover for delinquent clerics. The 1917 version required the laity to denounce any sexual solicitation that might occur during the course of confession under pain of excommunication, a concern that had become particularly pressing in the post-Tridentine church.[28] In 1983, however, this mandate disappeared altogether.[29] In the original 1917 code, the private correction of a clerical sinner was limited to two times before automatically going to trial, but this limitation has also disappeared.[30] Both the exercise of summary justice and the use of extrajudicial remedies are gone, eroding the bishop's independent capacity to discipline sinful clerics.[31]

Meanwhile, conditions still more conducive to the toleration of sex crimes have developed. The 1917 code had declared that priests guilty of grave sexual offenses, such as corrupting minors, "are suspended, declared infamous, and are deprived of any office, benefice, dignity, responsibility, if they have such, whatsoever, and in more serious cases they are to be deposed." The revised version is more equivocal: "the cleric is to be punished with just penalties, including dismissal from the clerical state if the case warrants."[32] The directions regarding miscreant religious are murkier still. While a member of a religious institution must be dismissed for murder, assisting in an abortion, or open concubinage, sexual infractions, including sex with a minor, are negotiable if "the superior judges that dismissal is not entirely necessary and that the correction of the member and restitution of justice and reparation of scandal can be sufficiently assured in some other way."[33] Since the current sexual abuse crisis first came to light, the church has been woefully slow to respond. The first substantive law to address the crisis is contained in Pope Francis's apostolic letter of May 7, 2019, ironically entitled "You are the light of the world" (Matt. 5:14). Catholic officials throughout the world are now legally bound to report cases of abuse and attempted cover-ups to their superiors. Yet, as victims' advocates were quick to point out, there were no fixed penalties assigned to the abusers or their abettors, nor was there any obligation to denounce offenders to the police. In short, Francis was advancing a toothless remedy that still relied upon the clergy to police itself.[34]

While the church continues to grapple with its troubled sexual legacy, the rest of the world has moved on. Since the 1960s, Western culture has seen the rise of a coherent gay and, more recently, LGBTQ movement, and a number of men who identify as gay are priests in the Catholic Church. Desperate for scapegoats, conservative Catholics, like Cardinal Viganò, have attempted to blame gay priests for the sexual abuse scandal.[35] Such a move is motivated by callous opportunism. The reality of today's abusive priest is a vestige of the past, and not contingent upon clerical homosexuality. Indeed, the church's own study has revealed that "most priests who had allegations of abuse were 'generalists' who did not target victims of a particular age and/or gender."[36]

Rather than looking for scapegoats, Catholic authorities need to understand and assume responsibility for what they have created—a system that not only enabled but, in many ways, created monsters like Donato Piermaria Bocco, the vicar-general of Pistoia, and William Presley, the defrocked priest from the diocese of Erie, Pennsylvania. The clergy's sexual abuse of minors preexisted modern understandings of sexual orientation by centuries. It is a sad by-product of compulsory celibacy, a discipline that enables predatory behavior and rewards its concealment—all in the service of avoiding scandal.

*   *   *

The reflexive fear of scandal has always been the church's Achilles' heel, urging the toleration of clerics guilty of the worst enormities. Even Alberic, our ten-year-old visionary, was apprised of the problem. He saw a vast subterranean chamber, abounding in hideous beasts, that was dominated by a fiery horse of momentous size. It was here that the bishops and superiors who were guilty of succoring evil priests dwelt. The only one way out of this terrible room was to enter into the stomach of the fiery horse and exit through its anus.[37]

Deathbed visions only spoke to justice in the afterlife, but the temporal realm was invariably more challenging. By the high Middle Ages, moreover, there were so many mechanisms in place protecting clerical privilege that it was often impossible to bring an unworthy cleric to justice. The higher the office, the more difficult this became. This is all too apparent in the lament of William of Auvergne (d. 1249), bishop of Paris for over twenty years, who had seen many things.

> There are certain kinds of offenses for which there is no reparation. Who can judge how many souls fall through the negligence or malice of one prelate? . . . The bishop should act on behalf of these souls and liberate the church. He should remove the offending prelate, who, as leader and abettor, is the reason that so many souls are lost. Wouldn't anybody who wished to save souls remove such a pastor? Yet it is difficult, often impossible, to follow this advice and remove bad clerics, replacing them with good ones. He who does not see this is blind.[38]

It is this grim reality that continues to render the incorrigible "corrupter of boys" virtually untouchable.

Works frequently cited have been identified by the following abbreviations.

AASS	*Acta Sanctorum* (Paris, 1865–)
ASDL, Criminale	*Tribunale Ecclesiastico, Sezione Criminale*, Archivio Arcives-covile, Archivio Storico Diocesano Lucca
CCCM	*Corpus Christianorum Continuatio Mediaeualis* (Turnhout, 1966–)
CCSL	*Corpus Christianorum Series Latina* (Turnhout, 1953–)
CSEL	*Corpus Scriptorum Ecclesiasticarum Latinorum* (Vienna, 1866–)
De apibus	Thomas of Cantimpré, *Bonum universale de apibus*
DEC	*Decrees of the Ecumenical Councils*
Dioc. Linc.	A. Hamilton Thompson, ed. and trans., *Visitations of Religious Houses in the Diocese of Lincoln*
EH	Orderic Vitalis, *Ecclesiastical History*
FCMC	*Fathers of the Church Medieval Continuation*, 15 vols. (Washington, DC, 1989–2014)
GO	*Biblia sacra cum glossa ordinaria nouisque additionibus*
GPA	William of Malmesbury, *Gesta pontificum anglorum*
GRA	William of Malmesbury, *Gesta regum anglorum*
HN	Eadmer, *Historia novorum in Anglia*
LG	Peter Damian, *Liber Gomorrhianus*, Ep. 31, to Leo IX (1049), *MGH, Briefe d. dt. Kaiserzeit* 4.1:284–330; trans. *Letters*, *FCMC* 2:3–53
MGH	*Monumenta Germaniae Historica* (Hanover, Prague, Leipzig, Berlin, 1826–)

Briefe d. dt. Kaiserzeit	*Die Briefe der deustchen Kaiserzeit*
Capit.	*Capitularia regum Francorum*
Capit. episc.	*Capitularia episcoporum*
Capit. N.S.	*Capitularia regum Francorum, Nova series*

Conc.	*Concilia*
Const.	*Constitutiones et acta publica imperatorum et regum*
Epp.	*Epistolae*
Epp. sel.	*Epistolae saeculi XIII e regestis pontificum Roman-orum selectae*
Fontes iuris	*Fontes iuris Germanici antiqui in usum scholarum separatim editi*
Ldl	*Libelli de lite imperatorum et pontificum*
LL	*Leges*
LL nat. Germ.	*Leges nationum Germanicarum*
Poetae	*Poetae Latini medii aevi*
QQ zur Geistesgesch.	*Quellen zur Geistesgeschichte des Mitteralters*
SS	*Scriptores*
SS rer. Merov.	*Scriptores rerum Merovingicarum*
SS rer. Germ.	*Scriptores rerum Germanicarum in usum scholarum*
SS rer. Germ. N.S.	*Scriptores rerum Germanicarum, Nova series*

NA	*Notarile antecosimiano*, Archivio di Stato di Firenze (State Archive of Florence)
NCE	*New Catholic Encyclopedia*, 14 vols. and index (New York, 1967)
PG	*Patrologia cursus completus . . . series Graeca*, ed. J.-P. Migne, 163 vols. (Paris, 1857–1866)
PL	*Patrologia cursus completus . . . series Latina*, ed. J.-P. Migne, 221 vols. (Paris, 1857–1866)
RB	Benedict of Nursia, *The Rule of Saint Benedict*. Ed. and trans. Justin McCann
Sacra concilia	G. D. Mansi, ed., *Sacrorum conciliorum nova et amplissima collectio*
SE	*The Standard Edition of the Complete Psychological Works of Sigmund Freud*, ed. James Strachey, 24 vols. (London, 1953–1974)
ST	Thomas Aquinas, *Summa Theologiae*
Stat. Ord. Cist.	Joseph-Marie Canivez, ed., *Statuta capitulorum generalium ordinis Cisterciensis*
Stat. Ord. Clun.	G. Charvin, ed., *Statuts, chapitres généraux et visites de l'ordre de Cluny*
UN	*Ufficiali di notte e conservatori dell' onesta' dei monasteri*, Archivio di Stato di Firenze
VA	Eadmer, *Vita sancti Anselmi*

The following abbreviations are used for citing the *Corpus Iuris Canonici*.

c.	canon
C.	Causa
D.	Distinctio
De pen.	De penitencia
d.p.c.	Dictum post canonem
q.	quaestio
X	*Liber Extra (Decretales Gregorii IX)*, in vol. 2 of *Corpus iuris canonici*

NOTES

INTRODUCTION

Note to epigraph: Pennsylvania's *40th Statewide Investigating Grand Jury: Report 1, Interim–Redacted* (2018), pp. 2–3, http://media-downloads.pacourts.us/InterimRedactedRe portandResponses.pdf?cb = 42148.

1. See the work by the investigative staff of the *Boston Globe, Betrayal: The Crisis in the Catholic Church* (Boston, 2002). The *Globe*'s initiative was recently the subject of the feature film *Spotlight* (directed Tom McCarthy, 2015), which was the name of the paper's investigative journalism unit. Those already apprised of the impending crisis prior to 2002 seem to have been either one-time members of the clergy (see Snipe, *Sex, Priests, and* Power) or cognoscenti, like Garry Wills, who had spent time in a seminary (*Papal Sin*).

2. Other researchers have pointed to this tactic in the premodern period. See, for example, the case of Stefano Cherubini, an abuser of boys who worked in a Catholic school in Naples run by the Piarist teaching order. When his abuse was revealed, he was first removed from the school and promoted to a prestigious administrative position, then in 1643 made the "universal superior" of the order by the pope (Podles, *Sacrilege*, 19).

3. "The Catholic Church's Unholy Stain," editorial, *New York Times*, September 13, 2018, https://www.nytimes.com/2018/09/13/opinion/pope-catholics-sexual-abuse.html?search ResultPosition.

4. *40th Statewide Investigating Grand Jury*, 2.

5. "Silenzio su quei peccati," *La Repubblica*, March 5, 1995, http://ricerca.repubblica.it/ repubblica/archivio/repubblica/1995/03/05/silenzio-su-quei-peccati.html?refresh_ce; John Preston, "The Vatican Archive: The Pope's Private Library," *Telegraph*, June 11, 2010, https:// www.telegraph.co.uk/culture/books/7772052/The-Vatican-Archive-the-Popes-private-library .html; Daniel J. Wakin, Associated Press, "Vatican Stirred Up over Book on Clerical Sins," *SFGate*, March 25, 1995, https://www.sfgate.com/news/article/Vatican-Stirred-Up-Over -Book-on-Clerical-Sins-3040171.php.

6. See *ST* 2a 2ae, q. 43, art. 1; and Bryan, "From Stumbling Block to Deadly Sin."

7. All biblical quotations are from the Douay-Rheims translation of the Latin Vulgate.

8. See Rocke, *Forbidden Friendships*, 87–88. Cf. similar patterns outlined by Christian Berco, who is nevertheless reluctant to take the veracity of such testimonies at face value, stating: "Although I could never ascertain whether the man appearing in a specific trial actually sodomized his adolescent accuser, the continued reappearance of this narrative in dozens of cases points to a conception of inter-generational sex that . . . is important in the mental-sexual makeup of homoeroticisim" (*Sexual Hierarchies*, 21). Also see Ruggiero, *Boundaries of*

Eros, 116–17, 121, 123–24, 137. Cf. Puff, *Sodomy in Reformation*, 75–76, which notes the designation of sodomites with the Greek term *paiderastes* by a sixteenth-century minister. There are also parallel relations that are hierarchically arranged, like master/servant or student/ teacher (Berco, *Sexual Hierarchies*, 97–98; Ruggiero, *Boundaries*, 115–116).

9. Ariès made this argument in his *L'Enfant et la vie familiale sous l'Ancien Régime*, translated as *Centuries of Childhood*.

10. Chrysostom, *Homily on Matthew* 62.4 (*PG* 58:600–601); as cited by Gillian Clark, "Fathers and the Children," 22.

11. Gregory of Tours, *Vitae patrum* 8.2, *MGH SS rer. Merov.* 1.2:242; trans. James, 51. See Van Dam, *Saints and Their Miracles*, 52–53.

12. For childhood as an extended period of irrationality and foolishness, see Gillian Clark, "Fathers and the Children," 20–22; Abraham, *Anticipating Sin in Medieval Society*, 52–55.

13. Augustine, *Confessiones* 1.7.11, *CSEL* 33: 9–10; trans. http://www.newadvent.org/ fathers/110101.htm.

14. Athanasius, *Vita Beati Antonii Abbatis*, c. 1, *PL* 73:127. The Latin translation was made by Evagrius of Antioch (before 384). Unless otherwise stated, translations are mine. For the politics driving this vita, see Brakke, *Athanasius and the Politics of Asceticism*, 201–265. On Athanasius's influence in the West, see Gwynn, *Athanasius of Alexandria*, 173–184.

15. *Visio Alberici*, 195. See Gardiner, *Medieval Visions of Heaven*, 31–34, which provides a summary of a given vision along with editions and bibliography. Alberic was a monk of Monte Cassino under Abbot Gerard (1111–1123). His vision was written down by the priest Guido and corrected under Abbot Senioretto with the help of Peter the Deacon (1127 × 1137).

16. English treatise on the Ten Commandments, British Library, Harleian MS 2396, fols. 93–94; trans. Horrox, *The Black Death*, 134–135.

17. Donatus of Besançon, *Regula ad virgines*, c. 32, *PL* 87:284; trans. http://monasticma-trix.osu.edu/cartularium/rule-donatus-besan%C3%A7. More typical are the concerns expressed in the late tenth-century Benedictine customary of Aniane, which warned monastic officials about the frivolous laughter of girls, their frequent conversations with friends and relatives, and the dangers of letting them be alone with men. *Monumenta aevi Anianensis*, ed. Hallinger, *Initia consuetudinis Benedictinae*, 279.

18. *Poenitentiale Vinniai*, cc. 27, 37–38 (written ca. 525–550), in Wasserschleben, *Bussord-nungen*, 114, 116–117.

19. *Capitula Theodori*, c. 145, in Wasserschleben, *Bussordnungen*, 158. This document first appeared in the *Dacheriana* (ca. 800).

20. *Poenitentiale Theodori* 1.2.4 (late seventh century), in Wasserschleben, *Bussord-nungen*, 186; also see *Capitula Theodori*, c. 27 (Wasserschleben, *Bussordnungen*, 147); and *Pae-nitentiale Pseudo-Theodori* 12.14, ed. Van Rhijn, *CCSL* 156B: 23.

21. *Poenitentiale Theodori* 2.12.35–36, in Wasserschleben, *Bussordnungen*, 217; note, how-ever, the manuscript variations regarding the age at which the *puella* has control over her body (217 n. 1).

22. *Poenitentiale Bedae*, c. 3 (early eighth century), in Wasserschleben, *Bussordnungen*, 221.

23. *Poenitentiale Hubertense*, c. 42 (ca. 850), in Wasserschleben, *Bussordnungen*, 383.

24. Payer, *Sex and the Penitentials*, 30–32 and appendix A (on works treating incest), 125–126.

25. *Poenitentiale Bedae* 3.17 (Wasserschleben, *Bussordnungen*, 222).

26. Gregory the Great, *Dialogues* 4.33.1, 3:110. The assault itself is circumlocutious: "and that night (what is wicked to say) he lost her"; it is possible that he even murdered her.

27. Hrabanus Maurus, *Poenitentiale*, c. 20, *PL* 110:487; Regino of Prüm, *Libri duo de synodalibus causis* 2.199, p. 340; Burchard of Worms, *Libri decretorum* 17.26, *PL* 140:924); Ivo of Chartres, *Decretum* 9.98, https://ivo-of-chartres.github.io/decretum/ivodec_9.pdf, p. 35.

28. On Boswell's use of the word "gay," see Hexter, "John Boswell's Gay Science," 37–44. See Boswell's effort to address some of this criticism in "Revolutions, Universals, and Sexual Categories," 1–33. For discussions of the book's context and quasi-polemical nature, see Kuefler's introduction to his edited volume *Boswell Thesis*, 1–31; and in the same volume, Hexter, "John Boswell's Gay Science"; Dinshaw, "Touching on the Past"; Schlager, "Reading *CSTH* as a Call to Action"; and Jordan, " 'Both as a Christian and as a Historian.' "

29. The homosexual allegedly "became a personage" in the nineteenth century as part of capitalism's "new persecution of peripheral sexualities" (Foucault, *The History of Sexuality*, 1:42–43). Also see Halperin, "Is There a History of Sexuality?" 257–274; Karras, "Active/ Passive, Acts/Passions," 1250–1257; Lochrie, "Presidential Improprieties and Medieval Categories"; Schultz, "Heterosexuality as a Threat to Medieval Studies."

30. Of course, such assumptions are challenged by writers like Judith Butler who argues in *Gender Trouble* that gender is performative, which would necessarily undercut any view of a stable sexual orientation.

31. This distinction is aptly captured in the subtitle of Karras's *Medieval Sexuality: Doing Unto Others*; for a useful summary of these issues, see *Medieval Sexuality*, 7–12.

32. The question of the abusers' orientation, or lack thereof, is discussed in the Conclusion.

33. See Brundage, *Law*, 213; Payer, *Sex and the Penitentials*, 40–41; Rocke, *Forbidden Friendships*, 11–12; Hergemöller, *Sodom and Gomorrah*, 6–25; Crawford, *European Sexualities*, 155–156.

34. Boswell, *Christianity*, chap. 9.

35. See ibid., pp. 231–232. For Burgwinkle's case for Richard's same-sex relations, see *Sodomy, Masculinity, and Law*, 73–82. Helmut Puff, in contrast, discounts a sexual interpretation ("Same-Sex Possibilities," 385). The key text is Roger of Hoveden's, *Gesta regis Henrici secundi*, 2:7 (formerly misattributed to Benedict of Peterborough). Also see Roger of Hoveden's *Annals*, 2:63–64.

36. Jaeger, *Ennobling Love*, 12–13.

37. Scandinavian culture did use rape as a way of degrading other men, however. See Gade, "Homosexuality and Rape of Males," 132–134.

38. Boswell, *Christianity*, 231–232, 298–300.

39. See, for example, the long-term relationship between a thirty-six-year-old and a seventeen-year-old in Rocke's *Forbidden Friendships*, 24–25.

40. Kuefler, "Sex with Eunuchs, Sex with Boys," 160–161.

41. Ruggiero, *Boundaries*, 117, 125–126; Rocke, *Forbidden Friendships*, 162–163; Berco, *Sexual Hierarchies*, 98; Berco, "Limits of Social Control," 343–344.

42. Boswell, "Dante and the Sodomites," 69–71; the sodomitical offenders are in Dante's *Inferno* 14 and *Purgatorio* 26.

43. Paul of Hungary, *Rationes penitentie*, 209b. As will be seen in Chapter 5, Paul is indebted to Peter the Chanter for the equation of sodomy and murder. Paul's explicit discussion of oppression takes the Chanter's argument one stage further.

44. *Stat. Ord. Clun.*, ann. 1292, 2:41.

45. Jordan, *The Silence of Sodom*, 128.

46. For an overview of his case, see Bill Chappell, "Penn State Abuse Scandal: A Guide and Timeline," NPR, June 21, 2012, https://www.npr.org/2011/11/08/142111804/penn-state -abuse-scandal-a-guide-and-timeline.

CHAPTER I

Note to epigraph: Cited in *Collectio Dacheriana*, preface, pp. 510–511.

1. See de Jong, "Transformations of Penance," 185–88; Uhalde,"Juridical Administration," 101–102. For a useful historiographical overview, see Hamilton, *Practice of Penance*, 2–23.

2. For different types of penitents in late antiquity, see Peter Brown, *Ransom of the Soul*, 99–102; and Uhalde, "Juridical Administration," 99–100. For the persistence of public penance in the high Middle Ages, see Mansfield, *Humiliation of Sinners*.

3. See Jerome's well-known description of the matron (d. 399 or 400) who divorced her whore-mongering husband and then remarried. After the death of her second husband, she engaged in dramatic public penance. Jerome, Ep. 77 (399), to Oceanus, c. 4, *CSEL* 55:40–41; trans. http://www.newadvent.org/fathers/3001077.htm. See Donnelly, "Penance and Justice," 49–50.

4. Tertullian, *De paenitentia*, c. 7, p. 363; trans. http://www.newadvent.org/fathers/ 0320.htm.

5. Lea, *History of Auricular Confession*, 1:34–35; Chadwick, *Church in Ancient Society*, 690.

6. De Jong, "Transformations of Penance," 190, 202. Although the mortal sin may have been expunged, the individuals who performed public penance had nevertheless incurred what later canonists termed "infamy of fact"—a situation in which a person's reputation is compromised whether or not he has been legally censured. Rodimer, *Canonical Effects of Infamy of Fact*, 10–15; Migliorino, *Fama e infamia*, 171–178. This condition is to be distinguished from someone who has legally been pronounced infamous and punished accordingly. See Tatarczuk, *Infamy of Law*, 13–33.

7. Council of Elvira (ca. 309?), c. 18, in Vives, *Concilios*, 5; trans. Laeuchli, *Power and Sexuality*, 128.

8. Council of Elvira, c. 30 (Vives, *Concilios*, 15; trans., 130). Note that the subdeacon was considered to be part of the minor orders until 1207 ("Minor Orders," *Oxford Dictionary of the Christian Church*, 1090).

9. Council of Elvira, c. 76 (Vives, *Concilios*, 15; trans., 135).

10. On this penalty, see "Lay Communion," *Catholic Encyclopaedia*, http://www.new advent.org/cathen/09093b.htm.

11. Meigne, "Concile ou collection d'Elvire?"

12. Council of Neocaesarea (315), c. 9, in Joannou, *Discipline générale antique*, 1.2:79; cf. c. 10 (p. 80), regarding the deacon; trans. http://www.newadvent.org/fathers/3803.htm.

13. Council of Nicaea (325), c. 9, *DEC*, 1:19.

14. Council of Nicaea, c. 10, *DEC*, 1:11.

15. De Jong, "Transformations of Penance," 196.

16. On the origins of the Donatist schism, see Frend, *Donatist Church*, 1–24.

17. Optatus, *S. Optati Milevitani libri VII* 2.24, *CSEL* 26:61; trans., 53. Despite the polemical nature of his writings, Optatus did his best to minimize the differences between the African Catholics and Donatists (Shaw, *Sacred Violence*, 62–64, 324–326). Bernhard Poschmann points out that Optatus's allusion to a Roman council in 313, which seems to condemn Donatus of Casa Nigra for reconciling a fallen bishop with the laying on of hands, is an earlier allusion to the prohibition of clerical penance rather than to reordination, as is often supposed (*Penance*, 110–111). See Optatus, *S. Optati Milevitani libri VII* 1.24, *CSEL* 26:26–27; trans., 24.

18. Optatus, *S. Optati Milevitani libri VII* 2.25, *CSEL* 26:65; trans., 55–56.

19. Augustine, *Contra epistolam Parmeniani* 2.13.28, *CSEL* 51:79. Elsewhere Augustine does make reference to a priest being reconciled through penance, but such an individual would cease to function as a priest unless "the interests of the Church require it" (*De baptismo contra Donatistas* 1.1.2, *CSEL* 51:146); trans. http://www.newadvent.org/fathers/14082.htm). See Poschmann, *Penance*, 111. For Augustine's indebtedness to Optatus, see Willis, *Saint Augustine and the Donatist Controversy*, 23–25, 105–110.

20. Siricius, *Ep.* 1, c. 14, *PL* 13:1145. This letter, which has the distinction of being the first papal decretal, emulates the imperial rescript of Gratian and Valentinian II from 378 or 379 (Jasper and Fuhrmann, *Papal Letters*, 10). Note that Siricius is also the first to assert that individuals who have done penance should not marry nor, if married, resume conjugal relations with their spouses. It is unclear if this represents tradition or innovation. If the latter, it may represent an effort to offset Donatist rigor (Siricius, *Ep.* 1, c. 4, *PL* 23:1136–1137). The ban on penitents entering the priesthood will be later restated in the Gallican *Statua ecclesiae antiquae* (475), in *Concilia Galliae*, *CCSL* 148:179–180.

21. Leo I, *Ep.* 167, to Rusticus, q. 2, *PL* 54:1203–1204; trans. http://www.newadvent.org/fathers/3604167.htm; Wessel, *Leo the Great*, 96. Leo I will further argue that former penitents should retreat from lawsuits, business, military service, and, if married, refrain from conjugal relations (*Ep.* 167, qq. 10–13, *PL* 54:1206–1207). This decretal was based on the version given in Dionysius Exiguus's canonical collection. It was widely cited in the early Middle Ages (Jasper and Fuhrmann, *Papal Letters*, 57–58).

22. Leo I also acknowledged that lesser offenses—such as eating the food of idols when in captivity—could be atoned for by fasting under the direction of the bishop (*Ep.* 167, to Rusticus, q. 19, *PL* 54:1209; cf. *Ep.* 159, to Nicaetas, bishop of Aquileia, c. 6, *PL* 54:1158; trans. http://www.newadvent.org/fathers/3604159.htm). See Wessel, *Leo the Great*, 167–168.

23. Hillner, *Prison, Punishment and Penance*, 298–306.

24. Adnès assumes the first position ("Pénitence," 965); Lea, the second (*History of Auricular Confession*, 1:43).

25. Leo I, *Ep.* 168, to the bishops of Campania, Samnium, and Picenum, c. 2, *PL* 54:1211; Wessel, *Leo the Great*, 129.

26. Wessel, *Leo the Great*, 176–178.

27. See Augustine, *Contra litteras Petiliani* 2.105.240, *CSEL* 52:155; trans. http://www.newadvent.org/fathers/14092.htm. For an overview of Augustine's controversy with the Donatists, see Willis, *Saint Augustine*, 36–92.

28. Note that in the Latin Vulgate, 1 Kings = 1 Samuel in the King James Bible.

29. It was noted by the sixteenth-century *Correctores Romani* of the *Corpus iuris canonici*, however (see the notes for D. 50 c. 67).

30. The Council of Orange (441), c. 4, states that penance should not be denied to any clerics desiring it (*Concilia Galliae, CCSL* 148:79); cf. Arles II (442–506), c. 29, which states that penance should be denied to no one—not "even to clerics" (*CCSL* 148:120). Arles II was not really a council but a compilation of canons. See Mathison, "'The Second Council of Arles'"; and Saint-Roch, *La pénitence*, 92–96. The Spanish Council of Lérida (546), c. 5, also allows the priest who erred sexually but "rushes to penance" to retain his position, albeit without possibility of promotion; he is, however, deposed in the case of a relapse (Vives, *Concilios*, 56–57). On the special sensitivity to penitential matters in Gaul, see Meens, *Penance in Medieval Europe*, 30–33.

31. Vaison II (442), c. 8, *Concilia Galliae, CCSL* 148:100. See Uhalde, "Juridical Administration," 109.

32. The Council of Epaon (517) was the first to require deposition and confinement to a monastery for mortal sins (c. 22, *Concilia Galliae, CCSL* 148A: 29). Guy Geltner argues that it was the church's use of penal cloistering that anticipated the secular use of imprisonment as punishment ("*Detrusio*").

33. Council of Marseilles (533), *Concilia Galliae, CCSL* 148A: 85; de Jong, "Transformations of Penance," 202; Uhalde, "Juridical Administration," 109; Hillner, "L'enfermement monastique au VIe siècle."

34. Council of Châlons (647–653), *Concilia Galliae, CCSL* 148A: 309–310.

35. Caesarius of Arles, Serm. 67.1, *Sermons au peuple*, 3:125; trans., 1:318. De Jong argues that Caesarius is distinguishing between two groups of public penitents, which does not seem very credible ("Transformations of Penance," 200). On the Gallic bishops' particular preoccupation with penitential matters, see Meens, *Penance*, 25–33.

36. Poschmann, *Penance*, 109. Authorities like Caesarius of Arles objected to postponing penance to the last moment, arguing that good Christians perform penance throughout their lives (Serm. 60.2, *Sermons au peuple*, 3:61; trans., 1:295).

37. Gerona I (517), c. 9, *Concilia Galliae, CCSL* 148:5. Cf. de Jong, who says explicitly that it was the publicity of penance for notorious sins that mattered ("Transformations of Penance," 198–199, 204); Uhalde, "Juridical Administration," 107.

38. Augustine, *Contra litteras Petiliani* 2.52.120, *CSEL* 52:89; trans. http://www.newadvent.org/fathers/14092.htm; cf. Augustine, *De baptismo contra Donatistas* 1.1.2, *CSEL* 51:145–147; trans. http://www.newadvent.org/fathers/14081.htm. Hence, the only possible choice would be to put your trust in God, not man: "Wherefore, whether a man receives the sacrament of baptism from a faithful or a faithless minister his whole hope is in Christ," *Contra litteras Petiliani* 3.42.51, *CSEL* 51:204; trans. http://www.newadvent.org/fathers/14093.htm. The Donatist position was in keeping with the tradition of the North African church, which held that a congregation in communion with an errant bishop risked contamination. See Carola, *Augustine of Hippo*, 75–77.

39. Augustine, *Contra litteras Petiliani* 1.2–4.3–5, *CSEL* 52:4–6; trans. http://www.newadvent.org/fathers/14091.htm.

40. Augustine, *Contra litteras Petiliani* 2.104.239, *CSEL* 52:154; trans. http://www.newadvent.org/fathers/14092.htm.

41. Augustine, *Contra litteras Petiliani* 3.31.36, *CSEL* 52:191; trans. http://www.newadvent.org/fathers/14093.htm.

42. Augustine, *Contra litteras Petiliani* 3.37.43, *CSEL* 52:197; trans. http://www.newadvent.org/fathers/14093.htm. Cf. his earlier allusion to the many deposed from office "on the

testimony of women whom they have seduced (since examples of this kind are not wanting anywhere)" (ibid., 2.26.61, *CSEL* 52:54; trans. http://www.newadvent.org/fathers/14092.htm).

43. Augustine, *Contra litteras Petiliani* 3.84.44, 3.36.42 *CSEL* 52:198, 196–97; trans. http://www.newadvent.org/fathers/14093.htm. See Willis, *Saint Augustine*, 117–118; Carola, *Augustine of Hippo*, 66ff. Elsewhere Augustine will argue that Judas was admitted among the disciples to give an example of how evil can be tolerated in the church (Carola, 222). Ironically, Augustine's view of the necessary coexistence of evil with good came from the great Donatist thinker Tyconius's *Book of Rules*. This work contained a chapter entitled "The Lord's Bipartite Body," which accommodated good and bad within the church (rule 2, pp. 14–15). Through its acknowledgment that the church militant could contain both saints and sinners, Augustine's *City of God* constituted just such a demonstration. For Tyconius's influence on Augustine, see O'Daly, *Augustine's "City of God,"* 57; Willis, *Saint Augustine*, 20–21.

44. Augustine, Serm. 82.8.11, *PL* 38:511. See Carola, *Augustine of Hippo*, 234–250; Clerici, *La Correzione Fraterna in S. Agostino*. Augustine's sermon is cited by Gratian, *Decretum*, C. 2 q. 1 c. 19; also see *ST* 2a 2ae, q. 33, http://www.newadvent.org/summa/3033.htm.

45. The third-century *Didascalia* relied upon the same text when instructing bishops how to proceed against criminal acts (2.37, p. 124), as did the likes of Gregory the Great (to John, bishop of Ravenna, *Registrum*, Ep. 3.54, *CCSL* 140:202–203; cf. Ep. 5.8, to Felix, bishop of Sardica, *CCSL* 140:274–275; trans., 1:328–329). See Hillner, *Prison, Punishment, and Penance*, 70.

46. Augustine, Ep. 211, c. 11, *CSEL* 57:364–365 (Augustine's rule is based on this letter, which was written to a community of nuns); *RB*, c. 23, pp. 72–73.

47. This discipline entails seven steps: secret admonition, public correction, excommunication, severe fasts, corporal punishment, prayer, and expulsion. Paul the Deacon (Warnefrid), *In sanctam regulam commentarium*, c. 28, p. 296; Hildemar of Corbie, *Expositio Regulae ab Hildemaro tradita*, c. 28, pp. 361–364; most of the *Expositio* has been translated at the Hildemar Project at http://www.hildemar.org. See Schroll, *Benedictine Monasticism as Reflected in the Warnefrid-Hildemar Commentaries*, 91–94. Also see Smaragdus of St.-Mihiel, *Commentary on the Rule of St. Benedict* 3.23, trans. Barry, 348–349.

48. *RB*, c. 46, pp. 108–109.

49. Isidore of Seville, *Regula monachorum*, c. 15, *PL* 103:568.

50. Isidore of Seville, *Sententiae* 2.20, *PL* 83:623; elsewhere, however, he excoriates hypocrites (*Sententiae* 3.24, *PL* 83:699–700).

51. Ward, *Sayings of the Desert Fathers*, Poemen, nos. 64, 114 (pp. 175, 183–184), and Paphnutius, no. 3 (pp. 202–203). The alphabetical collection is believed to have reached its final form by the end of the sixth century. Ward is translating from the Greek edition, printed in *PG* 65:71–440. Cf. "De eo quod non oporteat judicare quemquam" from the systematic collection of *Sayings*, translated from the Greek by Pelagius and John, *Verba seniorum*, bk. 9, *PL* 73:909–912.

52. Isidore of Seville, *Sententiae* 3.39.1–5, *PL* 83:709–710.

53. For an introduction to penitentials, see Vogel, *"Libri paenitentiales."* On their spread, see Meens, *Penance*, 37ff.; Meens notes that in the eighth and early ninth centuries, their influence was confined to the eastern and northern parts of the Carolingian Empire (116). According to Richard Price, the system of tariffs attributed to the Irish monks is indebted to the practice of the fourth-century Eastern church ("Informal Penance in Early Christendom," 32–33).

54. On the Carolingian reforms, see McKitterick, *Frankish Church*; Amann, "Pénitence publique et pénitence privée." On the ideological meaning of church reform for the Carolingian rulers, see de Jong, "The State of the Church." On efforts to reform the secular clergy, see Keefe, *Water and the Word*, 1:13–38.

55. The Council of Tours (813) expressed concern over the indiscreet manner in which different penances were ascribed, calling for a meeting of bishops to ensure greater homogeneity over what penitential texts were reliable (c. 22, *MGH Conc.* 2.1:289). But the Council of Châlons (813) calls for the outright elimination of penitentials (c. 38, *MGH Conc.* 2.1:281). The attack will continue at later councils. See the Council of Paris (829), cc. 32, 33, *MGH Conc.* 2.2:633–635. Also see Fournier and Le Bras, *Histoire des collections canoniques*, 1:98–100; Meens, *Penance*, 115–118. Despite the efforts of Carolingian councils, penitentials will continue to circulate. See Payer, *Sex and the Penitentials*, 58–59; and Peter Damian's extensive criticism of this genre, discussed in Chapter 3. On reformed penitential literature, see Meens, *Penance*, 132–135; Fournier and Le Bras, *Histoire des collections canoniques*, 1:108–112.

56. Theodulf of Orléans, *Zweites Kapitular*, c. 10.1–14, *MGH Capit. episc.* 1:172–176.

57. Theodulf of Orléans, *Zweites Kapitular*, c. 3.4, *MGH Capit. episc.* 1:157.

58. Council of Châlons (813), c. 33, *MGH Conc.* 2.1:280. The council equivocates, citing scriptural validation for both practices. On confession to God alone, see Vogel, *"Libri paenitentiales,"* 55–58.

59. Theodulf of Orléans, *Erstes Kapitular*, c. 30, *MGH Capit. episc.* 1:127–128.

60. Hrabanus Maurus, *Poenitentiale*, c. 10, *PL* 110:474–475. This work, written in 841, was dedicated to Heribald, bishop of Auxerre. Cf. Hrabanus's later *Liber poenitentium* dedicated to Otgar, archbishop of Mainz, which, although longer, contains almost identical canons (c. 1, *PL* 112:1399–1405). Hrabanus also invokes the problem of scandal in his discussion of satisfaction in *De institutione clericorum libri tres* 2.30, p. 376. The bulk of Hrabanus's deliberation from *Poenitentiale* will appear in Gratian's *Decretum* (D. 50 c. 34). Also note the penitential book of Halitgar, bishop of Cambrai (d. 831), written at the behest of his metropolitan bishop, Ebo of Reims. But while the first five books are written with careful attention to legitimate authority, the sixth book is an old-fashioned penitential. Halitgar claims that book 6 is from a "Roman penitential." But since there is no evidence of penitentials south of the Alps before the late ninth century, his claim was probably for purposes of authorization (Meens, "Historiography of Early Medieval Penance," 76–77). The books are divided up in *PL*: the first five books are entitled *De vitiis et virtutibus* (*PL* 105:651–694), while the sixth book is entitled *Liber poenitentialis* (*PL* 105:693–710). This edition contains some canons regarding the administration of penance that do not appear in all of the manuscripts, one of which concerns the procedure against an infamous priest (*PL* 105:706–707). The appearance of this protocol probably attests to its need. For a detailed examination of the sources, see Kottje, *Bussbücher Halitgars von Cambrai und des Hrabanus Maurus*.

61. Hrabanus Maurus, *De institutione clericorum libri tres* 2.29, p. 374. See Isidore of Seville, *De officiis ecclesiasticis* 2.17.6, *PL* 83:803. Hrabanus draws on this work throughout *De institutione clericorum*.

62. Hrabanus Maurus, *Poenitentiale*, c. 10, *PL* 110:476–477. This is buttressed by a compelling argument from a letter by Isidore of Seville answering a query from the bishop of Massio regarding the possibility of a lapsed priest's return to office. Isidore argues that any disagreement in authority on this question is more imagined than real. The priests who return to their pristine offices make satisfaction through sincere penance. Those who do not have not made amends (Hrabanus Maurus, *Poenitentiale*, c. 10, *PL* 110:478).

63. Hrabanus Maurus, *De vitiis et virtutibus*, c. 82, *PL* 112:1397.

64. Gregory the Great, Ep. 4.26, to Januarius, bishop of Cagliari (May 594), *Registrum*, *CCSL* 140:245–246; trans., 1:308. Earlier in May, Gregory had written to Januarius insisting that the cleric Paul, a frequent sinner who had reverted to the life of a layman and then fled to Africa, should first be punished corporally and then handed over to penance (Ep. 4.24, *CCSL* 140:243; trans., 1:306). Cf. the letter to Columbus, bishop of Numidia, regarding the appeal of a deacon who claims he was wrongfully deposed "due to bodily sin." Gregory determines that if the charges are upheld, the deacon should be forcibly brought back for penance (Ep. 12.3, September 601, *CCSL* 140A: 971; trans., 3:808). According to Carole Straw, Gregory believed that penance played an essential role in the taming of the carnal man (*Gregory the Great*, 213–235).

65. The authentic letter is Gregory the Great, Ep. 9.148, to Secundinus, *Registrum*, *CCSL* 140A: 698–704. The interpolated letter is given in the appendix, *CCSL* 140A: 1104–1111, esp. 1108ff.; trans., 2:630–635 and appendix 10, 3:889–895, esp. 892ff.

66. Pseudo-Isidore, *Decretales*, 142–143 (Callixtus, Ep. 2, c. 20); this collection, known as the False or Pseudo-Isidorian Decretals, is discussed below.

67. Southern, *Saint Anselm and His Biographer*, 125.

68. Gratian, *Decretum*, D. 82 c. 5.

69. Pseudo-Isidore, *Decretales*, 155 (Anterus, c. 1).

70. Augustine, Serm. 83.7, *PL* 38:519.

71. Vogel, *"Libri paenitentiales,"* 39–43; Hamilton, *Practice of Penance*, 5; Meens, *Penance*, 118–119; Meens, "Frequency and Nature of Early Medieval Penance," 47.

72. Arles (813), c. 26, *MGH Conc.* 2.1:253; Council of Châlons (813), c. 25, *Conc.* 2.1:278; cf. Council of Reims (813), c. 31, *Conc.* 2.1:256. See also the Council of Meaux-Paris (845 and 846), *MGH Conc.* 3:113; Council of Mainz (847), c. 31, *Conc.* 3:176. The Council of Meaux-Paris seems indebted to the comments of Hrabanus Maurus, discussed below.

73. Theodolf of Orléans, *Zweites Kapitular*, c. 8.1, *MGH Capit. episc.* 1:168–169. The example he gives is of a priest who is deposed and assigned ten years public penance for his open adultery. If his sin was secret, however, he can confess and do penance privately. In this case, it is up to him if he should withdraw from the ministry.

74. Hrabanus Maurus, *Poenitentiale*, c. 10, *PL* 110:474–475.

75. Council of Mainz (852), c. 8, *MGH Conc.* 3:245–246:

If any priest neglectful of his life were to permit himself to be suspected of evil things by depraved examples and the people bound by oath to the bishop or under penalty of the faith [*banno Christianitatis*] revealed his infamy, with certain accusers of his crime present, he would be admonished by the bishop, at first separately; then, with two or three witnesses. If he did not amend, the bishop would admonish him with public imprecation in the community of priests. But if he did not then correct himself, he would be suspended from office until he made fitting satisfaction, lest the faithful people should suffer scandal from him. If, moreover, his accusers were legitimate, and they insisted on proving his crimes with manifest signs, and he were to deny them [his crimes], then he with six companions of the same order should purge himself from the crime, if he is able.

This conciliar decree proved to be invaluable, giving rise to false attributions, particularly the Council of Agde (506) and the Council of Lérida (546). The pseudo-Agde version is closer to the original decree, while the pseudo-Lérida version makes an effort to align it with canonical rules regarding witnesses. Burchard of Worms cites it (*Libri decretorum* 2.181, *PL* 140:654–665), as does Ivo of Chartres (*Decretum* 6.226, https://ivo-of-chartres.github.io/decretum/ivodec_6.pdf, pp. 86–87; *Panormia* 5.1, https://ivo-of-chartres.github.io/panormia/pan_5.pdf, pp. 1–2). The pseudo-Agde appears in Gratian in a truncated form (*Decretum*, C. 2 q. 5 c. 12), while the pseudo-Lérida is repeated in its entirety in Gregory IX's *Decretals* (X.5.43.2). See Fiori, "*Probatio y purgatio* en el proceso canónico medieval," 83–86.

76. Booker, "*Iusta murmuratio*," 236–270. I am indebted to Melissa Vise for this reference.

77. De Jong, *Penitential State*, 232; Wagner, "*Cum aliquis venerit ad sacerdotem*," 204–205; Firey, "Blushing Before the Judge and the Physician," 173–174. On Louis the Pious's public penance in the wake of humiliating political defeat, see de Jong, *Penitential State*, esp. 228 ff.; Meens, *Penance*, 123–130.

78. Charles the Bald, for example, summoned Bishop Hincmar of Laon for secular judgment because the bishop was accused of having taken benefices that belonged to the king's men. The bishop refused to appear. Initially, he was supported by his uncle, Hincmar, archbishop of Reims, who would later accuse him of slighting royal authority. Kleinjung, "To Fight with Words"; also see Devisse, *Hincmar: Archevêque de Reims*, 2:752–785.

79. See particularly *Theodosian Code* 16.2.7, 16.2.12, 16.2.41; pp. 441, 442, 447. The code was issued under Theodosian II and published in 438.

80. Council of Chalcedon (451), c. 9, *DEC*, 1:91.

81. *Collectio Dacheriana*, preface, 510. This sole edition takes its name from the editor Luc d'Achery. (D'Achery's title was *Collectio antiqua canonum poenitentialium*.) For bibliography, see Kéry, *Canonical Collections of the Early Middle Ages*, 87–92. On the limitations of d'Achery's edition and some of the controversies surrounding it, see Firey, "Ghostly Recensions." Charlemagne based his reform on a collection he received from Pope Hadrian—an augmented form of the sixth-century collection of Dionysius Exiguus and thus called *Dionysio-Hadriana*. The *Collectio Dacheriana* united the *Dionysio-Hadriana* and a collection of canons from Spanish and Gallic councils to form a new collection known as *Collectio Hispana*. See Fournier and Le Bras, *Histoire des collections canoniques*, 1:94–104; on the significance and structure of the *Dacheriana*, see ibid., 1:104–107.

82. *Dacheriana* 2.1, p. 532; Council of Chalcedon (451), c. 18, *DEC*, 1:95.

83. *Dacheriana* 2.2, p. 532; Council of Elvira, c. 73 (Vives, *Concilios*, 14).

84. *Dacheriana* 2.3, p. 532; IV Carthage (ca. 475), c. 96, *Concilia Africae*, *CCSL* 149:352. The proceedings for this alleged council were generated in Gaul circa 475 by a priest named Gennadius of Marseilles (*Concilia Africae*, *CCSL* 149:342). Cf. *Dacheriana* 2.22 (p. 534); Council of Toledo VI (638), c. 11, in Vives, *Concilios*, 241.

85. *Dacheriana* 2.4–5, p. 532; Council of Carthage (419), c. 129, *Concilia Africae*, *CCSL* 149:231.

86. *Dacheriana* 2.6, pp. 532–533; Council of Carthage (419), c. 129, *Concilia Africae*, *CCSL* 149:231.

87. *Dacheriana* 2.7, p. 533, Council of Carthage (419), c. 131, *Concilia Africae*, *CCSL* 149:231.

88. *Dacheriana* 2.24, p. 535; Council of Chalcedon (451), c. 21, *DEC*, 1:97.

89. *Dacheriana* 2.23, p. 534; IV Carthage, c. 58, *Concilia Africae*, *CCSL* 149:349; *Dacheriana* 2.37, p. 536, from a collection of African canons, which appears in Munier's edition as *Registri ecclesiae Carthaginensis excerpta*, c. 59, in *Concilia Africae*, *CCSL* 149:196.

90. *Dacheriana* 2.10, p. 533; Carthage (390), c. 6, *Concilia Africae, CCSL* 149:14–15.

91. *Dacheriana* 2.19, p. 534; Council of Vaison (442), c. 7, in *Concilia Galliae, CCSL* 148:99–100.

92. *Dacheriana* 2.20, p. 534; Council of Arles (314), c. 15 (14), in *Concilia Galliae, CCSL* 148:12; cf. *Dacheriana* 2.25, p. 535; Council of Elvira, c. 74 (Vives, *Concilios*, 14).

93. *Dacheriana* 2.21, p. 234; IV Carthage (475), c. 55, *Concilia Africae, CCSL* 149:349.

94. *Dacheriana* 2.38, p. 536, from the collection of African canons, appearing in Munier's edition as *Registri ecclesiae Carthaginensis excerpta*, c. 62, *Concilia Africae, CCSL* 149:197; cf. *Dacheriana* 2.44, p. 537; Council of Antioch (341) c. 6, *Sacra concilia*, 2:1330.

95. *Dacheriana* 2.13, p. 533; Council of Carthage (390) c. 10, *Concilia Africae, CCSL* 149:17.

96. Pseudo-Isidore was using the *Collectio Hispana* as his base text into which he introduced his spurious interpolations (Paul Fournier, "La question des Fausses Décrétales," 23–26). Fournier argues that the forgers were members of the entourage of Alderic, bishop of Mons between 832 and 856 (ibid., 39–45). The inclusion of the capitularies was strategic because the authors were not sure which sources would best serve their ends—church canons or secular legislation (Paul Fournier, "De l'origine des Fausses Décrétales," 81). Klaus Zechiel-Eckes had argued that the forgery was made at the monastery of Corbie. For a recent reassessment of this claim, see the collection of essays in Ubl and Ziemann, *Fälschung als Mittel der Politik?* On the immense influence of these documents, see the exhaustive study by Fuhrmann, *Einfluss und Verbreitung der pseudoisidorischen Fälschungen*; for their influence on Gratian, see ibid., 2:563–85; on the *1917 Pio-Benedictine Code of Canon Law*, see ibid., 1:34–38. For their dissemination, see Schafer Williams, *Codices Pseudo-Isidoriani*.

97. See Paul Fournier, "Étude sur les Fausses Décrétales," pt. 1, in *Mélanges*, 1:88ff. These decretals could also be used by clerics against their bishops—especially with regard to their insistence on the validity of appeals to Rome. De Jong, "Hincmar, Priests and Pseudo-Isidore," 268–288. On Hincmar's vigorous defense of the rights of metropolitan bishops, see Devisse, *Hincmar: Archevêque de Reims*, 2:661–669.

98. Pseudo-Isidore, *Decretales*, 165 (Fabian, Ep. 2, c. 19).

99. Ibid., 166 (Fabian, Ep. 2, c. 23).

100. Ibid., 131–132 (Zeppherinus, Ep. 1, cc. 2, 5, 6); cf. Fabian, Ep. 3, c. 29, at p. 168.

101. Ibid., 131 (Zeppherinus, Ep. 1, c. 6).

102. Ibid., 133 (Zeppherinus, Ep. 2, c. 12).

103. Ibid., 138 (Callixtus, Ep. 2, c. 8).

104. Ibid., 150 (Pontianus, Ep. 2, c. 9); cf. Fabian, Ep. 3, c. 30, at p. 169. The False Decretals were also solicitous of simple priests who "are not to be molested, but honored." They cannot be arraigned or constrained by wicked laypeople or "men of evil life" (Pontianus, Ep. 1, c. 3, at p. 147; on accusers, also see Fabian, Ep. 1, cc. 5–7, at pp. 158–160, and Ep. 3, c. 1, at p. 167). Laypeople bringing charges against a priest must be lawfully married, with an exchange of dowry and a priest's blessing—conditions that would probably place them in the upper tier of society. Both accusers and witnesses also have to be above suspicion, untainted by any relationship—whether by friendship or through belonging to the same household (Callixitus, Ep. 2, c. 17, at pp. 140–41). Yet a conflicting decree maintains that only other members of the clergy can accuse. God has chosen "to reserve their cases to themselves"; hence those who injure priests through accusations "are marked with the stains of infamy, and go down into the pit" unless absolved by sacerdotal authority (Fabian, Ep. 2, c. 13, at p. 162). Moreover,

priests who have in some way lapsed into sin are readmitted to office, "after a proper satisfaction for their error" (Callixtus, Ep. 2, c. 20, at p. 142). The overall bias of our perspicacious forger is summarized by a citation from Deuteronomy cited in the epigraph to this section. The nebulous category of *doctor* (teacher) was also surrounded by heavy sanctions. He need not answer to an illiterate or any accuser who is not "trustworthy and recognized by law, and who leads also a life and conversation free of reproach" (Callixtus, Ep. 1, c. 3, at p. 136).

105. Hincmar of Reims, *De presbiteris criminosis*, c. 1, p. 65; Benedict the Levite, *Capitularia spuria* 1.35, *MGH LL* 2.2:48. The collection contains capitularies allegedly issued by Pepin, Charlemagne, and Louis the Pious. On Hincmar's opportunistic use of the False Decretals, see Devisse, *Hincmar: Archevêque de Reims*, 2:580–581, 794ff.; Devisse, *Hincmar et la loi*, 33–38.

106. Hincmar of Reims, *De presbiteris criminosis*, c. 21, pp. 90–91. Cf. "Excerpta quaedam ex synodalibus gestis sancti Silvestri papae," cc. 2–5, in Pseudo-Isidore, *Decretales*, pp. 449–450. See de Jong, "Hincmar, Priests, and Pseudo-Isidore," 273–275. Hincmar's rebellious nephew and namesake—Hincmar, bishop of Laon—also attempted to use some of the False Decretals to defend himself against conciliar action (Kleinjung, "To Fight with Words," 65).

107. Hincmar of Reims, *De presbiteris criminosis*, c. 22, pp. 91–92.

108. Gregory the Great, Ep. 12.10, to John, bishop of Prima Justiniana, March 602, *Registrum*, *CCSL* 140A: 983; trans. 3:616. Cf. the example of Archbishop Ebo of Reims, who was deposed for backing the revolt against Louis the Pious, imprisoned at the monastery of Fulda and ultimately ended up as bishop of Hildesheim. See McKeon, "Archbishop Ebbo of Reims"; de Jong, *Penitential State*, 252–259.

109. The original pope, John II, who had joined Caesarius in his condemnation of Contumeliosus, had died. The new pope wrote to Caesarius about the appeal (Ep. 16, Agapitus to Caesarius, in *Caesarius of Arles: Life, Testament, Letters*, 16–18).

110. Kleinjung, "To Fight with Words," 64, 68–69. On the various depositions with which Hincmar of Reims was involved, see ibid., 72 n. 2. The most successful depositions in the early Middle Ages seem to been joint endeavors between ecclesiastical and secular authorities. See Airlie, "'Not Rendering unto Caesar,'" 494–499.

111. De Jong translates the letter Burchard wrote about this case in the appendix to "Hincmar, Priests and Pseudo-Isidore," 282. Hincmar of Reims was more successful in deposing the priest Hunbert—who had conspired with his lover, the nun Duda, to overthrow her abbess and put Duda in her place—at the Synod of Douzy (874). See Hincmar's judgment against them, in *MGH Conc.* 4:587–96. Hunbert is deposed and perpetually exiled (ibid., 590, c. 4); Duda, out of deference to the fragility of her sex, received only a public beating in front of the other nuns and extensive penance (ibid., 592, 595, cc. 7, 8). I first heard about this case through Rachel Stone's paper "The Case of the Rebel Nun: Law and Gender Order in Ninth-Century France," delivered at the Berkshire Conference on the History of Women, Toronto, May 23, 2014.

112. See Hamilton, *Practice of Penance*, 27–44. On Regino, see Fournier and Le Bras, *Histoire des collections canoniques*, 1:244–268. For Burchard, see Austin, *Shaping Church Law Around the Year 1000*, esp. 15–31.

113. I have indicated in parentheses which authorities cite Leo and which Siricius. Dionysius Exiguus, *Collectio decretorum pontificum romanorum*, *PL* 67:237 (Siricius); Cresconius Africanus, *Die Concordia canonum des Cresconius*, 2:523 (Leo) and 2:707 (Siricius); Pope

Zachary, Ep. 8, to Pippin, mayor of the palace, c. 4, *PL* 89:935 (Leo); *Collectio Dacheriana* 1.25, 27, pp. 521–522 (Siricius and Leo); Pseudo-Isidore, *Decretales*, 522 (Siricius); Regino of Prüm, *Libri duo de synodalibus causis* 1.316, p. 172 (Leo); Burchard of Worms, *Libri decretorum* 19.71, *PL* 140:999 (Leo), and 19.49, *PL* 140:994 (Siricius); Anselm of Lucca, *Collectanea, PL* 149:480 (Siricius); Ivo of Chartres, *Decretum* 6.67, https://ivo-of-chartres.github.io/decretum/ ivodec_6.pdf, p. 27 (Leo), and 15.63, https://ivo-of-chartres.github.io/decretum/ivodec _15.pdf, p. 24 (Siricius); Gratian, *Decretum*, D. 50 c. 67 (Leo and Siricius). "Si sacerdos" is also cited in Gratian, *De poen.* D. 1 c. 59, but in the context of whether secret penance and satisfaction is possible without oral confession. Also see Bernold of Constance, *De vitanda excommunicatorum communione, PL* 148:1192–1193 (Leo).

114. See Ullmann, *Growth of Papal Government*, 180–184. The False Decretals had an immense impact on *The Collection in Seventy-Four Titles*—a work that imports the intricate procedural canons favoring the clergy and an urtext for the reformers. See *Diuersorum patrum sententie siue Collectio in LXXIV titulos digesta*, tit. 5–12, 44–71; trans., 97–125. For a detailed discussion, see Dusil, *Wissensordnungen des Rechts im Wandel*, 84–88. On procedure in Gratian, see Fraher, "Preventing Crime in the High Middle Ages," 217–219.

115. Hrabanus Maurus reiterated Pseudo-Gregory's reassurances on several occasions. See his *Liber poenitentium* c. 1, *PL* 112:1400–1402; also see the abbreviated version in idem *De videndo Deum, de puritate cordis et modo poenitentiae* 3.8, *PL* 112: 1314–1315. This canon was also deployed by: Burchard of Worms, *Libri decretorum* 19.43, *PL* 140:988–999; *Collectio canonum in V libris* 2.99, pp. 237–238 (between 1065 and 1085); Ivo of Chartres, *Decretum* 6.85, https://ivo-of-chartres.github.io/decretum/ivodec_6.pdf, pp. 34–45; *Panormia* 3.147, https://ivo-of-chartres.github.io/panormia/pan_3.pdf, pp. 95–96; and, most important, Gratian's *Decretum*, D. 50 c. 16. We also see evidence of it being applied in practice.

116. This is especially true of the later Middle Ages. See, for example, the hostile dynamics between local communities and papal representatives in Peterson, "Holy Heretics in Later Medieval Italy"; Augustine Thompson, "Lay Versus Clerical Perceptions of Heresy."

CHAPTER 2

1. This is Paul's most forceful condemnation since same-sex relations are singled out rather than included in lists of other vices. For various interpretations, see Brooten, *Love Between Women*, 203ff. For the ancient Hebraic association between idolatry and sexual sin, see Harper, "*Porneia*: The Making of a Christian Norm," 365, 370. While a number of scholars, including Bernadette Brooten, argue that the idolaters represent fallen humanity in general, Dale Martin rejects this view. See Martin, "Heterosexism and the Interpretation of Romans 1:18–32."

2. See, for example, Furnish, *Moral Teaching of Paul*, 52–83.

3. Suetonius, *Lives of the Caesars* 3.43–44, 1:372–373.

4. See Richlin, "Not Before Homosexuality," 566–71; Catharine Edwards, *Politics of Sexual Immorality in Ancient Rome*, 63–97, esp. 71. Craig A. Williams interprets the occasional trope of sex between mature men, appearing both in comic plays and the slurs by Greek historians against Romans, as evidence of actual practice (*Roman Homosexuality*, 77–82).

5. Laes, *Children in the Roman Empire*, 86–87, 94–95.

6. See the discussion of *Lex Scatinia* in Cantarella, *Bisexuality*, 106–114, 173; Craig A. Williams, *Roman Homosexuality*, 119–124.

7. Craig A. Williams, *Roman Homosexuality*, 113–119.

8. Laes, *Children in the Roman Empire*, 254; Gardner, *Women in Roman Law and Society*, 38–41.

9. Festugière, *Antioche païenne et chrétienne*, 201–206; Laes, *Children in the Roman Empire*, 251–252. According to Raffaella Cribiore, this was Libanius at his most daring (*Libanius the Sophist*, 110–111).

10. Although Eunapius's *Lives of the Philosophers and Sophists* mentions this charge after Libanius's death, Lieve Van Hoof notes that this was not simply a posthumous rumor, but one that Libanius himself addresses in his autobiography in an effort at damage control ("Libanius' Life and *Life*," 29–33; see also Libanius, *Autobiography*, c. 78, 1:142–145).

11. Note that the prohibitions against seducing a freeborn male were intensified by an edict against soliciting a *praetextatus*—anyone wearing the white tunic hemmed with purple, signifying the freeborn boy (Cantarella, *Bisexuality*, 115). Also see Harper, *From Shame to Sin*, 28–29, 148; Laes, *Children in the Roman Empire*, 42–44; Boswell, *Christianity*, 81. On nudity and social status, see Peter Brown, *Body and Society*, 315–316.

12. Boswell, *Christianity*, 144; Boswell, *Kindness of Strangers*, 51–137. Critics have pointed out that Boswell may be overoptimistic about the survival rate of exposed children.

13. Laes, *Children in the Roman Empire*, 256–257.

14. Ibid., 263.

15. *Didache* 2.2, pp. 4–5. This translates into the phrase "pueros non corrumpes" in *Doctrina duodecim apostolorum*, 9. Note, however, that it was not distinguished from other capital sins like murder, adultery, or fornication in any way, but was listed alongside of them. See Harper, *From Shame to Sin*, 98.

16. See Chapter 1, p. 19, above.

17. Cf. Harper, *From Shame to Sin*, 143. Note that while the adulteress-believer is denied communion even on her deathbed, the catechumen is permitted to be baptized on her deathbed (Council of Elvira, cc. 63, 68, in Vives, *Concilios*, 12, 13).

18. Doyle, Sipe, and Wall, for example, begin their scathing indictment of the contemporary church's sex scandal with the assumption that "the sexual abuse of children by priests is found condemned over and over again" in early councils, codified in twelfth-century canon law, and vigorously pursued by the popes (*Sex, Priests, and Secret Codes*, 4–5). As we shall see, things are not always as they appear.

19. See Foucault, *History of Sexuality*, vol. 3, *The Care of the Self*. Harper, however, resists this interpretation, attributing the turning away from same-sex relations to Christianization (*From Shame to Sin*, 141–143).

20. *Constitutiones apostolorum* 7.2.10, in *Didascalia et Constitutiones apostolorum*, ed. Funk, 391; trans. http://www.newadvent.org/fathers/07157.htm. Boswell notes that authors like Philo of Alexandria make parallel conflations (*Christianity*, 143 n. 31).

21. Tertullian, *Apologeticum*, c. 46, p. 141; trans. http://www.newadvent.org/fathers/0301.htm.

22. Laes, *Children in the Roman Empire*, 268.

23. Augustine, *Confessiones* 6.13, *CSEL* 33:137; trans. http://www.newadvent.org/fathers/110106.htm.

24. Morris, *"When Brothers Dwell in Unity,"* 123–125; Sozomen, *Historia ecclesiastica* 8.2, *PG* 67:1513–1514; trans. http://www.newadvent.org/fathers/26028.htm. Chrysostom borrowed liberally from Libanius, however, to subvert Libanius's defense of paganism. See Chrysostom's

Comparison Between a King and a Monk, 69–76; and Hunter's introduction, 25–29, which persuasively authenticates this treatise on the basis of this indebtedness. Also see Cribiore, *Libanius the Sophist*, 120–124.

25. Chrysostom, *Against the Opponents of the Monastic Life* 3.8, pp. 140–141. John's evocation of Roman law was presumably referring to the 390 edict of Theodosius I, discussed below. For the possible events prompting this treatise, see Schatkin, "John Chrysostom, *Adversus oppugnatores*," 373–376; on the educational responsibilities of the paterfamilias, see ibid., 378–380.

26. Chrysostom, *Against the Opponents of the Monastic Life* 3.8, p. 142. Regarding John's inclusion of Christian abusers, see Schatkin, "John Chrysostom, *Adversus oppugnatores*," 380.

27. Chrysostom, *Against the Opponents of the Monastic Life* 3.8ff., pp. 147ff.

28. Ibid., 3.18, p. 167. For Chrysostom's view of the advantages of a monastic education, see Festugière, *Antioche païenne et chrétienne*, 329–346. Also see Boswell, *Christianity*, 31–32. Chrysostom decries the "unnatural" aspects of same-sex relations at length in his *Homily 4 on Romans*, while his sermons on Genesis link the city of Sodom explicitly with same-sex relations. See Morris's analysis in *"When Brothers Dwell in Unity,"* 100–119, 125–129.

29. In fact, Boswell convincingly argues that Chrysostom saw same-sex desire as normal and "constantly juxtaposed homosexual and heterosexual desires as two faces of the same coin" (*Christianity*, 160).

30. Cassian, *Collationes* 13.5.4, *PL* 49:904–905; trans. p. 470.

31. Malalas, *Chronicle*, bk. 18, c. 18, p. 253. The pertinent passages from Justinian's Nov. 77 are translated at http://www.fordham.edu/halsall/pwh/just-novels.asp. See Dalla, *"Ubi Venus mutatur"*; Boswell, *Christianity*, 171–174; Laes, *Children in the Roman Empire*, 272–273; Brundage, *Law*, 121–122.

32. *Theodosian Code* 9.7.6, p. 232. The law in question is a condensed version of an edict issued by Theodosius the Great (I). See Cantarella, *Bisexuality*, 180–181, 186; Dalla, *"Ubi Venus mutatur,"* 165–184. For a detailed discussion, see Matthews, *Laying Down the Law*, esp. 277–279.

33. On the clash between such ascetic ideals and traditional Roman values, see Hunter, *Marriage, Celibacy, and Heresy*; Peter Brown, *Body and Society*, 341–365, 376–377.

34. Augustine, *Confessiones* 9.6.14, *CSEL* 33:207; trans. http://www.newadvent.org/fathers/110109.htm. See Peter Brown, *Body and Society*, 387–427.

35. Augustine, *De civitate Dei* 18.13, *CSEL* 40.2:284; trans. http://www.newadvent.org/fathers/120118.htm. Prudentius describes Ganymede as a minor as well (Harper, *From Shame to Sin*, 148). In his denunciation of pagan gods, St. Anthony conflates Jupiter's predations upon Ganymede with the rape of women. His later reference to Jupiter's assault on regal boys with the help of birds follows an allusion to his rape of Leda in the form of a swan (Athanasius, *Vita Beati Antonii Abbatis*, c. 46, *PL* 73:159). Cf. Arnobius, who uses the alternative name Catamitus for Ganymede, *Diputationes adversus gentes* 4.26, 5.22, *PL* 5:1055–1058, 1125–1127.

36. Cassian, *De institutis* 6.13, *CSEL* 17:122; trans., p. 158.

37. Athanasius, *Vita Beati Antonii Abbatis*, c. 4, *PL* 73:129–130.

38. See Morris, *"When Brothers Dwell in Unity,"* 19–33. For the unfortunate donkey herder, see John Climacus, *The Ladder of Divine Ascent*, c. 17, pp. 174–175.

39. Ward, *Sayings of the Desert Fathers*, Eudemon, no. 1 (p. 64). On women and ideas of femaleness among the desert fathers, see Brakke, *Demons and the Making of a Monk*, 182–212; Rousselle, *Porneia*, 147–148.

40. Ward, *Sayings of the Desert Father*, John the Dwarf, no. 4 (p. 86).

41. Ibid., Macarius the Great, no. 5 (p. 128).

42. Ibid., Matoes, Disciple of Abba Silvanus, no. 11 (p. 145).

43. Ibid., Poemen, no. 176 (p. 191).

44. Ibid., Carion, no. 2 (pp. 117–118).

45. John the Persian, no. 1 (p. 107).

46. On the monastic indifference to scandal, see Milis, *Angelic Monks*, 142.

47. On this transition, see Dunn, *The Emergence of Monasticism*.

48. Kolve, "Ganymede/Son of Getron," 1044.

49. De Jong, *In Samuel's Image*, 18–19.

50. *RB*, c. 59, pp. 134–135.

51. De Jong, *In Samuel's Image*, 23–27. Note the mixed efforts of Carolingian legislation at mitigating the absolute nature of oblation (ibid., 62–64).

52. *RB*, cc. 63, pp. 142–143.

53. *RB*, c. 70, p. 104.

54. *RB*, c. 37. pp. 92–93.

55. Pierre Riché sees Benedict's attitude as much more compassionate than his forebears' (*Education and Culture in the Barbarian West*, 452).

56. *RB*, c. 4, pp. 30–31.

57. *RB*, c. 30, pp. 80–81. This also pertained to certain adolescents as well as individuals with diminished understanding.

58. Smaragdus of St.-Mihiel, *Commentary on the Rule of St. Benedict* 3.30, p. 374.

59. On the sorry plight of the oblate, see Mary Martin McLaughlin, "Survivors and Surrogates," 129–132. On efforts to keep children separate from the other monks, see Riché, *Education and Culture*, 455–456. Note that in the St. Gall plan (the ideal Carolingian monastery that was never actually built), children were sequestered in the southeast cloister (Quinn, *Better Than the Sons of Kings*, 48–55).

60. Hildemar of Corbie, *Expositio*, c. 37, p. 419. See de Jong, "Growing Up in a Carolingian Monastery."

61. Hildemar, *Expositio*, c. 22, p. 332; trans. http://hildemar.org/index.php?option = com_content&view = article&id = 69&catid = 15&Itemid = 102.

62. Ibid., p. 334.

63. Ibid., c. 25, p. 350; trans. http://hildemar.org/index.php?option = com_content& view = article&id = 72&catid = 15&Itemid = 102. Smaragdus's concern over the molestation of boys becomes explicit in his citation of Fructuosus's rule, discussed below.

64. Hildemar, *Expositio*, c. 25, pp. 350–351; Coon, *Dark Age Bodies*, 119–120. The rape of a child is only treated after a discussion on the gravity of pilfering food.

65. The Council of Toledo (633) says explicitly: "Prona est omnis aetas ab adolescentia in malum, nicil [*sic*] enim incertius quam vita adolescentium." The canon goes on to say that if there are any clerics "puberes aut adulescentes," they must all live together under the direction of an older magister so that their "lubrica aetas" not be spent in wantoness but in ecclesiastical discipline. Council of Toledo (633), c. 24, in Vives, *Concilios*, 201. Such attitudes remain well into the high Middle Ages. See Brasington, "*Nihil incertius quam vita adolescentium,*" 41–43; Shahar, *Childhood in the Middle Ages*, 27–28.

66. Basil the Great, "Ascetical Discourse and Exhortation," p. 23; Quinn, *Better Than the Sons of Kings*, 156–157.

67. Riché perceives monastic legislators as much more severe with adolescents than with children, however. He also emphasizes the instability of the categories of *parvulus, adulescens, infans*, and so on (*Education and Culture*, 454, 448); cf. Innes, " 'A Place of Discipline,' " 61, 64–67, on the fluidity of categories regarding secular youths at court.

68. On increasing instances of monks becoming priests and how this is reflected in Hildemar's attitudes, see de Jong "Growing Up in a Carolingian Monastery," 120–122.

69. Hildemar, *Expositio*, c. 23, p. 346; trans. http://hildemar.org/index.php?option = com_content&view = article&id = 69&catid = 15&Itemid = 102. See de Jong, *In Samuel's Image*, 143.

70. Paul the Deacon (d. 796 × 799) likewise excused a culprit if he was drunk, instead preferring private penance of up to seven years (*In sanctam regulam commentarium*, c. 25, pp. 283–285; also see Chapter 5, pp. 125–126, below regarding the permeability of confession in this period).

71. Hildemar, *Expositio*, c. 60, p. 553. Here condemnation translates into flogging. Hildemar ultimately argues against this position, maintaining that bad priests often require more stringent disciplining. His source was either the False Decretals (*Excerpta quaedam ex synodalibus gestis sancti Silvestri papae*, c. 2, in Pseudo-Isidore, *Decretales*, 449) or one of their fonts: the *Constitutio Sylvestri*, a sixth-century forgery professing to be the canons of the alleged Council of Rome of 324 (*Sacra concilia*, 2:615–616). See Amann, "Pénitence," 803, 832.

72. Brooten, *Love Between Women*, 257.

73. De Jong, *In Samuel's Image*, 158–162.

74. Aristotle, *L'Éthique à Nicomaque* 7.6.1148b29–30, ed. Gauthier and Jolif, 1:198. In contrast, the later *Canon of Medicine* by the Muslim polymath Avicenna (d. 1037) will argue that same-sex attraction is psychological and, as such, untreatable. Even so, Avicenna concedes that incarceration or whips could act as powerful deterrents. See Cadden, *Nothing Natural Is Shameful*, 67–68. To be sure, Hildemar was writing long before the so-called rediscovery of Aristotle in the West, while Avicenna's *Canon of Medicine* had yet to be written, let alone translated from the Arabic. Even so, the theories and solutions proffered are not highly technical: they probably reflect pervasive cultural views that the Carolingians may well have shared. On the circulation of the *Nichomachean Ethics* in the later Middle Ages, see Cadden, *Nothing Natural Is Shameful*, 142–144.

75. Coon, *Dark Age Bodies*, 81, 120.

76. See Lockwood, *Prison Sexual Violence*; also see Mariner, *No Escape*, esp. 63–98.

77. Hildemar's monkish inmates were eagerly awaiting their release into paradise (Hildemar, *Expositio*, c. 7, p. 231). As the career of the hapless Gottschalk of Orbais (d. after 866) demonstrates, oblation could become something of a life sentence. A child oblate who attempted to leave the monastery when he came of age, Gottschalk was barred by his abbot, Hrabanus Maurus, whose treatise on oblation cited Abraham's willingness to sacrifice his son Isaac as a justificatory prefiguration of oblation—an apposite analogy (*Liber de oblatione puerorum*, PL 107:423). See translated excerpts of this treatise in Boswell's *Kindness of Strangers*, appendix, 438–444. Also see Quinn's summary in *Better Than the Sons of Kings*, 108–110. When the resigned Gottschalk turned to theology, here too he ran afoul of Hrabanus, who had him imprisoned. Gottschalk ended his life in prison. See Gillis, *Heresy and Dissent in the Carolingian Empire*.

78. See, for example, *St. Paul's Apocalypse*, which excoriates sins of the flesh, including same-sex relations, in *Visions of Heaven and Hell Before Dante*, ed. Gardiner, 40; Gardiner,

Medieval Visions, 179–196. For a useful chronological (but not comprehensive) list of medieval visions, see Dinzelbacher, *Revelationes*, 89–108. Also see Patch, *Other World*, 80–133.

79. Cf. the earlier vision of the Frankish monk Barontus in 678 or 679 (*Visio Baronti*, *MGH SS rer. Merov.* 5:368–394). Barontus does claim to have seen an immense number of clerics defiled with women but provides no other details. The two named bishops seem guilty of unrelated crimes of deception. This cursory treatment of hell is understandable, given all the smoke and shadow that the visionary complains obscures his vision (c. 17, pp. 390–391). Barontus's vision primarily stresses the presence of his confreres in heaven (cc. 13–16, 18, pp. 388–390, 392). See Contreni, "'Building Mansions in Heaven'"; Gardiner, *Medieval Visions*, 43–44.

80. Heito, *Visio Wettini*, c. 7, *MGH Poetae*, 2:270.

81. Ibid., c. 19, pp. 272–73. He does, however, state that this wickedness is not exclusive to males, but also afflicts the marriage bed—demonstrating the flexibility of the term "sodomy" in this period.

82. Ibid., cc. 24–25, p. 274.

83. Walafrid Strabo, *Visio Wettini*, lines 663–666, *MGH Poetae* 2:325. See the translation and commentary by Traill, *Walafrid Strabo's "Visio Wettini"*; and Gardiner, *Medieval Visions*, 228–231.

84. David Clark, *Between Medieval Men*, 203–205.

85. *Vita S. Euphrosynae*, *AASS*, February, 2:539. On the Old English version, see David Clark, *Between Medieval Men*, 195–203; and Frantzen, "When Women Aren't Enough," 463–464; on the Old French version, see Gaunt, "Straight Minds/'Queer' Wishes," 162–168.

86. Hildemar, *Expositio*, cc. 2, 31, 78, pp. 109, 363, 627.

87. Payer, *Sex and the Penitentials*, esp. 40–44; Brundage, *Law*, 152–160; Quinn, *Better Than the Sons of Kings*, 159–163.

88. *Liber Davidis*, cc. 5, 11, ed. Schmitz, *Bussbücher*, 1:492, 493.

89. Note that the eleventh-century Spanish *Paenitentiale Cordubense* also refers to boyish games (*de ludis puerilibus*), leading off with a light penance of twelve days for dirty conversations (c. 105, in Bezler, *Paenitentialia Hispaniae*, *CCSL 156A*:62). See Meens, "Children and Confession," 62–64. On the relation between age and increasing penance, see Abraham, *Anticipating Sin in Medieval Society*, 79–81.

90. *Cummean*, c. 9, in Bieler, *Irish Penitentials*, 128–129. Frantzen's analysis of this and related Anglo-Saxon canons suggests that the younger boy is held accountable for his effect on older men ("Where the Boys Are," 53–55). Abraham resists this interpretation, arguing that other canons would address the culpability of the predatory youth (*Anticipating Sin*, 78). The penitential attributed to Theodore of Tarsus adopts the Benedictine approach of whipping "boys who fornicate among themselves" (*Erster Theil des sog. Theodor'schen Bussbuches* 1.2.11, ed. Schmitz, *Bussbücher*, 2:547); note that earlier, however, Theodore does assign penance for same-sex relations: "if [the offender] is a boy, two years for the first offense; if he repeats it, four years" (ibid., 2.7, p. 546). An adult offender receives seven years. Similarly, Regino of Prüm's later compilation of penitential and other disciplinary material has a more aptly named section "On the Filth of Boys" (*De sordidatione puerorum*), also including the same assortment of voluntary, involuntary, and violent sexual experiences, in *Libri duo de synodalibus causis* 2.249, p. 366.

91. Elliott, *Bride of Christ*, 59.

92. See the eighth-century penitential attributed to Bede: "Si parvulus [*sic*] oppressus talia patitur, XL dies vel psalmis vel continentia castigetur" (*Poen. Bedae* 1.22, ed. Schmitz,

Bussbücher, 1:557); "Parvulus a majore puero oppressus, septimanam, si consensit, dies XX" (c. 32, ed. Schmitz, 1:558). See Frantzen, "Penitentials Attributed to Bede." Cf. the mid-eighth-century *Paenitentiale Parisiense simplex*—"Si quis puer paruulus obpraessus a seniori suo XX annos habens aetate, ebdomada peniteat. Si consentit, XX diebus peniteat" (c. 56, in Kottje, *Paenitentialia minora, CCSL* 156:79)—and the ninth- or possibly tenth-century *Paenitentiale Merseburgense a*—"Si puer paruulus oppressum a maiore habens X annos, XXVII ieiunit, si consenserit, XX dies peneteat [*sic*]" (c. 76, in Kottje, *Paenitentialia minora, CCSL* 156:148). Note that other manuscripts put the assailant at twenty years of age and lower the penance for the victim to seven days—providing he did not consent (ibid., c. 72/73). Also see the ninth-century Frankish *Paenitentiale Pseudo-Theodori*: "Parulus a maiore oppressus, peniteat ebdoma i. Si consenserit, dies xx" (22.7, ed. Van Rhijn, p. 65). And see the eleventh-century *Poenitentiale Vallicellanum I*: "Si quis puer parvus oppressus a majore habens XX, VII dies jejunet et si consenserit, XX dies peniteat" (1.68, ed. Schmitz, *Bussbücher*, 1:299); and "Puer parvus oppressus a majore per violentiam juxta aetatem suam poeniteat; si consensit, XL dies peniteat" (*Poenitentiale Vallicellanum II* 2.25, ed. Schmitz, *Bussbücher*, 1:360).

93. It specifies that this is the "irrational sin" of a man polluting himself with a man (*Capitula Franciae Occidentalis*, c. 8, *MGH Capit. episc.* 3:44).

94. Council of Paris (829), c. 34, *MGH Conc.* 2.2:634–635. The council's starting point is the Council of Ancyra, discussed below. Paris also claims that penitentials heighten the danger of such relations by downplaying their gravity.

95. Benedict the Levite, *Capitularia spuria*, Additio 2, c. 21, *MGH LL* 2.2:136. The spread of such corruption is associated with people who dabble in the dark arts. Note the elision of bestiality and sodomy, as well as the association between sodomy, heresy, and witchcraft, discussed in the Prologue to Part II.

96. Benedict the Levite, *Capitularia spuria*, Additio 4, c. 160, *MGH* 2.2:156.

97. Council of Ancyra (314) c. 15, *Sacra consilia*, 2:525.

98. See, for example, the capitulary of Abbot Ansegisus (780), *Collectio capitularum Ansegisi* 1.48, *MGH Capit. N.S.* 1:458; Theodulf of Orléans, *Zweites Kapitular*, c. 1, *MGH Capit. episc.* 1:168–169.

99. *Admonitio generalis*, c. 49, *MGH Fontes iuris* 16:204; Council of Ancyra (314), cc. 15, 16, *Sacra concilia*, 2:525 (numbered as canons 16, 17 elsewhere). The terminology of the council is quite confusing. The original Greek canons stigmatize *alogeusamenoi*, which means those guilty of shameless conduct. The several Latin traditions parse the canons differently. While there is a general consensus that same-sex practices and bestiality are being condemned, one tradition also includes incest. But apparently the conciliar fathers only intended to censure bestiality. Bailey, *Homosexuality*, 87–89; Boswell, *Christianity*, 178. Hence, a capitulary of Herard for the diocese of Tours (857) condemns those who sin irrationally, aligning it with those who have sex with their relatives (*MGH Capit. episc.* 2:130). Cf. Benedict the Levite, *Capitularia spuria* 1.82, *MGH LL* 2.2:50, which cites the pertinent canon of Ancyra but also aligns incest with bestiality and same-sex relations.

100. Hildemar, *Expositio*, c. 22, p. 333. Cf. Hincmar's presentation of the court as helping to restrain sin in the young (Innes, "'A Place of Discipline,'" 59–61).

101. *Capitulare missorum generale*, c. 17, *MGH Capit.* 1:93. See de Jong, "*Imitatio morum*," 52–54.

102. Synod of Aachen (816), c. 15, ed. Hallinger, *Initia consuetudinis Benedictinae*, p. 460. Note, however, that the later customary of Fleury mandates that children should be

flogged nude until they reach their fifteenth year (*Consuetudines Floriacenses antiquiores*, c. 18, ed. Hallinger, *Consuetudinum saeculi X/XI/XII*, p. 31).

103. Benedict the Levite, *Capitularia spuria*, c. 143, *MGH LL* 2.2:111.

104. Council of Aachen (816), c. 135, *MGH Conc.* 2.1:413. Chrodegang, bishop of Metz (d. 766), anticipated the Carolingian reforms by reorganizing the secular clergy into canons regular, insisting they live in common under the Rule of St. Benedict. See Clausen, *Chrodegang of Metz*. Chrodegang's initiative was continued by Carolingian councils.

105. As cited by Riché, *Education and Culture*, 453. Similar views were also expressed by Bede and Isidore of Seville (ibid., 453–454 n. 48).

106. Donald A. Bullough, *Alcuin*, 110–117; Boswell, *Christianity*, 188–191.

107. Schipper, "Secretive Bodies and Passionate Souls."

108. Alcuin, *Interrogationes et responsiones in Genesim*, interr. 191, *PL* 100:543. Note that there is the possibility that this treatise was written by one of his students.

109. On Alcuin's role in this legislation, see Boswell, *Christianity*, 178 n. 31. Note, however, that Boswell argues the opposite point: that Alcuin's homoerotic leanings translated as leniency. Regarding Alcuin's letter, see Frantzen, *Before the Closet*, 198–199.

110. *Regula Pachomii: Praecepta et Iudicia*, c. 7, in Boon, *Pachomiana Latina*, p. 66; cf. c. 18, p. 60. The rule was translated into Latin by Jerome.

111. *Regula orientalis* 17.18, ed. de Vogüé, p. 260; *Regula Tarnatensis* 13.4, ed. Villegas, p. 32. It is not at all clear where Tarn is, however, except the rule mentions it is on water (*Regula Tarnatensis* 4.5, p. 20). The *Regula orientalis* threatens that, after the third warning, the offending monk shall receive a severe correction (*correptio seuerrisma*) while the *Regula Tarnatensis* only specifies a rebuke (*increpatio*). The *Regula orientalis* also specificies that the *praepositus*, a senior monk who is second in command to the abbot and put in charge of discipline, be someone who is not influenced by the speech of little boys (*paruulorum*), nor does he laugh among boys (*pueros*) (17.22, 17.36, ed. de Vogüé, pp. 258, 259).

112. Isidore of Seville, *Regula monachorum*, c. 16, *PL* 103:569.

113. Fructuosus's anonymous life is one of the chief sources for Visigothic Spain. See the edition and translation by Nock, *Vita Sancti Fructuosi*. On the church in seventh-century Spain, see Collins, *Early Medieval Spain*, 88–145; for Fructuosus, ibid., 85–86. Also see Diaz y Diaz, "Fructueux de Braga."

114. Fructuosus of Braga, *Regula monachorum Complutensis*, c. 16, *PL* 87:1107. I have used my own more literal translation in this instance.

115. On the foundation of Compludo, see *Vita Sancti Fructuosi*, cc. 3–4, ed. Nock, pp. 90–93. The second rule is for a double monastery in which the monks and nuns are carefully segregated. See *Regula monastica communis*, cc. 16–17, *PL* 87:1123–1124.

116. Fructuosus, *Regula monachorum Complutensis*, c. 13, *PL* 87:1105; trans., p. 166.

117. Fructuosus, *Regula monachorum Complutensis*, c. 17, *PL* 87:1107; trans., p. 169.

118. Fructuosus, *Regula monachorum Complutensis*, c. 17, *PL* 87:1107; trans., p. 169.

119. Fructuosus, *Regula monachorum Complutensis*, c. 3, *PL* 87:1100; trans., p. 157.

120. Fructuosus, *Regula monachorum Complutensis*, c. 3, *PL* 87:1100; trans., p. 158.

121. Council of Toledo (693), c. 3, in Vives, *Concilios*, 500–501. Non-Christians, moreover, should receive one hundred blows, with their heads shaved, and be perpetually exiled.

122. This law, issued by King Chindasvindus (d. 653) differs from penitentials, however, insofar as it excuses anyone who was the victim of same-sex rape. The wife of someone so convicted gets her property back and is free to remarry (*Leges Visigothorum* 3.5.4, *MGH LL*

1.1:163); also see the legislation of King Egica (689–690), which explicitly extends castration to members of the clergy (*Leges Visigothorum* 3.5.7, *MGH LL* 1.1:165). This last law makes an oblique reference to the Sixteenth Council of Toledo, also convened under this monarch, in which clerics were degraded for sodomy, but not castrated (see ibid., 165 n. 5).

123. Boswell, *Christianity*, 175–176. Also note Rachel Stocking's argument that, after the Spanish conversion from Arianism, secular and religious authorities strove to find consensus (*Bishops, Councils, and Consensus*).

124. Smaragdus, *Commentary* 3.25, pp. 357–358.

125. Smaragdus's citation of the key passages from Isidore's rule, discussed above, has mixed results, however. On the one hand, in the category of graver offenses, he makes explicit the sexual innuendo of a monk "joking" with boys by adding "or if he kisses them"; the sexual implications of the graver offenses are reinforced by suitable passages from Paul condemning "the works of the flesh" (Gal. 5:19) and men and women who gave up "the natural use for that which is against nature" (Smaragdus, *Commentary* 3.25, p. 355). On the other hand, the potential severity is blunted by the fact that in the previous chapter he includes under lighter offenses "to exchange idle words with the juniors or have friendships [with those] of tender age" (3.24, p. 351). Although attributed to Isidore of Seville, this passage is, in fact, from the Frankish Rule of Tarn.

126. See Annette Grabowsky and Clemens Radl's forward to Ardo's life of Benedict of Aniane, in *Benedict of Aniane*, 7–8. In his early days, Benedict adhered to the stricter Eastern rules of Basil and Pachomius (Ardo, *Benedict of Aniane*, c. 5, pp. 68–69).

127. Benedict of Aniane, *Concordia regularum* 32.3, *CCCM* 168:282; Regino of Prüm, *Libri duo de synodalibus causis* 2.259, p. 372.

128. Burchard of Worms, *Libri decretorum* 19.35, *PL* 140:925; Ivo of Chartres, *Decretum* 9.93, https://ivo-of-chartres.github.io/decretum/ivodec_9.pdf, p. 34.

129. Burchard of Worms, *Libri decretorum* 19.36, 37, 47, *PL* 140:926, 929; Ivo of Chartres, *Decretum* 9.94, 95, 98, https://ivo-of-chartres.github.io/decretum/ivodec_9.pdf, pp. 34–35, 39–40. Also note Ivo's discussion of Lot's daughters, in Chapter 5, p. 111, below.

CHAPTER 3

Note to epigraph: Bayless, *Fifteen Medieval Latin Parodies*, 59.

1. See Laeuchli, *Power and Sexuality,* 88–113.

2. Council of Elvira (ca. 309?), cc. 8, 9, 10, 12, 13, 14, 44, 63, 64, 67, 68, 70, 72, in Vives, *Concilios*, 4–5, 9, 12–14.

3. Ibid., cc. 13, 15, 16, 17, pp. 4–5.

4. Ibid., cc. 61, 66, pp. 12–13.

5. Ibid., cc. 18, 27, 30, 33, 65, pp. 5– 7, 13.

6. Ibid., cc. 5, 81, pp. 2, 15.

7. Laeuchli, *Power and Sexuality*, 97.

8. There is a vast literature on clerical celibacy, much of which is partisan and contentious. For a recent overview of general issues of contention, see Hunter, "Married Clergy in Eastern and Western Christianity"; Parish, *Clerical Celibacy in the West*. Most scholars perceive clerical celibacy as an extra-scriptural Western innovation that began in the fourth century. See, for example, Lea, *History of Sacerdotal Celibacy*; Gryson, *Origines*; Lynch, "Marriage and Celibacy of the Clergy"; Dortel-Claudot, "Le prêtre et le mariage." Even Catholic

authorities, like Cardinal Alfons Maria Stickler, acknowledged that celibacy was an evolution-
ary process that began in earnest in the patristic era. See Stickler, "L'évolution de la discipline
du célibat." Stickler maintains this position in a later work written for a more general public,
The Case for Clerical Celibacy, which begins its inquiry at the Council of Elvira. As is clear
from the publication dates, much of this literature was produced in the wake of Vatican II,
the liberalizing tendencies of which spawned this kind of questioning. For an overview, see
Gryson, "Dix ans de recherches sur les origines de célibat ecclésiastique." There have been
more recent efforts to argue that this was the recommendation for clerics from the beginning.
See Cochini, *Apostolic Origins of Priestly Celibacy*; and Heid, *Celibacy in the Early Church*.
The discussion has become even more fraught in the wake of the church sex scandal. See, for
example, Phipps, *Clerical Celibacy*, with its conclusion that clerical celibacy is at odds with
the basic tenets of the Judeo-Christian tradition.

9. The traditional reason for why Nicaea made no such pronouncement was provided
by the historian Socrates Scholasticus, who claims that Paphnutius, identified as bishop of
Upper Thebes and confessor who had lost an eye during the persecutions, stood up during
the council and declared that celibacy was too heavy a burden to impose on the clergy, that
the marriage bed was honorable, and that it was sufficient to insist that clerics not marry
after ordination (*Historia ecclesiastica* 1.11, *PG* 67:101–104; trans. http://www.newadvent.org/
fathers/26011.htm; see Peter Brown, *The Body and Society*, 256). The reliability of this account
has been challenged. See Cochini, *Apostolic Origins*, 195–200.

10. Council of Nicaea, c. 3, *DEC*, 1:7.

11. The classic work on this subject is Achelis, *Virgines subintroductae*. Also see de Labriolle, "Le 'mariage spirituel.'"

12. For example, see the Pseudo-Cyprian's third-century *De singularitate clericorum*; and
Chrysostom's treatises *Instructions and Refutation Directed Against Those Men Cohabiting with
Virgins* and *On the Necessity of Guarding Virginity*. Also see Elizabeth A. Clark, "John Chrysos-
tom and the *Subintroductae*."

13. Council of Gerona (517), c. 7 (Vives, *Concilios*, 40); Council of Toledo (527), c. 3
(Vives, 43–44); Council of Lérida (546), c. 15 (Vives, 59); Council of Braga (561), c. 15 (Vives,
69); Council of Braga (572), c. 32 (Vives, 95); Council of Toledo (633), c. 43 (Vives, 207);
Council of Braga (675), c. 4 (Vives, 375).

14. Siricius, Ep. 1, to Himerius, bishop of Tarragona, c. 7, *PL* 13:1138. Also see the
council he presided over in Italy, the proceedings of which made their way to Africa (418),
where they were included in the Council of Telepte (Council of Telepte [418], c. 9, *Concilia
Africae*, *CCSL* 149:61–62). A third intervention attributed to Siricius likewise requires sexual
abstinence from bishops, priests, and deacons (Ep. 10.2.6, to the bishops of Gaul, *PL* 13:1184–
1186). See Gryson, *Origines*, 127–131, 136–142. Gryson is among a number of scholars who
ascribe Siricius's letter to the Gallican bishops to Pope Damasus on the testimony of Jerome.

15. Although arguing for clerical celibacy, Ambrose nevertheless acknowledges that in
"quite a number of out-of-the-way places, men who have been exercising the ministry—even,
in some cases, the priesthood itself —have fathered children" (*De officiis* 1.50, pp. 260–261).
See Gryson, *Origines*, 171–174. Ambrose was also one of the main architects of consecrated
virginity in the West. See Elliott, *Bride of Christ*, chap. 2.

16. Council of Toledo (589), c. 5 (Vives, *Concilios*, 126–127); cf. the Council of Seville
(590), which reiterates this decree and complains that some bishops are not complying with

this harsh mandate. In addition to priests and deacons, Seville also applies this to "clerics" (c. 3, Vives, 152–153). Also see Council of Toledo (633), c. 43 (Vives, 207); Council of Toledo (653), c. 5 (Vives, p. 279).

17. Council of Toledo (655), c. 10 (Vives, *Concilios*, 302–303). There were also efforts to impose celibacy on the minor clergy. The Council of Tarragona (516) mandated that a reader or doorkeeper who adhered to his female companion would be thrown out of the clergy (c. 9, Vives, 37).

18. Council of Gerona (517), c. 6 (Vives, *Concilios*, 40).

19. The Council of Agde (506) attempted to build in safeguards: the bishop was not to ordain anyone as deacon before the age of twenty-five. If the candidate for ordination was youthful, the wife had to consent to his ordination, after which she would be sequestered from the bedchamber (c. 16, *Concilia Galliae, CCSL* 148:201). Many councils repeated variations on Nicaea's interdict against clerics having familiarity with extraneous women; see the following in *Concilia Galliae, CCSL* 148A: Orléans (538), c. 4, p. 115; Châlons (647–653), c. 3, p. 303; specific to bishops, priest and deacons, Orléans (511), c. 29, p. 149; Pamiers (517), c. 20, p. 29; Clermont (535), c. 26, p. 109; Orléans (549), c. 3, p. 149; Aspasius (551), c. 2, p. 163; Mâcon (581–583), c. 1, p. 223; Lyon (583), c. 1, p. 232; specific to subdeacons, Tours (567), c. 10, p. 179; that clergy should abstain from wives and that those returning to the conjugal bed should be deposed and only receive communion on their deathbed, Orléans (549), c. 4, p. 149; Mâcon (581–583), c. 11, p. 22; specific to priests and deacons, Châlons (535), c. 13, p. 108; Lyon (583), c. 1, p. 232; specific to bishops, priests, deacons, Orléans (541), c. 17, p. 136; subdeacons, Orléans (538), c. 2, p. 114; Auxerre (561/605), cc. 20, 21, pp. 267–268; with regard to imprisoning priests who have extraneous women in their household and warning bishops to observe this ruling, Tours (567), c. 12, p. 180. Mâcon (581–583) also declared that any woman entering the bedroom of a bishop had to be accompanied by two priests (c. 3, p. 224).

20. Council of Tours (567), c. 20, *Concilia Galliae, CCSL* 148A: 183–184.

21. Council of Elvira, c. 45, in Vives, *Concilios*, 13; cf. c. 70, pp. 13–14.

22. Council of Toledo (380), c. 7, in Vives, *Concilios*, 22–23.

23. Council of Braga (572), c. 29, in Vives, *Concilios*, 94.

24. Ibid., c. 26, p. 94. The potential scandal from clerical offspring was also a matter of concern: a religiously dedicated daughter of a cleric who marries cannot be received by her parents on pain of excommunication, nor can she do penance until the death of her husband. If he is living, she still has the option of leaving and doing penance, though she will only be granted communion on her deathbed (ibid., c. 30, pp. 94–95). Cf. parallel measures in Gallican councils: No one should dare ordain a penitent, a digamist, or someone previously married to one. Whoever disobeys cannot say Mass for a year without forfeiting the love of his clerical brethren (Council of Orléans [524], c. 3, *Concilia Galliae, CCSL* 148A: 44). A later council bars digamists, bigamists, flat-nosed individuals (*simus corpore*—perhaps betokening someone with a broken nose?), or anyone who has been publicly arrested. Although the council notes that earlier statutes would have deposed the uncompliant bishop, it contents itself by suspending him from saying Mass for six months or risk forfeiting the love of his clerical brethren for an entire year (Council of Orléans [538], c. 6, *CCSL* 148A: 116–117).

25. Council of Braga (572), c. 38, in Vives, *Concilios*, 97.

26. McNamara, "Chaste Marriage and Clerical Celibacy."

27. Gryson, *Origines*, 101, 162, 166.

28. Elliott, *Spiritual Marriage*, 88–89.

29. On the connection between adultery, abortion, and infanticide, see Mistry, *Abortion*, 35–36, 44–45, 95–97. This set of associations will be carried forward in the canonical work of Burchard of Worms, *Libri decretorum* 17.51–54, *PL* 140:931.

30. Council of Lérida (546), c. 2, in Vives, *Concilios*, 55–56.

31. Mistry, *Abortion*, 122. This anxiety continues to be expressed much later. See the exemplum regarding a holy hermit, guardian to a young girl, who impregnates her and, on the advice of a demon disguised as a monk, murders her (Goscelin of St.-Bertin [d. after 1107], *Liber confortatorius*, bk. 4, pp. 104–105; trans. pp. 190–192).

32. *Penitential of Finnian*, c. 12, in Bieler, *Irish Penitentials*, 76–79. See Mistry's discussion of clerical sexual sin in this work (*Abortion*, 131–135).

33. *Penitential of Finnian*, cc. 10, 13, in Bieler, *Irish Penitentials*, 76–79; note, however, the situation of the cleric who was a secret fornicator for a long time who does lose his office "since it is not a smaller thing to sin before God than before men" (ibid., c. 11, pp. 76–77).

34. *Penitential of Columbanus*, cc. 2, 4, in Bieler, *Irish Penitentials*, 98–99, 100–101.

35. On provenance and dating, see Van Rhijn's introduction in *Paenitentiale Pseudo-Theodori*, *CCSL* 156B: ix–xiv.

36. *Paenitentiale Pseudo-Theodori* 12.5–6, ed. Van Rhijn, *CCSL* 156B: 20–21.

37. Ibid., 12.7, p. 21; cf. 12.10, p. 22.

38. Ibid., 12.8, p. 21.

39. Ibid., 12.16, 9, pp. 24, 22.

40. Council of Marseilles (533), *Concilia Galliae*, *CCSL* 148A: 86.

41. Pope John II wrote three letters, edited along with the proceedings of the council, with the canons being appended to the third letter (*CCSL* 148A: 86–89). The first appended canon, from Siricius's letter to Himerius, deals expressly with "lapsed" clerics who have returned to their wives (*CCSL* 148A: 88). Caesarius of Arles also wrote a letter adding his own Gallican precedents. The focus on uxorious clerics is confirmed by Caesarius's subsequent letter to his clearly resistant suffragan bishops, included with the Council of Marseilles of 533 (*CCSL* 148A: 92). On the Contumeliosus episode and the resistance that Caesarius encountered, see Klingshirn, *Caesarius of Arles: The Making of Community*, 247–250. Also see Chapter 1, p. 22, above. In penitential literature, for a cleric to sin with his wife after he is ordained is just as bad as for him to sin with a stranger. See, for example, *Penitential of Finnian*, c. 27, in Bieler, *Irish Penitentials*, 83.

42. *Theodorus Poenitentiale* 2.2, in Schmitz, *Bussbücher*, 1:526. Note, however, that the next canon assesses bestiality at fifteen years (2.3, p. 526). But a greater penalty for "irrational" intercourse is not invariably the case. *Poenitentiale Gildae* assigns a cleric the same penance for "natural fornication" and same-sex relations (c. 1, in Wasserschleben, *Bussordnungen*, 103).

43. Burchard of Worms, *Libri decretorum* 17.56, *PL* 140:932.

44. See Chapter 2, pp. 22–23, 34; Chapter 3, p. 62, above.

45. *Apostolic Constitutions* 7.2.9–11, http://www.newadvent.org/fathers/07157.htm.

46. *Ordo* 34.16 in Andrieu, *Ordines romani du haut moyen âge*, 3:607. *Arsenoquita* is from the Greek. It was used by Paul in 1 Cor. 6:9, although the Vulgate simply translates it as "adulterer." Damian makes oblique reference to these taboos when he cites a letter of Gregory the Great with regard to ordination. The candidate must be reputed to be a moral man and is only eligible if guilty of no crime that was punishable by death in the Old Testament (*LG*, pp. 289–290; trans., p. 9).

47. Gregory the Great, Ep. 10.2, to Sabinus, subdeacon of Regionaro (599), *Registrum epistularum*, *CCSL* 140A: 827–828; trans., 3:714–715. Yet Gregory recommends that a philandering archdeacon who persists in living with women be deposed (Ep. 4.26, to Januarius, bishop of Cagliari, *CCSL* 140: 245; trans., 1:307).

48. See Chapter 2, p. 37, above.

49. Odo of Cluny, *Occupatio*. See Christopher A. Jones's analysis of this complex work: "Monastic Identity and Sodomitic Danger." Odo's *Collationes* (*PL* 133:517–638) also reflect upon humanity's fallen sexuality and predilection for lust. See Jestice, "Why Celibacy?"

50. Bruce, *Silence and Sign Language in Medieval Monasticism*, 20–22. Also see Iogna-Prat, "Continence et virginité."

51. Odo of Cluny, *Occupatio*, bk. 7, lines 144–157, p. 153.

52. See Chapter 8, p. 194, below.

53. Odo of Cluny, *Occupatio*, bk. 7, lines 59–60, p. 153.

54. Odo's hagiographer, John, abbot of a monastery in Salerno, attempted to downplay this association. When he deploys imagery from the *Occupatio* to demonstrate Odo's opposition to such relations, it is deracinated from a monastic or even a clerical context. John simply presents Odo as a champion of virtue and enemy of vice, who, "to the effeminate and those who slept with males [*mollibus et masculorum concubitoribus*], he opposed the homicide of Herod whose slaying of bodies was less heinous than the seducer's destruction of souls." But the slayers of souls are not identified with any particular group or setting. Note, however, that the retention of the analogy regarding Herod and the slaughter of the innocents presupposes that the ones being seduced were young (John of Salerno, *Vita S. Odonis* 1.17, *PL* 133:51).

55. This is an epistle directed to Otto I's chancellor Ambrose, who apparently heard rumors that Rather and his clergy were at odds. Rather is quick to assure him that there was never any concord between them. Rather, Ep. 29 (968), *MGH Briefe d. dt. Kaiserzeit* 1:161; trans., 492. I have altered the translation slightly by reintroducing Rather's term *arsenoquita* (versus "homosexual"). See note 46, above. Also see Balzaretti, "Men and Sex in Tenth-Century Italy," 145–151.

56. *LG*, 284–330; trans., 5–53. In the early modern period, this treatise came to be known as the *Book of Gomorrah*. For an overview, see Goodich, *Unmentionable Vice*, 28–31. There has been considerable recent discussion of Damian's work and its rhetorical effects. Mark Jordan credits Damian with the creation of the term "sodomy" (*Invention of Sodomy*, 45–66). Conrad Leyser argues that, in contrast to the war on simony and greed associated with urbanization and its evils that could not be wiped out, the rhetoric of sodomy provided Damian with an unimpeachable sense of moral clarity ("Cities of the Plain"). For discussion of the way in which Damian destabilizes gender, see Burgwinkle, "Visible and Invisible Bodies"; cf. Boyd, "Disrupting the Norm." Also see Olsen, *Of Sodomites, Effeminates, Hermaphrodites, and Androgynes*, for historiographical background. Scholars used to divide Damian's works into treatises and letters, when, in fact, all his treatises were addressed as letters. I will be using the terms interchangeably.

57. On the significance of conversion in Damian's mind, see Little, "Personal Development," 330.

58. Fliche, *Réforme*, 1:178, 191; Lea, *History of Sacerdotal Celibacy*, 1:219.

59. Little, "Personal Development," 333.

60. See especially his ode to the eremitical life at the end of Ep. 28 to the hermit Leo of Sitria (1048–1053), in Damian, *Briefe*, 4.1:276–278; trans., 1:381–388.

61. Ilene Forsyth, for example, interprets Damian's deployment of the Pseudo-Basil/ Fructuosus passage as evidence that he was writing to protect the victimized young in monasteries, which, as we will see in the context of his larger argument, does not hold up. See Forsyth, "Ganymede Capital," 243.

62. Odo of Cluny, *Collationes* 2.28, *PL* 133:573; Odo, *Occupatio*, bk. 7, lines 208, 213–214, p. 155. See Jestice, "Why Celibacy?," 96ff.

63. Damian, Ep. 19, to John, bishop of Cesena, and Almeric, archdeacon of Ravenna (1046), *Briefe*, 4.1:189; trans., 1:182. See d'Avray, "Peter Damian, Consanguinity and Church Property," which takes Damian at his word regarding the extension of prohibitions promoting friendship among clans. The preoccupation with incest was not unique to Damian. See Brundage, *Law*, 191ff. In fact, the nobility took the rules of consanguinity very seriously and went to great lengths to find suitable brides who were not related. See Bouchard, *"Those of My Blood,"* 49–58. Lateran IV (1215) will eventually realize Damian's fear by mandating the reduction in forbidden degrees from seven to four (c. 50, *DEC*, 2:257–258).

64. Damian, Ep. 19, *Briefe*, 4.1:198, trans., 1:192.

65. *LG*, 295; trans., 15.

66. *LG*, 296; trans., 16. I have used my own more literal translation.

67. Burchard of Worms, *Libri decretorum* 17.26, 47, *PL* 140:924, 929. See Gregory the Great, *Dialogues* 4.33.1, 3:110. This is also cited by Regino of Prüm, *Libri duo de synodalibus* 2.199, p. 340.

68. *LG*, 317; trans., 39.

69. *LG*, 318; trans., 40. The irreparable effects of such impurity are demonstrated through an exemplum. A hermit tells a younger confrere that, whenever he feels the effects of sexual arousal, he rubs himself until he ejaculates, likening it to blowing his nose. After the hermit's death, his companion sees him in hell (*LG*, 319; trans., 40–41). Peter is indebted to Odo of Cluny for both the Isaiah passage and the exemplum (Odo of Cluny, *Collationes* 2.25–26, *PL* 133:570).

70. See Brundage, *Law*, 194.

71. Cushing, *"Pueri, Iuvenes,* and *Viri,"* 442–443.

72. *LG*, 308; trans., 29.

73. *LG*, 300–304; trans., 20–28. According to Cushing, Damian's critique of penitentials in the *Book of Gomorrah* was the first call for a revision of the canons (*Papacy and Law*, 23).

74. *LG*, 308, 309; trans., 29, 30. I have altered the latter translation to make it more literal.

75. *LG*, 287; trans., 6.

76. *LG*, 325–326; trans., 49.

77. Anselm of St.-Remy, *Historia dedicationis ecclesiae S. Remigii*, c. 14, *PL* 142:1431 (1st day).

78. Only Leclercq identifies the deacon with Damian (*Saint Pierre Damien*, 65). Other historians, however, have not made this connection. Cf. Fliche, *Réforme*, 1:137–141; Cushing, *Reform and Papacy*, 125–128; and William McCready's passing reference in *Odiosa sanctitas*, 214. Owen J. Blum even states that "there is little evidence that Damian was directly associated with Leo IX or that he made it his business to advise the Pope in person" ("Monitor of the Popes," 463).

79. Though many of these issues were on Peter's agenda, some of them also corresponded with actual cases. On the second day of the council, Hugh, bishop of Langres, was

charged with simony, bearing arms (which resulted in homicide), violating the laws of marriage, tyrannizing his clergy (including extortion and torture), and sodomy. Hugh confessed to simony and extortion but denied all the other charges (Anselm of St.-Remy, *Historia dedicationis ecclesiae S. Remigii*, c. 15, *PL* 142:1434–1435). When the assembly attempted to recall him on the third day, however, he had fled (ibid., c. 16, *PL* 142:1436).

80. Ibid. Sodomy seems to be downplayed, however, as it does not follow the formula of the other injunctions. The indictment is instead: "pari modo damnavit sodomitas."

81. *LG*, 286; trans., 6.

82. *LG*, 287–288; trans., 6–7.

83. Leo IX to Peter Damian, *Briefe*, 4.1:286; trans., 2:5. Leo's letter is appended to the beginning of most editions of Damian's treatise, as it appeared in the manuscripts.

84. Damian actually cites the biblical passage referring to the grievous sin of Sodom and Gomorrah (Gen. 18:20–21). A later letter to the pope, which maintains he is innocent against false charges, is probably fallout from the treatise. Damian, Ep. 33, to Leo IX (1050–1054), *Briefe*, 4.1:332–334; trans., 2:56–58; for other possibilities, see Blum's comments in *Letters*, 2:56 n. 2.

85. Damian, Ep. 156, to Archdeacon Hildebrand (1069), *Briefe*, 4.4:74–75; trans., 6:80. The pope could take such liberties because he knew Damian quite well. Prior to his elevation to the papal throne, Alexander II was Anselm of Lucca, Damian's companion in arms in the mission to Milan. Note this is Anselm the Elder—not be confused with his younger relative the canon lawyer, discussed below.

86. Little, "Personal Development," 334; Boswell, *Christianity*, 213; Brundage, *Law*, 212. McCready resists this view, reasoning that there is no evidence that the treatise was displeasing to Leo IX, nor should one suppose that it displeased Alexander II (*Odiosa sanctitas*, 214–215).

87. Although he condemned simony, this was not Damian's central issue. He believed that in most instances simoniacs could maintain their offices without being reordained. See Damian, Ep. 40, to Archbishop Henry of Ravenna (1052), *Briefe*, 4.1:384–509; trans., 2:111–214 (with an addendum from 1061). This work came to be known as the *Liber gratissimus*. McCready's *Odiosa sanctitas* focuses on an instance in which Damian defends a simoniac bishop.

88. Rather of Verona, Ep. 29, *Briefe, MGH Briefe d. dt. Kaiserzeit* 1:161; trans., 492.

89. On the extent of Leo IX's initiative, see n. 106, below.

90. On bishops misbehaving, see Megan McLaughlin, "Bishop in the Bedroom."

91. Damian, Ep. 61, to Nicholas II (1059), *Briefe*, 4.2:214; trans., 3:10. For Damian's theology of clerical celibacy, see de Chasteigner, "Célibat sacerdotal," esp. 173–177.

92. Damian, Ep. 61, *Briefe*, 4.2:214; trans., 3:4.

93. Blum, "Monitor of the Popes," 467–468.

94. Damian, Ep. 114, to Adelaide of Turin (1064), *Briefe*, 4.3:296; trans., 4:294. Note, however, that Damian was not an unequivocal misogynist and had warm spiritual relations both with his sisters and other select women. See Chapter 4, n. 140, below.

95. Damian, Ep. 138, to his brother Damianus (1065), *Briefe*, 4.3:138; trans., 5:98–99

96. *LG*, 294; trans., 15. I have rendered this translation more literal.

97. *LG*, 298; trans., 18. I have rendered this translation more literal.

98. Megan McLaughlin, "Bishop as Bridegroom," 222–224.

99. Meens, "Ritual Purity."

100. *Diuersorum patrum sententie siue Collectio in LXXIV titulos* 51.245, p. 151; trans., 209–210. On this collection and its wide influence, see Fournier and LeBras, *Histoire des*

collections canoniques, 2:14–20. Ivo of Chartres cites the same canon barring women from touching any fabric or vessels at the altar on two separate instances in one work (*Decretum* 2.72, 3.265, https://ivo-of-chartres.github.io/decretum/ivodec_2.pdf, p. 49; https://ivo-of -chartres.github.io/decretum/ivodec_3.pdf, p. 89). This canon, attributed to Pope Soter (d. ca. 174), is, in fact, one of the False Decretals. It made its way into Gratian's *Decretum*, D. 23 c. 25. There are also canons inhibiting women from approaching the altar in *Collectio canonum in V libris* 2.174.1–2, *CCCM* 6:282, also cited by Ivo of Chartres, *Decretum* 2.135–36, https://ivo-of-chartres.github.io/decretum/ivodec_2.pdf, p. 78. Cf. Bonizo of Sutri, *Liber de vita Christiana* 8.87–88, pp. 275–276. See Kéry, *Canonical Collections*, 234–237. Bonizo was one of Gregory VII's most loyal followers.

101. Damian, Ep. 61, *Briefe*, 4.2:215–216; trans., 3:11.

102. Maureen Miller has argued that clerical misogyny was really a side-effect of a struggle between the clergy and laymen over rival conceptions of masculinity in "Masculinity, Reform, and Clerical Culture," 49–52; cf. Cushing, *Reform and the Papacy*, 123. Also see Chapter 4, below.

103. *LG*, 310; trans., 31.

104. Damian, Ep. 112, to Bishop Cunibert of Turin (1064), *Briefe*, 4.3:278; trans., 4:276–277. On Damian's rhetoric, see Elliott, *Fallen Bodies*, 101–106; Cushing, *Reform and Papacy*, 120–125.

105. Damian, Ep. 114, *Briefe*, 4.3:299; trans., 4:297.

106. Damian, Ep. 112, *Briefe*, 4.3:280; trans., 4:277–278. Leo IX was clearly against clerical marriage and wrote to the canons of Lucca telling them to divest themselves of their wives (Fliche, *Réforme*, 1:155). According to Adam of Bremen (d. between 1081 and 1085), Leo held a synod at Mainz in 1051 where he condemned clerical marriages (*Gesta Hammaburgensis ecclesiae pontificum*, *MGH SS* 7:346; note the date is wrong in the margins of this edition). But if Leo did reintroduce the ordinance that clerical concubines be enslaved to the Lateran Palace at a full synod in Rome, we only have Damian's word for it (Ep. 112, *Briefe*, 4.3:280; trans. 4:278). Augustin Fliche finds it doubtful (*Réforme*, 1:134); Anne Llewellyn Barstow accepts this claim at face value (*Married Priests*, 43). Unfortunately the proceedings for the Roman Council of 1049, when this allegedly occurred, are no longer extant. There was, however, a council at Pavia in 1022 that did mandate that clerical children, and perhaps wives, become serfs to whatever manor they lived upon. Uta-Renate Blumenthal regards this law as more concerned with ecclesiastical property than clerical chastity ("Pope Gregory VII," 240–241). If Leo made no such pronouncement, however, subsequent reformers would. In Anselm of Lucca's canonical collection, it was stated unequivocally that clerical concubines be sold, but that their clerical husbands only receive penance, citing the Council of Toledo (633) as precedent (*Collectio canonum* 7.131, p. 418). See Chapter 2, above. For Anselm of Lucca, see Fournier and Le Bras, *Histoire des collections canoniques*, 2:25–33; Kéry, *Canonical Collections*, 218–226. On penance in this period, see Hamilton, "Penance in the Age of Gregorian Reform."

107. There was, however, a canonical collection (*Collectio 30 capitulorum*), containing a section entitled *De ratione matrimonii*; see Kéry, *Canonical Collections of the Early Middle Ages*, 81–82.

108. Damian, Ep. 19, *Briefe*, 4.1:198, trans., 1:192. Cf. his letter to the lay judge Bonushomo of Cesena, where he anticipates the end of the world when those indulging in earthly pleasure will be consumed by hellfire (Ep. 21 [before 1047], *Briefe*, 4.1:207; trans., 1:204). Also

note his comment that spouses who are not strong enough to give the conjugal debt "a bill of divorce" should at least have the decency to be "ashamed to yield the permanent place in their affection to it [sex] rather than to eternal life," in Ep. 23, to the lay judge Bonushomo (before 1047), *Briefe*, 4.1:223; trans., 1:222. Blum remarks upon the limited nature of his spiritual writings to laymen, focusing largely on the temptations of secular life (*St. Peter Damian*, 194, 197). On Damian's own attraction to women and his view of marriage, see Leclerq, "S. Pierre Damien," 50–51.

109. Damian, Ep. 172, to the clerics of the church of Faenza (no date), *Briefe*, 4.4:261–262; trans., 6:258–259. Unfortunately, this letter cannot be dated. Note, however, that Damian attacks the idea that a valid marriage required consummation, insisting that a couple is fully married after the marriage has been contracted, adducing the marriage of Mary and Joseph as evidence. This anticipates the spiritualized view of marriage that triumphed in the twelfth century. Damian differs by virtue of his emphasis on the wedding contract (*dotali foedere iungitur*), which for some reason he deems incompatible with Lent, rather than consent.

110. Damian, Ep. 172, *Briefe*, 4.4:262; trans., 6:259.

111. Augustine, *De bono coniugali* 1.1, *CSEL* 41:287–288; trans. http://www.newadvent .org/fathers/1309.htm. See Elliott, *Spiritual Marriage*, 43–47.

112. Damian, Ep. 19, *Briefe*, 4.1:184; trans., 1:176.

113. Damian, Ep. 114, *Briefe*, 4.3:304; trans., 4:302–303. There are a number of striking instances of nobles entering religious communities out of the conviction that they cannot be saved in this world. See, for example, the poignant example related by Herman of Tournai about his parents (*Liber de restauratione sancti Martini Tornacensis*, c. 61, *MGH SS* 14:302; Elliott, *Spiritual Marriage*, 107–108).

114. Damian, Ep. 28, *Briefe*, 4.1:264–265; trans., 1:272–273. The prohibition against bigamous clerics is repeated a surprising number of times in *Diuersorum patrum sententie siue Collectio in LXXIV titulos* (5.51; 15.118; 16.139, 143, 145, 150–152, 155–156; pp. 48, 77, 96, 97, 99–101; trans., 101, 132, 150–152, 154–157).

115. Damian, Ep. 112, *Briefe*, 4.3:260–261; trans., 4:259.

116. Leidulf Melve is under the impression that Damian first used this term in the *Book of Gomorrah* and that he applies it both to clerical same-sex relations and clerical marriage ("Public Debate," 689). Neither of these claims is correct.

117. Council of Tours (567), c. 20, *Concilia Galliae*, *CCSL* 148A: 183–184. When it came to the stigmatization of sexual vice, Spain was generally the forerunner. But it was some twenty years later at the Council of Toledo (589) that bishops, priests, or deacons who wished to continue having sex with their wives were pronounced heretical (c. 5, Vives, *Concilios*, 126–127). It is not clear that Damian was aware of this usage.

118. Clement of Alexandria, *Stromata* 3.4, *PG* 8:1129–1132, http://www.newadvent.org/ fathers/02103.htm. See Harnack, "Sect of the Nicolaitans." Maurice Goguel, however, argues that the ascetic account of Nicolas is but a legend designed to whitewash the deacon from responsibility for the sect (see "Nicolaïtes," 13–14).

119. Eusebius, *Historia ecclesiastica* 3.29, *PG* 20:275–278; trans. http://www.newadvent .org/fathers/250103.htm.

120. Augustine, *De haeresibus*, c. 5, *PL* 42:26. Cf. Jerome, who in his letter to the apostate deacon Sabinianus refers to Nicolas as "formerly of your order," crediting him with the heresy of the Nicolaitans, of "all unclean things," and of violating many virgins (Ep. 147, c. 4,

CSEL 56:319–320; cf. Ep. 14, to Heliodorus, c. 9, *CSEL* 54:57–58). John Cassian notes that just as Satan was a member of the rank of the angels, and Judas a member of the disciples, so Nicolas is the founder of a detestable heresy among the deacons. He entertains, but dismisses, the objection of others that the deacon from Acts is not the founder of the sect (*Collationes* 18.16, *PL* 49:1120–1121; trans., 651). Isidore of Seville (*Etymologiae* 8.5.1, *PL* 82:298) and Alcuin (*Commentaria in Apocalypsin* 2.2, v. 6, *PL* 100:1102) cite Augustine verbatim. Bede, however, stays truer to Clement, repeating the story of Nicolas and the renunciation of his wife, presenting the sectarians as infidels who distorted this instance (*Explanatio Apocalypsis* 1.2, *PL* 93:138).

121. Council of Tours (567), c. 20, *Concilia Galliae*, *CCSL* 148A:184.

122. Damian, Ep. 61, *Briefe*, 4.2:217; trans., 3:12.

123. Damian, Ep. 65, to Archdeacon Hildebrand (1059), *Briefe*, 4.2:230–231; trans., 3:25.

124. Damian, Ep. 112, *Briefe*, 4.3:286; trans., 4:282. On Cadalus, see Stroll, *Popes and Antipopes*, 133–150. In 1062, Damian addressed two letters to Cadalus urging his repentance. The second letter is more severe than the first (Eps. 88, 89, *Briefe*, 4.2:515–531, 531–572; trans. 3:325–369). According to I. S. Robinson, these open letters to the antipope were used to rally support around Alexander II ("Friendship Network of Gregory VII," 9). On Damian's perception of heresy, see Ryan, *Saint Peter Damiani and His Canonical Sources*, no. 107, pp. 63–65.

125. The anonymous life of Altmann (*Vita et res gesta S. Altmanni, PL* 148:878) was written in the late eleventh or early twelfth century; the anonymous thirteenth-century poem is quoted from Stehling, *Medieval Latin Poems of Male Love*, no. 125, pp. 138, 139.

126. See, for example, Manegold of Lautenbach's rubric "Testimonium Petri Damiani, quod iure vocentur heretici," *Manigoldi ad Gebehardum liber*, c. 76, *MGH Ldl* 1:428.

127. See Barstow, *Married Priests*, 67–75; Brundage, *Law*, 216–219.

128. On the charge of sodomy in the anti-reform treatises, see Boswell, *Christianity*, 216–217; Barstow, *Married Priests*, 112–114; Thibodeaux, "Defense of Clerical Marriage," 60–62; Thibodeaux, *Manly Priest*, 98–101. These treatises have recently been reedited by Erwin Frauenknecht in *Verteidigung*. Of course, we can never know the full extent of the resistance or its nuances since the reformers won. Witness the very sparse information we have of the anti-reform conciliar action. See Stoller, "Eight Anti-Gregorian Councils."

129. Dinshaw notes that such methods were especially common in cases of sodomy (*Getting Medieval*, 67ff.).

130. Fliche, *Réforme*, 3:3. For an overview of the defense of clerical marriage, see Parish, *Clerical Celibacy in the West*, 114–119.

131. For a summary of different theories of authorship, see Melve, "Public Debate," 690–691. Fliche argues that the treatise was written around 1060, but then reissued in an expanded version around 1074 (*Réforme*, 3:2–3). Recently, Frauenknecht has argued that it originated in Constance in 1075 (*Verteidigung*, 70); cf. Melve, *Inventing the Public Sphere*, 1:109.

132. For discussion of the treatise, see Barstow, *Married Priests*, 107–115; Fliche, *Réforme*, 3:2–11; Melve, "Public Debate," 694–704; Frauenknecht, *Verteidigung*, 84–98. For the critical role that Pseudo-Ulrich played in shaping the debate by the introduction of the apocryphal example of Paphnutius (the confessor who allegedly objected to mandatory celibacy for the clergy at the Council of Nicaea), see Melve, *Inventing the Public Sphere*, 1:109–116, and n. 9, above.

133. Damian alludes to the tradition that Gregory I mandated celibacy in his letter to Cunibert, bishop of Turin (Ep. 112, *Briefe*, 4.3:266; trans., 4:264).

134. Pseudo-Ulrich, *Rescriptio*, 208.

135. Barstow, *Married Priests*, 108. On the problem of finding the source for this story, see Frauenknecht, *Verteidigung*, introd., 92–93.

136. Robinson, *Authority and Resistance*, 32–33.

137. For biblical texts authorizing clerical marriage, see Pseudo-Ulrich, *Rescriptio*, 204–206.

138. Ibid., 209.

139. Ibid.

140. Ibid., 210–211.

141. Ibid., 205.

142. Ibid., 212.

143. Ibid., 214.

144. The Norman Anonymous, arguably, went much further, identifying the reform party with Satan (Barstow, *Married Priests*, 163–164). Others were more subtle, mentioning new or contrary doctrine. See, for example, Sigebert of Gembloux, *Apologia*, 220; *Tractatus pro clericorum conubio*, 254.

145. Letter from the canons of Cambrai to their brothers at Reims (ca. 1078), ed. Frauenknecht, *Verteidigung*, 245. On resistance to Gregory VII, see Cowdrey, "Gregory VII and Chastity," 278–279. Neither Cowdrey (ibid., 290–291) nor Blumenthal ("Pope Gregory VII," 248–249, 253) believe that clerical chastity was a priority for Gregory. Even so, the pressure on married priests certainly was intensified (Hunter, "Married Clergy," 136–137).

146. Landulf the Senior, *Historia Mediolanensis* 3.26, *MGH SS* 8:92. Landulf was himself a married priest who frequently put polemic before fact. Andrew may have been his fabrication. See Brian Stock's analysis of Landulf's history in *Implications of Literacy*, 174–215; and ibid., 208–210, for Andrew's speech. Also see Cowdrey, "Papacy, the Patarenes."

147. Serlo of Bayeux, *Defensio pro filiis presbyterorum*, *MGH Ldl* 3:581. See Barstow, *Married Priests*, 133–135. Cf. an anonymous poem written by another son of a cleric who cautions the reformer to

Leave us alone and chastise yourself, sodomite!
You draw up harsh laws, enact bitter statutes,
And make things generally impossible for us.

As cited in Barstow, *Married Priests*, 136 (which contains a translation of the entire poem).

148. Landulf the Senior, *Historia Mediolanensis* 3.22, *MGH SS* 8:88.

149. See Megan McLaughlin, "'Disgusting Acts.'" Kuefler notes that such strategies were probably allayed by a degree of projection, which seems likely ("Male Friendship and the Suspicion of Sodomy," 162). See the discussion of projection with respect to Anselm of Canterbury in Chapter 4, below.

150. Lampert of Hersfeld, *Annales*, ann. 1073, *MGH SS rer. Germ.* 38:140.

151. He does, however, note that Henry neglected his wife, as the many children born out of adultery would suggest. Wido of Ferrara, *De scismate Hildebrandi* 1.3, *MGH Ldl* 1:536. Originally in the reform camp, Wido later joined the entourage of Clement III, the emperor's antipope, and used much of the reformers' research against them. Although basically in favor

of reform, he disliked Gregory VII's methods. *De scismate* is a kind of *Sic et non* on Gregory VII's pontificate, with the *non* ultimately prevailing. See Fliche, "Guy de Ferrare." One of the points Wido makes against Gregory VII was his ill-treatment of Henry. Yet this charge is balanced by a description of Henry's vices, which, according to Fliche, was indebted to Manegold of Lautenbach's anti-Henrician polemic (ibid., pt. 1, pp. 112, 128–129). Also see Robinson, *Authority and Resistance*, 46–47, 96–98; Robinson, "Reform and the Church, 1073–1122," 278–279, 292–293.

152. Manegold of Lautenbach, *Ad Gebehardum*, c. 29, p. 362. On Manegold, see Megan McLaughlin, "'Disgusting Acts,'" 327–331; and Robinson, *Authority and Resistance*, 124–131.

153. Manegold of Lautenbach, *Ad Gebehardum*, c. 30, p. 365.

154. Ibid., c. 29, p. 362.

155. Bruno, *De bello Saxonico*, cc. 6, 8, *MGH Ldl* 5:331–332.

156. Bonizo of Sutri looks to the False Decretals to define infamy. The definition includes both the incestuous and adulterers. Another canon brands the children of incestuous unions as infamous. Bonizo of Sutri, *Liber de vita christiana* 3.45, 9.9, pp. 86, 280–281. Anselm of Lucca enlists a number of canons (many from Pseudo-Isidore) that detail the legal liabilities of the infamous—especially ensuring that they cannot accuse members of the clergy in *Collectio canonum* 3.1–9, pp. 119–122. See Peters, "Wounded Names."

157. Gregory VII, Reg. 4.1, to the faithful of the Roman church (1076), *MGH Epp. sel.* 2.1:290; trans., 206.

158. Robinson, *Henry IV*, 113.

159. *Walrami et Herrandi epistolae de causa Heinrici regis*, *MGH Ldl* 2:289. The chronicler is allegedly citing Herrand, bishop of Halberstadt, who was writing in response to the letter of the pro-Henrician bishop Walram (ca. 1090). Another twelfth-century chronicler displays his patristic savvy, relating that "in the manner of the Nicolaitans, he made a prostitute of his wife, subjecting her to the lust of others through force" (Helmold, *Chronica slavorum* 1.28, *MGH SS* 21:27).

160. Manegold of Lautenbach, *Ad Gebehardum*, c. 29, p. 362.

161. Damian, Ep. 102, to Abbot Desiderius and the monks of Monte Cassino (1063–1064), *Briefe*, 4.3:132–133; trans., 5:136–137.

162. *Epistola de sacramentis haereticorum*, ed. Sackur, *MGH Ldl* 3:16. It is unclear whether this work is from the late eleventh or late twelfth century. The lay boycott of Masses became papal policy under Nicholas II at the Lateran Council of 1059 (c. 3, *MGH Const.* 1:547). The canon was reissued by Gregory VII in 1075. According to Blumenthal, Gregory was responding to the Patarene uprising in Milan ("Pope Gregory VII," 244–45).

163. Gerhoh of Reichersberg, *Opusculum de edificio dei*, c. 36, *MGH Ldl* 3:160. Note that simoniacs are later aligned with the citizens of Sodom, clamoring against God (ibid., c. 59, 3:170). By the same token, the chronicler Helmold of Boss (d. 1177) would indirectly cast aspersions on the marriages of the anti-reform party by noting that Henry IV made a public prostitute of his wife "in the manner of the Nicolaitans"—reverting to apocryphal accounts of the deacon Nicolas (*Chronica slavorum*, c. 28, *MGH SS* 21:32).

164. *Diuersorum patrum sententie siue Collectio in LXXIV titulos* 21.170–173, pp. 108–109; trans., 164–166. See Dusil, *Wissensordnungen des Rechts im Wandel*, 140–141.

165. If the sexual infractions of nuns and consecrated women are included, the number rises to eighty-six.

166. The sins specified are homicide, adultery, fornication, sacrilege, theft or related vices arising from the principal ones (*Collectio canonum in V libros* 2.83, p. 230). "Fornication" is, however, a vague term that sometimes does accommodate sodomy. Other possible exceptions are in a letter of Gregory I, which refers to a deacon's grave and an unspecified *corporale delictum*, and a letter of Isidore of Seville that entertains the question of whether a cleric can be restored to office after a *carnale delictum* (ibid., 2.86, 100, pp. 232, 239; see Fournier and Le Bras, *Histoire des collections canoniques*, 2:131–135).

167. Heito, *Visio Wettini*, c. 6, *MGH Poetae* 2:270. The angel informs Wetti that guilty parties are beaten with sticks on their genitals for three days straight, with one day of reprieve before it starts again.

168. Bonizo of Sutri has a section meting out penance for sins of the flesh that drew heavily upon penitential literature, and so, unsurprisingly, there is one canon concerning penance for sodomy that distinguishes between penalties for someone in orders versus a layman (*Liber de vita Christiana* 10.73, p. 331). Another exception possibly occurs in Anselm of Lucca's collection, though it should be noted that Anselm may have been responsible for only the first seven of the twelve books that appear in some manuscripts (Cushing, *Papacy and Law*, 7). In the extended version of his work, book 12 also addresses "those who have sex with beasts and males" and "those who fornicate as the Sodomites," but with no special emphasis on the clergy (Anselm of Lucca, *Collectio canonum* 12.85–86, p. 509). Association with the clergy is further offset by the inclusion of a canon addressing the impossibility of a wife divorcing her husband "whether he is an adulterer or a sodomite"—a canon cited by Anselm (or his later continuator) and Bonizo alike (*Collectio canonum* 10.17, p. 489; *Liber de vita Christiana* 10.53, pp. 323–324). Both collections include a sizable proportion of canons addressing the sexual infractions of the secular and regular clergy with women; Bonizo includes a number of canons addressing the threats that male contact presents to nuns (Anselm, *Collectio canonum* 7.124–134, pp. 416–419; Bonizo of Sutri, *Liber de vita Christiana* 5.32–40, 48, 6.15–19, 31–34, 46, 48–49, 56, 58, pp. 185–187, 193–194, 214–215, 219–220, 213–214, 224–228; also see the discussion of "incestuous clergy" in Chapter 4, below). Note the incomplete Thaner edition only has the chapter headings for book 12.

169. The one exception was in Norman England where Anselm, archbishop of Canterbury, enacted legislation. See Chapter 4, below.

170. Burchard of Worms, *Libri decretorum* 19.30, *PL* 140:926–931.

171. Isidore Mercator, *Collectio decretalium*, c. 70, *PL* 130:420.

172. Cushing, *Papacy and Law*, 72–78.

173. The passage will continue to circulate in penitential literature into the twelfth century. See, for instance, the eleventh-century *Poenitentiale Valicellanum III*, under the rubric of "De clericis vel monachis, si fuerint masculorum insectatores" (c. 4, in Wasserschleben, *Bussordnungen*, 684). Its resurfacing in the later twelfth century is discussed in Chapter 5, below.

174. Bonizo of Sutri uses Augustine's *Against Julian* to make this point about original sin in his preamble concerning sin and baptism (*Liber de vita Christiana*, Praeambula 4, p. 5). Anselm of Lucca cites Gregory the Great's insistence that boys not be ordained lest "venality" be introduced into holy orders (*Collectio canonum* 7.39, p. 379; cf. *Collectio canonum in V libris* 1.76, p. 64). On the later augmented version of Anselm's collection, see Motta, "La redazione A 'aucta' della *Collectio Anselmi*."

CHAPTER 4

1. Honorius Augustodunensis, *De apostatis*, c. 13, *MGH Ldl* 3:60.

2. Honorius Augustodunensis, *De offendiculo*, *MGH Ldl* 3:38–57. See Megan McLaughlin, *Sex, Gender, and Episcopal Authority*, 221.

3. Honorius Augustodunensis, *De offendiculo*, c. 33, *MGH Ldl* 3:49; *De apostatis*, prol., 3:57; Gerhoh of Reichersburg, *Commentarius aureus*, pt. 2, Ps. 25, v. 4, *PL* 193:1159. The pronouncement of the marriage of the clergy as incestuous was helped along by a spurious canon attributed to a synod held at Chalcedon in 630, which appeared in eleventh-century penitentials like *Valicellanum III*, c. 1, in Wasserschleben, *Bussordnungen*, 682–684. The canon was picked up by authors like Bonizo of Sutri, who likewise attributed it to Chalcedon (*Liber de vita Christiana* 9.27, pp. 287–288). The canon is, in fact, a spurious addition to an already spurious set of decrees attributed to Pope Nicholas I (d. 867), *Epistolae*, *MGH Epp.* 6:688–689. In this context, it is ironic that immediately following this canon, Bonizo adds a comment warning against a misleading "apocryphal" canon on incest attributed to Isidore of Seville (which he nevertheless cites earlier; see *Liber de vita Christiana* 9.28, 9.15, pp. 289, 282).

4. Lateran II (1139), *DEC*, 1:198.

5. The graffiti in the first quotation was later added to a ninth-century manuscript; trans. Stehling, *Medieval Latin Poems of Male Love*, no. 104, pp. 98, 99. The second quotation is from Bernard of Cluny's, *Scorn for the World*, bk. 3, lines 409–418, pp. 160–161.

6. Boswell, *Christianity*, 243–266. Also see Curtius, *European Literature*, 113–117; for other expressions of same-sex sexuality and critiques, see ibid., 122–124.

7. The twelfth-century flourishing of homoerotic verse did not come out of nowhere. There are earlier instances of parallel works celebrating erotic relationships characterized by the same age dissymmetry found in twelfth-century verse. See, for example, the tenth-century *O admirabile Veneris idolum* that was written in Verona, probably by an older man to a younger boy (*puerulus*) in *Carmina Cantabrigiensia*, *MGH SS rer. Germ.* 40:105–107. Ronald Witt characterizes the author as "almost certainly a cleric" (*Two Latin Cultures*, 82).

8. Goodich, *Unmentionable Vice*, 6; Boswell, *Christianity*, 255–260; also see Boswell's translation of the text in the appendix, ibid., 381–389.

9. See Chapter 8, pp. 189–190, below.

10. Boswell, *Christianity*, 253. See the elaborate play on the word by Baudri of Bourgueil when he is urging his probable lover Peter to be discreet in love (ibid., 246).

11. Stehling, "To Love a Medieval Boy," 166.

12. Marbod of Rennes, "To an Absent Friend," in Stehling, *Medieval Latin Poems*, no. 45, pp. 30, 31.

13. Marbod of Rennes, "A Satire on a Young Boy's Lover in an Assumed Voice," in Stehling, *Medieval Latin Poems*, no. 46, pp. 31, 33.

14. Baudri of Bourgueil, "Avitus to Alexander," in Stehling, *Medieval Latin Poems*, no. 51, pp. 42, 43.

15. Baudri of Bourgueil, "Upon Alexander of Tours," in Stehling, *Medieval Latin Poems*, no. 52, pp. 44, 45. Baudri writes several poems for Alexander, one of which says: "He had scarcely reached nineteen years" ("For the Same Boy," no. 54, pp. 44, 45).

16. Baudri of Bourgueil, "To a Youth Too Proud," in Stehling, *Medieval Latin Poems*, no. 50, pp. 38, 39. Both Marbod and Baudri also wrote verse for women. But as Stehling

notes, both poets linger over the face of the woman versus the body of the boy—clearly the more familiar form ("To Love a Medieval Boy," 158–159).

17. Barbara Newman, *Making Love in the Twelfth Century*, 5–6.

18. Boswell, *Christianity*, 245 n. 7.

19. See Leclercq, *Monks and Love*.

20. See Turner, *Eros and Allegory*.

21. Jaeger, *Ennobling Love*, 71.

22. Baudri of Bourgueil, "To a Youth Too Proud," trans. Stehling, *Medieval Latin Poems*, no. 50, pp. 38, 39.

23. Baudri of Bourgueil, "Upon Alexander of Tours," ibid., no. 52, pp. 44, 45.

24. Baudri of Bourgueil, "For the Same Boy," ibid., no. 54, pp. 44, 45.

25. Fliche, *Réforme*, 2:115, 251–255; Cowdrey, *Pope Gregory VII*, 375–379.

26. Fliche, *Réforme*, 2:221–222; Cowdrey, *Pope Gregory VII*, 379–387. The deposition occurred at a council of Lyon where Manasses, once again, did not appear. Nor had he given up entirely: according to Hugh of Flavigny, Manasses sent a number of his subordinates with the resources to bribe Hugh of Die (Hugh of Flavigny, *Chronicon*, bk. 2, ann. 1098, ed. Wattenbach, *MGH SS* 8:421–422). According to Fliche, Hugh of Die exercised an absolute authority in the dioceses of northern and eastern France (*Réforme*, 2:223). Kriston Rennie stresses the clash between Hugh's exalted view of his office and Manasses's insistence on his prerogatives as archbishop (*Law and Practice*, 78–79). Also see John R. Williams's comparatively exculpatory analysis, arguing that Manasses was largely undone by his provincial outlook and inability to fathom legantine authority ("Manasses I of Rheims and Pope Gregory VII.") Manasses's deposition occurred in 1080. See Gregory VII, *Das Register Gregors VII*, Reg. 7.20, *MGH Epp. sel.* 2.1:496, trans., 350–351; Reg. 8.17, to the clergy and people of Reims (1080), *MGH Epp. sel.* 2.2:538–539, trans., 382–383; Reg. 8.18, to Count Ebolus of Roucy, *MGH Epp. sel.* 2.2:539–540, trans., 383–384; Reg. 8.19, to the bishops of the province of Reims, *MGH Epp. sel.* 2.2:540–541, trans., 384–385; Reg. 8.20, to Philip I of France, *MGH Epp. sel.* 2.2:542–543, trans., 385–386.

27. His full name is Hugh-Rainard of Tonnerre and, unlike Manasses, he was sympathetic to reform. See Bouchard, *Sword, Miter, and Cloister*, 239. He is not to be confused with the other Bishop Hugh of Langres who was accused of sodomy at the Council of Reims in 1049 and died the following year (see Chapter 3 n. 79, above).

28. Ep. 107, Manasses I, bishop of Reims, to Gregory VII (1077), in Erdmann, *Die Hannoversche Briefsammlung, MGH Briefe d. dt. Kaiserzeit* 5:179–180. See Gregory VII's letter to Hugh of Die, telling him to cooperate with the bishop of Langres in the matter of the council judging Manasses and others (Reg. 4.22 [1077], *MGH Epp. sel.* 2.1:332; trans., 234; the council was ultimately held in Autun, which is in Langres). Also see Gregory VII's letter to Manasses, which states that he would accept no excuses for his failure to attend the legatine council in Lyon—especially since he would be in the company of such excellent guides as Hugh of Die and Hugh of Langres (Reg. 7.12 [1080], *MGH Epp. sel.* 2.2:476; trans., 337).

29. Ivo of Chartres had encouraged the reappointment of Hugh as legate under Urban II and attempted (unsuccessfully) to have Hugh reappointed under Paschal II. In fact, Hugh was much less active than when he was legate under Gregory VII (Rennie, *Law and Practice*, 42–43, 207–208).

30. Philip was first crowned and consecrated king in 1059. But he repeated the ritual periodically in order to maintain power during his many excommunications. See Ivo of Chartres, *Correspondance*, 283 n. 7. Boswell, *Christianity*, 213–214; Fliche, *Règne de Philippe Ier*, 435.

31. Ivo of Chartres, Ep. 65, to Hugh of Die, archbishop of Lyon (1098), in *Correspondance*, pp. 282, 284 ("De hoc enim rex Francorum non secreto, sed publice mihi testatus est quod praedicti Joannis succubus fuerit; et hoc ita fama per Aurelianensem episcopatum et vicinias urbes publicavit ut a concanonicis suis famosae cujusdam concubinae Flora agnomen acceperit"). On the distinction of archdeacon, see Barrow, *Clergy in the Medieval World*, 49–50, 304–307.

32. Fliche, *Règne de Philippe Ier*, 435; Boswell, *Christianity*, 213–214, 435; Chiffoleau, "Dire l'indicibile," 297, follows Boswell.

33. Fliche, *Règne de Philippe Ier*, 46–48; 50–51. On Ivo's resistance to Philip I's marriage, see Rolker, *Canon Law and the Letters of Ivo of Chartres*, 230–247; and Duby, *Knight, the Lady, and the Priest*, 3–20.

34. Philip was excommunicated for his relations with Bertrade in 1094. The excommunication was temporarily lifted in 1096, when he agreed to repudiate her. The land was put under interdict when Philip failed to follow through (Rolker, *Canon Law*, 238–239).

35. *Succubare* is defined as "to lie under" in Lewis and Short's *Latin Dictionary* (http://www.perseus.tufts.edu/hopper/text?doc=Perseus%3Atext%3A1999.04.0059%3Aentry%3Dsuccubo1), though its usage is rare.

36. Ivo of Chartres, Ep. 66, to Urban II (1097–1098), *Correspondance*, 296 ("Persona est ignominiosa et de inhonesta familiaritate Turonensis archiepiscopi et fratris ejus defuncti [i.e., the elder John] multorumque aliorum inhoneste viventium").

37. Ivo of Chartres, Ep. 65, *Correspondance*, 283.

38. See Augustine, *De civitate Dei* 15.23, *CSEL* 40.2: 110; Isidore of Seville, *Etymologiae* 8.11.104, *PL* 82:326.

39. Lewis and Short, *Latin Dictionary*, http://www.perseus.tufts.edu/hopper/text?doc=Perseus%3Atext%3A1999.04.0059%3Aentry%3Dincubo1.

40. Unaware of the demonic pairing, scholars have attempted to normalize these terms. Hence, Leclercq's French translation of *succubus* is "il couchait avec," even as *incubus* is "gardien" (Ivo of Chartres, Ep. 65, *Correspondance*, 282, 283). But there does not seem to be any precedent for translating these words in this manner. *Concubinus*, though still unusual when applied to a male, would be more mainstream. Note that Ivo's association between promiscuous religious personnel and diabolism also occurs elsewhere. Apparently he heard from Countess Adelaide of Chartres that the nuns of the monastery of St.-Fara were acting like prostitutes and that the bodies of these demoniacal women were being put to the most filthy uses ("mulierum daemonialicum corpora sua ad turpes usus"), in Ep. 70, to Bishop Gautier of Meaux (1098), in *Correspondance*, 310.

41. Ivo makes note of this relationship in Ep. 65, to Urban II, *Correspondance*, 296. See *Gallia christiana*, 8:1441.

42. Ivo of Chartres, Ep. 65, *Correspondance*, 287. For administrative purposes, the diocese was divided into territories and an archpriest (usually the head of a collegiate church) was put in charge of the local clergy, supervising the implementation of the bishop's rule. See "Archpriest," *NCE*, http://www.newadvent.org/cathen/01697b.htm; Barrow, *Clergy in the Medieval World*, 334–335. Ivo seems to be implying that Ralph is using one of his archpriests to bully the younger John.

43. Ivo of Chartres, Ep. 65, *Correspondance*, 284.

44. Ibid., 286.

45. Ibid., 288; cf. Ep. 66, p. 296.

46. See, for example, his unflattering reference to the previous bishop of Chartres (Ep. 6 [1098], to a certain Geoffrey, *Correspondance*, 22 and n. 4). Geoffrey, Ivo's predecessor, refused to accept Urban II's deposition and continued to act as bishop, and his supporters resisted Ivo's consecration (Rolker, *Canon Law*, 14–15). Cf. Ivo of Chartres, Ep. 98, to the canons of Beauvais, *PL* 162:118. Ivo also uses *paedagogus* with respect to the redoubtable Stephen of Garland (Ep. 89, to Paschal II [1101], *PL* 162:111), who is discussed below.

47. Ivo of Chartres, Ep. 66, *Correspondance*, 296. On the phenomenon of the carnivalesque ritual of the boy bishop, see Mackenzie, *Medieval Boy Bishops*.

48. See Chapter 3, p. 64, above and Chapter 8, p. 194, below.

49. Boswell, *Christianity*, 214 n. 18. Even if Boswell is right, theoretically someone could not be made a bishop until he was at least thirty. See Gratian, *Decretum*, D. 77 c. 6, which cites the Council of Agde (506). Cf. the Council of Arles (524), c. 1, *Concilia Galliae*, CCSL 148A:43.

50. Note, however, that Ivo's *Decretum* gives the more traditional age of twenty-five for the deacon (Barrow, *Clergy in the Medieval World*, 40–41). This would be seconded by Lateran III (1179), c. 3, which requires bishops to be thirty (*DEC*, 1:212).

51. Barrow, *Clergy in the Medieval World*, 53.

52. Gregory VII, Reg. 4.4, to the people and clergy of Dol (1076), and Reg. 4.13, to Archbishop Ralph of Tours, *MGH Epp. sel.* 2.1:300, 316–317; trans., 213–214, 223–224.

53. This was not the only point of disagreement. Ivo also differed with Hugh of Die and papal reformers over the degree of papal intervention in local affairs and defended the role of the king in the election of bishops. These issues came to the foreground in the election of Daimbert as bishop of Sens. See Ivo of Chartres, Ep. 60, to Hugh of Lyon (1097), *Correspondance*, 238–255; Rolker, *Canon Law*, 19–21, 180, 196–204, 208. On the Gregorian conception of papal legate, see Rennie, *Law and Practice*, 53–85.

54. Wido of Ferrara, *De scismate Hildebrandi* bk. 2, *MGH Ldl* 1:557.

55. Boswell, *Christianity*, 216.

56. Guibert of Nogent, *Autobiographie* 1.11, pp. 62–65.

57. Ibid. 1.11, p. 64; Geoffrey of Vendôme, Ep. 17, to Archbishop Richard of Albanum, *PL* 157:57. Also see *Gallia christiana*, 14:70–76.

58. Fliche, *Réforme*, 2:223–224. In 1078, Gregory did lift Manasses's suspension, restoring him to his original dignity, provided he took an oath to submit to Gregory's legates and administer his diocese more judiciously (Reg. 5.17, memorandum of Gregory VII's revision of sentences passed by his legate, Bishop Hugh of Die, *MGH Epp. sel.* 2.2:379; trans., 266). Although Manasses took the oath, he proved incapable of adhering to it.

59. Guibert of Nogent, *Autobiographie* 1.11, p. 64.

60. *Gallia christiana*, 8:1148.

61. Ivo of Chartres, Ep. 68, to Hugh of Die (1097–1098), *Correspondance*, 302. The queen seems to have been the beneficiary. The same is true in Baudri's case, discussed below.

62. Ivo of Chartres, Ep. 65, *Correspondance*, 288. The queen apparently told Baudri to wait until she got the money from the successful candidate. Then she could have him deposed and elevate Baudri. It did not work out this way, however.

63. Unfortunately, much of the property associated with the see was eventually claimed by the bishop of Tours, and Baudri's see became merely personal, the right of wearing the episcopal pallium circumscribed (Fliche, *Règne de Philippe Ier*, 373–374).

64. Ivo of Chartres, Ep. 89, to Paschal II (1101), *PL* 162:110; also see Ep. 87 (1101), to Cardinals John and Benedict, *PL* 162:107–108; Ep. 95, to Paschal II (1101), *PL* 162:115–116; and Ep. 104, to Paschal II, *PL* 161:123. See Fliche, *Règne de Philippe Ier*, 411–412; Boswell, *Christianity*, 215. It was not unheard of for a cleric still to be in minor orders at the time of his elevation to a bishopric. This was the case when Hugh of Die received his first bishopric—at least according to Hugh of Flavigny (*Chronicon*, bk. 2, ann. 1073, *MGH SS* 8:411).

65. Christoph Rolker argues that Ivo did not compile the *Panormia*—an abbreviated version of Ivo's *Decretum* with a radically different organization—and that it was compiled by a canonist with very different priorities (*Canon Law*, 248–256). This helps explain the complete absence of any references to sodomy. Boswell had interpreted this absence as meaning that Ivo did not regard same-sex relations as much of a problem (*Christianity*, 226–227).

66. Ivo of Chartres, *Decretum* 9.93– 95, 109, https://ivo-of-chartres.github.io/decretum/ ivodec_9.pdf, pp. 34, 39–40. Most of these can also be found in Burchard of Worms (d. 1025), except for the edict from Elvira (*Libri decretorum* 17.35–37, *PL* 140:925–926). Note that both Ivo and Burchard have a rubric targeting *masculorum insectatores* (those who stalk males) versus the *parvulorum* (those who stalk little boys) within the text. Ivo's more generalized canons condemning acts against nature are taken from Augustine's writings. See Ivo, *Decretum* 9.105, 106, https://ivo-of-chartres.github.io/decretum/ivodec_9.pdf, p. 38. Neither of these canons are in Burchard, who cites Ancyra and its conflation of homosexuality and bestiality, and penitential condemnations of sodomy (*Libri decretorum* 17.30, 34, 56, *PL* 140:924–925, 932–933). On Ivo's use of Burchard, see Rolker, *Canon Law*, 109–112. Also note Ivo's discussion of Lot's daughters, in Chapter 5, below.

67. Slydini's quote is taken from Cavett, *Talk Show*, 210; Freud's, from "Notes Upon a Case of Obsessional Neurosis," *SE*, 10:230–231.

68. See Chapter 8, pp. 191, 192–194, below.

69. *Annales Ottenburani*, ann. 1083, *MGH SS* 7:7–8.

70. *VA* 2.1, p. 64.

71. Eadmer began taking notes about Anselm's activity sometime after 1093. He finished after the saint's death in 1109. At some point, however, this work got divided into two parts: *The Life of Anselm* and the *History of Recent Events in England*.

72. *HN*, 48–49; trans., 49–50. Cf. *VA* 2.7, p. 69. Here Anselm is less explicit, appealing "for the reform of morals which every day and in every class of people showed too many corruptions." The king's response, however, is basically the same.

73. *GRA* 4.312.1, 1:554–555. His description of Rufus is elsewhere less forgiving. See *GPA* 1.48ff.

74. *GRA* 4.314.4–6, 1:558–561.

75. *GRA* 4.315, 1:558–561.

76. *GRA* 4.316, 1:560–561. Henry I was apparently known for his antipathy to such behavior. In William's revision, instead of describing England as a "brothel for perverts," he has the wise man saying "that England would be fortunate if Henry were king"—arguing from Henry's passionate hatred of indecency from youth onward (*GRA* 4.314.5, 1:560–561). Even so, these fashions seem to have persisted throughout Henry's reign as well. The nightmare of a certain courtier, who dreamed that he was being strangled by his ringlets, was more effective than censures. Not only did the man cut his hair, but many other members of the aristocracy followed suit—at least for a time. William of Malmesbury, *Historia novella*, ann. 1030, pp. 5–6.

77. *EH* 5.10, 3:106–107. On Robert's estrangement from his father, William the Conqueror, and the preferment of his younger siblings, see A. M. Aird, "Frustrated Masculinity."

78. *EH* 8.4, 4:146–147. Orderic's homophobic bent has attracted particular attention. See Goodich, *Unmentionable Vice*, 4; Kuefler, "Male Friendship," 163; Mills, *Seeing Sodomy*, 182–183.

79. *EH* 8.10, 4:186–187.

80. *EH* 8.8, 4:178–179.

81. *EH* 8.10, 4:188–189.

82. *EH* 10.2, 5:202–203. Marjorie Chibnall translates *moechis* as "adulteries," but the term is more flexible. The penitentials use it for mother-son incest. Alan of Lille later applies it to any illicit form of sex: "*moechia* dicatur omnis illicitus concubitus" (*Distinctiones dictionum theologicalium*, s.v. *Moechari*, *PL* 210:861; emphasis added). I have altered Chibnall's translation to reflect this broader meaning.

83. Klaniczay, *Uses of Supernatural Power*, 60–64.

84. McNamara, "The *Herrenfrage*"; McNamara, "An Unresolved Syllogism"; Thibodeaux, *Manly Priest*, 32–40. Cf. the complementary argument that the clergy was simultaneously trying to cast itself as a third gender: Swanson, "Angels Incarnate"; Cullum, "Clergy, Masculinity and Transgression"; Jacqueline Murray, "One Flesh, Two Sexes"; Arnold, "Labour of Continence." See Karras's critique of this position in *From Boys to Men*, 160–162; and Karras, "Thomas Aquinas's Chastity Belt."

85. Kuefler, "Male Friendship," 148, 154, 161.

86. William did seem to have spent at least a year away from his monastery in Malmesbury collecting material. See Thomson, *William of Malmesbury*, 17–18. For Orderic, see Chibnall's introduction, *EH*, 1:23–29. On his travels, see Chibnall, *World of Orderic Vitalis*, 36–37, 107, and the map on 222.

87. On Orderic's acquaintance with Eadmer, see Chibnall's intro., *EH*, 1:61–62; Orderic's knowledge of William of Malmesbury is less clear (89–90). Also see Thomson's introduction and commentary to *GRA*, 2:15, 50, 144, 254–255. On their shared indebtedness to Eadmer, see Thomson, *William of Malmesbury*, 72–73; Barlow, *William Rufus*, 103–105.

88. *VA* 1.22, pp. 39–40.

89. Michael Staunton argues that one of Eadmer's chief purposes in writing was to justify Anselm's exile ("Eadmer's *Vita Anselmi*," 9–13). Eadmer does not attempt to suppress entirely the criticism, however. See the letter he cites at length that blames all the kingdom's corruptions on Anselm's exile. This was written during the reign of Henry I by a man "of no mean standing" (*HN*, 167; trans., 78).

90. *VA* 2.26, p. 102. See Vaughn, "St. Anselm of Canterbury."

91. *VA*, introd., x–xi.

92. Herbert of Clairvaux, *Liber miraculorum* 2.42, *PL* 185:1351–1352. No one seems to have told Herbert about Rufus's alleged sexual proclivities. Rather Herbert gives an extended account of how Rufus was about to violate a nun with the most beautiful eyes, and how the nun preserved her virginity by ripping them out and offering them to him (ibid.). This story may be a garbled representation of William Rufus's erstwhile desire to marry Mathilda of Scotland—an intent that Abbot Herman of Tournai claimed was reported to him by Anselm. Apparently Rufus went to see Mathilda at the female religious community of Wilton, where she was being educated. He left when he saw that she was wearing a veil, believing that she had already become a nun (Mason, "William Rufus," 7). Before marrying Henry I, Mathilda

had to convince the skeptical Anselm that she had not, in fact, taken the veil (Elliott, *Bride of Christ*, 115–118).

93. Southern, *Saint Anselm and His Biographer*, 336–43.

94. *VA*, c. 5, p. 67. When Anselm made the king a conciliatory present of five hundred pounds, however, the king was advised by his counselors to complain that it was not enough and refuse it (*HN*, 50–51; trans., 51–52). Cf. *GPA*, which claims that the king's exactions began on Anselm's first day in office (1.49.5, 1:126–127).

95. *GRA* 1.314.2–3, 1:558–559; cf. 4.318, 1:563. See Barlow, *William Rufus*, 180.

96. *HN*, 49; trans., 51.

97. *GPA* 1.49.1–2, 1:124–125.

98. According to Frank Barlow, William's behavior toward the bishoprics would be normal for the time (*William Rufus*, 182).

99. On the tensions over money with Rufus, see Southern, *Saint Anselm and His Biographer*, 155–160; Mason, "William Rufus," 6–7.

100. *VA* 2.17, pp. 88–89; cf. *HN*, 79–80; trans., 83. Also see *GPA* 1.49.7–10, 1:136–137.

101. *VA* 2.16, pp. 84–89; *HN*, 52ff.; 68, trans., 53ff.; 71–72. See Southern, *Saint Anselm and His Biographer*, 154–155.

102. *VA*, c. 20, pp. 91–93.

103. *VA*, c. 54, p. 132.

104. On Anselm's attitude toward the papacy, see Southern, *Saint Anselm and His Biographer*, 123–128. Anselm's resistance to legatine encroachment was one area of agreement with the king (Southern, *Saint Anselm and His Biographer*, 130–132).

105. Note that Anselm had sworn homage to Rufus, acknowledging the king as his feudal lord (*HN*, 41; trans., 42).

106. *VA* 2.45–46, pp. 122–123.

107. Barlow, *William Rufus*, 426.

108. Florence construed the very woods in which Rufus died as a judgment since this was the site where his father had burned villages, while Rufus's nephew had died in a hunting accident on the very spot where a church had once stood (Florence of Worcester, *Chronicon ex chronicis*, 2:45–46); the nephew would have been Richard, bastard son of Robert Curthose (Barlow, *William Rufus*, 419).

109. The king apparently had seen the bleeding fountain, but it did not make a particular impression on him because he was "a worldly man with no fear of God, given to desires of the flesh, given to pride and a despiser of God's precepts" (Hugh of Flavigny, *Chronicon*, bk. 2, ann. 1100, *MGH SS* 8:496).

110. Ibid. The priest's burial request is the standard curse associated with excommunication: "Let them be buried in the manner of an ass in a dung heap" (Vogel, Elze, and Andrieu, ed., *Pontifical Romano-Germanique*, no. 87, 1:314); see Vodola, *Excommunication*. The dating of Hugh's *Chronicon* is unclear. It breaks off in 1102, though Hugh probably lived until at least 1114. See Healy, *Chronicle of Hugh of Flavigny*, 92–95.

111. Hugh of Flavigny, *Chronicon*, bk. 2, ann. 1100, *MGH SS* 8:496.

112. Ibid., pp. 496–497. This series of monstrous marvels was rounded off by the birth of a formless fetus, possessing two heads and four horns. The fact that Hugh goes on to wonder how God can sustain such crimes with patience seems to imply that the monstrous birth was the result of bestiality. See Barlow, *William Rufus*, 408–409.

113. It is not inconceivable that Hugh might have met with Eadmer during his first visit to the English court in 1096 and may even have seen an incomplete version of his vita. For the dating of *VA*, see Southern's introduction, ix–xii.

114. Hugh of Flavigny, *Chronicon*, ann. 1096, *MGH SS* 8:475. See Healy, *Chronicle of Hugh of Flavigny*, 71; Barlow, *William Rufus*, 342–344.

115. *HN*, 68–69; trans., 71–72. Gerard also used the papal schism to ring a concession out of Urban II, the pope Anselm insisted on supporting: Rufus would acknowledge Urban II as true pope over his rival antipope, Clement III, provided that Urban would agree that no papal legate would enter England except at the king's request. Nor could there be any correspondence between the English clergy and the papacy without royal consent (*GPA* 1.49.16–22, 1:138–143). See Barlow, *William Rufus*, 342–344.

116. Southern, *Saint Anselm and His Biographer*, 146–147.

117. Barlow, *William Rufus*, 59, 146, 179, 359.

118. This time, Gerard deliberately misrepresented the pope's position in favor of the king, incurring a stern papal rebuke. See *VA* 3.133, 137, 139, 140; 4.179, 144–145, 147–148, 191; *GPA* 1.57.1–2, 1:174–175. Gerard would later, unsuccessfully, attempt to gain the archbishopric of York's equivalency with Canterbury, only to be rebuffed by the pope. For Gerard's submission to Anselm, see *HN*, 187; trans., 200. The primacy of Canterbury was so important to Eadmer that he ends his history with Paschal II's letter to Gerard affirming Canterbury's ascendancy (*HN*, 216; trans., 230–231). Cf. *GPA* 3.117.1–3, 1:392–393.

119. *GPA* 1.49.17, 1:140–141.

120. Gerard was eventually given a conspicuous tomb by his successor (*GPA* 3.118.1–3, 1:392–395).

121. Healy, *Hugh of Flavigny*, 82.

122. Brooke, "Gregorian Reform in Action,"14–15. The so-called Norman Anonymous is the most famous (see Chapter 3, n. 144, above).

123. Orderic does, however, note that priests were still "loath to part with their mistresses or to live chaste lives" (*EH* 5.12, 3:123).

124. While Lanfranc allowed parish priests to keep their wives, we shall see that Anselm attempted more rigorous legislation. Even so, Alexander III still frequently denounced both England's married clergy and their hereditary offices (Brooke, "Gregorian Reform in Action," 7, 10–11, 15).

125. *HN*, 193–195; trans., 207–208.

126. Cf. Kuefler, "Male Friendship," 162.

127. McGuire, "Love, Friendship and Sex"; Boswell, *Christianity*, 218–219. Also see discussion of Ailred of Rievaulx in Chapter 5, n. 23, below.

128. *VA* 1.10, pp. 16–17.

129. Lanfranc, *Monastic Constitutions*, c. 109, introd., xxxix–xl.

130. See Chapter 6, n. 10, below.

131. *VA* 1.15, pp. 23–24. The boy, who had made a vow to never touch his genitals, was being assailed by the devil. Because the boy refused to break his vow, Anselm examined the boy and found his genitalia perfectly intact. Eadmer presents Anselm's intervention as a miracle: "the mere fact that Anselm, inspired by a fatherly pity and reflecting that to the pure all things are pure [Titus 1:15], had looked on him freed him from so great a distress."

132. *VA* 1.10, p. 17. I have altered these translations slightly to render them more literal.

133. *VA* 1.10, pp. 18–19.

134. *VA* 1.10, p. 20.

135. McGuire, "Love, Friendship and Sex," 121.

136. Anselm of Canterbury, Ep. 130, to Gilbert, abbot of Westminster (ca. 1086–1089), *Opera omnia*, 3:273; trans., 1:305.

137. McGuire, "Love, Friendship and Sex," 143.

138. See esp. Anselm's letters to Gundulf, Ep. 16 (before 1077), Ep. 41 (1070 × 1077), and Ep. 68 (1075–1076), *Opera omnia*, 3:121–122, 152–153, 188, trans., 1:103–104, 144, 190; to Maurice, Ep. 42 (1073 × 1074), Ep. 69 (ca. 1076), Ep. 74 (ca. late 1076), Ep. 79 (ca. 1077), *Opera omnia*, 3:153–154, 189, 195–196, 202, trans. 1:145–146, 147–148, 190–191, 210. Gundulf, a former member of Anselm's household, had also entered religion relatively late. He was, in fact, ten years Anselm's senior (Southern, *Anselm and His Biographer*, 29, 69–70). This might explain Anselm's flagging interest. Gundulf went on to become bishop of Rochester. But Maurice's situation seemed especially plaintive. He had gone to Canterbury with Lanfranc and constantly beseeched Anselm to intervene so he could return to Bec where they could be together. See McGuire, "Love, Friendship and Sex," 128–140.

139. *VA* 1.11, p. 20. I have altered the translation slightly to render it more literal. To Gundulf, Ep. 4, *Opera omnia*, 3:104; trans., 1:81.

140. On Anselm's relations with women, see McGuire, "Love, Friendship and Sex," 143–145. He was especially withholding in his correspondence with the Anglo-Saxon royal women, including Mathilda, queen to Henry I (see n. 92, above); on Damian and Bernard of Clairvaux's comparatively warmer feelings toward women, see LeClercq, "S. Pierre Damien," 48–49; Elliott, *Bride of Christ*, 151, 158–160, 164. On the often symbiotic relationships between clerics and holy women in this period, see Griffiths, *Nuns' Priests' Tales*.

141. This is Southern's estimation (*Saint Anselm and His Biographer*, 46).

142. Anselm of Canterbury, Meditation 2, *Deploratio virginitatis male amissae*, *Opera omnia*, 3:80. See McGuire, "Love, Friendship and Sex," 117–119.

143. Alexander, a monk of Canterbury, *Dicta Anselmi*, c. 17, in *Memorials*, pp. 175–176; cf. c. 20, p. 190. Alexander succeeded Eadmer as the recorder of the archbishop's deeds ca. 1100.

144. Anselm of Canterbury, Meditation 2, *Deploratio virginitatis male amissae*, *Opera omnia*, 3:80, 81, 82. See McGuire's analysis in "Love, Friendship and Sex," 119–120.

145. *VA* 1.6, p. 11.

146. *VA* 1.21, p. 35; McGuire, "Love, Friendship and Sex," 120. I have followed McGuire's more literal translation of the movements ascribed to the denizens of the river. Note that in the previous chapter, Eadmer cites from Anselm's letter to the monk Lanzo where he describes the monastery as "a port in which to shelter from the storms and tossing of the world" (*VA* 1.20, p. 34).

147. Freud, "Psychoanalytic Notes on an Autobiographical Account of a Case of Paranoia," *SE*, 12:66; "Totem and Taboo," *SE*, 13:61–64. Also see this section's second epigraph, above.

148. Southern, *Saint Anselm and His Biographer*, 73.

149. Council of London (1102), cc. 28, 29, *Sacra concilia*, 20:1152; the council also has a separate canon stipulating that a man's hair should be cut so as not to cover his ears or eyes (c. 23). Also see Goodich, *Unmentionable Vice*, 41–42; Bailey, *Homosexuality*, 124–125. The edict of excommunication was not enacted immediately because Anselm thought it required more careful framing. See Anselm, Ep. 257, to Archdeacon William of Canterbury (1102–

1103), *Opera omnia*, 4:169–170. This is corroborated by William of Malmesbury, who lists all the various findings of the council but goes on to complain that the rules were broken immediately and that the rule about the sodomites being excommunicated every Sunday was later changed for good reason. Note that this latter point only appears in the earliest version of the work. William of Malmesbury, *GRA* 1.1.64.1–11, 1:191–194. Boswell argues it was suppressed altogether by Anselm (*Christianity*, 215). But the chronicle of Hugh of Flavigny suggests that there were excommunications regularly announced on Sundays and feast days nonetheless, as will be seen below.

150. Council of London (1102), cc. 4–7, *Sacra concilia*, 20:1151; Council of London (1108), *Sacra concilia*, 20:1229–1232.

151. *GRA* 4.313, 321, 1:556–558, 566–567. See Du Cange, *Glossarium*, ad *fenestratus,* 3:226. The sudden and undeniable influx of new fashion also worked against the king (Barlow, *William Rufus*, 105–108).

152. Mason, "William Rufus," 3–4. Barlow is more inclined to credit the rumors (*William Rufus*, 103–109).

153. Although critical of the king's humor, William was also aware that Rufus deployed it strategically to deflect or postpone dealing with problems (*GPA* 1.48.3, 1:118–119).

154. *GPA* 1.48.2, 1:116–119; cf. 1.48.7.3–4, 1:118–119.

155. *GRA* 4.33.2–3, 1:572–573. William of Malmesbury goes on to say that, despite this show of bravado, the king was nevertheless shaken. Cf. the king's quips about the possibility of winning certain Christian-Jewish disputations, which would necessitate his conversion to Judaism (*GRA* 4.317, 1:562–563).

156. *GRA* 4.305.1, 1:542–543.

157. See Bates, *William the Conqueror*, 77.

158. William of Poitiers is the first to mention the papal banner, but it is picked up by others, and then repeated by historians like William of Malmesbury (*GRA* 3.238.9, 1:449). See Bates, *William the Conqueror*, 221–222. Not everyone is convinced by William of Poitiers's account, however. See Morton, "Pope Alexander II." Gregory VII also highly esteemed William the Conqueror (Cowdrey, *Pope Gregory VII*, 459–467).

159. Southern, *Saint Anselm and His Biographer*, 163–164; cf. Mason, "William Rufus," 16–17.

160. Cowdrey, *Pope Gregory VII*, 21–26.

161. Cf. Barlow's parallel skepticism, in *William Rufus*, 109.

CHAPTER 5

Note to epigraph: Trans. Stehling, *Medieval Latin Poems*, no. 48, pp. 36, 37.

1. Boswell, *Christianity*, 226–227. Also see Brundage, *Law*, 251–252.

2. Gratian, *Decretum, De pen.* D. 1 cc. 12, 15. See Richlin, "Not Before Homosexuality," 562–563. On the later introduction of the majority of the canons drawn from Roman law, see Winroth, *Making of Gratian's "Decretum,"* chap. 5.

3. Gratian, *Decretum*, C. 32 q. 7 cc. 13, 14. The rubric for c. 14 claims that this passage is from Jerome's *Against Jovinian* when, in fact, it is from Augustine's *On Marriage and Concupiscence.*

4. Gratian, *Decretum*, C. 32 q. 7 c. 12; cf. Ivo, *Decretum* 9.115, https://ivo-of-chartres .github.io/decretum/ivodec_9.pdf, p. 42.

5. Ivo, *Decretum* 9.114, 9.117, 9.118, pp. 42–43. Another canon examines the question of the daughters' incest with their father (9.116, p. 42).

6. Gratian's lacuna is but an aspect of his disinterest. Children appear only fleetingly in the *Decretum* and are never the subject of sustained focus. See Goldberg, "The Legal Persona," esp. 18–25. Goldberg is concerned with Gratian 1—what Anders Winroth has proved to be the original recension of *Decretum* before the later additions of his followers (*Making of Gratian's "Decretum"*). In the thirteenth century, Gregory IX does dedicate a section to children in his *Liber Extra*, entitled "On the Sins of Children." It only contains two canons (Goldberg, "The Legal Persona," 23).

7. Gratian, *Decretum*, DD. 31–34; also see D. 51 c. 7, D. 82 cc. 2–4.

8. Gratian, *Decretum*, D. 81 cc. 10–11, 16–17, 19–33. The four that stigmatize fornication are D. 81 cc. 12, 13, 15, 18. Cf. D. 82 c. 5, which also only addresses procedure against fornication. On measures against clerical marriage, see Brundage, *Law*, 401–405.

9. See, for example, Boniface's account of the monk of Wenlock who saw the destiny of many souls when he was on his deathbed. This included a vision of King Ceolred of Mercia, who, though still alive at the time, was already overwhelmed by demons. Boniface, Ep. 10, to Eadburgh, *MGH Epp. sel.* 1:14. Also see the ninth-century vision of a "poor little woman" in which members of the circle around Emperor Louis the German are in torment, including his mother, Irmengarde (Houben, "*Visio cuiusdam pauperculae mulieris*," 41). Cf. the letter of 858 from Hincmar of Reims to Louis the German, attached to a series of capitularies. It reports the vision of Eucherius of Orléans (d. 743), who saw Charles Martel tortured in hell for his abuse of church property. After his rapture, moreover, Eucherius testified to the desecration of the tombs of both Charles Martel and his son Pepin (*MGH Capit.* 2:432–433). Wetti himself was not exempt from this pattern, having seen Charlemagne in purgatory long before the emperor was dead (Heito, *Visio Wettini*, c. 11, *MGH Poetae* 2:271). For an interesting recognition of the use of visions for posthumous revenge, see the eleventh-century case of Bernard, abbot of Peterhausen. Bernard was a visionary who was shown the destiny of good and evil souls. Soon after his death, one of the monks reported to Bishop Gebehard of Constance that another monk claimed to have seen Bernard tortured on a bed of coals. The bishop sagely told him not to worry: those who hated Bernard during his lifetime would continue to do so after his death. See *Chronik von Petrihusi*, c. 19, ed. Mone, 1:143. Cf. the vision of the Merovingian monk Barontus discussed in Chapter 2, n. 79, above.

10. Leclercq, "Redaction en prose de la *Visio Anselli*," 192. This vision was discovered amid a charter of 1063. See Gardiner, *Medieval Visions*, 35–38.

11. Leclercq, "Redaction en prose de la *Visio Anselli*," 193–194. The other sins are homicide, wrath, adultery, rape, and perjury.

12. Hugh of Flavigny, *Chronicon*, ann. 1011, *MGH SS* 8:381.

13. At the lowest point in hell is Judas, chained and surrounded by black and stinking flames until Judgment Day. The soul is terrified, calling on Peter, Paul, John the Baptist, and his own St. Vaast, until Michael takes pity and removes him to another place in hell. This one is not much better: the soul immediately recognizes the familiar face of Albert of Namur, the prefect of the county who had died the year before. The soul begins trembling with fear over his own fate, and Michael takes him to a different area of hell: a frigid lake of fetid, frosty waves, where, located in the deepest part, are the venial sinners—people "a little bit good" but nevertheless besmirched by worldly pursuits.

14. According to Kathleen Edwards, polyphony began growing in popularity in the tenth and first half of the eleventh century (*English Secular Cathedrals*, 309). See Chapter 7, n. 13. below.

15. Hugh of Flavigny, *Chronicon*, ann. 1011, *MGH SS* 8:382.

16. Ibid., p. 385. The previous archbishop of Cologne, Evergerus, is among them. His damnation, at least, was richly deserved since Evergerus was said to have buried his predecessor, Gero, alive, while the latter was lying helpless in a stupor. The visionary discreetly withholds the bishop's name and his offense, however. See *Catalogi Archiepiscoporum Colonensium*, ann. 984, *MGH SS* 24:339. Thietmar of Merseburg has a still more dramatic version in which the dead pontiff is awakened on the third day by a ringing bell and is freed by the people. When Evergerus confesses his crime, the resurrected bishop hits him with a big stick (*Thietmari Chronicon* 3.4, *MGH SS rer. Germ. N.S.* 9:101). There is also some confusion over whether the buried pontiff was Warinus, Evergerus's immediate predecessor, or Gero, the bishop before Warinus. The monks of St. Martin of Cologne benefit from this confusion by having Warinus bury Gero. This is a shrewd decision, considering that Evergerus was the monastery's benefactor. See *Chronicon S. Martini Coloniensis, MGH SS* 2:215. Other sources bypass this story, instead focusing on how Evergerus squandered church money. See *Chronicon Gladbacense*, c. 17, *MGH SS* 4:77.

17. Hugh of Flavigny, *Chronicon*, ann. 1011, *MGH SS* 8:385. Earlier in the vision, a couple of priests along with siblings of both sexes are described as burning, but the text is damaged, signified by ellipsis points in Wattenbach's edition: "draco ore, naribus auribusque flammas in faciem mortiferos u . . . [illegible] presbiteros Eucarium et Rainboldum, fratrem etiam suum puerulum nomine Petrum, sororem ex eius conspexit aduri latere" (ibid., p. 382).

18. Their clients endure a similar, but not as graphic, a fate (ibid., ann. 1012, 8:389). The monk is less discreet in other ways, claiming to have seen the earlier visionary's father in hell.

19. See, for example, John, monk of St.-Lawrence in Liège, *Visio de statu animarum* (ann. 1147), *PL* 180:184; Gardiner, *Medieval Visions*, 123. Cf. the vision attributed to William of Norwich by Heliland of Froidmont (d. 1212), *Chronicon*, ann. 1146, *PL* 212:1036–1037; see Gardiner, *Medieval Visions*, 50. In the visions by the Augustinian canon Peter of Cornwall (d. 1221), the one concerning sexual sinners in hell (allegedly occurring in 1170) mirrors this pattern. See "The Visions of Ailsi," c. 15, in *Peter of Cornwall's Book of Revelations*, 205; Gardiner, *Medieval Visions*, 29–30. But there is also a bizarre variation of this motif in the thirdhand account of a knight who allegedly visited St. Patrick's Purgatory (also in 1170). The knight accepts the demonic king's beautiful daughter in marriage, but she turns into a gnarled piece of wood, and his penis gets caught in a knot hole ("Peter of Cornwall's Account of St. Patrick's Purgatory," in *Revelations*, 136). On the many different visions of St. Patrick's Purgatory, see Gardiner, *Medieval Visions*, 151–178. The motif of skewering male and female sinners through their respective genitals is perhaps inspired by the way Phinees, son of Eleazar, punished the Israelites who entered a brothel: "perfodit ambos simul virum scilicet et mulierem in locis genitalibus" (Num. 25:7–8).

20. Both meanings are present in penitentials (Payer, *Sex and the Penitentials*, 40–41, 62). Also see Chapter 3, n. 54, above, and Chapter 5, p. 97, above.

21. *Visio Tnugdali*, 27–30; trans., 130–131. See Gardiner, *Medieval Visions*, 210–222. Vipers were, in fact, believed to rend the insides of their mothers, killing them as they are being born. See White, *Book of Beasts*, 170. Cf. Adamnán of Iona (d. 704), who saw a multitude of monks—either guilty of breaking their rule or deceiving the laity; the following

passage is suggestive, without being sexually explicit: "the children that are tearing the men in orders, are they who were committed to them for amendment, but they amended them not, neither reproved them for their sins" (*Irish Precursor of Dante*, c. 28, p. 42). See Gardiner, *Medieval Visions*, 23–28.

22. Constable, "Vision of Gunthelm," 110. In this earlier version, the monk is explicitly named William (ibid., 108), but will later be associated with Gunthelm. It is the source for Thurkill's vision (1206). See Gardiner, *Medieval Visions*, 118–122.

23. The visionary is prompted to tell the abbot to mend his lax ways (Constable, "Vision of Gunthelm," 108). One theory about the visionary is that he was a monk at Rievaulx during Ailred's abbacy (ibid., 103). Ailred's effusive writings to his monks have been construed by a number of scholars as homoerotic in nature. Boswell goes even further and says there is no doubt that Ailred was "gay" (*Christianity*, 222). For a different perspective, see Karras, "Friendship and Love in the Lives of Two Twelfth-Century Saints."

24. It is unclear how much importance should be attached to the fact that the vision is of purgatory versus hell. Certainly by the thirteenth century purgatory was seen as an upwardly mobile place that eventually led to heaven. The fate of the inhabitants in this purgatory seems less secure. When the narrator asks the sodomiticial lawyer, discussed below, whether he would ultimately be saved, the lawyer was uncertain ("Vision of the Monk of Eynsham," c. 26, p. 327. See Gardiner, *Medieval Visions*, 137–141).

25. "Vision of the Monk of Eynsham," c. 24, pp. 323–324.

26. Ibid., p. 325.

27. This scene anticipates Dante's recognition and conversation with his guardian and tutor, the philosopher and statesman Brunetto Latini (d. 1294), included with other sodomites in the seventh circle of hell (*Inferno* 15.82–87, *Divine Comedy*).

28. "Vision of the Monk of Eynsham," c. 26, p. 327.

29. Ibid., c. 25, p. 324; the editor, however, reproduced the rubrics from one manuscript, including "De vitio sodomitico" (see Salter's introduction, ibid., 277).

30. McGuire, "Lost Clairvaux Exemplum Collection," 34. McGuire gives a detailed summary of the manuscript in question with select exempla in Latin, of which this anecdote is one. He has a different theory about the excision, arguing that the subsequent editor may have deemed the lesson too harsh in view of the changing religious climate (ibid., 35).

31. Ibid., 27, 41–46.

32. Conrad of Eberbach, *Exordium magnum Cisterciense* 5.5, ed. Griesser, *CCCM* 138:309–312. The unconfessed sin loomed large among the Cistercians. Cf. the anecdote by Cistercian Caesarius of Heisterbach regarding a mature monk who seduced an adolescent member of his community in the course of hearing his confession. Out of shame, they resorted to the solution reviled by Peter Damian: confessing to and absolving one another. The elder monk confessed to the abbot on his deathbed, but his partner was too ashamed, despite the urgings of his ghostly partner in sin. It was his inability to approach the altar that was the catalyst for confession (*Dialogus miraculorum* 3.24, 1:139–141). The Cistercian abbot Richalm of Schöntal tells of a monk who waited thirty years to confess a sin; when he did, the demons made loud laments (*Liber revelationum*, c. 87, *MGH QQ zur Geistesgesch.* 24:105). Also see Thomas of Chobham's critique of the Cistercian insistence on a life confession when entering the order, discussed below.

33. Hildegard of Bingen, *Scivias* 2.6.76, *CCCM* 43:290; trans., 278. See Augustine Thompson, "Hildegard of Bingen on Gender and the Priesthood," 361, 363. This discussion

is preceded by a vision of the Mass and a celestial commentary emphasizing clerical celibacy (*Scivias* 2.6.62–63, *CCCM* 43:281–289; trans., 271–272).

34. See Allen, *Concept of Woman*, 292–315; Cadden, "It Takes All Kinds," 154ff.; Barbara Newman, *Sister of Wisdom*, 96–99.

35. Hildegard of Bingen, *Scivias* 2.6.77–78, *CCCM* 43:291–292; trans., 278–279. I have altered the translation slightly to render it more literal. In subsequent works, Hildegard hones her attack through adroit theological speculation about Satan's role in promoting this "contrary" fornication. *The Book of Life's Merits* (completed 1163) presents the devil as directly inciting men to desire one another "so that men polluted themselves in contrariety [*in contrarietate*]," thereby undermining female fecundity. Hildegard, *Liber vitae meritorum* 3.80, *CCCM*, 90:167. According to Barbara Newman, Hildegard perceived the devil as chronically jealous of humankind, harboring a special hatred for women because of their fertility (*Sister of Wisdom*, 107–110). Also see Hildegard, *Liber divinorum operum* 2.1.9, *CCCM* 92:277.

36. Hildegard, *Liber divinorum operum* 3.5.5, *CCCM* 92:412. In Hildegard's medical writings she discusses the way in which diabolical suggestion can make a person burn with such lust that s/he is oblivious to shame, which might also be a tacit reference to same-sex relations (*Causae et curae*, bk. 2, p. 140).

37. See, for example, the twelfth-century *Annales Stadenses*, c. 6, *MGH SS* 16:331.

38. See Barbara Newman, *Sister of Wisdom*, 3–4, 238–242.

39. Barbara Newman, "Divine Power Made Perfect in Weakness."

40. Hildegard of Bingen, Ep. 15r, to the shepherds of the church (1163?), in *Epistolarium*, *CCCM* 91:36; trans., 1:56. I have altered the translation slightly to make it more literal.

41. On the semantics of the unspeakable, see Blud, *Unspeakable*, esp. 4–9, 71–70; and Chiffoleau, "Dire l'indicibile."

42. David Clark, *Between Medieval Men*, 74.

43. Council of Chalcedon (451), c. 2, *DEC*, 1:88; Aldhelm, *De laudibus virginum*, bk. 1, *PL* 89:242; Abbo of Fleury, *Excerptum de vitis romanorum pontificium*, c. 56, *PL* 139:557.

44. Jerome, *Liber de nominibus Hebraicis*, *PL* 23:784. See Jordan, *Silence of Sodom*, 16; Jordan, *Invention of Sodomy*, 106.

45. Hrabanus Maurus, *Commentariorum in Genesim*, *PL* 107:539; cf. Hrabanus Maurus, *De universo*, *PL* 111:341, 380; cf. Remigius of Auxerre (d. 908), *Commentarius in Genesim*, v. 19, *PL* 131:83.

46. Haymo of Halberstadt (now thought to be Haymo of Auxerre), *Expositio in Apocalypsin*, *PL* 117:1074.

47. Guibert of Nogent, *Moralia in Genesin*, bk. 5, v. 16, *PL* 156:143.

48. Cf. Nicholas of Lyra, Gen. 18:20, no. 7, ad v. *Clamorem Sodomorum*, *GO*, 1:234.

49. Isa. 3:9, f. ad v. *Agnitio*, *GO*, 4:54; the citation of the Septuagint, *Confusio vultus eorum* (ibid.). Cf. Jerome, *Commentaria in Isaiam*, *PL* 24:65. The gloss also argues that such public turpitude does not even require an accuser for prosecution (interlinear gloss, Gen. 18:20, ad v. *Clamorem Sodomorum*, *GO*, 1:234–235).

50. Abelard, *Ethics*, 4–5, 42–43, 54–55, 98–101, 88–89. See Anciaux, *Théologie du sacrement de pénitence*, 176–186. For an overview, see Mann, "Ethics," 280–286. Also Marenbon, *Philosophy of Peter Abelard*, 255–264.

51. Abelard, *Ethics*, 40–41, 44–45.

52. Ibid., 43–45.

53. Abelard, *Sic et non*, q. 149, p. 509. This view is then trounced by citations from Augustine, Prosper of Aquitaine (d. 455), and especially Jerome, who argues that pretended

sanctity is far worse than flagrant sin. See Elliott, *Fallen Bodies*, 77–78. On Abelard's methodology and the way it differs from later scholastic methodology, see Geldsetzer, "'Sic et non' sive 'Sic aut non,'" On Isidore, see Chapter 1, pp. 25, 28, 29, above.

54. On Peter the Chanter's life, see Baldwin, *Masters, Princes, and Merchants*, 1:3–16.

55. Peter the Chanter, *Summa de sacramentis et animae consiliis*, c. 318, 3.2a: 373. The Chanter's *Summa* was left incomplete and later arranged by others. According to John Baldwin, the questions the Chanter addressed were based on disputations that he undertook throughout his career. The compilation probably began after 1191 and progressed until death intervened six years later (Baldwin, *Masters*, 1:13–14). By comparison, the canon law of the period lagged behind theology with respect to scandal. See Druwé, *Scandalum in the Early Bolognese Decretistic and in Papal Decretals*. I am indebted to Maryanne Kowaleski for this reference.

56. Peter the Chanter, *Summa de sacramentis*, c. 133, 2:293–294; c. 318, 3.2a:373. Aquinas would eventually differentiate between active scandal (when sinning or the appearance of sinning leads another to fall) and passive scandal (when an individual's words or deeds, however blameless, lead another to sin; *ST* 2a 2ae, q. 43, art.1). Later theologians are more specific still. An anonymous quodlibet of 1278 divides both passive and then active scandal into four distinct categories (see "Quodlibet anonyme IX," 317–319). The author relates that the question was suggested by John de Turno, prior of the Parisian Dominicans.

57. Peter the Chanter, *Summa de sacramentis*, c. 319, 3.2a: 376. See Bryan, "*Vae mundo a scandalis*," 56–69; and Bryan, "Peter the Chanter's Threefold Truth and the Sin of Scandal."

58. Peter the Chanter, *Summa de sacramentis* c. 320, 3.2a:378. He does not say this explicitly in the first case, but it is implied by his conclusion. Cf. Alan of Lille's rationale for imposing more penance for outer sins like lust, homicide (and so on) than for inner sins like jealousy, pride, and humility, arguing that inner sins are just sins against God, while outer sins are against God and one's neighbor (*Liber poenitentialis* 3.3, 2:128–129).

59. Peter the Chanter, *Verbum adbreviatum, textus prior*, c. 5, *CCCM* 196a:48. A sinning prelate cannot preach, however. Stephen Langton (d. 1228), another member of the Chanter's circle, would argue that even a flagrant fornicator could preach since the triple truth could not be ignored for the sake of scandal and preaching spoke to truth of life (Baldwin, *Masters*, 2:75–76 n. 38). *Verbum adbreviatum* exists in a long version and several abbreviated versions. Baldwin explores these variations in terms of expansion from a shorter original and abbreviation of a longer one, tending to regard the longer one as the original (*Masters*, 2:259–265, app. 2). Monique Boutry, however, challenges this theory, regarding the longer text as a conflation of earlier versions (see Peter the Chanter, *Verbum adbreviatum, textus prior, CCCM* 196a, introd.).

60. Peter the Chanter, *Verbum adbreviatum, textus prior*, c. 125, *CCCM* 196a:637. See Boswell's translation of the section on sodomy from Peter's *Verbum adbreviatum* in *Christianity*, app. 2, p. 375. Note that Honorius Augustodunensis may have been attempting to obfuscate such associations by referring to married priests as homicides. See Chapter 4, p. 85, above.

61. Peter the Chanter, *Verbum adbreviatum, textus prior*, c. 125, *CCCM* 196a: 638.

62. Ibid., 196a: 639–640.

63. He also entertains the possibility that this neglect is associated with avarice, perhaps implying some kind of graft (ibid., 196a: 639).

64. Matt. 18:6, ad v. *Qui autem scandali, GO*, 5:300; cf. Luke 17:2, ad v. *Si lapis molaris etc et proiictatur in mare* (ibid., 5:925).

65. Lateran III (1179), c. 11, *DEC*, 1:217. Laymen should be excommunicated and completely separated from the faithful. In detailing clerical punishment, the word used is *detrudantur*, which basically means imprisonment. See Geltner, "*Detrusio*," 90–91. This canon would make its way into Gregory IX's *Decretales* (X.5.31.4). See Brundage, *Law*, 398–401.

66. Cf. Boswell, *Christianity*, 277.

67. See, for example, Peter the Chanter, *Verbum adbreviatum, textus prior*, cc. 43, 46, 72, *CCCM* 196a:293, 305–306. Although the *Verbum adbreviatum* was probably written between 1191 and 1192, more than a decade after Lateran III, it is based on biblical matters that Peter had been engaging in his scriptural commentaries since the 1170s. See Baldwin, *Masters*, 1:12–13; on Alexander III and the Chanter, see ibid., 1:7.

68. Lateran IV (1215), c. 21, *DEC*, 1:245. Abelard did, however, regard the presence of the priest as helpful for inducing shame (*Ethics*, 100–101); Baldwin, *Masters*, 1:315ff. But Abelard's contemporaries were not entirely unsympathetic to his view. Gratian gives a detailed summary of the arguments for the contritionist versus noncontritionist view, without taking sides. See *De pen.* D. 1 c. 30 d.p.c.; D. 1 c. 37 d.p.c.; Larson, *Master of Penance*, 35–99. Peter Lombard (d. 1160) believed a priest was necessary for the sacrament, though he granted that sin was absolved with due contrition (*Sentences* 4.17.3–4, 4:100, 102–103; Rosemann, *Peter Lombard*, 163ff.). On the influence of Gratian and Peter Lombard, see Goering, "Scholastic Turn," 219–237.

69. On Robert of Courson, see Baldwin, *Masters*, 1:19–23. Robert's position is discussed further in Chapter 8, below. For an overview of confessors' treatments of sodomy, see Payer, *Sex and the New Literature of Confession*, 126–49.

70. On this genre, see Michaud-Quantin, "Á propos des premières *Summae confessorum*." Also see Goering, "The Internal Forum," 210–216. For the change from the old to the new system, see Payer, *Sex and the New Literature of Confession*, chap. 1; Payer, "Origins and Development of the Later *Canones Penitentiales*," 81–87. Goering, however, cautions against the tendency to exaggerate the rigidity of the old penitentials, perceiving the change more in terms of degree of clerical education ("Internal Forum, 199–200).

71. See Part II prologue, p. 143, below.

72. Robert of Flamborough, *Liber poenitentialis* 5.274, pp. 230–231; Thomas of Chobham, *Summa confessorum*, art. 7, dist. 21.19, pp. 401–402. On Thomas of Chobham, see Baldwin, *Masters*, 1:34–35; on Robert of Flamborough, ibid., 1:32–33. Their ultimate source for this passage was another Englishman, Bartholomew of Exeter (d. 1184); see Bartholomew, *Penitential*, c. 69, p. 236. Bartholomew seems to have taught in Paris, perhaps in Abelard's circle, before returning to England (see Morey, *Bartholomew of Exeter*, 4–5). The concern with predation on the young seems to have been kept alive mostly in England. Master Serlo, writing a confessor's manual "of English inspiration" after 1234, also includes the Pseudo-Basil/Fructuosus canon in an abbreviated form (Goering, "*Summa de penitentia*," p. 39). It is listed under the rubric *De sodomitis*, which also includes masturbation and bestiality.

73. Robert of Flamborough, *Liber poenitentialis* 5.272, ad fine, 5.275, pp. 230–231. Peter of Poitiers of St.-Victor is rather idiosyncratic, however. He categorizes sex between a married couple as "against nature" if done from behind, anally, or with the woman on top. With respect to the latter, he claims that Methodius (d. 311) cited this abnormal position as one of the reasons for the flood. Peter lumps sex between males or with beasts together as acts against nature, but without singling out these offenses as especially grave. He does note, however, that if someone had sex with an edible beast, he sh uld abstain from eating that kind of

animal—unless under necessity. But he seems particularly incensed by masturbation, describing this as "the sin he [the confessor] will not name further, because it is ignominious," but he can hint that it is the vice of *mollities*. Like the sodomitical vice, it is against nature. But because it only pertains to one person rather than two, the same person is rendered active and passive, male and female—like a hermaphrodite. Hence, it is more monstrous than sodomy (*Summa de confessione, compilatio praesens*, cc. 13–14, CCCM 51:16–19.) According to Thomas Tentler, the reference to women on top is, in fact, from Pseudo-Methodius's *Revelations* (*Sin and Confession on the Eve of the Reformation*, 192 n. 46). Aquinas briefly reviews something akin to Peter's view that masturbation's solitary nature renders it worse than sodomy only to quash it once and for all in *ST* 2a 2ae, q. 154, art. 12, ad 4 and resp. ad 4. Cf. Robert Grosseteste (writing 1214 × 1225), who argues that masturbation (a branch of sodomy) is worse than fornication or adultery, *De modo confitendi et paenitentias iniungendi* 2.17, ed. Goering and Mantello, "Early Penitential Writings of Robert Grosseteste," p. 96.

74. Alan of Lille, *Liber poenitentialis* 2.13, 2:54–55. Gavin Fort argues that Alan of Lille was the first of the new confessional writers to make this explicit condemnation of penitential canons in "Vicarious Middle Ages," 206 n. 99. Even so, Alan makes use of penitentials himself. See, for example, the punishments for clerics who fornicate *contra naturam*, taken from the Roman penitential (Alan of Lille, *Liber poenitentialis* 2.127, 2:111).

75. Peter of Poitiers, *Summa de confessione*, c. 50, CCCM 51:64–65. The likely association with Robert of Flamborough was first noted by Firth, "*Poenitentiale* of Robert of Flamborough," 551–552.

76. Robert of Flamborough, *Liber poenitentialis* 4.12.351, pp. 273–274.

77. Thomas of Chobham, *Summa confessorum* 5.6, pp. 205–206. Fortunately, the monk had confessed to someone else in extremis and the bishop allowed his body to be moved.

78. Robert of Flamborough, *Liber poenitentialis*, app. B, p. 298. This may be an anonymous addition to Robert's work. For a similar dialogue in the body of his work, see ibid. 4.222–230, pp. 195–200.

79. Thomas of Chobham, *Summa confessorum* 7.13.4, pp. 570–572.

80. Peter the Chanter, *Summa de sacramentis*, c. 134, 2:310. Over time, elaborate discussions would evolve surrounding the threats that female penitents presented to the confessor. See Elliott, "Women and Confession." One of the most scrupulous in this regard was Matthew of Cracow's *De modo confitendi et puritate conscientiae*. This text is unpaginated, but see the sections under the rubrics "De periculo familiaritatis dominarum et mulierum" and "De cautela in confessione habenda."

81. Peter the Chanter, *Summa de sacramentis*, c. 134, 2:310.

82. *Peniteas cito peccator*, ed. Goering, in *William de Montibus*, 128. On the identification with William de Montibus, see Goering, *William de Montibus*, 3–7, 109–112. Cf. Tristan Sharp's edition of an anonymous manual, "*Tractatus de confessione*," 51. Written in the the first quarter of the thirteenth century by someone who had studied at Paris, this work is aimed at monks with pastoral duties. It has parallels with some of the manuals produced in the Chanter's circle—particularly the English scholars (ibid., introd., 8–10, 4). The fear of introducing the penitent to new sins was anticipated by Theodulf of Orléans (see Chapter 1). See Jordan, *Invention of Sodomy*, 103–104, 111.

83. Robert of Flamborough, *Liber poenitentialis* 4.224, p. 196; app. B, p. 296.

84. Robert Grosseteste, *Templum Dei*, c. 17, 1, p. 61.

85. Robert Grosseteste, *Perambulavit Judas*, c. 15, ed. Goering and Mantello, p. 154. The editors make a compelling argument for Grosseteste's authorship; if he was the author, the

treatise would have been written between 1200 and 1230 (ibid., pp. 126–132). For Grosseteste's association with Peter the Chanter's students, see Baldwin, *Masters*, 2:12–13 n. 40. Grosseteste also makes reference to the Chanter toward the end of the treatise (*Perambulavit Judas*, c. 41, pp. 167–168). The second part of treatise, written for the "simpler brothers," is focused on specific sins. Sodomy appears under the category of lust (*luxuria*) as does the following: "you permitted little ones [*parvulos*] to become accustomed to irrational things, scurrilous curses, and things of this sort" (*Perambulavit Judas*, c. 34, p. 164). This may hark back to the early monastic rules that presented joking with young boys as a type of foreplay.

86. William de Montibus, *Speculum penitentis* 1.3, ed. Goering, in *William de Montibus*, 199. This was probably written between 1200 and 1213 (ibid., 183).

87. William de Montibus, *De penitentia religiosorum*, c. 7, ed. Goering, in *William de Montibus*, 217–218. This was probably written in the 1180s or early 1190s (ibid., 214).

88. Ibid., c. 9, p. 218. The penalty for sodomy is more or less the same as for adultery, though the number of prayers and genuflections are increased (ibid., c. 12, p. 219). The author does add, however, that even after the requisite penance is completed, someone guilty of these grave sins should undertake "some little penance" that lasts for the rest of his life (ibid., c. 13, p. 219).

89. For discussions of Paul of Hungary's treatment, see Jordan, *Invention of Sodomy*, 93–103; Johnson, "Paul of Hungary's *Summa de penitentia*"; Payer, *Sex and the New Medieval Literature of Confession*, 141–149. Payer also notes the Chanter's influence on Paul (ibid., 142).

90. Paul of Hungary, *Rationes penitentie*, 207b. He makes this point repeatedly, almost verbatim, throughout his diatribe (ibid., 208a, 208b).

91. Ibid., 207b.

92. Ibid., 208b

93. Ibid., 208a. On angelic horror in the face of sodomy, see Elliott, *Fallen Bodies*, 150–154.

94. Paul of Hungary, *Rationes penitentie*, 208a; cf. 209a.

95. Pennsylvania's *40th Statewide Investigating Grand Jury: Report 1, Interim–Redacted* (2018), p. 3, http://media-downloads.pacourts.us/InterimRedactedReportandResponses.pdf? cb = 42148.

96. Also see his discussion of the abbot who wishes to ordain someone guilty of one of the graver sins and what the confessor is permitted to say to warn him subtly (Hildemar, *Expositio*, c. 62, p. 85; Paul the Deacon, *In sanctam regulam commentarium*, c. 25, pp. 283–285).

97. Lea, *History of Auricular Confession*, 1:418ff.; Kurtscheid, *History of the Seal*, 90ff. The privacy of confession was, however, recognized earlier. See Abigail Firey's discussion of Empress Theutberga's confession in *Contrite Heart*, 18, 20, 24 n. 29.

98. Lanfranc, *De celanda confessione*, PL 150:628–629. A number of scholars have argued that Lanfranc's insistence on the seal was precocious for the period. See Kurtscheid, *History of the Seal*, 94; Alexander Murray, "Confession Before 1215," 53.

99. Peter the Chanter, *Summa de sacramentis*, c. 133, 2:293–294. Cf. the similar instance of two candidates under consideration: the confessor knows that the ostensibly less literate candidate is an honest man, while the well-born literate one is a great sinner. If the confessor is consulted, should he remain silent or counsel them to elect the less distinguished candidate? The confessor fears that he may, in fact, be disclosing the secrets of confession since he is diminishing the one man's reputation. As in the above case, Peter recommends neutrality (ibid., c. 133, 2:294)

100. Ibid., 2:302.

101. Ibid., 2:296–297, 304–305.

102. Kurtscheid, *History of the Seal*, 107. It would be interesting to know if this was extended to everyone, since Hugguccio famously argued that a pope who scandalized the people through public crime (such as fornication, robbery, or sacrilege) was basically a heretic who could be judged and deposed (Tierney, *Foundations of the Conciliar Theory*, 53–59; also see Hugguccio's gloss on this point in ibid., app. 1, pp. 227–228).

103. Thomas of Chobham, *Summa confessorum* 6.1.5, pp. 257–258. Thomas probably wrote the bulk of his treatise just before Lateran IV and only had a fragmentary knowledge of the council. See Broomfield's introduction, ibid., xl–lxii.

104. Lateran IV (1215), c. 21, *DEC*, 1:245. Even so there is resistance among canonists like Raymond of Peñafort (d. 1275) in cases of heresy (Elliott, *Proving Woman*, 28).

105. Bartholomew of Pisa, *Summa de casibus consciencie,* ad v. *confessio celacio.*

106. Kennedy, "Robert of Courson on Penance," c. 9, pp. 315–317. Grosseteste also treats the problem of appointing an unworthy to office in his treatise for monastic penitents (*Perambulavit Judas*, c. 35, p. 165). On the binding nature of conscience, even when erroneous, see Elliott, *Proving Woman*, 241–242.

107. For an introduction, see Wilson, "Henry of Ghent's Written Legacy."

108. Quodlib. 8, q. 29, in Henry of Ghent, *Quodlibeta Magistri Henrici Goethals a Gandauo doctoris solemnis*, fols. 336v–337r. Cf. the Franciscan Peter John Olivi and his parallel view about knowing as God (see Quodlib. 4, q. 9, in Olivi, *Quodlibeta quinque*, 234). In another question, however, Henry presents obstacles to the abbot's efforts to move the offending monk, should the opportunity arise. What if an abbot were to present a monk to the bishop for the care of souls, and he is then instated in a parish by the bishop, as standard procedure would dictate? Should the monk obey his abbot who recalls him to the cloister or the bishop who tells him to remain? The answer is that the monk is required to obey the one who has 'control over care of souls,' which is the bishop, not the religious superior—although the latter is doubtless better acquainted with the monk's personal habits (Quodlib. 4, q. 35, in Henry of Ghent, *Opera omnia*, 8:425).

109. Peter the Chanter, *Summa de sacramentis*, c. 319, 3.2a: 376.

110. Peter of Poitiers, *Summa de confessione*, c. 43, *CCCM* 51:53.

111. Aquinas, "On Fraternal Correction," art. 1, resp., and art 2, resp., in *Disputed Questions on Virtue*, 183–184, 197. Like the Chanter, Aquinas was also sensitive to the possibility of the corrected person being scandalized (ibid., art. 2, resp. ad 3, p. 188).

112. "Quodlibet anonyme IX," 308.

113. Ibid., 310.

114. Henry of Ghent, Quodlib. 9, q. 28, *Opera omnia*, 13:313; cf. Augustine, *Regula*, c. 7, *PL* 32:1381.

115. Henry of Ghent, Quodlib. 9, q. 28, *Opera omnia*, 13:313–314.

116. Cf. Augustine, *Regula*, c. 7, *PL* 32:1381.

117. Henry of Ghent, Quodlib. 9, q. 28, *Opera omnia*, 13:314–315.

118. See Chapter 1, pp. 24–25, above.

119. Henry of Ghent, Quodlib. 9, q. 28, *Opera omnia*, 13:314–316; cf. Augustine's Serm. 82, c. 7, *PL* 38:511.

120. Henry of Ghent, Quodlib. 9, q. 28, *Opera omnia*, 13:316; cf. Augustine, *Regula*, c. 7, *PL* 32:1381.

121. Henry of Ghent, *Quodlib.* 9, q. 28, *Opera omnia*, 13:317.

122. Ibid., 317–318. Henry emphasizes that these witnesses have to be legally viable: they cannot have learned of this offense through the admonisher, because no one should be condemned on the basis of one witness. If the original admonisher had coached the other witnesses, the alleged offender could take action against him for defamation.

123. Ibid., 31–319.

124. Ibid., 319.

125. Robert of Flamborough, *Liber poenitentialis* 3.90, pp. 111–113.

126. Thomas of Chobham, *Summa confessorum* 7.13.4, pp. 570–572. Cf. "Si nequeas caste, ne spernas vivere caute" (Abelard, *Carmen ad Astralabium Filium*, as cited by Dronke, *Poetic Individuality*, 149).

PROLOGUE TO PART II

1. Paul of Hungary, *Rationes penitentie*, 210a.

2. Hostiensis, *Summa*, bk. 5, 259v. But what he grants in one sentence, he arguably takes away in the next, ending with the reflection that a cleric ought not to brag publicly about his incontinence on account of scandal.

3. *ST* 2a 2ae, q. 154, art. 12, resp. See Goodich, "Sodomy in Ecclesiastical Law," 430–431.

4. *ST* 2a 2ae, q. 154, art. 12, resp. ad 1. Same-sex relations were only outstripped by bestiality in degree of grievousness (ibid., resp. ad 4).

5. John of Freiburg, *Summa confessorum*, bk. 2, tit. 5, q. 2, fol. 66v. See Boyle, "*Summa confessorum* of John of Freiburg."

6. Unnatural acts include sodomy, masturbation, inappropriate male-female relations, and bestiality. In keeping with Aquinas, Pseudo-Vincent of Beauvais assesses bestiality as worse than sodomy (*Speculum morale* 3.9.2.11, in *Speculum Quadruplex*, 3:1372–1373; although this work circulated as volume 3 of Vincent of Beauvais's *Speculum Quadruplex*, it was written after his death, sometime between 1310 and 1320). Cf. Vincent of Beauvais's similar conflation of masturbation, same-sex relations, and bestiality, in *Speculum historiale* 1.46, in *Speculum Quadruplex*, 4:18.

7. Thomas of Cantimpré, *De apibus* 2.30.7, p. 323. John Baldwin notes a variant of these myths, found in a Dominican compilation from the 1230s. The compiler alleges that Peter the Chanter discovered a passage by Jerome claiming that all the sodomites died on the night of Christ's birth (Baldwin, *The Language of Sex*, 44). Thomas manifests a particularly fierce commitment to the natural world. See, for example, his *Liber de natura rerum*, which opens with predictable Dominican homage to Aristotle (prol., 3). Thomas Aquinas and Thomas of Cantimpré studied under Albert the Great at the Dominican studium in Cologne around the same time. See Mulchahey, *"First the Bow Is Bent in Study,"* 56.

8. Thomas of Cantimpré, *De apibus* 2.30.11, p. 325. This is in spite of the fact that he notes elsewhere that old age is characterized by a cooling of lust (*Liber de natura rerum* 1.82, p. 81).

9. Thomas of Cantimpré, *De apibus* 2.30.10, p. 325. Thomas only learned this by hearsay from a trustworthy priest who walked behind the man in question. There is an exegetical rationale. Hugh of Fouilloy (d. ca. 1172) glossed Gomorrah as "dryness" and Sodom as "sterility." Metaphorically this represents those who are not moistened by the rain of compunction nor suffused by the celestial dawn, which is contemplation (*De claustro animae*, PL 176:1097).

10. Thomas of Cantimpré, *De apibus* 2.30.10, 2.30.12, pp. 325–326.

11. Ibid., 2.30.13, p. 326.

12. Thomas of Cantimpré, *Liber de natura rerum* 10.4, p. 316. He attributes this detail to the Jewish historian Josephus. Thomas likens the blighted apples that grow on the site, which look perfect but crumble at a touch, to hypocrites whose works seem good but are full of iniquity and deception. Cf. Vincent of Beauvais, *Speculum historiale* 1.106, in *Speculum Quadruplex*, 4:39.

13. Thomas of Cantimpré, *De apibus* 2.30.14, p. 326.

14. William Peraldus, *Summa aurea* 2.3.6c. Although primarily concerned with same-sex relations among men, William also includes "bestial" male-female sex. In this context, he includes the alleged opinion of Methodius: that women who mounted men in sexual inter-course precipitated the fall (cf. Peter of Poitiers, Chapter 5, n. 73, above). The reference is to the *Revelations* of Pseudo-Methodius. See Tentler, *Sin and Confession*, 192 n. 46. Peraldus did not consistently associate the flood with sodomy, however. See his discussion of clerical sins of the flesh in which the sons of God are indicted for mixing with the daughters of men (*Summa aurea* 3.2.12a). On the influence of Peraldus on Chaucer's Pardoner, see Lochrie, *Covert Operations*, 179–186.

15. Peraldus, *Summa aurea* 2.3.6c.

16. Astesanus d'Asti, *Summa de casibus conscientiae* 2.46.7, fols. 79v–80r.

17. Lateran III (1179), c. 11, *DEC*, 1:217. I have altered the translation to make it more literal.

18. Lateran IV (1215), c. 14, *DEC*, 1:242.

19. "Freers, freers, wo ye be!," in Duncan, *Medieval English Lyrics*, 303. The lyric is written half in Middle English and half in Latin.

20. Kuefler, "Male Friendship."

21. Baldwin, *Language of Sex*, 46–47. The poem in question is by Milon d'Amiens (*Du prestre et du chevalier*, in *Recueil général et complet des fabliaux*, ed. Montaiglon and Raynaud, 2:46–91; see esp. 81–82, 84, 88). For the frequency of other sexual offenses attributed to the clergy in fabliaux, see Baldwin's breakdown according to social group and sin perpetrated (*Language of Sex*, tables 1–2, pp. 252–254). The most famous example of a cleric clearly coded as effeminate who is, arguably, a sodomite is Chaucer's Pardoner. See Dinshaw, *Chaucer's Sexual Poetics*, chap. 6; and Holsinger, *Music, Body, and, Desire*, 176–187.

22. Andrew W. Miller, "To 'Frock' a Cleric," 278.

23. John of Salisbury, Ep. 307, Clerks of Archbishop Thomas Becket to William, Arch-bishop of Sens (1178), in *Letters of John of Salisbury*, 2:747–748.

24. Ibid., pp. 745, 747. There is also a letter from Roger of Pont l'Évêque himself, complaining of how the lies and slanders he endured led to a papal suspension (Ep. 306, Roger of Pont l'Évêque, archbishop of York, to Hugh du Puiset, bishop of Durham, et al., in *Letters of John of Salisbury*, 2:739–743). Although he does not specify what the rumors were, the terms of his compurgation make it clear that he was charged with inciting Becket's murder. See Alexander III's letter to the bishops of Rouen and Amiens (1171), in Robertson and Sheppard, *Materials for a History of Thomas Becket*, 7:501–502, no. 764. John, however, maintains that Roger went to Rome "to clear himself from the charge of leading a depraved life" (Ep. 307, in *Letters of John of Salisbury*, 2:746–747).

25. *De S. Conrado Nanuino, Wolfratshusii in Bavaria*, AASS, August, 2:214–215. Apparently, he was falsely accused by the judge, a certain Ganter, who was after Conrad's money.

26. See the account of the sermon preached by the patriarch of Constantinople preceding the Council of Nablus (1120), *Sacra concilia*, 21:261–262. For the influence of Justinian and later Byzantine law on the canons, see Kedar, "On the Origins of the Earliest Laws of Frankish Jerusalem," 313–320.

27. Council of Nablus (1120), cc. 9–11, *Sacra concilia*, 21:264.

28. *Annales Basileensis*, ann. 1277, *MGH SS* 17:201; *Annales Parmenses maiores*, ann. 1287, *MGH SS* 18:703.

29. Goodich, "Sodomy in Medieval Secular Law," 297–302. Also see Hergemöller, *Sodom and Gomorrah*, 31–33.

30. Boone, "State Power and Illicit Sexuality," 140.

31. *Bible Moralisée: Codex Vindobonensis 2554*, ed. and trans. Guest, fol. 36r (last register), with modern transcription, p. 108c. For context, see Guest's commentary, ibid., 18–27. Also see Guest, " 'The Darkness and the Obscurity of Sins,' " 95–97. The commentary on the errant bishops allegedly emerges in a discussion of 1 Kings. Even so, sodomy as a divinely visited punishment echoes Paul's depiction of same-sex relations being inflicted by God for humanity's religious disaffection (Rom. 1:25–27).

32. Dante, *Inferno* 15.106–108, *Divine Comedy*. The soul who imparts this information to Dante is his beloved teacher Brunetto Latini (*Inferno* 15.30ff.). The souls of the sodomites are significantly described as ogling passersby (*Inferno* 15.17ff.). The sodomites in hell are not tortured. Sexual torment is instead assigned to fraudulent thieves, who are sodomized by snakelike creatures (*Inferno* 25).

33. Boccaccio, *The Decameron*, 1st day, 2nd story; 2nd day, 3rd story, pp. 84, 132–33. The molested knight assumed that the abbot was in the grip of some "impure passion," but it turned out that the abbot was a noblewoman in disguise (132–133). Also see the 5th day, 10th story, where a young woman is married to a man with sodomitical inclinations who ignores her. When her youthful lover is discovered in the closet, the situation is amiably resolved with a ménage à trois (470–478).

34. See *Vernon Manuscript: A Facsimile*, fol. 126r. Also see Stones, "Miniatures in the Vernon Manuscript." I am indebted to Leanne MacDonald and Kathryn Kerby-Fulton for bringing this image to my attention.

35. The charges against Boniface VIII were framed by Philip IV's agent William of Nogaret during Boniface's lifetime, but the trial was posthumous (Boase, *Boniface VIII*, 327, 359–365; Coste, *Boniface VIII en procès*, introd., 91–106). For articles and testimony regarding sodomy (which were often lumped together with other sins of the flesh), see Coste, *Boniface VIII en procès*, September 7, 1304, no. 8, p. 243; May–June 1307, no. 6, p. 361; October 13–March 15, 1310, no. 10, p. 384, no. 7, p. 394; ca. 1309, no. 24, p. 415; no. 33, p. 418; no. 67, p. 430 (the preceding are various iterations of Nogaret's articles). Testimonies between April 5 and May 17, 1310, are given by Brother Berardus de Monte Nigro, no. 3, p. 489; Brother Petrus de Collevaccario, no. 6, pp. 491–492; Prior Vitalis of St. Geminus, nos. 8, 12, pp. 492, 496; the notary Petrus Oddarelli, no. 16, p. 498; the armorer Petruzolus, no. 21, p. 502; Brother Nicolaus of Rome, no. 54, p. 522; tertiary Franciscan Berardus of Soriano, no. 61, p. 528; Florianus Ubertini of Bologna, no. 63, p. 530; Nottus of Pisa, no. 78, p. 534; Lellus Thomassonis of Spoleta, no. 83, p. 536. Boniface was also accused of abusing women between the thighs "as with a boy" (Nottus of Pisa, nos. 68, 81, pp. 531, 535). Also see Coste's conclusion, pp. 899–902; and Bagliani, *Boniface VIII*, 363–366. Cf. the deposition of Ruggero dei Buondelmonti, abbot of Passignano and prior general of the Vallambrosan order, who got on

the wrong side of Florentine politics (Dameron, *Florence and Its Church in the Age of Dante*, 44).

36. See Gilmour-Bryson, "Sodomy and the Knights Templar," esp. 164ff. Also see Karras, "Knighthood, Compulsory Heterosexuality, and Sodomy," 275–279. For articles of prosecution involving homoerotic activities, see Gilmour-Bryson, *Trial of the Templars in the Papal State and the Abruzzi*, nos. 30–33, 40–44, pp. 76–77. On Philip's motivations, see Boswell, *Christianity*, 296–298. On the interchangeable use of the terms "sodomy" and "heresy" in secular sources, see Boone, "State Power and Illicit Sexuality," 135–153.

37. The clergy still used charges of sodomy to discredit monarchs; for example, the complicity of a papal canon and a French bishop in spreading rumors that Philip III of France had committed the sin against nature. See Kay, "Martin IV and the Fugitive Bishop of Bayeux." Secular princes would also use charges of sodomy against insubordinates. See Brundage, "Politics of Sodomy: Rex v. Pons Hugh de Ampurias (1311)"; Brundage cites Pons's resistance to the king's appropriation of Templar property as a salient factor in the charge. On the association of heresy and sodomy, see Vern L. Bullough, "Postscript," 213–214; Chiffoleau, "Dire l'indicibile," 300–302; Goodich, "Sodomy in Medieval Secular Law," 295–297. This pattern persists well into the early modern period. See Monter, "Sodomy and Heresy in Early Modern Switzerland."

38. Crawford, *European Sexualities*, 156.

39. Hudson, *Selections from English Wycliffite Writings*, 25. I have modernized the Middle English. Appended to this list was a poem that accused prelates of defending the crime of sodomy (Dinshaw, *Getting Medieval*, 55–57). On the ways in which the constitutions echo John Wycliffe, see Dinshaw, *Getting Medieval*, 69–70. Also see Hudson, *Premature Reformation*, 49 and nn. 225, 226; and Van Engen, "Anticlericalism Among the Lollards." On orthodoxy's deft use of reverse accusation in addressing this charge, see Dinshaw, *Getting Medieval*, 94–99. On the Lollards' perception of the clergy as a danger to the family, see Elliott, "Lollardy and the Integrity of Marriage and the Family." Reforming groups on the Continent also complained that clerical celibacy fostered sodomy. See Karras's discussion of the fifteenth-century reforming treatise *Reformatio Sigismundi* (*Unmarriages*, 123–124).

40. Karma Lochrie draws attention to how Chaucer's Pardoner makes a parallel claim that the word "sodomy" can only be used in the context of scripture, otherwise the individual is defiled (*Covert Operations*, 181).

41. The foundational work in this area is Paul Fournier's *Officialités au Moyen Âge*. Also see Donahue, "Ecclesiastical Courts"; and Donahue and McDougall, "France and Adjoining Areas." English ecclesiastical courts were more limited in scope than their continental counterparts. Clerics were subject to common law for certain civil actions, like debt, but still had the privilege of forum for serious crimes. See Helmholz, "Local Ecclesiastical Courts in England," 354–356; Helmholz, *Oxford History of the Laws of England*, 1:110–111. There is a greater rate of survival for ecclesiastical courts and bishops' registers in England than on the Continent. A number of these can be accessed online. See http://www.medievalgenealogy.org .uk/sources/church.shtml#bishops.

42. See Gratian, *Decretum*, C. 1 q. 8 c. 5; Fraher, "*Ut nullus describatur reus prius quam convincatur*"; Brundage, "Proof in Canonical Criminal Law," 330.

43. Fraher, "Theoretical Justification for the New Criminal Law," 587 and n. 50; Brundage, "Proof in Canonical Criminal Law," 331–332. The decretals in question are X.3.2.7 and X.3.2.8.

44. Archivio Arcivescovile di Pisa, *Atti straordinari* 1, ann. 1311–1312, fol. 184r. This series of records from the archiepiscopal criminal tribunal spans from 1304 to 1423. See Carratori, *Inventario dell'Archivio Arcivescovile di Pisa*, 1:51–52.

45. Geltner, "Patrolling Normative Boundaries," 179. This is not to say that there were no instances of false accusations against clerics. For England, see Storey, "Malicious Indictments of the Clergy," 221–238.

46. Helmholz, *Oxford History of the Laws of England*, 1:515–518. See Gregory IX's *Decretales*, X.5.1.10 and X.2.20.14 for the traditional strictures against bringing a case against a cleric.

47. Abelard, *Historia calamitatum*, 190; trans., 17. Although Fulbert was a cathedral canon, his quasi-parental relationship to Heloise renders his role in Abelard's castration effectively an act of lay vengeance. See "Bishop Alnwick's Court-Book," 216–218, for an account of the group effort at castration that occurred in mid-fifteenth century Huntingdon. The investigating bishop assumed that the wounded priest had slept with someone's wife or daughter, but the ringleader denied this, insisting that he was acting purely at the instigation of the devil. Also see a case in which a priest is mutilated out of jealousy in Clarke and Zutshi, *Supplications from England and Wales*, no. 1375, 2:29; and Lea, *Formulary*, no. 18 (2, 4, 5), pp. 29–30; no. 22, p. 32.

48. Lea, *Formulary*, no. 16, pp. 26–27. We learn this from the abbot's efforts to win the parishioners' pardon from the papal penitentiary, an institution discussed below. Orte is located in the province of Viterbo.

49. See Cullum, "Clergy, Masculinity and Transgression," 187; Karras, *Unmarriages*, 153–164.

50. Taglia, "On Account of Scandal," 60–61. Other scholars have emphasized the way in which the church, despite its theoretical hard line, also accommodated clerical bastards, even recruiting a sizable number into the clergy. See Rousseau, "Pope Innocent III and the Familial Relationships"; and Schimmelpfenning, "*Ex fornicatione nati.*"

51. In reality, a good deal of the work of the papal penitentiary was dispensations for clerical bastards so they could be ordained. See Schmugge, "Cleansing on Consciences," 358–359. On the basis of dispensations, Sara McDougall has argued that illegitimacy was more tolerable than other alleged prohibitions like deformities ("Bastard Priests," 145–147).

52. For an overview of the holdings for the archbishop's criminal court, see Geltner, "I registri criminali dell'Archivio Arcivescovile di Lucca." On Lucca, see Bratchel, *Medieval Lucca*; and Osheim, *An Italian Lordship*.

53. See Geltner, "Patrolling Normative Boundaries," 172–173.

54. For instances of clerical concubinage or affairs with women, see *ASDL, Criminale* 1, 1347, fols. 9r, 23r; *ASDL, Criminale* 2, 1350, fols. 12r, 18r; *ASDL, Criminale* 5, 1352, fols. 8r, 56r, 62r, 65r, 96r; *ASDL, Criminale* 9, 1357, fols. 8r–v, 153r; for abduction and rape, see *ASDL, Criminale* 5, 1352, fols. 38r, 42r; *ASDL, Criminale* 9, fols. 103r.

55. *ASDL, Criminale* 5, 1353, 126r–v.

56. Kuttner, "*Ecclesia de occultis non iudicat.*" Some did argue that simony and homicide were exceptions and constituted grounds for deposition.

57. The one instance of sodomy turned on a self-accusation. William Smyth had "publicly preached" that he committed sodomy with Thomas Tunley. The latter was cited but did not appear, and the case was suspended. In the defamation case, Agnes Andrew told Margaret Myler that her husband was a "woman" who grabbed priests between their legs. The case was sent to arbiters and dismissed (Wunderli, *London Church Courts*, 83–84). It is significant that

it was a woman who leveled this charge against the other's husband: uncontrolled male speech itself was associated with effeminacy. See Bardsley, *Venomous Tongues*, 90–95. Karras has argued that sodomy was not nearly as pressing a concern in England as it was on the Continent ("Lechery That Dare Not Speak Its Name"); and Janelle Werner notes that cases of sodomy are very rare in Hereford "as elsewhere" ("Just as Priests Have Their Wives," 186 n. 42). Also see Helmholz, *Oxford History of the Laws of England*, 1:629.

58. Ex officio c. Rector of Bordofale (Canterbury, 1408), Canterbury Cathedral Archives and Library, act book X.8.1, fol. 44v.

59. On canonical purgations, see Gregory IX's *Decretales*, X.5.34.1–6; and Fiori, *Il giuramento di innocenza nel processo canonico medievale*, 228–250, 255–267; Rodimer, *Canonical Effects of Infamy of Fact*, 18–24; Lévy, "Problème de la preuve dans les droits savants au Moyen Âge," 145–148.

60. Ex officio c. Benet (York, 1401) Borthwick Institute, BI D/C.AB1, fo Ml. fol. 21r. Note that the initial charge says that Benet had relations with men of "the same village," though Raper is clearly from Kyllam. This case is mentioned by Helmholz in his *Oxford History of the Laws of England*, 1:518.

61. Archivio Arcivescovile di Pisa, *Atti straordinari*, no. 1, ann. 1311–1312, fol. 205r.

62. See, for example, Rocke, *Forbidden Friendships*, 139.

63. For an introduction to the various types of sources, see Haskins, "Sources for the History of the Papal Penitentiary" (note, however, that this article predated any public access to the penitentiary proper); Schmugge, "Cleansing on Consciences." On the thirteenth-century evolution of the concept of bastardy, see McDougall, *Royal Bastards*.

64. Lea, *Formulary*, no. 18, p. 28. On the dating of the formulary, see Haskins, "Sources for the History of the Papal Penitentiary," 429–433. On successful seductions in the confessional, see Caesarius of Heisterbach's exemplum in Chapter 5, n. 32, above.

65. Tamburini, *Santi e peccatori*, no. 10, pp. 130–131. Also see the case of three adolescent clerics from Vicenza, who were apprehended for sodomy and punished. But because the episode became public, they wanted papal absolution to remove the stain of infamy (ibid., no. 14 [1463], p. 136). Cf. the abbot who kept a concubine but also committed the vice of sodomy—one assumes with men (ibid., no. 24 [1480], p. 155) and the Carmelite priest and master of theology from Toulouse who committed the vice of sodomy "in the front parts and the posterior parts with other clerics, laypeople, [and] servants" both inside and outside the convent (ibid., no. 39 [1492], 189–190).

66. See Gerson, Ep. 24, to an unknown bishop, in *Oeuvres complètes*, 2:90–93.

67. Schmugge, "Cleansing on Consciences," 350. The details of a sin were relayed via sealed letters. On the evolution of the penitentiary and its responsibilities, see Salonen and Schmugge, *Sip from the "Well of Grace."* Also note that the registry only records absolutions: in the event that the supplicant's sin was not absolved, his petition would not be recorded (Clarke and Zutshi, *Supplications from from England and Wales*, introd., xv).

68. Puff, "Localizing Sodomy," 177.

CHAPTER 6

1. *VA* 1.22, p. 37.

2. Othloh of St. Emmeram, *Liber visionum* vis. 3, *MGH QQ zur Geistesgesch.* 13:52–54. For the role that beating played in Othloh's conversion to religious life, see Chapter 8, pp.

194–195, below. According to Bernard of Cluny's customary, those entrusted with the care of youths cannot strike them, but only issue stern rebukes (*Ordo Cluniacensis* 1.28, p. 211).

3. Æthelwold, *Regularis concordia anglicae nationis*, c. 11, pp. 7–8.

4. See, for example, the tenth-century customs of Fleury, which further stipulate that boys should not be sent anywhere alone, but only go in groups of two. In the event that a lone child is compelled to go somewhere, the master should follow behind holding his stick. *Consuetudines Floriacenses antiquiores*, c. 18, ed. Hallinger, *Consuetudinum saeculi X/XI/XII*, pp. 30–31. Also see Joan Evans's description of the life of the oblate at Cluny (*Monastic Life at Cluny*, 47–48).

5. Bernard of Cluny, *Ordo Cluniacensis* 1.27, pp. 201–203; cf. Ulrich of Cluny, *Antiquiores consuetudines* 2.8, *PL* 149:742. Note that both Bernard and Ulrich recommend guardians for adolescents as well (Bernard, *Ordo Cluniacensis* 1.28, p. 210; Ulrich of Cluny, *Antiquiores consuetudines* 2.9, *PL* 149:748). These two customaries are roughly contemporaneous and have many passages in common, though it is not certain which came first. For a comparison, see Davril, "Coutumiers directifs et coutumiers descriptifs."

6. Bernard of Cluny, *Ordo Cluniacensis* 1.27, pp. 207–208; cf. Ulrich of Cluny, *Antiquiores consuetudines* 2.8, *PL* 149:744–745.

7. Bernard of Cluny, *Ordo Cluniacensis* 1.27, p. 208.

8. Ibid., p. 210; cf. Ulrich of Cluny, *Antiquiores consuetudines* 2.8, *PL* 149:747.

9. Bernard of Cluny, *Ordo Cluniacensis* 1.27, p. 206.

10. *The Monastic Constitutions of Lanfranc*, c. 109, pp. 170–173; cf. the treatment of older boys, ibid., c. 110, pp. 172–175.

11. Cochelin, "Besides the Book," 23.

12. Bernard of Cluny, *Ordo Cluniacensis* 1.27, p. 206; Ulrich of Cluny, *Antiquiores consuetudines* 2.8, *PL* 149:747.

13. Forsyth, "Ganymede Capital at Vézelay"; also see Chapter 3, n. 61, above. On sexual themes and nudity in Romanesque sculpture, see Wirth, *L'image à l'époque romane*, 272–286.

14. Kolve, "Ganymede/*Son of Getron*," 1043–1065.

15. Gilles of Corbeil, *Hierapigra*, 376.

16. Fortunately the ceremony was disrupted when a stranger at the back of the church threw an apple (Gilles of Corbeil, *Hierapigra*, 377).

17. Pennsylvania's *40th Statewide Investigating Grand Jury: Report 1, Interim–Redacted* (2018), p. 5, http://media-downloads.pacourts.us/InterimRedactedReportandResponses.pdf?cb = 42148.

18. Olsen, *Of Sodomites*, fig. 7.

19. Ibid., figs. 1 (Tayac, Aquitaine), 3 (San Juan Bautista, Villanueva de la Nie, Cantabria), 5 (Monprimblanc, Gironde, Aquitaine), 46 (St.-Gènes, Châteaumeillant, Cher, Centre). For pederasty, see the late twelfth-century example from Colegiata del Mar, Cantabria (figs. 8, 9; shown from two angles). Capitals also frequently feature naked youths; see figs. 10, 11, 13, 14 (St.-Pierre Mozat, Clermont-Ferrand), 15 (St.-Julien, Brioude), 16 (St.-Marcellin, Chanteuges). One trumeau depicts several youths wrestling with older, bearded men (fig. 50, Ste.-Marie, Souillac). Also see Weir and Jerman, *Images of Lust*, 84, 101, 153; for the possible apotropaic function of erotic images, see ibid., 10, 21, 29, 52, 146–148, 150.

20. Gilles of Corbeil, *Hierapigra*, 375.

21. Peter the Venerable, *De miraculis* 1.14, *PL* 189:877–878, as cited in Forsyth, "Ganymede Capital at Vézelay," 244.

22. Walter Map, *De nugis curialium* 1.24, pp. 80–81. See Joshua Bryan Smith's *Walter Map and the Matter of Britain*, 1–8. Note that Benedict prostrated himself on a dead boy, bringing him back to life. See Gregory the Great, *Dialogues* 2.32, 2:226–230.

23. This is from a thirteenth-century anonymous poem on the state of the clergy, appearing in Widmann, "Die Eberbacher Chronik der Mainzer Erzbischöfe," 142.

24. On the decline of oblation in the twelfth century, see de Jong, *In Samuel's Image*, 294–302. Note that canonists also reject oblation from Gratian onward on the basis of proper consent—a key issue in the twelfth century. The question of sexual abuse is never broached. See Berend, "La subversion invisible."

25. See Martha G. Newman, "Foundation and Twelfth Century."

26. *Stat. Ord. Cist.*, ann. 1134, c. 78, 1:31. The same statute dismantles the traditional monastic school, so there would be no children in the cloister. On the issue of age, see Lynch, "Cistercians and Underage Novices," 285–286. According to Constance Berman, who argues there was no real Cistercian "order" until the death of St. Bernard, there was purposeful obfuscation to make it seem as if the administrative framework for the order was in place earlier than it was (*Cistercian Evolution*, 48–54). Brian Patrick McGuire accepts the traditional view that the order took shape in the first couple of decades of the twelfth century (see "Constitutions and the General Chapter").

27. *Stat. Ord. Cist.*, ann. 1154, c. 16, 1: 57; Lynch, "Cistercians and Underage Novices," 286. There were a number of cases in which age seems indeterminate. See *Stat. Ord. Cist.*, ann. 1211, c. 5, 1:386; cf. ann. 1212, cc. 49, 53, 1:400, 401. The case surrounding the "little boy monk" (*puerulus monachus*) in Burgundy required an inquest (ann. 1205, c. 23, 1:312). Berman argues that the general chapter only began to take shape in the 1150s (*Cistercian Evolution*, 23–53, 93, 222–223). Even so, the general chapter was stipulated in the *Carta Caritatis*, one of the Cistercians founding documents. See Sayers, "Judicial Activities of General Chapters," 18–22.

28. *Stat. Ord. Cist.*, ann. 1157, c. 28, 1:62.

29. Ibid., ann. 1161, c. 12, 1:72.

30. Ibid., ann. 1175, c. 26, 1:26; ann. 1184, cc. 2–3, 1:93; ann. 1196, c. 65, 1:209; Lynch, "Cistercians and Underage Novices," 287.

31. *Stat. Ord. Cist.*, ann. 1191, c. 30, 1:139; ann. 1195, c. 55, 1:190. In this latter instance, the question of whether the boy could stay was remanded to the lord abbot. Also see the statutes of 1184, which punish the reception of too many adolescents (ann. 1184, cc. 2, 3, 1:95). On lighter faults, see ann. 1134, c. 65, 1:28.

32. Although the category of "graver faults" persists, these are designated as theft, conspiracy, and arson (*Stat. Ord. Cist.*, ann. 1134, c. 64, 1:27–28).

33. Ibid., c. 73, 1:30. On the conservative nature of Cistercian chant, see King, *Liturgies of the Religious Orders*, 93–96.

34. *Stat. Ord. Cist.*, ann. 1157, c. 23, 1:62; ann. 1181, c. 9, 1:89. Efforts to ban the customary kiss clearly were not effective. In Thomas of Cantimpré's life of the Cistercian nun Lutgard of Aywières (d. 1246), when the abbot who had hegemony over her community insisted on kissing the reluctant Lutgard, Christ interposed his hand so "so that she did not feel the taint of even the first carnal stirrings of a man's kiss" (Thomas of Cantimpré, *Vita S. Lutgardis virginis Cisterciensis* 1.2.21, *AASS*, June, 4:195). For Thomas's very vocal objections to this tradition, see Elliott, *Bride of Christ*, 203. Note that the Cistercian statutes also insisted that the abbot should not give the kiss of peace without a preceding prayer (*Stat. Ord. Cist.*, ann. 1157, c. 25, 1:62).

35. *Stat. Ord. Cist.*, ann. 1189, c. 16, 1:113. Later a form of damage control was attempted: it was ordained that an individual should do penance in his own house if this could be accomplished without danger or scandal (ibid., ann. 1224, c. 5, 2:31).

36. This reading is corroborated by a canon of 1195, the first explicitly addressing incontinence with women, which ordains that monks who have wives and concubines should be punished in the same way as those implicated in a "manifest contagion of the flesh" (*Stat. Ord. Cist.*, ann. 1195, c. 21, 1:185).

37. For reiterations, see ibid., ann. 1190, c. 10, 1:119; ann. 1191, c. 58, 1:143.

38. See Füser, *Mönche im Konflikt*, 184–190.

39. He was sent to another house outside the province where he would rank last of all, fasting on bread and water every Friday. The general chapter could lift these penalties if he were on the point of death (*Stat. Ord. Cist.*, ann. 1208, c. 16, 1:348).

40. He resurfaced as abbot of an Austrian community (ibid., ann. 1226, c. 15, 2:58). Cf. the Irish abbot who was deposed "propter nimiam dissolutionem et multa gravia et peremptoria" (ann. 1226, c. 37, 2:55; cf. also ann. 1232, c. 24, 2:104; ann. 1234, c. 28, 2:132).

41. Ibid., ann. 1230, c. 35, 2:91.

42. Ibid., ann. 1220, c. 42, 1:525. The abbot who ejected him was also assigned a three-day fast of bread and water for having acted without consulting higher authorities.

43. Ibid., ann. 1221, c. 9, 2:2; ann. 1224, c. 21, 2:34.

44. Ibid., ann. 1229, c. 6, 2:76; cf. ann. 1242, c. 13, 2:248.

45. Ibid., ann. 1242, c. 13, 2:248. Compare this with the comparatively light penalty meted out for "manifest contagion of the flesh" (ann. 1242, c. 12, 2:247–248).

46. Ibid., ann. 1267, c. 7, 3:38.

47. Ibid., ann. 1273, c. 9, 3:116–117.

48. Ibid., ann. 1201, c. 4, 1:264.

49. The finality of this statute was undercut by the acknowledgment that the general chapter could overturn the sentence (ibid., ann. 1202, c. 2, 1:275).

50. Sanctions were not uniformly applied, however. In 1205 it was discovered that a number of Frisian abbots had admitted underage students into the cloister—an offense for which "they deserved to be deposed," but were pardoned and given fasts (ibid., ann. 1205, c. 26, 1:313). The following year, however, the traditional sentence against educating underage boys was upheld, as was the presence of boys in the nuns' cloisters—both of which were considered to be sources of grave scandal (ann. 1206, 1:320–321). So when it was determined that an abbot in Mancy—who was "believed" to have admitted a little boy (*puerulus*) and "was said" to have taken an oath before a secular court and "other things "—should be corrected "according to the custom of the order," it is not entirely clear what this means or how admitting an underage novice should be weighed against the other alleged offenses (ann. 1205, c. 27, 1:313).

51. Ibid., ann. 1231, c. 12, 2:93–94. Whoever was responsible for receiving the underage novice was to fast every Friday on bread and water for the amount of time the boy had remained in the monastery. See Nancy Caciola's *Discerning Spirits*.

52. *Stat. Ord. Cist.*, ann. 1235, c. 14, 2:141.

53. Ibid., ann. 1191, c. 30, 1:139; ann. 1195, c. 15, 1:184.

54. Ibid., ann. 1241, c. 25, 2:234–235.

55. Ibid., ann. 1251, c. 1, 3:360; cf. ann. 1263, c. 7, 3:11, ann. 1264, c. 1, 3:17–18.

56. Ibid., ann. 1184, c. 10, 1:96. Cf. the interdict against boys carrying sharp knives (ann. 1215, c. 6, 1:435) and the stipulation that boys traveling with members of the order should not have sharp knives, variegated vests, silken caps, or gauntlets (ann. 1231, c. 9, 2:93).

57. Ibid., ann. 1239, c. 8, 2:204.

58. Ibid., ann. 1258, c. 22, 2:442–443.

59. Boynton and Cochelin, "Sociomusical Role of Child Oblates," 9.

60. Constable, *Reformation of the Twelfth Century*, 100–101. On the ambivalence toward children in monastic life in this period, see Riché, "L'enfant dans la société monastique," 692–693, who notes that efforts to restrict the admission of children in various capacities began in the eleventh century. At Cluny, there was already an effort to control the number of children. See Hunt, *Cluny Under Saint Hugh*, 96–97. Not all of the reasons for exclusion were disciplinary. In Ulrich of Cluny's dedicatory letter addressed to William, abbot of Hirsau, alongside whom he was educated, Ulrich characterized child oblates as children given up by their parents because they were deformed or ill: "half-humans or half-alive" (Ulrich of Cluny, *Antiquiores consuetudines*, PL 149:636). Boynton and Cochelin speculate that the number of oblates had already dropped to 9 or 10 percent of the community before Peter the Venerable's initiative ("Sociomusical Role of Child Oblates," 10).

61. *Statuta Petri Venerabilis*, no. 36, pp. 70–71. Cf. no. 35, which resists injudicious acceptance, including rustics, children, the old, the simple, or someone who cannot work (p. 70).

62. See Bruce, *Silence and Sign Language*, esp. 24–52.

63. *Statuta Petri Venerabilis*, c. 69, pp. 99–100. His purported motive for this statute, however, was because monks got into fights when they misplaced articles of clothing. The policing of the dormitory would continue over the years. See *Stat. Ord. Clun.*, Henry I, ann. ca. 1314, c. 44, 1:111; and the statutes of an unnamed fourteenth-century abbot (ibid., c. 52, 1:154). Also see the concern about the nude monks lying around during the visitation to St.-Orens d'Auch (ibid., ann. 1245, Gascony, 1:211; cf. ann. 1373, the Roman Monastery, Germany/Lorraine, 1:335). The ten Cluniac provinces were Auvergne, Gascony, Lyon (or Cluny), Poitou, Provence, France, Germany/Lorraine, England, Lombardy, and Spain.

64. *Statuta Petri Venerabilis*, c. 46, p. 78.

65. *Stat. Ord. Clun.*, c. 1, 1:53. Giles Constable is probably correct in his assumption that this would pertain to priors as well ("Cluniac Administration and Administrators," 423 n. 71).

66. This is in spite of the fact that the prohibition was repeated by some of his successors (*Stat. Ord. Clun.*, ann. 1200, Hugh V, c. 6, 1:42–43). See Constable's introductory notes to *Statuta Petri Venerabilis*, 23–24.

67. Valous, *Monachisme clunisien*, 1:41.

68. See, for example, *Stat. Ord. Clun.*, ann. 1335, Allex, Provence, 2:193–194; ann. 1336, Grazac, Auvergne, 3:231. With respect to the priory in Frontenayo, Germany/Lorraine, the visitors said explicitly that one of the monks was a youth who, on account of age, "was not able to be promoted for a long time" (ann. 1369, 4:63); cf. ann. 1379, Salm, Germany/Lorraine, 3:139. Also see the armed efforts to robe an individual described as an *infantulus* (ann. 1280, Santo Paolo, d'Argono, Lombardy, 1:391).

69. *Stat. Ord. Clun.*, ann. 1298, Relenges, Germany/Lorraine, 2:128; ann. 1335, Villaverde, Spain, 3:200.

70. Ibid., ann. 1308, Carénac, Gascony, 2:272. In this latter instance, the visitors showed no concern over the question of age: their main concern was that the little boys did not have

the proper monastic attire. Nor did the abbot seem to mind. In 1310, the visitors cautioned surrounding abbeys that greater care should be taken in correcting boys and youths (*juvenes et pueri*) and instructing them in monastic observances (2:305).

71. Bernard of Cluny, *Scorn for the World*, bk. 3, lines 77–78, 191, 199–200, pp. 146–147. Also note Bernard's complaint that "often a novice or a boy covered with a heap of blame presides over worship" (ibid., bk. 3, lines 391ff., pp. 158–159). This is an early reference to the carnivalesque tradition of the boy bishop (see Chapter 4, p. 93, above). In this latter instance, however, Bernard seems to be complaining about boys really being ordained as bishops.

72. See Chapter 3, pp. 63–64, above.

73. *Stat. Ord. Clun.*, ann. 1292, 2:41.

74. Ibid., Bertrand I, ann. 1309, c. 13, 1:71. Füser states that sodomy was a serious sin, but not a mortal sin, which is clearly not accurate ("Der Leib," 227).

75. *Stat. Ord. Clun.*, Bertrand I, ann. 1309, 1:71 n. 1. Later statutes will redouble Benedict's efforts to police the dormitory, targeting acts like monks lying around in their underwear (ann. 1399, John II, cc. 51–52, 1:153–154).

76. Ibid., ann. 1301, Bertrand I, c. 97, 1:84; cf. ca. 1314, Henry I, c. 8, 1:100; ann. 1399, John II, c. 36, 1:151. When later repeated at the general chapter, Bertrand's injunction will be rendered as condemning "the vice against nature which comprehends every touch of the two libidinous ones" (ibid., ann. 1391, 4:299).

77. This has given rise to the belief that Cluny was centralized prior to the thirteenth century, which Constable debunks ("Cluniac Administration and Administrators").

78. Valous, *Monachisme clunisien*, 2:70–76.

79. On the Cluniac provinces, see n. 63, above. Although yearly attendance of the general chapter was theoretically mandatory, exceptions were made for priors from Spain, Lombardy, England, and Germany who, owing to the distance, were only required to appear every two years.

80. On these two sets of officials, see Valous, *Monachisme clunisien*, 2:87–90, 96–111; Anger, "Chapitres généraux de Cluny," 126–142.

81. Füser has also examined these records for sexual activity in the cloister in "Der Leib"; for same-sex relations, see pp. 226–237.

82. *Stat. Ord. Clun.*, ann. 1279, St.-Nisius, Provence, 1:375.

83. Ibid., ann. 1279, Peaugres, Provence, 1:376. The monastery only contained the prior and Peter, which must have made life tense.

84. Ibid., ann. 1279, Podium, Provence, 1:378.

85. Ibid., ann. 1291, Bruillet, Poitou, 1:21.

86. Ibid., ann. 1385, St.-Gelasius, Poitou, 3:175.

87. Ibid., ann. 1326, Chante Merle, a dependent on the priory of Coincy, France, 3:32.

88. Ibid., ann. 1386, Bellevaux-en-Bauges, Provence, 3:212.

89. Ibid., ann. 1375, Provence, 3:103.

90. Ibid., ann. 1367, Namur, Germany/Lorraine, 3:32. Cf. ann. 1386, Savoy, Provence, 3:214.

91. Ibid., ann. 1280, Santo Paolo, d'Argono, Lombardy, 1:393.

92. Ibid., ann. 1310, Lihons-en-Santerre, France, 2:292.

93. Ibid., ann. 1316, Marmesse, France, 2:390. The offended couple were so in fear of the monk, however, that they denied that such incidents occurred.

94. Cf. Füser, who also suggests that this elision was in keeping with the use of *incontinentia* at Lateran IV ("Der Leib," 235, 228 n. 160).

95. See the examples of Brother Nicholas of Contamine-sur-Arve and Stephen of Romanus Monasterium, *Stat. Ord. Clun.*, ann. 1266, Provence, 1:299.

96. Ibid., Vosges, ann. 1274, Germany/Lorraine, 1:346.

97. Ibid., ann. 1266, Montleyry, Provence, 1:299; ann. 1292, Nogent, France, 2:35; also see the case of Oddo of Colombey-les-Deux-Églises (ibid.).

98. Ibid., ann. 1345, District of L'Ouche, Provence, 3:407; cf. the case of a monk accused of incontinence who committed "many excesses and enormities in the same place" (ann. 1358, Domène, Provence, 3:514).

99. Ibid., ann. 1301, Vaucluse, Germany/Lorraine, 2:175. Cf. the case of a monk who involved himself in "many enormities" (ann. 1303, St.-Lizier, Gascony, 2:193).

100. Ibid., ann. 1294, Ecclesiis, Provence, 2:71. The prior was given the opportunity to purge himself canonically. If he failed, he would be deposed. Even if he was successful, he was still defamed for poor administration, entailing an inquest to be sent under seal to the abbot. Canonical purgation was not always successful. See ibid., ann. 1291, Sardona, Germany, 2:23.

101. Ibid., ann. 1368, St.-Lizier, Gascony, 3:54.

102. Ibid., ann. 1313, Crespin, Poitou, 2:347–348.

103. Ibid., ann. 1280, Vertemate, Lombardy, 1:393.

104. The alleged witness is said to be the prior of Olzate, which possibly refers to Ozillac in southwestern France.

105. *Stat. Ord. Clun.*, ann. 1280, Vertemate, Lombardy, 1:393–394.

106. Ibid., ann. 1272, 1:327; ann. 1277, 1:368.

107. Ibid., ann. 1280, 1:394.

108. Ibid., ann. 1281, 1:402. The following year the visitors likened the priory's degree of corporeal and material dilapidation to a disease (ann. 1282, 1:419).

109. Ibid., ann. 1286, 1:439.

110. See Chapter 5, p. 120, above.

111. *Stat. Ord. Clun.*, ann. 1299, St.-Mayeul of Pavia, Lombardy, 2:140.

112. Ibid., ann. 1299, St.-Victor of Geneva, Provence, 1:131; ann. 1301, 1:169.

113. Ibid., ann. 1303, 2:204. Also see the discussion of this case in Füser, "Der Leib," 231–232.

114. *Stat. Ord. Clun.*, ann. 1303, St.-Victor of Geneva, Provence, 2:205 and n. a; 204 n. b.

115. Ibid., ann. 1200, Hugh V, c. 48, 1:49.

116. It was founded in 1130 (Valous, *Monachisme clunisien*, app. 3, 2:257).

117. Some small houses, like Chaux-les-Clerval, containing only the prior and one monk, seemed harmonious (*Stat. Ord. Clun.*, ann. 1270, Germany/Lorraine, 1:319; cf. ann. 1300, 2:150). In fact, the house was only intended for two, and things went awry when an additional monk was added (ibid., ann. 1273, 1:329; ann. 1304, 2:221). But others struggled. See ibid., ann. 1262, Nièvre, Lyon, 1:273–274. Then there were even some houses that had a prior but no monks at all. See ibid., ann. 1388, Locus Dei, Germany, 4:252.

118. On vagabond monks attempting to escape punishment, see Valous, *Monachisme clunisien*, 1:58–59; Füser, *Mönche im Konflikt*, 321–324. For the degrees of apostasy, see Logan, *Runaway Religious*, 9–34; also see the list of apostate Cluniacs (app. 5, pp. 199–203).

119. On the prior's seal, see *Stat. Ord. Clun.*, ann. 1200, Hugh V, c. 54, 1:49; ann. ca. 1204–1206, Hugh V, c. 13, 1:57.

120. Ibid., c. 49, 1:49. They did accept fugitives from other orders, however.

121. Ibid., c. 47, 1:48; ann. 1277, Yves II, c. 4, 1:67.

122. Very little is known about Cluny's liturgy, however. See Hiley, *Western Plainchant*, 574–578. Some of the earliest evidence comes from the *Liber tramitis*, assembled by Abbot Hugh of Cluny for the imperial monastery of Farfa. Although not a Cluniac priory, Farfa looked to Cluny for reform. See Boynton, *Shaping a Monastic Identity*, 106–143; Hunt, *Cluny Under Saint Hugh*, 99–103.

123. Valous, *Monachisme clunisien*, 1:353–354. For the dramatic rise in prayers for the dead, see Rosenwein, "Feudal War and Monastic Peace," 131, 140–145, and table 1 (pp. 134–135).

124. Cf. the house at St.-Nizier-l'Estra, which had only four monks—three of whom needed to be removed: two were boys not yet in orders who spent their time running around; the third (the sacristan) was incontinent (*Stat. Ord. Clun.*, ann. 1262, Lyon, 1:270).

125. McDougall, "Bastard Priests," 150–152.

126. Valous, *Monachisme clunisien*, 1:75.

127. *Stat. Ord. Clun.*, ann. 1301, Bertrand I, c. 2, 1:82; cf. ann. ca. 1314, Henry I, c. 86, 1:127; ann. 1399, John II, c. 49, 1:153; ann. ca. 1314, Henry I, cc. 86, 101, 1:127, 133; Cf. the general chapter's warning that it was dangerous for the secret statutes of the order to be revealed to the laity: there were those outside the order who wanted to be present at the chapter, which would have been scandalous (ann. 1353, 3:462).

128. Ibid., ann. 1276, Yves II, c. 4, 1:62. Cf. the Cistercians' comparable but earlier legislation (*Stat. Ord. Cist.*, ann. 1217, cc. 10, 11, 1:467–468). Also see the heavy sanctions against denigrating and defaming other brothers (ibid., ann. 1217, c. 9, 1:466–467).

129. *Stat. Ord. Clun.*, 1292, 2:41. It was issued as a formal statute under Bertrand I (ann. 1301, c. 24, 1:73). Cf. the 1265 case of Prior Nicholas of Lausitz, Germany/Lorraine, 1:293–294.

130. Ibid., ann. ca. 1314, Henry I, c. 101, 1:133.

131. The inquiry was made by Maurin de Monteclaio, prior of La Voûte-Chilhac and visitor of France (ibid., ann. 1386, 3:188). There was also a continuing problem with students who were basically illiterate and ill-suited for learning. See ibid., ann. 1383, Provence, 3:167.

132. Ibid., ann. 1391, John II, c. 124, 1:162.

133. Ibid., ann. 1259, Nogent, France, 1:233.

134. *Statuta Petri Venerabilis*, c. 48, p. 79; also see cc. 23, 35, pp. 60, 70.

135. *Stat. Ord. Clun.*, ann. 1291, Vasto, France, 2:15.

136. Ibid., ann. 1276, Yves II, c. 3, 1:62.

137. Ibid., ann. 1281, St. Paul de Argon, Lombardy, 1:402.

138. Ibid., ann. 1341, Ventadour, Auvergne, 3:307. In this case the prior seems to have forgotten that he denied that a particular monk was defamed for incontinence and slipped up by admitting it later in the visit. In another instance, the brothers took an oath that a given monk was not defamed. The *diffinatores* determined that an inquisition was only necessary if there was subsequent scandal (ibid., ann. 1260, Crespy, France, 1:245).

139. Ibid., ann. 1260, Provence, 1:246.

140. Ibid., ann. 1400, Diedenhofen, France, 4:414; ann. 1400, Grosbois, France, 4:416; ann. 1400, Ligny-sur-Canche, France, 4:417; ann. 1401, Dompierre-sur-Authie, France, 4:440–441.

141. See, for example, the case of the prior of St.-Germain of Montluel who had been deposed for many "wicked things and excesses" (ibid., ann. 1390, Lyon, 4:277); the infirmarian of Volta (ann. 1397, Poitiers, 4:392); or the prior of St.-Denis-de-la-Chartres in Paris who was defamed for "grave and enormous crimes" (ann. 1402, 4:458).

142. For instance, in 1375 the visitations to Provence were disbanded "out of fear for the British troops remaining there" (ibid., ann. 1375, 3:101). At the priory of Niger Stabulum the visitors reported that the church and all of the buildings were destroyed by war (ibid., ann. 1385, Auvergne, 3:178). Also see the statement made by the *diffinatores* on behalf of the abbot regarding the deleterious effects of "mortalities, wars, and pestilence" (ann. 1392, 4:313). The church belonging to the priory of St.-Racho of Autun, moreover, was polluted by an effusion of blood (ann. 1396, Lyon, 4:378–379).

143. Separate rooms as well as beds with curtains were outlawed explicitly at the general chapter meeting of 1389 (ibid., 4:275). But infractions continued. See, for example, ann. 1390, Nantua, Lyon, 4:278; ann. 1390, Grand-Champ, France, 4:281; ann. 1391, St.-Stephen, Nevers, France, 4:290; ann. 1394, Nantua, France, 4:364. Nantua is also cited a couple of years later, the infraction seemingly compounded by the presence of locks that required a key (ann. 1396, 4:373–374; cf. ann. 1402, Abbeville, France, 4:465). There were also instances of the light in the dormitory not being lit as ordained by the rule (ann. 1394, Thiers, Auvergne, 4:359).

144. Ibid., ann. 1293, Ronsenac, Poitou, 2:43.

145. But since the monks had already been imprisoned for three months, their sentence was ultimately more clement: one of the offenders was to be moved and the other was sent to Cluny to be subjected to regular discipline for a year. The prior was hardly blameless: he had a reputation for mistreating his subordinates, had long been excommunicated, and was eventually deposed. Yet the abusive monks are murkily likened to beasts touching a holy mountain (presumably the abbot), who must therefore be destroyed (cf. Heb. 12:20), which conjures up the fate of animals that had been subjected to bestiality (*Stat. Ord. Clun.*, ann. 1404, Autheuil-en-Valois, France, 4:505). If this was a case of sexual abuse, its prosecution would be fraught with difficulties. In modern instances, assailants and victims alike are frequently united in their denials that any such abuse occurred. See Mariner, *No Escape*; Stemple, "Male Rape and Human Rights," 608–614.

146. See the example of the prior of Ecclesiis, discussed in n. 100 above.

147. In one case, the material under seal was deemed so sensitive that the visitors insisted that only one of the more important priors could be entrusted with taking it to Cluny. If the monk was found guilty, he too must go to Cluny (*Stat. Ord. Clun.*, ann. 1342, Montchatain, Gascony, 3:334). Cf. the many unspecified charges brought against a certain Arnald, including civil charges. The charges had been proven, and Arnald even admitted to them, yet the *diffinatores* were unclear on some points and insisted a special inquiry be conducted. The results were sent under seal to Cluny and, if Arnald was, indeed, found guilty, he was also cited to appear (ibid., ann. 1334, Ronsenac, Poitou, 3:176).

148. *ST* III supp., art. 2, q. 20, rep. obj. 1.

149. *Stat. Ord. Clun.*, ann. 1301, Bertrand I, c. 97, 1:84; also see ann. ca. 1314, Henry I, c. 8, 1:100; and ann. 1399, John II, c. 36, 1:151. A statute of 1301, however, did provide some licit substitutes who were permitted to absolve a reserved sin if the abbot was not available, and this included the visitors themselves (ann. ca. 1314, Henry I, c. 8, 1:100). Other surrogates for the abbot would have been the *camerarius* (head official for a given province), the prior or cloister prior of Cluny or whoever was acting in their place, or the companions and chaplains accompanying the abbot during his visitations.

150. Ibid., ann. 1313, Chaux-lès-Cherval, Germany/Lorraine, 2:346.

151. Ibid., ann. 1263, Lenton, England, 1:279. On monastic prisons, see Lusset, "Entre les murs," 153–167; apparently 33 percent of the cases judged by the general chapter between 1236 and 1481 resulted in imprisonment (ibid., 163).

CHAPTER 7

Note to epigraph: William Peraldus, *Summa aurea de virtutibus et viciis* 3.2.18.

1. See Constable, *Reformation of the Twelfth Century*, 100–101. Peter the Venerable made some changes to the status of the choirboys, challenging the older tradition that they were ineligible to become monks (*Statuta Petri Venerabilis*, c. 66, p. 97). He also said that the boys need no longer share the same refectory as the monks, as they had in the past (ibid., c. 56, pp. 85–86). When Abbot Hugh V reiterated Peter the Venerable's statute regarding the age of admission, he added the exception of "those from the school at Cluny, without whom the service of God is not accustomed to be done." He noted, however, that a new chorister could not be introduced until the voice of one of the other boys had changed (*Stat. Ord. Clun.*, ann. 1200, c. 6, 1:42–43). For the liturgical role of boys in the eleventh century, see Boynton and Cochelin, "Sociomusical Role of Child Oblates," 13–17.

2. *Stat. Ord. Clun.*, ann. 1301, Bertrand I, c. 125, 1:93.

3. There were, however, even earlier instances of children singing in various offices. See Wright, *Music and Ceremony*, 165; Kathleen Edwards, *English Secular Cathedrals*, 308–309.

4. See Boynton, "Liturgical Role of Children"; and Boynton, "Training for the Liturgy."

5. *RB*, c. 45, pp. 106–107.

6. Bernard of Cluny, *Ordo Cluniacensis*, 201.

7. Boynton, "Liturgical Role of Children," 197. Also see the discussion of children in the choir in Lanfranc's *Constitutions*, cited in Chapter 6, p. 149, above.

8. Boynton, "Boy Singers in Monasteries and Cathedrals," 37–38. On the Corvey fresco, see McClendon, *Origins of Medieval Architecture*, 189–191. On the importance of liturgical reform in the Carolingian Renaissance and its impact on young singers, whose training began very early, see Witt, *Two Latin Cultures*, 34, 36, 49–50; also see Donald A. Bullough, *Alcuin*, 176ff.

9. Greatrex, "Almonry of Norwich Cathedral Priory," 172; Orme, *Medieval Schools*, 279. I am indebted to Kathryn Kerby-Fulton for drawing Norwich's physical requirements to my attention. Secular patrons sometimes imposed their own requirements. See the sixteenth-century instance in which a choirboy, solicited by a royal patron, was rejected for his height (Kirkman, "Seeds of Medieval Music," 118).

10. Rastall, "Choirboys in Early English Religious Drama," 78–80; Kirkman, "Seeds of Medieval Music," 111–112.

11. Harris, *Obscene Pedagogies*, 191–192; Orme, *Education in the West of England*, 42–55, esp. 44. Woods's work is discussed in the Chapter 8, below.

12. Holsinger, *Music, Body, and Desire*, 272–282; Boynton and Rice, *Young Choristers*, introd., 8–10.

13. On the Guidonian scale, see *Summa musice*, c. 8, ed. Page, pp. 157–162 (trans., 72–78); Berger, "Guidonian Hand"; Wright, *Music and Ceremony*, 176–177. Although some boys may have received rudimentary instruction in polyphony, advanced polyphony required

the ability to read musical notation. It was performed by a small group of highly skilled adult males for most of the medieval period. Jean Gerson's rule required knowledge of counterpoint and descant, but choirboys only began singing composed polyphony in the early sixteenth century (Gerson, *Pro pueris ecclesiae Parisiensis*, 687; Wright, *Music and Ceremony*, 177, 185); cf. "Ordinances and Statutes of the Choristers," in Watkin, *Dean Cosyn*, 99, 105. In England, the choirboys did not receive instruction in written polyphony until after the mid-fifteenth century (Roger Bowers, "To Chorus from Quartet," 12–13).

14. "Ordinances and Statutes of the Choristers," in Watkin, *Dean Cosyn*, 103.

15. Utley, "The Choristers' Lament," lines 45–52, p. 197. For the use of the Guidonian scale in the poem, see Holsinger, "Langland's Musical Reader," 117–120, appendix, p. 136.

16. "Lamentation of Boys Learning Prick-Song," in Halliwell, *Moral Play of Wit and Science*, 63.

17. Kirkman, "Seeds of Medieval Music," 115–116.

18. Wright, *Music and Ceremony*, 165–166.

19. Kathleen Edwards, *English Secular Cathedrals*, 314–315; cf. fifteenth-century Cambrai, where former choristers who did not receive a position were sent to school with a parting gift from the chapter (Planchart, "Choirboys in Cambrai," 124).

20. Witt, *Two Latin Cultures*, 89; Kirkman, "Seeds of Medieval Music," 116.

21. Gerson, *Expostulatio adversus correptionem juventutis*, 27. For Gerson's attitude toward children, see D. Catherine Brown, *Pastor and Laity*, 238–245. For the impact of images on the imagination and its susceptibility to the demonic, see Elliott, *Fallen Bodies*, 40–44.

22. Gerson, *Expostulatio adversus correptionem juventutis*, 27–28. Gerson is probably indebted to Quintilian here, who claimed that Alexander had inherited several bad, but unspecified, habits from Leonidas, who was his tutor prior to Aristotle. Quintilian cites the Stoic philosopher Diogenes of Babylon (fl. mid-second century BCE) as his source, whose works only remain in fragments. Marcus Fabius Quintilian, *Institutio oratoria* 1.1.9, 1:24–25.

23. Gerson, *Expostulatio adversus correptionem juventutis*, 28.

24. A large number of such badges were discovered in the Zeeland delta alongside more conventional religious badges (Koldeweij, "Lifting the Veil on Pilgrim Badges," 165–166, 185–188, and plates 1, 5, 10, 11). There have been parallel findings in the riverbeds of Paris and London, dating from ca. 1350–1450 (Gilchrist, *Medieval Life*, 105).

25. Gerson, *Expostulatio adversus correptionem juventutis*, 28. Cf. Gerson, *Pour le jour des morts*, 556. On Gerson's mistrust of servants, see McGuire, *Jean Gerson*, 144.

26. Gerson repeats a number of biblical and classical authorities, while adding others (*De parvulis ad Christum trahendis*, 669–672, 674). He offers a more systematic account of the ways in which children can be scandalized, distinguishing between active and passive scandal (ibid., 672–677). Gerson's preoccupation with lascivious writings and simulacra are also in evidence (ibid., 673–674).

27. Ibid., 676.

28. Ibid., 681.

29. Ibid., 679. Cf. Gerson, *De arte audiendi confessiones*, 12; and *De confessione mollitei*, 71.

30. *Poenitemini: Contre la luxure . . . Par le merveilleux et charitable advent*, 832. See Gregory the Great's *Dialogues* 4.19.

31. Gerson, *De cognitione castitatis*, 54. See D. Catherine Brown, *Pastor and Laity*, 239.

32. Gerson, *De confessione mollitie*, 71–73.

33. Gerson, *Poenitemini: Contre la luxure . . . En l'advent de N.S.J.C.*, 838; cf. *Poenitemini: Contre la luxure . . . Par le merveilleux et charitable advent*, 832. See also McGuire, *Jean Gerson*, 142–143.

34. Gerson, *De confessione mollitie*, 71–72.

35. Gerson, *De parvulis ad Christum trahendis*, 677.

36. Gerson, *En la fête de la Sainte Trinité*, 1124–1125. Intolerance for children's vices was hardly limited to Gerson. According to Marc Boone, nineteen of the ninety individuals burned for sodomy in fifteenth-century Burgundy were characterized by diminutives and, hence, were clearly not adults ("State Power and Illicit Sexuality," 151).

37. Gerson, *De parvulis ad Christum trahendis*, 669.

38. Gerson, *Pro pueris ecclesiae Parisiensis*, 686. I am indebted to Jessalynn Bird for referring me to this treatise. It is a partially translated in Wright, *Music and Ceremony*, 166–169.

39. Gerson, *Pro pueris ecclesiae Parisiensis*, 688–689.

40. Ibid., 687.

41. Ibid., 687–688. There was also more provision for the children's playtime (although a master was always to be present). Two boys to a bed was not unusual. See Kirkman, "Seeds of Medieval Music," 109 and n. 47, below.

42. Gerson, *Pro pueris ecclesiae Parisiensis*, 687.

43. Ibid., 689.

44. Ibid., 686. The magister is assisted by the *spe*—a former choirboy whose voice has broken. See Chartier, *L'Ancien chapitre de Notre-Dame*, 60–61; Wright, *Music and Ceremony*, 171. Gerson recommended simple switches that would do no real harm (*Pro pueris ecclesiae Parisiensis*, 689). But the potential for the master's correction becoming physically abusive was realized at the collegiate church of St.-Omer in northern France. Malin Alixandre was fired for his beating of the choristers (Kirkman, "Seeds of Medieval Music," 104–106.) Contemporaneous regulations for choirboys at the cathedral of Rouen stipulated that the rods for the little boys (*parvi pueri*) be kept behind the high altar (November 21, 1413, as cited by Collette, *Histoire de la maîtrise de Rouen*, 13–14 n. 3).

45. "Wenest thu, usch, with thi coyntyse," lines 1–6, in Duncan, *Medieval English Lyrics*, 307. Lincoln Cathedral MS 132, fol. 100r, was written between the school texts of *Accentuarius* and *Dictionarius*.

46. "Ordinances and Statutes of the Choristers," in Watkin, *Dean Cosyn*, 99, 102. On English cathedrals generally, see Orme, *History of England's Cathedrals*, esp. 66–68.

47. "Ordinances and Statutes," in Watkin, *Dean Cosyn*, 107–108. As at Notre Dame, the boys shared beds with one another, only here, the boys slept three in a bed, head to toe (108).

48. Orme, *Medieval Schools*, 280–281; Greatrex, "Almonry of Norwich Cathedral Priory," 172–173. On the different possibilities for living arrangements for choristers and their responsibilities, see Kathleen Edwards, *English Secular Cathedrals*, 310–317. Monasteries also had almonry schools, but they were not used to train professional choristers. See Roger Bowers, "Almonry Schools of the English Monasteries," 186.

49. "Ordinacio puerorum de choro ecclesie Lincoln.," in Bradshaw and Wordsworth, *Statutes of Lincoln Cathedral*, 3:162. This statute was entered into the cathedral's book of ordinances in 1525 (Bradshaw and Wordsworth, *Statutes*, 1:410). See A. Hamilton Thompson, "Notes on Colleges of Secular Canons," 144, 154–156.

50. *Liber Niger,* in Bradshaw and Wordsworth, *Statutes of Lincoln Cathedral,* 1:410; "Ordinacio puerorum de choro ecclesie Lincoln.," in Bradshaw and Wordsworth, *Statutes of Lincoln Cathedral,* 3:162. See Lepine, *Brotherhood of Canons,* 175–176. Prior to 1264, the supervision of the boys fell to the cantor. See Bradshaw's comments, in *Statutes of Lincoln Cathedral,* 3:161. The boys' choir becomes progressively prominent from the late fourteenth century, even as the prominence of adult voices declines. See Owen, "Lincoln Cathedral: Music and Worship," 57–58.

51. *Dioc. Linc.,* 1:139. The vicars choral, discussed below, received a similar rebuke (1:140). For the protocol for such visitations, see A. Hamilton Thompson's introduction, ibid., 1:ix–xii. On the interconnection between learning grammar, reading, and singing, see Zieman, *Singing the New Song,* 10–39.

52. *Dioc. Linc.,* 1:142.

53. Gray also attempted to clarify the process. The boys selected should be presented to the dean and chapter, provided they are found "fit and suitable in morals and birth and voice." Boys who were remiss or caught fooling around would receive light chastisement; more serious infractions were corrected by the dean and chapter or their delegates. *Novum registrum,* in Bradshaw and Wordsworth, *Statutes of Lincoln Cathedral,* 3:298–299. Note, however, that the dean and his retainers revolted against Gray's ruling, and it never came into effect. See Christopher Wordsworth's introduction to *Award of William Alnwick,* ed. and trans. Woolley, 23. The ordinance appears in Alnwick's so-called *Novum registrum,* which was intended to supplant earlier ones, but this work was never ratified by the chapter. See Wordsworth's introd., 35–47; Bradshaw's comments in *Statutes of Lincoln Cathedral,* 1:155–160; and Maddison, "Visitation of Lincoln Cathedral," 14–15.

54. On Alnwick's career, see A. Hamilton Thompson's introductory notes in *Dioc. Linc.,* 1:xviii–xix; 2.1:xiv–xxx.

55. *Detecta in visitacione* (1437), in Bradshaw and Wordsworth, *Lincoln Cathedral Statutes,* 3:366–392. See Maddison's summary in "Visitation of Lincoln Cathedral," 14–23; A. Hamilton Thompson, *English Clergy,* 91–93.

56. "Examinacio vicariorum chori" (1437), in Bradshaw and Wordsworth, *Lincoln Cathedral Statutes,* 3:402 (testimony of William Burn); note that the inquest regarding the vicars choral and choristers was undertaken by Alnwick's *officialis* Robert Thornton (ibid., 392). On the office of *officialis,* see Paul Fournier, *Officialités au Moyen Âge,* 3–24; Helmholz, *Oxford History of the Laws of England,* 1:140–142; A. Hamilton Thompson, *English Clergy,* 48–52; and Chapter 9, p. 216, below.

57. "Examinacio vicariorum chori" (1437), in Bradshaw and Wordsworth, *Lincoln Cathedral Statutes,* 3:404 (testimony of Thomas Darby).

58. Ibid., 415. Despite Bishop Alnwick's best efforts to arbitrate between the dean and the chapter, the two parties persisted in their hostilities, and in 1439 the bishop was again required to adjudicate. See *Award of William Alnwick,* 52ff.

59. "Examinacio choristarum" (1437), in Bradshaw and Wordsworth, *Lincoln Cathedral Statutes,* 3:413 (testimony of William Langholme, John Paronell).

60. Ibid., 413–414 (testimony of Robert Ford, John Woodcock, John Paronell).

61. Ibid. (testimony of John Woodcock, John Corbrig). The precentor was in debt and had already been charged with not feeding the choir properly (ibid., 392 [testimony of William Grantham, vicar and vice-chancellor]).

62. Ibid., 415 (testimony of John Twhyng).

63. John Bowers, "Performing Ensemble for English Church Polyphony," 176 n. 33.

64. Simony Darcy had fathered an illegitimate child and was promoted without a dispensation (see "Examinacio vicariorum chori" [1437] in Bradshaw and Wordsworth, *Lincoln Cathedral Statutes*, 3:394 [testimony of William Shipton], 3:402 [testimony of John Hamond]); John Skynner was widely known to be having an affair with the wife of a certain weaver (3:395 [testimony of Walter Proctour], 3:396 [testimony of Rogerus Nevel]). John Skynner retaliated by asserting that Thomas Savage, a canon, had fathered a child with two different married women—one in another parish and the other married to a servant of Thomas, Ricardus Ffydler; that a servant of the chancellor was fornicating with another servant; and that John Ouerton, a fellow vicar, was fornicating with a woman in another parish (3:398).

65. See the testimonies of William Grantham, Richard Coupeland, John Barkeworth, William Muskham, and Thomas Bentley (ibid., 3:392–393, 401, 413–414). Also see Zieman, *Singing the New Song*, 66–72.

66. "Examinacio vicariorum chori" (1437) in Bradshaw and Wordsworth, *Lincoln Cathedral Statutes*, 3:397 (testimony of Will'us Quentoñ).

67. "Vicars Statutes," in Watkin, *Dean Cosyn*, 144–147. On the evolution of this body, see Dobson, "English Vicars Choral"; and Barrow, "Origins of Vicars Choral." On their housing at Lincoln and the changes made by various bishops, including Bishop Alnwick, see Stocker, "Development of the College of the Vicars Choral."

68. A. Hamilton Thompson, "Notes on Colleges of Secular Canons," 148–149.

69. Maddison, *Short Account of the Vicars Choral*, 29. Cf. Robertson, *Sarum Close*, 52.

70. The fact that another errant vicar at Salisbury was sent to the grammar school with the charge of memorizing his psalter and book of antiphons as punishment suggests that many of them were quite young. See Robertson, *Sarum Close*, 57. In 1445, Thomas Beckynton, bishop of Wells, commissioned an inquest since so many of the vicars were accused "of many excesses insolences and abuses" and who, in times past, had created "seditions, discords, tumults, insults, conventicles, conspiracies, conjurations and confederacies," *Register of Thomas Beckynton*, no. 172, pp. 51–52. Four years later, Beckynton instituted statutes in an attempt to tame the unruly lot. The long list of sanctions includes prohibitions against swearing ($\frac{1}{4}$ d. for responding in kind to someone else's curse; $\frac{1}{2}$ d. for cursing by the spirit or members of Christ); arguing at table; keeping horses and hounds; making noise after curfew (20d.); abusing another verbally (7d.) or physically (20d.); leaving the door open after curfew (1d.); admitting women to their houses (with the threat of losing the house after the third offense); and hitting the servants (20d.) Some of the statutes have a distinctly monastic flavor. For instance, revealing anything to the prejudice of one's fellow clerics, either secretly or publicly, is punished with ostracism, while two vicars caught cohabiting were heavily fined (a hefty 40s.).

71. Robertson, *Sarum Close*, 52. Cf. Maddison, *Short Account of the Vicars Choral*, 28.

72. St. Mary's began as a hospital with simple chaplains and a warden but was transformed into a college of canons headed by a dean in the mid-fourteenth century. See A. Hamilton Thompson, *History of the Hospital*, 11–40. In 1450, St. Mary's was among the select sixty-five cathedral or collegiate churches that had a musical culture of polyphony, probably engaging adult professionals (Roger Bowers, "To Chorus from Quartet," 11 n. 19).

73. See the founding documents in A. Hamilton Thompson, *History of the Hospital*, 52, 71, 78.

74. *Dioc. Linc.*, 2.1:204; cf. his injunction regarding the boys themselves "that they mind the rod, learning [and] discipline" (2.1:194).

75. *Dioc. Linc.*, 2.1:188. On Alnwick's visit and injunctions, see A. Hamilton Thompson, *History of the Hospital*, 104–116; the case of John Dey is discussed at 111–112. It is also discussed briefly in Bryan, "*Vae mundo a scandalis*," 171–172; and Salih, "Sexual Identities," 23–24. Katherine Zieman's "Minding the Rod" is dedicated to this case. I learned of this study (which Dr. Zieman kindly shared with me in manuscript) subsequent to drafting this chapter.

76. See the testimony of Thomas Halywelle (canon), the only denunciation that alludes to sodomy (*Dioc. Linc.*, 2.1:191). Other accusations simply note Dey's tavern activity. See Richard Greve (vicar) and John Bramburghe (canon), 2.1:198.

77. *Dioc. Linc.*, 2.1:194.

78. Lincolnshire County Archives MS Vj/1 on fol. 103r. The folio was badly damaged by water, and I am indebted to Louisa Foroughi for her help with the transcription.

79. Secular courts developed similar grids. As Puff has shown, the presence or absence of ejaculation determined whether or not sodomy would be treated as a capital offense in Germany and Switzerland (*Sodomy*, 28).

80. See, for example, the case brought before the Bolognese podestà in 1435 concerning two Jews who violated a young girl of eleven and sodomized a youth, both of whom were also Jewish (Lett, "Genre, enfance et violence sexuelle.")

81. *Dioc. Linc.*, 2.1:198.

82. Lincolnshire County Archives MS Vj/1fol. 103r.

83. *Dioc. Linc.*, 2.1:194–195.

84. *Dioc. Linc.*, 2.1:197; he was still required to appear before the bishop or his *officialis* the following Saturday "to receive and do further in respect of the foregoing things [*prae-missis*] and by reason thereof what the sacred canons and holy father may prescribe and decree as regards the foregoing things [*praemissis*]." A. Hamilton Thompson translates *praemissis* as "premises," which does not make much sense. I am assuming the bishop is alluding to the canonical, penitential, and practical implications of John's sin and deposition. On canonries and prebends, see A. Hamilton Thompson, "Notes on Colleges of Secular Canons," 148–151.

85. According to A. Hamilton Thompson, Dey did resign the living soon after, however (*Dioc. Linc.*, 2.1: lx–lxi).

86. Lincolnshire County Archives MS Vj/1, fol. 102v.

87. Testimony of Dean William Whalesby, *Dioc. Linc.*, 2.1:189; cf. Sir John Bram-burghe's testimony, 2.1:198.

88. *Dioc. Linc.*, 2.1:191.

89. John Bramburghe (canon), *Dioc. Linc.*, 2.1:199.

90. He cleared himself alongside William Chelle (canon, whose offense is unspecified) and Shiryngham and Bedale, both canons (William Bedale, *Dioc. Linc.*, 2.1:190; cf. 2.1:194). Richard Spurnere (vicar) testifies that Bramburghe receives low women and even whores (*Dioc. Linc.*, 2.1:193); also see the testimony of Thomas Halywalle, who claims that Bram-burghe and Shiryngham both have recourse to the same woman, who also bakes their bread (2.1:192).

91. Dean William Walesby, *Dioc. Linc.*, 2.1:188; cf. William Bedale (canon) at 2.1:189; and the testimony of John Gaddesby (canon) at 2.1:192.

92. Dean William Walesby, *Dioc. Linc.*, 2.1:188–189. Both Shyringham and Welles were accused of relapsing into sins for which they had already been cited and corrected.

93. *Dioc. Linc.*, 2.1:194. He cleared himself with Bedale, Welles, and Gaddesby. With respect to the two other women, Robert asserted that he had already cleared himself of one of these charges and would produce his certificate of purgation. He claimed to have no knowledge of the other woman.

94. Robert Matfene (canon), *Dioc. Linc.*, 2.1:191. Richard maintained that he purged himself of this charge seven years earlier.

95. The exception may be Master John Atkynson, rector of a nearby church, boarding with one of the canons. He supposedly admitted suspect women into his chantry, especially one particular matron. Yet there is no mention of either his purgation or punishment (Dean William Walesby, *Dioc. Linc.*, 2.1:189). A. Hamilton Thompson suggests that Atkynson held one of the college's chantries before his preferment (*Dioc. Linc.*, 2.1:189 n. 3; cf. Robert Matfene, at 2.1:191).

96. See Donahue, "Proof by Witnesses," 130–131.

97. Ibid., 143.

98. John Fentone (prior), *Dioc. Linc.*, 2.2:220. Also see the visitation of Ramsey Abbey in 1439, at which it was found that both the infirmary and the cells of monks were overrun with extraneous boys (*Dioc. Linc.*, 2.2:315). See Cheney, *Episcopal Visitation of Monasteries*, 54–103.

99. Brother William Thorntone, *Dioc. Linc.*, 2.2:223.

100. Brother William Markeby, *Dioc. Linc.*, 2.2:224.

101. *Dioc. Linc.*, 2.2:222.

102. Brother John Yorke (cellarer), *Dioc. Linc.*, 2.2:221.

103. Brother William Saltfletby, Brother Robert Welle (subcellarer), *Dioc. Linc.*, 2.2:221–222.

104. *Dioc. Linc.*, 2.2:224.

105. Brother John Yorke (cellarer), *Dioc. Linc.*, 2.2:221.

106. The problem with choirboys continues well beyond the period under discussion. See Conclusion, below.

107. The documents for the case are in the Fondation des Archives de l'ancien Évêché de Bâle (Porrentruy), AAEB A 85/83. It has been edited by Bernd-Ulrich Hergemöller, in *Chorknaben und Bäckerknechte*, 103–118. See discussions by Puff, *Sodomy*, 38–40; Puff, "Localizing Sodomy," 171–175, 189–191; Albert, *Der gemeine Mann vor dem geistlichen Richter*, 139. Hergemöller also edits the 1416 case of the Dominican theologian Heinrich von Rheinfelden, who was accused of sexual overtures by various servants, in *Chorknaben und Bäckerknechte*, 29–59.

108. Hergemöller, *Chorknaben und Bäckerknechte*, doc. A, pp. 104–105.

109. Ibid., 105–106.

110. Ibid., 106.

111. Ibid., doc. B, pp. 107–108.

112. Ibid., 108.

113. Not all of the documents seem to be extant. But there is a letter of intervention by the governor that clarifies that situation (Hergemöller, *Chorknaben und Bäckerknechte*, doc. C, pp. 108–110), as well as a document signed by Stocker's allies, promising payment of the fine. This agreement is a chirograph, meaning that the document is written in duplicate and cut in half—one half for each party (ibid., doc. D, pp. 110–111).

114. Ibid., doc. E.c, p. 117.

115. *Basler Chroniken*, ann. 1475, ed. Vischer and Boos, 2:239. It is possible that the chronicler's mention of two victims somehow conflates the other children allegedly harmed by Stocker—mentioned by the canon who sought to warn Müller.

116. Puff, *Sodomy*, 35–43.

117. Albert, *Der gemeine Mann vor dem geistlichen Richter*, 193–196.

CHAPTER 8

Note to epigraphs: *VA* 1.11, 21 (I have adjusted this translation slightly for a more literal rendering); Augustine, *De libero arbitrio* 1.3, *PL* 32:1223 (I am indebted to Barbara Newman for this reference).

1. See Jaeger, *Envy of Angels*, chap. 4; Bynum, *Docere verbo et exemplo*, 77–98.

2. Hexter, *Ovid and Medieval Schooling*.

3. Woods, "Rape and the Pedagogical Rhetoric," 60–61, 66. For the tendency to highlight sex and violence, see Woods, "Teaching of Poetic Composition," 127–130; Woods, "Teaching of Writing," 88–91.

4. Carruthers, *Book of Memory*, 134.

5. Woods, *Classroom Commentaries*, 60.

6. Chronopoulos, "Ganymede in the Medieval Classroom." Similar changes occur in commentaries on Ovid. See Hexter, *Ovid and Medieval Schooling*, 74–75, 198.

7. Woods, "Rape and Pedagogical Rhetoric," 69.

8. Woods, "Weeping for Dido."

9. Stapleton, *Harmful Eloquence*, 58.

10. Ibid., 59–63.

11. Stehling, *Medieval Latin Poems of Male Love*, no. 91, pp. 94, 95. This poem was later added to a ninth-century manuscript. I have changed the translation slightly to make it more literal. See Boswell, *Christianity*, 261–262. Cf. Stehling, *Medieval Latin Poems*, nos. 92, 93, pp. 94, 95 (from the same manuscript), and no. 123, pp. 138, 139 (from a late thirteenth-century manuscript).

12. See Chapter 4, pp. 91–92, above.

13. Godrey of Winchester, in Stehling, *Medieval Latin Poems*, no. 43, pp. 26, 27. Note, however, that the phrase, "Tu peccare doces, peccandi ponis habenas"—translated by Stehling as "you teach sin and put curbs on sinning"—is translated by Boswell as "you teach them to sin, while you impose the penance" ("Dante and the Sodomites," 70).

14. Walter of Châtillon, in Stehling, *Medieval Latin Poems*, no. 79, pp. 80, 81.

15. John of Hauteville, *Architrenius* 3.1–16, pp. 60–79. William J. Courtenay's analysis of a *computus* recording the money exacted from masters and students on the basis of income suggests that this situation had improved by the fourteenth-century (*Parisian Scholars*, 95–96).

16. Karras, *From Boys to Men*, 69–70. For an introduction to the schools at Paris and Lincoln, see Goering, *William de Montibus*, 29–57.

17. Thomas of Chobham, *Summa confessorum*, art. 5, dist. 4, q. 7a, p. 298. In this instance, sodomy is evoked by innuendo since Thomas only identifies the temptation to take bribes and possible failure to inculcate good morals as dangers.

18. Baldwin, *Masters*, 1:139–140. For documents related to the Victorines' confessional responsibilities, see Peter of Poitiers, *Summa de confessione*, Longère's introd., lxxv–lxxxvii.

19. Baldwin, *Masters*, 1:337ff.

20. Robert of Courson, *Summa* 23.3, MS Paris BN 14524, fol. 84v, as quoted in Baldwin, *Masters*, 2:231–232 n. 219. Also see Baldwin's summary of Robert's position on clerical celibacy in ibid., 1:339–340. Robert anticipates parallel associations made by Wycliffe (Dinshaw, *Getting Medieval*, 62); and the fifteenth-century reformer Bishop Johann Schele of Lübeck (Karras, *Unmarriages*, 123). Robert also tells young girls who know that their confessor is either a revealer of confessions or likely to incite them to sin that they should either ask their parents or a close friend to be present at their confession (Kennedy, "Robert of Courson on Penance," 305). I am grateful to Barbara Newman for bringing this to my attention.

21. Thibodeaux, *Manly Priest*, 82.

22. Peter the Chanter, *Verbum abbreviatum, textus prior*, c. 25, p. 640.

23. Woods, *Classroom Commentaries*, 48; Woods, "Teaching of Writing," 90. One theory was that this work was commissioned as an indictment of the vices of Roger of Pont l'Évêque, the archbishop of York (see William Burgwinkle, *Sodomy, Masculinity, and Law*, 275 n. 17). Roger is discussed above, in the Prologue to Part II.

24. Alford, "Grammatical Metaphor."

25. Alan of Lille, *De planctu Naturae*, p. 806; trans., 67–68. For the place of grammar in the curriculum, see Orme, *Medieval Schools*, 171–75; Ziolkowski, *Alan of Lille's Grammar of Sex*, 77–107. For the association between grammar and nature, see Alford, "Grammatical Metaphor," 751–754. On the evolution of the persona of Nature and Alan's place in this discourse, see Curtius, *European Literature*, 106–113, 117–121; Barbara Newman, *God and the Goddesses*, 51–66; Economou, *Goddess Natura*, 58–72. Like the Chanter, Alan also believes that polyphony introduces homoerotic barbarisms into music (Alan of Lille, *De planctu Naturae*, 818; trans., 100. See Holsinger, *Music, Body, and Desire*, 139–140).

26. Gautier of Coincy, *De Sainte Léocade*, lines 1211–1315, pp. 171–74. On God's Book of Memory, see Elliott, "Violence Against the Dead," 1022–1023.

27. Gilles of Corbeil, *Hierapigra*, 362. The anonymous "Debate Between Ganymede and Helen" makes similar use of grammar. See Woods, "Teaching of Writing," 91–92.

28. The poet blames Innocent III for forcing the clergy into sodomy, regarding him not as "Innocentius" but "nocens" (harming) (Dobiache-Rojdesvensky, *Poésies des Goliards*, 127).

29. Baldwin, *Masters*, 1:6. Although Baldwin assumes most of the Chanter's responsibilities would have been delegated to the subchanter, there is, however, as Baldwin himself notes, an episode described in the fragmentary prologue to his *Summa* in which he has to adjudicate over two clerics who saw fit to duke it out in the choir (*Summa de sacramentis, Prolegomena*, 3:1, 311–332, 327–328 (the same story from two different manuscripts). This suggests a degree of involvement.

30. See *Summa musice*, c. 24, ed. Page, pp. 200–202 (trans., 124–126). Although basically a manual for plainchant, this is the first work to use the word "polyphony" (see Page's introd., p. 30). The names of the various aspects of polyphony differ from the ones traditionally used at Paris, hence Page argues that it was written in Germany (pp. 6–7).

31. Holsinger, *Music, Body, and Desire*, 157–175. This is very much in keeping with Peter the Chanter's proto-puritanical views on entertainment. See Baldwin, *Masters*, 1:200–203. John of Salisbury, who also studied at Paris, likewise associated the new music with effeminacy. See Knapp, "Polyphony at Notre Dame of Paris," 557.

32. Holsinger, *Music, Body, and Desire*, 141–152. On Leoninus, see Wright, *Music and Ceremony*, 281–288; on his influence, see 243ff.

33. Peter of Poitiers, *Summa de confessione*, c. 43, p. 53.

34. The composition for the Chanter's predecessor was written for three voices. See Wright, *Music and Ceremony*, 31–32. A *conductus* is a sacred but nonliturgical piece of music at which Notre Dame excelled. See Knapp, "Polyphony at Notre Dame," 626–628.

35. Gilles of Corbeil, *Hierapigra*, 362; and Vieillard, *Gilles de Corbeil*, 257–258; for a summary of the poem, see 79–95.

36. Gilles of Corbeil, *Hierapigra*, 364; Vieillard, *Gilles de Corbeil*, 429–432. On Gilles's debt to Peter the Chanter, see Baldwin, *Masters*, 1:41.

37. Davy, *Sermons universitaires parisiens*, 379–380; for a description of Bibl. Nat., Nouv. Acq. Lat. MS 338, from which the sermon is edited, see Davy, *Sermons*, 3–22. I am indebted to Jessalyn Bird for this reference. On the association between the clergy's sexual abuse of children and the Holy Innocents, see Chapter 3, p. 64 above, and Chapter 4, p. 93, above).

38. Davy, *Sermons universitaires parisiens*, 380–381.

39. Ibid., 381.

40. *Distichs of Cato* 4.6, pp. 34–35.

41. Augustine, *Confessiones* 1.9.14, *CSEL* 33:12–13; trans. http://www.newadvent.org/fathers/110101.htm.

42. Othloh of St. Emmeram, *Liber visionum*, vis. 3, *MGH QQ zur Geistesgesch.* 13:45–52.

43. Damian, Ep. 161, to the monks of Monte Cassino, *Briefe*, 4.4:135–144; trans., 7:131–141. He encouraged the monks to resume their public flagellations on Fridays after they had been mocked and forbidden by Cardinal Stephen of St. Chrysogonus (ibid., 138; trans., 134). For a discussion of Damian's initiative in promoting private and self-imposed floggings, see Largier, *In Praise of the Whip*, 75–100; Damian, Ep. 45, to the clerics of the church of Florence, ca. 1055, *Briefe*, 4.2:38; trans., 2:248.

44. Guibert of Nogent, *Autobiographie* 1.5, p. 34.

45. Ann. 1357, *ASDL*, *Criminali* 9, fol. 165v. On the trope of mothers objecting to pedagogical beatings, see Eve Salisbury, " 'Spare the Rod,' " 151.

46. "I wold fayn be a clarke," lines 21–25, in Duncan, *Medieval English Lyrics*, 306–307. See Harris, *Obscene Pedagogies*, 192.

47. As cited by Stewart, *Close Readers*, 88–89.

48. Parsons, "Beaten for a Book," 186; Orme, *Medieval Schools*, 146; Salisbury, " 'Spare the Rod,' " 144–146.

49. The birch was favored especially by English masters, but there was also the ferule—a wooden ruler with a wider end for hitting the hand used for minor offenses. It had a hole for the specific purpose of causing a blister (Orme, *Medieval Schools*, 144–145).

50. Parsons, "Beaten for a Book," 167–168.

51. At least on this occasion, the student was remunerated financially. See Stewart, *Close Readers*, 93.

52. Nelson, *Fifteenth Century School Book*, c. 118, p. 29. On these exercise books, including summaries of select ones, see Orme, *Education and Society*, 73–121; Parsons, "Beaten for a Book," 180–181.

53. Nelson, *Fifteenth Century School Book*, cc. 119–120, p. 29. Cf. Salisbury's discussion of a late fifteenth-century sermon preached by a boy bishop in which a boy, wishing to be spared the image of Jeremiah's "waking rod," fantasizes about compelling the master to commit suicide (" 'Spare the Rod,' " 147).

54. Nelson, *Fifteenth Century School Book*, c. 141, p. 34. I have modernized this text.

55. Ibid., c. 126, p. 31.

56. Ibid., c. 144, pp. 34–35.

57. Orme, *English School Exercises*, introd. 16–17.

58. On the manuscript tradition, see Orme's introductory notes, *English School Exercises*, 257–259.

59. Oxford and Winchester, ca. 1483, c. 10, in Orme, *English School Exercises*, p. 262.

60. Ibid., c. 42, p. 273.

61. Ibid., c. 59, p. 283.

62. Ibid., c. 48, c. 15, pp. 275–276, 264.

63. Ibid., c. 18, p. 265. Cf. similar self-congratulatory entries: "Although the discretion of the master will choose to give beatings rather than favour to those who are badly governed, he is nevertheless disposed to favour me, who at the solemn occasion yesterday was ruled the best-behaved boy according to his praise" (London, ca. 1450–1470, c. 61, in Orme, *English School Exercises*, 206).

64. Oxford and Winchester, c. 58, pp. 281–283.

65. Ibid., c. 55, pp. 280–281.

66. Ibid., c. 17, p. 265. Cf. "My schoolfellow is a glutton, a busybody, a worthless fellow and a lecher, and therefore it is hateful for me to sit with him at table" (ibid., c. 12, p. 263); and "Although my school fellow is large, he is childish" (ibid., c. 43, p. 274).

67. Ibid., c. 53, p. 279.

68. Ibid., c. 22, p. 266.

69. Ibid., c. 59, p. 283.

70. Ibid., c. 84, p. 291.

71. Abelard, *Historia calamitatum*, 183; trans., 10–11.

72. Barbara Newman, *Making Love in the Twelfth Century*, 44–48. On the authenticity of these letters, see Jaeger, *Ennobling Love*, 160–170; Mews, *Lost Love Letters of Heloise and Abelard*, 115–144; Mews, "Philosophical Themes," 37–38. Also see Jaeger's defense of their authenticity in "*Epistolae duorum amantium*"; Constable's skeptical reply ("Authorship of the *Epistolae duorum amantium*"); and Jaeger's response ("A Reply").

73. Ep. 29, trans. Barbara Newman, *Making Love in the Twelfth Century*, 126.

74. Epp. 59, 60, trans. Barbara Newman, in *Making Love in the Twelfth Century*, 160, 162; Mews, "Philosophical Themes," 47.

75. Abelard, Ep. 4, to Heloise, "Personal Letters Between Abelard and Heloise," 89; trans., 81. Cf. Barbara Newman, *Making Love in the Twelfth Century*, prol. 36–37. On Abelard's efforts to disparage sex generally, and their sexual past in particular, see Elliott, *Bride of Christ*, 128–130, 135–137, 147–148.

76. See Clanchy's timeline in *Letters of Abelard and Heloise*, ix and lxxiv. Also see how an older age concurs with Abelard's association of Heloise with the status of deaconess (Elliott, *Bride of Christ*, 343 n. 195).

77. Before her formal entrance into religion, Abelard hid Heloise among the nuns at Argenteuil, which Fulbert saw as forcing his niece into religion. This precipitated Abelard's castration (Elliott, *Bride of Christ*, 128). Heloise emphasizes repeatedly that she entered religion at his command (ibid., 126–127). If Barbara Newman is correct about Heloise's seduction, her voluntary subordination to Abelard corresponded to her sexual initiation.

78. Jean de Meun, *Romance of the Rose*, lines 8745ff., pp. 177ff.

79. Woods, "Rape and the Pedagogical Rhetoric," 60–64.

80. Jean de Meun, *Romance of the Rose*, lines 21539ff., pp. 459ff.

81. Otto of St. Blaise, *Chronici ab Ottone Frisigensi, Continuatio Sanblasiana*, ann. 1198, c. 47, *MGH SS* 20:329–330.

82. Roger Bacon, *Compendium studii philosophiae*, c. 2, 1:411.

83. Ibid., 412. I am indebted to Thomas Maloney, who is working on an edition and translation of this work, for drawing this to my attention. Bacon goes on to reflect grimly that those who, through God's grace, manage to reform themselves after the age of thirty, are prone to the even worse spiritual sins of cupidity and avarice. Their insatiable ambition leads to jealousy, hatred, litigation, and tedium. Despite their learning, they perform the divine offices by rote: "Just as boys, they bawl out the psalter which they had once taught and recite the divine offices like rural clerics and priests, who understand little or nothing, just like brutes" (ibid., 412–413).

84. In England, a criminous cleric could still be tried and fined in a secular court but had to be handed over to the ecclesiastical tribunal (which did not administer the death penalty) for more serious infractions (Helmholz, *Oxford History of the Laws of England*, 1:125). A cleric could, however, be tried and punished by a secular tribunal once he had been degraded and was no longer a cleric. See Elliott, "Dressing and Undressing the Clergy," 60–69.

85. The defendant, though found guilty, was released after a short bout in prison and payment of a fine (which was contested). See Courtenay, *Parisian Scholars*, 49–56.

86. Thijssen, *Censure and Heresy at the University of Paris*.

87. Guérard, *Cartulaire*, September 1205, no. 120, 1:113. The bishop was so shocked when the priest was wounded by a guard in the second prison that he pardoned him on condition of an oath of good behavior. This charter was witnessed by both Robert of Flamborough and Peter of Poitiers (Baldwin, *Masters*, 1:32, 33).

88. Robert Grosseteste, Ep. 10, to N., "Reprehensio grauis," ed. Mantello, app. 455; trans., 80.

89. Ibid., app., 456; trans., 81.

90. Thomas of Cantimpré, *De apibus* 2.30.8, pp. 323–324.

91. Le Roy Ladurie, *Montaillou*, 144–149. Arnold has also been discussed at length by Arnold, *Inquisition and Power*, 214–225. Arnold's trial appears in Duvernoy, *Registre*, 3:14–62. The bulk of it has been translated by Michael Goodich, in *Other Middle Ages*, pp. 119–142, but the translation contains errors and should be used with caution.

92. Duvernoy, *Registre*, 3:39 (Arnold of Verniolle). This could be because Arnold's (older?) brother was also in the bed.

93. Testimony of Peter Recort, in Duvernoy, *Registre*, 3:32. Cf. Elena Brizio's discussion of the alleged rapes of a twelve-year-old and an eight-year-old, both of whom were attending schools run by clerics ("Sexual Violence," 46–49).

94. We can estimate Arnold's age since he claimed that he was ten or twelve when he attended Master Pons's school some twenty years earlier.

95. Testimony of Arnold of Verniolle, in Duvernoy, *Registre*, 3:40.

96. Ibid., 40–41.

97. William Roux's testimony, in Duvernoy, *Registre*, 3:17.

98. Ibid., 18.

99. Ibid., 19; testimony of Arnold of Verniolle, in Duvernoy, *Registre*, 3:42.

100. Duvernoy, *Registre*, 3:41 (Arnold of Verniolle).

101. Ibid., 19 (William Roux) and 25 (William Bernard).

102. Ibid., 20 (William Roux).

103. Ibid., 41 (Arnold of Verniolle). Arnold would also use the story of the canon on others. See William Bernard's account, where it was a preliminary to seduction (ibid., 23), and Arnold's own account of what he told William Bernard (44). Interestingly, when an unnamed apprentice to a shoemaker (different from the one discussed below) needed a new master, Arnold told him about a different canon, one who was allegedly morally upright. When the boy made sexual advances, Arnold rebuffed him. Clearly he did not find the second boy attractive (45).

104. Ibid., 40, 42–43.

105. Ibid., 43; see also p. 31 (Peter Recort).

106. Ibid., 42, 49 (Arnold of Verniolle).

107. Ibid., 43.

108. See Arnold's testimony when he confessed to showing William Roux how to masturbate in the event that he did not have access to a male partner (ibid., 43).

109. Ibid., 32 (Peter Recort). His comment regarding sodomy and the religious orders is taken up below.

110. Ibid., 18 (William Roux), 44 (William Bernard), 39–40 (Arnold of Verniolle, regarding the apprentice). We don't know much about John Ioc, but he seems to have been one of William Bernard's companions, so was probably a student. Later in his testimony, Arnold will admit to having had sex with him (ibid., 43, 49).

111. Ibid., 22–23 (William Bernard). Note, however, that Arnold claims to have estimated his age as being between sixteen and eighteen (ibid., 44, 139).

112. Ibid., 18, 20–21 (William Roux). Arnold denies this, however (ibid., 46).

113. Ibid., 43 (Arnold of Verniolle).

114. Ibid., 25 (William Bernard). Arnold extracted a similar oath from the anonymous apprentice (ibid., 40) and the youth of Moissac, discussed below.

115. Ibid., 28–29 (William Pecs).

116. Ibid., 31 (Peter Recort).

117. Ibid., 26–28 (William Boyer).

118. Arnold attempted to deny it, saying that the young boy did not know what he was talking about (ibid., 27).

119. See the testimony of John Ferrié, whom Arnold not only tried to make confess but to whom he also boasted of already having heard the confessions of twelve other students (ibid., 14–15). Arnold also tried with William Pecs (ibid., 29). Cf. the testimony of Peter Recort (ibid., 31–33).

120. Arnold admitted to hearing confession, but denied performing Mass (ibid., 35–38). But see the testimonies by John Ferrié (ibid., 15–16) and Peter Recort (31, 33) which contradict Arnold on this point. See the series of questions about his sacerdotal fraud toward the end of his testimony (ibid., 46–47).

121. Arnold's confession appears in the Bibliothèque Nationale, Doat, vol. 23, fol. 23; trans., Goodich, *Other Middle Ages*, 142.

122. On Merton, see Rashdale, *Universities of Europe*, 3:191–201. Edmund's case is discussed in Karras, *From Boys to Men*, 81–82; and Elliott, "Church Sex Scandal," 96–97.

123. Salter, *Registrum annalium Collegii Mertoniensis*, 162. Richard Rawlins will eventually become warden of the college, only to be deposed in 1520 for abusing college funds, ignoring the statutes, and absenteeism (ibid., 502–508). Interestingly, this did not seem to hurt his career, since he was made bishop of St. David's two years later.

124. Ibid., 169. Ruth Karras thinks that Edmund was mentioned in the Merton register because he was formerly a fellow of the college.

125. Salter, *Registrum*, April 27, 1490, p. 132.

126. Ibid., December 19, 1491, p. 134.

127. Ibid., April 16, 1492, p. 156.

128. Ibid., July 27, 1492, p. 162.

129. Ibid., February 14, 1493, p. 170.

130. Ibid., August 1, 1496, p. 201.

CHAPTER 9

Note to epigraph: Boccaccio, *The Decameron*, 1st day, 2nd story, p. 84.

1. Herlihy and Klapisch-Zuber, *Tuscans and Their Families*, 203–214.

2. *Magnum Chronicon Belgicum*, ann. 1474, ed. Pistorius, 3:418. In the same year, a number of Lombard mercenaries were captured in Germany and burned for their sodomy (ibid., 150). The chronicle was written by an Augustinian canon in the fifteenth century.

3. Ibid., 300.

4. Italy's reputation, especially Florence, continues into the early modern period. See Monter, *Frontiers of Heresy*, 291–292; Berco, "Social Control and Its Limits," 346.

5. Rocke, *Forbidden Friendships*, 7, 22–23.

6. Ibid., 49.

7. See ibid., chap. 2. Cf. Ruggiero, *Boundaries of Eros*, chap. 6. For northern Europe, see Boone, "State Power and Illicit Sexuality"; and the work of Helmut Puff in Chapter 7, p. 187, above.

8. For cases in which clerics were apprehended by secular judiciaries, see Rocke, *Forbidden Friendships*, 163; Ruggiero, *Boundaries*, 127, 129–133, 142–144. Rocke has estimated that the clergy was only 2.3 percent of the people cited (*Forbidden Friendships*, table B.12, p. 249). This might seem like a low count, but one should take into account that the activities of the regular clergy lent themselves to concealment. It is also possible that the office's inability to take action against clerics might result in disaffection and low citations.

9. *UN* 11, 1465, fol. 42v. The layman Laurentio, the priest Venturo's sexual partner on the Guelph Bridge, was not charged because he was declared simple and mentally incapacitated. He was, however, banished. The Guelph Bridge probably refers to the Ponte Reale, which was begun in 1317 in honor of Robert of Anjou, head of the Guelphs, but never completed. So the act was not as flagrant as it would have been had it occurred near one of the other four bridges that were in use. On sex in holy places, see Elliott, *Fallen Bodies*, chap. 3.

10. *UN* 29, 1494, fol. 111r.

11. Ibid., fol. 105v.

12. *UN* 14, 1470, fol. 9v, partially translated in Rocke, *Forbidden Friendships*, 139. Cf. the frustration expressed by the Venetian authorities in Ruggiero, *Boundaries of Eros*, 142–43.

13. Trexler, "Episcopal Constitutions of Antoninus of Florence," 244–245. The appendix contains the salient statutes (ibid., p. 267, nos. 36–37).

14. *UN* 18, 1475, fols. 271v, 337r. Also see the brief entry that, while again excoriating Baldassarre's unabashed promiscuity, casts doubt on his clerical status (ibid., fol. 276r). This might imply he was using it opportunistically to escape penalty, as was the case with the youths who bribed Vicar-General Donato, discussed below. I am indebted to Kathleen Noll for these references. Chiasso was well known for its brothels. See Rocke, *Forbidden Friendships*, 160.

15. *UN* 27, 1492, fol. 17v.

16. Ibid., fol. 19v; cited and translated by Rocke, *Forbidden Friendships*, 297–298. This letter is dated August 3.

17. Peter the Chanter, *Summa de sacramentis*, cc. 319, 320, 3.2a: 377, 380.

18. Maureen C. Miller, *Bishop's Palace*, 89–97.

19. See Osheim, *An Italian Lordship*, 116–118.

20. For example, the household of the bishop of Ferrara had twenty-two persons named in particular posts in the 1430s. See Peverada, "La 'familia' del vescovo e la curia a Ferrara," 612–613. This probably did not include underlings or the kind of clerical apprentices discussed below.

21. Brentano, *New World in a Small Place*, 147–151.

22. On his career, see Gamurrini, *Istoria genealogica delle famiglie nobili toscone*, 5:118–120; Ughelli, *Italia sacra sive de episcopis Italiae*, 3:307–308.

23. Waldman, "Patronage of a Favorite of Leo X," 108–109. Also see his participation in the fraught commission of a monument for the late cardinal Niccolò Forteguerri in the cathedral of Lucca (Milner, "The Politics of Patronage.")

24. Waldman, "Patronage of a Favorite of Leo X," 112–115.

25. Herlihy, *Medieval and Renaissance Pistoia*, 214–231; Tanzini, "Tuscan States," 92, 95; Najemy, *History of Florence*, 366–367.

26. Milner, "Lorenzo and Pistoia," 245–246.

27. Pinto, *Storia di Pistoia*, 3:37–38.

28. Fioravanti, *Memorie storiche della città di Pistoia*, 407.

29. On bishops and their vicar-generals both in England and Italy, see Rusconi, "Vescovi e vicari generali."

30. Dougherty, "Vicar General," 13–20; Édouard Fournier, *Origine du vicaire général*, 333–351; A. Hamilton Thompson, *English Clergy*, 46–49. On the papacy's use of vicars, see Rocciolo, "Il cardinal vicario e il clero di Roma."

31. On visitations in Italy, see Meoni, "Visite pastorali a Cortona nel Trecento," 190ff.; Zarri, "Ordini religiosi e autorità episcopale"; Bornstein, "Parish Priests in Late Medieval Cortona."

32. Dougherty, "Vicar General," 19–20.

33. See Paul Fournier, *Officialités au Moyen Âge*, 17–24 and app. 2, pp. 398–400; David M. Smith, "'Officialis' of the Bishop"; A. Hamilton Thompson, *English Clergy*, 51–56.

34. On dioceses and parishes in Italy, see Hay, *Church in Italy*, 2–25.

35. Cagnin, "'Ad adiscendum artem et officium clericatus,'" 95–97. Also see Cossar, *Clerical Households*, 71–73.

36. Barrow, *Clergy in the Medieval World*, 41–42.

37. Rocke refers to Donato's case in passing in *Forbidden Friendships*, 163, 298 n.17, and 306 n. 91. It appears in *NA* 8604, 1504–1509. The trial covers thirty-two entire folios, but

these are not numbered and have been bound out of order. The folio numbers given here are the consecutive numbers assigned to the order in which the folios appear. All the testimony from this case is from Donato Bocco (whose last name in Latin is "de Bocchis") unless otherwise specified. I am deeply indebted to Elena Brizio, paleographer extraordinaire, for her help with this challenging document. On the formation of the diocese of Pistoia, see Herlihy, *Medieval and Renaissance Pistoia*, 18–26.

38. Notarial preamble, *NA* 8604, August 18, 1506, fol. 33v.

39. This is the date that Giovanni settled a dispute between two different religious orders. See Tamburinio de Marridio, *De iure abbatum et aliorum praelatorum*, 1:421.

40. For an account of this trial, see Polizzotto, "When Saints Fall Out," 501–503. I am indebted to Jennifer Shenk for drawing this article to my attention. Also see Valerio, "Domenica da Paradiso e Dorotea di Lanciuola," 133. The trial was sensational enough to be entered into at least one history of Pistoia. See E. Fazioni, *Delle historie di Pistoia*, 3:65.

41. *NA* 8604, April 18, 1507, fol. 23r; cf. fol. 2r.

42. Ibid., April 18, 1507, fol. 23v.

43. Ibid., April 19, 1507, fol. 26r.

44. Ibid., fol. 28r; on this dispute, see ibid., March 25, 1507, fol. 11r. On the origins of this conflict, see Herlihy, *Medieval and Renaissance Pistoia*, 200–207. On the politics of Italian factional warfare, see Muir, *Mad Blood Stirring*.

45. Pinto, *Storia di Pistoia*, 3:64–72; Milner, "Lorenzo and Pistoia," 237.

46. *NA* 8064, Testimony of Castellano di Castellani, April 18, 1507, fol. 2r.

47. Ibid., Donato, April 8, 1507, fols. 2v, 26r; April 20, 1507, fol. 1v.

48. Ibid., April 18, 1507, fol. 25v.

49. Ibid., April 19, 1507, fol. 28r.

50. Ibid., April 18, 1507, fol. 23r.

51. Ibid., April 19, 1507, fol. 27v.

52. Ibid, April 18, 1507, fol. 25v.

53. Ibid., April 19, 1507, fol. 27r.

54. Ibid., April 18, 1507, fol. 23v; April 19, 1507, fol. 26v. This move would not have been unusual. Antonio Ducci, another doctor of decretals hailing from Florence, was a career vicar-general who held the post first in Treviso in 1438, then Vicenza, then Padua, and then again Treviso (Rusconi, "Vescovi e vicari generali," 554).

55. *NA* 8604, April 18, 1507, fol. 23r.

56. Ibid., April 19, 1507, fol. 28r.

57. Ibid., April 18, 1507, fols. 25r–v. On the position of *gonfaloniere della giustizia*, see Najemy, *History of Florence*, 84–85. This officer represented the *popolo* over the magnates and was created in the late thirteenth century to enforce a new set of laws that favored the former. A parallel office emerged in Pistoia, following the Florentine model (Herlihy, *Medieval and Renaissance Pistoia*, 218).

58. *NA* 8604, April 19, 1507, fol. 26r.

59. Ibid., fol. 39r.

60. Ibid., April 26–28, 1507, fols. 20r, 21v.

61. Ibid., fols. 20r, 20v. More than half of Pistoia's territories were mountainous, and like many hill communities, the inhabitants were sometimes backward. See Herlihy, *Medieval and Renaissance Pistoia*, 35–36.

62. *NA* 8604, April 19, 1507, fol. 29r.

63. Ibid., April 26–28, 1507, fol. 21v.

64. Ibid., April 26, 1507, fol. 18r.

65. Ibid., April 26–28, 1507, fols. 18r, 19r.

66. Ibid., fol. 19v.

67. Ibid., fol. 21r.

68. Ibid., April 26, 1507, fol. 20v.

69. Ibid., April 26–28, 1507, fol. 19r.

70. Ibid., April 26, 1507, fols. 20v, 21r.

71. Ibid., 19v–20r.

72. Ibid., fols. 13v, 14r–v; April 22–26, 1507, fols. 17r–v, 18v, 19r. Donato additionally would charge any *operarius* involved in what he deemed a frivolous quarrel one florin (ibid., fol. 19v). Usually visitations were guided by lists of questions. Generally the first would be directed to the *operarius,* concerning ornaments, lights, books, or anything necessary for worship. See, for example, Moro, *Visitatio ecclesie capituli Utinensis (1346)*, no. 1, p. 43.

73. *NA* 8604, April 26, 1507, fol. 20v.

74. Ibid., April 19, 1507, fol. 28r.

75. Ibid., April 20, 1507, fol. 1r.

76. Ibid., April 26, 1507, fol. 21r.

77. Ibid., April 19, 1507, fol. 28r.

78. Ibid., April 26, 1507, fol. 21r.

79. If "nephew" was, in fact, a code word for clerical bastard, and it turned out that the abbess was the mother, this would add an unusual dimension to the euphemism.

80. *NA* 8604, April 18, 1507, fols. 23v–24r; also see fols. 2r–v.

81. Ibid., fols. 2v, 25r.

82. Ibid., fol. 2r.

83. Ibid., fol. 26r.

84. Ibid., April 26, 1507, fol. 26v.

85. Ibid., May 4, 1507, fol. 22v.

86. Will Storr, "The Rape of Men: The Darkest Secret of War," *Guardian*, July 16, 2011, https://www.theguardian.com/society/2011/jul/17/the-rape-of-men.

87. The hospital was founded in the thirteenth century but got caught up in the factionalism of the fifteenth century. See Pinto, *Storia di Pistoia*, 3:54–56.

88. *NA* 8604, Lorenzo Pietro Giovanni of Florence, April 22–26, 1507, fols. 14r–v.

89. Ibid., Iacopo Bernardino de Buti, March 15, 1507, fol. 10r.

90. Ibid., Niccolò, son of Piero Gori, April 22–26, 1507, fol. 13v.

91. Ibid., Bernardino, son of Bartholomeo di Pratese, March 15, 1507, fol. 10v.

92. Ibid., Donato, April 22–26, 1507, fols. 16r–17r. Donato's sexual conquests occur to him haphazardly. I have tried to arrange them into categories, which means that they are not necessarily in the sequence in which he mentions them.

93. Congar, "Clercs et laïcs au point de vue de la culture au Moyen Âge."

94. Augustine Thompson, *Cities of God*, 302.

95. *NA* 8604, April 26, 1507, fol. 21v.

96. Pennsylvania's *40th Statewide Investigating Grand Jury: Report 1, Interim–Redacted* (2018), pp. 8889, http://media-downloads.pacourts.us/InterimRedactedReportandResponses .pdf?cb = 42148.

97. Maureen C. Miller, *Bishop's Palace*, 68–70.

98. Herlihy, *Medieval and Renaissance Pistoia*, 246–248.

99. A copy of Donato's letter appears in the appendix to a life that Onesti was writing of the holy woman, Domenica da Paradiso—foundress of the Convento Crocetta di Varlungo (1511) and Dorotea's rival. See Convento Crocetta di Varlungo MS F, Biblioteca Domenica di Santa Maria Novella Florence, fols. 105r–106r. Onesti's description of the trial basically recapitulates Donato's account (fols. 40r–42v). I am grateful to Father Lucian Cinelli OP, director of the Biblioteca Domenicana di Santa Maria Novella "Jacopo Passavanti," and the director of its archives, Ughetta Sorelli and, once again, to Elena Brizio for providing access to these documents.

CONCLUSION

1. Swanson, "Angels Incarnate," 174.

2. *De rebus Alsaticis*, c. 1, *MGH SS* 17:232; the chronicler also notes that the canons and soldiers took turns sleeping with the nuns.

3. Bornstein, "Parish Priests in Cortona,"173–174.

4. See Goldberg, "The Legal Persona," esp. 18–25. Goldberg is concerned with Gratian 1—what Winroth has proved to be the original recension of *Decretum* before the later additions of his followers (*Making of Gratian's Decretum*). In the thirteenth century, Gregory IX does dedicate a section to children in his *Liber Extra*, entitled "On the Sins of Children." It only contains two canons (Goldberg, "The Legal Persona," 23). Gratian's relative indifference to children could explain his attitude to Lot's daughters, discussed in Chapter 5, above.

5. I recently discovered that Timothy Mitchell made that leap over two decades ago, describing sexual abuse in the church as a "transpersonal, transnational system that is centuries old and well entrenched" (*Betrayal of Innocents*, 20).

6. On clerical concubinage, see Session 25, Reform Decrees, c. 14, in *Canons and Decrees of the Council of Trent*, 246–248. For an overview of Trent, see O'Malley, *Trent: What Happened at the Council*. The emphasis on clerical relations with females versus males is also apparent in the early modern emphasis on sacerdotal solicitation of sex in the confessional. Stephen Haliczar notes that women were perceived as the main victims of solicitation and that sodomy was included some years later as an afterthought. As a result, he found only four male plaintiffs. In fact, there was confusion among the laity as to whether males could be victims. As late as the eighteenth century, male victims were not sure if they were obligated to denounce a confessor soliciting sex (*Sexuality in the Confessional*, 107). Cf. the Dominican apprehended for the solicitation of boys who told the Spanish inquisitors that it was none of their business since he was not approaching women (Monter, *Frontiers of Heresy*, 286).

7. Session 13, Reform Canons, c. 4, in *Canons and Decrees of the Council of Trent*, 83.

8. *Magnum Bullarium Romanum*, ed. Cherubino et al., 2:267.

9. Sherr, "A Canon, a Choirboy."

10. Ibid., 9–10.

11. The Spanish Inquisition was founded in 1478 by Ferdinand and Isabella to ensure Christian orthodoxy and persisted into the 1830s. See Henry Charles Lea's massive overview *A History of the Inquisition in Spain*. The office's expansion into nonheretical matters, like sodomy, met with some opposition (Monter, *Frontiers of Heresy*, 36–37, 276–282; Kamen, *Spanish Inquisition*, 80). There was also an unevenness concerning where the Inquisition appropriated control over sodomy (Kamen, *Spanish Inquisition*, 268).

12. As cited by Mitchell, *Betrayal of Innocents*, 16.

13. Haliczar, *Inquisition and Society*, 115, 303–304; Monter, *Frontiers of Heresy*, 115–116, 284–285. When a cleric was successfully prosecuted and subsequently degraded and executed, it was generally a function of poverty and class. See the case of Melchor Armengol (Haliczar, *Inquisition and Society*, 306–307). Cf. Kamen, *Spanish Inquisition*, 268; Monter, *Frontiers of Heresy*, 280.

14. Berco, "Social Control and Its Limits," 338–339, 345, 348–49. Also see the table 3, p. 337.

15. Carrasco, *Inquisición y represión sexual*, 174–175.

16. As cited by Monter, *Frontiers of Heresy*, 175–176 n. 32.

17. As cited by Berco, "Social Control and Its Limits," 345.

18. Monter, *Frontiers of Heresy*, 290.

19. Mitchell, *Betrayal of Innocents*, esp. chaps. 2–3.

20. Session 23, *Canons and Decrees of the Council of Trent*, 162–163.

21. Eugene Cullen Kennedy, "Did the Council of Trent Enable the Sex Abuse Scandal?" *National Catholic Reporter*, February 20, 2014, https://www.ncronline.org/blogs/bulletins -human-side/did-council-trent-enable-sex-abuse-scandal.

22. Massimo Faggioli, "Trent's Long Shadow: The Abuse Crisis and Seminaries, Dioceses, and the Laity," *La Croix*, August 27, 2018, https://international.la-croix.com/news/ trents-long-shadow/8295; cf. Mitchell, *Betrayal of Innocents*, 18–19, 29–31. See Reform regarding the Sacrament of Order, c. 18, *Canons and Decrees of the Council of Trent*, 175–179. On efforts to reform seminaries in the wake of the present crisis, see Coleman, "Seminary Formation."

23. See Junno Arocho Esteves, "Clericalism, Abuse of Power, at the Heart of Sex Abuse Crisis, Cardinal Says," Catholic News Service, February 21, 2019, https://www.catholicnews .com/services/englishnews/2019/clericalism-abuse-of-power-at-heart-of-sex-abuse-crisis-cardi nal-says.cfm. Also see Frawley-O'Dea, *Perversion of Power*, chap. 9.

24. See Rod Dreher, "Sins of the Fathers," *National Review*, August 15, 2018, https:// www.nationalreview.com/2018/08/sins-of-the-fathers/. Rather than behaving like salaried workers or privileged executives, Leon J. Podles seems more on track in his assessment that "the bishops suffered from a clericalism that identified the Church with the clergy. The laity were unimportant except insofar as they provided the opportunity for clerical careers" (*Sacrilege*, 489–490).

25. Indeed, A. W. Richard Sipe, a former priest and therapist who treated both abusers and the abused, maintains that "Clerical culture is *psychopathogenic*. That means that the elements that constitute the operation of the celibate culture favor, select, produce, and promote men who tend to be what were formerly termed psychopaths," "Scandal Versus Culture," 124.

26. *1917 Pio-Benedictine Code*, cc. 2312.2–3, 2290, 2288; *Code of Canon Law*, cc.1340, 1352, 1344. Cf. Elliott, "Sexual Scandal and the Medieval Clergy," 100–101.

27. *1917 Pio-Benedictine Code*, c. 890; *Code of Canon Law*, c. 984.

28. See Haliczar, *Sexuality in the Confessional*.

29. *1917 Pio-Benedictine Code*, cc. 904, 2368.2, 1935.2. See Doyle, Sipe, and Wall, *Sex, Priests, and Secret Codes*, 141–145.

30. *1917 Pio-Benedictine Code*, c. 1949.

31. Ibid., cc. 2183–2188, 2191.1; cf. cc. 2222.2, 2311.

32. Ibid., c. 2359.2; *Code of Canon Law*, c. 1395.2.

33. Ibid., c. 695.1.

34. Pope Francis, "*Vos estis lux mundi*," http://w2.vatican.va/content/francesco/en/
motu_proprio/documents/papa-francesco-motu-proprio-20190507_vos-estis-lux-
mundi.html. Also see Jason Horowitz, "Pope Issues First Rules for Catholic Church World-
wide to Report Sex Abuse," *New York Times*, May 9, 2019, https://www.nytimes.com/2019/
05/09/world/europe/pope-francis-abuse-catholic-church.html. The title of the letter is especially ironic if one considers that this was the title assigned to the book based on the interview
with Pope Emeritus Benedict XVI. See n. 35, below. Cf. Pope Francis's more recent abolish-
ment of the high level of secrecy associated with the clergy's abuse of children, allowing the
church to share charges of abuse with the secular authorities. Note, however, that such sharing
of information is voluntary as opposed to compulsory (https://www.nytimes.com/2019/12/17/
world/europe/pope-francis-secrecy-sexual-abuse.html?searchResultPosition = 1).

35. See Jason Horowitz, "The Man Who Took on Pope Francis: The Story Behind
Viganò's Letter," *New York Times*, August 28, 2018, https://www.nytimes.com/2018/08/28/
world/europe/archbishop-carlo-maria-vigano-pope-francis.html?searchResultPosition = 1.
Leon J. Podles points to the church's homosexual subculture and the high incidence of male
victims. He argues that most of the victims were postpubescent, hence the abusers were
essentially homosexual versus true pedophiles (*Sacrilege,* pp. 321 ff.). There is little doubt that
there is a high gay presence in the priesthood (see Wills, *Papal Sin,* ch. 13). Since 2005,
moreover, the church has attempted to exclude homosexuals as candidates for the priesthood
(Coleman, "Seminary Formation," 208–209). On the anxiety of gay Catholic priests regarding this vector of blame, see Elizabeth Dias, " 'It Is Not a Closet. It Is a Cage.' Gay Catholic
Priests Speak Out," February 17, 2019, *New York Times*, https://www.nytimes.com/2019/02/
17/us/it-is-not-a-closet-it-is-a-cage-gay-catholic-priests-speak-out.html. This response was in
many ways exacerbated by an interview with Pope Emeritus Benedict XVI in which he maintained that homosexuals be barred from ordination, positing some relation between their
orientation and the abuse of minors. This interview was released in a book entitled *Light of
the World.* See the summary by Brian Mullady, "Pope Benedict XVI on the Priesthood and
Homosexuality," at https://www.ncbi.nlm.nih.gov/pmc/articles/PMC6026964/. More recently, Benedict XVI has blamed the sexual revolution of the 1960s, however. See Benedict
XVI's essay "The Church and the Scandal of Abuse," trans. Anian Christoph Wimmer, Catholic News Agency, April 10, 2019, https://www.catholicnewsagency.com/news/full-text-of
-benedict-xvi-the-church-and-the-scandal-of-sexual-abuse-59639; and Jason Horowitz's article
"With a Letter on Sexual Abuse, Pope Benedict Returns to Public Eye," *New York Times*,
April 11, 2019, https://www.nytimes.com/2019/04/11/world/europe/pope-benedict-letter-sex
-abuse.html?searchResultPosition = 3. Benedict's eagerness to find a scapegoat is easily explained. When still Cardinal Ratzinger, he was appointed as prefect of the Congregation for
the Doctrine of the Faith in 1981 (the former Roman Inquisition)—the official body for
handling cases of sexual abuse by the clergy. This responsibility could only have increased
when he was elected pope in 2005.

36. Terry, Schuth, and Smith, "Incidence of Sexual Abuse," 22.

37. *Visio Alberici*, c. 8, in *Bibliotheca Casiensis*, 5.1:196–197. The worst offenders were
those who promoted priests whom they already knew to be corrupt. But the chamber also
accommodated prelates who only learned of their protégés' turpitude subsequent to their
promotion and did nothing.

38. William of Auvergne, *De sacramento poenitentiae*, c. 20, p. 505. As Richard Fraher suggests, the inquisitional procedure was introduced at Lateran IV to cut through some of the obstacles standing in the way of prosecuting clerics (Fraher, "Preventing Crime in the High Middle Ages," 222–229). Clearly this procedural innovation did little to address the problem, at least from William's perspective.

BIBLIOGRAPHY

PRIMARY SOURCES

Manuscript Sources

Archivio Arcivescovile, Archivio Storico Diocesano, Lucca. *Tribunale Ecclesiastico, Sezione Criminali* 1, 2, 5, 9.

Archivio Arcivescovile di Pisa. *Atti straordinari* 1.

Archivio di Stato di Firenze. *Notarile antecosimiano* 8604.

Archivio di Stato di Firenze. *Ufficiali di notte e conservatori dell'onesta dei monasteri* 11, 14, 18, 27, 29.

Bartholomew of Pisa. *Summa de casibus consciencie secundum compilacionenem Bartholomei de Pisis.* Oxford. Bodleian, MS 736.

Borthwick Institute of Historical Research, York. Dean and Chapter Act Book. D/C. AB1.

Canterbury Cathedral Archives and Library. Act book X.8.1.

Convento Crocetta di Varlungo. MS F. Biblioteca Domenica di Santa Maria Novella, Florence. MS F.

Fondation des Archives de l'ancien Évêché de Bâle (Porrentruy). AAEB A 85/83.

Lincolnshire County Archives. MS Vj/1.

Published Sources

Abbo of Fleury. *Excerptum de vitis romanorum pontificium. PL* 139:535–569.

Abelard, Peter. *Historia calamitatum.* Ed. J. T. Muckle. "Abelard's Letter of Consolation to a Friend (*Historia calamitatum*)." *Mediaeval Studies* 12 (1950): 163–213. Trans. Betty Radice, in *The Letters of Abelard and Heloise*, rev. ed., with introduction and notes by M. T. Clanchy, 3–43. Middlesex, 2003.

———. *Peter Abelard's "Ethics."* Ed. and trans. D. E. Luscombe. Oxford, 1971.

———. *Sic et non: A Critical Edition.* Ed. Blanche Boyer and Richard McKeon. Chicago, 1976.

Abelard, Peter, and Heloise. *The Letters of Abelard and Heloise.* Trans. Betty Radice. Rev. ed., with introduction and notes by M. T. Clanchy. Middlesex, 2003.

———. "The Personal Letters Between Abelard and Heloise." Ed. J. T. Muckle. *Mediaeval Studies* 15 (1953): 47–94. Trans. Betty Radice, in *The Letters of Abelard and Heloise*, rev. ed., 56–89. Middlesex, 2003.

Adam of Bremen. *Gesta Hammenburgensis ecclesiae pontificum.* Ed. M. Lappenberg. *MGH SS* 7:347–389. Hanover, 1846.

Adamnán. *An Irish Precursor of Dante: A Study on the Vision of Heaven and Hell Ascribed to the Eighth-Century Irish Monk Saint Adamnán.* Trans. C. S. Boswell. London, 1908.

Admonitio generalis Karls des Grossen. Ed. Hubert Mordek et al. *MGH Fontes iuris* 16. Hanover, 2012.

Æthelwold. *Regularis concordia anglicae nationis monachorum sanctimonialiumque.* Ed. Thomas Symons. New York, 1953.

Alan of Lille. *De planctu Naturae.* Ed. N. M. Häring. *Studi Medievali,* ser. 3, 19.2 (1978): 797–879. Trans. James J. Sheridan. *The Plaint of Nature.* Toronto, 1980.

———. *Distinctiones dictionum theologicalium. PL* 210:685–1012.

———. *Liber poenitentialis.* Ed. Jean Longère. 2 vols. Louvain and Lille, 1965.

Alcuin. *Commentaria in Apocalypsin. PL* 100:1087–1156.

———. *Interrogationes et responsiones in Genesin. PL* 100:515–570.

Aldhelm. *De laudibus virginum. PL* 89:237–280.

Alexander of Canterbury. *Dicta Anselmi.* In *Memorials of St. Anselm,* ed. R. W. Southern and F. S. Schmitt, 107–195. London, 1969.

Alnwick, William. *The Award of William Alnwick, Bishop of Lincoln, A.D. 1439.* Ed. and trans. Reginald Maxwell Woolley. With preface, introduction, and chronological table by Christopher Wadsworth. Cambridge, 1913.

———. "Bishop Alnwick's Court-Book." In *The English Clergy and Their Organization in the Later Middle Ages,* ed. A. Hamilton Thompson, 206–246. Oxford, 1947.

Ambrose. *De officiis.* Ed. Ivor J. Davidson. 2 vols. Oxford, 2001.

Andrieu, Michel, ed. *Les Ordines romani du haut moyen âge.* 5 vols. Louvain, 1931–1961.

Annales Basileensis a. 1266–1277. Ed. G. H. Pertz, *MGH SS* 17:193–202. Hanover, 1861.

Annales Ottenburani a. 727–1113. Ed. G. H. Pertz. *MGH SS* 7:1–9. Hanover, 1844.

Annales Parmenses maiores a. 1165–1335. Ed. G. H. Pertz. *MGH SS* 18:664–790. Hanover, 1868.

Annales Stadenses auctore M. Alberto ab O. c.–1256. Ed. I. M. Lappenberg. *MGH SS* 16:271–379. Hanover, 1858.

Ansegisus. *Collectio capitularum Ansegisi.* Ed. G. Schmitz. *MGH Capit. N.S.* 1. Hanover, 1996.

Anselm of Canterbury. *Epistolae.* In *Opera omnia,* ed. F. S. Schmitt, 3:93–294, and vols. 4, 5. Edinburgh, 1946. Trans. Walter Fröhlich. *Letters of Saint Anselm of Canterbury, 1033–1109.* 3 vols. Kalamazoo, MI, 1990–1994.

———. *Meditationes.* In *Opera omnia,* ed. F. S. Schmitt, 3:76–91. Edinburgh, 1946.

Anselm of Lucca. *Anselmi episcopi collectio canonum una cum collectione minore.* Ed. Friedrich Thaner. Innsbruck, 1915.

———. *Collectanea. PL* 149:475–484.

Anselm of St. Remy. *Historia dedicationis ecclesiae S. Remigii. PL* 142:1411–1440.

Aquinas, Thomas. "On Fraternal Correction." In *Disputed Questions on Virtue.* Trans. Jeffrey Hause and Claudia Eisen Murphy, 183–203. Indianapolis, 2010.

———. *Summa Theologiae.* http://www.newadvent.org/summa/.

Ardo. *Benedict of Aniane: The Emperor's Monk; Ardo's Life.* Trans. Allen Cabaniss. Forward by Annette Grabowsky and Clemens Radl. Kalamazoo, MI, 2008.

Aristotle. *L'Éthique à Nicomaque.* Ed. and trans. René Antoine Gauthier and Jean Yves Jolif. 2nd ed. Louvain, 1970.

Arnobius. *Disputationes adversus gentes. PL* 5:713–1288.

Astesanus d'Asti. *Summa de casibus conscientiae.* Strassbourg, before 1469.

Athanasius. *Vita Beati Antonii Abbatis. PL* 73:127–169.

Augustine. *Confessionum libri XIII.* Ed. P. Knöll. *CSEL* 33. Vienna and Leipzig, 1896. Trans. http://www.newadvent.org/fathers/1101.htm.

———. *Contra epistolam Parmeniani.* Ed. M. Petschenig. In *Scripta contra Donatistas.* Vol. 1 of 2. *CSEL* 51:19–41.

———. *Contra litteras Petiliani libri tres.* Ed. M. Petschenig. In *Scripta contra Donatistas.* Vol. 2 of 2. *CSEL* 52:3–227. Trans. http://www.newadvent.org/fathers/1409.htm.

———. *De baptismo contra Donatistas.* Ed. M. Petschenig. In *Scripta contra Donatistas.* Vol. 1 of 2. *CSEL* 51:145–375. Vienna and Leipzig, 1908. Trans. http://www.newadvent.org/fathers/14082.htm.

———. *De bono coniugali.* Ed. J. Zycha. In *Opera omnia, CSEL* 41:187–231. Vienna, 1900.

———. *De civitate Dei libri XXII.* Ed. Emanuel Hoffmann. 2 vols. *CSEL* 40.1–2. Prague and Vienna, 1899–1900. Trans. http://www.newadvent.org/fathers/120108.htm.

———. *De haeresibus. PL* 42:22–50.

———. *De libero arbitrio. PL* 32:1221–1310.

———. *Ep.* 211. To an anonymous community of nuns. In *Epistulae,* ed. Al. Goldbacher, *CSEL* 57:356–371. Vienna and Leipzig, 1911.

———. *Regula. PL* 32:1378–1384.

———. *Sermones de scripturis. PL* 38:24–994.

Bacon, Roger. *Compendium studii philosophiae.* Ed. J. S. Brewer. *Rerum Britannicarum Medii Aevi Scriptores,* 1:393–519. London, 1859.

Barontus of Lonrai. *Visio Baronti, Monachi Longoretensis.* Ed. W. Levinson. *MGH SS rer. Merov.* 5:368–394. Hanover, 1910.

Bartholomew of Exeter. *The Penitential.* In *Bartholomew of Exeter: Bishop and Canonist,* ed. Adrian Morey, 175–300. London, 1937.

Basil the Great. "An Ascetical Discourse and Exhortation on the Renunciation of the World and Spiritual Perfection." In *Saint Basil: Ascetical Works,* trans. M. Monica Wagner, 15–31. Fathers of the Church 9. New York, 1950.

Basler Chroniken. Ed. Wilhelm Vischer and Heinrich Boos. 7 vols. Leipzig, 1872–1915.

Bayless, Martha, ed. *Fifteen Medieval Latin Parodies.* Toronto, 2018.

Beckynton, Thomas. *The Register of Thomas Beckynton, Bishop of Bath and Wells, 1443–1465.* Ed. H. C. Maxwell-Lyte and M. C. B. Dawes. Somerset Record Society, no. 49. London, 1934.

Bede. *Explanatio Apocalypsis. PL* 93:129–206.

Benedict of Aniane. *Concordia regularum.* Ed. Pierre Bonnerue. 2 vols. *CCCM* 168, 168A. Turnhout, 1999.

Benedict of Nursia. *The Rule of Saint Benedict.* Ed. and trans. Justin McCann. London, 1952.

Benedict the Levite. *Capitularia spuria.* Ed. G. H. Pertz. *MGH LL* 2.2:17–158. Hanover, 1837.

Bernard of Cluny [the elder]. *Ordo Cluniacensis sive Consuetudines.* Ed. M. Herrgott. In *Vetus disciplina monastica,* 133–364. Paris, 1726. Reprint, Sieburg, 1999.

Bernard of Cluny [the younger]. *Scorn for the World: Bernard of Cluny's "De Contemptu Mundi."* Ed. and trans. Ronald E. Pepin. Woodbridge, 1991.

Bernold of Constance. *De vitanda excommunicatorum communione, de reconciliatione lapsorum. PL* 148:1181–1218.

Bezler, Francis, ed. *Paenitentialia Hispaniae. CCSL* 156A. Turnhout, 1998.

Bible moralisée: Codex Vindobonensis 2554, Vienna, Österreichische Nationalbibliothek. Ed. and trans. Gerald B. Guest. London, 1995.

Biblia sacra cum glossa ordinaria nouisque additionibus. 6 vols. Venice, 1603.

Bieler, Ludwig, ed. *The Irish Penitentials.* Dublin, 1963.

Boccaccio, Giovanni. *The Decameron.* Trans. G. H. McWilliam. Middlesex, 1972.

Boniface. *S. Bonifatii et Lulli epistolae.* Ed. Michael Tangl. *MGH Epp. sel.* 1. Berlin, 1916.

Bonizo of Sutri. *Liber de vita Christiana.* Ed. E. Perels. Berlin, 1930.

Boon, Amand, ed. *Pachomiana Latina.* Louvain, 1932.

Bradshaw, Henry, and Christopher Wordsworth, eds. *Statutes of Lincoln Cathedral.* 2 pts. in 3 vols. Cambridge, 1892–1897.

Bruno of Magdeburg. *De bello Saxonico liber.* Ed. Wilhem Wattenbach. *MGH SS rerum Germ.* 15. Hanover, 1880.

Burchard of Worms. *Libri decretorum. PL* 140:537–1057.

Caesarius of Arles. *Caesarius of Arles: Life, Testament, Letters.* Trans. William E. Klingshirn. Liverpool, 1994.

——. *Sermons au peuple.* Ed. Marie-José Delage. 3 vols. Sources chrétiennes, nos. 175, 243, 330. Paris, 1978–1986. Trans. Mary Magdalene Mueller. *Saint Caesarius of Arles: Sermons.* 2 vols. New York, 1956.

Caesarius of Heisterbach. *Dialogus miraculorum.* Ed. Joseph Strange. 2 vols. Cologne, 1851.

Canivez, Joseph-Marie, ed. *Statuta capitulorum generalium ordinis Cisterciensis ab anno 1116 ad annum 1786.* 8 vols. Louvain, 1933–1941.

Canons and Decrees of the Council of Trent. Ed. and trans. H. J. Schroeder. London, 1955.

Capitula episcoporum. Ed. Rudolf Pokorny. *MGH Capit. episc.* 3. Hanover, 1995.

Capitulare regum Francorum, I. Ed. A. Boretius. *MGH Capit.* 1:91–99. Hanover, 1883.

Carmina Cantabrigiensia. Ed. Karl Strecker. *MGH SS rer. Germ.* 40. Berlin, 1926.

Cassian, John. *Collationes. PL* 49:477–1328. Trans. Boniface Ramsey. *The Conferences.* New York, 1997.

——. *De institutis coenobiorum.* Ed. M. Petschenig. In *Iohannis Cassiani opera. CSEL* 17:3–231. Prague, Vienna, and Leipzig, 1888. Trans. Boniface Ramsey. *Institutes.* New York, 2000.

Catalogi archiepiscoporum Coloniensium. Ed. H. Cardauns. *MGH SS* 24:332–367. Hanover, 1879.

Cato, Dionysius. *Distichs of Cato: A Famous Medieval Textbook.* Ed. and trans. Wayland Johnson Chase. Madison, WI, 1922.

Charvin, G., ed. *Statuts, chapitres généraux et visites de l'ordre de Cluny.* 9 vols. Paris, 1965–1982.

Chronicon Gladbacense a. 973–974. Ed. G. Waitz. *MGH SS* 4:74–77. Hanover, 1846.

Chronicon S. Martini Coloniensis a. 756–1021. Ed. D. Ildephonso. *MGH SS* 2:214–215. Hanover, 1879.

Chronik von Petrihusi. Ed. Franz J. Mone. Vol. 1 of 4. In *Quellensammlung der badischen landesgeschichte.* Karlsruhe, 1848–1867.

Chrysostom, John. *A Comparison Between a King and a Monk/Against the Opponents of Monastic Life: Two Treatises.* Trans. David G. Hunter. Lewiston, NY, 1988.

——. *Instructions and Refutation Directed Against Those Men Cohabiting with Virgins.* In *Jerome, Chrysostom, and Friends,* trans. Elizabeth A. Clark, 164–208. New York, 1979.

——. *On the Necessity of Guarding Virginity.* In *Jerome, Chrysostom, and Friends,* trans. Elizabeth A. Clark, 209–248. New York, 1979.

Clarke, Peter D., and P. N. R. Zutshi, eds. *Supplications from England and Wales in the Registers of the Apostolic Penitentiary, 1410–1503*. 3 vols. Canterbury and York Society series, nos. 103–105. Rochester, NY, 2012–2015.

Clement of Alexandria. *Stromata*. *PG* 8–9. Trans. http://www.newadvent.org/fathers/02103.htm.

Climacus, John. *The Ladder of Divine Ascent*. Trans. Colm Lubheid. New York, 1982.

Code of Canon Law. Trans. Canon Law Society of America. Washington, DC, 1983.

Collectio canonum in V libris. Ed. M. Fornasari. *CCCM* 6. Turnhout, 1970.

Collectio Dacheriana. Ed. Luc d'Achery. In *Spicilegium sive Collectio veterum aliquot scriptorum qui in Galliae bibliothecis delituerant*, 1:509–564. 2nd ed. Paris, 1723.

Concilia aevi Karolini, 742–782. Ed. Albert Werminghoff. *MGH Conc.* 2.1–2. Hanover and Leipzig, 1906–1908.

Concilia aevi Karolini, 843–859. Ed. Wilfried Hartman. *MGH Conc.* 3. Hanover, 1984.

Concilia aevi Karolini, 860–874. Ed. Wilfried Hartman. *MGH Conc.* 4. Hanover, 1998.

Concilia aevi Merovingici, 511–695. Ed. Frideric Maassen. *MGH Conc.*1. Hanover, 1893.

Concilia Africae, a. 345–525. Ed. Charles Munier. *CCSL* 149. Turnhout, 1974.

Concilia Galliae. Ed. Charles Munier and Charles de Clercq. 2 vols. *CCSL* 148, 148A. Turnhout, 1963.

Conrad of Eberbach. *Exordium magnum Cisterciense sive Narratio de initio Cisterciensis ordinis*. Ed. Bruno Griesser. *CCCM* 138. Turnhout, 1994.

Constable, Giles, ed. "The Vision of Gunthelm and Other Visions Attributed to Peter the Venerable." *Revue Bénédictine* 92 (1956): 92–114.

Corpus iuris canonici. Ed. Emil Friedberg. 2 vols. 2nd ed. Leipzig, 1879. Reprint, Graz, 1955.

Coste, Jean, ed. *Boniface VIII en procès: Articles d'accusation et dépositions des témoins, 1303–1311*. Rome, 1995.

Cresconius Africanus. *Die Concordia canonum des Cresconius: Studien und Edition*. Ed. Klaus Zechiel-Eckes. 2 vols. Frankfurt am Main, 1992.

Damian, Peter. *Die Briefe des Petrus Damiani*. Ed. Kurt Reindel. *MGH Briefe d. dt. Kaiserzeit* 4.1–4. Munich, 1983–1993. Trans. Owen J. Blum and Irven M. Resnick. *The Letters of Peter Damian*. 6 vols. *FCMC* 1–3, 5–7. Washington, DC, 1989–2005.

Davy, M. M., ed. *Les sermons universitaires parisiens de 1230–1231*. Paris, 1931.

Decrees of the Ecumenical Councils. Ed. Norman P. Tanner et al. 2 vols. London and Washington, DC, 1990.

De rebus Alsaticis ineuntis saeculi xiii. Ed. Ph. Jaffé. *MGH SS* 17:232–237. Hanover, 1861.

De S. Conrado Nantuino, Wolfratshusii in Bavaria. *AASS*, August, 2:214–215.

The Didache: Text, Translation, Analysis and Commentary. Ed. and trans. Aaron Milavec. Collegeville, MN, 2003.

Didascalia et Constitutiones apostolorum. Ed. F. X. Funk. Paderborn, 1905.

Dionysius Exiguus. *Collectio decretorum pontificum romanorum*. *PL* 67:229–316.

Diuersorum patrum sententie siue Collectio in LXXIV titulos digesta. Ed. John Gilchrist. Vatican City, 1973. Trans. John Gilchrist. *The Collection in Seventy-Four Titles: A Canon Law Manual of the Gregorian Reform*. Toronto, 1980.

Dobiache-Rojdesvensky, Olga, ed. and trans. *Les poésies des Goliards*. Paris, 1931.

Doctrina duodecim apostolorum. Ed. F. X. Funk. Tübingen, 1887.

Donatus of Besançon. *Regula ad virgines*. *PL* 87:273–298. Trans. John E. Halborg and Jo Ann McNamara. *The Ordeal of Community: The Rule of Donatus of Besançon*. http://monasticmatrix.osu.edu/cartularium/rule-donatus-besan%C3%A7.

Doyle, Ian, ed. *The Vernon Manuscript: A Facsimile of Bodleian Library, Oxford, MS. Eng. Poet. A.1.* Cambridge, 1987.

Du Cange, Charles du Fresne, et al. *Glossarium mediae et infimae Latinitatis.* 7 vols. Paris, 1840–1850.

Duncan, Thomas G., ed. *Medieval English Lyrics and Carols.* Woodbridge, 2013.

Duvernoy, Jean, ed. *Le registre d'inquisition de Jacques Fournier, évêque de Pamiers (1318–1325).* 3 vols. Toulouse, 1965.

Eadmer. *Historia novorum in Anglia, et opuscula duo de vita sancti Anselmi et quibusdam miraculis ejus.* Ed. Martin Rule. Rerum Britannicarum Medii Aevi Scriptores 81. London, 1884. Trans. Geoffrey Bosanquet. *History of Recent Events in England.* London, 1964.

———. *Vita sancti Anselmi archiepiscopi Cantuariensis.* Ed. and trans. R. W. Southern. *The Life of St. Anselm, Archbishop of Canterbury.* London, 1962.

Epistola de sacramentis haereticorum. Ed E. Sackur. *MGH Ldl* 3:12–20. Hanover, 1897.

Erdmann, C., ed. *Die Hannoversche Briefsammlung.* In *Briefsammlungen der Zeit Heinrichs IV,* 1–187. *MGH Briefe d. dt. Kaiserzeit* 5. Weimar, 1950.

Eusebius. *Historia ecclesiastica. PG* 20:45–910. Trans. http://www.newadvent.org/fathers/250103.htm.

Eynsham Cartulary. Ed. H. E. Salter. 2 vols. Oxford, 1907–1908.

Friedberg, Emil, ed. *Decretalium collectiones.* In *Corpus iuris canonici,* 2nd ed., vol. 2. Leipzig, 1879. Reprint, Graz, 1955.

Fructuosus of Braga. *Regula monachorum Complutensis. PL* 87:1099–1110. Trans. Claude W. Barlow as "Rule for the Monastery of Compludo," in *Iberian Fathers,* 2:156–175. Fathers of the Church 63. Washington, DC, 1969.

———. *Regula monastica communis. PL* 87:1111–1130. Trans. Claude W. Barlow as "General Rule for Monasteries," in *Iberian Fathers,* 2:176–206. Fathers of the Church 63. Washington, DC, 1969.

Gallia christiana, in provincias ecclesiasticas. Congregation of St. Maur. 10 vols. Paris, 1715–1865.

Gautier of Coincy. *De Sainte Léocade au tans que sainz Hyldefons estoit arcevesques de Tholete cui Nostre Dame donna l'aube de prelaz: Miracle versifié par Gautier de Coinci.* Ed. Eva Vilamo-Pentti. Helsinki, 1950.

Geoffrey of Vendôme. *Epistolae. PL* 157:33–212.

Gerhoh of Reichersberg. *Commentarius aureus in Psalmos et cantica ferialia. PL* 193:619–1814.

———. *Opusculum de edificio dei.* Ed. E. Sackur. *MGH Ldl* 3:136–202. Hanover, 1897.

Gerson, Jean. *De arte audiendi confessiones.* In *Oeuvres complètes,* 8:10–17.

———. *De cognitione castitatis.* In *Oeuvres complètes,* 9:50–64.

———. *De confessione mollitiei.* In *Oeuvres complètes,* 8:71–75.

———. *De parvulis ad Christum trahendis."* In *Oeuvres complètes,* 9:669–686.

———. *En la fête de la Sainte Trinité.* In *Oeuvres complètes,* 7.2:1123–1137.

———. *Expostulatio adversus correptionem juventutis.* In *Oeuvres complètes,* 10:27–28.

———. *Oeuvres complètes de Jean Gerson.* 10 vols. Ed. Palémon Glorieux. Paris, 1960–1973.

———. *Pour le jour des morts.* In *Oeuvres complètes,* 7.2:549–560.

———. *Pro pueris ecclesiae Parisiensis.* In *Oeuvres complètes,* 9:686–689.

———. *Poenitemini: Contre la luxure . . . En l'advent de N.S.J.C.* In *Oeuvres complètes,* 7.2:810–821.

————. *Poenitemini: Contre la luxure . . . Par le merveilleux et charitable advent.* In *Oeuvres complètes*, 7.2:822–832.

Gilles of Corbeil. *Hierapigra ad purgandos prelatos* (excerpts). Ed. C. Vieillard. In *Gilles de Corbeil: Médecin de Philippe-Auguste et chanoine de Notre-Dame, 1140–1224?*, 360–410. Paris, 1909.

Gilmour-Bryson, Anne, ed. *The Trial of the Templars in the Papal State and the Abruzzi.* Vatican City, 1982.

Goodich, Michael, ed. and trans. *Other Middle Ages: Witnesses at the Margins of Medieval Society.* Philadelphia, 1998.

Goscelin of St.-Bertin. *Liber confortatorius.* Ed. C. H. Talbot. In *Studia Anselmiana*, fasc. 37. *Analecta Monastica*, 3rd ser. Rome, 1955. Trans. W. R. Barnes and Rebecca Hayward. In *Writing the Wilton Women*, ed. Stephanie Hollis, 99–207. Turnhout, 2004.

Gratian. *Decretum Magistri Gratiani.* Ed. Emil Friedberg. Vol. 1 of *Corpus iuris canonici.* 2nd ed. Leipzig, 1879. Reprint, Graz, 1955.

Gregory I (the Great). *Dialogues.* Ed. Adalbert de Vogüé. 3 vols. Sources chrétiennes, nos. 251, 260, 265. Paris, 1978–1980.

————. *S. Gregorii Magni registrum epistularum.* Ed. Dag Norberg. *CCSL*, 140, 140A. Turnhout, 1982. Trans. John R. C. Martyn. *The Letters of Gregory the Great.* 3 vols. Toronto, 2004.

Gregory VII. *Das Register Gregors VII.* Ed. E. Caspar. *MGH Epp. sel.* 2.1–2.2. Berlin, 1920–1923. Trans. H. E. J. Cowdrey. *The Register of Pope Gregory VII, 1073–1085.* Oxford, 2002.

Gregory of Tours. *Liber vitae patrum.* Ed. Bruno Krusch. *MGH SS rer. Merov.* 1.2:211–294. Trans. Edward James. *The Life of the Fathers.* Liverpool, 1985.

Grosseteste, Robert. Ep. 10, to N. "Reprehensio grauis, amica tamen, magni cuiusdam fornicatoris: Letter 10." Ed. F. A. C. Mantello. In *From Learning to Love: Schools, Law, and Pastoral Care in the Middle Ages; Essays in Honour of Joseph W. Goering*, ed. Tristan Sharp, 443–457. Toronto, 2017.

————. *The Letters of Robert Grosseteste, Bishop of Lincoln.* Trans. F. A. C. Mantello and Joseph Goering. Toronto, 2010.

————. *Perambulavit Judas.* In Joseph Goering and F. A. C. Mantello, "The 'Perambulauit Iudas . . .' (Speculum confessionis) Attributed to Robert Grosseteste." *Revue Bénédictine* 96 (1986): 125–168.

————. *Templum Dei.* Ed. Joseph Goering and F. A. C. Mantello. Toronto, 1984.

Guérard, M., ed. *Cartulaire de l'église de Notre-Dame de Paris.* 4 vols. Paris, 1850.

Guibert of Nogent. *Autobiographie.* Ed. Edmond-René Labande. Paris, 1981.

————. *Moralia in Genesin. PL* 156:19–337.

Halitgar of Cambrai. *De vitiis et virtutibus. PL* 105:651–694.

————. *Liber poenitentialis. PL* 105:693–710.

Hallinger, Kassius, ed. *Consuetudinum saeculi XI/ XII/ XII monumenta non-Cluniacensia, Consuetudines Floriacenses antiquiores, saec. X. ex.* Corpus consuetudinem monasticarum 7.3. Sieburg, 1984.

————, ed. *Initia consuetudinis Benedictinae: Consuetudines saeculi octavi et noni.* Corpus consuetudinum monasticarum 1. Sieburg, 1963.

Halliwell, James Orchard, ed. *The Moral Play of Wit and Science and Early Poetical Miscellanies.* London, 1848.

Haymo of Halberstadt. *Expositio in Apocalypsin. PL* 117:937–1220.

Heito. *Heitonis visio Wettini.* Ed. E. Dümmler. *MGH Poetae* 2:268–275. Berlin, 1884.

Heliland of Froidmont. *Chronicon. PL* 212:771–1082.

Helmold. *Helmoldi presbyteri chronica Slavorum a. 800–1172.* Ed. I. M. Lappenberg and G. H. Pertz. *MGH SS* 21:1–99. Hanover, 1869.

Henry of Ghent. *Henrici de Gandavo: Opera omnia.* Vol. 8, *Quodlibet IV.* Ed. Gordon A. Wilson and Girard J. Etzkorn. Louvain, 2011. Vol. 13, *Quodlibet IX.* Ed. R. Macken. Louvain, 1983.

———. *Quodlibeta Magistri Henrici Goethals a Gandauo doctoris solemnis: Socii Sorbonici: & archidiaconi Tornacensis cum duplici tabella.* Louvain, 1518.

Herbert of Clairvaux. *Liber miraculorum. PL* 185:1273–1384.

Hergemöller, Bernd-Ulrich, ed. *Chorknaben und Bäckerknechte: Homosexuelle Kleriker im mittelalterlichen Basel.* Hamburg, 2004.

Herman of Tournai. *Liber de restauratione monasterii sancti Martini Tornacensis.* Ed. G. Waitz. *MGH SS* 14:274–317. Hanover, 1883.

Hildegard of Bingen. *Causae et curae.* Ed. Paul Kaiser. Leipzig, 1903.

———. *Epistolarium.* Ed. L. Van Acker. 3 vols. *CCCM* 91, 91A, 91B. Turnhout, 1991–1993. Trans. Joseph L. Baird and Radd K. Ehrman. *The Letters of Hildegard of Bingen.* 3 vols. New York, 1994–2004.

———. *Liber divinorum operum.* Ed. A. Derolez and P. Dronke. *CCCM* 92. Turnhout, 1996.

———. *Liber vite meritorum. CCCM,* 90. Ed. Angela Carlevaris, Turnhout, 1995.

———. *Scivias.* Ed. Adelgundis Führkötter and Angela Carlevaris. 2 vols. *CCCM* 43, 43A. Turnhout, 1978. Trans. Columba Hart. *Scivias.* New York, 1990.

Hildemar of Corbie. *Expositio Regulae ab Hildemaro tradita.* Ed. Rupert Mittermüller. Regensburg, 1880. In progress translation at the Hildemar Project, http://www .hildemar.org.

Hincmar of Reims. *De presbiteris criminosis: Ein Memorandum Erzbischof Hinkmars von Reims über straffällige Kleriker.* Ed. G. Schmitz. *MGH Studien und Texte* 34. Hanover, 2004.

———. *Epistola synodi Carisiacensis ad Hludowicum regem.* Ed. A. Boretius and V. Krause. *MGH Capit.* 2:427–441. Hanover, 1897.

Honorius Augustodunensis. *De apostatis.* Ed. J. Dieterich. *MGH Ldl* 3:57–63. Hanover, 1897.

———. *De offendiculo.* Ed. J. Dieterich. *MGH Ldl* 3:38–57. Hanover, 1897.

Horrox, Rosemary, ed. and trans. *The Black Death.* Manchester, 1994.

Hostiensis. *Summa.* Lyon, 1537. Reprint, Aalen, 1962.

Houben, Hubert. "*Visio cuiusdam pauperculae mulieris*: Überlieferung und Herkunft eines frühmittelalterlichen Visionstextes." *Zeitschrift für die Geschichte des Oberrheins* 124 (1976): 31–42.

Hrabanus Maurus. *Commentariorum in Genesim. PL* 107:439–670.

———. *De institutione clericorum libri tres.* Ed. Detlev Zimpel. Frankfurt, 1996.

———. *De universo. PL* 111:9–614.

———. *De videndo Deum, de puritate cordis et modo poenitentiae. PL* 112:1261–1332.

———. *De vitiis et virtutibus. PL* 12:1333–1397.

———. *Liber de oblatione puerorum. PL* 107:419–440.

———. *Liber poenitentium. PL* 112:1397–1424.

———. *Poenitentiale. PL* 110:467–494.

Hudson, Anne, ed. *Selections from English Wycliffite Writings.* Cambridge, 1978.

Hugh of Flavigny. *Chronicon.* Ed. W. Wattenbach. *MGH SS* 8:280–503. Hanover, 1848.

Hugh of Fouilloy. *De claustro animae. PL* 176:1017–1183.

Isidore Mercator. *Collectio decretalium. PL* 130:7–1177.

Isidore of Seville. *De ecclesiasticis officiis. PL* 83:737–826.

———. *Etymologiae PL* 82:73–728.

———. *Regula monachorum. PL* 103:555–572.

———. *Sententiae. PL* 83:537–738.

Ivo of Chartres. *Correspondance.* Vol. 1, *1090–1098.* Ed. Jean Leclercq. Paris, 1949.

———. *Decretum.* Ed. Martin Brett and Bruce Brasington. https://ivo-of-chartres.github.io/decretum/ivodec.html.

———. *Epistolae. PL* 162:11–288.

———. *Panormia.* https://ivo-of-chartres.github.io/panormia.html.

Jean de Meun. *The Romance of the Rose.* Trans. Harry W. Robbins. New York, 1962.

Jerome. *Commentaria in Isaiam. PL* 24:17–678.

———. *Epistulae.* Ed. Isidore Hilberg. 3 vols. *CSEL* 54, 55, 56. Vienna and Leipzig, 1910–1918.

———. *Liber de nominibus Hebraici. PL* 23:1297–1306.

Joannou, Périclès-Pierre, ed. *Discipline générale antique, IVe–IXe s.: Les canons des synodes particuliers.* 2 vols. Rome, 1962–1964.

John of Freiburg. *Summa confessorum.* Rome, 1518.

John of Hauteville. *Architrenius.* Ed. and trans. Winthrop Wetherbee. Cambridge, 1994.

John of Salerno. *Vita S. Odonis. PL* 133:43–86.

John of Salisbury. *The Letters of John of Salisbury.* Ed. W. J. Miller and C. N. L. Brooke. 2 vols. Oxford, 1955–1979.

John, monk of St. Lawrence, Liège. *Visio de statu animarum. PL* 180:177–186.

Kennedy, V. L., ed. "Robert of Courson on Penance." *Mediaeval Studies* 7 (1945): 291–336.

Kottje, Raymund, ed. *Paenitentialia minora Franciae et Italiae saeculi VIII–IX. CCSL* 156. Turnhout, 1994.

Lampert of Hersfeld. *Annales.* Ed. Oswald Holder-Egger. *MGH SS rer. Germ.* 38:1–304. Hanover and Leipzig, 1894.

Landulf the Senior. *Historia Mediolanensis.* Ed. L. C. Bethmann and W. Wattenbach. *MGH SS* 8:32–100. Hanover, 1848.

Lanfranc. *De celanda confessione. PL* 150:625–632.

———. *The Monastic Constitutions of Lanfranc.* Ed. and trans. David Knowles. Revised C. N. L. Brooke. Oxford, 2002.

Lea, H. C., ed. *A Formulary of the Papal Penitentiary in the Thirteenth Century.* Philadelphia, 1892.

Leclercq, Jean, ed. "Une redaction en prose de la *Visio Anselli* dans un manuscrit de Subiaco." *Benedictina* 16 (1969): 188–195.

Leges Visigothorum. Ed. K. Zeumer. *MGH LL nat. Germ.* 1. Hanover, 1902.

Leo I. *Epistolae. PL* 54:581–1213. Trans. http://www.newadvent.org/fathers/3604.htm.

Libanius. *Autobiography and Select Letters.* Ed. and trans. A. F. Norman. 2 vols. Cambridge, MA, 1992.

Lombard, Peter. *Sentences.* Trans. Giulio Silano. 4 vols. Toronto, 2007–2010.

Magnum Bullarium Romanum. Ed. Laertius Cherubino et al. Rev. ed. Lyon, 1703.

Magnum Chronicon Belgicum. 3 vols. Ed. Ioannes Pistorius. Frankfurt, 1607.

Malalas, John. *The Chronicle of John Malalas.* Trans. Elizabeth Jeffreys et al. Melbourne, 1986.

Manegold of Lautenbach. *Manigoldi ad Gebehardum liber.* Ed. K. Francke. *MGH Ldl* 1:300–430. Hanover, 1891.

Mansi, G. D., ed. *Sacrorum conciliorum nova et amplissima collectio*. 53 vols. in 60. Paris, 1901–1927.

Map, Walter. *De nugis curialium: Courtiers' Trifles*. Ed. and trans. M. R. James. Revised C. N. L. Brooke and R. A. B. Mynors. Oxford, 1983.

Matthew of Cracow. *De modo confitendi et puritate conscientiae*. Antwerp, 1486.

Milon d'Amiens. *Du prestre et du chevalier*. In *Recueil général et complet des fabliaux des XIIIe et XIVe siècles*, ed. Anatole de Montaiglon and Gaston Raynaud, 2:46–91. Paris, 1877.

Moro, Cristina, ed. *Visitatio ecclesie capituli Utinensis (1346)*. Udine, 1994.

Nelson, William, ed. *A Fifteenth Century School Book: From a Manuscript in the British Museum, MS. Arundel 249*. Oxford, 1956.

Newman, Barbara, trans. *Making Love in the Twelfth Century: "Letters of Two Lovers" in Context; A New Translation with Commentary*. Philadelphia, 2016.

Nicholas I. *Epistolae*. Ed. E. Perels. *MGH Epp.* 6:257–690. Berlin, 1925.

Nicholas II. *Concilium Lateranense (1059)*. Ed. L. Weiland. *MGH Const.* 1:537–549. Hanover, 1893.

The 1917 or Pio-Benedictine Code of Canon Law. Ed. and trans. Edward N. Peters. San Francisco, 2001.

Nock, Frances Clare, ed. and trans. *The Vita Sancti Fructuosi*. Catholic University of America Studies in Medieval History, n.s., 7. Washington, DC, 1946.

Odo of Cluny. *Collationes. PL* 133:517–638.

———. *Occupatio*. Ed. Antonius Swoboda. Leipzig, 1900.

Olivi, Peter John. *Quodlibeta quinque*. Ed. Stephan Defraia. Rome, 2002.

Optatus. *S. Optati Milevitani libri VII*. Ed. C. Ziwsa. *CSEL* 26. Prague, Vienna, and Leipzig, 1893. Trans. Mark Edwards. *Optatus: Against the Donatists*. Liverpool, 1997.

Orderic Vitalis. *Ecclesiastical History*. Ed. and trans. Marjorie Chibnall. 6 vols. Oxford, 1973.

Orme, Nicholas, ed. *English School Exercises, 1420–1530*. Toronto, 2013.

Othloh of St. Emmeram. *Liber visionum*. Ed. Paul G. Schmidt. *MGH QQ zur Geistesgesch.* 13. Weimar, 1989.

Otto of St. Blaise. *Chronici ab Ottone Frisingensi episcopo conscripti continuatione auctore, uti videtur, Ottone S. Blasii monacho*. Ed. Roger Wilmans. *MGH SS* 20:302–337. Hanover, 1868.

Paul of Hungary. *Rationes penitentie composite a fratribus predicatorum*. In *Bibliotheca Casinensis*, vol. 4, part 2, pp. 191–215. Monte Cassino, 1880.

Paul the Deacon (Warnefrid). *In sanctam regulam commentarium*. Monte Cassino, 1880.

Pelagius and John, trans. [from the Greek]. *Verba seniorum. PL* 73:851–1062.

Peraldus, William. *Summa aurea de virtutibus et viciis*. Brescia, 1498.

Peter of Cornwall. *Peter of Cornwall's Book of Revelations*. Ed. and trans. Robert Easting and Richard Sharpe. Toronto, 2013.

Peter of Poitiers of St.-Victor. *Summa de confessione, compilatio praesens*. Ed. Jean Longère. *CCCM* 51. Turnhout, 1980.

Peter the Chanter. *Summa de sacramentis et animae consiliis*. Ed. Jean-Albert Dugauquier. 3 parts in 5 vols. Louvain and Lille, 1954–1963.

———. *Verbum adbreviatum, textus prior*. Ed. Monique Boutry. *CCCM* 196A. Turnhout, 2012.

Peter the Venerable. *De miraculis. PL* 189:857–954.

———. *Statuta Petri Venerabilis*. Ed. Giles Constable. In *Consuetudines Benedictinae Variae, Saec. XI–Saec. XIV*, 1–106. Vol. 6 of *Corpus consuetudinem monasticarum*, ed. Kassius Hallinger. Siegburg, 1975.

Fazioni, E. *Delle historie di Pistoia*. 3 vols. Venice, 1662

Pinto, Guiliano, ed. *Storia di Pistoia*. 4 vols. Florence, 1999.

Pseudo-Cyprian. *De singularitate clericorum*. In *S. Thasci Caecili Cypriani opera omnia*, ed. G. Hartel. *CSEL* 3.3:173–220. Vienna, 1871.

Pseudo-Isidore. *Decretales pseudo-Isidorianae et Capitula Angilramni*. Ed. Paul Hinschius. 1863. Reprint, Aalen, 1963.

Pseudo-Ulrich. *Rescriptio*. Ed. Erwin Frauenknecht. In *Die Verteidigung der Priesterehe in der Reformzeit*, 203–215. *MGH Studien und Texte* 16. Hanover, 1997.

"Quodlibet anonyme IX (1278)." In *La littérature quodlibétique de 1260 à 1320*, ed. Palémon Glorieux, 1:307–347. Paris, 1925.

Quintilian, Marcus Fabius. *Institutio oratoria*. Trans. H. E. Butler. 4 vols. Cambridge, MA, 1961–1966.

Rather of Verona. *Die Briefe des Bischofs Rather von Verona*. Ed. Fritz Weigle. *MGH Briefe d. dt. Kaiserzeit* 1. Weimar, 1949. Trans. Peter L. D. Reid. *The Complete Works of Rather of Verona*. Binghamton, NY, 1991.

Regino of Prüm. *Libri duo de synodalibus causis et disciplinis ecclesiasticis*. Ed. F. G. A. Wasserschleben. Revised Wilfried Hartmann. Stuttgart, 2004.

Regula orientalis. Ed. Adalbert de Vogüé. In "La *Regula orientalis*: Texte critique et synopse des sources." *Benedictina* 23 (1976): 241–272.

Regula Tarnantensis. Ed. Fernando Villegas. In "La *Regula Monasterii Tarnantensis*: Texte, sources et datation." *Revue Bénédictine* 84 (1974): 7–65.

Remigius of Auxerre. *Commentarius in Genesim*. *PL* 131:51–134.

Richalm of Schöntal. *Liber revelationum*. Ed. Paul Gerhard Schmidt. *MGH QQ zur Geistesgesch.* 24. Hanover, 2009.

Robert of Flamborough. *Liber poenitentialis*. Ed. J. J. Francis Firth. Toronto, 1971.

Roger of Hoveden. *Annals of Roger de Hoveden: Comprising the History of England and of Other Countries of Europe from A.D. 732 to A.D. 1201*. Ed. and trans. Henry Riley. 2 vols. London, 1853.

———(formerly attributed to Benedict of Peterborough). *Gesta regis Henrici et Gesta regis Ricardi: The Chronicle of the Reigns of Henry II and Richard I, A.D. 1169–1192*. Ed. William Stubbs. 2 vols. London, 1867.

Salter, H. E., ed. *Registrum annalium Collegii Mertoniensis, 1483–1521*. Oxford, 1923.

Schmitz, Hermann Joseph, ed. *Die Bussbücher und die Bussdisciplin der Kirche*. 2 vols. Mainz and Düsseldorf, 1883–1898.

Serlo of Bayeux. *Defensio pro filiis presbyterorum*. Ed. E. Dümmler and H. Böhmer. *MGH Ldl* 3:579–583. Hanover, 1891.

Sharp, Tristan, ed. "*Tractatus de confessione: 'Activus contemplatio'*: A Thirteenth-Century Guide to Confession for Monks." *Mediaeval Studies* 76 (2014): 1–56.

Sigibert of Gembloux. *Apologia contra eos qui calumniantur missas coniugatorum sacerdotum*. Ed. Erwin Frauenknecht. In *Die Verteidigung der Priesterehe in der Reformzeit*, 219–247. *MGH Studien und Texte* 16. Hanover, 1997.

Siricius. *Epistolae et decreta*. *PL* 13:1131–1196.

Smaragdus of St.-Mihiel. *Commentary on the Rule of St. Benedict*. Trans. David Barry. Kalamazoo, MI, 2007.

Socrates Scholasticus. *Historia ecclesiastica*. *PG* 67:29–842. Trans. http://www.newadvent.org/fathers/2601.htm.

Sozomen. *Historia ecclesiastica*. *PG* 67:843–1592. Trans. http://www.newadvent.org/fathers/26028.htm.

Stehling, Thomas, ed. and trans. *Medieval Latin Poems of Male Love and Friendship*. New York, 1984.

St. Paul's Apocalypse. In *Visions of Heaven and Hell Before Dante*, ed. Eileen Gardiner, 13–50. New York, 1989.

Strabo, Walafrid. *Visio Wettini*. Ed. E. Dümmler. *MGH Poetae* 2:301–333. Berlin, 1884. Trans. David A. Traill. *Walafrid Strabo's "Visio Wettini": Text, Translation, and Commentary*. Bern and Frankfurt am Main, 1974.

Suetonius. *Lives of the Caesars*. Ed. and trans. J. C. Rolfe. 2 vols. Cambridge, MA, 1913–1914.

Summa musice: A Thirteenth-Century Manual for Singers. Ed. and trans. Christopher Page. Cambridge, 1991.

Tamburini, Filippo, ed. *Santi e peccatori: Confessioni e suppliche dai Registri della Penitenzieria dell'Archivio Segreto Vaticano, 1451–1586*. Milan, 1995.

Tertullian. *Apologeticum*. In *Opera omnia, editio minor*, ed. F. Oehler, 58–213. Leipzig, 1854. Trans. http://www.newadvent.org/fathers/0301.htm.

———. *De paenitentia*. In *Opera omnia, editio minor*, ed. F. Oehler, 354–368. Leipzig, 1854. Trans. http://www.newadvent.org/fathers/0320.htm.

The Theodosian Code. Trans. Clyde Pharr. Princeton, NJ, 1952.

Theodulf of Orléans. *Erstes Kapitular*. Ed. Peter Brommer. *MGH Capit. episc.* 1:73–142. Hanover, 1984.

———. *Zweites Kapitular*. Ed. Peter Brommer. *MGH Capit. episc.* 1:142–184.

Thietmar of Merseburg. *Thietmari Chronicon*. Ed. Robert Holtzmann. *MGH SS rer. Germ. N.S.* 9:2–532. Berlin, 1935.

Thomas of Cantimpré. *Bonum universale de apibus*. Ed. George Colvener. Douai, 1627.

———. *Liber de natura rerum*. Ed. H. Boase. Berlin, 1973.

———. *Vita S. Lutgardis virginis Cisterciensis*. *AASS*, June, 4:189–210.

Thomas of Chobham. *Summa confessorum*. Ed. F. Broomfield. Louvain, 1968.

Thompson, A. Hamilton, ed. and trans. *Visitations of Religious Houses in the Diocese of Lincoln*. 3 vols. Canterbury and York Society series, nos. 17, 24, 33. London, 1915–1929. Reprint, London, 1969.

Tractatus pro clericorum conubio. Ed. Erwin Frauenknecht. In *Die Verteidigung der Priesterehe in der Reformzeit*, 254–266. *MGH Studien und Texte* 16. Hanover, 1997.

Tyconius. *The Book of Rules*. Ed. and trans. William Babcock. Atlanta, 1989.

Ulrich of Cluny. *Antiquiores consuetudines Cluniacensis monasterii*. *PL* 149:635–778.

Utley, Francis Lee, ed. "The Choristers' Lament." *Speculum* 21 (1946): 194–202.

Van Rhijn, Carine, ed. *Paenitentiale Pseudo-Theodori*. *CCSL* 156B. Turnhout, 2009.

Vincent of Beauvais. *Speculum Quadruplex sive Speculum maius*. 4 vols. Douai, 1624. Reprint, Graz, 1965.

Visio Alberici. Ed. Order of St. Benedict. In *Bibliotheca Casinensis*, vol. 5, part 1, pp. 191–206. Monte Cassino, 1894.

Visio Tnugdali. Ed. A. Wagner. Hildesheim, 1989. Trans. Jean-Michel Picard. *The Vision of Tnugdal*. Dublin, 1989.

"The Vision of the Monk of Eynsham." In *Eynsham Cartulary*, ed. H. E. Salter, 2:255–371. Oxford, 1908.

Vita et res gesta S. Altmanni. PL 148:867–894.

Vita S. Euphrosynae. AASS, February, 2:537–541.

Vives, José, ed. *Concilios Visigóticos e Hispano-Romanos*. Barcelona, 1963.

Vogel, Cyrille, Reinhard Elze, and Michel Andrieu, eds. *Le Pontifical Romano-Germanique du dixième siècle*. 3 vols. Vatican City, 1963.

Walrami et Herrandi epistolae de causa Heinrici regis conscriptae. Ed. E. Dümmler. *MGH Ldl* 2:285–291. Hanover, 1892.

Ward, Benedicta, trans. *The Sayings of the Desert Fathers: The Alphabetical Collection*. Rev. ed. Kalamazoo, MI, 1984.

Wasserschleben, F. W. H., ed. *Die Bussordnungen der abendländischen Kirche*. Halle, 1851. Reprint, Graz, 1985.

Watkin, Aelred, trans. *Dean Cosyn and Wells Cathedral Miscellanea*. Somerset Record Society, no. 56. Frome and London, 1941.

White, T. H., trans. *The Book of Beasts: Being a Translation from a Latin Bestiary of the Twelfth Century*. New York, 1984.

Widmann, Simon, ed. "Die Eberbacher Chronik der Mainzer Erzbischöfe." *Neues Archiv der Gesellschaft für ältere deutsche Geschichtskunde* 13 (1888): 119–143.

Wido of Ferrara. *Wido episcopus Ferrariensis de scismate Hildebrandi*. Ed. E. Dümmler and R. Williams. *MGH Ldl* 1:529–567. Hanover, 1891.

William of Auvergne. *De sacramento poenitentiae*. In *Opera omnia*, 1:451–511. Paris, 1674. Reprint, Frankfurt am Main, 1963.

William of Malmesbury. *Gesta pontificum anglorum*. Ed. and trans. M. Winterbottom. 2 vols. Oxford, 2007.

———. *Gesta regum anglorum*. Ed. and trans. R. A. B. Mynors, R. M. Thomson, and M. Winterbottom. 2 vols. Oxford, 1998.

———. *Historia novella*. Ed. and trans. K. R. Potter. London, 1955.

William de Montibus. "The Writings of William de Montibus." In Joseph Goering, *William de Montibus (c. 1140–1213): The Schools and the Literature of Pastoral Care*, part 2. Toronto, 1992.

Zachary. *Epistolae et decreta. PL* 89:917–960.

SECONDARY SOURCES

Abraham, Erin V. *Anticipating Sin in Medieval Society: Childhood, Sexuality, and Violence in the Early Penitentials*. Amsterdam, 2017.

Achelis, Hans. *Virgines subintroductae: Ein Beitrag zum VII. Kapitel des I. Korintherbriefs*. Leipzig, 1902.

Adnès, Pierre. "Pénitence." In *Dictionnaire de spiritualité*, ed. Marcel Viller et al., 12:943–1010. Paris, 1984

Aird, W. M. "Frustrated Masculinity: The Relationship Between William the Conqueror and His Eldest Son." In *Masculinity in Medieval Europe*, ed. D. M. Hadley, 39–55. London, 1999.

Airlie, Stuart. " 'Not Rendering unto Caesar': Challenges to Early Medieval Rulers." In *Der frühmittelalteriche Staat—Europäische Perspektiven*, ed. Walter Pohl and Veronika Wieser, 489–502. Vienna, 2009.

Albert, Thomas D. *Der gemeine Mann vor dem geistlichen Richter: Kirchliche Rechtsprechung in Diözesen Basel, Chur und Konstanz vor der Reformation.* Stuttgart, 1998.

Alford, John A. "The Grammatical Metaphor: A Survey of Its Use in the Middle Ages." *Speculum* 57 (1982): 728–760.

Allen, Prudence. *The Concept of Woman: Vol. I. The Aristotelian Revolution, 750 BC–AD 1250.* Montreal, 1985.

Amann, É. "Pénitence publique et pénitence privée à l'époque de la réforme Carolingienne." In *Dictionnaire de théologie catholique,* 12.1:862–886. Paris, 1933.

Anciaux, Paul. *La théologie du sacrement de pénitence au XIIe siècle.* Louvain, 1940.

Anger, P. "Chapitres Généraux de Cluny." *Revue Mabillon* 8 (1912–1913): 105–147, 213–252.

Arnold, John. *Inquisition and Power: Catharism and the Confessing Subject in Medieval Languedoc.* Philadelphia, 2001.

———. "The Labour of Continence: Masculinity and Clerical Virginity." In *Medieval Virginities,* ed. Anke Bernau et al., 102–118. Toronto, 2003.

Austin, Greta. *Shaping Church Law Around the Year 1000: The "Decretum" of Burchard of Worms.* Farnham, 2009.

Bagliani, Agostino Paravicini. *Boniface VIII: Un pape hérétique?* Paris, 2003.

Bailey, Derrick Sherwin. *Homosexuality and the Western Christian Tradition.* London, 1955.

Baldwin, John W. *The Language of Sex: Five Voices from Northern France Around 1200.* Chicago, 1994.

———. *Masters, Princes, and Merchants: The Social Views of Peter the Chanter and His Circle.* 2 vols. Princeton, NJ, 1970.

Balzaretti, R. "Men and Sex in Tenth-Century Italy." In *Masculinity in Medieval Europe,* ed. D. M. Hadley, 143–159. London, 1999.

Bardsley, Sandy. *Venomous Tongues: Speech and Gender in Late Medieval England.* Philadelphia, 2006.

Barlow, Frank. *William Rufus.* New Haven, CT, 2000.

Barrow, Julia. *The Clergy in the Medieval World: Secular Clerics, Their Families and Careers in North-Western Europe, c. 800–c. 1200.* Cambridge, 2016.

———. "The Origins of Vicars Choral to c. 1300." In *Vicars Choral at English Cathedrals: "Cantate Domino"; History, Architecture and Archaeology,* ed. Richard Hall and David Stocker, 11–16. Oxford, 2005.

Barstow, Anne Llewellyn. *Married Priests and Reforming Papacy: The Eleventh-Century Debates.* New York, 1982.

Bates, David. *William the Conqueror.* New Haven, CT, 2016.

Berco, Christian. *Sexual Hierarchies, Public Status: Men, Sodomy, and Society in Spain's Golden Age.* Toronto, 2007.

———. "Social Control and Its Limits: Sodomy, Local Sexual Economies, and Inquisitors During Spain's Golden Age." *Sixteenth Century Journal* 36 (2005): 331–358.

Berend, Nora. "La subversion invisible: La disparition de l'oblation irrévocable des enfants dans le droit canon." *Médiévales* 26 (1994): 123–136.

Berger, Karol. "The Guidonian Hand." In *The Medieval Craft of Memory: An Anthology of Texts and Pictures,* ed. Mary Carruthers and Jan M. Ziolkowski, 71–82. Philadelphia, 2002.

Berman, Constance. *The Cistercian Evolution: The Invention of a Religious Order in the Twelfth Century.* Philadelphia, 2000.

Blud, Victoria. *The Unspeakable, Gender and Sexuality in Medieval Literature, 1000–1400.* Woodbridge, 2017.

Blum, Owen J. "The Monitor of the Popes: St. Peter Damian." *Studi Gregoriani* 2 (1947): 459–473.

———. *St. Peter Damian: His Teaching on the Spiritual Life.* Washington, DC, 1947.

Blumenthal, Uta-Renate. "Pope Gregory VII and the Prohibition of Nicolaitism." In *Medieval Purity and Piety: Essays on Medieval Clerical Celibacy and Religious Reform*, ed. Michael Frassetto, 239–268. New York, 1998.

Boase, T. S. R. *Boniface VIII.* London, 1933.

Booker, Courtney M. "*Iusta murmuratio:* The Sound of Scandal in the Early Middle Ages." *Revue Bénédictine* 126 (2016): 236–270.

Boone, Marc. "State Power and Illicit Sexuality: The Persecution of Sodomy in Late Medieval Bruges." *Journal of Medieval History* 22 (1996): 135–153.

Bornstein, Daniel. "Parish Priests in Late Medieval Cortona: The Urban and Rural Clergy." In *Preti nel medioevo*, ed. Maurizio Zangarini, 165–194. Verona, 1997.

Boston Globe Investigative Staff. *Betrayal: The Crisis in the Catholic Church.* Boston, 2002.

Boswell, John. *Christianity, Social Tolerance, and Homosexuality: Gay People in Western Europe from the Beginning of the Christian Era to the Fourteenth Century.* Chicago, 1980.

———. "Dante and the Sodomites." *Dante Studies* 112 (1994): 63–76.

———. *The Kindness of Strangers: The Abandonment of Children in Western Europe from Late Antiquity to the Renaissance.* New York, 1988.

———. "Revolutions, Universals, and Sexual Categories." In *Hidden from History: Reclaiming the Gay and Lesbian Past*, ed. Martin Duberman, Martha Vicinus, and George Chauncey Jr., 1–33. New York, 1989.

Bouchard, Constance Brittain. *Sword, Miter, and Cloister: Nobility and Church in Burgundy, 980–1198.* Ithaca, NY, 1987.

———. *"Those of My Blood": Constructing Noble Families in Medieval Francia.* Philadelphia, 2001.

Bowers, John. "The Performing Ensemble for English Church Polyphony, c. 1320–1390." In *Studies in the Performance of Music*, ed. Stanley Boorman, 161–192. Cambridge, 1983.

Bowers, Roger. "The Almonry Schools of the English Monasteries." In *Monasteries and Society in Medieval Britain: Proceedings of the 1994 Harlaxton Symposium*, ed. Benjamin Thompson, 177–219. Stamford, 1999.

———. "To Chorus from Quartet: The Performing Resource for English Church Polyphony, c. 1390–1559." In *English Choral Practice, 1400–1650*, ed. John Morehen, 1–48. Cambridge, 1995.

Boyd, David. "Disrupting the Norm: Sodomy, Culture, and the Male Body in Peter Damian's *Liber Gomorrhianus.*" *Essays in Medieval Studies* 11 (1994): 63–72.

Boyle, Leonard. "The *Summa Confessorum* of John of Freiburg and the Popularization of the Moral Teaching of St. Thomas and Some of His Contemporaries." In *St. Thomas Aquinas 1274–1974: Commemorative Studies*, ed. Armand A. Maurer et al., 2:245–268. Toronto, 1974.

Boynton, Susan. "Boy Singers in Monasteries and Cathedrals." In *Young Choristers, 650–1700*, ed. Susan Boynton and Eric Rice, 37–48. Woodbridge, 2008.

———. "The Liturgical Role of Children in Monastic Customaries." *Studia Liturgica* 28 (1998): 194–209.

————. *Shaping a Monastic Identity: Liturgy and History at the Imperial Monastery of Farfa, 1000–1125.* Ithaca, NY, 2006.

————. "Training for the Liturgy as a Form of Monastic Education." In *Medieval Monastic Education,* ed. George Ferzoco and Carolyn Muessig, 7–20. New York, 2005.

Boynton, Susan, and Isabelle Cochelin. "The Sociomusical Role of Child Oblates at the Abbey of Cluny in the Eleventh Century." In *Musical Childhoods and the Cultures of Youth,* ed. Susan Boynton and Roe-Min Kok, 3–24. Middletown, CT, 2006.

Boynton, Susan, and Eric Rice, eds. *Young Choristers, 650–1700.* Woodbridge, 2008.

Brakke, David. *Athanasius and the Politics of Asceticism.* Oxford, 1995.

————. *Demons and the Making of a Monk: Spiritual Combat in Early Christianity.* Cambridge, MA, 2006.

Brasington, Bruce C. "*Nihil incertius quam vita adolescentium*: Adolescence in the *Decretum* and Decretist Commentary." *Zeitschrift der Savigny-Stiftung für Rechtsgeschichte Kanonistische Abteilung* 94 (2008): 38–65.

Bratchel, M. E. *Medieval Lucca and the Evolution of the Renaissance State.* Oxford, 2008.

Brentano, Robert. *A New World in a Small Place: Church and Religion in the Diocese of Rieti, 1188–1378.* Berkeley, CA, 1994.

Brizio, Elena. "Sexual Violence in the Sienese State Before and After the Fall of the Republic." In *Sex, Gender and Sexuality in Renaissance Italy,* ed. Jacqueline Murray and Nicholas Terpstra, 35–52. London, 2019.

Brooke, C. N. L. "Gregorian Reform in Action: Clerical Marriage in England, 1050–1200." *Cambridge Historical Journal* 12 (1956): 1–21.

Brooten, Bernadette J. *Love Between Women: Early Christian Responses to Female Homoeroticism.* Chicago, 1996.

Brown, D. Catherine. *Pastor and Laity in the Theology of Jean Gerson.* Cambridge, 1987.

Brown, Peter. *The Body and Society: Men, Women and Sexual Renunciation in Early Christianity.* New York, 1988.

————. *The Ransom of the Soul: Afterlife and Wealth in Early Western Christianity.* Cambridge, MA, 2015.

Bruce, Scott. *Silence and Sign Language in Medieval Monasticism: The Cluniac Tradition, c. 900–1200.* Cambridge, 2007.

Brundage, James A. *Law, Sex, and Christian Society in Medieval Europe.* Chicago, 1987.

————. "The Politics of Sodomy: Rex v. Pons Hugh de Ampurias (1311)." In *Sex in the Middle Ages: A Book of Essays,* ed. Joyce E. Salisbury, 239–246. New York, 1991.

————. "Proof in Canonical Criminal Law." *Continuity and Change* 11 (1996): 329–336.

Bryan, Lindsay. "From Stumbling Block to Deadly Sin: The Theology of Scandal." In *Scandala,* ed. Gerhard Jaritz, 7–17. Vienna, 2008.

————. "Peter the Chanter's Threefold Truth and the Sin of Scandal." In *From Learning to Love: Schools, Law, and Pastoral Care in the Middle Ages; Essays in Honour of Joseph W. Goering,* ed. Tristan Sharp et al., 29–47. Toronto, 2017.

————. "*Vae mundo a scandalis*: The Sin of Scandal in Medieval England." PhD diss., University of Toronto, 1998.

Bullough, Donald A. *Alcuin: Achievement and Reputation.* Leiden, 2004.

Bullough, Vern L. "Postscript: Heresy, Witchcraft, and Sexuality." In *Sexual Practices and the Medieval Church,* ed. Vern L. Bullough and James Brundage, 206–217. Buffalo, NY, 1982.

Burgwinkle, William. *Sodomy, Masculinity, and Law in Medieval Literature: France and England, 1050–1230.* Cambridge, 2004.

———. "Visible and Invisible Bodies and Subjects in Peter Damian." In *Troubled Vision: Gender, Sexuality, and Sight in Medieval Text and Image,* ed. Emma Campbell and Robert Mills, 47–62. New York, 1994.

Butler, Judith. *Gender Trouble: Feminism and the Subversion of Identity.* London, 1990.

Bynum, Caroline Walker. *"Docere verbo et exemplo": An Aspect of Twelfth-Century Spirituality.* Missoula, MT, 1979.

Caciola, Nancy. *Discerning Spirits: Divine and Demonic Possession in the Middle Ages.* Ithaca, NY, 2003.

Cadden, Joan. "It Takes All Kinds: Sexuality and Gender Difference in Hildegard of Bingen's *Book of Compound Medicine." Traditio* 40 (1984): 149–174.

———. *Nothing Natural Is Shameful: Sodomy and Science in Late Medieval Europe.* Philadelphia, 2013.

Cagnin, Giampaolo. "'Ad adiscendum artem et officium clericatus': Note sul reclutamento e sulla formazione del clero a Treviso (sec. XIV)." In *Preti nel medioevo,* ed. Mauricio Zangarini, 93–124. Verona, 1997.

Cantarella, Eva. *Bisexuality in the Ancient World.* Trans. Cormac Ó Cuilleanáin. New Haven, CT, 1992.

Carola, Joseph. *Augustine of Hippo: The Role of the Laity in Ecclesial Reconciliation.* Rome, 2005.

Carrasco, Rafael. *Inquisición y represión sexual en Valencia: Historia de los sodomitas, 1565–1785.* Barcelona, 1985.

Carratori, Luigina. *Inventario dell'Archivio Arcivescovile di Pisa.* Pisa, 1986.

Carruthers, Mary. *The Book of Memory: A Study of Memory in Medieval Culture.* Cambridge, 1990.

Cavett, Dick. *Talk Show: Confrontations, Pointed Commentary, and Off-Screen Secrets.* New York, 2010.

Chadwick, Henry. *The Church in Ancient Society: From Galilee to Gregory the Great.* Oxford, 2001.

Chartier, E.-L. *L'ancien chapitre de Notre-Dame de Paris et sa maîtrise.* Paris, 1897.

Chasteigner, Jean de. "Le célibat sacerdotal dans les écrits de Saint Pierre Damian." *Doctor Communis* 24 (1971): 169–183.

Cheney, C. R. *Episcopal Visitation of Monasteries in the Thirteenth Century.* Manchester, 1931.

Chibnall, Marjorie. *The World of Orderic Vitalis: Norman Monks and Norman Knights.* Oxford, 1984.

Chiffoleau, Jacques. "Dire l'indicibile: Remarques sur la catégorie du *nefandum* du XIIe au XVe siècle." *Annales: Histoire, Sciences Sociales* 45 (1990): 289–324.

Chronopoulos, Tina. "Ganymede in the Medieval Classroom: Reading an *Ode* by the Roman Poet Horace." *Medium Aevum* 86 (2017): 224–248.

Clark, David. *Between Medieval Men: Male Friendship and Desire in Early Medieval English Literature.* Oxford, 2009.

Clark, Elizabeth A. "John Chrysostom and the *Subintroductae." Church History* 46 (1977): 171–184.

Clark, Gillian. "The Fathers and the Children." In *The Church and Childhood,* ed. Diana Wood, 1–28. Oxford, 1994.

Clausen, M. A. *Chrodegang of Metz and the "Regula canonicorum" in the Eighth Century.* Cambridge, 2004.

Clerici, Agostino. *La Correzione Fraterna in S. Agostino.* Palermo, 1989.

Cochelin, Isabelle. "Besides the Book: Using the Body to Mould the Mind—Cluny in the Tenth and Eleventh Centuries." In *Medieval Monastic Education,* ed. George Ferzoco and Carolyn Muessig, 21–34. New York, 2005.

Cochini, Christian. *Apostolic Origins of Priestly Celibacy.* Trans. Nelly Marans. San Francisco, 1990.

Coleman, Gerald D. "Seminary Formation in Light of the Sexual Abuse Crisis: *Pastores Dabo Vobis.*" In *Sexual Abuse in the Catholic Church: A Decade of Crisis, 2002–2012,* ed. Thomas G. Plante and Kathleen L. McChesney, 205–219. Santa Barbara CA, 2011.

Collette, A. *Histoire de la maîtrise de Rouen.* Rouen, 1892. Reprint, Paris, 2000.

Collins, Roger. *Early Medieval Spain: Unity in Diversity, 400–1000.* New York, 1983.

Congar, Yves. "Clercs et laïcs au point de vue de la culture au Moyen Âge: 'Laicus' = sans lettres." *Antonianum* 45 (1970): 309–322.

Constable, Giles. "The Authorship of the *Epistolae duorum amantium*: A Reconsideration." In *Voices in Dialogue: Reading Women in the Middle Ages,* ed. Linda Olson and Kathryn Kerby-Fulton, 167–178. Notre Dame, IN, 2005.

———. "Cluniac Administration and Administrators in the Twelfth Century." In *Order and Innovation in the Twelfth Century: Essays in Honor of Joseph R. Strayer,* ed. William Chester Jordan, Bruce McNab, and Teofilo F. Ruiz, 17–30, 417–424. Princeton, NJ, 1976.

———. *The Reformation of the Twelfth Century.* Cambridge, 1996.

Contreni, John J. "'Building Mansions in Heaven': The *Visio Baronti,* Archangel Raphael, and a Carolingian King." *Speculum* 78 (2003): 673–706.

Coon, Lynda L. *Dark Age Bodies: Gender and Monastic Practice in the Early Medieval West.* Philadelphia, 2010.

Cossar, Roisin. *Clerical Households in Late Medieval Italy.* Cambridge, MA, 2017.

Courtenay, William J. *Parisian Scholars in the Early Fourteenth Century.* Cambridge, 1999.

Cowdrey, H. E. J. "Gregory VII and Chastity." In *Medieval Purity and Piety: Essays on Medieval Clerical Celibacy and Religious Reform,* ed. Michael Frassetto, 269–301. New York, 1998.

———. "The Papacy, the Patarenes, and the Church of Milan." *Transactions for the Royal Historical Society* 18 (1968): 25–48.

———. *Pope Gregory VII, 1073–1085.* Oxford, 1987.

Crawford, Katherine. *European Sexualities, 1400–1800.* Cambridge, 2007.

Cribiore, Raffaella. *Libanius the Sophist: Rhetoric, Reality, and Religion in the Fourth Century.* Ithaca, NY, 2013.

Cullum, P. H. "Clergy, Masculinity and Transgression in Late Medieval England." In *Masculinity in Medieval Europe,* ed. D. M. Hadley, 178–196. London, 1999.

Curtius, Ernst. *European Literature and the Latin Middle Ages.* Trans. Willard R. Trask. New York, 1953.

Cushing, Kathleen G. *Papacy and Law in the Gregorian Revolution.* Oxford, 1998.

———. "*Pueri, Iuvenes,* and *Viri*: Age and Utility in the Gregorian Reform." *Catholic Historical Review* 94 (2008): 435–449.

———. *Reform and Papacy in the Eleventh Century: Spirituality and Social Change.* Manchester, 2005.

Dalla, Danilo. *"Ubi Venus mutatur": Omosessualità e diritto nel mondo romano*. Milan, 1987.

Dameron, George W. *Florence and Its Church in the Age of Dante*. Philadelphia, 2005.

d'Avray, D. L. "Peter Damian, Consanguinity and Church Property." In *Intellectual Life in the Middle Ages: Essays Presented to Margaret Gibson*, ed. Lesley Smith and Benedicta Ward, 71–80. London, 1992.

Davril, Anselme. "Coutumiers directifs et coutumiers descriptifs d'Ulrich à Bernard de Cluny." In *From Dead of Night to End of Day: The Medieval Customs of Cluny / Du coeur de la nuit à la fin du jour: Les coutumes clunisiennes au moyen âge*, ed. Susan Boynton and Isabelle Cochelin, 23–28. Turnhout, 2005.

de Jong, Mayke. "Growing Up in a Carolingian Monastery: Magister Hildemar and His Oblates." *Journal of Medieval History* 9 (1983): 99–128.

———. "Hincmar, Priests and Pseudo-Isidore: The Case of Trising in Context." In *Hincmar of Rheims: Life and Work*, ed. Rachel Stone and Charles West, 268–288. Manchester, 2016.

———. "*Imitatio morum*: The Cloister and Clerical Purity in the Carolingian World." In *Medieval Purity and Piety: Essays on Medieval Clerical Celibacy and Religious Reform*, ed. Michael Frassetto, 49–80. New York, 1998.

———. *In Samuel's Image: Child Oblation in the Early Medieval West*. Leiden, 1996.

———. *The Penitential State: Authority and Atonement in the Age of Louis the Pious, 814–840*. Cambridge, 2009.

———. "The State of the Church: *Ecclesia* and Early Medieval State Formation." In *Der frühmittelalteriche Staat—Europäische Perspektiven*, ed. Walter Pohl and Veronika Wieser, 241–254. Vienna, 2009.

———. "Transformation of Penance." In *Rituals of Power from Late Antiquity to the Early Middle Ages*, ed. Frans Theuws and Janet Nelson, 185–224. Leiden, 2000.

Devisse, Jean. *Hincmar: Archevêque de Reims, 845–882*. 3 vols. Paris, 1975–1976.

———. *Hincmar et la loi*. Dakar, 1962.

Diaz y Diaz, Manuel C. "Fructueux de Braga (saint)." In *Dictionnaire de spiritualité*, 5:1541–1546. Paris, 1964.

Dinshaw, Carolyn. *Chaucer's Sexual Poetics*. Madison, WI, 1989.

———. *Getting Medieval: Sexualities and Communities, Pre-and Postmodern*. Durham, NC, 1999.

———. "Touching the Past." In *The Boswell Thesis: Essays on "Christianity, Social Tolerance, and Homosexuality,"* ed. Mathew Kuefler, 57–73. Chicago, 2006.

Dinzelbacher, Peter. *Revelationes*. Typologie des sources du moyen âge occidental, fasc. 57. Turnhout, 1991.

Dobson, Barrie, "The English Vicars Choral: An Introduction." In *Vicars Choral at English Cathedrals: "Cantate Domino"; History, Architecture and Archaeology*, ed. Richard Hall and David Stocker, 1–10. Oxford, 2005.

Donahue, Charles, Jr. "The Ecclesiastical Courts: Introduction." In *The History of Courts and Procedure in Medieval Canon Law*, ed. Wilfried Hartmann and Kenneth Pennington, 3–30. Washington, DC, 2016.

———. "Proof by Witnesses in the Church Courts of Medieval England: An Imperfect Reception of Learned Law." In *On the Laws and Customs of England: Essays in Honor of Samuel E. Thorne*, ed. Morris Arnold, 127–158. Chapel Hill, NC, 1981.

Donahue, Charles, Jr., and Sara McDougall. "France and Adjoining Areas." In *The History of Courts and Procedure in Medieval Canon Law*, ed. Wilfried Hartmann and Kenneth Pennington, 300–343. Washington, DC, 2016.

Donnelly, Doris K. "Penance and Justice." In *Sacraments and Justice*, ed. Doris K. Donnelly, 45–65. Collegeville, MN, 2014.

Dortel-Claudot, Michel. "Le prêtre et le mariage: Évolution de la legislation canonique des origines au XIIe siècle." *L'Année canonique* 17 (1973): 319–344.

Dougherty, T. David. "The Vicar General of the Episcopal Ordinary." PhD diss., Catholic University of America, Washington, DC, 1966.

Douglas, Mary. *Purity and Danger: An Analysis of Concepts of Pollutions and Taboo*. London, 1966.

Doyle, Thomas P., A. W. Richard Sipe, and Patrick J. Wall. *Sex, Priests, and Secret Codes: The Catholic Church's 2,000-Year Paper Trail of Sexual Abuse*. Los Angeles, 2006.

Dronke, Peter. *Poetic Individuality in the Middle Ages: New Departures in Poetry, 1100–1150*. Oxford, 1970.

Druwé, Wouter. *Scandalum in the Early Bolognese Decretistic and in Papal Decretals, ca. 1140–1234*. Louvain, 2018.

Duby, Georges. *The Knight, the Lady, and the Priest: The Making of Modern Marriage in Medieval France*. Trans. Barbara Bray. New York, 1983.

Dunn, Marilyn. *The Emergence of Monasticism: From Desert Fathers to the Early Middle Ages*. Oxford, 2000.

Dusil, Stephan. *Wissensordnungen des Rechts im Wandel: Päpstlicher Jurisdiktionsprimat und Zölibat zwischen 1000 und 1215*. Louvain, 2018.

Economou, George D. *The Goddess Natura in Medieval Literature*. Notre Dame, IN, 2002.

Edwards, Catharine. *The Politics of Sexual Immorality in Ancient Rome*. Cambridge, 1993.

Edwards, Kathleen. *The English Secular Cathedrals in the Middle Ages: A Constitutional Study with Special Reference to the Fourteenth Century*. 2nd ed. Manchester, 1967.

Elliott, Dyan. *The Bride of Christ Goes to Hell: Metaphor and Embodiment in the Lives of Pious Women, 200–1500*. Philadelphia, 2012.

———. "The Church Sex Scandal: Medieval Blueprint for Disaster." In *Why the Middle Ages Matter: Medieval Light on Modern Injustice*, ed. Celia Chazelle, Simon Doubleday, Felice Lifshitz, and Amy G. Remensnyder, 90–105. London, 2011.

———. "Dressing and Undressing the Clergy: The Rites of Ordination and Degradation." In *Medieval Fabrications: Dress, Textiles, Cloth Work, and Other Cultural Imaginings*, ed. E. Jane Burns, 55–69. New York, 2004.

———. *Fallen Bodies: Pollution, Sexuality, and Demonology in the Middle Ages*. Philadelphia, 1999.

———. "Lollardy and the Integrity of Marriage and the Family." In *The Medieval Marriage Scene: Prudence, Passion, Policy*, ed. Sherry Roush and Cristelle Baskins, 37–54. Tempe, AZ, 2005.

———. *Proving Woman: Female Spirituality and Inquisitional Culture in the Later Middle Ages*. Princeton, NJ, 2004.

———. *Spiritual Marriage: Sexual Abstinence in Medieval Wedlock*. Princeton, NJ. 1993.

———. "Violence Against the Dead: The Negative Translation and *Damnatio memoriae* in the Middle Ages." *Speculum* 92 (2017): 1020–1055.

————. "Women and Confession: From Empowerment to Pathology." In *Gendering the Master Narrative: Women and Power in the Middle Ages*, ed. Mary Erler and Maryanne Kowaleski, 31–51. Ithaca, NY, 2003.

Evans, Joan. *Monastic Life at Cluny, 910–1157*. London, 1931.

Festugière, André-Jean. *Antioche païenne et chrétienne: Libanius, Chrysostome et les moines de Syrie*. Paris, 1959.

Fioravanti, Jacopo Maria. *Memorie storiche della città di Pistoia*. Lucca, 1758.

Fiori, Antonia. *Il giuramento di innocenza nel processo canonico medievale: Storia e disciplina della "purgatio canonica."* Frankfurt am Main, 2013.

————. "*Probatio* y *purgatio* en el proceso canonico medievale, entre rito acusatorio e inquisitorio." In *Procesos, inquisiciones, pruebas*, ed. Mario Sbriccoli, 77–96. Buenos Aires, 2009.

Firey, Abigail. "Blushing Before the Judge and the Physician: Moral Arbitration in the Carolingian Empire." In *A New History of Penance*, ed. Abigail Firey, 173–200. Leiden, 2008.

————. *A Contrite Heart: Prosecution and Redemption in the Carolingian Empire*. Boston, 2009.

————. "Ghostly Recensions in Early Medieval Canon Law." *Legal History Review* 68 (2000): 63–82.

Firth, J. J. Francis. "The *Poenitentiale* of Robert of Flamborough." *Traditio* 16 (1960): 541–556.

Fliche, Augustin. "Guy de Ferrare: Étude sur la polémique religieuse en Italie à la fin du XIe siècle." 2 parts. *Bulletin Italien* 16 (1916):105–140; 18 (1918): 114–131.

————. *La réforme grégorienne*. 8 vols. Louvain and Paris, 1924–1946.

————. *Le règne de Philippe Ier, roi de France, 1060–1108*. Paris, 1912.

Florence of Worcester. *Chronicon ex chronicis*. 2 vols. London, 1848–1849.

Forsyth, Ilene H. "The Ganymede Capital at Vézelay." *Gesta* 15 (1976): 241–246.

Fort, Gavin. "The Vicarious Middle Ages: Penitents and Their Proxies in Medieval Europe." PhD diss., Northwestern University, 2017.

Foucault, Michel. *The History of Sexuality*. Vol. 1, *An Introduction*. Vol. 3, *The Care of the Self*. Trans. Robert Hurley. New York, 1978, 1988.

Fournier, Édouard. *L'origine du vicaire général et des autres membres de la curie diocésaine*. Paris, 1911.

Fournier, Paul. "De l'origine des Fausses Décrétales." In *Mélanges de droit canonique*, ed. Theo Kölzer, 1:65–82. Aalen, 1983.

————. "Étude sur les Fausses Décrétales." In *Mélanges de droit canonique*, ed. Theo Kölzer, 1:83–201. Aalen, 1983.

————. *Les officialités au Moyen Âge: Étude sur l'organisation, la compétence et la procédure des tribunaux ecclésiastiques ordinaires en France de 1180 à 1328*. Paris, 1880. Reprint, Aalen, 1984.

————. "La question des Fausses Décrétales." In *Mélanges de droit canonique*, ed. Theo Kölzer, 1:23–64. Aalen, 1983.

Fournier, Paul, and Gabriel Le Bras. *Histoire des collections canoniques en occident depuis les Fausses Décrétales jusqu'au Décret de Gratien*. 2 vols. Paris, 1931.

Fraher, Richard M. "Preventing Crime in the High Middle Ages: The Medieval Lawyers' Search for Deterrence." In *Popes, Teachers, and Canon Law in the Middle Ages*, ed. James Ross Sweeney and Stanley Chodorow, 212–233. Ithaca, NY, 1989.

———. "The Theoretical Justification for the New Criminal Law of the High Middle Ages: *Rei publicae interest, ne crimina remaneant impunita.*" *University of Illinois Law Review*, no. 3 (1984): 577–595.

———. "*Ut nullus describatur reus prius quam convincatur*: Presumption of Innocence in Medieval Canon Law?" *Proceedings of the Sixth International Congress of Medieval Canon Law*, ed. Stephan Kuttner and Kenneth Pennington, 493–506. Vatican City, 1985.

Frantzen, Allen. *Before the Closet: Same-Sex Love from "Beowulf" to "Angels in America."* Chicago, 1998.

———. "Penitentials Attributed to Bede." *Speculum* 58 (1983): 573–597.

———. "When Women Aren't Enough." *Speculum* 68 (1993): 445–471.

———. "Where the Boys Are: Children and Sex in Anglo-Saxon Penitentials." In *Becoming Male in the Middle Ages*, ed. Jeffrey Cohen and Bonnie Wheeler, 43–66. New York, 1997.

Frauenknecht, Erwin. *Die Verteidigung der Priesterehe in der Reformzeit. MGH Studien und Texte* 16. Hanover, 1997.

Frawley-O'Dea, Mary Gail. *Perversion of Power: Sexual Abuse in the Catholic Church.* Nashville, 2007.

Frend, W. H. C. *The Donatist Church: A Movement of Protest in Roman North Africa.* Oxford, 1952.

Fuhrmann, Horst. *Einfluss und Verbreitung der pseudoisidorischen Fälschungen: von ihrem Auftauchen bis in die neuere Zeit.* 3 vols. *MGH Schriften* 24.1–3. Stuttgart, 1972–1974.

Furnish, Victor Paul. *The Moral Teaching of Paul.* Nashville, 1979.

Füser, Thomas. "Der Leib ist das Grab der Seele: Der Institutionelle Umgang mit sexueller Devianz in Cluniazensischen Klöstern des 13. und frühen 14. Jahrhunderts." In *Vita regularis: Ordnungen und Deutungen religiosen Lebens im Mittelalter*, ed. Gert Melville, 187–245. Munster, 2014.

———. *Mönche im Konflikt: Zum Spannungsfeld von Norm, Devianz und Sanktion bei den Cisterziensern und Cluniazensern (12. bis frühres 14. Jahrhundert).* Munster, 2000.

Gade, Kari Ellen. "Homosexuality and Rape of Males in Old Norse Law and Literature." *Scandinavian Studies* 58 (1986):124–151.

Gamurrini, Eugenio. *Istoria genealogica delle famiglie nobili toscone et umbre.* 5 vols. Florence, 1668–1685.

Gardiner, Eileen. *Medieval Visions of Heaven and Hell: A Sourcebook.* New York, 1993.

Gardner, Jane F. *Women in Roman Law and Society.* Bloomington, IN, 1989.

Gaunt, Simon. "Straight Minds/'Queer' Wishes in Old French Hagiography." In *Premodern Sexualities*, ed. Louise Fradenburg and Carla Freccero, 153–174. New York, 1996.

Geldsetzer, Lutz. "'Sic et non' sive 'Sic aut non': La methode des questions chez Abélard et la stratégie de la recherche." In *Pierre Abélard: Colloque international de Nantes*, ed. Jean Jolivet and Henri Habrias, 407–415. Rennes, 2003.

Geltner, Guy. "*Detrusio:* Penal Cloistering in the Middle Ages." *Revue Bénédictine* 118 (2008): 89–108.

———. "I registri criminali dell'Archivio Arcivescovile di Lucca: prospettive di ricerca per la storia sociale del Medioevo." In *Il patrimonio documentario della Chiesa di Lucca. Prospettive di ricerca*, ed. Sergio Pagano and Pierantonio Piatti, 331–340. Florence, 2010.

———. "Patrolling Normative Boundaries After the Black Death: The Bishop of Lucca's Criminal Court." In *Center and Periphery: Studies on Power in the Medieval World in*

Honor of William Chester Jordan, ed. Katherine L. Jansen, G. Geltner, and Anne E. Lester, 169–180. Leiden, 2013.

Gilchrist, Roberta. *Medieval Life: Archaeology and the Life Course.* Woodbridge, 2012.

Gillis, Matthew Bryan. *Heresy and Dissent in the Carolingian Empire: The Case of Gottschalk of Orbais.* Oxford, 2017.

Gilmour-Bryson, Anne. "Sodomy and the Knights Templar." *Journal of the History of Sexuality* 7 (1996): 151–183.

Goering, Joseph. "The Internal Forum and the Literature of Penance and Confession." *Traditio* 59 (2004): 175–227.

———. "The Scholastic Turn (1100–1500): Penitential Theology and Law in the Schools." In *A New History of Penance*, ed. Abigail Firey, 219–237. Leiden, 2008.

———. "The *Summa de penitentia* of Master Serlo." *Mediaeval Studies* 38 (1976): 1–53.

———. *William de Montibus (c. 1140–1213): The Schools and the Literature of Pastoral Care.* Toronto, 1992.

Goering, Joseph, and F. A. C. Mantello. "The Early Penitential Writings of Robert Grosseteste." *Recherches de théologie ancienne et médiévale* 54 (1987): 52–112.

Goguel, Maurice. "Les Nicolaïtes." *Revue de l'histoire des religions* 115 (1937): 5–36.

Goldberg, Jessica. "The Legal Persona of the Child in Gratian's *Decretum.*" *Bulletin of Medieval Canon Law* 10 (2000): 11–53.

Goodich, Michael. "Sodomy in Ecclesiastical Law and Theory." *Journal of Homosexuality* 1 (1976): 427–434.

———. "Sodomy in Medieval Secular Law." *Journal of Homosexuality* 1 (1976): 295–302.

———. *The Unmentionable Vice: Homosexuality in the Middle Ages.* Santa Barbara, CA, 1979.

Greatrex, Joan. "The Almonry of Norwich Cathedral Priory in the Thirteenth and Fourteenth Centuries." In *The Church and Childhood*, ed. Diana Wood, 169–181. Oxford, 1994.

Griffiths, Fiona J. *Nuns' Priests' Tales: Men and Salvation in Medieval Women's Monastic Life.* Philadelphia, 2018.

Gryson, Roger. "Dix ans de recherches sur les origines de célibat ecclésiastique: Réflexion sur les publications des années 1970–1979." *Revue théologique de Louvain* 11 (1980): 157–185.

———. *Les origines du célibat ecclésiastique du premier au septième siècle.* Gembloux, 1970.

Guest, Gerald B. "'The Darkness and the Obscurity of Sins': Representing Vice in the Thirteenth-Century *Bibles moralisées.*" In *The Garden of Evil: The Vices and Culture in the Middle Ages*, ed. Richard Newhauser, 74–104. Toronto, 2005.

Gwynn, David M. *Athanasius of Alexandria: Bishop, Theologian, Ascetic, Father.* Oxford, 2012.

Haliczar, Stephen. *Inquisition and Society in the Kingdom of Valencia.* Berkeley, CA, 1990.

———. *Sexuality in the Confessional: A Sacrament Profaned.* New York, 1996.

Halperin, David M. "Is There a History of Sexuality?" *History and Theory* 28 (1989): 257–274.

Hamilton, Sarah. "Penance in the Age of Gregorian Reform." In *Retribution, Repentance, and Reconciliation*, ed. Kate Cooper and Jeremy Gregory, 47–73. Woodbridge, 2004.

———. *The Practice of Penance, 900–1050.* Woodbridge, 2001.

Harnack, Adolf von. "The Sect of the Nicolaitans and Nicolaus, the Deacon of Jerusalem." *Journal of Religion* 3 (1923): 413–422.

Harper, Kyle. *From Shame to Sin: The Christian Transformation of Sexual Morality in Late Antiquity.* Cambridge, MA, 2013.

———. "*Porneia:* The Making of a Christian Norm." *Journal of Biblical Literature* 131 (2012): 363–383.

Harris, Carissa M. *Obscene Pedagogies: Transgressive Talk and Sexual Education in Late Medieval Britain.* Ithaca, NY, 2018.

Haskins, Charles Homer. "The Sources for the History of the Papal Penitentiary." *American Journal of Theology* 9 (1905): 421–450.

Hay, Denys. *The Church in Italy in the Fifteenth Century.* Cambridge, 1977.

Healy, Patrick. *The Chronicle of Hugh of Flavigny: Reform and the Investiture Contest in the Late Eleventh Century.* Aldershot, 2006.

Heid, Stefan. *Celibacy in the Early Church: The Beginnings of a Discipline of Obligatory Continence for Clerics in East and West.* Trans. Michael J. Miller. San Francisco, 2000.

Helmholz, R. H. *Canon Law and the Law of England.* London, 1987.

———. "Local Ecclesiastical Courts in England." In *The History of Courts and Procedure in Medieval Canon Law,* ed. Wilfried Hartmann and Kenneth Pennington, 344–391. Washington, DC, 2016.

———. *The Oxford History of the Laws of England.* Vol. 1, *Canon Law and Ecclesiastical Jurisdiction from 597 to the 1640s.* Oxford, 2004.

Hergemöller, Bernd-Ulrich. *Sodom and Gomorrah: On the Everyday Reality and Persecution of Homosexuals in the Middle Ages.* Trans. John Phillips. London, 2001.

Herlihy, David. *Medieval and Renaissance Pistoia: The Social History of a Medieval Town, 1200–1430.* New Haven, CT, 1967.

Herlihy, David, and Christiane Klapisch-Zuber. *The Tuscans and Their Families.* New Haven, CT, 1985.

Hexter, Ralph J. "John Boswell's Gay Science: Prolegomenon to a Re-Reading." In *The Boswell Thesis: Essays on "Christianity, Social Tolerance, and Homosexuality,"* ed. Mathew Kuefler, 35–66. Chicago, 2006.

———. *Ovid and Medieval Schooling: Studies in Medieval School Commentaries on Ovid's "Ars Amatoria," "Epistulae ex Ponto,"and "Epistulae Heroidum."* Munich, 1986.

Hiley, David. *Western Plainchant: A Handbook.* Oxford, 1993.

Hillner, Julia. "L'enfermement monastique au VIe siècle." In *Enfermements: Le cloître et la prison (VIe–XVIIIe siècle),* ed. Isabelle Heullant-Donat, Julie Claustre, and Élisabeth Lusset, 39–56. Paris, 2011.

———. *Prison, Punishment and Penance in Late Antiquity.* Cambridge, 2015.

Holsinger, Bruce. "Langland's Musical Reader." *Studies in the Age of Chaucer* 21 (1999): 117–120.

———. *Music, Body, and Desire in Medieval Culture.* Stanford, CA, 2001.

Hudson, Anne. *Premature Reformation: Wycliffite Texts and History.* Oxford, 1988.

Hunt, Noreen. *Cluny Under Saint Hugh, 1049–1109.* London, 1967.

Hunter, David G. Introduction to *A Comparison Between a King and a Monk/Against the Opponents of the Monastic Life: Two Treatises,* by John Chrysostom, 1–68. Trans. David G. Hunter. Lewiston, NY, 1988.

———. *Marriage, Celibacy, and Heresy in Ancient Christianity: The Jovinianist Controversy.* New York, 2007.

———. "Married Clergy in Eastern and Western Christianity." In *A Companion to Priesthood and Holy Orders in the Middle Ages,* ed. Greg Peters and C. Colt Anderson, 97–139. Leiden, 2016.

Jasper, Detlev, and Horst Fuhrmann. *Papal Letters in the Early Middle Ages.* Washington, DC, 2001.

Innes, Matthew. "'A Place of Discipline': Carolingian Courts and Aristocratic Youth." In *Court Culture in the Early Middle Ages*, ed. Catherine Cubitt, 59–76. Turnhout, 2003.

Iogna-Prat, Dominique. "Continence et virginité dans la conception clunisienne de l'ordre du monde autour l'an mil." *Académie des Inscriptions et Belles-Lettres: Comptes rendus des séances de l'année 1985*, 127–146. Paris, 1985.

Jaeger, Stephen C. *Ennobling Love: In Search of a Lost Sensibility*. Philadelphia, 1999.

———. *The Envy of Angels: Cathedral Schools and Social Ideals in Medieval Europe, 950–1200.* Philadelphia, 1994.

———. "*Epistolae duorum amantium* and the Ascription to Heloise and Abelard." In *Voices in Dialogue: Reading Women in the Middle Ages*, ed. Linda Olson and Kathryn Kerby-Fulton, 125–166. Notre Dame, IN, 2005.

———. "A Reply to Giles Constable." In *Voices in Dialogue: Reading Women in the Middle Ages*, ed. Linda Olson and Kathryn Kerby-Fulton, 179–186. Notre Dame, IN, 2005.

Jestice, Phyllis G. "Why Celibacy? Odo of Cluny and the Development of a New Sexual Morality." In *Medieval Purity and Piety: Essays on Medieval Clerical Celibacy and Religious Reform*, ed. Michael Frassetto, 81–116. New York, 1998.

Johnson, Mark. "Paul of Hungary's *Summa de penitentia*." In *From Learning to Love: Schools, Law, and Pastoral Care in the Middle Ages; Essays in Honour of Joseph W. Goering*, ed. Tristan Sharp, 402–418. Toronto, 2017.

Jones, Christopher A. "Monastic Identity and Sodomitic Danger in the *Occupatio* by Odo of Cluny." *Speculum* 82 (2007): 1–53.

Jordan, Mark D. "'Both as a Christian and as a Historian': On Boswell's Ministry." In *The Boswell Thesis: Essays on "Christianity, Social Tolerance and Homosexuality,"* ed. Mathew Kuefler, 88–107. Chicago, 2006.

———. *The Invention of Sodomy in Christian Theology*. Chicago, 1997.

———. *The Silence of Sodom: Homosexuality in Modern Catholicism*. Chicago, 2000.

Kamen, Henry. *The Spanish Inquisition: A Historical Revision*. New Haven, CT, 1998.

Karras, Ruth Mazo. "Active/Passive, Acts/Passions: Greek and Roman Sexualities." *American Historical Review* 105 (2000): 1250–1265.

———. "Friendship and Love in the Lives of Two Twelfth-Century Saints." *Journal of Medieval History* 14 (1988): 305–320.

———. *From Boys to Men: Formations of Masculinity in Late Medieval Europe*. Philadelphia, 2003.

———. "Knighthood, Compulsory Heterosexuality, and Sodomy." In *The Boswell Thesis: Essays on "Christianity, Social Tolerance, and Homosexuality,"* ed. Mathew Kuefler, 275–279. Chicago, 2006.

———. "The Lechery That Dare Not Speak Its Name: Sodomy and the Vices in Medieval England." In *In the Garden of Evil: The Vices and Culture in the Middle Ages*, ed. Richard Newhauser, 193–205. Toronto, 2005.

———. *Medieval Sexuality: Doing Unto Others*. 3rd ed. London, 2017.

———. "Thomas Aquinas's Chastity Belt: Clerical Masculinity in Medieval Europe." In *Gender and Christianity in Medieval Europe: New Perspectives*, ed. Lisa Bitel and Felice Lifshitz, 52–67. Philadelphia, 2008.

———. *Unmarriages: Women, Men, and Sexual Unions in the Middle Ages*. Philadelphia, 2012.

Kay, Richard. "Martin IV and the Fugitive Bishop of Bayeux." *Speculum* 40 (1965): 60–83.

Kedar, Benjamin Z. "On the Origins of the Earliest Laws of Frankish Jerusalem: The Canons of the Council of Nablus, 1120." *Speculum* 74 (1999): 310–335.

Keefe, Susan A. *Water and the Word: Baptism and the Education of the Clergy in the Carolingian Empire.* 2 vols. Notre Dame, IN, 2002.

Kéry, Lotte. *Canonical Collections of the Early Middle Ages, ca. 400–1140: A Bibliographical Guide to the Manuscripts and Literature.* Washington, DC, 1999.

King, Archdale A. *Liturgies of the Religious Orders.* London, 1955.

Kirkman, Andrew. "The Seeds of Medieval Music: Choirboys and Musical Training in a Late-Medieval Maîtrise." In *Young Choristers, 650–1700*, ed. Susan Boynton and Eric Rice, 104–122. Woodbridge, 2008.

Klaniczay, Gábor. *The Uses of Supernatural Power: The Transformation of Popular Religion in Medieval and Early-Modern Europe.* Ed. Karen Margolis. Trans. Susan Singerman. Cambridge, 1990.

Kleinjung, Christine. "To Fight with Words: The Case of Hincmar of Laon in the Annals of St.-Bertin." In *Hincmar of Rheims: Life and Work*, ed. Rachel Stone and Charles West, 60–75. Manchester, 2015.

Klingshirn, William E. *Caesarius of Arles: The Making of a Christian Community in Late Antique Gaul.* Cambridge, 1994.

Knapp, Janet. "Polyphony at Notre Dame of Paris." In *The New Oxford History of Music*, vol. 2, *The Early Middle Ages to 1300*, ed. Richard Crocker and David Hiley, 557–635. 2nd ed. Oxford, 1990.

Koldeweij, A. M. "Lifting the Veil on Pilgrim Badges." In *Pilgrimage Explored*, ed. J. Stopford, 161–188. Woodbridge, 1999.

Kolve, V. A. "Ganymede/Son of Getron: Medieval Monasticism and the Drama of Same-Sex Desire." *Speculum* 73 (1998):1014–1067.

Kottje, Raymund. *Die Bussbücher Halitgars von Cambrai und des Hrabanus Maurus: Ihre Überlieferung und ihre Quellen.* Berlin, 1980.

Kuefler, Mathew, ed. *The Boswell Thesis: Essays on "Christianity, Social Tolerance, and Homosexuality."* Chicago, 2006.

———. "Male Friendship and the Suspicion of Sodomy in Twelfth-Century France." In *Gender and Difference in the Middle Ages*, ed. Sharon Farmer and Carol Braun Pasternack, 145–181. Minneapolis, 2003.

———. "Sex with Eunuchs, Sex with Boys, and the Implications of Sexual Difference." In *Atti del 53 Congresso Internazionale di studi sull'alto Medioevo: Comportamenti e immaginario della sessualità nell'alto medioevo*, 139–172. Spoleto, 2006.

Kurtscheid, Bertrand. *A History of the Seal of Confession.* Trans. F. A. Marks. London, 1927.

Kuttner, Stephan. "*Ecclesia de occultis non iudicat*: Problemata ex doctrina poenali decretistarum et decretalistarum a Gratiano usque ad Gregorium PP. IX." In *Acta congressus iuridici internationalis*, 3:225–246. Rome, 1936.

Labriolle, Pierre de. "Le 'mariage spirituel' dans l'antiquité chrétienne." *Revue historique* 137 (1921): 204–225.

Laes, Christian. *Children in the Roman Empire: Outsiders Within.* Cambridge, 2011.

Laeuchli, Samuel. *Power and Sexuality: The Emergence of Canon Law at the Synod of Elvira.* Philadelphia, 1972.

Largier, Niklaus. *In Praise of the Whip: A Cultural History of Arousal.* New York, 2007.

Larson, Atria A. *Master of Penance: Gratian and the Development of Penitential Thought and Law in the Twelfth Century.* Washington, DC, 2014.

Lea, Henry Charles. *A History of Auricular Confession and Indulgences in the Latin Church.* 3 vols. Philadelphia, 1896.

———. *A History of the Inquisition in Spain.* 4 vols. New York, 1906–1907.

———. *History of Sacerdotal Celibacy in the Christian Church.* 3rd rev. ed. 2 vols. London, 1907.

Leclercq, Jean. *Monks and Love in Twelfth-Century France: Psycho-Historical Essays.* Oxford, 1979.

———. *Saint Pierre Damien, ermite et homme d'église.* Rome, 1960.

———. "S. Pierre Damien et les femmes." *Studia monastica* 15 (1973): 43–55.

Lepine, David. *A Brotherhood of Canons Serving God.* Woodbridge, 1995.

Le Roy Ladurie, Emmanuel. *Montaillou: The Promised Land of Error.* Trans. Barbara Bray. New York, 1979.

Lett, Didier. "Genre, enfance et violence sexuelle dans les archives juridiciaires de Bologne au XVe siècle." *Âge et sexualité* 42 (2015): 202–215.

Lévy, Jean-Philippe. "Le problème de la preuve dans les droits savants du Moyen Âge." In *La preuve*, vol. 2, *Moyen Âge et temps modernes*, 136–167. Recueils de la Société Jean Bodin pour l'histoire comparative des institutions 17. Brussels, 1965.

Leyser, Conrad. "Cities of the Plain: The Rhetoric of Sodomy in Peter Damian's *Book of Gomorrah*." *Romanic Review* 86 (1995): 191–211.

Little, Lester K. "The Personal Development of Peter Damian." In *Order and Innovation in the Middle Ages: Essays in Honor of Joseph R. Strayer*, ed. William Chester Jordan, Bruce McNab, and Teofilo F. Ruiz, 317–341. Princeton, NJ, 1976.

Lochrie, Karma. *Covert Operations: The Medieval Uses of Secrecy.* Philadelphia, 1999.

———. "Presidential Improprieties and Medieval Categories: The Absurdity of Heterosexuality." In *Queering the Middle Ages*, ed. Glenn Burger and Steven F. Kruger, 87–96. Minneapolis, 1999.

Lockwood, Daniel. *Prison Sexual Violence.* New York, 1980.

Logan, Donald. *Runaway Religious in Medieval England, c. 1240–1540.* Cambridge, 1996.

Lusset, Élisabeth. "Entre les murs: L'enfermement punitive des religieux criminels au sein du cloître (XIIe–XVe siècle)." In *Enfermements: Le cloître et la prison, VIe–XVIIIe siècle*, ed. Isabelle Heullant-Donat, Julie Claustre, and Élisabeth Lusset, 1:153–167. Paris, 2011.

Lynch, John E. "The Cistercians and Underage Novices." *Cîteaux* 24 (1973): 283–297.

———. "Marriage and Celibacy of the Clergy: The Discipline of the Western Church; An Historico-Canonical Synopsis." *Jurist* 32 (1972): 14–38, 189–212.

Mackenzie, Neil. *The Medieval Boy Bishops.* Leicester, 2012.

Maddison, A. K. *A Short Account of the Vicars Choral, Poor Clerks, Organists, and Choristers of Lincoln Cathedral.* London, 1878.

———. "A Visitation of Lincoln Cathedral Held by William Alnwick, Bishop of Lincoln, A.D. 1437." *Journal of the British Archaeological Organization* 47 (1891): 12–24.

Mann, William E. "Ethics." In *The Cambridge Companion to Abelard*, ed. Jeffrey E. Brower and Kevin Guilfoy, 279–304. Cambridge, 2004.

Mansfield, Mary. *The Humiliation of Sinners: Public Penance in Thirteenth-Century France.* Ithaca, NY, 1995.

Marenbon, John. *The Philosophy of Peter Abelard.* Cambridge, 1997.

Mariner, Joanne. *No Escape: Male Rape in U.S. Prisons.* Human Rights Watch report. New York, 2001.

Martin, Dale B. "Heterosexism and the Interpretation of Romans 1:18–32." In *The Boswell Thesis: Essays on "Christianity, Social Tolerance, and Homosexuality,"* ed. Mathew Kuefler, 130–151. Chicago, 2006.

Mason, Emma. "William Rufus: Myth and Reality." *Journal of Medieval History* 3 (1977): 1–20.

Mathisen, Ralph. "'The Second Council of Arles' and the Spirit of Compilation and Codification in Late Roman Gaul." *Journal of Early Christian Studies* 5 (1997): 511–554.

Matthews, John F. *Laying Down the Law: A Study of the Theodosian Code.* New Haven, CT, 2000.

McClendon, Charles B. *The Origins of Medieval Architecture: Building in Europe, A.D. 600–900.* New Haven, CT, 2005.

McCready, William D. *Odiosa sanctitas: St. Peter Damian, Simony, and Reform.* Toronto, 2011.

McDougall, Sara. "Bastard Priests: Illegitimacy and Ordination in Medieval Europe." *Speculum* 94 (2019): 138–172.

———. *Royal Bastards: The Birth of Illegitimacy, 800–1230.* Oxford, 2017.

McGuire, Brian Patrick. "Constitutions and the General Chapter." In *Cambridge Companion to the Cistercian Order,* ed. Mette Birkedal Bruun, 87–99. Cambridge, 2013.

———. *Jean Gerson and the Last Medieval Reformation.* University Park, PA, 2005.

———. "A Lost Clairvaux Exemplum Collection Found: The *Liber visionum et miraculorum* Compiled Under Prior John of Cornwall." *Analecta Cisterciensia* 39 (1983): 26–62.

———. "Love, Friendship and Sex in the Eleventh Century: The Experience of Anselm." *Studia Theologica* 28 (1974): 111–152.

McKeon, Peter R. "Archbishop Ebbo of Reims (816–35): A Study in the Carolingian Empire and Church." *Church History* 43 (1974): 437–447.

McKitterick, Rosamond. *The Frankish Church and the Carolingian Reforms, 789–895.* London, 1977.

McLaughlin, Mary Martin. "Survivors and Surrogates: Children and Parents from the Ninth to the Thirteenth Centuries." In *The History of Childhood,* ed. Lloyd deMause, 101–181. New York, 1974.

McLaughlin, Megan. "The Bishop as Bridegroom: Marital Imagery and Clerical Celibacy in the Eleventh and Early Twelfth Centuries." In *Medieval Purity and Piety: Essays on Medieval Clerical Celibacy and Religious Reform,* ed. Michael Frassetto, 208–237. New York, 1998.

———. "The Bishop in the Bedroom: Witnessing Episcopal Sexuality in an Age of Reform." *Journal of the History of Sexuality* 19 (2010): 17–34.

———. "'Disgusting Acts of Shamelessness': Sexual Misconduct and the Deconstruction of Royal Authority." *Early Medieval Europe* 19 (2011): 312–331.

———. *Sex, Gender, and Episcopal Authority in an Age of Reform.* Cambridge, 2010.

McNamara, Jo Ann. "Chaste Marriage and Clerical Celibacy." In *Sexual Practices and the Medieval Church,* ed. Vern L. Bullough and James A. Brundage, 22–33. Buffalo, NY, 1982.

———. "The *Herrenfrage*: The Restructuring of the Gender System, 1050–1150." In *Medieval Masculinities: Regarding Men in the Middle Ages,* ed. Clare Lees, 3–29. Minneapolis, 1994.

———. "An Unresolved Syllogism." In *Conflicted Identities and Multiple Masculinities: Men in the Medieval West,* ed. Jacqueline Murray, 1–24. New York, 1999.

Meens, Rob. "Children and Confession in the Early Middle Ages." In *The Church and Childhood,* ed. Diana Wood, 53–65. Oxford, 1994.

———. "The Frequency and Nature of Early Medieval Penance." In *Handling Sin: Confession in the Middle Ages,* ed. Peter Biller and A. J. Minnis, 35–62. Woodbridge, 1999.

———. "The Historiography of Early Medieval Penance." In *A New History of Penance*, ed. Abigail Firey, 73–96. Leiden, 2008.

———. *Penance in Medieval Europe, 600–1200*. Cambridge, 2014.

———. "Ritual Purity and the Influence of Gregory the Great in the Early Middle Ages." In *Unity and Diversity in the Church*, ed. R. N. Swanson, 31–43. Oxford, 1996.

Meigne, Maurice. "Concile ou collection d'Elvire?" *Revue d'histoire ecclésiastique* 70 (1975): 361–387.

Melve, Leidulf. *Inventing the Public Sphere: The Public Debate During the Investiture Contest, ca. 1030–1122*. 2 vols. Turnhout, 2007.

———. "Public Debate on Clerical Marriage in the Late Eleventh Century." *Journal of Ecclesiastical History* 61 (2010): 688–706.

Meoni, Noemi. "Visite pastorali a Cortona nel Trecento." *Archivio storico italiano* 129 (1971): 181–256.

Mews, Constant J. *The Lost Love Letters of Heloise and Abelard: Perceptions of Dialogue in Twelfth-Century France*. New York, 1999.

———. "Philosophical Themes in the *Epistolae duorum amantium*: The First Letters of Abelard and Heloise." In *Listening to Heloise: The Voice of a Twelfth-Century Woman*, ed. Bonnie Wheeler, 35–52. New York, 2000.

Michaud-Quantin, Pierre. "À propos des premières *Summae confessorum*." *Recherches théologie anciennes et médiévale* 26 (1959): 264–306.

Migliorino, Francesco. *Fama e infamia: Problemi della società medievale nel pensiero giuridico nei secoli XII e XIII*. Catania, 1985.

Milis, Ludo R. J. *Angelic Monks and Earthly Men: Monasticism and Its Meaning to Medieval Society*. Woodbridge, 1992.

Miller, Andrew W. "To 'Frock' a Cleric: The Gendered Implications of Mutilating Ecclesiastical Vestments in Medieval England." *Gender and History* 24 (2012): 271–291.

Miller, Maureen C. *The Bishop's Palace: Architecture and Authority in Medieval Italy*. Ithaca, NY, 2000.

———. "Masculinity, Reform, and Clerical Culture: Narratives of Episcopal Holiness in the Gregorian Era." *Church History* 72 (2003): 25–52.

Mills, Robert. *Seeing Sodomy in the Middle Ages*. Chicago, 2015.

Milner, Stephen J. "Lorenzo and Pistoia: Peacemaker or Partisan?" In *Lorenzo the Magnificent: Culture and Politics*, ed. Michael Mallett and Nicholas Mann, 235–252. London, 1996.

———. "The Politics of Patronage: Verocchio, Pollaiuolo, and the Forteguerri Monument." In *Artistic Exchange and Cultural Translation in the Italian Renaissance City*, ed. Stephen J. Campbell and Stephen J. Milner, 221–245. Cambridge, 2004.

Mistry, Zubin. *Abortion in the Early Middle Ages, c. 500–900*. Woodbridge, 2015.

Mitchell, Timothy. *Betrayal of Innocents: Desire, Power, and the Catholic Church in Spain*. Philadelphia, 1998.

Monter, E. William. *Frontiers of Heresy: The Spanish Inquisition from the Basque Lands to Sicily*. Cambridge, 1990.

———. "Sodomy and Heresy in Early Modern Switzerland." In *The Gay Past: A Collection of Historical Essays*, ed. Salvatore J. Licata and Robert P. Petersen, 41–55. Binghamton, NY, 1985.

Morey, Adrian. *Bartholomew of Exeter, Bishop and Canonist: A Study in the Twelfth Century*. London, 1937.

Morris, Stephen. *"When Brothers Dwell in Unity": Byzantine Christianity and Homosexuality.* Jefferson, NC, 2016.

Morton, Catherine. "Pope Alexander II and the Norman Conquest." *Latomus* 34 (1975): 362–382.

Motta, Guiseppe. "La redazione A Aucta' della *Collectio Anselmi episcopi Lucensis.*" In *Studia in honorem eminentissimi cardinalis Alphonsi M. Stickler,* ed. Rosalio Josepho Castillo Lara, 375–449. Rome, 1992.

Mulchahey, M. Michèle. *"First the Bow Is Bent in Study": Dominican Education Before 1350.* Toronto, 1998.

Muir, Edward. *Mad Blood Stirring: Vendetta and Factions in Friuli During the Renaissance.* Baltimore, 1993.

Murray, Alexander. "Confession Before 1215." *Transactions of the Royal Historical Society* 3 (1993): 51–81.

Murray, Jacqueline. "One Flesh, Two Sexes, Three Genders." In *Gender and Christianity in Medieval Europe: New Perspectives,* ed. Lisa Bitel and Felice Lifshitz, 34–51. Philadelphia, 2008.

Najemy, John M. *A History of Florence, 1200–1575.* Oxford, 2006.

Newman, Barbara J. "Divine Power Made Perfect in Weakness: St. Hildegard on the Frail Sex." In *Peace Weavers,* vol. 2 of *Medieval Religious Women,* ed. J. A. Nichols and Lillian Thomas Shank, 103–122. Kalamazoo, MI, 1987.

———. *God and the Goddesses: Vision, Poetry, and Belief in the Middle Ages.* Philadelphia, 2003.

———. *Making Love in the Twelfth Century: "Letters of Two Lovers" in Context; A New Translation with Commentary.* Philadelphia, 2016.

———. *Sister of Wisdom: St. Hildegard's Theology of the Feminine.* Berkeley, CA, 1987.

Newman, Martha G. "Foundation and Twelfth Century." In *The Cambridge Companion to the Cistercian Order,* ed. Mette Birkedal Bruun, 25–37. Cambridge, 2013.

O'Daly, Gerard. *Augustine's "City of God": A Reader's Guide.* Oxford, 1999.

Olsen, Glenn W. *Of Sodomites, Effeminates, Hermaphrodites, and Androgynes: Sodomy in the Age of Peter Damian.* Toronto, 2011.

O'Malley, John W. *Trent: What Happened at the Council.* Cambridge, MA, 2013.

Orme, Nicholas. *Education and Society in Medieval and Renaissance England.* London, 1989.

———. *Education in the West of England, 1066–1548.* Exeter, 1976.

———. *The History of England's Cathedrals.* Toronto, 2017.

———. *Medieval Schools from Roman Britain to Renaissance England.* New Haven, CT, 2006.

Osheim, Duane J. *An Italian Lordship: The Bishopric of Lucca in the Late Middle Ages.* Berkeley, CA, 1977.

Owen, Dorothy. "Lincoln Cathedral: Music and Worship." In *A History of Lincoln Minster,* ed. Dorothy Owen, 47–76. Cambridge, 1994.

Parish, Helen. *Clerical Celibacy in the West, c. 1100–1700.* New York, 2010.

Parsons, Ben. "Beaten for a Book: Domestic and Pedagogic Violence in *The Wife of Bath's Prologue.*" *Studies in the Age of Chaucer* 37 (2015): 163–194.

Patch, Howard Rollin. *The Other World: According to Descriptions in Medieval Literature.* New York, 1970.

Payer, Pierre J. "The Origins and Development of the Later *Canones Penitentiales.*" *Mediaeval Studies* 61 (1999): 81–105.

———. *Sex and the New Literature of Confession, 1150–1300.* Toronto, 2009.

———. *Sex and the Penitentials: The Development of a Sexual Code, 550–1150.* Toronto, 1984.

Peters, Edward. "Wounded Names: The Medieval Doctrine of Infamy." In *Law and Mediaeval Life and Thought,* ed. Edward B. King and Susan J. Ridyard, 43–89. Sewanee, TN, 1990.

Peterson, Janine. "Holy Heretics in Later Medieval Italy." *Past and Present* 204 (2009): 3–31.

Peverada, Enrico. "La 'familia' del vescovo e la curia a Ferrara." In *Vescovi e diocesi in Italia dal XIV alla mèta del XVI secolo,* ed. Giuseppina de Sandre Gasparini et al., 1:601–660. Rome, 1990.

Phillips, Chris. "Medieval Source Material on the Internet: Church Records and Religious Houses." In *Some Notes on Medieval English Genealogy,* http://www.medievalgenealogy .org.uk/sources/church.shtml#bishops.

Phipps, William E. *Clerical Celibacy: The Heritage.* New York, 2004.

Planchart, Alejandro Enrique. "Choirboys in Cambrai in the Fifteenth Century." In *Young Choristers, 650–1700,* ed. Susan Boynton and Eric Rice, 123–145. Woodbridge, 2008.

Podles, Leon J. *Sacrilege: Sexual Abuse in the Catholic Church.* Baltimore, 2008.

Polizzotto, Lorenzo. "When Saints Fall Out: Women and the Savonarolan Reform in Early Sixteenth-Century Florence." *Renaissance Quarterly* 46 (1993): 486–525.

Poschmann, Bernhard. *Penance and the Anointing of the Sick.* Trans. Francis Courtney. New York, 1964.

Price, Richard. "Informal Penance in Early Christendom." In *Retribution, Repentance, and Reconciliation,* ed. Kate Cooper and Jeremy Gregory, 29–38. Woodbridge, 2004.

Puff, Helmut. "Localizing Sodomy: The 'Priest and Sodomite' in Pre-Reformation Germany and Switzerland." *Journal of the History of Sexuality* 8 (1997): 165–195.

———. "Same-Sex Possibilities." In *The Oxford Handbook of Women and Gender in Medieval Europe,* ed. Judith M. Bennett and Ruth Mazo Karras, 379–395. Oxford, 2013.

———. *Sodomy in Reformation Germany and Switzerland, 1400–1600.* Chicago, 2003.

Quinn, Patricia A. *Better Than the Sons of Kings: Boys and Monks in the Early Middle Ages.* New York, 1989.

Rashdale, Hastings. *The Universities of Europe in the Middle Ages.* Rev. ed. 3 vols. Oxford, 1936.

Rastall, Richard. "Choirboys in Early English Religious Drama." In *Young Choristers, 650–1700,* ed. Susan Boynton and Eric Rice, 68–85. Woodbridge, 2008.

Rennie, Kriston R. *Law and Practice in the Age of Reform: The Legatine Work of Hugh of Die (1073–1106).* Turnhout, 2010.

Riché, Pierre. *Education and Culture in the Barbarian West: Sixth Through Eighth Centuries.* Trans. John J. Contreni. 3rd ed. Columbia, SC, 1976.

———. "L'enfant dans la société monastique." In *Pierre Abélard—Pierre le Vénérable: Les courants philosophiques, littéraires et artistiques en Occident au milieu du XIIe siècle,* 659–701. Paris, 1975.

Richlin, Amy. "Not Before Homosexuality: The Materiality of the *Cinaedus* and the Roman Law Against Love Between Men." *Journal of the History of Sexuality* 3 (1993): 523–573.

Robertson, Dora H. *Sarum Close: A History of the Life and Education of Cathedral Choristers for 700 Years.* London, 1938.

Robertson, James Craigie, and J. Brigstocke Sheppard, eds. *Materials for the History of Thomas Becket, Archbishop of Canterbury.* 7 vols. London, 1875–1885.

Robinson, I. S. *Authority and Resistance in the Investiture Contest: The Polemical Literature of the Late Eleventh Century.* Manchester, 1978.

———. "The Friendship Network of Gregory VII." *History* 63 (1978): 1–22.

———. *Henry IV of Germany, 1056–1106.* Cambridge, 1999.

———. "Reform and the Church, 1073–1122." In *The New Cambridge Medieval History*, vol. 4, part 1, ed. David Luscombe and Jonathan Riley-Smith, 268–334. Cambridge, 2004.

Rocciolo, Domenico. "Il cardinal vicario e il clero di Roma nella seconda metà del cinquecento." In *Per il Cinquecento religioso italiano: Clero cultura società*, ed. Maurizio Sangalli, 1:243–254. Rome, 2004.

Rocke, Michael. *Forbidden Friendships: Homosexuality and Male Culture in Renaissance Florence.* New York, 1996.

Rodimer, Frank. *The Canonical Effects of Infamy of Fact: A Historical Synopsis and Commentary.* Washington, DC, 1954.

Rolker, Christoph. *Canon Law and the Letters of Ivo of Chartres.* Cambridge, 2010.

Rosemann, Philipp W. *Peter Lombard.* Oxford, 2004.

Rosenwein, Barbara H. "Feudal War and Monastic Peace: Cluniac Liturgy as Ritual Aggression." *Viator* 2 (1971): 129–158.

Rousseau, Constance. "Pope Innocent III and the Familial Relationships of the Clergy and Religious." *Studies in Medieval and Renaissance History* 14 (1993): 105–148.

Rousselle, Aline. *Porneia: On Desire and the Body in Antiquity.* Trans. Felicia Pheasant. Oxford, 1988.

Ruggiero, Guido. *The Boundaries of Eros: Sex Crime and Sexuality in Renaissance Venice.* New York, 1985.

Rusconi, Roberto. "Vescovi e vicari generali nel basso medioevo." In *Vescovi e diocesi in Italia*, ed. Giuseppina de Sandre Gasparini et al., 1:547–568. Rome, 1990.

Ryan, J. Joseph. *Saint Peter Damiani and His Canonical Sources: A Preliminary Study to the Antecedents of the Gregorian Reform.* Toronto, 1956.

Saint-Roch, Patrick. *La pénitence dans les conciles et les lettres des papes des origines à la mort de Grégoire le Grand.* Vatican City, 1991.

Salih, Sarah. "Sexual Identities: A Medieval Perspective." In *Sodomy in Early Modern Europe*, ed. Tom Betteridge, 112–130. Manchester, 2002.

Salisbury, Eve. "'Spare the Rod and Spoil the Child': Proverbial Speech Acts, Boy Bishop Sermons, and Pedagogical Violence." In *Speculum Sermonis: Interdisciplinary Reflections on the Medieval Sermon*, ed. Georgiana Donavin, Cary J. Nederman, and Richard Utz, 141–155. Turnhout, 2004.

Salonen, Kirsi, and Ludwig Schmugge. *A Sip from the "Well of Grace": Medieval Texts from the Apostolic Penitentiary.* Washington, DC, 2009.

Sayers, Jane. "The Judicial Activities of General Chapters." *Journal of Ecclesiastical History* 15 (1964): 18–32, 168–185.

Schatkin, M. A. "John Chrysostom, *Adversus oppugnatores vitae monasticae*: Marriage in Light of Greek Political Philosophy, Roman Law, and the Agonistic Exegesis of Scripture." In *Il matrimonio dei cristiani: Esegesi biblica e diritto romano, XXXVII Incontro di studiosi dell' antichità cristiana*, 373–383. Rome, 2009.

Schimmelpfenning, Bernhard. "*Ex fornicatione nati*: Studies on the Position of Priests Sons from the Twelfth to the Fourteenth Century." *Studies in Medieval and Renaissance History* 12 (1979): 3–50.

Schipper, W. "Secretive Bodies and Passionate Souls: Transgressive Sexuality Among the Carolingians." In *Conjunctions of Mind, Soul, and Body from Plato to the Enlightenment*, ed. Danijela Kambaskovic, 173–201. Heidelberg, 2014.

Schlager, Bernard. "Reading *CSTH* as a Call to Action: Boswell and Gay-Affirming Movements in American Christianity." In *The Boswell Thesis: Essays on "Christianity, Social Tolerance, and Homosexuality,"* ed. Mathew Kuefler, 74–87. Chicago, 2006.

Schmugge, Ludwig. "Cleansing on Consciences: Some Observations Regarding the Fifteenth-Century Registers of the Papal Penitentiary." *Viator* 29 (1998): 345–361.

Schroll, Alfred M. *Benedictine Monasticism as Reflected in the Warnefrid-Hildemar Commentaries on the Rule*. New York, 1967.

Schultz, James A. "Heterosexuality as a Threat to Medieval Studies." *Journal of the History of Sexuality* 15 (2006): 14–29.

Shahar, Shulamith. *Childhood in the Middle Ages*. Trans. Chaya Galai. London, 1990.

Shaw, Brent D. *Sacred Violence: African Christians and Sectarian Hatred in the Age of Augustine*. Cambridge, 2011.

Sherr, Richard. "A Canon, a Choirboy, and Homosexuality in Late Sixteenth-Century Italy: A Case Study." *Journal of Homosexuality* 21 (1991): 1–22.

Sipe, A. W. Richard. "Scandal Versus Culture: Mother Church and the Rape of Her Children." In *Sexual Abuse in the Catholic Church: A Decade of Crisis, 2002–2012*, ed. Thomas G. Plante and Kathleen L. McChesney, 117–129. Santa Barbara CA, 2011.

———. *Sex, Priests, and Power: Anatomy of a Crisis*. New York, 1994.

Smith, David M. "The 'Officialis' of the Bishop in Twelfth- and Thirteenth-Century England: Problems of Terminology." In *Medieval Ecclesiastical Studies: In Honour of Dorothy M. Owen*. Ed. M. J. Franklin and Christopher Harper-Bill, 201–220. Woodbridge, 1995.

Smith, Joshua Bryan. *Walter Map and the Matter of Britain*. Philadelphia, 2017.

Southern, R. W. *Saint Anselm and His Biographer: A Study of Monastic Life and Thought, 1059–1130*. Cambridge, 1963.

Stapleton, M. L. *Harmful Eloquence: Ovid's "Amores" from Antiquity to Shakespeare*. Ann Arbor, MI, 1993.

Staunton, Michael. "Eadmer's *Vita Anselmi*: A Reinterpretation." *Journal of Medieval History* 23 (1997): 1–14.

Stehling, Thomas. "To Love a Medieval Boy." *Journal of Homosexuality* 8 (1983): 151–170.

Stemple, Lara. "Male Rape and Human Rights." *Hastings Law Journal* 60 (2008): 605–646.

Stewart, Alan. *Close Readers: Humanism and Sodomy in Early Modern Europe*. Princeton, NJ, 1997.

Stickler, Alfons Maria. *The Case for Clerical Celibacy: Its Historical Development and Theological Foundations*. Trans. Brian Ferme. San Francisco, 1995.

———. "L'évolution de la discipline du célibat dans l'église en occident de la fin de l'âge patristique au Concile de Trente." In *Sacerdoce et célibat*, ed. Joseph Coppens, 373–442. Gembloux and Louvain, 1971.

Stock, Brian. *The Implications of Literacy: Written Language and Models of Interpretation in the Eleventh and Twelfth Century*. Princeton, NJ, 1983.

Stocker, David. "The Development of the College of the Vicars Choral at Lincoln Minster." In *Vicars Choral at English Cathedrals: "Cantate Domino": History, Architecture and Archaeology*, ed. Richard Hall and David Stocker, 76–92. Oxford, 2005.

Stocking, Rachel L. *Bishops, Councils, and Consensus in the Visigothic Kingdom, 589–633*. Ann Arbor, MI, 2000.

Stoller, Michael. "Eight Anti-Gregorian Councils." *Annuarium Historiae Conciliorum* 17 (1985): 252–321.

Stones, Alison. "The Miniatures in the Vernon Manuscript." In *The Making of the Vernon Manuscript: The Production and Contexts of Oxford, Bodleian Library, MS Eng. poet.a.1*, ed. Wendy Scase, 149–169. Turnhout, 2013.

Straw, Carole. *Gregory the Great: Perfection in Imperfection*. Berkeley, CA, 1988.

Storey, R. L. "Malicious Indictments of the Clergy in the Fifteenth Century." In *Medieval Ecclesiastical Studies in Honour of Dorothy M. Owen*, ed. M. J. Franklin and Christopher Harper-Bill, 221–240. Woodbridge, 1995.

Stroll, Mary. *Popes and Antipopes: The Politics of Eleventh-Century Church Reform*. Leiden, 2012.

Swanson, R. N. "Angels Incarnate: Clergy and Masculinity from Gregorian Reform to Reformation." In *Masculinity in Medieval Europe*, ed. D. M. Hadley, 160–177. London, 1999.

Taglia, Kathryn Ann. "On Account of Scandal: Priests, Their Children, and the Ecclesiastical Demand for Celibacy." *Florilegium* 14 (1995–1996): 57–70.

Tamburinio de Marradio, Ascanio. *De iure abbatum et aliorum praelatorum tam regularium, quam saecularium episcopis inferiorum*. 4 vols. London, 1640.

Tanzini, Lorenzo. "The Tuscan States: Florence and Siena." In *The Italian Renaissance State*, ed. Andrea Gamberini and Isabella Lazzarini, 90–111. Cambridge, 2012.

Tatarczuk, Vincent A. *Infamy of Law: A Historical Synopsis and a Commentary*. Washington, DC, 1954.

Tentler, Thomas N. *Sin and Confession on the Eve of the Reformation*. Princeton, NJ, 1977.

Terry, Karen J., Katarina Schuth, and Margaret Leland Smith. "Incidence of Clerical Sexual Abuse over Time: Changes in Behavior and Seminary Training Between 1950 and 2008." In *Sexual Abuse in the Catholic Church: A Decade of Crisis, 2002–2012*, ed. Thomas G. Plante and Kathleen L. McChesney, 17–30. Santa Barbara, CA, 2011.

Thibodeaux, Jennifer D. "The Defense of Clerical Marriage: Religious Identity and Masculinity in the Writings of Anglo-Norman Clerics." In *Religious Men and Masculine Identity in the Middle Ages*, ed. P. H. Cullum and Katherine J. Lewis, 46–63. Woodbridge, 2013.

———. *The Manly Priest: Celibacy, Masculinity, and Reform in England and Normandy*. Philadelphia, 2015.

Thijssen, J. M. M. H. *Censure and Heresy at the University of Paris, 1200–1400*. Philadelphia, 1998.

Thompson, A. Hamilton. *The English Clergy and Their Organization in the Later Middle Ages*. Oxford, 1947.

———. *The History of the Hospital and the New College of the Annunciation of St. Mary in the Newarke, Leicester*. Leicester, 1937.

———. "Notes on Colleges of Secular Canons in England." *Archaeological Journal* 17 (1917): 140–199.

Thompson, Augustine. *Cities of God: The Religion of the Italian Communes, 1125–1135*. University Park, PA, 2005.

———. "Hildegard of Bingen on Gender and the Priesthood." *Church History* 63 (1994): 349–364.

———. "Lay Versus Clerical Perceptions of Heresy: Protests Against the Inquisition in Bologna, 1299." In *Praedicatores, inquisitores*, vol. 1, *The Dominicans and the Medieval Inquisition: Acts of the First International Seminar on the Dominicans and the Inquisition, Rome, 23–25 February 2002*, 701–730. Rome, 2004.

Thomson, R. M. *William of Malmesbury*. Woodbridge, 2003.

Tierney, Brian. *Foundations of the Conciliar Theory: The Contribution of the Medieval Canonists from Gratian to the Great Schism*. Rev. ed. Leiden, 1998.

Trexler, Richard C. "The Episcopal Constitutions of Antoninus of Florence." *Quellen und Forschungen aus italienischen Archiven und Bibliotheken* 59 (1979): 244–272.

Turner, Denys. *Eros and Allegory: Medieval Exegesis of the Song of Songs*. Kalamazoo, MI, 1995.

Ubl, Karl, and Daniel Ziemann, eds. *Fälschung als Mittel der Politik? Pseudoisidor im Licht der neuen Forschung: Gedenkschrift für Klaus Zechiel-Eckes*. Wiesbaden, 2015.

Ughelli, Ferdinando. *Italia sacra sive de episcopis Italiae*. 10 vols. Venice, 1717–1722.

Uhalde, Kevin. "Juridical Administration in the Church and Pastoral Care in Late Antiquity." In *A New History of Penance*, ed. Abigail Firey, 97–120. Leiden, 2008.

Ullmann, Walter. *The Growth of Papal Government in the Middle Ages*. 3rd ed. London, 1970.

Valerio, Adriana. "Dominica da Paradiso e Dorotea di Lanciuola: un caso Toscano di simulata santità degli inizi del '500." In *Finzione e santità tra medioevo ed età moderna,* ed. Gabriella Zarri, 129–144. Turin, 1991.

Valous, Guy de. *Le monachisme clunisien des origines au XVe siècle*. 2 vols. Paris, 1970.

Van Dam, Raymond. *Saints and Their Miracles in Late Antique Gaul*. Princeton, NJ, 1993.

Van Engen, John. "Anticlericalism Among the Lollards." In *Anticlericalism in Late Medieval and Early Modern Europe*, ed. Peter A. Dykema and Heiko A. Oberman, 53–64. Leiden, 1993.

Van Hoof, Lieve. "Libanius' Life and *Life*." In *Libanius: A Critical Introduction*, ed. Lieve Van Hoof, 7–38. Cambridge, 2014.

Vaughn, Sally N. "St. Anselm of Canterbury: The Philosopher-Saint as Politician." *Journal of Medieval History* 1 (1975): 279–306.

Vieillard, C. *Gilles de Corbeil: Médécin de Philippe-Auguste et chanoine de Notre-Dame, 1140–1224?* Paris, 1909.

Vodola, Elisabeth. *Excommunication in the Middle Ages*. Berkeley, CA, 1986.

Vogel, Cyrille. *Les "Libri paenitentiales."* Typologie des sources du moyen âge occidental, fasc. 27. Turnhout, 1978.

Wagner, Karen. "*Cum aliquis venerit ad sacerdotem*: Penitential Experience in the Central Middle Ages." In *A New History of Penance*, ed. Abigail Firey, 201–218. Leiden, 2008.

Waldman, Louise A. "The Patronage of a Favorite of Leo X: Cardinal Niccolò Pandolfini, Ridolfo Ghirlandaio and the Unfinished Tomb by Baccio Da Montelupo." *Mitteilungen des Kunsthistorischen Institutes in Florenz* 48 (2004): 105–128.

Weir, Anthony, and James Jerman. *Images of Lust: Sexual Carvings on Medieval Churches*. London, 1986.

Werner, Janelle. "'Just as the Priests Have Their Wives': Priests and Concubines in England, 1375–1549." PhD diss., University of North Carolina, 2009.

Wessel, Susan. *Leo the Great and the Spiritual Rebuilding of a Universal Rome*. Leiden, 2008.

Williams, Craig A. *Roman Homosexuality*. New York, 1999.

Williams, John R. "Manasses I of Rheims and Pope Gregory VII." *American Historical Review* 54 (1949): 804–824.

Williams, Schafer. *Codices Pseudo-Isidoriani: A Palaeographico-Historical Study.* New York, 1971.

Willis, Geoffrey Grimshaw. *Saint Augustine and the Donatist Controversy.* London, 1950. Reprint, Eugene, OR, 2005.

Wills, Garry. *Papal Sin: Structures of Deceit.* New York, 2000.

Wilson, Gordon A. "Henry of Ghent's Written Legacy." In *A Companion to Henry of Ghent*, ed. Gordon A. Wilson, 3–23. Leiden, 2011.

Winroth, Anders. *The Making of Gratian's "Decretum."* Cambridge, 2000.

Wirth, Jean. *L'image à l'époque romane.* Paris, 1999.

Witt, Ronald. *Two Latin Cultures of Medieval Italy.* Cambridge, 2012.

Woods, Marjorie Curry. *Classroom Commentaries: Teaching the "Poetria nova" Across Medieval and Renaissance Europe.* Columbus, OH, 2010.

———. "Rape and the Pedagogical Rhetoric of Sexual Violence." In *Criticism and Dissent in the Middle Ages*, ed. Rita Copeland, 56–86. Cambridge, 1996.

———. "The Teaching of Poetic Composition in the Later Middle Ages." In *A Short History of Writing Instruction: From Ancient Greece to Modern America*, ed. James J. Murphy, 123–143. 2nd ed. Mahwah, NJ, 2001.

———. "The Teaching of Writing in Medieval Europe." In *A Short History of Writing Instruction: From Ancient Greece to Modern America*, ed. James J. Murphy, 77–94. Davis, CA, 1990.

———. "Weeping for Dido: Epilogue on a Premodern Rhetorical Exercise in the Postmodern Classroom." In *Latin Grammar and Rhetoric: From Classical Theory to Medieval Practice*, ed. Carol Dana Lanham, 284–294. London, 2002.

Wright, Craig M. *Music and Ceremony at Notre Dame of Paris, 500–1500.* Cambridge, 1989.

Wunderli, Richard M. *London Church Courts on the Eve of the Reformation.* Cambridge, MA, 1981.

Zarri, Gabriella. "Ordini religiosi e autorità episcopale: Le visite pastorali a chiese esenti e monasteri." In *Fonti ecclesiastiche per la storia sociale e religiosa d'Europe, XV–XVIII secolo*, ed. Cecilia Nubola and Angelo Turchini, 347–368. Bologna, 1999.

Zieman, Katherine. "Minding the Rod: Sodomy and Clerical Masculinity in Fifteenth-Century Leicester." *Gender and History* 31 (2019): 60–77.

———. *Singing the New Song: Literacy and Liturgy in Late Medieval England.* Philadelphia, 2008.

Ziolkowski, Jan. *Alan of Lille's Grammar of Sex: The Meaning of Grammar to a Twelfth-Century Intellectual.* Cambridge, MA, 1985.

INDEX

Abbo of Fleury, 118

Abelard, Peter, 118–19, 141, 198–200, 291n68, 299n47, 319n77

Abraham, Erin V., 260n90

accusations and accusers, 32–35, 79–91, 253n104

Adam of Bremen, 270n106

Adamnán of Iona, 287n21

Adelaide, Countess of Chartres, 278n40

Adelaide, Duchess of Turin, 71–73

Ælfric Bata, 49–50

age dissymmetry, 37–38, 40–41, 53, 64–65, 86, 93. *See also* pederasty, culture of

Ailred, Abbot of Rievaulx, 288n23

Alan of Lille, 122, 192–93, 290n58, 292n74, 317n25

Alberic of Settefrati, visionary monk of Monte Cassino, 6, 238

Alcuin, 53–54, 63, 117, 262n109

Alderic, Bishop of Mons, 253n96

Alexander II, Pope, 69, 269n85, 272n124

Alexander III, Pope, 120, 283n124

Alexander the Great, 174, 310n22

Alnwick, William, Bishop of Lincoln, 178, 179, 182–84

Altmann, Bishop of Passau, 76, 272n125

Ambrose, Bishop of Milan, 42, 59, 111, 264n15

Ansellus, scholasticus of Fleury, 112

Anselm, Archbishop of Canterbury: anti-sodomy legislation of, 107, 275n169; corporal punishment, resistance to, 147; exile of, 99, 281n89; *Lament over Virginity Wickedly Lost*, 106; relationships with monks Osbern, Gilbert, Gundulf, and Maurice, 103–5, 284n138; on unchaste priests, 29; William Rufus and, 96–97, 99–100, 108; young males, affection for, 103–7

Anselm of Lucca, canonist, 83, 269n85, 270n106, 275n168, 275n174

Anthony, St., 43, 257n35

Antonino, Archbishop of Florence, 213

Antonino (Pierozzi), Archbishop of Florence, St., 213

Apostolic Constitutions, 63

Aquinas, Thomas, 129–30, 135–36, 290n56, 292n73

Ariald, reforming deacon of Milan, 79–80

Aristotle, 48, 135–36, 310n22

Arnold of Verniolle, apostate friar, 202–7, 216

Astesanus d'Asti, Franciscan theologian, 137

Athanasius, 6

Augustine, Bishop of Hippo: beaten at school, 194; on children, 5–6, 42; cited by Pseudo-Ulrich, 78; on fraternal correction, 25, 131; on hidden and tolerated sin, 17, 31; on living with sin and justification of secrecy, 23–25, 249n43; on marriage, 73; on Nicolas, 75; ordination as indelible, 20; original sin, doctrine of, 42; on penance, 247n19; on sodomy, 136; on teachers, 189; on unnatural acts, 111; on virginity, 42; wife chosen at age ten, 40

Ausonius, Roman poet, 39

Avicenna, 259n74

Bacon, Roger, 200–201, 320n83

Baldwin, John, 290n59, 295n7

Baldwin II, King of Jerusalem, 139

Barontus, visionary monk of Lonray, 260n79

Barstow, Anne Llewellyn, 270n106

Bartholomew, Bishop of Exeter, 291n72

Basil the Great, 46

Bates, David, 108

Baudri of Bourgueil, Bishop of Dol, 87–88, 94, 190–91, 199, 279nn62–63

Bec Abbey, 103–4

Becket, Thomas, Archbishop of Canterbury, 139, 296n24

Beckynton, Thomas, Bishop of Wells, 313n70

Benedict of Aniane, 56, 244n17

Benedict of Nursia, 45–46. *See also* Rule of St. Benedict

Benedict the Levite, 33–34, 51–52

ACKNOWLEDGMENTS

———————

A historian's job is to make sense of the past, but there are times when the past refuses to cooperate. And yet sometimes we get lucky, stumbling upon something—call it a key, a code, a password—revealing a hidden corridor that leads to where we are longing to go. Although I have experienced this kind of historical grace in the past, it was by and large withheld from me in the course of writing this book. Most of the time I was confronted with the full extent of the past's intractability. Although dismayed, I can't say I was surprised. The religious authorities who recorded and controlled the information I sought were intensely scandal-averse, and generally inclined to conceal something as repugnant as the sexual abuse of adolescents and minors. This experience with so unyielding a past has made me all the more thankful for the help I encountered along the way. First and foremost there is the paleographic assistance I received from Elena Brizio and Louisa Foroughi. I am especially indebted to Elena, not only for her finely honed paleographic skill, but also for the depth of her historical understanding of premodern Italy. I am appreciative of the extremely helpful personnel at the Archivio di Stato di Firenze, the Archivio Arcivescovile di Lucca, the Archivio Arcivescovile di Pisa, the Biblioteca Domenicana di Santa Maria Novella "Jacopo Passavanti" di Firenze, the Borthwick Institute of Historical Research at York, the Canterbury Cathedral Archives, the Fondation des Archives de l'ancien Évêché de Bâle (Porrentruy), and the Lincolnshire County Archives. Jessalyn Bird, Guy Geltner, Ruth Mazo Karras, Kathryn Kerby-Fulton, Richard Kieckhefer, Thomas Maloney, Andrew Miller, Barbara Newman, and Kathleen Noll all provided me with invaluable leads of one sort or another. And then there is the ongoing support of friends and colleagues like Caroline Walker Bynum, John Van Engen, Maryanne Kowaleski, Robert Lerner, and my long-suffering editors at the University of Pennsylvania Press—Jerry Singerman and Ruth Mazo Karras. Although I may revel in their generosity, I hope they know that I never take it for granted. I am grateful to Zoe Senecal and Johnna Sturgeon, who assisted me in the preparation of the manuscript, and Scott Smiley for his painstaking work on the index. But special plaudits go out to Jennifer

Shenk of the University of Pennsylvania Press, the most diligent and learned of manuscript editors, and Lily Palladino, the most tactful and patient of managing editors. Nor could this book have been written without the generous institutional support of the National Humanities Center, the ACLS, University of Connecticut's Charles Owen Visiting Professorship, and Northwestern University—my home institution.

There are also the crucial zones of emotional support that were central to this project. First, there is the canine faction—Maggie Comestor; Roo the Irascible; Brenda Stellae; and the late great Dydo, queen of Carthage—whose very existence ensured that I never sat at a desk for too punishing a length of time. Then there are my friends and colleagues, particularly the late Paula Blank, Donald Gray, and Susan Gubar, whose unflagging interest in my work sustained my sometimes flagging spirits. And last, but not least, comes the debt to my family. I would like to thank my siblings, Dori, Geordie, Robbie and my parents, Helga and the late George Elliott, for their love. I am especially obliged to my mother for my intense, albeit unconventional, religious education, which I am still, in my own way, pursuing. But above all, I thank my husband, Rick Valicenti, for his devotion to all things in the Middle Ages, especially me.